THE EAGLE AND THE RISING SUN

ALSO BY ALAN SCHOM

Napoleon Bonaparte: A Life

Trafalgar: Countdown to Battle 1803–1805

One Hundred Days

Emile Zola: A Biography

THE EAGLE AND THE RISING SUN

The Japanese-American War 1941–1943

PEARL HARBOR THROUGH GUADALCANAL

ALAN SCHOM

W. W. NORTON & COMPANY

New York London

Printed in the United States of America
First published as a Norton paperback 2004

For information about permission to reproduce selections from this book, write to Permissions, W. W. Norton & Company, Inc., 500 Fifth Avenue, New York, NY 10110

Manufacturing by The Maple-Vail Book Manufacturing Group
Book design by JAM Design
Production manager: Andrew Marasia

Library of Congress Cataloging-in-Publication Data

Schom, Alan.
The Eagle and the Rising Sun : the Japanese-American war, 1941–1943, Pearl Harbor through Guadalcanal / Alan Schom.
p. cm.
Includes bibliographical references and index.
ISBN 0-393-04924-8 (hard)
1. World War, 1939–1945—United States. 2. World War, 1939–1945—Japan. 3. World War, 1939–1945—Campaigns—Pacific Area. 4. Pacific Area—History, Military. 5. Pacific Area—History, Naval. I. Title.
D767 .S3515 2003
940.54'25—dc21 2002015941

ISBN 0-393-32628-4 pbk.

W. W. Norton & Company, Inc.
500 Fifth Avenue, New York, N.Y. 10110
www.wwnorton.com

W. W. Norton & Company Ltd.
Castle House, 75/76 Wells Street, London W1T 3QT

1 2 3 4 5 6 7 8 9 0

I dedicate this work to Admiral Richmond Kelly Turner, who gave his life to the U.S. Navy and developed and headed the extremely difficult amphibious operations throughout the war; General A. A. Vandegrift, USMC, for his courageous leadership in Guadalcanal, turning what MacArthur predicted would be a U.S. defeat into a glorious victory; Commander Joseph Rochefort, the head of the U.S. Navy Intelligence unit at Pearl Harbor, whose wisdom and intelligence made possible the battle of Midway, a great victory and a turning point in the war; Admiral Chester Nimitz, whose unrelenting and bold leadership took over the forces of the Pacific while Pearl Harbor was still burning, and who confidently and wisely built up the U.S. Navy in the Pacific, making it the most powerful naval force ever created; and General Robert Eichelberger and his troops, along with General George Kenney's new air force, which saved the situation in New Guinea and the Philippines, thereby halting the Japanese advance and reversing it in that theater, which in turn saved MacArthur's reputation. Finally, I dedicate this tome to Françoise Marie Jeanne Coménie, who, alas, died just before completion of the work.

Contents

List of Maps

Foreword

From time to time, we are privileged to be given extraordinary insights into the history of our age. This volume is one such occasion. Alan Schom has given us a tapestry, into which he has woven figures of immense proportions, yet he has not lost sight of their humanity. In the space of these pages, he has highlighted the ideologies, personal aspirations, and leadership challenges faced by the protagonists on the world's stage, welding them all into a gripping story. Yes, we know the outcome, but, as happens infrequently, he has given us new insights, refreshing assessments, and trenchant judgments on those who made history in their time, and made our world what it has become today.

In the grand tradition of Barbara Tuchman's *The Guns of August,* he has assembled the main actors, reviewed their cultures and beliefs, and traced the almost inexorable path to war that led to conflicting civilizations, the deaths of millions, and a new order of peace in the Pacific that has endured to our day. Throughout, his lucid explanation of misperceptions and internal politics, the dangers of an overly domestic focus, and an emerging world mission, guides us to an understanding of the outcome that now seems preordained. Yet, as his memorable text makes clear, it was nothing of the sort. Despite the education of key Japanese leaders in the United States, and the awareness of economic issues driving Japanese concerns in the US government, the dialogue of the deaf, to adopt a French phrase, seemed inevitable.

Once the conflict had been joined, despite the celebration of victory we recall today, the issue was far from clear. Leadership, the sine qua non of success in battle, was in short supply on both sides. Resources, in the main dedicated to the outcome of events in Europe, were even more in doubt in the vast reaches of the Pacific where, from the beginning, Japanese forces held the upper hand. From the first moments of Pearl Harbor to the demise of the Asiatic Fleet, from Midway to Guadalcanal, the issue, and the balance, were always in doubt. Valor, self-sacrifice, intelligience, and judgment—all would be required to turn the tide of what seemed in the first years of this global struggle an almost impossible task. In hindsight, we might say the issue was never in doubt. For those who lived it, it ws, in so many painful ways, the effort of a lifetime.

Through these pages, the reader is privileged to learn the causes for which men fought and died, the objectives sought and lost, the role of intelligience, and the cost of misapplied force. The emerging role of airpower is made clear. In every conflict since then, it has made a predominant difference. Yet, in those days, as great civilizations struggled for preeminence, it was not fully appreciated. The losses of the ships on battleship row may have transformed the U.S. Navy in ways no modern administration could have foreseen, with profound effect. When the final curtain rang down, the shape of combat at sea for the next sixty years had been defined. We live it today, as our battle groups range the world, in support of U.S. policy.

Above all, Alan Schom has given us history in its most precise form—readable and relevant. We, of course, know now how the war evolved, but his insights illuminate our understanding and appreciation in a way no mere reading of dispatches possible could. Through his eyes we are present on the ships' bridges, in the bunker, at the White House, as decisions are made that will bring a new era into being. In the world of writing history, this is no mean task. Schom does not hesitate to judge, to assess, and to ask the difficult questions. No figure, from MacArthur to Nimitz, from Fletcher to Eichelberger, is exempt from his searching judgment. Consequently, this history is a nice change from the often bland assessment of the purely academic and reflects what the practitioner knows—there must be accountability for the responsibility of leadership. When leaders send men and women into war, history will judge them, as it has here. Let us pray that the judgment is kind, and the risks worth the candle.

Too often, history is recounted as a series of events. Alan Schom's talent is to relate it as a series of interactions among human beings, driven by ego, or worldview, or politics, to make choices, or take risks.

And so we have the marvelously flawed leadership of General MacArthur, the "come from behind coaching" of Admiral Nimitz, and the signal contributions of a host of lesser characters who, at the right time and place, made a distinct difference in a conflict that raged over thousands of miles of ocean, involving the risk of national objectives on which all depended.

Above all, the reader will see that this volume is a testimony to the nearness of the game. As Wellington is reputed to have said after Waterloo, "It was a near run thing." The risks and the political gains were so far disproportionate on both sides that the fundamental issue was always in doubt. Neither side held back. All was on the table. In the event, as Schom's riveting recounting of the battle of Midway shows, it came down to a few seconds. History can be like that—in retrospect. For those on its front lines, it is a kaleidoscope of decisions and actions taken in rapid succession. For the forces in action that June day, a world hung in the balance. And from that time, the clock ticked on with ineluctable determination.

While Waterloo determined the shape of Europe for a century, the collision between the eagle and the rising sun would reshape the Pacific, give rise to a new economic power, and provide an umbrella of peace that would profoundly transform our world. The result, born of hard lessons learned in the searing battle for supremacy at sea, forged in the teeming jungles of the Pacific Islands, and ultimately won in the shipyards and industrial vastness of the United States, paved the way for a post empire world that would give birth to another generation of conflict, smaller in scale, yet no less violent.

Mariners learn early about the forces of tide and wind—or they do not long survive. The Pacific War was driven by forces far greater, yet once the economic tide had begun to flood against the dwindling resources of Japan, the ultimate result, Schom shows us, could not have been in doubt. How and why that came to be are recalled here, to our current advantage and understanding. It is the duty of historians, from Herodotus to the present day, to recall the events and leaders who made a difference in their time. Alan Schom has done so, with vigor.

Thomas F. Marfiak
Annapolis, Maryland

Acknowledgments

I am most grateful to my secretary Mrs. Wooldridge for deciphering my manuscript, to Admiral J. L. Holloway III, and to the Naval Historical Foundation. Rear Admiral Tom Marfiak and his U.S. Naval Institute, including Mr. Paul Stillwell, have helped time and again. Very special thanks to Admiral of the Fleet, former First Sea Lord, Sir Henry Leach, for kindly and bravely reading my entire manuscript and correcting several errors while explaining various points; Professor Alex Deconde for also going through the entire text with his equally useful suggestions; John Greenwood, a former artillery commander, for taking the trouble to explain many aspects of guns; Major Burt Bank, USAC, a survivor of the Bataan Death March; Mr. Theodore Taylor; Sir Martin Gilbert; Lord [Hugh] Thomas; Mr. Donald Perlroth; Dr. George Mitchell; Professor B. Mitchell Simpson III; and Mrs. Marilyn Bargteil. In addition, I must thank Mr. Gary La Valley, Nimitz Library Archives, U.S. Naval Academy; the archivists at the MacArthur Memorial Library, Norfolk; Brigadier General John Brown, Office of the Chief of Military History, U.S. Center of Military History; Miss Catherine Lloyd, Naval Historical Center, Washington, D.C.; Mr. Selwyn Eagle, for carrying out research for me in far-flung libraries and archives; Mr. Barry L. Zerby, Modern Military Records and Archives at the National Archives; Dr. Piers Brendon, Churchill Archives, Cambridge University; A. A. Bell, Director of the London Library; and also Christopher Hurley of that library for the extraordinary effort he made to get me the rare books I needed; Dr. Hamish Todd, Curator, Oriental Department, the British Library; U.S. Department of the Navy for releasing various illustrations to me; the Hoover Institution with its large holdings on the Far East; and a variety of other libraries, including those of the University of California, the Library of Congress, the National Archives, the Nimitz Library, the British Library, the Public Record Office, and the London Library. I thank Ann Adelman and Patricia Chui for their editorial assistance, and in particular my late friend, the historian Byron Farwell, for his early encouragement of this project.

Author's Note

This book begins with the Japanese attack on Pearl Harbor on December 7, 1941, and concludes with the conquest of Guadalcanal in February 1943.

I attempt to explain the historical background in twentieth-century Japan in order to better understand the conditions that led to an attack against America. By describing some of the main events and characters in that country as well as its ideological outlook, I hope to fill a void existing in most general histories. This war was not inevitable, nor was it necessary. Hostilities might have been avoided had the Japanese government ended the veritable civil war within its own country and desisted from trying to enslave its Asian neighbors by sheer force. The last thing the vast majority of Americans wanted was to enter another international war, whether in Europe or Asia. But when attacked, they had to defend themselves. Ignorance and distrust of the unknown, that is, of one another, helped lead to this cataclysm.

Japan, which had begun to intimidate and conquer Asian countries for half a century prior to its attack on the United States, had clearly established a continuous, brutal expansionism, so that the United States had no excuse for being caught unawares or for thinking it was untouchable. The American military at the highest level had been forewarned, in fact, by Richmond Kelly Turner, who was in charge of Naval Planning throughout 1941; but his warnings were either ignored or toned down by his superiors. Furthermore, both the U.S. Army and Navy had been negligent in instructing their men and women for a real war, a failure that was, alas, only remedied when those forces finally came under live fire in the Pacific and Europe. And yet the U.S. Navy had successfully "attacked" Pearl Harbor in simulations conducted in 1928, 1932, and 1938, employing the very strategy and tactics that Admiral Yamamoto Isoroku for one had followed closely and imitated. Part of the blame for this lack of preparation to defend the nation must be laid firmly on the U.S. Congress between wars, which failed to bring the U.S. military up to a reasonable degree of readiness and strength by withholding the funds required.

I hope that my history will in some small measure clarify the interplay of the many complex factors and military actions taken to achieve victory for the Allies.

•

It should be noted that the Japanese use the family name followed by the first name. The reader should also be alerted to the fact that all American commanders during the war, including President Roosevelt on occasion, referred to the Japanese as "Japs," just as during World War I many people referred to the Germans as "the Boches." Some of the quotes in this book include that terminology, which as a professional historian I am unable to alter. Fortunately, these usages gradually disappeared over the years.

THE EAGLE AND THE RISING SUN

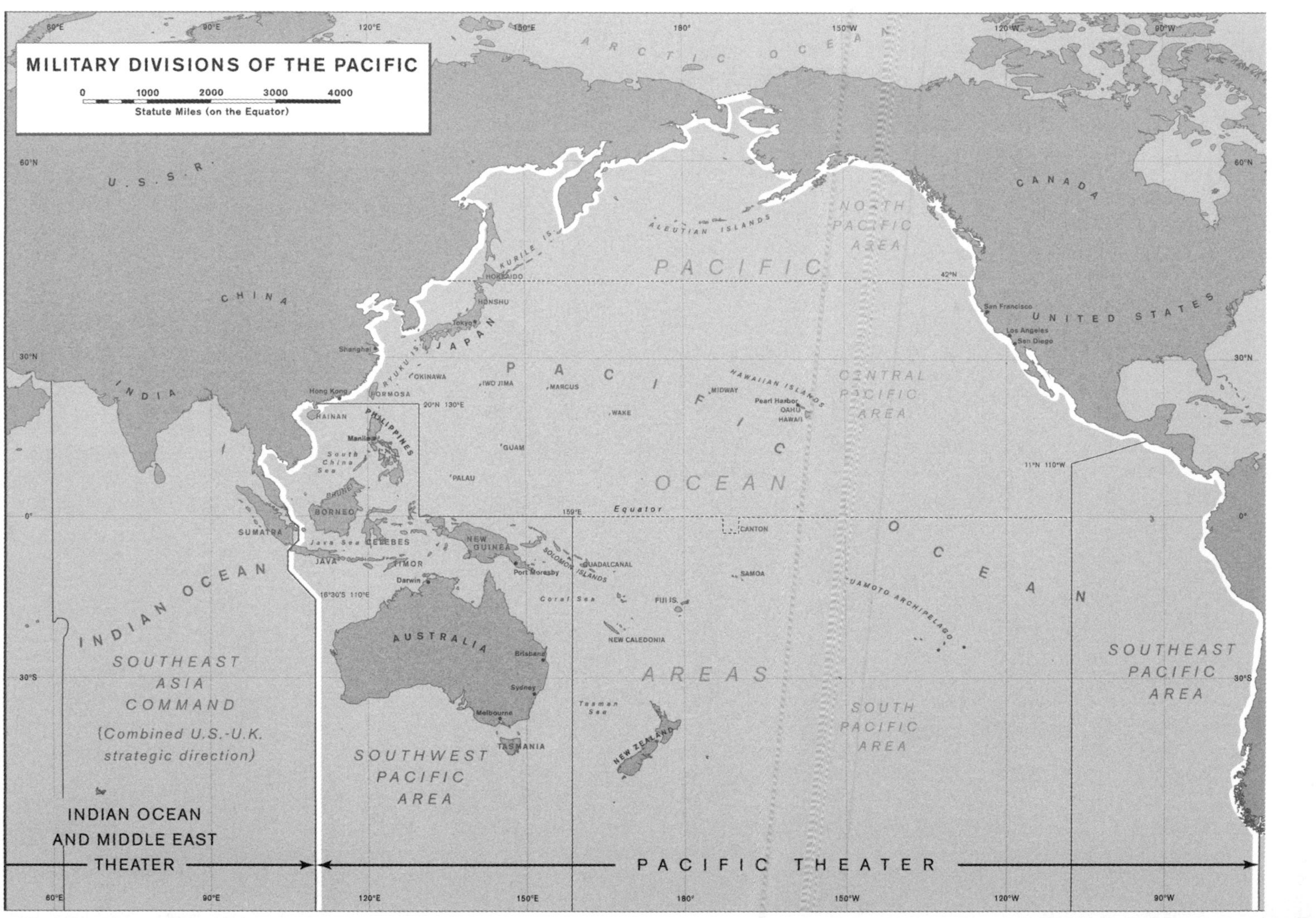
MILITARY DIVISIONS OF THE PACIFIC
0 1000 2000 3000 4000
Statute Miles (on the Equator)
ARCTIC OCEAN
U. S. S. R.
CHINA
INDIA
CANADA
UNITED STATES
San Francisco
Los Angeles
San Diego
NORTH PACIFIC AREA
CENTRAL PACIFIC AREA
SOUTH PACIFIC AREA
SOUTHEAST PACIFIC AREA
SOUTHWEST PACIFIC AREA
PACIFIC OCEAN AREAS
PACIFIC OCEAN
INDIAN OCEAN
SOUTHEAST ASIA COMMAND
(Combined U.S.-U.K. strategic direction)
INDIAN OCEAN AND MIDDLE EAST THEATER
PACIFIC THEATER
ALEUTIAN ISLANDS
KURILE IS.
HOKKAIDO
HONSHU
Tokyo
JAPAN
Shanghai
RYUKU IS.
OKINAWA
IWO JIMA
MARCUS
Hong Kong
FORMOSA
HAINAN
PHILIPPINES
Manila
South China Sea
BRUNEI
BORNEO
SUMATRA
Java Sea
CELEBES
JAVA
TIMOR
Darwin
NEW GUINEA
Port Moresby
SOLOMON ISLANDS
GUADALCANAL
Coral Sea
AUSTRALIA
Brisbane
Sydney
Melbourne
TASMANIA
Tasman Sea
NEW ZEALAND
NEW CALEDONIA
FIJI IS.
SAMOA
CANTON
WAKE
GUAM
PALAU
MIDWAY
HAWAIIAN ISLANDS
Pearl Harbor
OAHU
HAWAII
TUAMOTO ARCHIPELAGO
Equator
42°N
20°N 130°E
159°E
11°N 110°W
16°30'S 110°E
60°N
30°N
0°
30°S
60°E
90°E
120°E
150°E
180°
150°W
120°W
90°W

PRELUDE

A Cherry Blossom Funeral

Pale blossoms greet you
Seaman from afar
Who brings him home
Where all his memories are.

—*Ode to Captain Richmond Kelly Turner by Yone Nogushi, 1939*[1]

The armed U.S. Marine Guards snapped to attention as the miniature orange and white flag bearing the Rising Sun flying on the fender of Ambassador Kensuke Horinouchi's black limousine passed through the Maryland Avenue Gate of the United States Naval Academy at Annapolis. The funeral cortège then slowly crossed beneath ancient magnolias and elms, past throngs of busy midshipmen going to their classes, until it reached the long pier. Here where the waters of the Severn River spilled into Chesapeake Bay, the procession stopped before a marine honor guard and the imposing gray hull of Heavy Cruiser 34, the USS *Astoria,* on this bleak eighteenth day of March in the troubling year 1939.

Rear Admiral Wilson Brown, Superintendent of the Academy, briefly presented Ambassador Saitō Hiorshi's widow and Secretary of State Cordell Hull to the ship's captain, Richmond Kelly Turner, Class of '08, in his full dress blue uniform with two gold epaulettes. Saitō's young daughters came next, followed by some one hundred senior naval officers and government officials. Marine Corps drums rolled the traditional lament accompanied by a nineteen-gun salute as the small lacquered box containing the ashes of the former ambassador was piped aboard the *Astoria*, accompanied by the third secretary of the Japanese Embassy, for the long voyage to Tokyo.[2]

The choice of the popular aristocrat, Saitō, by Emperor Hirohito for this important post in Washington, D.C., had been significant: he represented the first generation of young English-speaking Japanese, many of them educated in American schools. The political and military upheavals of the 1930s had required a very special individual to represent the imperial Japanese house to help bridge over the continuing period of difficult relations between the two nations.

The decision in turn by President Franklin Delano Roosevelt to accord such honors to the late ambassador was taken after great deliberation. It was intended as an act of goodwill to help reduce tensions between Tokyo and Washington.

Completing the 10,000-mile journey and now escorted by three Japanese destroyers, the *Astoria* entered Yokohama Harbor on April 17 with the Stars and Stripes at half-mast. Turner ordered a twenty-one-gun salute. It was a solemn moment, as any ritual for the dead inevitably is. It also marked the symbolic funeral of peace, for during this voyage across the Pacific, German armies had invaded Czechoslovakia and created German "protectorates" of Bohemia and Moravia, while annexing the port of Memel. In September, Germany would invade Poland, to be followed by the Soviet Union's unprovoked attack against Finland. Meanwhile, in the Far East, Japan already had some 700,000 troops fighting Chiang Kai-shek in the prolonged war with China, the ally of Britain and America. Another Japanese army had seized Manchuria back in 1931, where those troops now in 1939 faced powerful units of the Soviet army across the Amur River in Siberia.

Hence the selection of Kelly Turner, a specialist in the Far East, for this delicate diplomatic mission. During his nine-day sojourn in Japan, day after day filled with special ceremonies, a shower of cherry blossoms and ritual teas, Turner had an opportunity to study the mighty Japanese navy's latest fast carriers and ships of the line. He also met the Japanese war minister, General Itagaki Seishirō; the blustery foreign minister, Arita Hachiro, who bestowed a silk Daimyō robe on the American captain; the naval minister, Admiral Yonai Mitsumasa, who presented Turner with a cloisonné vase; and the deputy chief of the

Naval General Staff, Admiral Koga Mineichi. It was to prove a unique opportunity for Turner both to talk with and observe major Japanese officers. But of all the dinners in his honor, the most interesting was the one given by the fluent English-speaking, Harvard-educated deputy naval minister, Admiral Yamamoto Isoroku, the architect of Japan's new navy, with whom Turner would one day return to the Pacific to do battle.[3]

CHAPTER I

A Distinguished Visitor

"We cannot forget the frightful recent past, but we cannot but realize that we must pass from recollection to action and attention if we are to grapple successfully with the problems of the present."

—*the Hon. George Harvey, Ambassador Designate to the Court of St. James's, May 10, 1921*[1]

Admiral Sir Charles Madden, commander of the Royal Navy's Atlantic Fleet, looked on as the order to "DRESS SHIP" was given and as dozens of flags broke out over his flagship, the battleship *Queen Elizabeth*, and *Royal Oak*. A special ensign appeared over the mainmast in honor of the visiting squadron that emerged through a squall near Spithead, firing a twenty-one-gun salute to its waiting hosts. The British flotilla's lead ship and eight destroyers that had escorted it up the Channel now peeled off as a squadron of seaplanes performed maneuvers high above, then suddenly swept down to water level.

At eight o'clock on Tuesday morning, May 9, 1921, the ships of the visiting Crown Prince received a resounding royal salute from the guns of Spitbank Fort, the King's Bastion, and of course from the battle-worn 12-pounders of Horatio Nelson's *Victory*. As his two battleships steamed into Portsmouth Harbour, "The Empire's greatest arsenal," all active warships were ablaze with flags flapping in the brisk breeze, and by ten o'clock, the Crown Prince's flagship* was secured along the south rail-

*His flagship is described as both a "battleship" and a "battle-cruiser," though officially classed as a pre-Dreadnought battleship.

way jetty opposite Portsmouth. Everywhere along the sea route to England his ships had been greeted by the bastions and outposts of the British Empire, and nowhere more superbly than at Valetta, where Governor General Plumber had ordered another resounding salute from Malta's guns, the illumination against the night sky of the warships in the harbor, and a reception in the subtropical gardens of San Antonio Palace, a welcome that was repeated as the royal visitor reached Gibraltar, where he was fêted by its Governor General at the Convent.

But if the twenty-year-old prince and heir to the imperial throne of his country had been impressed by the elaborate preparations laid at every stage of the voyage, it was as nothing compared to what now awaited him. The reception in England was to leave him dazzled by its magnificence, as he later acknowledged, and created memories that would remain with him until his next visit to England as an old man.

The jetty was lined by the Royal Marines, a guard of blue-jackets, and the band playing the Imperial Prince's national anthem. The twenty-seven-year-old Prince of Wales, the future Edward VIII, as slender as his guest, if taller and fairer, attired in the uniform of a captain in the Royal Navy, was piped aboard the foreign warship that, like its sister escort, had been designed and built in these very British Isles. After an exchange of courtesies by the two princes and their immediate entourages, they returned to shore. Earlier showers had given way to sunny skies.

The Prince of Wales's senior military officers, the Lord Lieutenant of Hampshire and the Lord of Portsmouth, were now duly introduced, the latter welcoming His Imperial Highness to his fair port and country. The visiting Crown Prince, in the uniform of a lieutenant commander of his own navy, thanked him briefly, through an interpreter. Following an inspection of the guard, the entire combined party, including the thirty-four naval, army, and court officers of the visitor, crossed the jetty to the special royal train already under steam waiting to whisk them up to London.[2]

If the approach to Victoria Station's blackened brick walls looked bleak even in the sun, not so the welcome waiting within. Indeed, scarcely had the Crown Prince descended upon the brilliant red carpet specially laid for this event than he was warmly greeted by a smiling King George in the uniform of an Admiral of the Fleet of the Royal

Navy, flanked by the Dukes of York and Connaught. Behind them the station's pillars had been sheathed in scarlet bunting bearing the flags of the two nations adorned with palms, lilies, and exotic flowers. The crowd of celebrities about to be introduced was indeed daunting, both in title and number. In addition to members of the royal family and diplomatic corps, included were the Marquis of Crewe, in the uniform of Lord Lieutenant of the County of London; Foreign Secretary Lord Curzon of Kedleston in levee dress; the Earl of Chesterfield, Master of the Horse; Earl Beatty, First Sea Lord; Field Marshal Sir Henry Wilson, chief of the Imperial General Staff; and Air Marshal Sir Hugh Trenchard; not to mention the lieutenant general of London and that city's lord mayor and sheriffs, commissioner of police, and many others. Opposite the tunnel roadway stood the guard of honor, the 1st Scots Guards, in brilliant scarlet tunics and towering bearskins.

Following more speeches and introductions, which already appeared too much for the rather hesitant, bespectacled Crown Prince, at one o'clock precisely a state coach, drawn by six horses with mounted postillions in a livery of scarlet and gold lace, drew up opposite the train. The king, the Crown Prince, his ambassador, and the Prince of Wales boarded the coach as the band of the Scots Guards played the visitor's anthem followed by "God Save the King." A sovereign's escort of the 1st Life Guards and the King's Guard of the 1st Battalion of the Coldstream Guards, with gleaming breastplates, swords, and mirrorlike boots, preceded the carriage. The procession passed packed crowds, tens of thousands strong, waving flags of both countries, and cheering all along the circuitous route heading via Grosvenor Place to Hyde Park Corner, then back through Green Park along the sweep of tree-lined Constitution Hill, around the Victoria Memorial and through the wrought-iron gates before Buckingham Palace, where the Crown Prince was to be guest of honor for the next week, before moving into Lord Chesterfield's Mayfair mansion.[3]

Ushered into the Bow Room, the Crown Prince was introduced to Queen Mary. The British royal family for its part found the young visitor tongue-tied, obviously overwhelmed by this display of imperial pageantry and elaborate court etiquette, the likes of which he had never before experienced. That he could only respond most briefly, and then through an embassy interpreter, hardly helped. But George V, in a smart naval uniform, with his well-trimmed white beard, was hardly a stickler for rigid court etiquette, and despite the setting addressed the young man in a warm, avuncular manner, trying to put him at his ease: "I hope, me boy, that everyone is giving you everything you want while you are here."

The royal family, indeed the nation as a whole, did its best to welcome the state visitor, with two sumptuous feasts the first day, beginning with a luncheon at Buckingham Palace. That evening an even more splendid feast was held in the palace's nineteenth-century Banqueting Hall. Yeomen of the King's Bodyguard in scarlet and gold Tudor costumes were stationed at intervals round the magnificent hall, with footmen behind every crimson chair. The guests were seated at two long tables, resplendent with the royal goldplate, while the string band of the Royal Artillery played in the gallery.

At this great dinner King George spoke of the Crown Prince's visit as a "symbol of the friendship which has for long united our two Empires," acknowledging his "gratitude for our Ally's loyal support and for the gallant conduct of her Army and Navy during the Great War, and our conviction that the friendly cooperation of our respective countries is one of the essential factors in the maintenance of the world's peace." The king was of course referring to the protective naval escorts provided for British troop transports between Australia and the Middle East, and the cruiser and fifteen destroyers dispatched to escort other British and Allied shipping across the Mediterranean between 1917 and 1918.

Rising in turn, the Crown Prince spoke out in a strong, almost staccato voice, expressing his "deep and heartfelt gratitude" for the welcome and "most bountiful hospitality" he had received since his arrival. "I feel most happy that, as the very first step in my European tour of study and observation, I set my foot upon these beautiful shores of this great country, whose invariable friendship and goodwill are prized very highly by the whole [of my] nation. . . . It is extremely gratifying to me that the happy relations existing between our two countries have well stood the strain and stress of our times, and will continue, as your Majesty has just observed, as one of the essential factors in the maintenance of the world's peace."[4]

Given the traumatic drama presented by World War I and the consequences since its conclusion nearly three years earlier, it is hardly surprising to find this great emphasis on and concern regarding world peace, which was even now being echoed in Southampton as the new American ambassador-designate to the Court of St. James's, George Harvey, upon landing from the luxury liner *Aquitania*, spoke before the delegation sent to receive him. He reminded the assemblage not only of his country's "good will . . . but of [its] good cheer and good hope. We cannot forget the frightful recent past, but we cannot but realize that we must pass from recollection to action and attention if we are to grapple successfully with the problems of the present. You of England, as all the world knows, are striving manfully to do your part. We of America want to help. . . . Acting together the Great Empire and the Great Republic, shoulder to shoulder, arm in arm, cannot and must not fail to save themselves, and with themselves to save the world" from the great international postwar challenges facing them.[5]

On the home front, meanwhile, a besieged Prime Minister Lloyd George, recently returned from the peace conference at Versailles, was now pleading for another sort of peace, as Great Britain faced coal mine and transport strikes that threatened to paralyze the country and its still feeble economy. "I must appeal here and now to the nation, to endure with the patient and stubborn courage which has piloted it throughout much worse troubles."[6] The war was over, but the peace, in all its forms—political, financial, social, and military—had yet to be won.

•

The visit of the Crown Prince, Hirohito, could hardly have come at a less propitious time, it would seem, with Britain deeply in debt and its economy in a state of nearly complete disruption, during the period of demobilization and transition to the postwar realities, including the fading memory of a once powerful empire. Among the very real ghosts of the past, of course, were the continued "troubles" in Ireland that had been bedevilling relations for centuries, as a fresh proposal was now submitted to accept "in principle the status of a self-governing Dominion for Ireland," provided that the "Ulster Unionists and the rest of Ireland are in accord," which would include the creation of a Constituent Assembly to frame a new constitution, even as Sinn Fein reputedly offered a truce for such elections.

Hostilities with Germany and its wartime allies may have ceased on November 11, 1918, but not the seemingly insurmountable postwar problems. Under great pressure from Britain, America, and their Allies, for instance, the Reichstag had just given in to their ultimatum of May 5 regarding final disarmament, including that of Bavaria's *Einwoherwehr* (home guard), as the newly elected German chancellor, Dr. Karl Wirth, took office. But there was still no sign of an armistice in Silesia, where the Inter-Allied Commission was attempting to bring a halt once and for all to the heavy artillery exchanges between Germans and Poles in the contested sectors of Kosel and Rosenberg as final borders between the two countries were negotiated. Far to the north, however, at least Finland and Sweden were nearing agreement over a settlement concerning the disputed Aaland Islands. Such were but a few of the problems facing the international conference at Versailles, which included the ramifications of the newly launched League of Nations, espoused by President Woodrow Wilson, but rejected by his own Congress. Meanwhile, Britain and France were still demanding greater reparations from the defeated Reich in order to meet their own debt obligations. Washington, while publicly calling for reconciliation and a more moderate approach to the Versailles process, was privately pressuring Britain in particular very hard to honor its own war debts to the United States. Pressure was occurring at a time when Britain was facing a shortage not only of coal with which to heat the homes and stoke the fires of industry (due to a devastating national coal miners' strike) but also of raw materials of all kinds, and jobs for the millions of demobbed servicemen.

Nor was the once great British Empire, now but a shaken image of its former self, able to help. Lord Buxton, the former Governor General of South Africa, for example, was in the midst of publishing his report supporting the creation of a "responsible Government for Southern Rhodesia," in brief, independence. And this situation was typical of an empire unraveling everywhere. The dominions of the British Empire, tried, bled, and utterly exhausted financially and reduced in manpower as a result of the long European war, were now politically astir, more independent-minded and more demanding, while lacking the political pride and cohesion of the empire of yore. Nowhere was this unease more evident than now in May 1921 as the premiers of the dominion members prepared for the annual Imperial Conference to be held in London the following month. Indeed, the very convening of these conferences was a source of controversy. Prime Minister William F. Massey of New Zealand, supported by Australia, was highly critical of such annual reunions in the first place, and equally resentful of their being held invariably in the capital of the empire. There should instead be a rotating venue if they were to continue to meet, with only occasional conferences in London. After all, those two countries alone had suffered 269,000 casualties in the recent war, and they were not about to let England forget that sacrifice. An old Canadian recruitment slogan of 1914—"E is the Empire for which we would die"—no longer held the same allure in this postwar era.[7]

Nor was Britain's new Secretary of State for Colonies, the forty-six-year-old firebrand Winston Churchill, MP, any more popular, coming under withering fire from the vast stretches of empire, including publications such as the *Montreal Gazette* and the *Winnipeg Free Press*, as he called for changes in the structure and work of this international union of dominions. These changes would require a tightening of its working mechanism that would among other things render the annual meeting of dominion premiers the equivalent of an "Imperial Cabinet," which he could control de facto and wield to achieve Downing Street's objectives. This "new drive for centralization" frightened everyone. If changes were to be adopted, they insisted, then they would have to be authorized first by each of the dominions' national parliaments, and not decreed unilaterally by London. They had fought hard for their independence and were not about to be manipulated for the rubber-stamping of Britain's programs.[8]

Among specific proposals, for instance, Colonial Secretary Churchill now called for a total revamping of the administration of the Middle East, as he had recently pointed out in March at the Cairo Conference, to organize the governing of the newly mandated countries assigned to both Britain and France in that region. Among other things he hoped to cut the draining costs of government by handing over much more political power to the Arabs themselves, until so recently still under the yoke of the Ottoman Empire. Thus Iraq would be made into an independent kingdom ruled by the present Emir Feisal, one of the sons of King Hussein of the Hijaz, but with the stipulation that the large Kurdish minority in the north of that country would in turn be granted its independence as well. Other new kingdoms would emerge in Jordan and Saudi Arabia. The entire British zone of the Middle East would be administered by a specially created British force policed by Indian troops.

The growing Middle Eastern problem between Jews and Muslims was also coming to the fore. France's prime minister, Alexandre Millerand, roundly criticized Britain, and Lord Balfour in particular, for having encouraged "Zionism," which Millerand denounced. He demanded an end to all Jewish immigration to the British Mandate of Palestine, although of course it was none of his business and had nothing whatsoever to do with France.

Churchill, although hardly a lifelong friend of the Jews, had been astonished and much impressed by the young Jewish farmers he had just visited in the Palestine Mandate following the Cairo Conference. He protested before the House of Commons: "I defy anybody, after seeing work of this kind, achieved by so much labour, effort and skill, to say that the British Government" should give in to the French government and renounce British policy, thereby bringing an end to Jewish immigration to the Holy Land. Such a reversal of policy would, Churchill insisted, inevitably result in this agricultural achievement being "rudely and brutally overturned by the incursion of a fanatical attack by the Arab populations from outside."[9] He had, it will be recalled, witnessed one *jihad*, or Muslim holy war, during the clash of Kitchener's army with the Mahdi's Arab forces, as the British sought to avenge the brutal death of General Gordon and to reoccupy the Sudan. Arab ferocity had shaken him. He did not want to see it repeated against the Jewish farmers he had so admired.

Nevertheless, the problems in the parts of the Middle East arising from the transformation of the recently dismantled Ottoman Empire into the new states of Lebanon, Syria, Iraq, Jordan, Palestine, Saudi Arabia, and the Yemen would continue. More British and dominion troops would be required in that vast region, and not fewer, as Winston Churchill had envisioned.

Churchill's support later in the year for the creation of "an Irish State" for Southern Ireland was not much more welcome to Westminster itself, although it finally passed the following the year. The dominions as a whole, including Australia and New Zealand, could not but be aware of the very real global disruptions and threats facing them, including the necessity of a final peace treaty with the newly created state of Turkey, Wilhelm II's ally during the previous war. If they failed to work together, they might have to send troops once more.

Germany's former colonial empire, too, required dismemberment, but the dominions strongly opposed—in vain—the handover of Berlin's Far Eastern island possessions to Japan. The "Yellow Peril" that had so raised the fears and hackles of the West in the first years of the new century continued to cause grave disquiet, especially in the Antipodes. The two "white islands" of Australia and New Zealand were isolated in a "yellow sea," thousands of miles from Europe, protected only by a very thin line of Royal Navy warships. And yet Japan, as a loyal ally during World War I—its navy having escorted these very Australians and New Zealanders in their transports to Europe—was demanding payment for services rendered, and thus German islands in the western Pacific effectively passed into Japanese hands at Versailles, over all objections.

For Japan itself the future seemed equally uncertain, even as to the most elementary question of who qualified as an ally, for the Anglo-Japanese Defence Alliance, initiated nearly two decades earlier and up for renewal within a matter of months, was still under review. Should the British decline to sign now, where would that leave Tokyo?

●

But back in London in 1921, all these vexing issues were far from almost everyone's thoughts during the ensuing swirl of events surrounding the hectic royal schedule and one of the most comprehensive tours of the capital ever experienced by a state visitor. It began at Westminster Abbey and the call by the Black Rod to attend Parliament, where the Crown Prince was given his first glimpse of the inner workings of a true democracy, the key to the British Empire, in both the House of Lords and the Commons. The lord mayor of London, accompanied by the city's lord lieutenant, naturally had their turn to welcome the royal guest at Guildhall followed by the inevitable hearty dinner at Mansion House. Across the way at Threadneedle Street the governor of the Bank of England gave the visiting entourage the half-crown tour of the vaults of the empire, including a rare glimpse of its fabled bullion rooms. A little downriver at the Tower of London, manned by its "Beefeaters" in their traditional garb, they viewed the historic prison cells where Mary Queen of Scots and Sir Walter Raleigh had awaited the executioner's sword. They saw the famed crown jewels, and then climbed up to the Tower's loftiest ramparts to see the royal ravens. A weekend visit was made to the country estate of Chequers, which Lord Lee of Fareham had placed at the disposal of the British prime minister and which he was shortly to donate to the country permanently. There a haggard, much-troubled Lloyd George did his best to entertain the royal prince, complimenting him and his country as England's "gallant ally."

The Crown Prince, already noted for his intensive military studies, would of course have to visit some of Britain's major military establishments, including Aldershot for a review of the Coldstream Guards, Sandhurst Military Academy for a trooping of the colors, and nearby Camberley where eight hundred British and Indian cavalry paraded in front of the prince before demonstrating their martial and equestrian skills. But to the surprise of the Duke of York, now his guide, it was the No. 24 RAF Squadron at Kenley Aerodrome (near London) and its three hundred aircraft that really took the prince's fancy. There he witnessed aerial acrobatics, intricate maneuvers, Bristol fighters bombing trenches, and others involved in realistic dogfights complete with spiraling planes and parachuting pilots. The tour was delayed as the prince insisted on studying the different kinds of aircraft, their armament, and the newest navigational devices, and on having long talks with their pilots. The official schedule was now well out of joint, but the prince had his aides take plenty of notes, notes he was to review carefully after returning to his country.

Back in London there were embassy receptions, a dinner hosted by the Prince of Wales at St. James's Palace, a respondent reception by the foreign minister, Lord Curzon of Kedleston, whose mansion at 1 Carlton House Terrace entertained a veritable *Who's Who* of the empire within its towering walls. The haughty Curzon, with his wealth and power, was one of the most influential statesmen of his times. The Crown Prince could not but be impressed by all that he had seen thus far, representing the height of imperial attainments, a dazzling display unmatched in any other capital of the world.

On the other hand, there were more relaxing moments as King George invited the royal visitor to the inevitable game of golf, the prince appearing in his newly tailored tweed plus fours for the first time in his life. But for all the practice he had taken, teeing off from the deck of his battleship as he crossed the Mediterranean, he was hardly a match for the king, who did his best to slice and hook to reduce the gap in their scores. The awkward, embarrassing twitches of the Crown Prince's shoulders and head, remarked upon during earlier receptions and put down to nervousness, now recurred on the fairway, hardly helping his game. These physical problems were to plague him the rest of his life.

The king saw to it that the young prince had an opportunity to visit London's theaters. In spite of his lack of fluent English, the young man seemed to enjoy thoroughly the comedy *Sybil* at Daley's Theatre starring Jose Collins, and a musical comedy, the *League of Notions*, with the delightful Dolly Sisters at the New Oxford. The prince laughed to his heart's delight for the first time since his arrival in England. If the West End had by now almost returned to its former fame, glory, and patronage, its postwar fare was still mainly on the light side, offering *The Naughty Princess* at the Adelphi, a special performance of Mary Pickford at the Palace, *Faust on Toast* at the Gaiety, Somerset Maugham's more serious *The Circle* at the Haymarket, and the "play of adventure," *Bull-Dog Drummond*, at Wyndham's, starring the popular Gerald du Maurier.

Before Hirohito left England for a visit to Scotland and France, George V bestowed upon him the Knight's Grand Cross of the Most Honoured Order of the Bath, and had him gazetted a general in Great Britain's army. The prince was almost overcome by emotion as his tailor prepared this impressive uniform. His long sojourn in the heart of the British Empire now drawing to a close, the prince made the most important symbolic visit of his official tour, arriving at Britain's greatest war memorial, the Cenotaph on Whitehall, where he was greeted by the Second Sea Lord, Admiral Sir Henry Oliver. An equerry laid a wreath of laurel, palm, and red and white carnations on the plinth, and the Crown Prince, bareheaded in army uniform, bowed deeply twice before the monument representing the blood spilt by more than 1 million men.

Hirohito's almost entirely military entourage now moved on to France. Two of that body in particular were to remain with him in senior positions over the next two decades: his cousin Prince Kan'in Kotohito and Lieutenant General Nara Takeji. While in France, Hirohito was joined by his close and favorite uncles, Princes Asaka and Higashikuni, both of whom were also to play dominant roles in his future and that of the Imperial Japanese Empire.

•

Given Hirohito's habitual diffidence and awkwardness during state and religious ceremonies in the past—due in part to the childhood meningitis that had caused a curvature of the spine, in turn resulting in the gradual sloping of one shoulder—the imperial court had been hoping that the young prince, as the first representative of the imperial Japanese family ever to appear in the West, would execute this official tour, if not with élan, then at least with dignity. The glowing praise of the international press had come as both a surprise and a relief. If some of his remarkable success had been achieved due to the rigid formality surrounding this very special Japanese envoy, a good measure was likewise due to the jovial bonhomie of his host, King George V, who was also most interested in making this sensitive occasion a success.[10]

On the other hand the purpose of this state visit, in addition to its obvious instructional nature for the future ruler of Japan, was to secure the renewal of the Anglo-Japanese Defence Alliance; but for all the smiles and hearty welcomes, it was not to be. This setback was to have complex repercussions over the next two decades. Behind the scenes, the Americans—Britain's single most important creditor between 1914 and 1918—joined by the Australians—who, like the Americans themselves, were continuing to experience a genuine "Yellow Peril" hysteria—had put pressure on the British. Money was a significant factor, for as the Americans were exerting undiplomatic pressure on London to repay its staggering war debt, Great Britain was forced to demand, in addition to war reparations from Germany, its own £2 billion war loan owed by France in particular, but also by Belgium, Italy, and Japan. Winston Churchill regretted the demise of this Anglo-Japanese alliance. "Many links were surrendered," he reflected, "which might afterwards have proved of decisive value to peace."[11] And thus it was that an almost intimate amity reverted to a more traditional suspicion and mutual distrust which would finally culminate in war.

The West did not intend to drop Japan into some diplomatic abyss, however, but rather to redirect Japanese-Western ties through a new international disarmament conference, which opened in Washington, D.C., late in 1921. This conference was led by aggressive American statesmen intent on defusing future international confrontations, by arms reduction, at the expense of the world's major navies in particular. Two of the American spokesmen, Secretary of State Charles Evans Hughes and Theodore Roosevelt, Jr., called for dramatic naval reductions of existing warships by the Allies—that is, the United States, Britain, Japan, France, and Italy—while drastically curtailing future naval construction. It sounded very sensible *if* all the "Allies" played by the same ground rules, and *if* the defeated enemies, chiefly Germany, also cooperated. Germany, on the other hand, was not a signatory, its navy instead limited by the Versailles Peace Treaty.

Many months of negotiations held in the American capital were concluded by the signing of new treaties in 1922: the Four Power Treaty, signed on February 6, 1922, by Charles Evans Hughes, Lord Balfour, Aristide Briand, and Baron Katō; and a Limitation of Armaments Treaty. The latter, proclaimed Hughes, would "end absolutely the race in competition of naval armament. At the same time it leaves the relative security of the great naval Powers unimpaired. . . . We are taking the greatest forward step in history to establish the reign of peace."[12] The aim was to reduce warships to the ratio 10:10:6, or 100 million tons for the United States, another similar amount for Great Britain, and 600,000 tons for Japan. These new limits were shortly to be reduced again by one half, much to the outrage of both American and British naval officers who had never been properly asked about their countries' defense requirements. Hughes, Roosevelt Junior, and the other civilian American team members simply acted in a vacuum, bypassing and even failing to consult the U.S. Navy's General Board, which was responsible for advising and establishing naval policy and plans for the protection of the country. The 5:5:3 ratio now required the United States to scrap or sink many of its newest battleships and cruisers, and cancel construction on fifteen others. New, powerful battleships such as the USS *Washington*, 32,500 tons and three-quarters completed, were used for *target practice* by the U.S. military and sunk off the Virginia Capes. With the exception of one or two capital ships, the entire remainder of the U.S. Navy was of pre–World War I vintage, already outgunned and well out of date. Japan in return was required to destroy eight new warships but instead merely "destroyed" eight such vessels that were still on the drawing boards. As far as aircraft carriers were concerned, they were new in concept and existence to any navy, and no restriction was put on their numbers. This same logic also applied to the better established and proven category of submarines. The only consolation for the United States was the saving of two ships under construction, the *Saratoga* and *Lexington*, which were to be converted from battle cruisers to aircraft carriers.[13]

The treaties of 1922, resulting from the Washington Conference, would in time prove to be a considerable Japanese triumph. This imbalance was particularly true of the Limitations of Armaments Treaty, which further required the United States and Great Britain to refrain from further fortification of existing defenses and naval facilities in the Pacific, including those at Singapore, the Philippines, Wake, and Guam, and from building any new facilities. Furthermore, Japan assumed control of former German islands in the Pacific, including the Marianas.

The Republican congressional majority had fought U.S. intervention in World War I and rejected America's participation in the League of Nations. Now the same interests had scuppered the most modern warships in the U.S. Navy and greatly reduced its personnel. The process of further reductions would continue throughout the 1920s and 1930s. "We are taking the greatest forward step in history to establish the reign of Peace," Charles Evan Hughes had proclaimed. In fact, the Washington Arms Limitation Conference of 1922 was to make another world war possible, thanks to the incompetence of American and British "statesmen."

•

"British General" Prince Hirohito was altogether pleased with the reception he had received in Britain; after visiting France, and finally the Vatican and King Victor Emmanuel, he boarded the battleship *Katori* and made the homeward voyage via the Indian Ocean.

This journey to the West, was of great significance both for Hirohito and the empire he would soon inherit. Clearly he could not be expected to understand very much: his tour was brief; he saw things only from the official level as a state guest; and he was further restricted by his practically nonexistent knowledge of English. Nevertheless he was to continue to follow Western affairs in far greater detail hereafter, indeed until the day of his death, and read works and newspapers in both French and English (when his skills improved). There was much he secretly admired about Britain and "the English way of life," including golf, "English" horse races, and Western jazz (otherwise forbidden everywhere in the country, even in his father's palace). Every day he ate a cooked English breakfast with fried eggs, grilled tomato, bacon (or sausage when it could be obtained), and toast. "English tea" would be served every afternoon. He had a golf course specially built on the palace grounds, and he even played his rounds in plus fours. He and his wife, Nagako,* and their children wore only European clothes (except for special Shinto or state ceremonies), while his government ministers were ordered to appear in English morning suits (tails and gray top hat).

As Prince Regent, and finally emperor, Hirohito withdrew more and more from society, and by the age of thirty that exclusion included most of the imperial family as well. Much of his leisure time was spent tinkering in a special marine laboratory he had built at the palace. He and his wife were very close, however, and had breakfast, lunch, and supper together almost every day of their lives, for unlike his predecessors, Hirohito refused to keep concubines. But although he may have played cards and enjoyed dabbling in other Western diversions, deep down, Hirohito was not only Japanese, but a Japanese emperor, whose earliest education had instilled in him the values of Meiji history and the philosophic concepts of Shintoism, Confucianism, and Zen Buddhism. His life was spent in the Far East, and his responsibilities were rooted there. He was expected to become a soldier (the royal princes all bore army and naval rank), and was brought up and educated by soldiers. Lieutenant General Nogi had conducted and supervised his primary education at the Peers' School; then Fleet Admiral Tōgō

*They were married on January 26, 1924.

Heichachirō had assumed responsibility for the equivalent of his high school studies, all of which had been dominated by military history and related subjects.[14]

When General Nogi had committed ritualistic suicide following the death of Hirohito's grandfather, the Meiji emperor whom he served, the boy cried for perhaps the only time. He had very much admired this rigid, upright disciplinarian, a Samurai of yesteryear who had lived as simply as a monk, and who had dedicated his entire life to the imperial crown.

On July 18, 1920, General Nara Takeji, a celebrated soldier in his own right and a diplomatist as well, had been appointed Hirohito's official mentor and adviser on all things military, and along with the older Admiral Tōgō would hold this position for the rest of his life. Flanked by a sailor and a soldier, both of whom he sincerely admired, Hirohito had been guided on a straight military road, with the aging but influential Field Marshal Yamagata Aritomo ever in the background as well.[15] These three men reminded Hirohito daily of the greatness of his forebears, and in particular of his grandfather, the Meiji emperor, and his military exploits. Having spent his childhood summers at army camps and naval bases, Hirohito's outlook had been well set before he left for his visit to London in 1921. It is hardly surprising that upon his return, apart from his taste for certain trappings of Western culture, Hirohito's worldview mirrored the code of the Samurai.

Two of Hirohito's younger brothers were to play roles of responsibility during his reign, beginning with Chichibu (or Yasuhito), born a year after him in 1902 and raised with him. Unlike the sickly Hirohito, whose childhood meningitis had left him bedridden or weak for many years, Chichibu was much taller, stronger, and generally more athletic. The boys were educated together, with a military emphasis, of course, but not always with the same views. Just as Hirohito was brought up in adoration of the Meiji emperor, a warrior, Chichibu, to the contrary, had found his grandfather cold and distant, and was more dismissive of the old man's person and achievements. Hirohito and Chichibu were so close in age that scuffles between them occurred from time to time. Chichibu was chastised strictly, however, and informed from the tenderest age that his elder brother was to rule the land of their forefathers one day, and therefore had to be treated with special respect. "The

Emperor is Heaven descended, divine, and sacred. He is preeminent above all his subjects. He must be reverenced and is inviolable . . . [and] the law has no power to hold him accountable to it. . . . He shall not be made a topic of derogatory comment nor [even] one of discussion," as one counsellor reminded Chichibu, a strong-minded, rebellious, and defiant young man.[16] On the other hand, the younger sibling was given greater freedom and latitude in his personal life than Hirohito, the heir apparent, who was constantly "in training" preparing for the great role that awaited him one day. But both boys continued to be trained for the highest military positions and received the traditional basic military education. It is not clear whether or not they, like all other Japanese soldiers, were required to execute bayonet practice on live pigs. (In later years the Japanese used Korean, Chinese, British, American, and Australian POWs.) While Hirohito was never considered strong, had a problem controlling involuntary muscular twitches, and became stoop-shouldered on one side, Chichibu excelled in all sports, including swimming and skating.

Hirohito's grand European tour had been deemed such a success for both the Japanese government and the imperial family that a similar, if more extensive, program was then prepared for Chichibu. As the latter was brought up speaking fluent English, it was intended that he pass a year of study at Oxford University.

Upon his arrival in England early in 1925, he too was warmly greeted by King George, and like his brother before him, given a fairly extensive tour of the realm and then of the Continent, after which he settled in at Magadalen College, Oxford, with its expansive deer park. Chichibu dressed like the other students, arrived punctually at his tutorials, and no doubt donned the inevitable boater when punting on the Cherwell. Despite the anti-Japanese steps taken at Versailles, and by both the United States and Great Britain, the Japanese imperial family nevertheless remained strongly pro-British and pro-Western at this stage, and those roots might have continued to develop had not Chichibu been recalled to Japan after just a few weeks because his father, Yoshihito, Emperor Taisho, was gravely ill. Leaving abruptly, Chichibu sailed from Southampton, but even before reaching America was informed of his father's death.[17]

In New York, Prince Chichibu was greeted by Ambassador Matsudaira Tsuneo, a close friend of the imperial family. In Washington, D.C., the prince was introduced to President Calvin Coolidge. A thoroughly modern young man, Chichibu was naturally attracted by Ambassador Matsudaira's seventeen-year-old daughter, Setsuko, who was "Westernized" down to modern dress, bobbed hair, and education at the Quaker Sidwell Friends School. She enjoyed dancing and tennis, as did the prince.

Chichibu then had to resume his return journey to Japan to take up his new official position at court while continuing with his military studies. His elder brother, Hirohito, was now de facto emperor of Japan, though his coronation was delayed for the time being. Meanwhile, Chichibu and Setsuko were married and moved into a wing of the Asaka Palace within the sprawling grounds of the Imperial Palace's 240-acre site in Tokyo. The young couple danced the Charleston, outraged their relatives by roller-skating down palace corridors, wore the latest Western clothing, drank whiskey and soda, and built Japan's first squash court.[17] But they had less and less contact with Hirohito.

The new emperor's second brother, Prince Takamatsu, was born in 1905, and given the usual court/military education before entering the Naval Academy, followed by intensive courses at the Imperial Navy's Torpedo, Aviation, and Gunnery schools. He too was brought up in a "Western"-oriented manner, including music, dress, and the custom of afternoon tea. Although Takamatsu was a homosexual, as an imperial prince he was required to marry. His bride, the spoiled and temperamental Kikuko, was no doubt a match for him. In 1930 the young couple duly made their tour of the West, which included the by now traditional reception at Buckingham Palace, where Prince Takamatsu presented King George with the Order of the Rising Sun.

Following an extensive tour of many of the European capitals, Takamatsu and his bride boarded the luxury liner *Aquitania* for America, a country that had long interested him and about which he had read a good deal. Unlike his brothers, who neither liked the United States nor were at ease with the press, Takamatsu chatted easily with journalists upon reaching New York, explaining, "I look forward to seeing all of the things that make for the greatness of America. . . ."[18]

But here he broke from the traditional tour and for the first time became the instrument of American political and financial interests.

He no doubt was startled to learn from his ambassador that he was to be given a traditional American ticker-tape parade down Fifth Avenue, accompanied by a band and the U.S. Cavalry. All of this was laid on by the House of Morgan and the president of the United States, both of whom had strong financial investments in Japan and in some of its recent colonial conquests. Indeed, upon reaching Washington, D.C., Prince Takamatsu found President Herbert Hoover waiting at Union Station to welcome him to the capital and to escort him to an official state banquet at the White House. An even larger and more splendid reception awaited Takamatsu at the Mayflower Hotel, where the dinner was attended by fifty of the nation's most influential men. There he had an opportunity to chat with America's highly decorated and colorful, if already controversial, army chief of staff, the fifty-one-year-old Douglas MacArthur. They were not destined to meet again for another fifteen years, and then under very different circumstances indeed.[19]

A third brother, Mikasa, was born in 1914, thirteen years after Hirohito, and was educated for a traditional military career. Despite the usual family poor eyesight, he completed the Military Staff College course in 1941 and was to serve in the air force through the later war years.

As far as the West was concerned, the effect of the combined tours of the imperial princes had been most positive. They had certainly given the leaders of the West the impression of a courteous, very traditional and stable royal family. And this image of the royal family—and, by extension, of Japan—continued to be cultivated when Joseph Grew arrived in Tokyo as the new American ambassador in June 1932.

•

The recently commissioned fast aircraft carriers, the 815-foot *Kaga* and the 817-foot *Akagi*, the pride of the fleet and of the emperor, stood out amongst the other 206 warships and 39 submarines assembled for this unique occasion. At 43,700 tons and 42,800 tons, respectively, and with a total of 153 aircraft, these ships were the giants of the fleet and of the world. Only the American carriers *Lexington* and *Saratoga* equaled them in size. The two Japanese carriers would become famous—or infamous—thirteen years hence on a Sunday morning off the Hawaiian Islands. Forty-five thousand crewmen—more than half the entire Imperial

Navy—and their flag officers stood rigidly at attention in their dress uniforms on this December 2, 1928: 130 modern warplancs flew over the imperial reviewing stand in Yokahama where the newly enthroned Shōwa Emperor, Hirohito, stood on the dais.[20] Below him stood the princes Chichibu, Takamatsu, and the young Mikasa; other key members of the imperial family, including Prince Asaka Takahiko, Prince Higashikuni, Prince Takeda, Prince Kan'in, and Prince Konoe; Admirals Nagumo, Yamamoto, Katō, Nagano, Nomura, and the aging Tōgō; and Generals Yamagata, Nara, and Tōjō. This was one of the rare occasions when these men, all to be associated with the war to come, were seen together.

Hitherto largely dependent on the British, Germans, French, and Americans for warships and planes, Japanese industry was already producing its own carriers, battleships, cruisers, destroyers, submarines, and aircraft.[21] Two days earlier, the Japanese air force and army had presented the emperor with an equally impressive exhibition of collective might during a 40,000-man troop review at the Yoyogi Parade Ground in Tokyo—most of these were veterans of foreign campaigns—accompanied by a flyover of hundreds of fighters and bombers.[22]

These events to commemorate the enthronement and deification of Hirohito as the 124th emperor of Japan now concluded the ceremonies that had begun weeks before. Earlier, addressing 2,700 civil and military officials, most of them hearing, if not seeing, the twenty-seven-year-old Hirohito for the first time, he pronounced his philosophy of rule for the land:

> From the viewpoint of national affairs, I sincerely wish to bring harmony to the people by guiding them benevolently to the goal of good, thus promoting the further prosperity of the country. As for foreign relations, I sincerely wish to maintain world peace abroad and advance goodwill among the nations through diplomacy, thereby contributing to the welfare of humanity.[23]

Words of hope and peace . . . before a backdrop of a massive arms display. Earlier, at the age of nineteen, he had dwelt on the same issue, writing privately: "I must fulfill this important duty [working with the League of Nations] to establish permanent peace in the world." But he followed this with the question: "How shall I go about carrying out this duty? Without military preparedness, profitable diplomatic negotiations will be difficult. Also, we cannot become a rich country unless we make industry and transportation flourish. . . . If we do not achieve this, we will be unable to keep up with the Great Powers."[24] Hirohito's Japan had to be a great power, on an equal footing with the other world giants. That was his vision of "peace."

Now no longer a mere prince-in-waiting but the director of an empire, he had to make major decisions to match his words. He had listened carefully to statesman Prince Konoe Fumimaro expound on the solution of Japan's dramatic economic problems, and the concomitant issues of "war" and "real peace." "Unequal distribution of land and natural resources cause war," Konoe had said. "We cannot achieve real peace until we change the present irrational international state of affairs. . . . As a result of our one million annual increase in population, our national economic life is heavily burdened. We cannot [afford to] wait for a rationalizing adjustment of the world system."[25] Therefore, Japan would have to expand overseas, which would then solve so many of these problems. If in 1928 Hirohito was not yet fully in agreement with all that Prince Konoe said, nevertheless he had been educated since birth by the military, for a military life, based on military values. He had already begun to fill his own primary requirement by establishing Japan on the road to full "military preparedness" as he looked out over his powerful fleet, a fleet that would soon be doubled, then doubled again under his reign.

To the serious foreign observers present during his famous discourse before the nation's highest officials, Hirohito's précis of future domestic and foreign policies was most disturbing in light of the problems besetting the country. As Prince Konoe had rightly observed, the Japanese birth rate was soaring out of control, and no one had proposed a way to resolve the dual problems of feeding and employing this burgeoning population. Nor were there sufficient health facilities available for the masses. A large number of highly educated people would be required for the economic and industrial expansion envisioned, and yet that problem had not been addressed by Hirohito or anyone else. Most of the country's arable land lay in the hands of a few powerful men, chiefly representing the old aristocratic families, and those few peasants who retained land were taxed into poverty while the government failed to provide food for the nation. It was becoming apparent that given the present crisis, most of the food and raw materials needed would have to be imported. As Emperor Hirohito saw it, Konoe's solution of foreign conquest to gain access to these products was the only feasible one.

Hirohito could hardly forget the tumult that rocked Japan between 1918 and 1921, prior to his tour of Europe. It began with the upheaval of 1918, which along with famine resulted in thousands of deaths and nationwide riots. But instead of turning over more land to the peasants for rice production, for instance, the government called in 57,000 troops to suppress them. Instead of aiding the farmers and production, the government was imprisoning or killing agricultural producers. The ensuing bloody riots over workplace issues at the Tokyo Artillery Arsenal, at the Kamaishi iron mine, at the Ashio copper mine, at the Yawata Steel Company, and at the Kawasaki-Mitsubishi Shipyards, were hardly sanguine harbingers for either the people or the economy. More troops were brought in to crush every one of those strikes.[26]

Instead of recognizing the urgent necessity of introducing reforms to the whole of the nation's economy and institutions, the government chose to crush all problems—economic, political, and above all, human. In so doing, it crushed any possibility of improvement in society and the economy in the foreseeable future. What was already manifestly bad could only worsen, given the imperial government's attitude to reform. Japan's grave economic problems would spill over to affect the entire Far East, for Japan's solution to its own economic and social woes would be to expand and conquer abroad and inflict those same woes upon the peoples of neighboring countries . . . at bayonet point.

The problems of prewar Japan—famine, riots, strikes, unemployment, ineffective forms of government and administration—occurred in part because the big commercial, financial, and industrial conglomerates known as *zaibatsu* (e.g., Mitsui, Iwasaka, Yasuda, Mitsubishi, Sumitomo, and later Nissan) that dominated the entire economy were inviolable, protected by the state and the emperor himself. Several members of the imperial family were linked directly or indirectly to the *zaibatsu*, as were the *genrō*, or senior statesmen of the past, and many very senior military officers. The emperor himself was traditionally under the influence of the *genrō*.

The banking system was equally corrupt, and worse, incompetently managed. Indeed, the Japanese banking system was built on quicksand: the president of the Bank of Japan, Inoue Junnosuke, an adviser to the emperor, seems to have been ignorant of the most elementary principles of sound banking. There was no shortage of Anglo-American investments and loans to Japan, including those made by Baring Brothers, Kuhn & Loeb, J. P. Morgan, John D. Rockefeller, Schiff, and Warburg.[27] But much of that money was siphoned off by the heads of the powerful financial conglomerates, military and government officials. As one expert later summed up the situation, then and in postwar Japan, "Corruption in Japan is legitimatized by its systematic penetration. It is so highly organized and has become so much a part of the extra-legal ways of the Japanese system that most citizens do not [and did not] recognize it for what it was."[28] Bribes were considered to be a basic part of doing business in the country, including among the banks themselves. The loans made by the banks to industry, railways, large commercial enterprises, or simply to important individuals—"honorable friends"—were not secured. Collateral was rarely required or even mentioned, and credit checks almost never made. It was hardly surprising then that some eight hundred Japanese banks—more than half of the total—collapsed in 1927, two full years before the crash on Wall Street. To save the entire national economy from disintegration, the government had to intervene with an injection of some 2 billion yen.[29] Banks were not solvent and the entire system so defective as to equal a gaping hole in the side of a rapidly sinking ship, one which even the most powerful pumps could not save. The aftereffects may be seen to this day.

But any attempt at economic or political reform was literally outlawed, as was any criticism of the government and of the emperor himself. Such criticism was tantamount to "revolt," treated as treason and punishable by the death penalty, thanks to legislation known as the "Peace Preservation Law."[30] Hirohito himself, despite the information laid before him and his own personal knowledge of the inefficiency and corruption riddling the system, was for all that terrified of any major change in society at any level. Real reform meant sweeping aside the entire "system" and beginning from scratch, and that would inevitably involve the crown itself.

There was no hope of addressing these many issues by political means. The Japanese parliament, the Diet, itself far too often simply reflected imperial wishes. In theory, the governing ministers only remained in office as long as the emperor himself so agreed. The granting of universal male suffrage in 1925 had in reality been meaningless. Nothing had changed, apart from appearances. One party controlled politics, and one emperor controlled all.

And now in the year of his coronation, 1928, Hirohito himself authorized the extension of the Peace Preservation Law and the application of the death penalty (without the right to trial by jury) to include any protests or agitation against private property in any form—whether in industry or on the land—or for criticizing government ministers and policy. Opposing political parties literally were not permitted to "oppose" the government, question, or debate. The nation's press was equally muzzled. The enactment of the "deification" of Emperor Hirohito now, which utterly amazed the Western heads of government who had recently entertained this young man, further reinforced the suppression of opposition in Japan. It would now be considered sacrilegious to attack, in any form whatsoever, the Shinto-appointed god-ruler of Imperial Japan, much as had been the case of attacks against the Vatican and the Catholic Church during the Spanish Inquisition (1478–ending in the nineteenth century). The formerly diffident, seemingly good-natured Crown Prince of 1921 had within a matter of seven years become unapproachable, unreproachable, and as infallible as the pope, no longer a mere human being but a god beyond the reach of any authority. "All religions are extremely weak and none furnishes a foundation of the State," the political sage Itō Hiōrohumi had declared in 1921. Therefore, Hirohito replaced that missing element, he argued, reminding the people of the emperor's "divinity" and position above all laws.[31] And the Meiji constitution of Hirohito's grandfather had long before established that "the Emperor is sacred and inviolable."[32]

The Crown Prince's most influential teacher in international law, Professor Tachi Sakutarō of the Tokyo Imperial University Law Faculty, had brought him down from the heavenly realm when it came to inculcating realpolitik views regarding international conflicts. War in general, Tachi had taught the young prince, was always legal, never illegal, and that in fact "established international law" had been an invention of the West to subvert the interests of the state. He had also taught young Hirohito that the right of self-defense permitted the launching of a war in order to expand the country's territory (to deal with excess population) or to protect the lives and property of the Japanese living in other countries.[33] Hirohito had been instructed by several other university professors as well, including those in the fields of philosophy and economics, science and history. But it was the lasting memory of his mentor General Nogi and the legal teachings and interpretations of Professor Tachi that remained with Hirohito now in 1928 and in the future. According to them, the state, Japan, had the right to do *anything* it required to protect its interests, and when such a policy was officially espoused by an emperor who was at once "sacred and inviolable," the populace must follow his lead, wherever it might take them, without troubling doubts. Japan was not a democracy, but rather an authoritarian state, blessed by the gods.

If the system did not allow for any real dissonance or discord by the masses, protest could nevertheless be felt within the small ruling elite, by respected aristocratic ministers, or more importantly by factions of military officers opposing state policy and aims. And however illegal it was, such factions were about to demonstrate their real force, with the ability of bringing down the walls of the empire once and for all.

But there were also challenges beyond Japanese shores in the Far East. As has been seen, some Japanese leaders, such as Konoe, had insisted upon the right to expand, to conquer neighboring states in order to meet the economic, industrial, and social requirements of the Japanese state. This contention had already brought them into conflict with Western powers who were also vying for positions in the Far East, including the Dutch, the French, and the British. But it was the Russians who had proven the most actively aggressive by the turn of the nineteenth century. Tsar Nicholas II had pushed the Trans-Siberian Railway to the rim of the Pacific, and this act led ultimately to the Russo-Japanese War of 1904–05, and the overwhelming Japanese naval victory. The Russians, every bit as stubborn as the Japanese, persisted in the Far East, attempting to expand southward into China and Manchuria, the very places Japan coveted for itself. With Soviet garrisons now lining the frontiers of the Mongolian People's Republic and Siberia, and given Japanese interests in that same region, Hirohito was about to find himself forced to take actions he had never anticipated.

CHAPTER II

The World in Flux

"It is almost impossible that there should not be an armed clash between two such different civilizations."

—*Henry Stimson, U.S. Secretary of War, 1928*[1]

"You didn't have to tell Turner much. He was usually one jump ahead of you."

—*U.S. Admiral Royal Ingersoll (recalled after the war)*[2]

"Captain Turner handled the extensive entertainment program while in Japan with commendable ease, skill and grace. He spoke well and was a credit to the Navy," Rear Admiral Royal Ingersoll reported to Washington, where the president had followed Turner's mission with unusual interest.[3] Given Japanese sensibilities and unpredictability, one faux pas on Turner's part might very well have provoked an international crisis, or even a military clash. After his tour of duty aboard the heavy cruiser *Astoria*, and partly in recognition of his excellent work on this delicate mission in Japan, Kelly Turner was ordered to Washington, D.C., in October 1940.

There he was informed that he was to assume the direction of the navy's influential War Plans Division, and was being promoted to flag rank on Roosevelt's personal orders. He would be serving under the new secretary of the navy, Frank Knox, and would report directly to Chief of Naval Operations (CNO) Admiral Harold "Betty" Stark.[4] Turner would now be responsible for distilling the actual state of affairs throughout the world, and for recommending the role to be played by the U.S. Navy in coordination with the rest of the military. In brief, he was responsible to the CNO and to the president of the United States for anticipating and preparing the navy for the next threat to America and the West. These were no longer the war games carried out at the Naval War College at Newport, where he had taught, or the annual "fleet problems" (or exercises). He would now be dealing with events that might require U.S. military intervention in the very near future. Working alongside Turner in Stark's office were Rear Admiral Leigh Noyes, director of Communications; Rear Admiral Walter Anderson, director of Naval Intelligence; as well as Turner's former commanding officer and now CNO Stark's second in command, Admiral Roy Ingersoll.[5]

These officers were hardly strangers to one another, and if they had very little in common in private life, here they were bound by their dedication to the U.S. Navy and by the necessity of preparing it to meet any threat facing the nation. Intelligent and strong-minded, they were not easy men to work with. Turner had been selected by Stark for this prestigious post on the basis of his exceptional, proven abilities, and not for a "politically correct" personality or attitude. Kelly Turner had never been noted for his charm and humor.

Official Washington was in the grip of war fever following Germany's startlingly successful blitzkrieg, which resulted in the conquest of most of Western Europe in May and June of 1940 and concluded with the unexpected surrender of France and its entire armed forces on June 22. The United States, like Great Britain, was stunned and caught completely off guard. This was one eventuality they had not anticipated. The France that had fought so valiantly for nearly forty-nine months during World War I had given up after less than two months this time around. Britain was in the worst position, of course, suddenly isolated against the combined armed forces of Germany and Italy, with German artillery and warplanes now on the cliffs of Calais, a mere twenty-two miles from English shores.

The situation in the Mediterranean was hardly more encouraging. British troops in North Africa were thrown back into Egypt, and the Germans threatened both Cairo and the vital Suez Canal. At the other end of the Mediterranean, the bastion of Gibraltar, too, was in grave danger. The British feared the advance of a German army through Spain and Portugal, aided possibly by German bombers in French Morocco. Malta was under almost daily siege and Alexandria, also, under attack. To the northeast, Greece was under threat, bringing Axis troops and aircraft even closer. If the Germans and Italians were to succeed in closing off the Mediterranean at both ends, they could easily link their forces to the Japanese navy in the Indian Ocean, thus cutting Britain's lifeline to the Orient and to its own forces in the Mediterranean.

The fall of France had much more immediate significance for the United States. In June 1940, Roosevelt had succeeded in convincing a major conference of Latin American Republics held at Havana, Cuba, to adopt a policy of "non-neutral neutrality," in hopes of shoring up and enforcing the Monroe Doctrine that prescribed North and South America as American preserves to the exclusion of European interference. The intention was to deny the Axis military machine access to, and domination of, "American" skies and waters, both north and south. This was no mere theoretical threat, for the Germans were already very active in South America, where they had large, well-established and highly influential communities from Brazil to Argentina.

The German menace was at once doubled when the French abandoned the British in mid-battle in June 1940, for unlike the conquered Czechs and the Poles, the French did not fly their air force over to Britain,* and there was a very real fear of Paris handing over its pristine French navy to the Axis powers. France also caused considerable anxiety in Washington now because of the proximity and strategic position of its colonies and possessions across the world, in particular its naval ports and warships in the Caribbean, a mere stone's throw from the American states bordering the Gulf of Mexico, the U.S. base at Guantánamo, Cuba, and installations in the American territory of Puerto Rico. If the Germans controlled these French possessions, they had the capability of destroying or seizing the Panama Canal, at once dividing the U.S. Navy in two and playing havoc with commerce. The large, unprotected Dutch oil refineries on the islands of Aruba and Curaçao could easily be seized by a fuel-hungry German navy.

*Later, French pilots, flying recently purchased U.S. warplanes, bombed and strafed American and British troops in North Africa and in Syria.

Should France open its port at Martinique to German submarines and warships, and permit the Luftwaffe to operate from that island, all of America would be vulnerable to attack. Washington, of course, could not even be sure that French warships at Martinique might not "collaborate" with the Axis in such attacks.

Far to the north, the tiny French islands of St. Pierre and Miquelon, just off the southern coast of Newfoundland, could pose similar problems threatening the main northern shipping lanes between North America and the British Isles. If the Japanese then entered the war, joining the Axis, all American coasts could be threatened simultaneously. Indeed, so critical was the situation that even Colonel Charles Lindbergh, recently decorated by the Nazi government and strongly anti-British—the first among many powerful isolationists recommended to Congress the necessity of quickly building an air force of at least ten thousand warplanes with which to protect U.S. shores, including the isolated territories of Alaska, Hawaii, and the Philippines. As for the even more vulnerable Australia and New Zealand, defending them would prove a nightmare; indeed, they might have to be abandoned altogether.

•

The question of a possible war with Japan was hardly new. In fact, the U.S. Navy had been carrying out fleet problems and war games based on just such an assumption since the turn of the century, at the strong prompting of a vigilant President Theodore Roosevelt. The basic strategy for such a war, a drive across the central Pacific, was laid down in "War Plan Orange" (orange being the color designated for Japan in war games, blue for the United States). Although no such war plan was ever officially acknowledged in writing by either the president or the Congress, the secretary of the navy had prepared these maneuvers since 1924. Each year different fleet problems presented different threats, including attacks against the West Coast, the Panama Canal, or the Philippines; but little attention was paid to the South Pacific until 1939. During maneuvers in 1928, American carriers under the command of Admiral Joseph "Bull" Reeves, including the *Langley* and *Lexington*, took Pearl Harbor by complete surprise and "bombed" and "destroyed" U.S. naval and air force installations there.[6] Captain Jack Towers, commanding the *Langley*, had helped prepare the master plan and was pleased with the results: the "attackers" had achieved what so many of the flag officers had called an impossibility. As for Lieutenant Marc "Pete" Mitscher, the senior flight officer aboard the *Lexington*, he was left in a most reflective mood, for carriers were his very life.[7]

Then on Sunday, September 7, 1932, Towers once again participated in launching a predawn attack on Pearl Harbor from the northwest, directed by Admiral Harry E. Yarnell and Captain Ernest King, and once again the U.S. Navy and Air Force were caught napping. In Honolulu, a Japanese spy made notes of everything and passed them on to general headquarters in Tokyo, which later duplicated the 1932 simulated attack and that of 1938—this time in earnest—on another Sunday, three years hence.[8]

Clearly the American military had a very short memory. As early as 1925, Towers had called for an effective long-range aviation policy, arguing that aviation was "not only the eyes of the Navy, but also its good right arm." It did not take much imagination, he continued, "to see the day when it may be *both* arms."[9] Turner, along with Admiral William Moffett, studied the 1928 Fleet Problem and was greatly impressed. As he was to play a major role as a commander in the Pacific during World War II, a brief sketch of his career might prove of some interest at this point.

•

Richmond Kelly Turner was born in Portland, Oregon, on May 27, 1885, the scion of pioneers who had emigrated from England to the colony of Maryland early in the eighteenth century. As prosperous members of the Church of England, they had received a land grant of twelve square miles in Caroline County, some fifty miles from the present American capital. When Kelly Turner's great-great-grandfather abandoned the Church of England for the Methodist Church, it caused a split within the clan; Kelly Turner's branch broke away, moving west until it reached Portland, where the admiral's father, Enoch, met and married Laura Kelly, the daughter of a prosperous farmer. Like the Turners, the Kellys had come to the colonies in the eighteenth century, but as Methodists in their case, from Northern Ireland.

After the birth of Kelly Turner in Oregon, Enoch Turner soon moved his family to the Stockton area of California, where Richmond Kelly

Turner—one of seven surviving children—was educated. Education was in fact a hallmark of the family and given high priority by his parents. Enoch had taught school and later edited a small newspaper, the first of the Turners to leave the land. Five of the seven Turner siblings later became teachers as well.[10] It was a somber but close and loyal family, brought up as strict Methodists. If later in life Admiral Kelly Turner rarely smiled, and was not noted for a sense of humor, nevertheless the brothers and sisters were dedicated to one another throughout their lives.

Turner was a good student in high school and easily passed the entrance exams to the U.S. Naval Academy. At the age of nineteen he was one of 297 midshipmen to arrive at Annapolis, Maryland, on June 13, 1904. Among the new friends he made there were Marc "Pete" Mitscher and Tom Kinkaid, both of whom he would be working with closely during World War II. He followed the usual courses in math, engineering, history, literature, and seamanship. During the annual "Summer Practice Cruise" aboard a fleet comprising battleships, cruisers, monitors, and the Academy's sailing ship USS *Severn*, the midshipmen applied their seamanship previously learned at anchor, including navigation and gunnery. Turner, who later was to prove one of the finest gunnery officers of the navy, was taught this art by Lieutenant Ernest King. Kelly Turner graduated fourth in the Class of 1908, the Academy's yearbook summing up the young Californian as enjoying a "love of adventure and . . . a game of 'draw' [poker]. . . . He has served the class well in different capacities and is . . . a busy man with hardly time to catch a smoke."[11] Apart from the interest in cards, it was to prove a surprisingly accurate picture of the future admiral.

After graduating from the Academy "with distinction," Kelly Turner served aboard several cruisers in the Atlantic, including the *Milwaukee* and finally the *West Virginia*. He was transferred to the Armored Cruiser Squadron of the Pacific and sailed past the Solomon Islands to New Guinea and the Admiralty Islands in the Bismarck Archipelago. The squadron's mission was to establish new coaling stations. Turner was assigned to the fleet's Intelligence Board, where he helped prepare the first chart ever of Narest in Western Marus Island. This proved a good introduction to the western and southern Pacific waters, which Turner was later to get to know very well indeed.

"Let me tell you," he wrote his mother, "it gets hot down there."[12] For a young man from central California, where temperatures were frequently well above 100° Fahrenheit, that was quite a complaint. It was also a typical Turner understatement, brief and to the point. He was interested in the basic facts, not color or drama; and he rarely left the ship when in port. When not preparing charts, he served as a gun division officer. From Manila, the squadron made its way to Japan, and it was at Nagasaki that Kelly Turner first came into contact with the Japanese—"a really civilized people," as he described them to his mother. But since leaving Honolulu, "except for one day in Manila, I have spent every bit of time on board ship, doing nothing but stand my watches and work on my guns. It has been mighty interesting too. . . ." In August 1910, as an ensign earning $170 a month, Turner got married. When he was not working, he was usually reading the works of classical naval enthusiasts such as Mahan, Darriers, Knapp, and Bogan, along with the various books required for a series of naval correspondence courses. Within a few years he would be ranked number one for the Class of 1908 on the official *Naval Register*, a position he would hold for the rest of his career.

Turner's subsequent postings included a stint of postgraduate work at the Academy in 1914; a special assignment aboard a gunboat for police work in the Dominican Republic (including an armed landing party involved in a firefight); and terms as a gunnery officer on an impressive list of battleships, including Admiral Henry Mayo's Atlantic Fleet flagship, the *Pennsylvania*, and Captain William Moffett's *Mississippi*, which resulted in a close friendship between Turner and that captain. Rear Admiral Crayson Carter later recalled the young officer at this time: "Kelly had the admiration and respect of all on board, which generated complete confidence in his leadership. His great industry (he came closer to working 18 hours a day than any person I have ever known) and brilliant intellect justified beyond a doubt the high regard in which we held him." And as for his character, "I don't recall his ever showing any mean or petty streak when [someone's] shortcoming came to his notice. He was unselfish, the good of the Navy was his only thought. . . . As I have said, he was all serious business."[13]

Vice Admiral Newton McCully fully confirmed this positive view, for the most part. "His judgment is extraordinarily sound," he pronounced, but added, "Very tenacious of his opinions. . . . Individual ability too strong to make a good subordinate." McCully concluded however that "in actual war, he would be invaluable," describing Turner as "thoroughly capable, resolute and bold."[14]

Turner's career mirrored that of many of his classmates. He passed the Naval War College course and was named head of the Naval Gun Factory at Washington, D.C., and later worked at the Bureau of Ordnance there. Turner commanded the destroyer *Mervine*, drawing the criticism of one young ensign, who complained of Kelly Turner's "invincible determination to make a happy efficient destroyer over into a taut battleship,"[15] which Turner naturally took for a compliment.

At the age of forty-two Turner did the unexpected when he decided to go into naval aviation. After earning his golden wings at Pensacola, he was promoted and named the commanding officer of the recently created Naval Aircraft Squadron of the U.S. Asiatic Fleet in China, making him responsible for an enormous area comprising Japan, China, and the Philippines. Arriving at Manila in January 1928, he was disturbed to learn that this "squadron" in fact consisted of thirty-two aircraft of all classes, including trainers and seaplanes, and only five other pilots. The planes for the most part lacked basic spare parts and were given a very meager fuel allowance. It was hardly encouraging; but the navy's budget was dwindling annually—and this was even before the Wall Street Crash of 1929. Realities were realities.

Turner had been fascinated by the Far East ever since his first tour of duty after leaving the Academy. Although he had been too young to serve aboard Theodore Roosevelt's Great White Fleet visit of nineteen American battleships to Japan in 1907, he had followed events there closely, including the earlier Russo-Japanese War of 1904–05 in which Admiral Tōgō had destroyed Tsar Nicholas II's entire navy. He had also followed the continuing competition between Russia and Japan for control of northern territories in the Far East, after Russia's Trans-Siberian Railway reached the sea and began consolidating holdings there.

As early as the 1890s the Japanese military had demonstrated unusual aggression in every direction, beginning with the seizure of Formosa (or Taiwan), which China ceded to Tokyo in 1895 by the Treaty of Shimonoseki, followed by Japan's annexation of Amami and the Ryukyu Islands (including Okinawa), and finally by Japan's invasion and occupation of Korean in 1905, which gave Japan the foothold on the Asian continent it had long wanted. It was no coincidence that an anxious President Theodore Roosevelt decided to "show the flag" with the American fleet in 1907, in order to protect the recently acquired American territory of the Philippines. "I am exceedingly anxious to impress upon the Japanese that I have nothing but the friendliest possible intentions towards them, but I am not afraid of them and that [they must learn that] the United States will no more submit to bullying than it will [itself] bully," Roosevelt declared at that time.[16] The voyage of the world's largest, most modern fleet—10,000 miles to Tokyo and ultimately 46,000 miles around the world—was a startling achievement in itself. It was a demonstration that even a very distant "enemy" could now be reached, that a large naval force could master the very complicated logistics of such an undertaking, including the coaling and victualing involved, all without a major breakdown or mishap. Roosevelt had every right to be anxious about Japanese intentions concerning the Philippines, but after impressing them by the circumnavigation of the world, he then weakened his stance by deciding not to maintain a major Pacific Fleet at Manila Bay for fear of provoking Tokyo with the excuse for escalating violence in that direction. It would prove a very great error on the president's part, because that weakness itself eventually encouraged Tokyo to further escalations.

The Japanese continued to make their presence felt everywhere, literally in every direction in the Far East, even in the Philippines, where American troops expected an invasion. One recent West Point graduate on a surveying exercise in Luzon, Second Lieutenant Henry "Hap" Arnold, was astonished at their arrogance, as Japanese army surveyors literally followed his own team, taking photos and making their own surveys. "We really expected Japan to invade the Philippines at any minute. . . . Men slept with two hundred rounds of ammunition at the foot of their beds. This feeling was not the hysteria of greenhorns or recruits. . . . The Japanese, methodically and almost openly, *were* making war preparations all around us."[17] Japanese teams were also to be found in Hong Kong, Singapore, the Dutch East Indies, and elsewhere. Teddy Roosevelt's well-intended quid pro quo—abandoning Manila as a major base to encourage Japanese cooperation—had been a failure. On the other hand, the president's decision to take up the building of the Panama Canal, where France had not succeeded, was more than a saving grace. When the canal was opened in August 1914, on the very eve of a world war, it completely redefined U.S. naval logistics and strategy, cutting thousands of miles and weeks of sailing time to and from the Pacific.

•

Kelly Turner had of course followed all these events closely over the years and knew what to expect when he took over the command of the Naval Aircraft Squadron in 1928, and he intended to keep his eyes open as he prepared the squadron for its new role in the Far East. His few pilots were always in the air so long as the gasoline allowance lasted, observing Tokyo's Kwantung Army pouring over the frontier from North Korea, scouting the Chinese coastline and the rivers inland. As a result of Japanese aggression and growing military might, so anxious was Admiral Mark Bristol, in command of the U.S. Asiatic Fleet by 1928, that he placed the entire fleet on alert and prepared to evacuate American nationals in China if necessary.[18] After the revelation of Prime Minister Tanaka's orders to assassinate a powerful Chinese warlord, Chang Tso-lin, that year, anything seemed possible.[19]

Turner trained his pilots to accustom themselves to the unusual weather conditions in the Far East, including erratic typhoon schedules, which limited the amount of flying possible. There were also severe problems with radio comomunications due to frequent heavy thunderstorms.

Among Turner's innovations were aerial surveillance and the preparation of aerial charts, starting from his base in China at Chefoo (Yentai) and moving along the Chinese coast. Although his primary responsibility was covering Kwantung troop movements flowing northward from Korea and Japan, Turner paid close attention to mapping of the long, complicated coastlines of the major islands of the Philippines. His squadron photographed Mindoro, Mindanao, the west coast of Luzon from Lingayen Gulf to San Bernardino Strait, and the east coast of Luzon. In addition, he mapped the country's principal ports and possible sites of amphibious landings by an enemy force. In particular, he studied and focused on Lingayen Gulf and Lopez Island in Lamon Bay, 125 miles southeast of Manila, which were likely to be targeted by the Japanese in the event of an invasion.

Having shown these new air charts and his personal analyses to Admiral Bristol—who fully concurred in every respect—Turner reported his conclusions officially in 1929: "It is customary among Naval officers [i.e., himself and Bristol] to consider it practically settled that the ORANGE forces will be landed on the shores of the Lingayen Gulf."[20] As both aviator and sailor, Turner had taken into consideration weather patterns, currents, tides, water depth, underwater obstacles, possible ports for seaplane tenders, and so on. And he was right on the mark when it came to anticipating where the Japanese landings of December 1941 and early 1942 would take place. Turner included twenty intelligence reports in his Annual Report and strongly recommended that the Office of Naval Intelligence issue his findings and maps to the appropriate naval authorities as a part of an updated "intelligence portfolio for the Far East."[21] A few years later these aerial reconnaissance maps were to prove invaluable to General MacArthur, the air force, and especially to Admirals Bill Halsey, Raymond Spruance, Marc Mitscher, and Turner himself, saving them many months of work as they prepared for fresh campaigns in that region.

Kelly Turner also insisted on a state of combat readiness for his squadron and stressed gunnery practice and night flying, at a time when both were largely ignored, apart from one or two other prescient commanders including Jack Towers and Hap Arnold. And he felt it necessary for army and navy planes to work together in combined operations involving ground forces. Setting yet another precedent at the Asiatic station, Turner noted that "it is believed [that] for the first time in [U.S. military] history, Army and Navy planes in a single formation, under a unified command, performed a simulated attack on an assumed hostile fleet [preparing to land in the Philippines]," a prelude to the joint air operations that were to take place throughout the Pacific during World War II based on the Turner model. "This manoeuver marks a distinct advance in the efficiency of the defense of the Philippine Islands," he concluded.[22]

Although Major General Douglas MacArthur, a future army chief of staff who was at this time serving as the head of the army's Philippine Department, endorsed these joint air exercises, he adamantly refused to comply with similar joint land and sea operations by the army and navy repeatedly requested by Turner and his commanding officer

Admiral Bristol in 1929.[23] MacArthur successfully quashed any such cooperation by the army. Alas, the long, senseless, occasionally bitter, and most unprofessional contest that blighted relations between the army and navy after World War I was to continue through the war to follow. This rivalry was later extended to the air as well, affecting the selection of types of planes to be developed and ordered, and the definition of their deployment over Hawaii, the Panama Canal, and American coastal waters. Who should guard the coast and when should the navy take over from the army? The outspoken Brigadier General Billy Mitchell then complicated matters by demanding the consolidation of all aircraft under one single permanent command, similar to the Royal Air Force in Britain, although the size and geographical positions of the two countries were totally different, requiring different solutions.

At the conclusion of his tour of duty, despite having greatly enhanced the efficiency and capabilities of his squadron, Turner was now even more aware of just how unprepared the U.S. Navy was to meet an enemy on the field of battle. The lack of congressional funding was further crippling the navy every year and there was nothing he could do about it. But, in his valuable Annual Reports, he had at least gone on record as to what was needed and to be expected, for as one of his junior officers later remarked, "He could foresee war with Japan . . . [and had] demanded hard work and efficiency from others, while driving himself still harder." He had done his best. As a flag officer later wrote, "It was my opinion that Kelly was tops in all respects as a Squadron Commander," and would soon be contributing much more at a higher level.[24]

•

Admittedly, the various international conferences held to date had not been encouraging. The Kellogg-Briand Pact of 1928 had officially renounced all war, an inspiring ideal that was never to be realized. The following year the Young Plan succeeded in reducing German war reparations, which did little to assuage Berlin, although the French withdrawal of the last of their troops from the Rhineland in 1930 was greeted with more enthusiasm.

That same year another Naval Disarmament Conference was held in London, from which Germany, as usual, was excluded. The Treaty of Versailles had limited that vanquished country's navy to a maximum of six armored ships of 10,000 tons each and six light cruisers, with no allowance either for battleships or submarines. Now at London Japanese cruiser strength was limited to 69 percent of that of Britain and America each, with no limits whatsoever on submarines. Senior Japanese admirals denounced this London Naval Treaty out of hand; Katō, Suetsugu, and Tōgō had demanded the lifting of all restraints.

Winston Churchill roundly denounced this same treaty for placing limits on American and British naval size because rogue states such as Germany and Japan were simply ignoring all restrictions, despite the fact that Japan at least had been a signatory in April 1930. Both the United States and Britain were limited to battleships of only 35,000 tons each, whereas Germany was building two giant Dreadnoughts, the *Bismarck* and *Tirpitz*, of 45,000 tons each. The Japanese were to go one better, and soon began preparing plans for the construction of two 57,400-ton super Dreadnoughts, the *Yamato* and *Musashi*, whose 18.1-inch guns, the mightiest afloat, were to completely surpass even those of the *Bismarck* class.

As a cynical Churchill summed up the new arms race, so far as Germany alone was concerned, "There was therefore no practical limitation or restraint of any kind. . . . They could build as fast as was physically possible," and did so.[25]

Three years hence, in 1935, Prime Minister James Ramsay MacDonald would aggravate matters still further, breaking the Versailles Treaty by secretly signing an Anglo-German Naval Agreement allowing the Germans to start rebuilding their navy to up to one third the size of Great Britain's. He also unilaterally authorized the construction of German submarines, for the first time since 1918, up to 60 percent of current British submarine strength. So much for Versailles and the League of Nations, and for that matter, any international cooperation. Churchill was fed up with this naval appeasement, "which has crippled us in building the kind of ships we wanted," and not only with Ramsay MacDonald's part in this affair—"the acme of gullibility," Churchill fumed—but also with the London Naval Limitations Treaty of 1930 which had placed such disastrous constraints on the law-abiding British and Americans. Churchill would no doubt have agreed with Hirohito's later "reflection" that the world was "deeply troubled everywhere and disorder seems endless," a truth that was soon to be magnified many times over.[26]

CHAPTER III

"Spreading Imperial Virtue"

"They brandish the Covenant of the League of Nations, and holding up the No-War [Kellogg-Briand] Treaty before them as their shield of self-righteousness, dare to censure us. . . . They are not qualified to judge us!"

—*Prince Konoe, 1933*[1]

"Not one of the lessons of the past has been learned, not one of them applied. . . ."

—*Winston Churchill,*
February 7, 1934[2]

Officers of a unit of the Kwantung Army assigned to protect the Japanese-controlled South Manchurian Railway at Liut'iaokou, near Mukden, finally staged the incident they had long sought, the pretext for invasion and conquest of the whole of Manchuria, with its rich deposits of coal and iron and its great agricultural capacity that would permit the creation of new industries and work for hundreds of thousands of unemployed Japanese.

On September 18, 1931, Japanese troops, disguised as Chinese soldiers, set off an explosion along the railway at Liut'iaokou. In "retaliation," Japanese troops attacked, quickly overwhelming and slaughtering to a man the unsuspecting Chinese troops in a nearby army barracks. There would be no witnesses. Simultaneously, another Japanese officer at Ryojun (Port Arthur) transmitted a prearranged report of this "Incident" to Tokyo. Within forty-eight hours, thousands of reinforcements on standby alert were on their way. Or, as Foreign Minister Shidehara Kijūro explained to the international press, "When the Chinese attacked, they [the Japanese troops] could not but perform the duty for which they had been stationed there—namely, to repel such an attack and prevent its repetition."[3] Thus Hirohito's government simply turned reality on its head, much as Hitler was to do eight years hence when Germany invaded Poland under a similar pretext of foreign attack.

When informed of the "Manchurian Incident" the following day, Emperor Hirohito and Prime Minister Wakatsuki Reijirō were greatly irritated, the prime minister complaining that he was "not being kept informed either by the foreign ministry or the army" of what they were doing. This was "an irresponsible action," Wakatsuki insisted, for the Chinese had a couple hundred thousand men in their Manchurian territory, whereas the Japanese "had only 10,000 men." It was madness. Quite the contrary, the army minister assured him, for "we'll send in troops from Korea," a response that had been arranged well in advance. The answer was not what the prime minister was hoping to hear, and he was further informed that this was not the first time that Japanese troops had crossed the frontier "without government authorisation." "Under the circumstances," he shrugged with surprising resignation, "I am quite powerless to restrain the military. But how can His Majesty's military act without his orders?"[4] A seemingly peeved Hirohito wanted to quash the situation then and there before it got out of hand, though he said nothing for the moment. Back at Army GHQ, the senior commanders responsible for the "Manchurian Incident" were equally unhappy . . . because of the lack of appreciation they were receiving for their efforts from Hirohito's ministers and personal advisers, including the aging Prince Saionji, who instead counseled caution and withdrawal. Still, Hirohito said nothing.

In reality, the army that was in charge of events, and General Hayashi Senjūrō, commanding Japan's Kwantung Army in Korea, were already *unilaterally* launching several divisions across the frontier by the afternoon of September 21, 1931. Although privately miffed at the army's arrogance in having acted without confiding in him, Hirohito—through his spokesman, General Nara—announced that the emperor had accepted this large-scale invasion as a fait accompli. "This time it couldn't be helped," Hirohito said, but they "had to be more careful in the future." Privately, he praised the army for "mowing down like weeds large numbers of the enemy." That was the real Hirohito speaking.[5]

As Winston Churchill so rightly surmised, certain Japanese leaders were still unsure of themselves, including Hirohito, who would tend to vacillate from one view to another on a variety of issues over the next several years. But invariably after such swings in mood, with very few exceptions, he sided with the military. In the final analysis, Hirohito, basically weak-minded and surrounded by the military from childhood, was steeped in the military exploits and mystique of the warrior-emperors of yore, and was determined to walk in the footsteps of his revered Meiji ancestors.

And so began the "Manchurian Incident," as the Japanese government officially referred to their invasion. Despite an uncomfortably loud international uproar, Hirohito stepped up operations, authorizing air strikes in support of the Japanese army's attack against Chinchou (Kinchow), a city situated along the railway link between Peking (Beijing) and Mukden.

Meanwhile, a sense of emergency pervaded the Council of the League of Nations, and the General Disarmament Conference convening in Geneva, which unanimously denounced this latest aggression in Manchuria, protesting the violation of both the League's founding principles and the Kellogg-Briand Pact of 1928 renouncing all war—treaties to which Japan was a signatory. President Hoover's secretary of state, Henry Stimson, joined in the League's condemnation of both China and Japan, presenting Japan with an ultimatum: to withdraw from Chinese Manchuria by November 16, 1931.

That date came and went, and the Japanese invasion continued unabated. They claimed to have seized northern Manchuria for reasons of self-defense, before the Soviets got there. Not once did Hirohito state that the invasion of Manchuria was wrong. Prime Minister Wakatsuki's government was made the scapegoat for this incursion. Wakatsuki, furthermore, had no effective policy to cope with the collapsing national economy, and was obliged to resign on December 11, 1931.

Inukai Tsuyoshi, who replaced Wakatsuki as prime minister, simply went on reinforcing Japanese troops in Tientsin, near Peking, as well as the units in Manchuria proper. By January 4, 1932, after briefly condemning the fighting around Chinchou to assuage foreign criticism,

Hirohito praised his army for its "self-defense" of national interests and its "loyalty." The Kwantung Army continued to occupy that city and to spread over the land in all directions like a swarm of all-devouring locusts, successfully completing the occupation of Manchuria by March 1 of that same year. In less than five months' time it was all over.[6]

Manchuria was declared to be independent of China and was to be known thereafter as Manchukuo, Tokyo informed the dismayed delegates of the Geneva Disarmament Conference. Herbert Hoover, among others, announced that the United States would not recognize this new Japanese puppet state, and threatened to begin rebuilding the U.S. Navy if Japan did not withdraw forthwith. But knowing full well that the Hoover administration had consistently blocked the increase of the American Navy by even a single ship over the past several years, Japan simply dismissed his "threat" as the usual empty American rhetoric, which indeed it was.[7]

Then, to the delight of Tokyo, a veritable unplanned "incident" did unexpectedly occur down in Shanghai in January 1932, thereby upping the stakes: a local Chinese newspaper in that large international city condoned a recent attempt on Hirohito's life. A Japanese army officer then provoked a Chinese mob in Shanghai to attack a group of Japanese "Nichiren priests" (in reality, Japanese soldiers in disguise, yet again), some of whom were killed, providing Japan with the double excuse it sought.[8]

On January 28, 1932, a Japanese naval force already at anchor in the Whangpoo River duly landed marines at Shanghai. Greatly outnumbered by a modern Chinese force of 34,000 men, the small Japanese contingent was wiped out. An astonished imperial Japanese high command then dispatched a powerful "Shanghai Expeditionary Force" to teach the Chinese a lesson. After more bloody battles and the retreat of the Chinese army, however, international pressure on Hirohito became too great and he agreed to a British-mediated truce on May 5, 1932, in large part to assuage the international outcry at Geneva, where Japanese representatives were finding the situation rather uncomfortable.[9]

•

But Japanese aggression was not limited to military operations abroad, as contesting cliques of Japanese army and naval officers at home took advantage of the growing rebellion within the military while a more martial environment was gradually enveloping the Japanese people and its leaders, further destabilizing the country. This was best reflected in a spate of murders that had begun with the assassination of Prime Minister Hamaguchi Osachi by an irate politician of the extreme left back in November 1930. It was followed by the assassination of two wealthy corporate leaders—a former finance minister, Inoue Junnosuke, and Baron Dan Takuma, the director of the powerful Mitsui Corporation—in February and March 1932, by extremist civilians.[10] Prime Minister Inukai Tsuyoshi himself was the next to fall victim to assassins, this time young naval officers who also threw bombs at his party's headquarters. And yet, to further bewilder foreign observers, this same Inukai, the second head of government to die in the streets of the capital, was hardly a moderate, having denounced the London Naval Limitations Treaty of 1930 and the League of Nation's condemnation of the Japanese occupation of Manchuria. Further bomb attacks were launched by naval officers against public buildings, including the Bank of Japan and the Metropolitan Police office. Ironically, these officers had demanded the same annulment of the London Naval Treaty and any further limits on the Imperial Japanese Navy's building program as had some of their victims.

Hirohito, angered by these murders, bombings, and the general reign of terror within the very heart of his empire, disassociated himself and his government more and more from party influence, relying instead on his court advisers. His answer to the immediate problem was to appoint a new prime minister, one not involved in party politics, the elderly Admiral Saitō Makoto, with instructions to restore order and discipline in society and in the military. Accordingly, Saitō formed a cabinet comprising very tough career officers who favored fresh foreign conquests and the development of Manchukuo, precisely as Hirohito had insisted.[11] Such was the answer to the country's problems.

When the League of Nation's report by Lord Lytton's commission was released, condemning the Japanese invasion of Manchuria, Admiral Saitō retaliated by demanding the immediate withdrawal of Japan from the League. The most outspoken members of Saitō's new government included Army Minister General Araki Sadao, Naval Minister Admiral Okada Keisuke, and Foreign Minister Uchida Ryōhei. On

August 25, 1932, Uchida announced Hirohito's support of the "most just and appropriate . . . measure we have adopted toward China," describing the establishment of Manchukuo as representing "the autonomous will of the people who live there."[12] On September 15, Japan officially recognized the illegal state of Manchukuo, sealed by the "Japan-Manchukuo Protocol," preparing the way for the future annexation of that state by Tokyo. So intensively was Japan to concentrate on the "development" of Manchuria that by 1939 it had already invested over $1 billion in enterprises manned by some 900,000 Japanese civilian colonists, all under the direction of the chief executive of the new Nissan Corporation, Kishi Nobusuke.[13]

Hirohito had long straddled the fence in an attempt to avoid a break with Britain and America. Ever prone to influence by the military and those immediately surrounding him, he was only now just beginning to assert himself, but still not sufficiently to control the army. Indeed, it was his army that informed him in November 1932 that it had decided to incorporate the large Chinese province of Jehol within Manchukuo, which it intended to invade early in 1933. Hirohito's response: "We have been very lucky so far in Manchuria. It would be regrettable if we should make a mistake now. So go carefully when taking Jehol."[14]

Hirohito, however, did try to bring some semblance of stability to the government and strengthen his own hand by the inclusion of members of his own family in positions of importance, including Prince Kan'in as chief of the Army General Staff and Prince Fushimi as chief of the Naval General Staff.

Against the advice of Makino, Lord Keeper of the Privy Seal, Hirohito authorized his government to withdraw from the League of Nations on March 27, 1933, although he was anxious about the League's attitude to the mandated islands Japan had received from Germany after Versailles.[15] Less than two months later, Japan officially annexed Jehol province. Prince Konoe Fumimaro, frequently called in to advise the emperor at this stage, also fully endorsed further expansion of Japan's empire and a complete break with the West. The momentum was growing.

"Unequal distribution of land and natural resources cause[s] wars," Konoe wrote in 1933. "We cannot achieve real peace until we change the present irrational international state of affairs." He demanded an abolition of tariffs across the world, while calling for the "freedom of immigration," a euphemism for the right of the Japanese to occupy and colonize foreign countries when it behooved them to do so. "Few possibilities exist for the implementation of these principles in the near future, however," and that means a continued burden on a country which is growing by a million people annually. "We cannot wait for a rationalizing adjustment of the world system. Therefore we have chosen to advance into Manchuria and Mongolia as our only means of survival." Here in a few sentences Konoe succinctly summed up Japan's attitude to the world, and what he considered to be his country's inalienable rights, thereby declaring Japan's intentions in the future. If the country needed land for its surplus population, Japan had the right to conquer and suppress other countries for that purpose. If Japan needed minerals and raw materials, unavailable or lacking in sufficient quantity in its own land, then it had the right to invade and seize whatever countries provided them. (It did not appear to occur to him that the same objective might have been achieved more cheaply and with less difficulty through expansion of Japan's international trade, a course adopted by most civilized countries across the world.) Indeed, he openly scorned Western nations when they then denounced Japan's adventurism abroad. "They brandish the Covenant of the League of Nations, and holding up the No-War [Kellogg-Briand] Treaty before them as their shield of self-righteousness, dare to censure us. . . . They are not qualified to judge us!" The white races of the West were clearly inferior to the yellow races of Japan and China, he concluded. When would they learn their lesson?[16]

Konoe's "declaration of rights" was certainly one of the most startlingly unambiguous documents coming out of Japan in this decade preceding the outbreak of World War II; but how many senior Western officials and career officials even knew of its existence, or if they did, fathomed its deep but obvious significance? The West was always looking for Oriental caution and subtlety, and therefore tended to overlook the obvious. There was nothing subtle about the Japanese. Of Hirohito's entire family, his younger brother, Prince Takamatsu, alone at this particular moment at least seemed to want something else, something very different of Japan, for a more positive future, as he confided to his diary while serving in the fleet in June 1933. "We must somehow restore harmony, end the bullying by the military, and restrain the selfishness of big business [*zaibatsu*] interests."[17]

•

Following his tour of service in the Orient, Kelly Turner had been called to Washington to take up the post as director of planning under Rear Admiral William Moffett, the head of the navy's air arm, the Bureau of Aeronautics, replacing Jack Towers, who became Moffett's new deputy.[18] In the meantime, the spiraling decline in the state of international relations both in Europe and Asia resulted in the League of Nations' hastily summoning the General Disarmament Conference in Geneva, beginning in 1932. The American naval representatives there, led by three distinguished admirals—Mark Bristol, Charles McVay, and A. J. Hepburn—required an expert on all aspects of naval aviation, and in the autumn of 1931 Commander Turner found himself on a plane bound for Switzerland.

Even before the official opening of the conference, the head of the U.S. delegation, Ambassador Hugh Gibson, found it pretty heavy going in an ambiance of intrigue, distrust, and pervading pessimism. Given the relative failure of the previous naval disarmament agreements of London and Washington, no one was unduly sanguine about prospects here, where talks were destined to extend throughout the spring and summer of 1932. In Europe, Germany's growing aggressiveness was already a major source of anxiety, while in the Far East, Japan's invasion and seizure of Manchuria in 1931 was, if anything, of even more immediate concern for the United States. But when, on the eve of the opening of this conference in January 1932, Japanese troops invaded Shanghai, the complexities were compounded until the British had successfully negotiated a truce between Japan and China, the latter agreeing to halt its crippling boycott that had cut Japanese imports by 90 percent.[19]

•

Given European apathy vis-à-vis the threats bristling everywhere, if there was any sign of hope at all in the West, it lay in the as yet untested hands of the newly elected American president, Franklin Delano Roosevelt. With several divisions of Japanese troops in the northern Chinese territory of Manchuria, there was little reason for optimism in diplomatic and political circles, as the statements of Prince Konoe made clear. The net yield of the international conferences since the end of World War I had been meager at best, and the League of Nations was bereft of American support. This diplomatic impotence had encouraged the scorn of the League's most belligerent members, Germany, Italy, and Japan. The Japanese had demonstrated their sense of mission. As government spokesman Mori Tsutomu announced, "The new Manchukuo is a declaration to the world that our diplomacy has become autonomous and independent. . . . This action is akin to a declaration of diplomatic war."[20]

Hardly happy with the legacy he had inherited upon entering the White House in March 1933, President Roosevelt was determined to check the deteriorating world situation. Franklin Roosevelt, "a hard-nosed Dutchman," as he once referred to himself, put more trust in military strength than in the State Department's ditherings and moral indignation. He also knew that unsupported threats to foreign countries were not only useless but dangerous, undermining the authority of the individual or country espousing them. But he made no secret of his full support for Henry Stimson's earlier declaration, made when still Hoover's secretary of state, that the United States would recognize "no situation, treaty or agreement" made under intimidation or by the force of arms.[21] The "Stimson Doctrine," as it was dubbed by the press, implied the threat of economic and even military sanctions against any transgressor, a clear reference to the Japanese. FDR endorsed the Stimson Doctrine wholeheartedly.

In reality, as Japan well knew, although both Britain and America could impose economic sanctions on Tokyo, neither was in a position to take military action to intervene in the Orient. As Churchill later admitted, "We have never been able to provide effectively for the defense of the Far East against an attack by Japan." Instead, it had been British policy "at almost all costs to avoid embroilment" with that country until such time as they could work effectively with the United States to be able to act.[22] Under Hirohito, the Japanese economy was dedicating larger and larger resources to naval and military manufacturing, including large new naval yards, public and private. Herbert Hoover's administration had not only insisted on keeping out of foreign ventures but had also cut back U.S. Navy personnel by some 5,000 men, reducing it to a total strength of just under 80,000 officers and men.

Franklin Roosevelt—like his cousin, Theodore Roosevelt, before him—was an advocate of a strong military and national defense. He found, upon taking office, that his country was in its weakest state since 1918. Hoover had slashed the navy's budget so ruthlessly that Admiral Moffett's Bureau of Aeronautics' sub-budget was reduced from $53 million to $35 million overnight.[23] Naval air development and production, the key to any naval confrontation in a new war, were seriously undermined in consequence. As if these hard realities were not enough to harm overall naval effectiveness in the event of a serious military flare-up, morale too was plummeting, sinking lower still when naval officers had been informed by the lame-duck Hoover administration that the navy's already modest pay was to suffer a further reduction of 20.8 percent over the next two years.[24]

•

Now at Geneva, in 1932, the British fully supported the American delegation's demand for Japanese military reductions, including the scrapping of all their aircraft carriers, present and future. Britain's largest carrier, the 22,500-ton *Furious*, commissioned in 1925 and capable of carrying all of thirty-six aircraft, was hardly a match for Japan's two giants, the eighty-one-plane *Kaga* and the seventy-two-plane *Akagi*. The keel of the U.S. Navy's first purpose-built carrier, the diminutive *Ranger*, only laid down in September 1931 and due to be commissioned in 1934, was already too small, too slow, and generally out of date, and of course was less than half the size of the two Japanese purpose-built carriers.[25]

The Republican Congress, admittedly in the circumstances of the Great Depression, was responsible for suppressing military expenditure on four other authorized carriers and another five 20,000-ton warships recommended back in the 1920s.[26] The decision was supported by several influential senior naval officers of the old school who were bitter about the carrier's replacement of the battleship as the heart of the fleet.

But worse was to come when President Hoover had demanded—in defiance of his own irate army chief of staff, General Douglas

MacArthur—that the conference here at Geneva reduce all land forces by one third while abolishing all "offensive weapons," including submarines, tanks, heavy mobile guns, and aerial bombardment.[27]

Hence Kelly Turner's further frustration at Geneva in the summer of 1932 as he came face to face with his very determined Japanese opposites, who were anything but cooperative. The United States had the core of skilled personnel to design, build, and man the new large carriers so badly needed, but the money was not available, as Congress continued to insist that the country could not afford to defend itself.

Commander Turner was only too pleased to be released from the fruitless talks in July 1932 to return to the United States, as the conference came to a confused and uneventful end a few weeks later. Putting to sea as executive officer of the converted carrier *Saratoga* permitted him to put some sea room between himself and the haze of the Geneva talks, but not enough room to blind him to the fact that the United States was still putting more ships in mothballs, as a demonstration of "goodwill," or using them for target practice. As a result, the entire fleet was now reduced to four converted carriers, with only fifteen first-line battleships and fourteen heavy cruisers in service worldwide. Meanwhile, Japanese shipyards would soon be working round the clock to churn out warships of every category.

●

This latest League of Nations–sponsored conference had achieved only one thing: the isolation of Japan, Germany, and Italy from that world organization and any future meetings. Prime Minister Prince Konoe berated the League of Nations for disdainfully "brandishing" its Covenant before the people of Japan as some sort of pious shield. He summed up his country's view in 1933: "We cannot achieve real peace until we change the present state of international affairs," and declared that Japan was fully prepared to do just that, unilaterally.[28]

A dithering Hirohito reluctantly agreed to what he considered a partial break with the West. Japan withdrew from the League of Nations and dismissed the constraints of the Washington and London agreements, along with the Kellogg-Briand Pact's renunciation of war. He had not prevented his Kwantung Army from annexing Jehol province, which provided a major source of revenue from its lucrative opium production. Backed by the defiant Konoe Doctrine of expansion in April 1933, the Japanese army next broke through the Great Wall of China and entered the provinces of North China proper. Much to his chagrin, however, General Honjō Shijeru was ordered to halt his advance temporarily by an angered Hirohito, who feared a possible full-scale war with China. "The Emperor does not intend to obstruct the operation," Honjō temporized in his diary in May 1933, "but neither can he permit decisions to be made for [his] supreme command [without his approval or knowledge]."

The Tanghu Truce of May 31, 1933, recognized the consolidation of greater Manchukuo and the neutralization of the region around the Great Wall, thus separating Manchuria/Jehol from North China proper while retaining land from Japan's fresh inroads made in Hopei province south of the Great Wall.[29] Simultaneously, in a surprising bid to placate Tokyo, the Soviet Union agreed to sell Japan its Chinese Eastern Railway, hoping to defuse the tension between Japanese and Soviet forces facing one another across the Amur River separating Manchuria from Siberia. The supreme commander of the Chinese army, General Chiang Kai-shek, who had been defeated at the hands of the Japanese, now attempted to consolidate his position elsewhere by crushing China's growing Communist forces. Aboard a warship far out at sea, Prince Takamatsu reflected on the situation at home and the Japanese army's staggering arrogance in every sphere of life, and what he termed its "fascist mood." His observations were perhaps tinged by jealousy of his brother the emperor, who was falling more and more under the influence of that very army.

There was discontent within the Japanese army as well, just as there was in civilian circles. Army Minister Araki attempted to unite some of the opposing factions by inciting the Japanese people through a semidocumentary propaganda film entitled *Japan in the National Emergency*. It played upon a traditional, deep-seated xenophobic fundamentalism by denouncing all things Western—the wearing of Western clothes by women, cosmetics, smoking in public, playing golf, and dancing—clearly an attack on Hirohito's friends and members of the imperial family itself. "We have lost our hold on the autonomous ideals of the Japanese race," the film preached. The people had to return to "the Imperial Way," respecting the emperor, while expanding frontiers abroad in order to secure "the defence of the nation." Backing this extraordinary propaganda with quasiphilosophy and metaphysics, General Araki insisted that "the imperial forces exist as moral entities," not only to defend "Japan's responsibility abroad" but to instill "the enterprising spirit of the immortal State, which is coeval with heaven and earth." The Japanese armed forces, he insisted, formed "a great embodiment of our national virtue. . . . The spirit of the Japanese military manifests the sacred spirit of His Majesty who commands the Japanese armed forces. . . . *Ninety million people must become one and join the emperor in spreading the imperial virtue* . . . in order to secure the glory of final victory [in China]."[30]

Araki's documentary was followed in 1934 by a book published by the army, *Essays on the Time of Emergency Confronting the Nation*, reinforcing the film's doctrine, stressing the necessity for Japan to concentrate the entire nation's workforce and industry on the "fulfillment of war preparations." The state, General Tōjō is quoted as saying, must "monolithically control . . . ideological warfare [and] spread [these] moral principles across the world." He was in fact espousing a sort of Oriental "New Order" to justify future conquests.[31] If the much-lambasted West needed proof of Japan's public intentions over the coming years, it now had it in moving images and printed doctrine.

Hirohito "accepted" these latest propaganda efforts more or less ex post facto: they were undertaken without his prior authorization. But he was not yet prepared to commit the nation to total war, or to make a total break with the West. The emperor, with his predilection for golf, Harris tweeds, and afternoon tea, was deeply torn, one foot in the Western world and the other here in Japan. He would soon have to make up his mind.

On the other hand, Hirohito was hardly fainthearted when it came to suppressing Communist doctrine and its growing supporters in Japan. He therefore ordered the mass arrest of some eighteen thousand people, and would later seal the act by signing the Anti-Comintern Pact with Germany and Italy in November 1936. This document was also riddled with anti-Semitic propaganda, which soon spread through Japan, a country without a Jewish population.

Meanwhile, through 1935, the emperor's Kwantung Army strengthened its garrisons and grip on Peking-Tientsin, forcing Chiang Kai-shek and his army to withdraw once again.[32] The Japanese army set up an "Autonomous Committee for Defence Against Communism" in Hopei province; this puppet government took a hard line about its role there, to the point of ordering officers and men alike never to dishonor their country by being taken alive in the battles to come.[33]

Within Japan itself, political and military unrest continued unabated. Back in 1934, officers at the army's elite Military Academy had been discovered plotting a coup d'état to "reform the government." They were duly arrested, but punishment was light.[34] The following year, an irate lieutenant colonel of the "Imperial Way" group of army officers entered the office of the Military Affairs Bureau chief, General Nagata Tetsuzan, and hacked him to death with his Samurai sword because Nagata was planning to restore badly needed discipline to the army, as the incident itself well demonstrated.[35]

But just how grave the situation was within the army officer corps no one quite realized until a few months later when, on February 26, 1936, nearly thirty officers, commanding three regiments as well as a unit of the Imperial Guards, mutinied. The snow-covered streets of Tokyo were swathed in trails of Vlaminckian red as the officers carried out a series of assassinations that was to astound the world.

The first to go was Saitō Makoto, Hirohito's Lord Keeper of the Privy Seal; then Finance Minister Takahashi Korekiyo, followed by General Watanabe Jōtarō, an army Inspector General who favored the maintenance of the constitutional status quo. Hirohito's grand chamberlain, Suzuki Kantarō, was wounded, and both Prime Minister Okada Keisuke and Privy Seal Makino Nobuaki barely escaped the assassins. Several soldiers and police were killed during these deadly forays: army officers stormed the Metropolitan Police Headquarters in the heart of Tokyo; others overran the Army Ministry building and ransacked the offices of two major newspapers that had opposed the overthrow of constitutional government. The mutineers were unsuccessful, however, in taking the well-defended Imperial Palace.[36]

Unlike the previous rash of isolated assassinations and murder attempts against high officials over the years, the massacre of February 1936 had been well organized by a very determined group of officers and coordinated on a large scale. Surprisingly, never before had murderers had so many well-placed friends and sympathizers to support them, including the commander of the military police of Tokyo, General Kashii Kōhei, and General Honjō, the emperor's own senior aide-de-camp. Even the army minister, General Kawashima, pleaded the mutineers' cause before an impatient Hirohito. Instead, he ordered Kawashima personally to place the capital under military law and put down this army mutiny, and rejected appeals by his brothers, Chichibu and Takamatsu, to soften the action taken to quell "the disorders." In fact, Hirohito very nearly did not get his way, for the Supreme Military Council, later convened by the army minister, was itself largely composed of pro–"Imperial Way" generals supportive of the reforms demanded by the mutineers, and among their number were to be found Generals Araki, Mazaki, Tamashita, General Prince Higashikuni Naruhiko, Admiral Prince Fushimi, and Lieutenant General Prince Asaka Yasuhika.

Hirohito, who had lost so many trusted old servants in this bloodbath, was in no mood for compromise. On February 29, after three more days of fighting and negotiating, the mutiny came to an end, and the defeated officers returned to their barracks, advised by the palace to commit suicide. Although they declined this honor, the court-martial that followed was less lenient, and seventeen of the conspirators were executed before a firing squad.[37]

These were not good times for Japan, the coup aside. Vice President of the Privy Council Hiranuma Kiichirō had warned in January 1931, "The depression in the business world is reaching its height. Unemployment is increasing daily. The family is breaking up. Starving people fill the streets. Do you think people are satisfied with this situation? . . . To conceal this reality and pretend that everything is peaceful would be an act of the greatest disloyalty."[38]

Now, in 1936, the truth of these words rang more forcefully than ever before. Society was indeed breaking down. Over the decade, impoverished fathers sold hundreds of thousands of daughters into prostitution and economic slavery of one sort or another. Army and naval officers were constantly plotting against the state and their emperor and were desperate enough not merely to bring down an entire government but to murder every minister in it.

Facing "this reality," as Hiranuma called it, this latest attempt to convulse society in a national revolution—one supported by many members of the imperial family itself—Hirohito decided to act. He began by shifting alliances, associating himself now more decisively with the extreme right of the army high command known as the Control Faction, the only group that had opposed the "reformist" mutineers. This turning point for the emperor would result in even greater aggression abroad and an ultimate break with the West.

In spite of the presence of Japanese troops in various parts of China, that country was nevertheless not Hirohito's main objective so far as the future and fresh expansion were concerned. Rather, the presence of a large Soviet army along the Siberian-Manchurian frontier was of particular concern to Hirohito, and so he signed the Anti-Comintern Pact with Germany later in 1936. And when Japan's "China Garrison Force" in the five northern Chinese provinces was increased to secure these coal- and iron-rich areas and ultimately detach them from China, Hirohito did not oppose the move, although this act confirmed that it was the army that was continuing to dictate Japanese foreign policy, and not the Imperial Palace.

The cumulative effect of all these disturbing events over the past few years had finally shaken the emperor, who now convened a series of ministerial conferences on August 7, 1936. The result was two crucial documents—"The Criteria for National Policy" and the "Foreign Policy of the Empire"—which at last spelled out Japan's future objectives at home and abroad. Manchukuo was to be developed intensively, with massive investment in mining, industry, and agriculture; China's occupied northern provinces (south of the Great Wall) were to be secured more directly to the Japanese government by means of puppet regimes, similar to that of Manchukuo; the military would have to make substantial long-term preparations for an anticipated war with the Soviets; and Japan was to gain control of Southeast Asia and nothing less than the entire "South Seas Region . . . a natural region for our future racial development," or development by conquest. Achieving this last objective would in turn require a major naval construction program and the development of dozens of military airfields and radio stations in the Marianas, Carolines, and on Taiwan.[39]

Needless to say, the military was delighted. There was something in this package for everyone: the army, navy, and air force. In 1936, the Japanese army totaled only seventeen divisions, or 233,365 officers and men, while the navy roster reached a mere 107,467. The latter would have to be doubled over the next four years, and the army multiplied manyfold.[40]

Noticeably absent from the list of Japan's long-term foreign policy and military objectives, however, was any reference to invading and conquering the whole of China. The single most powerful foreign opponent envisaged now in 1936 was the Soviet Union, not China, which was still regarded as a temporary sideshow. It was evident, of course, that these foreign policy moves would inevitably result in a clash of interests with the United States, Great Britain, the Netherlands, and France, due to their vested commercial and historical interests in the Far East and the South Pacific. One of these new government papers explicitly stated that the aim was to "eliminate the hegemonistic policies of the Great Powers in East Asia." The vast waters of the Orient were to be cleansed of the West altogether to become Japan's "Mare Nostrum." This required that the Japanese "secure our footing on the East Asian continent, and . . . advance and develop in the Southern Oceans by combining diplomacy and national defence." There "we must . . . strive to dispel their fears of our Empire by advancing peacefully and gradually."[41] In brief, the new master plan for the Far East called for Japan's complete domination of that entire region, beginning with subterfuge, followed by force.

Even if such a policy, or series of policies, had been undertaken by a closely knit, stabilized Japanese society with thriving industry and substantial financial resources, there was no avoiding the fact that the country lacked the population and ability to conquer and control an area covering millions of square miles, nor did it possess the industrial might to take on the combined forces of Great Britain and the United States. But to have committed Japan to such a policy given its present destabilized state, where prime ministers, corporate leaders, and senior officers could be hacked to death or gunned down in their own homes and offices, was utter madness.

In order to implement this grandiose scheme of conquest, Japanese military leaders demanded complete, direct control of all national industrial production, which Hirohito rejected. They also demanded the trebling of the military budget of 1937, and got their way: *69 percent of the government's entire annual budget* for that year was duly handed over to the military. To Western observers like Kelly Turner, it was simply astonishing. The Japanese economy was wobbling along, rife with inflation; wages—when there was work—were low, and now taxes would have to be raised considerably to meet these military increases for a people already barely able to cope with the existing burden. Policy makers who were calling for "gradual and peaceful expansion" of the Japanese Empire to the north and south now also boasted of Japan as the "stabilising force in East Asia."[42]

Japan's senior military officers and political advisers could have saved all the trouble they were about to heap upon themselves, and indeed on much of the world, simply by having asked a few elementary questions:

1. For such massive conquests, where were they to find enough educated men in Japan to provide the officers that this expanded military would require, not to mention the troops to fill the ranks? As early as 1937, before the new navy had begun to add hundreds of new ships, that service lacked 1,021 officers. The situation for the much larger army was even more severe.[43]
2. Preparations for the war anticipated with the Soviet Union or the United States and Great Britain (for the Japanese still failed to recognize a full-scale war with China) required the stockpiling of oil and the continuing of the same effort for scrap iron, iron ore, and coal. If coal and iron ore deposits available in China and Manchuria were sufficient, transport vessels to haul them were not, and Japan was always to suffer a shortage of shipping, including the transports needed for troops during the war. As for scrap metal, most of that had been coming from the United States, and when tensions reached a certain level, an American boycott would halt the flow overnight. This was a constant worry for Hirohito, who discussed it on several occasions.
3. Vast reserves of aviation and diesel fuel had to be prepared, sufficient to meet the needs of warships, the merchant marines, and warplanes. (This excluded the consideration of the needs of industry.) Eighty to 90 percent of all Japanese aviation fuel and oil now came from the United States.[44] Once that source was cut off, what was Japan to do? As early as the mid-1930s petroleum products,

and the lack thereof, became the navy's most nagging logistical problem. It is not that the chiefs of the Japanese navy had overlooked the necessity of anticipating oil reserves for a growing navy; they simply miscalculated the extent of the reserves needed, and then how to top them up.[45] By 1936, the Imperial Japanese Navy was importing 1.2 million tons of oil a year and would soon have 3.5 million tons stockpiled, but was already burning 800,000 tons a year. And this was *before* the war in China had escalated. The aircraft that were to play such a dominant role in that war would consume large amounts of 100-octane gasoline, which would require emergency imports of as much as 43,000 additional tons of this fuel from America in 1938.[46]

When the United States began restricting high-octane aviation fuel after 1939, the enormity of their future problems began to dawn on the leaders of the Japanese navy's planning department. The navy scrambled to stockpile even more petroleum products, and by December 1, 1941, the country as a whole would have 6.5 million tons of petroleum reserves for all uses. The navy's share of those reserves would meet its requirements (for ships and planes) for a two-year period. This was a maximum storage figure, one that was going to drop rapidly thereafter. By 1940, the navy would be consuming one quarter of all the petroleum used in the whole of Japan. Although the country possessed 300,000 tons of oil tanker capacity, the navy alone required 270,000 tons of that. The army and industry had somehow to make do with a mere 30,000 tons, an utter impossibility.

In August 1940, senior naval officers would convene another emergency meeting when they came to the conclusion that at the current rate, Japan could not fight for more than *another twelve months*, and the war with the United States, anticipated in its 1936 policy document, had not even begun. Once a complete cutoff of all American oil was in effect, Japan would have to seize the massive oil reserves in the Dutch East Indies and British North Borneo. As they were to discover by 1943, however, that did not quite work out as expected, due to the heavy toll of oil tankers sunk by American submarines. The result was that by 1943, the Japanese Fleet would have lost considerable strategic and tactical maneuverability when it found itself "tethered to its Southeast Asia oil spigot."

Thus, ironically, by 1941 oil would prove to be "the single most important reason for undertaking the risk of war."[47] The Japanese navy reckoned that in any single major battle at sea it would be consuming a maximum of 500,000 tons of fuel. But three major battles—Midway, the Philippine Sea (the Marianas), and the battles off the Philippines—surpassed even that figure. All prewar navy calculations proved overly optimistic. So lacking in the strategic appreciation of petroleum and fuel were the Japanese planners that when Pearl Harbor was struck, they ignored and left untouched the U.S. Navy's huge, vulnerable oil and fuel storage depots. Within a matter of minutes Japanese bombers could have destroyed the U.S. Navy's entire oil reserves, thereby crippling all air and sea operations for months to come.[48]

4. Japan's military would require enormous stockpiles of aluminum, especially for the manufacture of warplanes. These stockpiles did not exist now, nor would they in the future. And once hostilities began, where could Japan turn?
5. Spare parts for the army's many mechanized divisions and artillery would be needed, ditto for the warplanes and warships; but no sufficient provision was made for this. Stockpiles remained low or nonexistent, which would compromise any major military operation in the future.
6. Apart from radio, modern electronics technology was lacking and not even considered a top priority by most of the Japanese military chiefs. In 1937, this was a very small, poorly developed industry in Japan, and thus proved quite incapable of providing for the country's military needs. New inventions, such as the various types of radar Britain was currently secretly developing, were not even taken into consideration. Only once war had begun with the United States would the Japanese hastily send a team of scientists to the Third Reich for the basic instructions on that project, which the Germans were not altogether happy about revealing even to an "ally." When the first elementary radar was eventually installed in wartime Japan, there were very few units available, and they were grossly inferior to the gradually more sophisticated radar employed by the Americans and the Royal Navy.

These are but a few examples of the most elementary questions that serious professional military officers should have been considering. After even a single day's study, they would have realized that the wars they were soon expecting to launch with so much bravado would never be feasible, or at least not for decades to come. But Japan's senior war leaders were neither realistic enough, nor sufficiently open-minded, and in consequence were intent on blind military adventurism, confident that the superiority of their genius and the aid of their gods would bring them victory as they had in Korea and Manchuria.

In brief, even as early as 1936, the Japanese military could have calculated with some degree of precision that their policy of foreign expansion, leading in turn to conflict with the Soviet Union, the United States, and Great Britain, could never have succeeded in victory because of the lack of manpower, manufacturing potential, and access to oil. But a society constantly on the brink of revolution from within its own military ranks is not living in a realistic world. The only remotely comparable examples of such underlying social and political upheaval are to be found in the long years of chaos wrought by the French Revolution of 1789, and the Soviet Revolution of 1917.

Japan was experiencing a catastrophe as great and as dangerous as any of its periodic geological cataclysms, such as the devastating earthquake of 1923 that had leveled most of Tokyo, leaving millions homeless across the land. The Japanese, at the highest levels, were living in a world of military make-believe as fantastic as any to be found in their own mythological past, beginning with the legend of their god-emperors. Examples here would be their reliance on the "emperor's ideological and spiritual role" as the finest model of "national benevolence and morality" and their faith in the superiority of the Japanese race over all other peoples.[49]

If the nation's military and civilian leaders were incapable of forecasting such basic requirements as manpower, manufacturing output, and available oil resources, it should come as no surprise that they were equally incapable of understanding or dealing with the complexities of China that were about to suck the life out of the Japanese military.[50]

CHAPTER IV

"The Eight Corners of the World"

"If the United States does not understand the position of Japan, Germany and Italy . . . and if it constantly adopts a confrontational attitude, then we three countries will fight [America] resolutely."

—*Prince Konoe, October 4, 1940*[1]

"We sincerely hope to bring about a cessation of hostilities and a restoration of peace. . . . [Hence the government's decision] to ally itself with [Nazi] Germany and Italy, nations that share the same good intentions as ourselves."

—*Emperor Hirohito, September 27, 1940*[2]

One might say that it all began at Marco Polo Bridge—some twenty miles south of Peking—where on July 8, 1937, Japanese troops clashed unexpectedly with the Chinese garrison guarding that bridge. Tokyo quickly intervened, ordering the fighting to be contained, and a truce soon followed.

The matter might have ended there had it not been for a clique of zealous extremists in the Japanese officer corps bent on expanding "the Incident." During an emergency audience with the emperor, they used as pretext for their ambitions the fact that China had still refused to recognize the new state of "Manchukuo" and that the demilitarized zone between North China and Manchukuo had often been violated (in fact, chiefly by the Japanese themselves). If the Japanese military were to act quickly and vigorously, they argued, the Chinese would be brought into submission once and for all, allowing Tokyo to seize Peking and thereby to protect its "citizens and property." The whole idea was at first overruled by the Konoe government, but by July 11 Prime Minister Konoe had changed his mind and a full-scale invasion of northern China was launched by the Kwantung Army, the Korean army, and reinforcements from Japan.[3]

Hundreds of miles to the north, just days before the Marco Polo Bridge incident, Japanese troops had seized the island of Kanchazu in the Amur River, which separated Japanese Manchukuo from the Soviet Union's Siberian frontier. Although the troops came under Soviet fire, the Soviets did not push the matter, and the fighting ceased for the moment. But what if it flared up again? an anxious Hirohito asked his uncle, Prince Kan'in, the army's general chief of staff. "What will you do if the Soviets attack us from the rear?" "We will have no choice [but to fight]," Kan'in replied.[4] Alas, Hirohito did not reveal the same qualms when dealing with the situation in the south, where Japanese forces were again advancing toward Peking. Kan'in had assured Hirohito, his former protégé, that "Even if war with China came . . . it would be over within two or three months," and neither Kan'in nor the army's General Staff deviated from that estimate.[5]

Things did not quite work out as planned, however, as Tokyo ordered in more troops, ultimately even transferring entire divisions from the Siberian border. From now on, supreme headquarters would be constantly looking over its shoulder to ensure that the Soviet army did not take advantage of Japan's full-scale battle with the Chinese. In fact, the situation within China proper was escalating out of control, despite the additional assurances of both Army Minister Sugiyama Hajime and Naval Minister Yonai Mitsumasa that they would be in a position to wind up operations within three months' time. Still fully confident in his advisers, the emperor himself was counting on what he called "one decisive battle"—a knockout blow—that would put an end to the "China Incident" by the end of July 1937, concluding with the seizure of Peking and Tientsin.

But then a small city by the name of Tungchow rebelled against its Japanese occupiers, slaughtering over 250 of them, including local Japanese residents. When word of this massacre reached Tokyo, the attitude of the Japanese government hardened dramatically. The mood of the army was "that we're really going to smash China so that it will be a good ten years before they'll be able to get to their feet again," Prince Takamatsu boasted.[6] With Hirohito's full support, Japanese troops pushed on, forcing Chiang Kai-shek to abandon the north altogether, his 110,000-man army regrouping along the lower Yangtze River at Shanghai. It was a move that was to alter the parameters of the war drastically.

As China's most populous city, Shanghai, with its inordinately large foreign community including 25,000 Japanese and some 60,000 Europeans, proved an enticing prize for the enemy. Now for the second time in five years the Japanese army launched its attack against Chiang's defenses and the city proper on August 13, 1937. The Japanese navy bombarded the city and its environs indiscriminately with its big guns, while in the skies far above, yet another dimension of terror was added to the battle as Admiral Yamamoto's two new stars made their debut.

The sleek, powerful (500 hp) Mitsubishi A5M (type 96), the navy's latest carrier-launched fighter, tore through the antiquated Chinese air force at 280 miles per hour, its two 7.7mm machine guns "shredding" what remained of their planes. Based on earlier versions developed in the 1920s by a team of brilliant British aeronautical engineers brought to Japan following World War I, the A5M remained unmatched, untouchable as it strafed the civilian population and Chiang's armies. The skies quickly cleared of all opposition. The Japanese navy then launched another pristine new Mitsubishi masterpiece, the G3M twin-engine, 230 mph long-range (2,300 miles) bomber all the way from Nagasaki. Flying at a ceiling of 29,000 feet, it was unmatched by what few Chinese planes remained, dropping its 800-kilo bombloads first over the heart of Shanghai and then on Nanking.[7]

Yamamoto's field-testing of his latest aircraft, like that of Hitler's Luftwaffe over Spain, proved so successful as to give the Nipponese complete air superiority. Chinese casualties, civilian and military, soon reached staggering levels, leaving Tokyo and Hirohito in particular hopeful of the quick victory his General Staff had earlier promised. Take "resolute measure . . . [to] spur the Nanking government to reflect a bit," Hirohito ordered; "destroy the enemy's will to fight."[8]

But this Far Eastern blitzkrieg did not have the immediate effect expected, and by early September a frustrated army minister called for "total war."[9] Because of continuing dependence on American copper, scrap iron, oil, and even cotton, however, Japan could not afford to declare an actual state of war; hence all future documents referred to the conflict merely as the "China Incident."

The United States, for its part, was more than war-wary—it was prickly. Its Neutrality Acts of 1935, 1936, and 1937 were designed to insulate and isolate the country from any foreign conflicts, and they further tied Roosevelt's hands from sending arms as aid. Hoping to counter the Neutrality Acts, FDR gave a speech in October 1937 in Chicago before tens of thousands of people. In it he discussed the "haunting fear of calamity" that had beset the world, the fear of the "reign of terror and international lawlessness" that was threatening "the very foundation of civilization. . . . There is a solidarity and interdependence about the modern world, both technically and morally, which makes it impossible for any nation completely to isolate itself from economic and political upheavals in the rest of the world." Nations such as the United States had to act, for "the epidemic of world lawlessness is spreading. When an epidemic of physical disease starts to spread, the community approves, and joins in, a quarantine of the patients in order to protect the health of the community against the spread of the disease," he argued, clearly referring to Germany, Italy, and Japan. "It is my determination to adopt every practicable measure to avoid being involved in war . . . yet we cannot insure ourselves against the disastrous effects of wars and the dangers of involvement. . . . Most important of all, the will for peace on the part of peace-loving nations must express itself to the end that nations that may be tempted to violate their agreements and the rights of others will desist from such a course. . . ." Although this "Quarantine Speech" was warmly received by the audience, and initially so by much of the press, the isolationist viewpoint gradually built in momentum in direct defiance of FDR's plea.[10]

Germany, Italy, and Japan ignored the speech altogether. Indeed Hirohito, far from being cowed by Roosevelt's challenge, took another definitive step that was to alter greatly all future military operations: he ordered the transfer of supreme military headquarters directly to his Imperial Palace, where they would remain for the next eight years. Hereafter the prime minister would have much less control over military decisions. The policy decisions made at the Liaison Conference were reviewed by Hirohito, then passed on to the Imperial War Conferences, now held in the palace itself. Here, those decisions were passed, confirmed, modified, and rejected. Conducted before the emperor's dais against the backdrop of a yellow silk screen, the Imperial War conferences were attended by Hirohito, who in fact directly controlled their proceedings. It was a system that would be finely tuned by the time of the outbreak of World War II.

By the second week of November, the Japanese navy's heavy land, sea, and air bombardment of Shanghai had forced Chiang Kai-shek once again to retreat—this time nearly two hundred miles along the Yangtze River to Nanking, leaving behind nearly a million Chinese dead, most of them civilians. Reinforced Japanese army units converged on Nanking with orders to take no prisoners, military or civilian; General Nakajima alone executed all 323,000 POWs that he had taken so far.

Prince Asaka Yasuhito, Hirohito's uncle, took personal charge of the siege of Nanking, a city of more than 400,000 people. Laying waste to the city, he had it occupied with Japanese troops by December 13. And yet despite the tragic toll on life and a series of major battles, the Chinese refused to surrender. The slaughter—for there is no other word for it—continued: in preparation for his victory march through the rubble of Nanking, Prince Asaka ordered the roundup and summary mass murder of seventeen thousand boys and men found hiding in the ruins of that city the preceding night. This was just the beginning of the genocide Japan was to carry out until the very end of the war. Meanwhile, the sadistic Asaka now installed himself in Nanking while General Matsu, the ailing nominal commander, proclaimed victory and "Banzai for His Majesty the Supreme Commander!"[11]

Many other members of the imperial family were already involved in these atrocities, including Prince Higashikuni (uncle of Empress Nagako) with the air force and Prince Kan'in commanding massacres on the ground. Prince Asaka now personally supervised the looting of Nanking's treasury, banks, and temples, accumulating 6,000 metric tons of gold. Hirohito's brother Chichibu, and his deputy, Prince Takeda, directed the looting under Asaka in similar operations in Shanghai, Peking, Canton, the rest of China, and most of Asia, which would ultimately net them 100 metric tons of gold—including large solid gold Buddhas and other valuable religious and historic artistic works.[12]

More important, however, was the human price of this invasion. The conquest of Nanking alone had cost China some 200,000 civilian lives, approximately one half the city's entire population. Twenty thousand Chinese civilian men and boys of military age were used for live bayonet practice by the troops as officers looked on, even participating in the beheading of some of the wounded and bound prisoners—"cutting them down like weeds," as Hirohito put it. This practice was to be extended throughout conquered China and later during World War II. Prince Asaka personally gave the order to "teach our Chinese brothers a lesson they will never forget. . . . Kill all captives."

Nor was that all, as the post–World War II War Crimes Tribunal established that some one thousand women and girls had been raped daily over the first several weeks of the occupation, after which those who survived were forced to serve in permanent "Comfort Stations" (brothels) for Japanese troops. Ultimately the number would reach at least 200,000 such women. No Japanese soldier or officer was ever executed or punished for his actions, actions which were frequently ordered by members of the imperial Japanese household. In fact, Hirohito publicly praised his officers, including General Matsui and Prince Asaka, the latter eventually receiving the Order of the Gold Eagle. But at least one Japanese Foreign Office official was horrified by such barbaric acts, recording in his diary, "My god, is this how our imperial army behaves?"[13] In any event the situation in Nanking was hardly a state secret, thanks to the large presence of Europeans in both Shanghai and Nanking. U.S. Ambassador Joseph Grew, for his part, valiantly protested the pillaging of American property in the war zone.[14]

In addition to inflicting Chinese casualties, the Japanese shelled and sank the U.S. gunboat *Panay* (formerly under the command of one Ensign Chester Nimitz) as it lay at anchor on the Yangtze twenty-seven miles from the fighting. Two British gunboats, *Ladybird* and *Bee*, and two Standard Oil tankers filled with Chinese refugees seeking shelter also went down, their survivors strafed by Japanese fighters as they attempted to swim to shore. More Americans perished when another U.S. gunboat, the *Tutuila*, was bombed by the Japanese at Chungking.[15] Although mere footnotes to the widespread slaughter occurring at this time, these sinkings nevertheless received considerable attention in the Western press.

Despite the vivid accounts of witnesses and the rousing headlines in both the British and American press, the international community yet again failed to take effective action. A Nine-Power Treaty Conference was hastily convened at Brussels in November 1937, but Japan naturally refused to attend, and in the end no sanctions were taken against Tokyo. Instead, a perversely outraged Prime Minister Konoe denounced the Chinese government for its "actions . . . [and] its anti-Japanese movement," and what's more, he added that "they show no sign of reflection [remorse]." Nor for that matter did Konoe or Hirohito show remorse throughout the "China Incident"[16] as fresh Japanese divisions, aided by heavy naval aerial bombardment, attacked Canton and the three Wuhan cities (Wuchang, Hankow, and Hanyang).

•

Far to the north, along the border of desolate Manchurian-Siberian outposts, the situation remained tense—and on at least one occasion, the inevitable occurred. On July 11, 1938, without orders from Tokyo, Japanese troops of the 19th Division attacked the Soviets holding a hill along that northern frontier. This time the Nipponese were repulsed with heavy losses.

In May the following year, the Japanese clashed again with Soviet troops near the village of Nomonhan, on the northwestern frontier between Manchukuo and the USSR's Mongolian Republic. The fighting was fierce from the outset, both sides backed by major forces. Casualties quickly mounted. With the arrival of substantial Soviet reinforcements—thirty-five infantry battalions, twenty cavalry squadrons, five hundred modern warplanes, and a like number of tanks, all under the command of General Georgi Zhukov—the odds turned heavily against the unprepared Japanese. In the battles that ensued, Kwantung's entire 23rd Division was annihilated in the first major Japanese defeat in modern times. Ultimately the Japanese suffered some nineteen thousand casualties, exclusive of those of their Manchurian "allies." The fighting ended in September 1939 with a full Japanese retreat, followed by the signing of a humiliating truce with Moscow on the 15th of that same month.[17]

One special Japanese army unit stationed in the bleak wastes of the north, in Manchuria to be precise, was to play a critical role in a variety of military engagements not only against the Soviets but against the Chinese as well. In fact, very few individuals were ever to learn of the existence of the top-secret Unit 731 of the Imperial Japanese Army, established to develop biological and chemical warfare at Pingkiāng (Harbin), Changchun, and other locations in 1933, later expanding to Peking, Kwangchow (Guangzhou), and Singapore.

"Colonel Miyata Tsuneyashi," alias Ishii Shiro—a career army officer in charge of the biochemical institute, which was disguised as the Epidemic Prevention Research Laboratory in the Imperial Army Hospital of Tokyo—was given this command to create basic experimentation centers in Manchuria for the development of toxic gases as well as variants of plague, anthrax, typhoid, dysentery, smallpox, and cholera. This unit was unlike any other in the armies across the world, for the Japanese the use of any such "products" against an enemy in the field was closely controlled by Hirohito himself. Ishii could experiment as much as he liked in Manchuria on thousands of Chinese POWs placed at his disposal, but only the *emperor himself* could authorize the use of these agents on the battlefield. Thus a precise record was maintained of each such authorization by the Imperial Palace in Tokyo. Later, this growing concentration of power for all military actions, regardless of the location or the subject, was to cripple the imperial chain of command as Hirohito increasingly dictated battle actions on his own, whether or not they included the use of poisonous gases and agents.

Unit 731 was very much a family enterprise. It was financed directly by the Japanese army, for instance, of which Hirohito's cousin, Prince Takeda Tsunehisa, was the senior financial officer, thus responsible for Unit 731's annual budget and payroll. Hirohito's uncle Prince Kan'in Kotohito, as chief of the Army General Staff, had to receive Hirohito's personal authorization before he could order the use of any toxic gas or agent. And this applied to *each gas attack*. In 1938, 375 such attacks were launched between August and the end of the year, and each time the personal imperial sanction from the palace had to be received. This included those carried out during the Wuhan offensive. Later, Hirohito authorized the release of plague-infested fleas over certain Chinese cities, and during the 1939 war against General Zhukov's Soviet forces, he allowed the use of various biological agents to poison rivers and wells. In 1939, fifteen thousand canisters of poisonous gas were released. Hirohito's reliance on this brand of warfare reflected in part the vastly superior size of the Chinese fighting force, for which poison gas, capable of killing large numbers of people at once, could compensate. (Japan's use of gas attacks was later addressed by the War Crimes Tribunal following World War II, where U.S. General Douglas MacArthur, in conjunction with the White House, intervened to cover up the role played by Hirohito and members of the imperial family.)[18]

Although Japan had signed the Versailles Treaty, whose Article 171 banned the use of poison gas, Hirohito had later declined to ratify the Geneva Convention on the Treatment of Prisoners of War in 1929. In any event, he chose to ignore both agreements, using Chinese civilians and POWs as human guinea pigs during Unit 731's "experiments." These tests were often filmed; upon viewing one such army film sent to Tokyo, a disturbed young Prince Mikasa complained to Hirohito, recording in his diary how he watched "large numbers of Chinese prisoners of war . . . [who] were made to march on the Manchurian plain for poison gas experiments, carried out on live subjects . . . [while others were] tied to posts in a wide field, gassed and shot." It was, he said, "a massacre."[19]

Hirohito's attitude toward the entire subject of treatment of POWs was greatly influenced by a Tokyo University professor of international law, Tachi Sakutarō, who scorned any international (Western-inspired) constraints. Indeed, Hirohito even went so far as to forbid the designation "prisoner of war" when applied to Chinese troops captured in battle. To Japanese eyes, these POWs were less than human and required no special or even minimal treatment or consideration.

That the Japanese used Chinese, Korean, and Western POWs for bayonet practice is common knowledge, as photo archives attest, but the extent of Japan's use of poison gases and lethal biological cultures against even major Chinese cities is less well known. On August 5, 1937, "Uncle Kan'in" issued the following top-secret directive to the Japanese army:

> In the present situation, in order to wage total war in China, the empire will neither apply nor act in accordance with, all the concrete articles of the Treaty Concerning the Laws and Customs of Land Warfare, and Other Treaties concerning the Laws and regulations of Belligerency.[20]

On July 28 of that same year, Hirohito had allowed the use of chemical weapons in Manchuria. In 1940, Hirohito was first to introduce biological weapons in China, perhaps encouraged by the failure of the League of Nations in 1938 to condemn his previous use of poisonous gas elsewhere. Nor did Hirohito discourage the high command from launching large-scale bombing raids against Shanghai, Nanking, and the capital of Chungking. These attacks included the use of incendiary explosives (each of which caused widespread fires) and antipersonnel explosives (which scattered hundreds of pieces of metal) against civilian populations, a program largely executed by the navy's long-range bombers from Nagasaki.

In the final analysis, the mass gassing of hundreds of thousands of Chinese POWs captured during the eight-year war in China had dramatic impact, similar to what the Germans were doing in their concentration camps against Jews and other prisoners. At the conclusion of World War II, only fifty-six Chinese POWs were found alive.

The "China Incident" was clearly out of control, despite all the drastic measures taken: by the end of the 1930s, Hirohito had already committed some 700,000 Japanese troops to the battlefields and ultimately would treble that number. "Strengthen the containment of the enemy and destroy his will to continue fighting," the emperor ordered. On his instructions the Japanese military would murder 2.7 million Chinese noncombatants as well, but the stubborn Chinese never surrendered. Hirohito's policy of *sankōsakusen*—"burn all, kill all, steal all"—proved a true demonstration of Japan's "New Order in East Asia."[21]

•

The year 1939 had proven to be a disastrous one for Japan. It was not winning the war in China, thereby requiring the deployment of many more troops than ever anticipated. It had lost its first large-scale battle with a well-equipped modern Soviet military and for the first time had been forced to withdraw and sign a humiliating truce. It had also used, with little success at this stage at least, biological warfare against the Russians. Then, in July, President Roosevelt's government informed the Japanese that it would not be renewing the U.S.-Japan Treaty of Commerce and Navigation in January 1940. This was by far the worst and most vital blow so far as Japan's future was concerned. It meant the cutting off of oil and metal products, without which Hirohito's expanding military forces could not continue. "Even if we can purchase [oil and scrap metal] for the next six months, we will have difficulties immediately thereafter," an anxious Hirohito acknowledged.[22] This had been among his greatest fears ever since the invasion of Manchuria back in 1931, and now they were about to be realized. To be sure, the country and its armed forces had been gradually building up reserves of metal and oil, but now Tokyo would have to act very quickly to ensure alternative sources. Compounding Hirohito's bad year was Germany's betrayal by its signing of a Non-Aggression Pact with Japan's great enemy, Moscow, on August 23, 1939. This pact nullified the Japan-German Anti-Comintern Pact of 1936, leaving the Soviets free to build up substantial military forces in the Far East. Hence Japan's quick decision to sign a truce with the Soviets over the Mongolian issue.[23] Once again the emperor would be looking over his shoulder.

•

In 1940, important decisions by Hirohito and his military leaders ensued, along with a general hardening of the line that would escalate the number of problems facing Japan. On June 1, Hirohito selected Kido Kōichi as his new Lord Keeper of the Privy Seal. Although only fifty-one, a very young age at which to hold such a major post, Kido was a man of great influence, a member of the senior aristocracy and a traditional militarist. In his new position, Kido met with the emperor daily—indeed, more frequently than anyone else apart from Hirohito's private secretary—and was able to use his position to bring Hirohito around to supporting a deeper commitment to the war in China. He even persuaded the emperor to overcome his deep suspicions and wariness of Germany.[24]

Kido's presence now seemed timely, for Germany's startling triumphs in Europe throughout May and June 1940 were bound to influence Hirohito's actions. Mesmerized not only by Germany's "Samurai" might but also by the Reich's lightning victories over Denmark, the Netherlands, Belgium, and France—the very sort of success he had been hoping in vain to achieve in China—Hirohito was convinced that Britain would be next to fall. If that occurred, Japan would suddenly be free to move into all the Far Eastern colonies of those conquered nations with impunity. At one fell blow Japan would have all the oil, rubber, and tin it needed.

But no Westerner could have readily discerned what Hirohito's intentions were when he asked Prince Kan'in, "As soon as peace comes to Europe [with the defeat of Britain] will there be a deployment of [Japanese] troops to the Netherlands Indies and French Indochina?" (Hirohito traditionally gave his opinions and orders in the form of a question.) Hirohito further disguised his ambitions by distancing himself from past conquerors. Napoleon and Frederick the Great, he claimed, had carried out illegal invasions, "Machiavellian acts," as he called them, but "our country does not wish to imitate them." Instead, "shouldn't we always bear in mind the true spirit of *hakkō ichiū* [benevolent rule], which has been our policy ever since the age of the gods?"[25] Hirohito was anticipating full-scale invasions of several countries, but describing them instead as acts of "benevolent rule." It is little wonder that the emperor's words and actions were rarely understood in London and Washington. In fact, his plans were even grander still: in case of a British rejection of his request to cut off all supplies to Chiang Kai-shek, he continued, "We shall then be forced to occupy Hong Kong [as well] and might, ultimately, even have to declare war [against Britain]."[26]

When Prince Konoe was called upon to form a new government in July 1940, he selected two very militant individuals for key cabinet posts: General Tōjō Hideki—the brutal former head of the dreaded secret police in Manchuria—as army minister, and Matsuoka Yōsuke as foreign minister. Four days later, Matsuoka gave one of the most extraordinary interviews on record for a diplomat, declaring that "without question in the battle between democracy and totalitarianism the latter will triumph and control the world. The era of democracy is finished," he asserted, and "Fascism will develop in Japan through the people's will. It will evolve through love of our Emperor."[27]

This was followed by a top-level secret Liaison Conference to discuss a new policy paper entitled "Main Principles for Dealing with the

Situation Accompanying Changes in the World." This document argued that in order to facilitate the conquest of China, the Japanese military had to move south, and then still further into the region of the Dutch East Indies, while incorporating British Malaya. At the same time it recommended allying Japan with the Germans and applying a "New Order" doctrine to the whole of Asia.[28] If successful, these invasion plans would ensure major sources of oil, rubber, tin, and timber for Japan. Admiral Prince Fushimi assured Hirohito that the navy was not at all worried about the lack of progress in China, which would not interfere with the navy's ability to move against the anticipated foreign targets mentioned. Nevertheless he was fearful of provoking a war with the United States. Konoe, too, supported the drive into East Asia and the South Pacific, including French Indochina.

At another strategy meeting held in the palace on July 29, 1940, Hirohito asked his military chiefs if they were planning "to occupy points in India, Australia and New Zealand?" In other words, these territories were to be added to the agenda. But he suddenly interjected with a most pertinent question: in the event of war, could Japan "obtain a victory in a major naval battle with the United States as we once did in the Battle of the Japan Sea [against the Russians in 1905]?"[29] Hirohito was considering a non-aggression pact with Moscow in order to neutralize a threat from the north, but on whom could Japan really depend? "Both Germany and the Soviet Union are untrustworthy," he sighed. "Don't you think there would be a problem if one of them betrays us . . . at a moment when we might be fighting the United States?" Irritated by the evasive answers he was receiving, including the stock reply that they might be able to act or win in the event "a favorable opportunity presented itself," Hirohito finally snapped. "I take it then that you people are trying to resolve these problems by availing yourselves of today's 'good opportunities'!"[30]

Time was running out for Japan, and the pressure was mounting on Hirohito, who wanted rock-bottom assurances from his military chiefs that they could indeed succeed in any of these scenarios. In war, however, there are never rock-bottom assurances for anyone. He certainly did not receive them now, and with the announcement that the U.S. Congress had passed the Export Control Act, Hirohito was more tense than ever, for this officially meant that all chemicals, minerals, oil, copper, tin, aircraft parts, and tools still theoretically available could not be bought by anyone without "licenses." On that same date, July 5, Vichy chief Henri Philippe Pétain broke off diplomatic relations with Britain, while opening negotiations with the Japanese Foreign Office.

•

Less than a month after surrendering an army of over 1.5 million men to the Germans in June 1940, Pétain's government was already beginning to feel the consequences of that unpropitious act, not merely in France but everywhere across its far-flung empire. Nowhere was that more evident than in the long troublesome colony of Indochina, where the results of the surrender were to unleash a tidal wave across Asia and the waters of the Pacific, ultimately striking the shores of the United States itself.

Until August 1940, Indochina's Governor General, Georges Catroux —although having long encountered difficulties with the government of Thailand over counterclaims to the buffer zone of Laos, which lay between the two countries—had enjoyed generally friendly commercial relations with General Chiang Kai-shek's army in southwestern China, near Indochina's northern frontier. The Chinese supreme commander, more and more battered and limited in action by the Japanese and even by the Communists, depended heavily at this stage on the flow of supplies, such as rice, that reached him by ship and French railway, traveling from Haiphong on the Gulf of Tonkin to Kunming. Catroux's French Indochina shared the same anxieties and the same foes as Chiang's China. Indeed, within Indochina proper, Nationalists and Communists were pressing Catroux's 40,000-man army (soon to be reinforced by up to 20,000 additional men) to the limit.

And yet that situation was hardly new. Joseph-Simon Galliéni had faced similar "pacification problems" within Indochina in the nineteenth century, in addition to attacks by the Chinese demanding the return of this land. The fighting in Indochina had hardly relented ever since, and in consequence Indochina,[31] unlike its neighboring British and Dutch colonies, became dominated by the military rather than by a large French civilian commercial population. Indochina's financial balance sheet had always been in the red and the colony had long been a drain on the coffers of Metropolitan France, as had other French holdings throughout Africa, north and south of the Sahara. Major French communities—excluding government personnel and the military—failed to develop except in Tunisia (where Italian immigrants made up most of the population) and some cities in Algeria and Morocco; hence there was a constant need for injections of fresh cash and subventions from Paris. Nor was the French colonial empire—one vast military operation—generally popular either in the country or in the French National Assembly: apart from a few businesses, only the great Parisian banks had profited from these colonial misadventures. Thus, whereas most British colonies thrived by relying heavily upon local, indigenous peoples to fill the lower echelons of colonial administration and the military, nothing even remotely similar existed in French possessions.

Given this background and the traditional Parisian anticolonial attitude, General Catroux's attempt to contain a difficult situation worsened sharply in 1940 as news of France's defeat and subjugation by the Germans—before the battle for France had even begun—caused its international prestige to plummet. Catroux had been attempting to strengthen ties with the British in Singapore and India while appealing to the American State Department directly for arms. The British, while sympathetic, were for their part greatly overextended, incapable (as Churchill acknowledged) of defending properly even their own widespread Asian possessions. Nor was Sumner Welles of the U.S. State Department any more helpful, for Washington, although supportive of a pro-China policy, was not yet militarily prepared for a confrontation with Japan.[32]

Unlike Pétain and his future deputy, Admiral Jean-François Darlan, Catroux was no defeatist. He was determined to defend Indochina with its limited forces, including six artillery groups and five dozen fighters and bombers and a few warships. But Catroux, who was finally to join the Gaullists in July, was very unpopular with Pétain and especially with Admiral Darlan's close friend, Foreign Minister Paul Baudoin—all of them collaborators with the Third Reich—not to mention the new colonial minister, Charles Platon. The result was the announcement of Catroux's replacement on June 25, 1940, as Governor General by Pétain's man, Admiral Jean Decoux.[33] From this point on everything went downhill rapidly, as the Japanese moved to take full advantage of French frailty at home.

Tokyo immediately went in for the kill, beginning with the first of a series of ultimatums in Paris/Vichy: a demand that France sever its rail links with China and Chiang Kai-shek's forces. Meanwhile, a Japanese "Control Unit" arrived to supervise the scene at Haiphong to ensure that supplies and arms were being stopped by sea and rail. The French gave in, and the original thirteen-man "Control Team" soon multiplied to 260 (mostly soldiers) as a Japanese destroyer cruised through the Gulf of Tonkin to register the government's serious intentions. The French foreign minister's call for "a very wide-ranging collaboration between Indochina and Japan" was rejected out of hand by an impatient Japanese Foreign Minister Matsuoka, whose "bizarre attitudes and unstable character" greatly disturbed Pétain and his advisers.[34]

This was just the beginning, however. Matsuoka soon demanded French participation in the war against China, as well, requiring northern Indochina to host Japanese airports, transit points (port facilities), and free passage for the Japanese Army of Canton. The French gradually caved in after several more ultimatums, including one by General Nishihara for the "stationing" of 5,000 (later 25,000) Japanese troops in the region. (They of course were not to be referred to as "troops of occupation.")

Although an accord was signed on September 22, 1940, agreeing to all the principal demands, Japan's Army of Canton nonetheless advanced that same night, attacking the French at Langson in a battle lasting four days. Also that day, Japanese warships arrived at Haiphong Harbor and began landing troops. The Japanese now had a solid base in northern Indochina, all legally sanctioned by Vichy.[35]

•

Three days earlier, Hirohito had taken another major step toward bringing Japan closer to war with the West: an urgent Liaison Conference was convened, at which, after much discussion, he agreed to sign a Tripartite Pact with Nazi Germany and Fascist Italy. The pact was duly executed on September 27, 1940. Clearly, the passing of the American Export Control Act had been a critical factor in bringing Japan to this decision,[36] although given Foreign Minister Matsuoka's high praise of fascism, this should hardly have come as a surprise to anyone. And as Hirohito confided to Prime Minister Konoe after signing the Tripartite

Pact, "If there is no other way of handling America, then it cannot be helped." But he also asked apprehensively, "What will happen if Japan should be defeated [in a war with America]?" Konoe remained silent. Never before had he heard Hirohito mention the word "defeat." "Will you, prime minister, bear the burden with me?" the emperor pressed.[37] Perhaps Hirohito had forgotten General Araki's earlier definition of "command," when Araki had stated, "The spirit of the Japanese military manifests the sacred spirit of His Majesty who in turn commands the Japanese military itself. I believe our spirit expresses the emperor's heart, which is why *the imperial forces move only at the emperor's command.*"[38]

"The great principle of the eight corners of the world under one roof is the teaching of our imperial ancestors," an imperial rescript of September 27, 1940, began. "Today, however, the world is deeply troubled everywhere and disorder seems endless. As the disasters that mankind may suffer are immeasurable, We sincerely hope to bring about a cessation of hostilities and a restoration of peace," and hence the government's decision "to ally itself with Germany and Italy, nations that share the same good intentions as ourselves. . . ."[39]

As Winston Churchill would soon conclude, "Well, when heads of states become gangsters, something has got to be done!"[40] Prince Konoe even upped the ante with another masterpiece of logic. "If the United States does not understand the position of Japan, Germany and Italy . . . and *if it constantly adopts a confrontational attitude,* then we three countries will fight [America] resolutely."[41] Nevertheless, it was Hirohito who got in the last word on Anniversary Day, November 11, 1940. As Japan celebrated its 2,600th birthday, he enjoined the Japanese people "to promote at home and abroad the grand principle of the Way of the Gods, thereby contributing to the welfare of mankind."[42] And that same month Hirohito demonstrated his benevolence by forcing his puppet regime in China to sign the Japan-China Basic Treaty at bayonet point, as the fighting expanded. The pendulum continued to swing faster and faster.

CHAPTER V

Unlimited National Emergency

"The president is determined that we shall win the war together."

—Harry Hopkins to Winston Churchill, January 10, 1941[1]

"Since it is inexcusable for [U.S.] military forces to be unprepared for an attack . . . it is recommended that steps be taken to place our Army and Navy forces in the Far East in an Alert status. . . ."

—Rear Admiral Kelly Turner to CNO Harold Stark, July 11, 1941[2]

Many thousands of miles away, in Washington, D.C., Rear Admiral Kelly Turner was, as usual, working round the clock. Turner's career had suffered a severe setback in December 1937, as he was completing a two-year stint on the faculty of the Naval War College. After his annual physical, doctors had informed him that due to a deterioration in his eyesight, his flying days, at least as a solo pilot, were over.[3] Therefore instead of being given the command of a carrier as promised, he had found himself captain of the heavy cruiser *Astoria*—a post that concluded in 1939 with the delicate diplomatic mission of returning Ambassador Saitō's remains to Tokyo. That assignment, it was hoped, would help slow the burning Asian fuse, buying time for the United States while permitting Captain Turner to assess the state of the Japanese military. Upon his return in 1940, Turner had been called to Washington as director of Naval Planning under CNO Harold Stark and promoted to flag rank. Thus by 1941 the future actions of the U.S.

Navy, to a considerable extent, lay in his hands. It was up to him to apprise a very frustrated Franklin Roosevelt of when the navy would be in a position to defend itself and the interests of the country.

•

Unlike Admiral Ernest King, Kelly Turner detested cocktail parties, but he was ordered by his superiors to attend one on March 11, 1941, given in honor of the new Japanese ambassador, Admiral Nomura Kichisaburō. Although a distinguished sailor in his own right, Nomura had seen his reputation somewhat tarnished in 1932 after he commanded the Japanese naval forces attacking Shanghai and other parts of China. On this particular evening, the sixty-four-year-old Nomura mentioned in passing that he should like to speak with Turner privately, and the next day arranged for a meeting. Informing Admiral Stark of the situation, the CNO encouraged Turner to meet Nomura, to take full notes, and to get back to him. It was to be the first of several important such encounters.

Turner reported of his March meeting that Nomura began by emphasizing that it was in "the best interests of the two countries . . . to maintain peace" and that he was seeing Turner now in order to explore "the ground . . . to find a basis on which the two nations could agree" to some sort of accommodation. Nomura personally denounced the war in China and blamed it on a "younger radical element" of the Japanese army. Turner of course had a fairly detailed knowledge of the series of assassinations and attempted coups in Japan over the past several years, and thus had a pretty good idea of the type of people Nomura was now referring to (though he was unfamiliar with Nomura's own earlier actions in China). Senior Japanese naval officers had no wish for a war with the United States, Nomura stressed, any more than they had "any desire to extend control over the Philippines." Nomura therefore thought it wise for the United States and Britain to maintain a strong naval presence in the Pacific in order to help stabilize the situation, thereby impressing upon the Japanese army the realities of the forces with which it would have to contend should its leaders push matters too far. In his report to Stark, Turner concluded, "I believe he is fully sincere and that he will use his influence against further aggressive moves by the military forces of Japan."[4]

By the middle of 1941, events were hurtling forward around the eight corners of the world. Britain was blockading German and French ports, and on June 22, Hitler unleashed another surprise attack, this time against the Soviet Union. The maneuver at once relieved Hirohito's considerable anxiety that the Soviets might attack the Japanese in Manchuria, even though Tokyo had signed a so-called Neutrality Pact with Moscow back in April. The Japanese military could now commit itself more forcefully in its drive across Asia and the South Pacific.[5] As for the war in China, there the Japanese were now mired down in the fourth year of the "Incident." If in 1937 Hirohito had committed only a quarter of a million troops to that country, by the end of this year, 1941, he would have over 2 million on Chinese soil.[6] So much for his promised "three-month campaign."

On July 2, 1941, the emperor convened another historic war council at the palace to discuss immediate policy, confirming Japan's advance southward to "establish a solid basis for our national preservation and security," and to create the much-vaunted "Greater East Asia Co-Prosperity Sphere" that would restore the health of the entire Far East. "In order to achieve the above objectives [driving south and ending the China war] *preparations for war with Great Britain and the United States will be made* . . . ," Hirohito announced. "Our empire will not be deterred by the possibility of being involved in a war with Great Britain and the United States."[7] He then authorized the occupation of southern Indochina in three weeks' time, from which troops could more easily launch still further invasions.[8]

Under extreme Japanese pressure, the French in Indochina had at last signed a peace treaty with their longtime nemesis Thailand at Tokyo back on May 9, 1940, thus putting an end to years of fighting in the west. Yet this still left Indochina facing the full brunt of a frontal diplomatic attack from the east by Tokyo.[9] The Japanese would first seize all Chinese merchandise blocked in the Tonkin area by the end of May, and by July would be demanding to occupy the whole of southern Indochina, or Cochin-China.

If the original pretext for entering Indochina the previous year had been to deny Chiang Kai-shek access to provisions and war matériel via Hanoi-Haiphong, Tokyo now hoisted its true colors, demanding major military bases in this area—army, air, and naval—for the launching of fresh attacks on Indochina's neighboring countries. Japanese troops began pouring into southern Indochina by July 20 and Admiral Decoux, as that colony's new administrator, was obliged to sign a convention with General Sumita on July 23, ceding the remaining southern half of Indochina to Japan as well. On the 29th of the month, at Vichy, Darlan duly signed a protocol to this effect and exchanged letters with the new Japanese ambassador, Admiral Katō Kanji. The document now referred to the Franco-Japanese "joint defense of Indochina" (*défense commune de l'Indochine*) against any foreign aggression, that is, American or British. Once again it was stressed that Japanese troops permanently occupying the country—the figure varied from 30,000 to 80,000—were neither "permanent" nor "occupying" the land, but were in fact simply "stationed" there alongside some 100,000 French citizens (administrators, soldiers, and businessmen).[10] Another convoy of 50,000 Japanese troops already en route would be arriving shortly as Tokyo prepared for the next phase of its "gradual and peaceful expansion" into British Malaya and the Dutch East Indies, a further implementation of its "Greater East Asia Co-Prosperity Sphere."

Admiral Turner heard nothing from Nomura again until July 20, when the ambassador's black limousine pulled up before Turner's modest residence late on a hot, steamy Washington afternoon. Nomura informed Turner that Japan was about to strike, moving into the southern part of Indochina with large military forces occupying new military bases there. (In fact, the Signal Intelligence Service, or SIS, of the U.S. Army intercepted this news earlier and had decoded it just the day before.) Nomura had been sent here now to try to justify Japan's position, stating that it had to have "uninterrupted access to necessary raw materials," for the economic situation in Japan proper was very bad indeed, and one of the reasons for the present war with China. Moreover, he explained to Turner, it was necessary "to break the connection between Russia and China," hence the reason for Japanese troops in Inner Mongolia. And although Nomura justified the occupation of southern Indochina as "essential," he added that Japan was planning on no further moves southward "for the time being." His country had the right to defend itself, Nomura repeated uncomfortably.

Concluding his report to Stark about this extraordinary meeting, Turner warned: "The occupation of Indo-China by Japan is particularly important for the defense of the United States, since it might threaten the British position in Singapore and the Dutch position in the Netherlands East Indies," and the Americans in the Philippines.[11] Stark sent Turner's latest warning over to the White House and to General George Marshall, chief of staff of the army.

As usual, Turner got to the crux of the problem immediately. Indochina was necessary to Japan not for the throttling of China, as Nomura now claimed, but as a jumping-off point for major air and sea strikes throughout the Far East. In Indochina, Japanese forces were hundreds of miles closer to objectives such as the English fortress of Singapore at the bottom of the Malay Peninsula—"the Gibraltar of the Far East"—and were better able to guard commercial interests and the flow of commodities, including rubber, tin, and oil. Their new position also increased protection of the vital shipping lanes between the South China Sea and the Indian Ocean, while leaving the Philippines fully exposed. In a year's time, the further seizure of Singapore and the oil-rich Dutch East Indies would prove a very grave blow indeed to the West and would expand Japan's own military opportunities considerably. (Turner was of course totally unfamiliar with Japan's top-secret long-term military policies drawn up since 1936.)

Nor had the rest of the news reaching Washington been any more encouraging. A German U-boat had sunk another U.S. merchant ship back on May 21, and yet Admiral Stark still had not provided escort convoys in the Atlantic to prevent such attacks now or in the future. Then, on July 30, the Japanese air force bombed an American gunboat, this time the *Tutuila*, at Chungking. If Turner could not control those actions, he could make recommendations to the White House thanks to his periodic meetings with Roosevelt's personal confidant, Harry Hopkins—a man who was to play an important role, both directly and indirectly, in the country's preparations for war.

•

About the only normal thing in Harry Hopkins's brief life was his having been born into a reasonably normal family, on August 17, 1890, in the reasonably normal town of Sioux City, Iowa. He was the son of David Hopkins, an incompetent businessman—sometime traveling salesman, sometime harness store owner—from Bangor, Maine, and of

Anna Picket, a schoolteacher born in Hamilton, Ontario, and raised in South Dakota.[12]

Harry Hopkins was the fourth of five children: one girl and four boys. His mother, a fervent Methodist and supporter of the Methodist Missionary Society of Iowa, was evidently the driving force in a family that was always trying unsuccessfully to make ends meet. After high school, young Harry Hopkins attended the Methodist-sponsored Grinnell College, where he achieved some notoriety as a perpetual rebel against the authorities, Grinnell College's greatest practical joker, and, most unlikely of all for someone so thin and badly coordinated, the college's star basketball player. He was close and even devoted to two of his professors, one of sociology, the other of political science. He was an extroverted, hardworking, puritanical young man, who challenged everything and participated in so many extracurricular activities that he managed with considerable ease to graduate in the lower half of his class. The fact that he even graduated almost shocked his mother, who admitted, "I can't ever make Harry out," a sentiment no doubt shared by many of his friends and enemies throughout the tempestuous career to follow.

With BA in hand, Harry set out for New York City. There he began a long career in social work, in which capacity he met his future wife, fellow social worker Ethel Gross. (The fact that she was Jewish does not seem to have proven too great an obstacle to their relationship.) They would have three sons and were both deadly earnest about their work, both politically involved in the city, and both very independent people. Hopkins attended political conventions and worked in various New York City welfare departments, where he quickly proved an extraordinary administrator capable of finding apples even at the bottom of seemingly empty barrels. Yet when it came to his own finances, his pockets were always empty well before the end of the month—perhaps owing in part to the fact that, when not at work, Hopkins could often be found in the two-dollar line at the race track, or, when he could afford it, at nightclubs.

It was through politics that his career moved away from general social work to administering welfare through government organizations. He had attended the Republican National Convention in Chicago when Theodore Roosevelt had complained about the "thieves" running the Republican Party, and he had first met Franklin Roosevelt in 1928 during FDR's campaign for the governorship of New York. "Our Government is not the master but the creature of the people. The duty of the State toward the citizens is the duty of the servant to its master. . . . One of these duties of the State is that of caring for those of its citizens who find themselves the victims of . . . adverse circumstance, poverty, and unemployment."[13] After that speech, a profoundly moved Hopkins was Roosevelt's man. Once in Albany, Hopkins was named to the Temporary Emergency Relief Administration, chaired at first by Roosevelt himself. Harry Hopkins also continued to work for the Tuberculosis and Health Association, where one of his colleagues, a physician, summed up this tall, slender, curious young man in a few sentences: "You could mark him down as an ulcerous type. He was intense, seeming to be in a perpetual nervous ferment—a chain smoker and black coffee drinker. He was always careless in his appearance." Many years later, a dismayed British prime minister was to give Hopkins his own hat after seeing the battered one his American visitor was wearing. "Most of the time," his former colleague continued, "he would show up in the office looking as though he had spent the previous night sleeping in a hayloft." Still another friend, Joseph Davies, once remarked, "He had the purity of St. Francis of Assisi combined with the sharp shrewdness of a race track tout."[14]

As for Franklin Roosevelt, he had no greater admirer than Harry Hopkins, who wrote to his brother, "I am convinced that Roosevelt is not only fearless, but a very able executive. All this business about his health is utter nonsense. I have seen a great deal of him within the past few months, and the amount of work that he can carry out is perfectly amazing."[15] This was no mean praise coming from the most demanding Hopkins.

When Roosevelt went to the White House in 1933, Hopkins did so too, at first to cope with the evils of the Great Depression as head of the Public Works Administration (PWA, later the WPA, or Works Progress Administration). Once, as a hesitant Congress debated granting the funds he demanded, a frustrated Hopkins replied, "Hunger is not debatable," and when told that everything would work out in the end, Hopkins snapped back, "People don't eat in the long run—they eat every day." Back at his new office, Hopkins put through 180,000 public works projects in less than four months, at a cost of $933 million.[16]

During these early White House years, Roosevelt and Hopkins got to know and respect one another at a close, personal level. By this time Hopkins was long divorced and had discovered that he was seriously ill with a rare malady destroying his ability to digest food. Hopkins was to spend the rest of his days in and out of hospitals. When his second wife, Barbara Duncan, died, Eleanor Roosevelt herself took in Diana, Hopkins's six-year-old daughter.[17]

In 1940, Roosevelt offered the ailing Hopkins two rooms on the second floor of the White House, formerly a large, single study where Abraham Lincoln had written the Emancipation Proclamation freeing the nation's slaves.[18] In addition to his bedroom with its large four-poster bed (inevitably covered with heaps of files and scattered notes), Hopkins had a second, smaller room that was used as his secretary's office, his secretary having to make do with a folding card table as a desk for several years. Hopkins never was one for pomp. Opposite him, in the southwest corner of that wing, Eleanor Roosevelt had a sitting room and a small bedroom, whereas the northeast corner of the floor was set aside for guests such as Queen Elizabeth and Winston Churchill. Nearby was the president's study, and off it Roosevelt's bedroom and bath. This section of the White House reflected the Hyde Park touch—old, dark, comfortable, and informal—and it was from this long, dingy corridor that the U.S. government was run.

Robert Sherwood, who got to know FDR and Harry Hopkins very well during the ensuing years, once remarked that "Roosevelt and Hopkins were alike in one important way: they were thoroughly and gloriously unpompous. The predominant qualities in both were unconquerable confidence, courage and good humor."[19] They were going to need every one of those three attributes in the trying days ahead as they coped with the problems of the approaching war. They also shared an absolute, unshakable trust in one another, something rarely witnessed in history at any time.

•

During Admiral Kelly Turner's several meetings with Harry Hopkins at the White House in 1941, the two men seemed to understand one another perfectly. Both were serious, both were single-minded, both were very determined . . . and the word "impossible" never passed their lips.

At one such working lunch in April, Hopkins asked Turner abruptly, "What steps might be taken on the assumption that the United States might be in the war on August first?" The admiral recommended that "a detachment of the Pacific Fleet be sent at an early date to the Atlantic [where U-boats were taking a heavy toll on British merchantmen]; that enough anti-aircraft guns and pursuit aircraft be diverted from deliveries to the British and assigned to the United States Army . . . [to] outfit the ground and air defense units which would protect [future] United States bases in the British Isles." He also recommended that the president immediately requisition "approximately thirty transports, freighters and tankers," while increasing naval and Marine Corps personnel to bring all units, including the additional crews for these new ships, up to full strength.[20] Just the week before, Roosevelt had, under a "Limited National Emergency" declared earlier, already increased naval strength to 232,000 officers and men.[21]

Within a week following this April meeting, Admiral Turner had drawn up and presented the proposal known as the Project for Western Hemisphere Defense Plans. It called for the creation of a two-ocean navy by transferring an aircraft carrier, battleships, and cruisers from Hawaii to the Atlantic, and the acquisition or requisitioning of 550,000 tons of transports, freighters, and tankers to bolster the existing six "battle-fitted" naval transports. Even these additions would prove scarcely sufficient. Despite the gravity of his illness, underscored by weeks at a time spent in the old naval hospital, Hopkins somehow got an enormous amount of work done on the Lend-Lease program and Turner's new "Project." Both Turner and Hopkins worked vigorously to implement Turner's vast plan quickly, and by mid-May it was authorized by FDR.[22]

It was ironic that two such seriously ill men as Roosevelt and Hopkins were the dynamic political force behind the staggeringly immense and complicated war preparations that would be undertaken over the next four years. Both of them were living on very limited bursts of energy . . . and indeed on borrowed time. That Hopkins—who time and time again was nearly given up for dead by both his battery of physicians and FDR—somehow managed to hang on really did qualify as a miracle, albeit one aided by an extremely specialized diet and periodic blood transfusions.*

Hopkins had first been dispatched to Britain on a secret mission back in January 1941 with personal letters of introduction from Roosevelt to King George V and Prime Minister Churchill, explaining that "Mr. Hopkins is a very good friend of mine in whom I repose the utmost confidence," and asking them to confide in him as they would in the president himself.[23] During this sojourn Hopkins was to spend a lot of time with Churchill, who first received him at a dust-covered No. 10 Downing Street where a bevy of workmen were in the midst of repairing the latest bomb damage. Hopkins himself did not appear to be in much better shape than the prime minister's residence, arriving there in his usual crushed hat and wrinkled suit after having narrowly escaped a heavy air raid by the Luftwaffe—his train had passed through Clapham Junction amid dozens of bombs bursting all about him. The meeting with Churchill was pivotal because the two men, so very different in just about every possible manner, got on well and respected and trusted one another. This in turn was to aid greatly the close relationship Churchill and Roosevelt later developed.

Churchill's own impressions of Harry Hopkins's first visit were vivid. "On January 10 a gentleman arrived to see me at Downing Street with the highest credentials. . . . His was a soul that flamed out of a frail and failing body." Churchill's physician, Sir Charles Wilson (later Lord Moran), upon meeting the stooped, skeletal Hopkins, described him more clinically. "His lips are blanched as if he had been bleeding internally, his skin yellow, like stretched parchment and his eyelids contracted to a slit so that you can just see his eyes moving about restlessly, as if he was in pain. He looks like a Methodist but one capable of enjoying whisky and oysters."[24] Or as the inimitable Churchill summed up: "He was a crumbling lighthouse from which there shone the beams that led great fleets to harbour. . . . It was evident to me that here was an envoy from the President of supreme importance to our life. With gleaming eye and quiet constrained passion he said: 'The

*The new Bethesda Naval Hospital would open the following year, and Hopkins had an almost permanent "suite" where he could work between blood transfusions and intravenous feedings. But he was frequently too weak for any work. Reduced to a skeleton as he was, the doctors desperately attempted to get him to gain weight.

president is determined that we shall win the war together. Make no mistake about it. He has sent me here to tell you that at all costs and by all means he will carry you through, no matter what happens to him—there is nothing that he will not do so far as he has human power.' " Harry Hopkins, the prime minister concluded, "was the most faithful and perfect channel of communication between the President and me. But far more than that, he was for several years the main prop and animator of Roosevelt himself."[25] Hopkins's friendship with Churchill was to prove close and steady, as indeed was his relationship with most of Churchill's family.

Although the government put Hopkins up at Claridge's, centrally located in the heart of Mayfair, Hopkins spent nearly every weekend with the prime minister at Dytchley or Chequers, and frequently accompanied him on journeys across Britain touring factories and bombed-out cities, including Southampton, Portsmouth, Plymouth—the entire city already nearly leveled to the ground, leaving Hopkins almost in tears—Bristol, Birmingham, Manchester, and Glasgow. The whole time, Hopkins was taking copious notes of what he saw, and, more important, of the recommendations made by heads of industry and the military. In February, he filled out some thirty pages of telegram forms with lists of Britain's immediate needs, ranging from fifty-eight Wright-model 1820 airplane engines to 20 million rounds of 50-caliber ammunition.

Before leaving after a little over a month, he also had to quash false rumors circulating in London—deliberately spread previously by Joseph Kennedy, prior to his having been fired as U.S. ambassador to the Court of St. James's—including that Churchill disliked Americans and Roosevelt in particular. Sowing lies, distrust, hatred, and defeatism, Joe Kennedy had done considerable harm to the Allied cause before his abrupt dismissal, even denouncing Roosevelt himself and socializing with the pro-Nazi Cliveden set. Harry Hopkins did his best to undo these machinations to set the record straight.

By the conclusion of his long, busy sojourn in Britain, Hopkins, hardly a political sycophant, was much impressed with the British leader, upon whom he felt British victory ultimately depended. Churchill was the one indispensable individual in the entire British Isles and a real leader under all circumstances, Hopkins emphasized to FDR. In one of his final telegrams to Roosevelt, Hopkins wrote: "I was with Churchill at 2 A.M. Sunday night when he got word of the loss of the [cruiser] *Southampton*—the serious damage to the new aircraft carrier [*Illustrious*]—a second cruiser knocked about—but he never falters or displays the least despondence—till four o'clock he paced the floor telling me of his offensive and defensive plans. . . . [Nevertheless] the battering continues and Hitler does not wait for Congress [to come to Britain's aid]. . . . *Churchill* is the gov't in every sense of the word," he stressed; "he controls the grand strategy and often the details—labor trusts him—the army, navy, air force are behind him to a man. This island needs our help now Mr. President with everything we can give them. . . ."[26] But the nation had suffered almost beyond human endurance, and Churchill and the British people could not be expected to carry on alone in Europe unaided much longer. Between April 1940 and March 1941, German U-boats sank 1,677,000 gross tons of British merchant shipping in the Atlantic. This could not continue, and it was imperative that Roosevelt and Churchill meet to see what joint action could be undertaken—"the sooner the better," Hopkins wrote in February.[27]

If Roosevelt could not yet aid Britain openly, however—this was still February, and the Lend-Lease Bill, which would provide for the sale, transfer, or lease of war materials to U.S. Allies, would not be passed until March 8, 1941—at least the two countries could prepare for future cooperation.[28] Joint Anglo-American staff talks were begun in Washington even while Hopkins was in Great Britain, with Admirals R. L. Ghormley and Turner among others representing the U.S. Navy. These talks continued for the next two months and in March would produce what was termed the ABC-1 Plan, establishing the basic strategy of a war against Germany and Japan if and when the United States were to get involved. The defeat of Germany was to be given top priority over that of Japan, while the war against Japan was to be continued until the situation in Europe was stabilized enough to permit the transfer of more military forces to the Pacific. For, as Churchill explained, "There never has been a moment . . . when Great Britain or the British Empire single-handed, could fight Germany and Italy, could wage the Battle of Britain, the Battle of the Atlantic, and the Battle of the Middle East," while simultaneously fighting in the Far East "against the impact of a vast military empire like Japan." Therefore Britain, like America, was attempting to avoid a clash with Japan "at almost all costs . . . until we were sure that the United States would also be engaged" in the war.

As Churchill assured Australia's equally concerned prime minister, John Curtin, the safety of the Pacific "and ultimate victory" in that region could only be achieved by the United States after it had time to build up sufficient military forces to conquer Japan. "To be safe everywhere," Churchill pointed out, "is to be strong nowhere"—that is, spreading oneself too thin to cover every point on the compass would merely ensure widespread defeat.[29] And thus he later told Roosevelt, "Of course it is for you to handle this business [in the Far East]," while expressing his personal anxiety that "we feel that the Japanese are most unsure of themselves. Therefore one never really quite knows what they would do next."[30]

The ABC-1 Plan also spelled out the primary steps to be taken against Germany, including a blockade, intensified aerial bombing, and subversive activities and propaganda. And a permanent British Joint Staff Mission in Washington was finally agreed to; when the United States entered the war, it would eventually become the Combined Chiefs of Staff (of Britain and America).[31]

Nevertheless, several more hurdles remained to be overcome before the United States could become a much more effective ally to Britain. The isolationist right wing in America was powerful indeed, with the Lend-Lease Bill encountering considerable opposition in a 60–31 Senate vote on March 8. Roosevelt hailed the passage as "the end of compromise with tyranny,"[32] and that very night Hopkins rang up a sleeping Churchill to give him the good news. "The strain has been serious," the prime minister confessed in an unusually solemn tone, "so I thank God for your news." He went on to praise FDR as "a brilliant and great leader."[33]

A huge new organization was set up overnight, overseen by Hopkins and General James Burns as official executive director. The organization and its hundreds of employees moved into the old Federal Reserve Building with an opening budget of $7 billion, a figure that would ultimately total $60 billion. The passage of the bill—and its effects—came just in time, for the British Purchasing Commission had already paid the United States $1.337 billion in cash for supplies received, promising another $400 million by the end of 1941, leaving the vaults of the

Bank of England completely empty.[34] Thus the Lend Lease Act passed on March 8, 1941, was signed by the president on March 11, and went into effect immediately. "We the American people are writing new history today," a much-relieved FDR proclaimed before the nation. And of course the year before Britain had leased strategically important bases from the Caribbean to Newfoundland to Washington, and in September 1940 fifty reconditioned World War I–vintage destroyers had been transferred to Great Britain.

Roosevelt's planned speech celebrating Pan-American Day in 1941 was delivered on May 27, a sweltering Washington day. Ambassadors from various Latin American countries arrived at the White House in black tie and were led to the East Room, where they were seated in gilded Louis XV chairs; behind them, radio and newsreel crews crowded to hear this mysterious speech which had been so built up in the media and had aroused so much speculation. They did not have to wait long. "I hereby proclaim that an unlimited national emergency exists," FDR began before a startled audience. "From the point of view of strict naval and military necessity, we shall give every possible assistance to Britain and to all who, with Britain, are resisting Hitlerism or its equivalent with force of arms. Our patrols are helping now to insure delivery of the needed supplies to Britain. *All additional measures necessary to deliver the goods will be taken. Any and all further methods or combination of methods, which can or should be utilized, are being devised. . . .*"[35]

If it was not the full declaration of war that Churchill, for one, had been praying for, it was the next best thing. Roosevelt's announcement greatly increased the amount of war matériel and shipping required to assist the British, while permitting him a freer hand in building up the American military. Following the speech and the diplomatic reception on the South Lawn, Eleanor Roosevelt invited those who remained—including Irving Berlin—upstairs to the Monroe Room, where Roosevelt, a fan of the popular composer, begged him to play Sigmund Romberg's "Alexander's Ragtime Band." The president had every reason to celebrate that night.

•

With the German surprise attack on the Soviet Union, Lend-Lease aid would have to be made available to Moscow as well, for that country was now fighting for its very existence against well over two hundred German divisions. Late in July, Franklin Roosevelt decided to risk Hopkins's life again, albeit at the latter's insistence, by flying him to the Soviet Union via Britain. "Tell him [Stalin], tell him," Churchill insisted during Hopkins's stopover there, "Tell him that Britain has but one ambition today, but one desire—to crush Hitler. Tell him that he can depend upon us. . . . Good-bye—God bless you, Harry."[36] An unheated, unpressurized American PBY Catalina W (a large, amphibious navy plane) then flew Hopkins on the next leg of his long journey to the Soviet Union, where it was hoped he could break the ground for talks and cooperation with Stalin.

The two men had a frank and most fruitful series of têtes-à-têtes in the Kremlin, talks that were very long and very detailed. Hopkins and Stalin went down the list of Soviet military requirements and discussed the best air and sea routes required for the delivery of these supplies from the United States and Britain. The logistics alone were to prove a nightmare over the next three and a half years. Hopkins also discussed Japan with Stalin, a subject that he later reported to Roosevelt was "of very considerable concern to him and . . . he felt the Japanese would not hesitate to strike [the Soviet Union] if a propitious time occurred. Hence his great interest in the attitude of the United States toward Japan."

Their discussions were clearly enhanced by the fact that Hopkins and Stalin were both blunt, down-to-earth men. As Hopkins put it, "It was like talking to a perfectly co-ordinated machine, an intelligent machine. Joseph Stalin knew what he wanted. . . . The questions he asked were clear, concise, direct." Hopkins described Joseph Stalin for FDR as "an austere, rugged, determined figure in boots that shone like mirrors, stout baggy trousers, and snug-fitting blouse. He wore no ornament, military or civilian. . . . He's about five foot six, about a hundred and ninety pounds. His hands are huge, as hard as his mind. His voice is harsh but ever under control. . . . [H]e never wastes a syllable. . . . He's a chain smoker. . . . He laughs often enough, but it's a short laugh, somewhat sardonic, perhaps. There is no small talk in him. His humor is keen, penetrating. . . ."[37]

At the end of his brief but profitable visit, Harry Hopkins flew twenty-four hours back to Scapa Flow in Scotland, where an anxious

Prime Minister Churchill was awaiting his arrival, his bags already in the barge alongside that was to take them to the *Prince of Wales*.

Back in Washington, Roosevelt was facing the next formidable obstacle—convincing Congress to extend the Selective Service Act (SSA), which would provide the manpower to rebuild the still minuscule American armed forces. Over the weeks to come this bill would be fought as fiercely as any piece of legislation in American history. Its opponents were largely Republican isolationists, some of them with considerable national influence; they included Charles Lindbergh and his America First Committee; General Robert E. Wood; union leader John L. Lewis; Charles Leonard; businessmen Jay Hormel of Hormel Meatpacking and James D. Mooney of General Motors; various women's organizations including Catharine Curtis's Women's National Committee to Keep the U.S. Out of War; Father Charles Coughlin; and Henry Ford, all of whom shared one other common trait: a blinding anti-Semitism. Backed by the Patterson and Hearst newspaper chains, they called on U.S. servicemen to desert in October when the present Selective Service Act would expire. Their new theme: OHIO, "over the hill in October." This bitterly contested battle in Congress would become the cliff-hanger of all cliff-hangers, a decision that would ultimately hinge on a single vote when the final tally was taken in August.[38]

Throughout this time the Turner-Hopkins meetings continued to provide the means for coordinating the needs of the nation's defenses. Robert Sherwood, the White House communications chief and Pulitzer Prize–winning playwright, noted one such instance. "Roosevelt and Hopkins read a remarkably prescient memorandum prepared in the Navy Department. It was written by Admiral Richmond Kelly Turner . . . [who] foresaw the ominous possibility that by June [1941], the British might have been driven out of the Mediterranean"—this at a time when heavy fighting in Greece was still taking place and the British army in North Africa had been hurled back deep into Egypt, threatening Cairo and the Suez Canal.[39]

Turner's prediction, which was very close to being realized, was not the only grim warning to come from that admiral's desk. Back in January 1941, Turner had submitted a report through CNO Stark for Roosevelt in which he stated that "it is believed easily possible that hostilities would be initiated by a surprise [Japanese] attack upon the Fleet or the Naval Base at Pearl Harbor."[40] Turner of course realized that if the Japanese were to put the U.S. Navy out of commission, the most effective place to do so was at the point of its primary concentration, at its largest base in the Pacific, in Hawaii. Then, too, as a former naval air squadron commander, Kelly Turner was mindful of the previous maneuvers and naval war games conducted in 1928 and 1932, when planes from U.S. carriers directed by Admiral Reeves and Jack Towers, and later by Admirals Harry Yarnell, King, and again Towers, had caught Pearl Harbor by complete surprise and "destroyed" both the naval and air installations there.[41] Then it was a fleet exercise; now it could become a reality.

Nor was this the last of Turner's prognostications of just how and when war would come to the United States. After his initial talks with Admiral Nomura in Washington, he had warned Stark (and hence the secretary of the navy and FDR) that the U.S. Navy was not yet ready for a confrontation with Japan, and recommended simply "sustaining the status quo in the southern position of the Far East" for the time being.[42] In July, Turner repeated this warning, requesting that "trade with Japan not be embargoed at this time," and that American troops not be committed in a Chinese campaign against Tokyo. "To prevent her [Japan] from severing the Burma Road [which was to be used to supply General Chiang Kai-shek]," he insisted, "would lead to war," and he reiterated that no ultimatum be handed to Japan just yet.[43] Neither the army nor the navy was yet prepared to enforce such an ultimatum, he argued.

With the Third Reich's surprise attack on the Soviet Union on June 22, 1941, at once many of the factors involved changed. Turner prepared a fresh analysis on July 11, stating that the Japanese, who had been facing the real possibility of a new northern clash with Soviet forces in Siberia and Mongolia, could instead now be expected to concentrate on the south. He further warned: "*Since it is inexcusable for (US) military forces to be unprepared for an attack, even if the chances for attack be small,* it is recommended that steps be taken to place our Army and Navy forces in the Far East in an alert status to be achieved as far as practicable within about two weeks."[44] Ten days later the Japanese invaded southern Indochina, just as he had predicted. The threat against the Americans, British, and Dutch in Asia and the South Pacific was now at once greatly magnified.

As Admiral Stark himself admitted, "Probably nobody in Washington had a better understanding of the Japanese situation than Kelly did."[45] Unfortunately for the U.S. Navy, Stark chose to ignore some of Turner's prognostications and to soften the wording of others; as a result, five months later the navy was still not on proper "alert status" as defined by Turner.

With the occupation of Indochina completed by the end of July 1941, Japanese intentions were very clear as their troops concentrated around military airports and ports. Everyone from Singapore to Manila was threatened. Following a long telephone conversation with Prime Minister Churchill on July 25, Roosevelt summoned Admiral Ernest "Ernie" King, commander of the U.S. Atlantic Fleet, to his Hyde Park estate for an urgent meeting—one so secret that Admiral Stark himself was not informed for the moment. On July 26, General Marshall sent a dispatch to Douglas MacArthur ordering him to take command of the U.S. Army Forces in the Far East. That same day President Roosevelt froze all Japanese assets in the United States and closed the Panama Canal to their shipping.[46]

CHAPTER VI

"We Cannot Speculate with the Security of This Country"

"Japan has historically shown that she can misinterpret a pacifistic policy of the United States for weakness."

—*Secretary of War Henry Stimson, October 2, 1940*[1]

"If other peoples obstruct world peace and the welfare of mankind, we must be prepared to display our nationalism in a grand manner. . . ."

—*Hiranuma Kiichirō, justice minister and later prime minister of Japan*[2]

On Saturday, August 2, 1941, Admiral Ernest King ordered his flagship, the heavy cruiser *Augusta*, and her sister ship, the cruiser *Tuscaloosa*, to put to sea from their port at Newport, Rhode Island. In the nation's capital, the *Washington Post* announced a different sort of voyage: "ROOSEVELT OFF FOR SECLUDED REST ON YACHT."[3] Indeed, the lights on the second floor of the White House were burning unusually late that Saturday night as Franklin Roosevelt and his staff attempted to clear his desk of all outstanding work so as to permit him, Major General "Pa" Watson, Captain John Beardall, and the president's physician, Admiral "Doc" McIntire, to leave "for a real vacation, however brief." It had been a most hectic year, in which FDR had successfully battled Congress for the passage of the Lend-Lease Bill and was now awaiting the results of even more critical pending legislation that would allow the extension of national conscription.

That the president should wish to take a sea excursion with his aides, all equally keen fishing enthusiasts, was hardly unusual. But despite the oppressive August heat that everyone from government employees to foreign diplomats tried to escape at this time of year, the tense situation worldwide—in Europe the German army and air force were pounding the Ukraine and advancing on Moscow, while some 2 million Japanese troops advanced across China—made the president's timing seem curious, if not downright questionable.

Earlier that afternoon, Navy Secretary Frank Knox had left his office at the usual time, as had CNO Admiral Stark, who was planning to check in the following morning. Everyone was working seven days a week now. It was thought a bit strange, however, that Admiral Kelly Turner, accompanied by his aide, Commander Forrest Sherman, left work hours earlier than usual. Next door at the Munitions Building, the War Department's chief of staff, General George Marshall, left his office for a "do" at the fashionable Chevy Chase Country Club where his socialite wife and friends were awaiting him. As for the air force chief, General Hap Arnold, he was in the Deep South on a tour of inspection of various bases and factories.[4]

While Roosevelt's armored train was heading up the Connecticut coast to join the presidential yacht, *Potomac*, at New London on Sunday, August 3, a special army flight took off at noon from the Gravell Point Washington Airport, landing in New York less than an hour later. Generals Marshall, Burns, and Arnold, along with Colonel McGeorge Bundy, descended from the plane into army cars that were waiting for them. "At the 125th Street docks on the Hudson River, we were met by Commander Forrest Sherman of the Navy, an old friend of mine," Hap Arnold later recalled. "There, too, Admiral Stark and Admiral Turner joined us. We went by barge to a destroyer leader set out in the river, then down the Hudson through Hell's Gate to College Point where the *Augusta* and *Tuscaloosa* were anchored. General Marshall and Admiral Stark went aboard King's flagship; [Turner] and I to the *Tuscaloosa*."[5] Looking at one another questioningly, they wondered why they had been whisked away without notice and where they were going.

Immediately weighing anchor, the flotilla, preceded by four destroyers, steamed out to sea. Proceeding via Montauk Point and Block Island, they anchored off Martha's Vineyard on August 4. That same day President Roosevelt, aboard the *Potomac* moored off the New Bedford Yacht Club, received his guests Princess Martha of Norway and Prince Carl of Denmark (future king of Norway) while an anxious Colonel Edward W. Starling, head of the Secret Service and the person in charge of guarding the president, looked on from a respectable distance. The smiling FDR wore a Panama hat and light beige tropical suit, his cigarette holder at its usual jaunty angle as he greeted his guests beneath the sun awning of the main deck of the white yacht. In spite of the elaborate security established around the yacht club, this was dangerous behavior on the president's part, considering all the death threats he had received and the very real possibility of attack by German agents. The risk would be still greater in a few hours' time, when the *Potomac* was due to pass through the narrow Cape Cod Canal before reaching the open waters of the bay where the president intended to get in some serious fishing.

Needless to say, the next day Colonel Starling was greatly relieved to see the *Potomac* emerge from the canal encircled by a small flotilla of naval ships, the president and "Pa" Watson streaming their fishing lines in the blue water. But all was not as it appeared. The previous night, instead of proceeding on a northeasterly course toward the canal, the *Potomac* had altered course to the southeast in the direction of Martha's Vineyard. There, according to Hap Arnold, "the *Potomac* joined us during the night and discharged its passengers aboard the *Augusta*. We were under way at 6.30 next morning [the 5th]," even as the presidential yacht, complete with look-alike Roosevelt and friends, had returned to its original course and was entering Cape Cod Bay.[6] So strict was the secrecy surrounding this event—Admiral Stark had not even been apprised of King's visit to Hyde Park earlier in July when these plans were finalized—that Colonel Starling of the Secret Service was himself left totally in the dark and still under the assumption that it was indeed Roosevelt seen fishing from the stern of the *Potomac* for the next several days. The two cruisers, attended by destroyers and naval aircraft, proceeded at full speed (if on a zigzag course because of U-boat warnings) through dense banks of summer fog in some of the busiest maritime waters of the world, reliant only on a radar system that was still very far from perfect. Their destination: Newfoundland.

If the deception was complete, nevertheless both the *Washington Post* and the *New York Times* noticed that something was up. For one thing, none of the chiefs of staff could be found over the next several days. And their wives had been left without an explanation, including Harriet Turner, who had been preparing for that couple's long-overdue vacation. Even the most enterprising newspaper reporters failed to track down Marshall, Arnold, Stimson, Knox, Sumner Welles, or Ed Stettinius, who was shortly to replace Welles as deputy secretary of state. Why had just about every important member of the Roosevelt administration and the military disappeared overnight? the papers asked. There was no lack of conjecture: the president was going to meet returning Harry Hopkins in the mid-Atlantic to bring him up to date on his recently concluded secret talks with Stalin; the president was going to have a mid-Atlantic rendezvous with Prime Minister Churchill; Roosevelt was on a tour of inspection of American convoys and the new U.S. military installations on Iceland. Others speculated that the president was indeed on vacation, as were his chiefs of staff during his absence.[7]

Meanwhile, during the course of this voyage, all the chiefs of staff and the few assistants who had accompanied them were summoned aboard the *Augusta*, where Arnold did in fact find FDR fishing: the president had somehow landed on the high deck of that big cruiser a toadfish, a dogfish, and even a halibut. Roosevelt's lifelong love of fishing was no hoax. But it was only when Stark, Marshall, and Arnold were assembled that the purpose of this extraordinary convocation on the high seas was finally revealed—there was to be a rendezvous with the British prime minister in Placentia Bay off Argentia, Newfoundland, in a few days' time.

The purpose of this maritime summit was to coordinate British and American defense efforts, that is, to establish their joint policies, determine both countries' priorities, and ascertain what the United States could actually achieve in aiding the hard-pressed British.[8] Alas, due to Roosevelt's absolute insistence on stringent secrecy, the American side had prepared nothing in advance—no position papers, no summaries, no analyses. Arnold later related that when he had suddenly been summoned over the weekend without explanation, he had simply selected a handful of his most immediate files pertaining to the state of the army air corps and the industrial production related to it. Stark had done the same regarding the navy, hence his decision to bring Turner, who had the most complete assessment of the state of the navy, Naval Intelligence, and war plan contingencies. Marshall, who had been in on the secret for some days, was in better shape. But compared with the British, who were always thoroughly laden with portfolios on every aspect of every subject to be discussed, the American military chiefs were left in a lamentable position. FDR now ordered them to return to their cabins to put together reports covering their present strength: in personnel, war matériel, military manufacturing, production in the various fields, and what was planned for the near future.

At an early conference on board the *Augusta*, according to Arnold, "It was brought out that (1) We had a responsibility to the people of the United States for what we had been doing with the money they had appropriated for building up our Army and Air Force. We had had the money, we had had the time, and they, the people would demand results. (2) Such items as we could make available to the British, by all means should be sent to them"—clearly Roosevelt had taken heed of Hopkins's plea from London back in February. Arnold continued: "(3) We, the United States, must be prepared to put a military force into the war, if and when we entered it, as the people of the United States would want action, not excuses. . . . Time, then, would be just as important to us as it was to the British, now."[9] Roosevelt also discussed the necessity of protecting convoys, which, given the severe U-boat toll on Allied shipping thus far, would be a key to British survival and to the American ability to get supplies, food, and munitions across the Atlantic. Furthermore, U.S. Army troops would now have to relieve American marines who had replaced British troops in Iceland. In regard to the threat from Japan, the president "said he would turn a deaf ear if Japan went into Thailand but not if they went into the Dutch East Indies,"[10] a territory with enormous oil refineries so desperately needed by the Japanese military. Enough was enough. America, "the arsenal of democracy," as Roosevelt called it, simply had to be ready.

Even as the *Augusta* was entering the green, glacial waters off Argentia on the morning of August 7, strikes in shipyards, defense plants, and coal mines across the United States were crippling the very production of war matériel upon which FDR and the country's military leaders were now depending. On that day the Congress of Industrial

Organizations (CIO) labor union announced it was shutting down the Federal Shipbuilding & Dry Dock Co. yards in Kearny, New Jersey, in order to consolidate the union's hold over its sixteen thousand workers there and better dictate to the U.S. government the conditions acceptable to them. With $493 million worth of ships under construction, the navy had much at stake at Kearny, including production of the new prototype antiaircraft cruiser *Atlanta*. The first of eleven of this class to be built, it was due to be launched within a few days; six destroyers, three tankers, and two cargo ships were also at various stages of completion. But George W. Wright, the financial secretary of Local 16 of the Industrial Union of Maritime and Shipbuilding Workers of America, was absolutely determined to "completely shut down tonight" this major shipyard, and he threatened the U.S. Navy and the plant that it would "stay shut down" until they caved in to the unions. Roosevelt retaliated by putting Wright and Local 16 on notice that he would order the U.S. Navy to take over the entire operation and dismiss the workers, who no doubt would instead receive call-up papers to serve in the army.[11] This strike and dozens of others—including a series led by John L. Lewis (the founder of the CIO) and the United Mine Workers, not to mention those that halted operations at aircraft or aircraft accessory plants nationwide during the first six months of 1941—left 204,000 men and women refusing to work, thereby paralyzing FDR's and the government's effort to arm and defend the nation. As Air Force Chief Hap Arnold put it, "with national defense production barely beginning, these lost production days . . . were days gained by Hitler when he was calculating his time advantage in terms of hours."[12]

The *Prince of Wales*, Britain's mightiest and newest battleship, commanded by Captain John Leach and bearing Winston Churchill, the Imperial General Staff, dozens of aides and specialists, as well as the ailing Harry Hopkins, entered Placentia Bay at 9 A.M. on August 9 while the Americans were still in a staff conference. The imposing British warship, her bridge completely repaired after her recent battle with the *Bismarck* (in which she had left the *Bismarck* wounded), now approached the *Augusta*, the two ships exchanging salutes with flags flying. "It was," said airman Arnold, "an inspiring sight."

By 9:30 A.M. everyone aboard the *Tuscaloosa* had been ferried over to the *Augusta* where Roosevelt, supported by his two sons Captain Elliott

Roosevelt and Lieutenant (j.g.) Franklin Roosevelt, was standing on deck along with General Marshall, Major General Watson, Sumner Welles, Averell Harriman (who was directing Lend-Lease in London and had just flown in), and others. Harry Hopkins was among the first to join the American cruiser. "He did not look well; certainly the reports concerning his poor health were not exaggerated," reported Churchill's physician, Lord Moran, later. "The band started playing 'God Save the King,' side boys saluted and sailors paraded as Winston Churchill, wearing a Navy cap and Navy uniform [in fact the uniform of the Elder Brothers of Trinity House] came up the ladder and saluted the President."[13] Churchill handed Roosevelt a letter from King George:

> This is just a note to bring you my best wishes and to say how glad I am that you have an opportunity at last of getting to know my Prime Minister. I am sure that you will agree that he is a very remarkable man, and I have no doubt that your meeting will prove of great benefit to our two countries in the pursuit of our common goal.[14]

Churchill in turn was followed by Sir Dudley Pound, the First Sea Lord (the British equivalent of the American CNO) and Admiral of the Fleet; General Sir John Dill, chief of the Imperial Army Staff; Air Vice Marshal Sir Wilfrid Freeman; Sir Alexander Cadogan, representing the Foreign Office; and Churchill's close aides Colonel Ian Jacob and Professor Frederick Lindemann (Lord Cherwell).

At four-thirty that afternoon an exchange visit was made and, as Arnold noted, "we went aboard the *Prince of Wales* to pay our respects. I had an opportunity to become acquainted with Captain John Leach, her commander, who had fought her against the *Bismarck* in which the *Hood* was sunk. We had sherry in the Captain's lounge. The Prime Minister came in and joined me and we talked about the changes that had taken place in the war situation since my [earlier] visit to England. Then we went into the war room where the complete records were maintained for the Prime Minister of all ships, convoys, bombings, sinkings, and other items of interest."[15] That was followed by a big dinner aboard the *Augusta* with a chicken course as the *pièce de résistance*, a meal later grandly surpassed at a reciprocal luncheon, hosted by Churchill aboard his flagship, that featured grouse flown in from Scotland and some choice bottles of vintage French wine.

After dinner Churchill spoke, explaining that this war was unlike World War I, where millions of men lined up facing one another in trenches for months at a time. This was instead a modern, scientific, mobile war, he stressed. But after fourteen months of fierce fighting over British cities, in the Atlantic and the English Channel, and in the Mediterranean and Middle East, the British were by now short of planes, ships, tanks, and antiaircraft guns. The prime minister explained that they were stretched to the very limit, and he now asked the U.S. Navy to aid the Royal Navy by taking over convoy duty in the North Atlantic, thereby releasing fifty British warships and their crews for combat duty around Britain and in the Mediterranean. He also called for the United States, Britain, and the Soviet Union to send, in Arnold's recollection, "an ultimatum to Japan . . . a statement that if Japan went south into the Malay Peninsula, or into the Dutch East Indies they would use all means necessary to make her withdraw."[16]

The next day, Sunday religious services for the combined British and American forces were held beneath the towering 14-inch guns of the *Prince of Wales*. The president and prime minister stood behind a pulpit bearing the Stars and Stripes and Union Jack as hundreds of American and British sailors shared prayer books before them. Churchill had personally selected the three hymns—"O God Our Help in Ages Past," "Eternal Father Strong to Save," and "Onward Christian Soldiers"—and the reading taken from the book of Jonah. "You would have had to be pretty hard-boiled not to be moved by it all—hundreds of men from both fleets all mingled together. . . . It seemed a sort of marriage service between the two navies, already in spirit allies."[17]

Detailed sessions followed the services, as they would over the next few days of this Atlantic Conference. Roosevelt and Churchill conferred at one level, the chiefs of staff at another; and the State Department's Sumner Welles and the deputy minister of the Foreign Office, Sir Alexander Cadogan, met separately to begin drafting a joint document of policies and aims.

Arnold and Marshall were staggered by the requests of the British, who needed many thousands of airplanes and airplane engines and hundreds of tanks immediately. The British, in turn, were even more astonished to learn how poorly the Americans were prepared for war and how little they had available even for themselves. For example, the entire U.S. Army had only forty heavy tanks and would only have light and medium tank production, up to 1,400 units a month, early the following year. As for bombers, the United States was not yet producing five hundred per month. When Air Vice Marshal Freeman asked for six thousand heavy bombers, he was informed that that amounted to the total U.S. production for an entire year. He was speechless.[18]

The British had been made fully aware of American industrial potential, especially by Lord Beaverbrook, but had failed to comprehend and take into consideration the powerful war resistance lobby across the American heartland; in consequence, the United States was still very far from being on a wartime footing. The resistance FDR had been encountering in his own country seemed quite unfathomable to the British, as their own cities came under almost daily bombing raids. In between Hopkins's blood transfusions, Arnold had an opportunity to talk with him and found him, as Arnold later put it, "very bitter about the American public toward our all-out industrial production. He talked about the 600,000 automobiles produced [annually]. . . . All those automobiles rolling out for pleasure-seeking people when we needed airplanes and engines and tanks so badly."[19]

On the other hand, the American chiefs of staff could report that facilities were being prepared to train 4,000 Royal Air Force flying cadets in the United States and that within a year's time American factories would be producing 2,500 warplanes a month.[20] By 1944 they projected the annual production of some 26,000 combat planes and 37,000 trainers, this exclusive of another 17,000 aircraft on order for the RAF. The British made their preference clear: the Boeing four-engine B-17, modified and far better armed then than originally planned, over the B-25s and B-26s. As for those badly needed tanks, Roosevelt could assure Churchill that the Chrysler Corporation alone was already retooling many of its plants for war production; this included its enormous new Midwest "Tank Arsenal" that would be producing one hundred M-3 tanks per week before the autumn was out. Henry Ford, on the other hand, continued to be a headache for the U.S. military. Having signed an earlier government contract worth $122 million for Liberty airplane engines, Ford was now asked to produce another $67 million worth of army trucks. These instead would have to be offered to Chrysler, since Ford—as a good Irishman—refused to hand over a single vehicle to the English.* His open opposition to the war and his personal vendetta against Roosevelt were no secret. But if Henry Ford was not loyal to the needs of his country with the threat of war, he was loyal to one thing, money; and after a strong push by the U.S. Supreme Court, a bitter Henry Ford finally conceded, taking back the truck contract from Chrysler and allowing Walther Reuther's United Automobile Workers to unionize all 140,000 Ford employees.[21]

Hundreds of other contracts were being awarded for war production to Dodge, General Motors, Westinghouse, General Electric, Bethlehem Steel, Reynolds Aluminum, Dupont (after the government promised to build a new plant), and many additional large corporations. In brief, there was hope for major American contributions if the British could just hold on a little longer, for it would take a good year before these moves would begin to see results.

Nevertheless, the British were alarmed to learn that the Americans had continued to sell plane parts and high-octane airplane fuel to the Japanese until 1940, and that only now was the federal government beginning to introduce gasoline rationing in the United States for civilian vehicles. And yet army and navy air squadrons had been suffering from insufficient gasoline allowances for the past two decades, which had in turn curtailed their training and exercises at a time when Americans at home had, until that very month, unlimited access to high-octane gasoline.[22]

Once again the British had failed to comprehend the power and influence that American isolationists held in obstructing the government's efforts to rearm and defend the country. Among their number were former president Herbert Hoover, Chicago University president Robert Maynard Hutchins, and Senators Burton Wheeler, David Walsh, Robert Taft, Robert LaFollette, Gerald Nye, William Borah, and Hiram Johnson, all backed by the *Chicago Tribune*, the *Washington Times-Herald*, the *New York Daily News*, and the entire Hearst chain. Thus, when the government submitted the supplemental Defense Arms Appropriation Bill for a total of $8,063,238,478, the Senate

*Far from limiting his bias to the English, Ford also refused to hire Jews at any level and barred the unions from organizing his works.

Appropriations Committee slashed $1,347,053 of that intended for the army, explaining, "This amount represents requests made by [War] Department over and above the requirements to equip and maintain an Army of three million men." Eventually the army mobilized nearly 9 million men.[23] The cuts made by the Senate affected production of tanks, antitank guns, antiaircraft weapons, and artillery.

Undersecretary of the War Department Robert Patterson replied to the Senate's decision by stating that "it would be most unfortunate if we were caught short in maintaining them [the equipment and artillery included in the request] because of the shortsightedness of the Senate Committee."[24] But as Roosevelt could reassure an anxious Churchill, over the 1940–41 period Congress had in the long run already authorized some $64 billion for defense spending alone, exclusive of separate appropriations for the Lend-Lease program.

The American military for its part required greater air, sea, and ground forces, and many new bases in Labrador, Greenland, Iceland, the West Indies, Brazil, and the Azores.[25] All these plans depended on the House of Representatives extending the current conscription law for military service for another thirty months, a law that would otherwise expire by October 1 of that year.

The meetings between the chiefs of staff of the U.S. and British armed forces were somewhat cool, if not distant. While Britain's Admiral Pound and Field Marshal Dill were generally respected by all the American chiefs (including the usually prickly Ernie King, who sat in on some sessions), the British in turn found Arnold, Marshall, and Stark agreeable but nevertheless unable (or unwilling) to commit the United States to any long-term course of action. King's coldness, arrogance, and open disdain for anything English hardly helped matters.

Colonel Ian Jacob, Churchill's personal aide, noted wearily in his diary that "not a single American officer has shown the slightest keenness to be in the war on our side. They are a charming lot of individuals but they appear to be living in a different world from ourselves." Colonel Jacob also acknowledged that the U.S. Navy was "further ahead [in war preparations] than their Army," both in thought and resources, but he grimly concluded: "The Americans have a long way to go before they can play any decisive part in the war."[26]

For all that, these discussions held aboard ship in Placentia Bay did achieve several things required for the execution of the war in the future: Churchill and Roosevelt got to know, like, and understand one another, which was absolutely essential for the future close collaboration between their two countries. Moreover, joint military missions were to continue on a more expanded basis and be coordinated with Lend-Lease which, thanks to Harry Hopkins, General Burns, and Ed Stettinius, was already reaping great harvests. The U.S. Navy would take over convoying British ships from the United States as far as Iceland, freeing several dozen British warships to fulfill more critical duty around the British Isles and in the Mediterranean; and the great "Atlantic Alliance," or Charter, was formed along with the drafting of a declaration of principles for which the now openly proclaimed alliance between Britain and America would stand.

On August 12, the final day of meetings, news reached them that Japanese minister Hiranuma Kiichirō had narrowly escaped yet another assasination attempt. And back in Washington, a final site was being announced for the new Department of Defense building: a grass airstrip known as Hoover Field, sandwiched between an amusement park and a rubbish dump. The projected five-sided building complex, the future Pentagon, would consolidate several existing military offices currently scattered over several square miles, providing office space for more than forty thousand people and parking for some ten thousand vehicles, military and civilian.[27]

Also on this day, the *Augusta* received news via navy radio about the results of the congressional vote on the bill to extend national conscription. It had earlier passed the Senate thanks in part to General Marshall's testimony before the Senate Military Affairs Committee, in which he quietly stated: "It may clarify the atmosphere for me to explain that I made the specific recommendations regarding the extension of the twelve-month period of service [without consultation with the president] . . . purely on the basis of a military necessity for the security of the country. . . . We must not make the mistake of going on the short side. The hazards are too great. We cannot speculate with the security of this country."[28] Everywhere from Alaska to Hawaii and the Panama Canal, the United States was vulnerable, openly exposed to enemy attack. American armed forces were already reduced to such a low level of readiness that they were incapable of repelling an enemy or preventing the seizure and destruction of American territory. Pearl Harbor, as well as the Gatun Dam and the locks of the Panama Canal, seemed particularly at risk. Thus George Marshall stated dramatically that if the U.S. Congress now voted against an extension of the Selective, or National, Service Act, his greatest fear was that "the [military] institutions would melt away," and that there would no longer be an army or navy. The news reaching the *Augusta* now announced the passing of this bill by a single vote: 203–202. One vote less and the United States would have been left virtually undefended.

Similarly, Marshall had earlier fully supported FDR's declaration of an unlimited national emergency, defending it before the House Military Affairs Committee. When one of the committee members rather boorishly criticized the president's declaration, the normally phlegmatic George Marshall turned roundly on him and snapped, "The declaration of an emergency does not create it. An emergency exists whether or not the Congress declares it. I am asking you to recognize the fact—the fact that the national interest is imperiled and that an emergency exists. I am not asking you to manufacture a fact."[29] Congress concurred, voting thereafter to declare a state of national emergency in the first week of August. Vocal opponents of this action included William Randolph Hearst and Colonel Robert McCormick, whose *Chicago Tribune* later went on to publish top-secret U.S. military plans, an act tantamount to aiding and abetting the enemy. The transgression would outrage Secretary of the Interior Harold Ickes, who would state: "I believe that the charge of treason should have been thrown at McCormick immediately." Attorney General Francis Biddle agreed, charging the publisher of the *Chicago Tribune* with having violated the Espionage Act.[30]

Hearst and McCormick were not the only Americans to cross the line in criticizing their country's move toward war. Democratic senator Burt Wheeler of Montana, after telling the press that Roosevelt was going "to bury every fourth American boy" in the forthcoming war, designed and printed a crude cartoon defaming the president on some 1 million postcards and mailed them to soldiers, sailors, marines, pilots, and civilians alike. For the hawkish, silver-haired, seventy-three-year-old lawyer Henry Stimson, now serving as secretary of war, this was simply too much. He called a press conference of his own, denouncing the unpatriotic Wheeler and declaring that this latest action, one of a series, "comes very near the line of subversive activities against the United States—if not treason."

Indeed, war was nearer than McCormick, Hearst, or Wheeler realized. Even while the Atlantic Conference had been taking place in Newfoundland, Admiral Nagano Osami had advised Hirohito, "If we are going to fight [the U.S. and Britain], then the sooner the better because our supplies [fuel and oil] are fast running out."[31] And at a dinner party given for some senior military officers in Tokyo, Admiral Tagaki Sōkichi starkly predicted before the assembled guests, "As time passes and this situation continues, our empire will either be totally defeated or forced to fight a hopeless war"; he then confided to Matsudaira Yasumasa (Kido Kōichi's chief secretary), "if we make our attack now the war is militarily calculable and not hopeless."[32]

All the while, the Germans were sinking a few more U.S. merchantmen and naval vessels, even as the Japanese were drawing up the final draft of their planned surprise attacks against the United States—plans first tentatively broached by Emperor Hirohito himself some five years earlier. But despite the obvious threat of action by both the Germans in the Atlantic and the Japanese in the Far East, Churchill advisers Jacob, Dill, and Pound all agreed that the Americans seemed to be living in "another world." With few exceptions, Americans seemed to have no sense of urgency, no sense of what Nimitz was to call "battle alertness." That lack of battle alertness was to continue months after hostilities had begun, even as late as Guadalcanal. Somehow this dialogue seemed to be just another prewar "war game" or "fleet problem," not the real thing. Indeed, Americans appeared to consider themselves not only immune from war and attack but safe mentally, which baffled the British, who had quite literally been fighting for their lives, homes, and families since May 1940.

By the time the *Augusta* and *Prince of Wales* finally put to sea later on the 12th, President Roosevelt and Prime Minister Churchill had signed what would become the Atlantic Charter: a document summarizing their achievements and principles, linking the two nations morally to their overall objective of defeating Nazi Germany while listing eight principles highly reminiscent of Woodrow Wilson's celebrated Fourteen Points. The press release introducing the document denounced "the dangers to world civilization arising from the politics of military domination by conquest upon which the Hitlerite government of Germany and other governments associate therewith. . . ." The document itself declared the steps necessary to be taken in order to maintain the safety of Britain, the United States, and the free world. Among the points delineated were those arguing that all people had the right to choose their form of government; that the rights of sovereignty and self-government that had been stripped from many countries should be restored; and that all countries should have equal access to the trade and raw materials required for their economic prosperity. All nations would have to collaborate to improve labor standards, economic adjustments, and social security. The Atlantic Charter further demanded "the final destruction of the Nazi tyranny," the establishment of international peace, and the right of every nation to cross the world's seas unhindered; and it was agreed that all nations must abandon the use of force in all arenas pending the creation of a permanent system of general world security. The system envisioned was eventually to become the United Nations.[33]

Berlin and Tokyo immediately denounced the Newfoundland talks and the Atlantic Charter, dismissing them as a "propaganda bluff." Back in the United States, the *New York Times* enthusiastically endorsed the creation of the Atlantic Alliance and the principles it encompassed. That paper had also supported the earlier creation of the Lend-Lease program which would now result in more intensified and coordinated efforts to ensure the immediate increase in the open "shipment of tanks, planes and foodstuffs in the largest possible quantities" to Britain and the Allies.[34] "The Statement of principles and objectives [of the new alliance] will have the enthusiastic support of all peoples of the world who believe in freedom and democracy," Senate Majority Leader Alben Barkley declared.[35]

Nevertheless, privately, the final report of Churchill's chiefs of staff did not share this enthusiasm: "To sum up, we neither expected nor achieved startling results. The American Chiefs of Staff are quite clearly thinking in terms of the defence of the Western Hemisphere and have so far not formulated any joint strategy for the defeat of Germany in the event of their entry into the war."[36]

Fortunately, Churchill was a man of great vision and understanding, a man of strong will and determination, and above all, a leader endowed with inordinate optimism. He, for one, well realized the ultimate achievement of this first transoceanic summit. The governments of the United States and Britain had bridged the Atlantic and initiated the coordination of joint efforts that were to continue to develop unhindered until the end of the war. If his chiefs of staff saw only silent, noncommittal faces at their conferences, their American counterparts had been under strict orders from the president of the United States to make no commitments. FDR alone would say what had to be said. As for this first face-to-face contact between the two world leaders, Roosevelt and Churchill,[37] it was a basic step for the close wartime relationship that was to follow—in fact, a declaration to the world, to the Axis powers and Japan, that everything had now changed and that America was committed to the struggle. And all the positive changes that were to take place in Congress were a sure sign that deep down the country understood the path it would have to take to achieve victory. The establishment of mutual U.S.-British principles and objectives would allow sufficient time for American industry to put the nation on a firm war footing.

Churchill was now absolutely confident of Roosevelt's sincerity in wishing to destroy the German and Japanese hordes. On the other hand, Churchill, for all his optimism in the ultimate outcome, was at the same time a tough, practical realist and fully cognizant of future possible congressional pitfalls. As he informed his War Cabinet on August 19, "Clearly he [Roosevelt] is skating on pretty thin ice in his relations with Congress," and they would have to accept the fact that the American president could push Congress no further at this time.[38] But at least the United States was openly committed to the cause. Vast amounts of war matériel would soon be churned out, and it was merely a matter of time until Congress would at last prove Senator Burt Wheeler wrong by providing the one remaining piece of legislation required before America could act: a declaration of war. Churchill would just have to be patient.

•

On the far western shores of the Pacific, the clock was ticking faster and faster. Despite the negotiating ploys of the Konoe administration and those to follow, Hirohito and his military advisers were bent on one path only—war and expansion—regardless of the consequences. All elementary priorities had clearly been established by August 1941, independent of whatever action Roosevelt would take. This policy was formulated around a major drive "to the south," and thus inevitably destined to clash with the great Western powers. It would seem as if Japanese leaders were accepting the very strong probability not merely of conflict, but of a conflict which they knew they could not survive. Indeed, there was something almost suicidal in this basic philosophy that Hirohito himself appeared to embrace, publicly and privately.

Konoe's "negotiations" with Cordell Hull's State Department came to nought. The United States was adamant that Japan withdraw from French Indochina and most of China; Manchuria was not mentioned. "We remain deadlocked," General Tōjō informed Prime Minister Konoe. "If by early October we cannot thoroughly achieve our demands through negotiations," there would be no choice but war. "We are mobilizing hundreds of thousands of soldiers . . . and have requisitioned two million tons of shipping. . . . The heart of the matter is [their insistence on our] withdrawal [from Indochina and China]. . . . If we yield to America's demands, it will destroy the fruits of the China Incident. Manchukuo will be endangered and our control of Korea undermined." Japan would not only be unable to undertake the further invasions already planned but would also lose its entire empire. "If hostilities erupt this time [with the U.S.], I think I may have to issue a declaration of war," Hirohito told Kido on October 13.[39] "What are you going to provide by way of justification?" the emperor asked Tōjō. "The matter is presently under examination," he replied.[40] On October 16, 1941, Prime Minister Konoe resigned.

The clock ticked on relentlessly. "I understand you are going to attack Hong Kong after Malaya," Hirohito said to the new army minister, General Sugiyama. "Well, what about the foreign concessions in China?" "We are studying the confiscation of concessions by right of belligerency," Sugiyama replied. "You are going to attend to the concessions after Hong Kong?" Hirohito next asked. "Indeed, Your Majesty. If we don't our surprise attack in Malaya will fail." Then addressing Admiral Nogano, Hirohito asked: "When does the navy plan to open hostilities [against Hawaii]?" "We are planning for December 8 [Tokyo time—December 7 at Pearl Harbor]," the naval director informed him. "That is the best time because [everyone] will be exhausted after the long weekend."*[41]

On November 5, 1941, Kido recorded in his diary: "Our policy toward the United States, Britain, and the Netherlands was decided upon at the imperial conference that convened in the emperor's presence at 10.30 a.m."[42] At that top-secret imperial conference, held at the palace, Hirohito sanctioned the finalization of "preparations for our operations" and the termination of further talks with Washington, which had been tentatively scheduled for midnight on December 1. Also on November 5, Admiral Yamamoto issued secret operation Order No. 1: "To the east, the American fleet will be destroyed. The American lines of operation and supply to the Far East will be severed. Enemy forces will be intercepted and annihilated. Victories will be exploited to smash the enemy's will to fight."[43] Japan's reputedly finest carrier commander, Vice Admiral Nagumo Chuichi, continued to object to the attack on Hawaii as being far too risky, coming after a 6,000-mile voyage. His carriers were too vulnerable and bound to be spotted. But Admiral Yamamoto overruled him, and Nagumo finally conceded.

On November 7, Yamamoto Isoroku issued his next orders to the Combined Fleet: "The Task Force will launch a surprise attack at the outset of the war upon the U.S. Pacific Fleet reported to be in Hawaiian waters and destroy it." The following day, Hirohito was given the complete details of the proposed attack on Pearl Harbor, which had been prepared back in January. He studied them with great interest and approval, although as late as November 30 his brother, Takamatsu, was still attempting to talk him out of any attack against America.[44]

The U.S. Navy searched in vain for Yamamoto's principal carrier force, which had begun to assemble secretly on November 22 at Tankan Bay (or Hitokappu), north of Hokkaido in the Kurile Islands. The countdown had begun. On November 25, the Japanese Strike Force, or *Kido Butai*, was given its sailing orders and then went on radio silence. At 0900 hours the following morning, the six carriers—*Akagi*, *Kaga*, *Hiryu*, *Shokaku*, *Soryu*, and *Zuikaku*—slipped their moorings, steaming out of the fog-covered bay on a bearing that would take

*Every weekend, two thirds of American seamen were given two-day passes.

them into the North Pacific, just south of the Great Northern Circle. Their destination: Hawaii.

On November 27, another Liaison Conference held decided on the "procedures to be taken regarding the declaration of war," while two days later the "senior statesmen" were again debating the final decision to unleash the war. Hirota Tosuke, Hayashi Senjūrō, and Abe Nobuyuki, among the most aggressive proponents for war, encountered no strong opposition. "The decision this time [due to be made on December 1] will be enormously important," Kido Kōichi advised the emperor. "Once you grant the imperial sanction there can be no going back."[45]

CHAPTER VII

General Quarters!

"If war eventuates with Japan, it is believed easily possible that hostilities would be initiated by a surprise attack upon the Fleet or the Naval Base at Pearl Harbor."

—Rear Admiral Kelly Turner to CNO Admiral Stark, January 24, 1941[1]

"The coming war will be protracted and dirty. . . ."

—Admiral Yamamoto Isoroku, Autumn 1941[2]

Throughout 1941, Admiral Kelly Turner, as head of the navy's War Plans Department, had been keeping CNO Stark and the White House abreast of the growing Japanese threat. In January, he had predicted the possibility of a "surprise attack" by the Japanese not only against the Philippines but also against Pearl Harbor before the year was out. In mid-April, he had drafted the "Project for Western Hemisphere Defense Plans" creating, among other things, the two-ocean navy.[3]

And on July 11, Turner had warned Stark that "during July or August, the Japanese will occupy important points in [the southern half of] Indo-China, and will adopt an opportunistic attitude toward the Siberian Maritime provinces" of the Soviet Union. He recommended that steps be taken to place the U.S. Army and Navy in the Far East on "an alert status."[4] "He may be right," Stark wrote his friend, Captain Charles "Savvy" Cooke, Jr.; "he usually is."[5] Ten days later the Japanese did indeed invade southern Indochina (today's Vietnam), and Roosevelt and Churchill met urgently in Newfoundland.

On October 16, 1941, Turner sent another memorandum to Admiral Stark warning that there was a "distinct possibility that Japan will attack Britain and the United States in the near future." Stark toned this down in his official communiqué to senior naval commanders in Panama, the Philippines, and Hawaii, stating that "there is *a possibility* that Japan *may attack*." As for the situation in Siberia, Turner indicated that for the moment Japanese and Soviet forces were too evenly matched "to warrant an [Japanese] offensive"—until the war between Germany and the Soviet Union had been decided.[6] If the Soviets were ultimately defeated in that campaign, Japan's present plans for "the south" would be modified and hundreds of thousands of its troops moved north to the Siberian frontier.

•

Admiral Husband "Mustapha" Kimmel, whose mind, according to his intelligence chief, Edwin Layton, "worked with a well-ordered precision," had long been uneasy about the lack of information CNO Stark had been sending him. The issues Kimmel so clearly stated were not being addressed; instead, Layton later recalled, "the overwhelming vagueness of Stark's communications . . . boiled to a head" in 1941. Unlike General MacArthur and Admiral Thomas Hart at CAST (code name for Cavite), Kimmel had no Purple machine to decode and decipher Japanese diplomatic intercepts, messages that were known as Ultra or Magic.[7] Nor indeed were either Kimmel or General Short even cleared to receive these messages when intercepted via Guam. Thus, out of desperation, in June 1941 Admiral Kimmel had written a powerful, pleading letter to Stark, stating (while referring to himself in the third person) that as Commander in Chief, U.S. Pacific Fleet, he was "in a very difficult position. He is far removed from the seat of government, in a complex and rapidly changing situation. He is, as a rule, not informed as to the policy, or change of policy, reflected in current events and naval movements, and as a result is unable to evaluate the possible effect upon his own situation. . . . This lack of information is disturbing and tends to create uncertainty." Kimmel had been sent to Hawaii to carry out extensive new training programs preparatory to expanding the fleet, but this "must be carefully balanced against the desirability of interruption of this training by strategic dispositions, or otherwise, to meet impending eventualities," he stressed. Moreover, "the C-in-C, Pacific Fleet [should be] guided by a broad policy rather than by categorical instructions," or specific, inflexible instructions tying his hands. He closed by "suggesting" that "it be made a cardinal principle that the Commander-in-Chief, Pacific Fleet, *be immediately informed of all important developments as they occur* and by the quickest secure means available."[8]

Instead of addressing the issues so clearly stated by Kimmel, Stark continued to deny him access to these Purple intercepts; and when he did communicate with Kimmel, it was not by the "quickest secure means available" (navy radio) but by informal letters sent via the U.S. Post Office, which took ten days to reach Pearl Harbor.[9] What is more, Kimmel was left largely in the dark about the Nomura-Hull negotiations and was equally uninformed about the sixty-eight Purple messages exchanged between Honolulu's Japanese vice consul, Takeo Yoshikawa, and Tōgō in 1941. These intercepts contained detailed information on almost all U.S. military dispositions on Oahu, including all ship movements, and revealed the use of a new grid system employed by Tokyo that would have proven invaluable to Joseph J. Rochefort's Pearl Harbor intelligence station.[10] Most of these Purple messages from Hawaii were instead deemed so unimportant when they were received by SIS in Washington that they were simply filed, only to be discovered later during the inquiries on the Pearl Harbor debacle. Even those top-secret Purple messages that were translated never reached Admiral Kimmel, and as a result, as one frustrated intelligence officer, Lieutenant Jaspar Holmes, later summed it up, "secrecy constipated the flow of information." According to Commander Layton, even Roosevelt was kept at least a month behind in reaching these intercepts.* Had Marshall and Stark decided to provide Kimmel and Short with a Purple cipher machine instead of giving the only one in the

*In February 1939, William Friedman, the head of the army's SIS, was given the headache of cracking the new Japanese diplomatic code "Purple" which was then introduced. Frank Rowlett and a team of cryptanalysts finally solved many of the problems, but it was a young MIT engineer, Leo Rosen, who actually invented the "Purple machine" itself required to decipher the new code. He produced the decrypts code called "Magic" or "Ultra" on the third floor of the Munitions Building in 1940. See Stephen Budiansky, *Battle of Wits: The Complete Story of Codebreaking in World War II* (New York: Free Press, 2000), pp. 164–67.

Pacific to MacArthur and Hart, things might have turned out very differently. After all, Hawaii—not Manila—was the main army, air force, and navy base for the entire Pacific. But Chief of Staff Marshall had insisted that it go to MacArthur at Cavite, and Stark went along with the decision.[11] It was not the first time that the much-lauded George Marshall had made a grave error of judgment, nor would it be the last, especially concerning Douglas MacArthur.

•

More and more uneasy about the deteriorating situation vis-à-vis Japan and what little he was being told, Admiral Kimmel at last took matters into his own hands on November 25, 1941. Accompanied by Vice Admiral Claude Bloch, the commandant of the Fourteenth Naval District in Hawaii—for whose administration he was responsible—Kimmel suddenly appeared in the basement of the newly completed wing of the Makalapa Administration Building at the headquarters of Naval Intelligence's Fleet Radio Unit, Pacific (FRUPac), which was listed under the naval directory as "Combat Intelligence Unit." This operation, code-named HYPO, was otherwise so hush-hush that even most of the senior naval officers at Pearl Harbor had no idea of its real work.

HYPO's chief, Commander Joseph Rochefort, one of the three most experienced intelligence veterans in the military, directed a mere ten officers and twenty enlisted men who were responsible for intercepting, decrypting, decoding, translating, and analyzing only one thing: Japanese naval communications. (His interception station was located thirty miles away on higher ground.) Rochefort, who had been with Naval Intelligence since 1925, when the Naval Communication Intelligence Center (OP-20-G) was created in Washington, was appointed head of HYPO in May 1941. His colleagues considered him the finest cryptanalyst in the entire navy, and the small team he had selected the finest anywhere—better than those at Cavite and Washington, D.C. This operation centered on three junior cryptanalysts, two (radio) traffic analysts, and two translator analysts.[12]

Admiral Kimmel's rare appearance at these secluded offices hidden behind the Supply Department surprised everyone, for he generally received all pertinent information from Rochefort via Kimmel's fleet intelligence officer, Lieutenant Commander Edwin Layton. But today was different. Kimmel, along with Claude Bloch, disappeared behind the door of Commander Rochefort's office. Everyone at HYPO had realized earlier that something unusual was going on when the quiet, eccentric Rochefort had exchanged his red silk smoking jacket and old bedroom slippers for a uniform jacket. The tall, slender, poker-faced Rochefort, who could at times be quite caustic, was never known to have raised his voice and was respectful to all his men, officers and enlisted men whose rare qualities he clearly appreciated. He in turn was highly esteemed by his unique team. Admiral Kimmel, as Commander in Chief, U.S. Pacific Fleet, now asked Commander Joe Rochefort three questions: Where was every unit of the entire Imperial Japanese Navy? What were they doing at this very moment? And what did Rochefort think their intentions were?[13] Joe Rochefort was literally the only person in the U.S. Navy who could provide the answers, given the special tasks of Station HYPO; and Kimmel had bypassed Layton to deliver these queries in person. So much depended on the outcome. Kimmel was promised a full written report the next day.

Meanwhile, Washington intercepted at least three Purple communications between the Japanese Foreign Office and the Japanese consul general in Honolulu from November 15 to November 18, and laboriously translated them by December 6. They concerned just one subject: the location and movement of all U.S. warships in Pearl Harbor. Alas, Washington refused to share this information with an already anxious Kimmel.[14] But there had been even more directly disturbing diplomatic exchanges between Tokyo and Ambassador Nomura on November 5 instructing Nomura that it was "absolutely necessary that all arrangements for the signing of this agreement [the result of negotiations between Japan and the U.S.] be completed by the 25th of this month."[15] When Nomura requested a delay, the Japanese foreign minister replied on November 16 (translated in Washington on the 17th): "I am awfully sorry to say that the situation renders this out of the question. . . . There will be no change . . . you know how short time is."[16] Nomura still argued with the Foreign Office, which replied on November 22: "There are reasons beyond your ability to guess why we wanted to settle Japanese-American relations by the 25th, but if within the next three or four days you can [settle this satisfactorily] we have decided to wait until that date."[17]

None of this information was passed on to either Admiral Kimmel or General Short in Hawaii, although MacArthur had access to it through his own Purple machine. Admiral Stark had seen all the above intercepts, as had Kelly Turner, who prepared an alert for naval Chief of Staff, CNO Stark to send out. In a meeting with Marshall on November 24, they agreed the alert should be sent to the navy commanders in the Pacific that same day:

> There are very doubtful chances of a favourable outcome of negotiations with Japan. The situation coupled with statements of [the Japanese] government and movements of their naval and military forces indicate in our opinion that *a surprise aggressive movement in any direction*, including an attack on the Philippines or Guam is a possibility.[18]

Hence Admiral Kimmel's urgent request to Rochefort. Following the departure of his rare visitors, Commander Rochefort called in the members of Station HYPO one at a time and gave each his special assignment. Responding to Kimmel's order would require the collation of all intercepts, decodings, and translations of Japanese naval communications over the past month, involving thousands of documents. Rochefort himself remained at his desk the rest of the day and all night, as did everyone else. He finally emerged the next morning, November 26, to wash and shave. He left HYPO's windowless offices by the sole door and climbed the stairs into the blinding Hawaiian sunlight. Walking around the building, he entered the main entrance of the two-story Administration Building and went up to Kimmel's office, where the commander in chief was awaiting him. Silently, Rochefort handed him his report.

According to the most recent information, the commander of the Japanese Second or "Scouting" Fleet was assembling in Formosa and Indochina an impressive task force that included most of the Third Fleet (specializing in blockades and transport) and the First Fleet—including one battleship division and two cruiser divisions—along with several destroyer squadrons. Moreover, most of the Combined Air Force—consisting of shore-based naval aircraft—was also attached. Some units had already entered the South China Sea. Rochefort indicated that there had been an unusual amount of radio traffic between the Second Fleet and the island of Palau (due west of Truk on the

Philippine Sea). At least one third of their navy's submarines were participating in this operation, as were Air Squadron 24 and one or two carriers of the First Air Fleet, all in the Marshall Islands. Looking up from the report, Admiral Kimmel asked the solemn Rochefort what conclusions he drew from all this activity. Rochefort replied that it looked as if a strong Japanese naval force based in Hainan and Formosa, with components in Indochina, Palau, and the Marshalls (near Truk), was about to attack Southeast Asia, including Malaya and the Dutch East Indies.[19]

A by now very worried Kimmel immediately sent this report to Cavite and Washington, D.C., for feedback. Compounding Kimmel's concern was the fact that even Rochefort had been unable to locate three Japanese carrier divisions (up to seven aircraft carriers). Cavite Naval Intelligence thought—incorrectly, as it proved—the entire carrier force was at Kure in the Inland Sea. Rochefort could not confirm that conclusion.

The day before Rochefort's report reached Washington, Rear Admiral Turner had been drafting an independent analysis based on the intercepts the Office of Naval Intelligence (ONI) had given him over the previous several weeks. In his memorandum, which he prepared for CNO Stark and ultimately the White House, Turner advised that the "Japanese are strongly reinforcing their garrisons and naval forces in the Mandates [the Carolines and Marianas, i.e., at Truk] and thus threatening U.S. possessions [e.g., the Philippines]." There was a southerly movement of troop transports and warships from Shanghai and Japan to Formosa. "Preparations are becoming apparent in China, Formosa and IndoChina for an early aggressive movement," though he could not predict exactly where, suggesting "Thailand, the Malay Peninsula, the Netherlands East Indies or the Philippines. . . . I consider it probable"—Roosevelt soon changed this to "possible"—that this next Japanese aggression may"—the president altered this to "might"—"*cause an outbreak of hostilities between the US and Japan*."[20] So convinced were Stark, Roosevelt, and Marshall after reading first Turner's analysis of the 25th and then Rochefort's assessment of the 26th that they instructed Turner to prepare another memo to be sent to Admirals Hart in Manila and Kimmel in Pearl Harbor. Turner promptly did so on November 27.

> This despatch is to be considered a war warning. . . . [An] *aggressive move by Japan is expected in the next few days* . . . [including] an amphibious expedition against either the Philippines, Thai[land] or Kra Peninsula or possibly toward Borneo. Execute an appropriate defensive employment preparatory to carrying out the tasks assigned in WP146. . . . [Also] take appropriate measures against sabotage.[21]

At the same time, Marshall notified Major General Walter Short:

> Japanese future action unpredictable but *hostile action possible at any moment*. If hostilities cannot, repeat, cannot be avoided the United States desires that Japan commit the first overt act. This policy should not, repeat, *not be construed as restricting you to a course of action that might jeopardize your defense*. Prior to hostile action you are directed to undertake such reconnaissance and other measures as you deem necessary. . . . Should hostilities occur you will carry out the tasks assigned in Rainbow Five.[22]

A similar warning had been sent to General MacArthur at Manila. MacArthur replied immediately to the War Department that he was prepared for anything, and Stimson acknowledged that he and Marshall "were highly pleased to receive your report that your command is ready for any eventuality."[23]

On November 28, Marshall dispatched a final warning. "Critical situation demands that all precautions be taken immediately against subversive actions. . . ."[24] In particular, Washington worried about Hawaii, with its nearly 200,000 Japanese residents with work visas; the Philippines, too, had a similarly large community. There were many American military bases—navy, army, air—in both places and never enough troops to defend them. The U.S. mainland also had to take elaborate precautions, especially against German sabotage. In Hawaii the threat was real not only because of the large number of military installations, but also because of the activities of the Japanese consul general, Nagao Kita, and his vice consul, Takeo Yoshikawa (a naval officer).

Following the attack on Pearl Harbor, the FBI and Office of Naval Intelligence discovered that Nagao had been sending from Honolulu precise maps of military facilities, including Pearl Harbor, which showed the regular berths of every U.S. battleship and the location of every submarine, seaplane tender, torpedo net, machine work, drydock, and artillery battery. Over the course of a few weeks alone, very detailed reports including data of arrivals and departures had been sent to the Japanese foreign minister concerning every vessel entering or leaving Pearl Harbor. Indeed, so precise was the information received in Tokyo that naval headquarters had been able to construct a large-scale mock-up of every ship, mooring, building, gun emplacement, and airfield on Oahu, even noting the lack of barrage balloons. It was later discovered that a well-known, long-established German national by the name of Otto Kuehn living in Honolulu had also been providing information to the consul general and was preparing to participate in the attack of Pearl Harbor by sending signals from land to the approaching enemy aircraft and submarines. Although unaware of the depth of Japanese intelligence, both Kimmel and Short acted promptly to prevent sabotage of their bases and airfields.[25]

In addition, as a result of the reports submitted by Rochefort and Turner, a few more army warplanes were dispatched urgently to Wake and Midway islands on the only two carriers available. But George Marshall, who authorized this operation, was no pilot, and he had not taken into consideration the elementary fact that army pilots did not receive instruction and training on how to land on, and take off from, aircraft carriers. After a last-minute delay, all the army planes had to be replaced by marine corps planes and pilots. Similar warplanes, especially the long-distance B-17s, were promised MacArthur while the army fighters were put in crates and sent by ship. Yet there would be no U.S. carriers at all in Pearl Harbor on December 7.[26]

On December 1, Rochefort reported the disturbing news to Kimmel's fleet intelligence office, Lieutenant Commander Layton, that the Japanese navy had again just changed its radio "call signs"—initials identifying to and from whom all naval messages were sent. The HYPO unit at Pearl Harbor could no longer identify individuals, units, cities, or even the islands involved. This was grave news, rendering all plotting of Japanese ships, for instance, impossible. On December 3, CNO Stark warned Kimmel that Tokyo had just ordered Japanese embassies in Washington, London, and throughout the Far East, including Hong Kong, Batavia, Singapore, and Manila, to destroy codes, ciphers, and important documents. On December 4, Commander Rochefort bore even more bad news: the Japanese had suddenly changed their entire naval code, "JN-25."[27] Pearl Harbor could no longer decipher or decode any of the Japanese naval signals. And there was still no trace of Japan's "lost" carrier force, not to mention a large number of fleet submarines.

There certainly was a steady flow of information reaching army and navy headquarters on Constitution Avenue; but no one at the senior command level seemed unduly worried about the fact that such a large number of carriers and subs had completely disappeared at a time when the rest of the Japanese Combined Fleet was loudly visible and apparently involved in a massive series of operations. That alone should have told Kimmel and Stark something, but they failed to comprehend the seriousness of the gap in information. Unlike King and Nimitz, Stark and Kimmel were representative of the old navy, officers afraid of taking a chance or of harming their careers by making errors. Lacking the ability and the mentality to make quick, important decisions when the moment required it, they instead followed, and depended entirely upon, written orders. Every "i" had to be dotted, every "t" crossed and sanctioned by the Navy Department or the Joint Chiefs of Staff before they would act. Individual initiative still had not been encouraged by the end of 1941, despite the grave situation worldwide.

On Friday, December 5, the officer of the watch aboard the destroyer *Talbot* noted the sonar detection of a large unidentified submarine just up the channel leading into Pearl Harbor. He requested immediate permission from his squadron commander aboard the destroyer *Selfridge* to drop depth charges. His commander laughed, saying it was nothing more than a big fish, and refused the use of depth charges. At about the same time, another enemy sub was spotted by an army observation post on Kahala Beach, east of Diamond Head; the submarine was apparently in the process of charging its batteries behind a reef. Unfortunately, the two 8-inch guns at Black Point were unable to fire at it because of a colony of beach houses that had been recently built, inhibiting the command post's field of fire. The Japanese submarine made a leisurely escape. Neither Kimmel nor Stark drew any apparent conclusions from these unusual reports.[28]

Meanwhile, General Marshall and Admiral Stark continued to withhold from Kimmel and Short most of the important Purple (Magic/Ultra) intercepts they were receiving in Washington. During the first week of December, Kelly Turner warned Captain Arthur McCollum, the head of the Office of Naval Intelligence's Far Eastern Section, "of the danger of imminent war." Yet when Turner next met with the director of ONI, Admiral Theodore Wilkinson, on December 6, a misguided Wilkinson assured him that he was "mistaken in the belief that Japan would attack a United States objective."[29] Turner warned Stark that the Japanese were about to strike at U.S. territory, and Stark's chief of Naval Intelligence, Wilkinson, thought the whole idea quite preposterous.

On the morning of that December 6, a Saturday, Franklin Roosevelt received word from London that the day before, British pilots had discovered three large Japanese convoys—forty-six troop transports, escorted by a battleship and seven cruisers—entering the Gulf of Siam and headed either for Siam (Thailand) or British Malaya. This confirmed the earlier assessments of both Commander Rochefort and Admiral Turner: the attack was about to begin. Roosevelt, for his part, was firmly convinced that under no circumstances would Hirohito be so foolish as to risk all by attacking the Philippines, or indeed any other U.S. territory, when Japan was already heavily committed in a major war with China. As FDR reiterated to Hopkins and Robert Sherwood, it simply did not make sense to add another important enemy to the list. Indeed, the president felt strongly that the emperor would go to great lengths to avoid just such a confrontation. Given the information he had received to date, Roosevelt believed that the real Japanese target was the Netherlands East Indies and its rich oil refineries, which Tokyo so desperately needed. At the same time, he also thought that such an attack would probably be the means by which the United States would get involved in the war. Secretary of State Cordell Hull, on the other hand, completely disagreed with him. In any event, Roosevelt, who had earlier that morning made a final appeal to Hirohito—"This son of man has just sent his final message to the Son of God," he grimly quipped—was still awaiting a response from Tokyo.[30]

That evening, the Roosevelts gave their usual large weekend dinner, but FDR excused himself early from his thirty-two guests and returned to his study. At 9:30 P.M. he and Harry Hopkins were discussing the situation in the Far East when there was a knock at the door. Commander L. R. Schulz entered with an urgent Magic translation for the president. Unlocking his leather dispatch pouch, he handed Roosevelt fifteen pages containing the first thirteen parts of a fourteen-part set of instructions, intercepted, deciphered, decoded, and translated by Army Intelligence's Signal Intelligence Service (SIS, equivalent to the navy's OP-20-G). This Purple intercept was addressed by Foreign Minister Tōgō to Admiral Nomura in Washington. Hopkins as usual paced the floor nervously, Schulz later recalled, while FDR carefully studied the long document. He remained emotionless as he handed it to Hopkins. "This means war," the president said quietly.[31]

Roosevelt tried to contact Admiral Stark, but when informed that he was attending a production of *The Student Prince* at the National Theater, he decided not to have him paged, fearing it might attract too much attention.[32] The president finally reached Stark later that evening after Stark had returned to his official residence at the Naval Observatory. Both agreed that the message, which indicated Japanese naval movement toward the Dutch East Indies and Malaya, meant an attack was likely very soon; they would cover their options more fully at a War Cabinet meeting the following day.[33] But an important figure was missing from the preliminary discussions: George Marshall. Did Roosevelt ever try to contact him? If not, why the omission of such an important person as the army chief of staff? Or did the White House attempt to reach him unsuccessfully? Marshall claimed he spent that evening at his official residence at Fort Myer, where there was always a duty officer present to take and log calls.[34]

Messengers were dispatched to deliver the vital thirteen-part cable to other members of the cabinet and the military. Lieutenant Commander Kramer personally handed one such copy to Naval Secretary Frank Knox at his apartment in the Hotel Wardman Park, and Knox instructed him to tell the president that he would hold a special meeting with Secretary of State Hull and Secretary of War Stimson at the State Department at ten o'clock the next morning. Meanwhile, Colonel Rufus Bratton, the head of the War Department's Far Eastern Section, of G-2, Army Intelligence, was responsible (along with his assistant, Colonel Carlisle Dusenbury) for delivering the Purple messages to the chief of staff, the chief of intelligence, the chief of war plans, and the secretary of state. Bratton decided to wait until the fourteenth part of the message was received before delivering the entire text to General Marshall. But when at 10:00 P.M. he was informed that the last part would not be ready until the following morning, Bratton consulted with the head of Army Intelligence, Major General Sherman Miles, who said he had already seen the intercepts and found nothing alarming in them. Miles advised Bratton not to disturb the chief of staff and instead to lock the message in Marshall's safe and show it to him early the next morning. No further effort was made to see George Marshall during the night.

When the rest of the intercept was available the next morning, Bratton did attempt to ring Marshall sometime after 9:00 A.M., but he was informed that the general was riding his horse and would not be back before 10:00 A.M. Bratton left a message with the orderly for Marshall to contact the War Department, but without indicating the urgency of the moment. Therefore, no one was dispatched to look for the chief of staff, who rode every morning on the same trail along the Virginia side of the Potomac.[35] And yet Stark had considered the situation so grave that on the 6th he had notified Kimmel that "in view of the international situation and the exposed position of our outlying Pacific islands," Kimmel was to authorize appropriate personnel to destroy "secret and confidential documents."[36]

Just before three o'clock on the morning of the 7th, SIS had begun receiving several more radio intercepts from Tokyo to Nomura, including "Purple 902," containing the fourteenth part of the ambassador's instructions. Another message, "Purple 907," directed Nomura to deliver Tōgō's previous fourteen parts to Cordell Hull at one o'clock in the afternoon that same Sunday, December 7, when Hull would be informed that Tokyo was breaking off all negotiations. The ambassador was also instructed to destroy the one remaining Purple cipher machine along with various codes and documents.[37] These latest messages were all decoded by Army Intelligence by seven o'clock Sunday morning and translated sometime between 9:00 and 10:00 A.M. (according to different sources).

The fourteenth part of Tōgō's message, the order to break off all negotiations, was handed to President Roosevelt before ten o'clock Sunday morning.

As for Colonel Bratton, he was finally able to speak with Marshall himself between ten and ten-thirty Sunday morning. Even then, Bratton's words apparently lacked the sense of urgency required, for Marshall took a leisurely shower before changing and driving to the War Department.[38]

While Marshall had been riding along the Potomac River, a much more concerned Admiral Stark had arrived at the Main Navy Building on Constitution Avenue and was at his desk by 9:00 A.M. There he found his chief of Naval Intelligence, Ted Wilkinson, and Wilkinson's assistant, Commander Arthur McCollum, already waiting for him with the complete translations of Foreign Minister Tōgō's instructions. They urged Stark to ring Kimmel and Hart at once, to alert them to the grave situation. "Betty" Stark started to reach for the phone, but then stopped. The CNO, a superb commanding officer in many respects, had one failing: he was indecisive and was now quite flummoxed. Stark did not like to make a major decision without the support of others; Stimson described him as "a little bit timid and cautious when it comes to a real crisis."[39] What is more, Kelly Turner, who had pushed Stark in the past, had been working nonstop for weeks, had at last been given half a day off, and was not there to help. Stark had less confidence in Wilkinson and could not make up his mind. He finally rang the White House, only to be told that the president was not available at the moment. Stark then rang Fort Myer but was told that General Marshall was out. The admiral believed the Japanese would attack somewhere by the 1:00 P.M. deadline, but he was paralyzed. He never did clarify his astonishing inaction, except once, when he explained that everything he did "was in accordance with orders from higher authority,"[40] but he was not able to elaborate further on that rather hollow-sounding remark. Indeed, for two hours Admiral Harold R. "Betty" Stark sat frozen at his desk, in effect doing nothing, not even phoning Pearl Harbor and Manila. Apparently overwhelmed by the immensity of the event, he instead dithered, unable to make any logical decision.

Much to Stark's presumed relief, Marshall finally returned to his office, and the two service chiefs met shortly before noon. They drafted a brief—but, under the circumstances, totally inadequate—message that Marshall would issue to all commands:

> The Japanese are presenting at 1 P.M. Eastern Standard Time, today, what amounts to an ultimatum. Also they are under orders to destroy their code machine immediately. Just what significance the hour set may have we do not know, but be on the alert accordingly. Inform naval authorities of this communication.[41]

At such a historic moment as this, one might inevitably wonder what a leader such as Admiral Lord Horatio Nelson would have done under similar circumstances. That English admiral's entire naval career is answer enough if one only recalls his many decisive acts, sometimes against orders, in his long campaign against Napoleon's navy. For example, no sailor can forget Nelson's most remarkable pursuit of Admiral Villeneuve first in the Mediterranean, then across the Atlantic to the Antilles, and back across the Atlantic again (with his "Mediterranean Fleet") without orders, a pursuit that finally ended in the battle of Trafalgar in October 1805. Nelson had a clear mind and understood the importance of the moment. He could make firm decisions and was not afraid of the responsibility he would bear. Marshall and Stark evidently were not made of the same stuff, and hence their lamentable loss of precious time, followed by a totally inadequate "warning." But this was just the beginning of a colossal historic foul-up.

Marshall prepared to send this alert to the Philippines, Hawaii, and Panama. Stark suggested using the navy's communications system, which was notably faster and more reliable than that of the army, but Marshall declined. As Bratton rushed out with the message, War Plans Director Leonard T. Gerow called out, "If there is any question of priority, give the Philippines first priority!" All the while, Admiral Nagumo's warplanes were nearing Hawaii; on Formosa, other Japanese squadrons were waiting for the weather to clear to strike at the Philippines.

As George Marshall had ruled out notifying the bases in the Pacific by his electronically scrambled telephone—he was fearful that the enemy was tapping the underwater cables, an irrelevant concern at such a critical moment—Colonel Bratton had to run to the army's message center. There Colonel Edward French told him that it would take at least thirty minutes to encode those three sentences. In less than half that time that message could have been delivered by telephone to

Panama, Hawaii, and the Philippines. It was already past twelve o'clock in Washington.

At around the same time, USS *Antares* was nearing the channel leading into Pearl Harbor when an officer spied the conning tower of a Japanese submarine and immediately radioed the nearby destroyer *Ward* for help. Unlike the commanders of the *Selfridge* and *Talbot*, the *Ward*'s captain ordered the crew to General Quarters at 6:40 A.M. (Hawaiian time) and opened fire on the sub, blasting away at the conning tower. The *Ward* then finished the vessel off with depth charges. The alert Captain William Outerbridge of the *Ward* immediately radioed a report of this attack to Pearl Harbor, and the news reached Admiral Kimmel just after 7:00 A.M. He ordered that it first be verified. Until that happened he would not alert anyone, and would continue instead with his plans to play golf with General Short that Sunday morning. Kimmel, for one, would not be accused of failing to dot his "i"s. Like Stark and Marshall, it did not seem to occur to him that given the present critical situation it might be better to err on the side of preparedness than to follow the old, slow, methodical prewar procedures guaranteed to ensure a good fitness report.

In Washington, the army's message center in the Munitions Building was sending Marshall's warning to Panama, to MacArthur in the Philippines, and to the commanding general of the Presidio's Fourth Army headquarters at San Francisco. Because of "atmospheric problems" between California and Hawaii, however, all army radio communications to and from those two points had been stopped since 10:20 A.M. EST that day. Instead, Colonel French sent the message to Hawaii by Western Union over RCA's far more powerful radio transmitter, which had no trouble in reaching the island. Despite these delays—deadly ones, as it turned out—Marshall still refused to call Hawaii or the Philippines with the news.

Back in Hawaii at Kahuku Point, at 7:00 A.M. that Sunday (after noon Washington time), the privates in charge of the U.S. Army's only mobile radar unit in the islands were just about to close down for the morning because of limited budget when the radar picked up more than fifty planes, some 132 miles north of Oahu and closing rapidly. The two enlisted men present immediately reported this to the Air

Force Information Center, where a nonchalant Lieutenant Kermit Tyler assumed their radar had picked up U.S. Army or Navy planes. "Well, don't worry about it," he instructed them, and did nothing further about the matter. It was a Sunday, after all. It was now 7:20 A.M., and Lieutenant Tyler's poor judgment had put Hawaii at risk.

George Marshall's alert to General Short finally reached Hawaii at 7:33 A.M. But because the teletype line between the RCA facilities and Fort Shafter was down, a clerk handed the coded telegram to a messenger, who set out on his motorbike. Meanwhile, the two enlisted men at Kahuku Point who should have—if they had followed orders—shut down their radar unit instead remained at their station, following the approaching first wave of enemy bombers until 7:30 A.M., when radio interference broke up the images. At 1:09 P.M. in Washington, D.C., General Marshall was returning to Fort Myer for lunch, as usual. President Roosevelt had called a "war conference" at the White House, scheduled for 3:00 P.M.[42]

Back at the Munitions Building, "At 1:30 P.M. an enlisted man from the Navy rushed into the office out of breath," according to Colonel John R. Deane, secretary to the army's General Staff and the only officer then on duty at the chief of staff's office in Washington. "[He had] a pencil note which was supposed to have been a message from the Navy radio operator at Honolulu and which said, as I recall: 'Pearl Harbor attacked. This is no drill.' I immediately telephoned General Marshall at his quarters at Fort Myer where he was having lunch and told him of the message that had been received."[43] Marshall rushed back to the War Department. A naval courier delivered the same message to the secretary of the navy at Hotel Wardman Park.

"I lunched with the President today at his desk in the Oval Room," Robert Sherwood recorded in his diary.

> We were talking about things far removed from war when at about 1:40 Secretary Knox called and said that they had picked up a radio [message] from Honolulu from the Commander-in-Chief of our forces there [Kimmel] advising all our stations that an air raid attack was on and that it was "no drill."
>
> I expressed the belief that there must be some mistake and that surely Japan would not attack in Honolulu. . . .

The President thought the report was probably true and thought it was just the kind of unexpected thing the Japanese would do. . . .[44]

Secretary of War Stimson's telephone rang at 2:00 P.M. "The President called me up . . . in a rather excited voice to ask me—'Have you heard the news?' " Stimson thought he was referring to fresh Japanese advances in the Gulf of Siam. " 'Oh no. I don't mean that. They have attacked Hawaii. They are now bombing Hawaii.' Well, that was an excitement, indeed." Stimson, a former army colonel, immediately held the U.S. commanders at Pearl Harbor responsible. "The outpost commander," he was later to tell a Joint Committee of Congress, "is like a sentinel on duty in the face of the enemy. His fundamental duties are clear and precise. . . . It is not the duty of the outpost commander to speculate or rely on the possibilities of the enemy attacking at some other outpost instead of his own. It is his duty to meet him at the post at any time and to make the best possible fight that can be made against him with the weapons with which he has been supplied."[45]

"At 2:28 Admiral Stark called the President and confirmed the attack," Sherwood noted, "stating that it was a very severe attack and that some damage had already been done to the fleet and that there was some loss of life." Roosevelt then instructed Stark to execute his existing orders—the Rainbow 5 Plan—drawn up for just such an eventuality.[46] Unlike his chiefs of staff, Roosevelt was immediately decisive.

Air Corps chief Hap Arnold was in California traveling in the car of Donald Douglas, the aircraft manufacturer, when the news of the Japanese attack was announced on the radio. "I couldn't believe it," Arnold later recalled. "The Japanese had sunk our battleships, destroyed our airplanes . . . they had made a mess of things in general in and around Pearl Harbor and Honolulu. The war was on. Looking back on it, I doubt very much if there were many officers in the Army or Navy who really expected the Japanese to start the war by attacking where they did . . . the general assumption seemed to have been that they would hit the Philippines first."[47] Arnold jumped to the conclusion that it was the fault of the navy, which he felt should have had warships constantly cruising around the islands to intercept any Japanese intruders. He had not realized the very limited number of cruisers available for such service, and of course battleships were not used for that purpose. On the other hand, the navy did have a few long-range PBY seaplanes that could have searched the seas over several hundred miles and given a warning. These were not in the air.

Arnold refused to accept responsibility for the fact that the air force was equally to blame, as it had failed to send its dozens of B-17s on long-range search missions, which if directed as far out as six hundred miles to the north or northwest of Hawaii might have seen the enemy. Indeed, when a few B-17s had been used earlier for surveillance, they were dispatched hundreds of miles to the *south and southwest* of the islands. This was hardly the most logical decision, as the planes would have detected an attack only if the entire Japanese carrier force had sailed a much more circuitous route, or one moreover that followed the main sea and air routes used regularly by the U.S. Navy and Air Force.

Arnold immediately got in touch with Brigadier General Frederick Martin, the air force commander at Honolulu, to find out what had happened. He then contacted General Lewis Brereton, the air force chief in the Philippines, "to try to give him some idea of what had occurred at Pearl Harbor, so that he would not be caught the same way, and his entire air force destroyed . . . but in spite of all the precautions taken . . . within a few hours we also lost most of our airplanes in the Philippines—practically all of the B-17s and most of our fighters on the ground." What Arnold did not know was that MacArthur refused to let Brereton attack Japanese air bases in Formosa. More incredible still, MacArthur refused even to see his air corps chief for the next *nine hours*. "In any event," Arnold concluded, "I have never been able to get the real story of what happened in the Philippines."[48]

Admiral Chester Nimitz was serving in the nation's capital that year as the head of the Bureau of Navigation, a misleading name for Office of Naval Personnel. He was responsible for assigning all the officers of the fleet to the quickly expanding navy, and had earlier been considered for the Hawaiian command that had gone to Admiral Kimmel in February 1941. As Nimitz was not involved in either diplomatic or military operations, he had not been apprised of any information revealed by Naval Intelligence or the army's Purple intercepts. Nevertheless, he had kept himself informed generally about the quickly deteriorating position in the Pacific, when the Japanese had invaded southern

Indochina in July. Having served several years in the Far East, he had a good idea what the implications were.

Nimitz was spending Sunday, December 7, with his wife and daughters at their 2222 Q Street apartment. His son Chester Junior was serving aboard a submarine off the Philippines. After their usual Sunday afternoon meal, the Nimitzes settled down to read and listen to the three o'clock New York Philharmonic Orchestra concert conducted by Arthur Rodzinski. Nimitz's daughter Catherine was walking Freckles, the family cocker spaniel, down Massachusetts Avenue when she saw a huge bonfire in front of the Japanese Embassy: the embassy staff, surrounded by reporters and photographers, were burning ciphers and box after box of official papers. She rushed back to the apartment to tell her father. But even before she returned, just as the radio concert began, the broadcast was interrupted with a flash announcement stating that the Japanese had bombed Pearl Harbor. Nimitz leaped from his chair to grab an overcoat when the telephone rang. His assistant, Captain John Shafroth, was driving to the Navy Department and would collect his chief at the apartment. Mrs. Nimitz went to the kitchen to prepare sandwiches, a thermos of coffee, and another of hot soup for the hard work ahead.[49]

The previous day, Admiral Ernie King, commander of the Atlantic Fleet, had been aboard his flagship the *Augusta* at her buoy in Narragansett Bay, preparing to return to Washington for the usual biweekly meeting at naval headquarters. "Well," he commented, according to biographer Thomas Buell, "I've got to go down to Washington and straighten out those dumb bastards again," as he typically referred to the secretary of the navy and that service's governing General Board. At sunset the ship's bugler sounded the colors, and the watch lowered the flag on the forecastle and fantail; after a movie, King retired for the night.

On Sunday, King's steward awakened him as usual at 7:00 A.M. as the cook prepared breakfast in the flag pantry. He then went to his desk, working until lunch, where he was joined by Rear Admiral Olaf Hustvedt, King's chief of staff. Ernie King was taking his afternoon nap when a marine orderly brought a message to Rear Admiral Hustvedt, stating that Japan was attacking Pearl Harbor. Hustvedt immediately woke King to give him the news; the admiral read the message without comment. For the remainder of the day the staff routine was unchanged, but King was on the telephone much of the time attempting to obtain further information.

The next morning King's aide, Harry Sanders, gathered the admiral's papers. King, traveling in civilian clothes, boarded the black barge that was waiting to take him ashore. There the marine driver held the door of his sedan open and they were soon off to the railway station at Kingston, Rhode Island, where they would take the train to Washington.[50]

●

"When the first bombs fell on Pearl Harbor I was fourteen miles away at home in bed, the best place for a naval intelligence officer to be that Sunday morning," the modest Jaspar Holmes recalled. A former submarine commander, Lieutenant Holmes had developed a severe case of spinal arthritis, forcing him to abandon a naval career a few years earlier. He had been appointed assistant professor of engineering at Honolulu University when he was called back to active service in 1941, working under Joe Rochefort's top-secret Combat Intelligence Unit on Makalapa Hill.

Lieutenant Holmes was awakened by his young son telling him, "Mr. Herndon says to get up, the Japs are taking the island. . . ." "The Japs aren't taking the island," Holmes reassured him. "They are thousands of miles away, taking an island in the Dutch East Indies." Just then the telephone rang. "This is the District Intelligence duty officer. General Quarters!" a voice said, and the phone was hung up abruptly. "In the few minutes required to get into my uniform," Holmes continued, "I had time to reflect that the sadistic high brass would probably pick this as the ideal time for a practice alert. . . . On the other hand, war was expected at any moment. It might already have exploded in the South China Sea or the East Indies, as we expected. This might be the first real all-hands alert, in which case information I had been carefully collecting during the past few months [plotting Japanese warships] would immediately be needed to provide protection for [our] ships at sea in the eastern Pacific." Instructing his wife to move in with friends—their house at Black Point was just one street away from the beach and a major artillery battery—Holmes jumped into his Studebaker and started on his way. He later recalled the events of that day:

> The coast artillery company that manned the Diamond Head batteries were assembling for muster at Fort Ruger as I drove through. When I topped the rise and looked down on Waikiki I saw a string of black bursts of antiaircraft fire out over the reef. I took it as an indication that this was all part of a realistic practice alert, for the bursts appeared to be placed only over the water, where there would be no danger of anyone being hit by shell fragments. . . . I was near the center of town [Honolulu] before cars started streaming in from the side streets. Then the traffic clotted rapidly, all headed in the direction of Pearl Harbor.
>
> By the time we reached Kalihi, the traffic bound for Pearl Harbor preempted the right of way, ignoring all traffic lights. . . . In the distance, above the cane fields, a great pillar of ominous black smoke arose, advertising disaster at our destination. A car pulled out into the left lane, followed immediately by a string of others until quickly all four lanes were packed into a solid and unmoving mass headed toward Pearl Harbor. . . . On the rough left shoulder of the road a convoy of cars came bumping along from the Pearl Harbor direction. In some of them we could see obviously injured people. For the first time I knew for sure that this was not a drill. . . . I sped on with the others to the main gate of the Navy Yard. The Marine sentry recognized the identifying sticker on my car and waved me on in. This must have been the brief lull in the battle, about nine o'clock. . . . Thousands of men had died and thousands of others were then manning guns or desperately trying to save their burning and sinking ships. . . . I reported to my boss, Joseph J. Rochefort. . . . "Japanese air attack on battleship row," Rochefort informed me. "It looks bad."

"I saw *Oklahoma* hit by torpedoes and roll completely over," the chief petty officer told him, and someone else added, "*Arizona* blew up about the same time." Firing resumed as the second wave of enemy bombers struck. "Several heavy explosions rocked the solid earth, and our basement trembled," Holmes remembered. "The lights went out plunging us into darkness."[51] Meanwhile, Admiral Kimmel had abandoned his game of golf with General Short.

●

Admiral Stark, General Marshall, War Secretary Stimson, Naval Secretary Knox, and Secretary of State Cordell Hull met in the Oval

Room at 3:00 P.M. "The conference met in not too tense an atmosphere because I think that all of us believed that in the last analysis the enemy was Hitler and that he could never be defeated without force of arms; that sooner or later we were bound to be in the war and that Japan had given us an opportunity," eyewitness Robert Sherwood recalled. "Everybody, however, agreed on the seriousness of the war and that it would be a long, hard struggle. During the conference the news kept coming in, indicating more and more damage to the fleet. The President handled the calls personally. . . . Most of them came through the Navy."[52]

Roosevelt gave a general review of the history of relations with Japan leading to Pearl Harbor, and Hull discussed his long negotiations with Nomura. When Churchill called from England, "The President told him that we were all in the same boat now and that he was going to Congress tomorrow," Sherwood recorded. "Churchill apparently told him that the Malay Straits had been attacked and that he too was going to the House of Commons in the morning and would ask for a declaration of war. . . . Marshall was clearly impatient to get away." The general said that he had "ordered General MacArthur to execute 'all the necessary movement required in event of an outbreak of hostilities with Japan.'" Although Marshall announced that the army would guard the War Department from now on, Roosevelt refused to have troops surround the White House. He announced another conference to be held at 8:30 P.M., this one with the full cabinet; a third would include Speaker Sam Rayburn, Majority Floor Leader John McCormack, Minority Floor Leader Joseph Martin, Foreign Affairs Chairman Sol Bloom, Tom Connally and Charles Eaton of the Foreign Relations Committee, Warren Austin of the Military Affairs Committee, and Representative Charles McNary. Sherwood observed that "The President was in a very solemn mood" that evening when he convened "the most serious Cabinet session since Lincoln met with the Cabinet at the outbreak of the Civil War. . . . At this time we [still] did not know whether or not Japan had actually declared war on us." Afterward Roosevelt met with the congressional leaders who were waiting outside. The president announced that he would appear before Congress at 12:30 P.M. on Monday, December 8.[53]

Earlier that afternoon, just before the three o'clock meeting in the

White House, General Marshall had radioed message number 736 to General MacArthur in Manila:

> Hostilities between Japan and the United States, British Commonwealth and Dutch have commenced. Japanese made air raid on Pearl Harbor this morning December 7th. Carry out tasks assigned in Rainbow 5 as they pertain to Japan.

MacArthur received this message at 5:35 A.M., December 8, Manila time.[54]

●

On December 7, Admiral Yamamoto, who as far back as January had prepared a complete set of plans for an attack against Pearl Harbor, waited anxiously aboard his flagship, the mighty *Yamato*. Vice Admiral Nagumo edged the Pearl Harbor Strike Force, or *Kido Butai*, to a fix at latitude 26° north, longitude 158° west, 275 miles due north of his target. In addition to six carriers—*Akagi*, *Kaga*, *Hiryu*, *Shokaku*, *Soryu*, and *Zuikaku*—Yamamoto was escorted by a light cruiser and nine destroyers and preceded by twenty-five submarines, including five bearing two-man midget subs. A Support Force comprising two battleships, two cruisers, three reconnaissance subs, two destroyers, eight tankers, and eight supply ships followed.[55] Although Nagumo and Yamamoto had hoped to find and destroy all the American carriers in Hawaii, aerial pilots launched by eleven of the big submarines confirmed on the evening of December 6 that the carriers were no longer in these waters. The wind picked up to gale force, jeopardizing the air launch scheduled for the following day. The five midget subs were launched at 0100 on December 7, with orders to get into Pearl Harbor itself if possible. They were never to be seen again.

The sea was still very rough at 0500 on the 7th, and two more floatplanes were catapulted to establish the feasibility of a full attack. Despite the dangerous pitching of the big ships, Nagumo began the launch of the first wave at 0530 and by 0615 had sent 183 aircraft (49 high-level bombers each carrying a 1,600-pound armor-piercing bomb, 40 planes carrying shallow-running torpedoes, and 51 dive-bombers with 500-pound bombs, all protected by 43 Zeroes) right on schedule and on course for their targets. Earlier Admiral Yamamoto had issued his battle order, reminding the task force that "the rise or fall of the Empire depends upon this battle," as Admiral Tōgō's had once famously pronounced just before the battle of Tsushima. These words now rang in the ears of another generation of warriors.

Their targets were the U.S. Fleet in Pearl Harbor—some ninety ships, among which were eight battleships, two heavy cruisers, six light cruisers, twenty-nine destroyers, and several submarines. They were also to attack six airfields: Hickham, Wheeler, Kaneohe, Ewa, Bellows, and the Ford Island field. Admiral Nomura had been ordered to present his final diplomatic message, ending negotiations, to Secretary Hull at 0800 Honolulu time (1300 hours in Washington) so as to coincide with, but not precede, the attack. At 0755 Japanese dive-bombers dropped down to attack the airfields, strafing those planes that were not already destroyed by bombs. Torpedo planes and high-level bombers struck simultaneously. The Japanese achieved total surprise and met no initial resistance from American gunners on land or aboard warships for the first quarter of an hour. Neither Admiral Kimmel nor General Short, both of whom were still on the golf course when the first attack came, had sounded the full level of alert required by the war warning of November 27 and the information provided by Rochefort. Most American soldiers, sailors, and pilots were literally asleep. No guns were manned, no ammo at the ready.

The planes swept across Pearl Harbor at wave level with deadly accuracy. At 0810 the *Arizona* was struck several times, disappearing in a massive explosion. By now there was some sporadic return of fire, but only a handful of U.S. Army and Navy planes managed to get into the air to challenge the intruders. At 0915, as Lieutenant Holmes reached the Naval Yard, a second wave of 167 warplanes struck the port and airfields again; they failed to attack the machine sheds and the 4.5 million gallons of oil and fuel stored around the military bases and harbor, however, for the simple reason that those were not included in their orders.[56]

By noon, in addition to the *Arizona*, which had blown up with heavy loss of life, the *Oklahoma* and *Utah* had capsized, the *California* and *West Virginia* had been sunk, the *Nevada* had been wrecked and beached, and the *Tennessee* and the *Pennsylvania* had been badly dam-

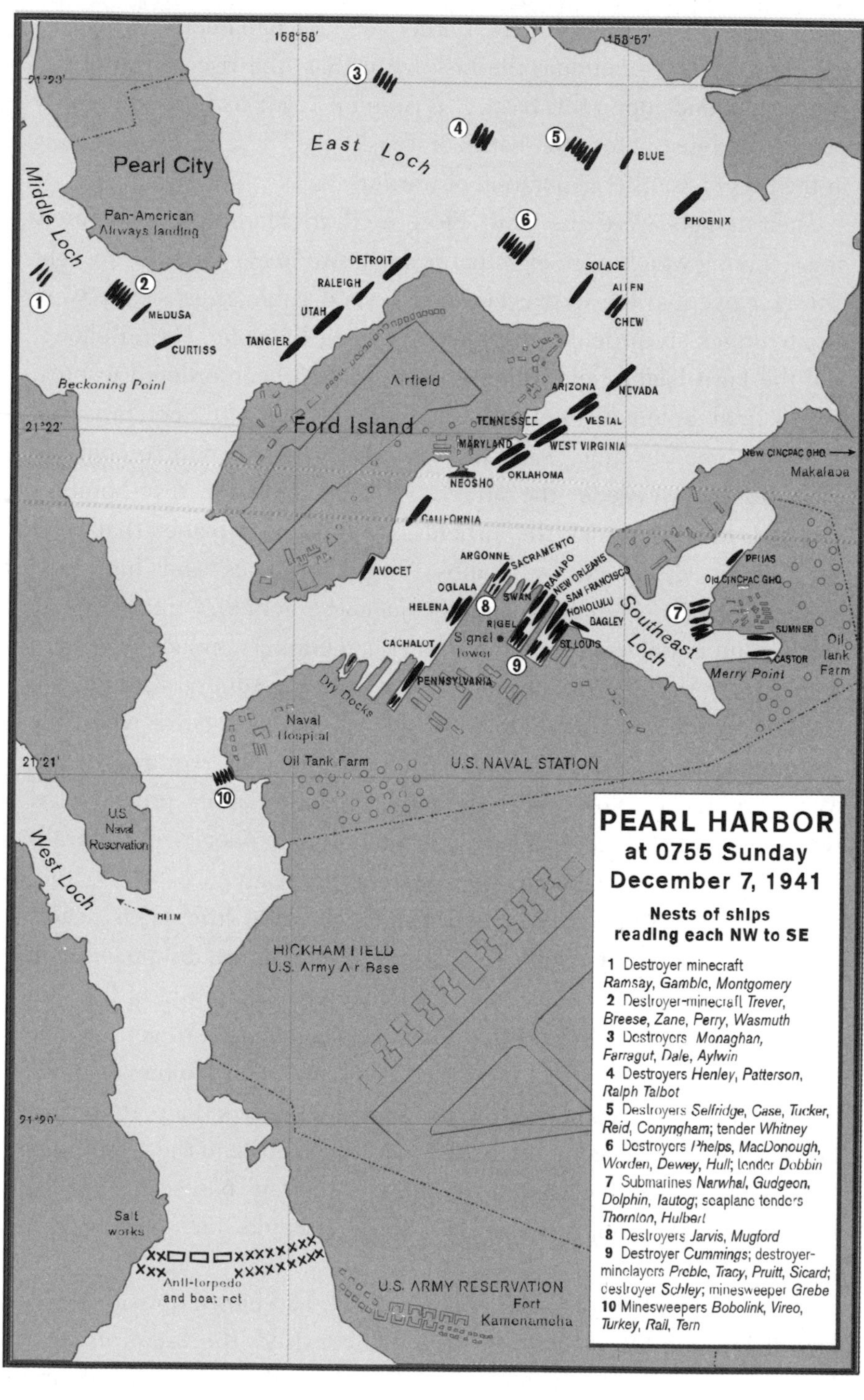

PEARL HARBOR
at 0755 Sunday
December 7, 1941
Nests of ships reading each NW to SE
1 Destroyer minecraft Ramsay, Gamble, Montgomery
2 Destroyer-minecraft Trever, Breese, Zane, Perry, Wasmuth
3 Destroyers Monaghan, Farragut, Dale, Aylwin
4 Destroyers Henley, Patterson, Ralph Talbot
5 Destroyers Selfridge, Case, Tucker, Reid, Conyngham; tender Whitney
6 Destroyers Phelps, MacDonough, Worden, Dewey, Hull; tender Dobbin
7 Submarines Narwhal, Gudgeon, Dolphin, Tautog; seaplane tenders Thornton, Hulbert
8 Destroyers Jarvis, Mugford
9 Destroyer Cummings; destroyer-minelayers Preble, Tracy, Pruitt, Sicard; destroyer Schley; minesweeper Grebe
10 Minesweepers Bobolink, Vireo, Turkey, Rail, Tern
158°58'
158°57'
21°23'
21°22'
21°21'
21°20'
Pearl City
Pan-American Airways landing
Middle Loch
East Loch
BLUE
PHOENIX
DETROIT
RALEIGH
UTAH
TANGIER
MEDUSA
CURTISS
SOLACE
ALLEN
CHEW
Beckoning Point
Airfield
Ford Island
ARIZONA
NEVADA
TENNESSEE
VESTAL
MARYLAND
WEST VIRGINIA
NEOSHO
OKLAHOMA
New CINCPAC GHQ
Makalapa
CALIFORNIA
ARGONNE
SACRAMENTO
AVOCET
OGLALA
HELENA
SWAN
RAMAPO
NEW ORLEANS
SAN FRANCISCO
HONOLULU
RIGEL
DAGLEY
Signal tower
ST. LOUIS
CACHALOT
PENNSYLVANIA
Dry Docks
PELIAS
Old CINCPAC GHQ
SUMNER
CASTOR
Southeast Loch
Merry Point
Oil Tank Farm
Naval Hospital
Oil Tank Farm
U.S. NAVAL STATION
U.S. Naval Reservation
West Loch
HELM
HICKAM FIELD
U.S. Army Air Base
Salt works
Anti-torpedo and boat net
U.S. ARMY RESERVATION
Fort Kamehameha

aged. The *Maryland* was lightly damaged, as were the light cruisers *Raleigh*, *Helena*, and *Honolulu*. Three destroyers were also crippled along with one seaplane tender.

If the naval toll was tragic, military aircraft destruction was equally devastating: 188 (army and navy) planes completely destroyed on the ground and another 159 severely damaged, leaving only 43 planes untouched. Upon learning of the total destruction of the U.S. Air Force on Oahu, a staggered FDR slammed his fist down on the table and exclaimed, "Our planes were destroyed on the ground, by God, on the ground!"[57] In all, 2,402 Americans were killed outright and 1,178 wounded; ambulance sirens screamed across the rubble of the port and back to the U.S. Naval Hospital, and to the city of Honolulu for the next twenty-four hours. Of the 350 warplanes launched by Nagumo, all but 29 returned safely. But the midget submarines had not reached their targets and were destroyed, while one I-class sub had been sunk.[58] Clearly, Admiral Kimmel and General Short had learned nothing from the maneuvers of 1928, 1932, and 1938. Clearly, they had not done their homework, and in consequence, men had to die.

●

The clock in Washington, D.C., had already struck noon on Monday, the 8th, as Franklin Delano Roosevelt stood in the Capitol Building to address both houses of Congress. Somberly he announced, "Yesterday, December 7, 1941—a date that will live in infamy—the United States of America was suddenly and deliberately attacked by naval and air forces of the Empire of Japan. . . . Very many American lives have been lost." At the same moment Tokyo had also, he told them, "launched an attack against Malaya.

"Last night Japanese forces attacked Hong Kong.

"Last night Japanese forces attacked Guam.

"Last night Japanese forces attacked the Philippine Islands.

"Last night Japanese forces attacked Wake Island.

"This morning the Japanese attacked Midway Island.

"Japan has, therefore, undertaken a surprise offensive extending throughout the Pacific area. . . .

"Hostilities exist. There is no blinking at the fact that our people, our territory, and our interests are in grave danger. . . . I ask that the Congress declare that since the unprovoked and dastardly attack by Japan on Sunday, December 7, 1941, a state of war has existed between the United States and the Japanese Empire."

The two houses then voted, with the Senate voting unanimously for a declaration of war against Japan. Everyone in the House of Representatives also gave their approval, with one exception, Jeannette Rankin of Montana.[59]

On December 11, Germany, followed by Italy, declared war against the United States. The nation was finally at General Quarters. It was time to man battle stations.

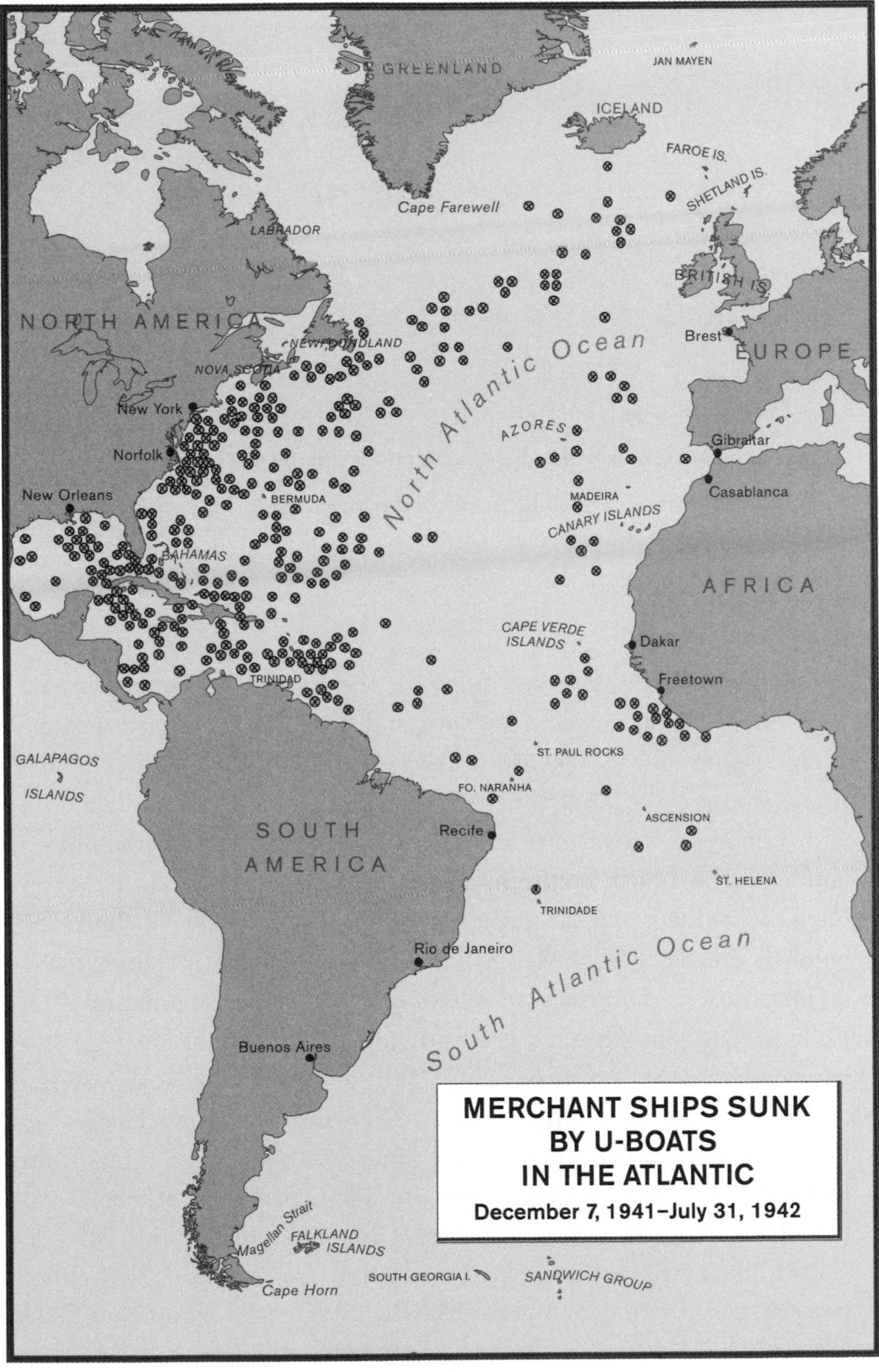

MERCHANT SHIPS SUNK BY U-BOATS IN THE ATLANTIC

December 7, 1941–July 31, 1942

CHAPTER VIII

Two Admirals

"Historically, despite Washington's (and others') experienced and cogent advice to make due preparations for war, it is traditional (and habitual) for us to be inadequately prepared."

—*Captain Ernest King, 1932*[1]

Between December 7 and 14, 1941, the Far East suddenly exploded as the Imperial Japanese Army, Navy, and Air Force unleashed massive simultaneous attacks against Malaya, Thailand (then Siam), Hong Kong, Borneo, the Philippines, Wake, Guam, Midway, and Hawaii, with hundreds of warships and troop transports making amphibious landings. The British battleship *Prince of Wales* and the battle cruiser *Repulse,* without any air cover, were sunk by dozens of Japanese bombers off the coast of Malaya with heavy loss of life, including those of John Leach, the *Prince of Wales*'s captain, and Rear Admiral Tom Phillips. The long-expected war with Japan was a reality at last, and nowhere were the U.S. Army, Navy, and Air Force ready. A devastated Navy Secretary Frank Knox, who had flown out to Pearl Harbor on December 9, returned to the White House with a very grim report on December 15. As he met with the president, Secretary Stimson, and the chiefs of staff, Prime Minister Churchill crossed the Atlantic aboard the newly commissioned battleship *Duke of York* with Lord Beaverbrook, Admiral Pound, Air Marshal Sir Charles Portal, and Field Marshal Dill to consult with their new wartime Allies in Washington.

Supreme Court Justice Owen J. Roberts was appointed to head a commission of inquiry to study the causes of the disaster at Pearl Harbor. Roosevelt had already demanded the recall of Admiral Kimmel and Generals Short and Martin. On the 16th, a solemn Admiral King was summoned to the office of Knox on the second deck (or floor) of the Navy Building. Vice Admiral Nimitz would be fleeted up to full admiral and would relieve Kimmel forthwith, Knox informed him, and King would become Commander in Chief, U.S. Fleet (CINCUS, an unfortunate acronym he was shortly to change to COMINCH), a position that FDR had initially eliminated back in January. He would also assume most of Stark's powers, although that admiral would remain CNO (Chief of Naval Operations), at least in title, for the time being.[2] That same day, Army Chief of Staff Marshall rang up General Delos Emmons ordering him "to take command of the Hawaiian Department relieving Short. You are to leave immediately, tonight if possible. . . . Meanwhile our issue is the security of Hawaii."[3]

In the Philippines, General Lewis Brereton was falsely accused of gross incompetence as MacArthur ordered him to take what was left of his air force to Australia. Following the "surprise attack on MacArthur's forces on the 8th of December, on the land, in the air and at sea," most of Brereton's warplanes had been destroyed on the ground.

In reality it was Douglas MacArthur who had been given nearly a nine-hour warning because of the Japanese attack on Pearl Harbor—but instead of taking action according to the plans he himself had earlier prepared, the stunned general had sealed himself off from everyone except his chief of staff, Major General Richard Sutherland. General Brereton had rushed over to MacArthur's office at 5:00 A.M., but was turned back. Despite two more attempts, MacArthur still refused to see the anguished Brereton, who had his planes armed, fueled, and ready to take off; yet he could not launch them without Douglas MacArthur's authorization. Sutherland informed Brereton that MacArthur would not permit his warplanes to attack Japanese airfields on Formosa, and declined even to send out reconnaissance planes.[4] Despite Douglas MacArthur's later denial of much of this, it was established that it was Brereton, and not his commander MacArthur, who had been telling the truth. For his role in the greatest twin U.S. military disasters in history, Douglas MacArthur nonetheless received only the highest praise from General George Marshall, who congratulated him on "the resolute and effective fighting of you and your men in the air and on the ground" which has "made a tremendous impression on the American people and confirms our confidence in your leadership."[5]

Army Chief of Staff George Marshall was guilty of initiating one of the greatest cover-ups in American history, concealing MacArthur's total failure to act, to take preventative measures in the hours before the first Japanese attack, or in the end to protect the Philippines, for whose defense *he alone was ultimately responsible.* More dismaying and bewildering, General Marshall refused to have MacArthur fired once the enormity of the debacle was known. Instead, Marshall successfully employed all his personal influence to quash any attempt to convene a full board of inquiry, similar to Justice Roberts's commission in Hawaii, that would have investigated the events in the Philippines. Clearly George Marshall was acting prejudicially so as to protect the name of the army as well as his own responsibility in this affair. The old-boy network was hard at work, protected by the ultimate authority, the president of the United States.

Stark, unlike Marshall, was automatically held responsible for the failure of the U.S. Navy in Hawaii, and he had promptly relieved his admiral, Kimmel, of duty there. Stark's head was next to roll. Why?[6] That is to say, why was the chief of the navy found wanting but not the head of the army, when they had both given more or less identical instructions to their commanding officers in Hawaii and the Philippines? Why was Brereton made MacArthur's scapegoat in the Philippines? If Marshall had recalled MacArthur, as he should have done, other future problems in the Pacific would almost certainly have been avoided. But then of course Marshall would have had to accept his share of the responsibility, and thus instead hushed the whole unsavory truth up. He did not wish to be dismissed in ignominy like Admiral Stark.

Nor did Roosevelt ever explain his own failure to act. But it bears remembering that upon MacArthur's retirement as army chief of staff in 1935, Roosevelt had informed him that in the event of war breaking out, the president would recall him "to the colors" immediately. MacArthur's abuse of power was to grow and continue to the end of his career, when he unfathomably protected Hirohito's role regarding crimes committed during World War II by destroying documentation, including papers tying Hirohito directly to the use of biological and chemical weapons. Finally, in Korea, MacArthur was to overstep the mark with the one president who would not tolerate his behavior: Harry Truman, who would fire him.

Nevertheless, the men who were to be responsible for the conduct of the coming war in the Pacific had been named. No understanding of the events and military campaigns that were about to take place in that vast region can be achieved without first looking at the two admirals and the general who would lead U.S. military forces in both Washington and the Far East: Admirals King and Nimitz, and General MacArthur.

●

When on December 30 Admiral Ernest King entered the Main Naval Building as the new commanding officer of the entire U.S. Fleet, he entered a nightmare. His office, on the third deck, consisted of nothing more than a vacant room, as the post he now held had been suppressed at the beginning of the year and the entire staff had been disbursed elsewhere. The presidential executive order appointing him stated that he was to have "supreme command of the operating forces comprising the several fleets of the United States Navy and the operating forces of the Naval Coastal Command," and that he was directly responsible to one person only, the president of the United States. The single empty office he was shown into was as bereft of furniture as he was of "staff." As King put it, "nothing was ready, I had to start with nothing," which was literally true. "Upon my arrival in Washington . . . I found Admiral King enthroned in the most disreputable office I have ever seen," Rear Admiral Richard Edwards, former commander of the Atlantic submarine force and recently named deputy chief of staff for operations for King, later recalled. "Someone had moved out in a hurry, taking the furniture with him, but not the dirt. The Admiral had liberated a flat top desk from somewhere and a couple of chairs; opposite him sat Russell Willson [formerly Superintendent of the Naval Academy and now King's new chief of staff]. I and my assistant [Francis "Frog" Low, the new operations officer] borrowed a broken down table from a friend who was out to lunch and set up shop in a corner of the Admiral's office." This was "the headquarters of the greatest navy in the world; it fell somewhat short of being impressive." Nothing had been prepared for the most important officer of the U.S. Navy, not even a telephone.

Yet Roosevelt had selected King for this very post because of his amazing energy, resilience, decisiveness, and positive thinking. He was a man intimidated by no obstacle and no individual, no matter how high his title. King now had a staff of three and soon sequestered more from Stark and other senior officers, sometimes without even asking their permission. As far as King was concerned, Stark had had his opportunity and failed. Stark protested when King took Kelly Turner (who would head Planning), Willis Lee, and Roland Brainard, and then he fought when King also took Roy Ingersoll. "You cannot keep him," King informed the CNO. "He is needed at sea." Ingersoll was promptly put in command of the Atlantic Fleet. Captain Charles Cooke, Jr., was commanding the battleship *Pennsylvania* when he received orders to report promptly to King's office. He did.

Then Ernie King needed transport. He wanted a black Cadillac and got it. He instructed CNO Stark to provide him with a twin-engine Lockheed Lodestar, and the following day the chief of the Bureau of Aeronautics found his Lodestar missing, permanently. King also demanded a very special flagship—one comfortable enough to live in and large enough for conferences. The Dodge family of automobile manufacturers soon found its 1,200-ton, 257-foot luxury yacht *Delphine* requisitioned by the U.S. Navy, refitted with the latest naval technology, a coat of camouflage, and a gun mounted on the foredeck. She arrived at her new berth in the Washington Naval Yard, where she was rechristened USS *Dauntless* (King thought it a more martial name). She was to serve as King's personal living quarters throughout the duration of the war. *Dauntless* was manned by Commander Charles Grisham's crew of one hundred and was also used for training purposes. But as more than one irate congressman complained, King's floating "bedroom" cost the U.S. taxpayers $250,000 a year to maintain. Shortly thereafter Stark was removed as CNO; King assumed his title along with the CNO's official mansion, the Naval Observatory. But King was to prove a very rare visitor at that house where his estranged wife and several children lived, preferring as he did the relative peace and quiet of the *Dauntless*.[7]

Who, then, was this rough, complex character Ernest King, selected by the president himself to command ultimately some 3.4 million men?

●

Throughout his naval career, Ernie King went out of his way to be rude to the English and generally took an anti-British attitude when it came to cooperation with them as wartime Allies. It puzzled many people, but his antagonism might have come from his origins as a son of immigrants: a nearly illiterate working-class Scottish father from Renfrewshire and an English mother of similar background but with some education. His father, James King, had been put to work as a very young lad and had come to the United States to serve as a merchant seaman on the Great Lakes. He then worked at an oil refinery and next repairing bridges before finally marrying and settling down with Elizabeth Keam in Lorain, Ohio, repairing railway locomotives. And it was there that Ernest King was born on November 23, 1878, followed by several siblings. The marriage was not a great success, and when his mother became quite ill, she moved to Cleveland to stay with her sister while Ernie alone of the children remained with his father. The father was a loud, boastful man, a socialist who was strongly anti-British. He drank heavily and was, in the words of King's biographer, Thomas Buell, "profane, opinionated, blunt, outspoken . . . stubborn and self-righteous," attributes his son would inherit. He was also brutal, but his son preferred to remain with him rather than to go with his mother (who would die during Ernie's second year of high school). Young King had to work every day after school and had no time for sports. He spent his summer vacations working on locomotives with his father, perfecting skills involving metalwork and engines that would hold him in good stead years later in the navy. He was even forced to quit school for one year to work and earn money. King finally graduated at the top of his class—out of thirteen classmates—and successfully crammed to pass the entrance exam to the Naval Academy.

When he first walked through the Maryland Avenue Gate at Annapolis on August 15, 1897, he found the Naval Academy "decrepit," long starved of congressional appropriations. Cadet King was one of 290 young men at various stages in the four-year course. The students were mostly lower-middle or working-class, white and Protestant. Life was rigid and disciplined. Six feet tall and 135 pounds, King was lean, handsome, and sociable—if bereft of the usual social graces—and a good, serious student. He was a very poor athlete, although he loved ice skating, at which he excelled. He worked conscientiously and was determined to come out at the top of his class, but as his teachers noted, deep down there was a rage in him; he was at war, with himself and the world. He always had a chip on his shoulder and over the years this internal war simmered, despite his having achieved one remarkable success after another. Although everything he achieved should have given him a foundation of self-confidence, his inner turmoil would continue to intensify over the following decades. Like his father, he was stubborn and tenacious, with a violent temper (during World War II, he nearly physically attacked a British chief of staff). He was cocky, and as Buell put it, "an egoist, intellectually arrogant and supremely confident" in naval matters and in his views on every subject. But he had a social inferiority complex, due no doubt to his humble origins. While "he sought to be omnipotent and infallible," he was a poor loser, whether in sports or in being proven wrong in an argument. Later as a father he was even angry when his children beat him in a game of Monopoly. According to Buell, "There were few men whom he regarded as his equal as to 'brains'; he would acknowledge no mind as superior to his own."[8]

He graduated fourth in his class in June 1901, with the rank of battalion commander. Vice President Teddy Roosevelt gave the commencement address as King became a "passed midshipman" ("naval cadet" had been discarded since his arrival at the Academy). Little did the bristling King realize the significance of Roosevelt's succession to the presidency that autumn, which greatly expanded naval funds and created a vast new building program that included ten new battleships, four armored cruisers, and seventeen other ships, while calling for an increase in naval officers.

In spite of his considerable success at the Academy, once his career began, King's cockiness got out of control, as did his heavy drinking (which would plague him until the outbreak of World War II). One fitness report after another listed his failure to obey orders, his rudeness to superior officers, and his constant tardiness in returning to his ship.

After completing a short course at the Naval Torpedo Station, he served in a variety of ships, including a wooden geodetic survey vessel, where he was navigator, and the battleship *Illinois*, where he was an aide to the admiral and in charge of visual communications (whose machinery he improved). Aboard the cruiser *Cincinnati*, he traveled most of the seven seas, through the Suez Canal and into the Indian Ocean to Singapore and Shanghai—a voyage he would never forget because the ship's commander restricted the ever tardy King to his quarters. Its next captain, Commander Hugo Osterhaus, put a drunk and (again) tardy King "under hatches" for six days. He was never late again.[9]

Amazingly enough, despite his deplorable fitness reports, King was promoted to ensign on June 7, 1903, and immediately got into trouble again when he ordered a senior officer, in fact the cruiser's executive officer, out of his cabin. Osterhaus now threatened him with ten days under hatches. But King never did learn to govern his temper or recognize the limits of his own self-importance.

In 1905 he transferred back to the United States, marrying Martha (Mattie) Lamkin Egerton in the Cadet Chapel at the U.S. Military Academy on October 10. Given King's social inferiority complex, his marriage to a young woman from an old, upper-middle-class family was doomed from the start.

His career, however, was beginning to advance. In the fall of 1906, Lieutenant King was assigned to the Naval Academy to teach ordnance, gunnery, and seamanship. He was next assigned to the Executive Department there and soon got into a flaming row with his superiors, failing to obey their orders: in consequence, he was roundly chastised by the Superintendent of the Academy.

Thanks to King's wife's money—which he deeply resented—the couple was able to buy a house on Franklin Street at Annapolis, complete with servants. But he preferred work to married life: for the next three years King did not take a single day of leave, spending as little time as possible at home. His relationship with his wife would steadily deteriorate over time, and he was never anything but cold and distant toward his many children.

King next became a gunnery officer, engineering officer, and flag secretary. When he did return to the Academy, it was to serve as executive officer under Tom Kinkaid at the Experimental Engineering Department, and to edit and write for the Naval Institute's magazine *Proceedings*. In 1912 he visited the adjacent naval air station near Annapolis where Jack Towers, the future architect of the navy's new air arm, gave him his first flight in an airplane.

In the spring of 1914, at the age of thirty-five, Lieutenant Commander King was given his first command at sea, as skipper of a destroyer assigned to seek out German merchantmen in coordination with the British Royal Navy. King was no fan of the alliance. "The British were very nice to us," he later commented, "to let us use the high seas."

In December 1915 he was appointed to the staff of Vice Admiral Henry Mayo, commander of the Atlantic Battleship Force. But as usual, King, first weighing his possibilities, was slow in accepting the post. He did not like the idea of being considered a specialist and then getting stuck in a rut, and the position with Mayo was as staff engineering officer. He finally accepted, however, and worked with a staff that included William Pye, Russell Willson, and Leigh Noyes. Much to his surprise, Ernie King was greatly impressed with his new quiet, modest commanding officer, Henry Mayo, a distinguished sailor of the highest order.

When the United States joined in the war against Germany in 1917, King was given the enormous task of converting the U.S. fleet power from coal to oil. When Mayo was promoted to command all U.S. Naval Forces operating in Europe, King was again assigned to his staff. This time he did not hesitate to accept the honor. In this capacity he attended numerous high-level conferences with British officers, and occasionally diplomats, all of whom he was highly contemptuous of. Among these was Admiral Sir David Beatty, who had invited King aboard his flagship during maneuvers. King being King, he loudly criticized Beatty, who in turn furiously complained to Admiral Mayo about the young man's remark before his officers. Nevertheless, King was invited by Sir John Jellicoe, First Sea Lord, to observe a bombardment of German-occupied Ostend from a British destroyer. Although he continued to find nothing good to say about the Royal Navy, he did learn a great deal about naval operations at the highest levels, drafted reports, minutes, and policy papers, and visited battlefields, bases, airfields, and foreign fleets. He saw a major war firsthand.

Just before the conclusion of World War I, in early September 1918, Ernie King—in spite of his long list of delinquencies ever since leaving the Academy—was promoted to the rank of captain.

The following year he was ordered to reopen the Naval Post Graduate School, which had been closed for some time. He and two other officers were to draw up a report of recommendations for the new school's curriculum. They suggested a two-tier system of courses, one for junior, one for senior officers; these recommendations were adopted and highly praised. King, now quite bald, was still a heavy smoker and drinker and continued to like loud parties, where he was known as "Uncle Ernie." As for his six daughters and one son, he preferred to avoid them when possible, remaining forever a stranger to his own family.

Requesting sea duty again, he first attended the submarine school, and although he never took the final qualifying exam as a sub commander, he was afterwards given command of a division of four subs. He never particularly liked this service and was frequently seasick aboard submarines; nevertheless, he was then appointed commander of the principal U.S. submarine base at New London, Connecticut. Subs at this time were still restricted to protecting American shores and possessions and were not yet used for offensive operations.

Later King again disobeyed orders, this time in Panama when he ordered his submarines to leave the U.S. Fleet's scouting vessels despite Vice Admiral John McDonald's furious barrage of blinking signals to return. Once again King was nearly court-martialed, adding yet another negative report to his personnel record. When it came to taking orders, King simply did not give a damn. But when he was in command of ships, he was the strictest of disciplinarians and would brook no nonsense from his own officers.

After several years as a submariner, King next requested flight instruction at Pensacola, Florida. Among other "student aviators" there at the time were Alva Bernhard and Kelly Turner, who were among the oldest taking the course. King had been so detested by some of his junior officers at New London, however, that some of them took the highly unusual step of writing a joint letter to the C.O. of the flight school, recommending that he fail King or else suffer the consequences of bringing chaos to naval aviation. King, when not flying, was at parties, womanizing and playing poker. "He was the damndest party man in the place," one officer later recalled. But King was no more a natural pilot than he was a submariner, and after successfully completing the course and making the final solo flight required to gain his wings, he rarely soloed again.

Admiral Moffett next ordered Captain King to serve as his assistant in the Bureau of Aeronautics, a decision he was soon to regret. As usual King tried to take control of everything, infuriating Moffett. "Maybe you want me to quit so you can have my job!" he rebuked Ernie King,[10] and soon had him transferred elsewhere.

In June 1930 King was given command of the carrier *Lexington*, which like the *Saratoga* had been converted from a battle cruiser. But unlike the *Saratoga*, "*Lex*" had no admiral aboard, hence King's selection of her instead. She was a large ship, 900 feet long, displacing 33,000 tons, with turbo-electric engines producing 180,000 horsepower; she carried a complement of 60 aviators and 2,000 men. The notorious King—his reputation had preceded him—ran a taut ship, as an equally difficult Captain John Hoover soon discovered. The two men were well matched, but King outranked Hoover, which did not stop Hoover from telling King off in private. "Still, he gets results. He always did," Hoover admitted. Nor was King subtle or dignified in giving orders, which he literally shouted out, regardless of the rank of the officers whom he was addressing. "He didn't need a megaphone. He'd just stand on the edge of that bridge . . . he could really bellow when he was mad," one recipient recalled.

The relentless King drove his officers and men hard, and did indeed get results. He was detested by most of his pilots, whom King found to be the most undisciplined officers in the navy, or as he elegantly put it, "Unless they get a kick in the ass every six weeks, they slack off." Ever impatient, King very much disliked losing time by having to refuel accompanying destroyers, and one day when one destroyer captain greeted him on the bridge with "Good morning, captain," King snapped, "Good morning Hell!" That was vintage Ernie King, the angriest man in the U.S. Navy.

"King conned the *Lexington* with imperious disdain for nearby ships," one of his officers complained, and one day off Long Beach, California, when warships automatically fell in astern of the senior flagship—now under the command of Admiral "Bull" Reeves—King once again passed the entire fleet and "disappeared over the horizon." Clearly he had learned nothing from that previous Panama escapade. When Reeves's fleet later reached port, the *Lexington* was already there, but Ernie King's pennant was absent. He had been invited to a party and was not about to waste his time dawdling at sea behind his commanding officer. The next day King received a peremptory summons to appear before Reeves forthwith. Reeves, not known for his sweet temper, read the "Riot Act" to King. "When the Commander in Chief issues an operation order, he doesn't have to include in it the rules of etiquette at sea!" the livid Reeves upbraided King. Ernie King gave one of the few apologies of his life . . . or he would have been ordered ashore. But when King was in command aboard his own ship, "he lived on the bridge" and never let up.

At the age of fifty-four he was assigned to take a senior course at the Naval War College, for which he wrote his thesis entitled *The Influence of the National Policy on the Strategy of a War*. Japan, he argued, was to be America's most likely enemy, but what were we doing about it? "Historically, despite Washington's (and others') experienced and cogent advice to make due preparations for war, it is traditional (and habitual) for us to be inadequately prepared."[11] The year was 1932, and he was, of course, quite right.

Of his thirty-five years in the navy, King had spent twenty-two at sea, openly boasting that he intended to became chief of naval operations, running the entire U.S. Navy and reforming it, he hoped, in his own image. There was probably no more ruthlessly ambitious officer in a navy filled with very ambitious line officers. Every step of his career had been calculating. Every time a superior officer offered him a promotion, he considered it from every possible viewpoint before making his decision. He had chosen to become a submariner because it added another notch to his already impressive qualifications. He had no real interest in naval aviation, but had simply concluded that it, too, was necessary for his dossier as a well-rounded commander. But a few years later he would criticize Pat Bellinger, who was carefully weighing a position King had just offered him: "I don't need to tell you that we cannot tolerate in the Naval service people who think they are entitled to pick and choose what they will do or what they will work with." It was perfectly all right for Ernie King to do it, but how dare a junior officer do that to him. In any event, he did not want to be known as a specialist in just one field but rather as a line officer who was an expert in every aspect of his profession.

Next it was necessary to become chief of all naval aviation, he decided, and he openly lobbied his best contacts in order to replace Moffett, who was due to retire in the summer of 1933. But then Admiral Moffett was killed aboard the dirigible *Akron* when it crashed in

April 1933. "You never get a job unless you ask for it," King told his friends. And now he wrote to influential Senator Harry Byrd of Virginia, asking him to intervene on his behalf; and Byrd indeed spoke personally to the new president, Franklin Roosevelt, recommending him. Leaving nothing to chance, King called on CNO Admiral William Pratt, who in turn recommended him to the secretary of the navy, Claude Swenson, listing King's merits:

> (a) He is highly intelligent.
> (b) He is extremely active and energetic.
> (c) He is very forceful.
> (d) He is a flyer and pilot.
> (e) He is a man of great decision of character.
> (f) He is a good strategist and tactician.
> (g) He is not as tactful as some men but he is very direct.
> (h) He is due for promotion to the position of Rear Admiral.[12]

And of course Ernie King won again, named the new chief of the Bureau of Aeronautics and promoted to flag rank in November 1933. As he acknowledged, "I had a proper ambition to get to the top," and he was well on his way. He held this post until June 1936, by which time the navy had four carriers and one thousand aircraft of all kinds.

His new billet in the summer of 1936 was as Commander, Aircraft, Base Force, which meant commanding a dozen squadrons of seaplane patrols around the world. In fact, this time King had lost. His bridling arrogance and flagrant incivility had ended his chance of being given the command he really wanted, which would have been over the navy's entire force of aircraft carriers. He got down to work, however, training his flyers intensively in preparation for the war he knew was coming. Further, he urged the creation of new, strategically situated seaplane bases throughout the Pacific—a wise stroke, as it turned out. He trained his pilots in all weathers and in all conditions, and several dropped out because of the constant grind and the dangers encountered. "Anyone who won't take a chance now and then," King countered, "isn't worth a damn." King himself had taken one chance after another, and was in at least one serious plane crash off the Mexican coast while en route to the Panama Canal.

As a commanding officer, King also had detrimental qualities. He had fixed ideas about things and would not change; he did not like to delegate authority (unlike Chester Nimitz, Spruance, and Marc Mitscher), and he did not at all like to take advice or be criticized. Therefore he was unable to take full advantage of possible contributions by his own staff. Moreover, he so intimidated those around him that he stifled initiative. His foul temper did not help matters. He was ruthless and, according to Commander Walter Boone, would on more than one occasion humiliate junior officers before their peers when he considered them incompetent. And as seaplane commander he never once called a staff conference or meeting of his main commanders to discuss operations, tactics, or schedules. Ernie King supposedly knew it all. These factors alone should have rendered his nomination for the supreme command of the U.S. Navy an obvious impossibility.

On the other hand, on rare occasions he could protect his own men. When his flagship USS *Wright* ran aground in Seattle, its captain would have automatically been denied another sea command. King intervened on his behalf. "Grounding? I was up here and I didn't see any grounding." The incident was never logged and the captain was duly promoted. On another occasion when a plane was presumed lost at sea, King personally went over that pilot's home to comfort his wife and children, as well as to the homes of the other crewmen. Ernie King was a complex man, and few around him even pretended to understand him.

Once, when interviewing a captain he was promoting to a new position, he passed along the standard King advice: "Experience has led me to the conviction that if anyone succeeds by hard work or rare good fortune, or both, to raise his head far above the herd [here King held his forefinger half an inch above his thumb], there are untold numbers of sons-of-bitches standing by ready and willing to knock him down."[13]

Fleeted up to vice admiral in January 1938, King was finally given command of three carriers (*Saratoga*, *Lexington*, and *Ranger*), and then two more newly commissioned carriers, *Yorktown* (1938) and *Enterprise* (1939). King developed new tactics and means of deploying his ships, separating his fast carriers (capable of 33 knots) from the slower battleships (maintaining 21 knots); but he was then overruled by the CNO, who was not sympathetic to aviation. Aboard his flagship, *Saratoga*, King was part of a minority of officers—among them Towers and Mitscher—

who insisted on intensive night flying. In 1938 King practiced Fleet Problem XIX using four carriers to execute a successful surprise attack on Pearl Harbor, similar to the exercises of 1928 and 1932.

If King did not often consult his staff when preparing fresh orders, he did always write them himself in his own hand, and as Squadron Commander Boone noted, "His directives were the ultimate in clarity, brevity, and incisiveness, the meaning and intent of every word unmistakable," as compared to Admiral William Halsey's later very sloppy instructions. Time and again King criticized his officers. "Let me say that working for Admiral King was not always a pleasant pastime," one carrier officer, James Russell, confirmed. And as King confided to Captain John McCrea, "You know, McCrea, I regard you as a good officer, but you could be a lot better. The trouble is, you have one outstanding weakness . . . you are not a son-of-a-bitch, and a good naval officer has to be a son-of-a-bitch." Needless to say, many superior flag officers fully disagreed with King, including Bill Halsey, Chester Nimitz, Jack Towers, Marc Mitscher, and Kelly Turner. And Arleigh Burke, then a destroyer captain, commented: "Admiral King himself was an expert seaman and he expected everybody else to be the same. If some destroyer captain was a poor shiphandler, he would really raise hell." (Burke of course achieved flag rank later and ultimately became CNO.)

When Admiral William Leahy was due to retire as CNO in the summer of 1939, King announced his interest in the job, but lost out to Admiral Stark. Instead, a dejected King was directed to Washington to serve on the ten-man General Board governing the navy. This was usually the last appointment one received prior to automatic retirement, but King muttered, "They're not done with me yet. . . . No fighter ever won by covering up," he insisted, "by merely fending off the other fellow's blows. The winner hits and keeps on hitting even though he has to take some stiff blows in order to be able to keep hitting."[14] King's internal war was still continuing at the age of sixty.

The General Board had sweeping governing powers, from the formulation of policy and strategy to ship design. Naval Secretary Charles Edison now asked King, as a member of this elite board, to completely modernize the U.S. Fleet's antiaircraft capability, which the admiral undertook with his usual fervor and thoroughness. But then on a long tour of inspection with Edison to Panama and Hawaii, King drank a great deal too much, saying and doing some fairly offensive things. Word got back to the White House. FDR had once teased King, to the latter's considerable discomfort, "I hear, Ernie, that you use a blowtorch to shave with in the morning," and chuckled. But when in June 1940 Edison recommended that Roosevelt promote Ernie King to commander in chief of the U.S. Fleet, the president flatly refused. This may have been the reason for King's resolve now to give up hard liquor.

By 1940, the political scene everywhere was changing, including in Washington. The ailing Charles Edison was replaced by the publisher of the *Chicago Sun Times* newspaper and former Republican vice presidential candidate Frank Knox, while Herbert Hoover's former Republican secretary of state, Wall Street lawyer Henry Stimson, joined the Roosevelt administration as secretary of war.[15]

Despite Ernie King's most curious personnel file, Frank Knox was still impressed by the admiral and backed his promotion to full admiral, as did CNO Stark, who then gave him command of the U.S. Atlantic Fleet effective February 1, 1941.[16] This is the bewildering story of King's meteoric career in the U.S. Navy. In spite of grave personal drawbacks, his merits as a thoroughgoing seaman apparently outweighed his grievous demerits. But immediately upon assuming the role as commander in chief of the entire U.S. Navy in December 1941—to which he was soon to add Stark's title as chief of naval operations—Roosevelt, Knox, and just about everyone else were already beginning to regret this choice. King had refused to work with Knox and sometimes even ignored personal orders of the president of the United States, but even that paled in comparison to the considerable damage he was to inflict on inter-Allied relations with Churchill and Britain throughout the war.

•

Secretary of the Navy Frank Knox's other choice for a senior command was to prove far more sound. In one of those pivotal decisions that would significantly affect the outcome of the war, Knox selected Admiral Chester Nimitz as Commander in Chief, Pacific (CINCPAC), replacing the unfortunate Kimmel, his fellow classmate. And no two equally talented men could have been more different than Chester Nimitz and Ernie King.

Nimitz's ancestral family had, as members of the lower aristocracy and the Order of Teutonic Knights, served the crown since the Middle Ages but lost much of their wealth and position gradually over the centuries. They were living in Hannover when, in the nineteenth century, the future admiral's great-grandfather squandered what remained of the family's fortune.

An ocean away, Fredericksburg, Texas, was founded in 1846 when a German nobleman bought several thousand acres west of Austin and just north of San Antonio, and named the town he created there after his patron, Prince Friedrich of Prussia. It was here that Chester Nimitz's grandfather, the young merchant seaman Karl Heinrich Nimitz, Jr., decided to settle after first immigrating to Charleston, South Carolina, in 1845.

Changing his name to Charles Henry Nimitz (the "von" having been long discarded), he bought a parcel of land—formerly Comanche territory—and, in the best American tradition, built a log cabin. The community was entirely German, and that language was spoken as much as English, the latter admittedly retaining a heavy German accent for that first generation. Indeed, Fredericksburg remained a "little Germany" with its language and love of traditional classical music—one of the few places in nineteenth-century Texas where Bach, Beethoven, and Haydn were an integral part of the popular culture, along with the inevitable bierfests.

Charles Henry Nimitz, now a bookkeeper, married Sophie Dorothea Miller in April 1848, and the two ultimately had twelve children. Advancing socially, Nimitz briefly joined the Texas Rangers and then built a small adobe brick hotel, named the Steamboat Hotel in reference to his earlier seafaring days. "Captain" Nimitz's hotel became one of the waystations between southwestern Texas and San Diego, California, boasting its own smokehouse, a brewery, bathhouse, saloon, and dance hall. The affable blond, blue-eyed proprietor entertained some famous guests there, including Colonel Robert E. Lee, Phil Sheridan, James Longstreet, and the writer O. Henry.[17]

In 1884, Chester Bernard Nimitz, the future admiral's father, married a young woman of the same town, Anna Henke, also of German descent. And on February 24, 1885, Chester William Nimitz was born and later christened in the local Lutheran church. His father, who had taken over the family hotel, died when his son was only five months old. Five years later, Anna Nimitz married her late husband's brother, Willie Nimitz, an engineer and graduate of Worcester Polytechnic Institute, Massachusetts. But work even for a qualified engineer was scarce, and the family moved to nearby Kerrville, Texas, on the Guadalupe River, where they bought and ran the Charles Hotel (a wooden boardinghouse). Anna and Willie had two children of their own, Dora and Otto.

Chester Nimitz walked to school barefoot as a child, chopped wood to earn money, hunted, and learned to swim in the Guadalupe. The family spent many pleasant hours at the ranch of his mother's father, where the "cowboys" spoke German and young Chester dodged scorpions while hunting for specimens for his impressive rattlesnake collection. The hotel was hardly a thriving affair, and Nimitz had to start working regularly after school from the age of eight. At fifteen, he began to work in the family hotel; yet he never ignored his studies, and he was an excellent student. The family was close, and although Chester rarely spoke German, his aunts always did, and he understood the language well. As his stepfather had little money, it was decided to prepare the boy for the Naval Academy. He easily passed the entrance exams.

On September 7, 1901, Chester William Nimitz was sworn in as a cadet at the U.S. Naval Academy at Annapolis. He was never to regret this decision. The Academy, which had been founded in 1845, had an entering class of 131 cadets in 1901. Ernest King and William Pye had graduated three months earlier. Nimitz's own class, which would graduate in 1905, included an unusually long list of future flag officers, most of whom he would work with closely in the decades to come: Wilson Brown, Frank Jack Fletcher, Bill Halsey, Kent Hewitt, Tom Kinkaid, John McCain (father of the future U.S. senator), Raymond Spruance, Jack Towers, and Richmond Kelly Turner—indeed, a veritable *Who's Who* of World War II.

Tall, blond, blue-eyed, and broad-shouldered like his father and grandfather before him, Chester Nimitz was a handsome, amiable, self-confident young man. He participated fully in the activities of the Academy and proved himself an excellent student, though known as an inveterate prankster, even later in life. Occasionally on a Saturday afternoon he would slip away from the Academy to disappear into the backroom of the tailor's shop on Maryland Avenue, returning with a heavy suitcase. Once upstairs in his dormitory, he would open the suitcase and distribute a provision of beer (prohibited by the Academy).

As a student, his best subjects were modern languages (French and Spanish), ordnance, mathematics, and navigation. He graduated early in January 1905, seventh in a class of 114 passed midshipmen. The Academy's yearbook, the *Lucky Bag*, described Nimitz as a man "of cheerful yesterdays and confident tomorrows," noting that he possessed that "calm and steady-going Dutch way that always gets to the bottom of things," which proved to be very accurate over the next four decades as well.

His first posting found him in the battleship *Ohio*, the flagship of the U.S. Asiatic Fleet, bound for the Orient. Arriving in Tokyo just after the great Japanese victory over the Russian Fleet at Tsushima in May 1905, some of the young officers, including Midshipman Nimitz, were invited to a victory party given in the gardens of the Imperial Palace. There Nimitz was fortunate enough to meet and briefly speak with Admiral Tōgō himself, who, to Nimitz's surprise, addressed him in fluent English. The scene made a deep impression on the midshipman, as did the Japanese and their country.

Nimitz next served aboard the cruiser *Baltimore* (which had fought with Dewey at the battle of Manila Bay), and then in February 1907 the twenty-two-year-old passed ensign was given his first command: the gunboat *Panay*, whose name would appear in the world's headlines many years later following a Japanese attack. After completing that roving commission along the shores of the southern Philippines, Nimitz was made the captain of a small coal-burning destroyer, the USS *Decatur*. He was surely one of the youngest men in modern U.S. naval history to be given such a command. It was also in 1907 that Theodore Roosevelt's Great White Fleet of nineteen battleships steamed into Tokyo Bay.

Nimitz's tour of duty took him through a powerful typhoon ("and I hope it may be my last"), through the South China Sea to Indochina. But on July 7, 1908, his career almost came to an abrupt halt when he grounded the *Decatur* as it approached Batangas Harbor (south of Manila). Although the *Decatur* was successfully refloated, Nimitz was court-martialed and found guilty of "neglect of duty"; the ruling called for a public reprimand by the Commander in Chief, U.S. Naval Forces in Philippine waters. Instead, a very decent Admiral J. N. Hemphill simply had the findings "promulgated" and never personally reprimanded the fortunate young man. The standing rule in the U.S. Navy was that once a commander grounded his ship, he was never to be promoted or given command of another vessel. Nimitz was one of the very rare cases where this rule was overlooked.[18]

Back in the States, Nimitz's next stint in the service took him to submarine school in 1909. After passing his exam, he was given the command of three successive subs. Lieutenant Nimitz was then ordered to Boston to take command of the 3rd Submarine Division. While overseeing the installation of diesel engines in one of his subs at Quincy, Massachusetts, he met his future wife, Catherine Freeman, the daughter of a shipbroker Nimitz knew there. It was a period not just of romance but heroics: during a trial run in a newly launched sub, *Skipjack*, one of the sailors fell overboard and went down quickly. Nimitz dived in and was able to save him.

In June 1912 the twenty-seven-year-old Nimitz was invited to address the Naval War College on "Defensive and Offensive Tactics of Submarines." Meanwhile, he continued to receive excellent fitness reports, and that same year he was promoted to Commander, Atlantic Submarine Flotilla. The following year Chester Nimitz and Catherine Freeman were married, despite some strong protests by members of the Nimitz clan that she was neither German nor Lutheran. What is more, she was a "Yankee." Nimitz was now earning $215 a month.[19]

By May 1913, Nimitz was already considered one of the foremost diesel experts in the navy, and as such sailed with his wife to Hamburg to study German naval construction at the Blohm und Voss Naval Yards, where he later observed the launching of the battle cruiser *Derfflinger*. Although he and Catherine very much enjoyed their stay in Hamburg, which he in particular found to be "the most beautiful city" he had ever seen, he also found the German officers with whom he had to associate arrogant and pushy. He spoke only English to them, but unfortunately he could understand the sometimes rather uncomplimentary remarks that they made among themselves. Chester Nimitz's distaste for the Germans was hardly unique at that time, something he shared, for instance, with both Franklin Roosevelt and King George V. In the summer of 1918 when Roosevelt, in his capacity as U.S. assistant secretary of the navy, was on an official visit to England, he fell into conversation with King George about the war (World War I) and Germany. Roosevelt mentioned that he spoke fluent German and had gone to school in that country, and the king remarked that he, too, had been educated in Germany. "You know," he added, "I have a number of relations in Germany [e.g., Kaiser Wilhelm II], but I can tell you frankly that in all my life I have never seen a German gentleman."[20]

In any event, the Nimitzes did at least enjoy the local bierkellers and public gardens, which they were able to take in during Lieutenant Nimitz's visits to various engineering firms (including Rudolf Diesel's famed Augsburg plant). After touring Bruges, Kiel, Copenhagen, and southern Sweden, the Nimitzes sailed back to New York, where Nimitz was assigned to supervise the construction of two powerful diesel engines for the 14,500-ton oiler, *Maumee*.[21] Unlike Ernie King's marriage, that of the Nimitzes was to prove a true and lasting love match. The first of their four children was soon born. Around this time, Nimitz was offered a job by a major American diesel manufacturer that would have paid $40,000 a year, but although he was earning all of $2,880 annually at the time, he readily turned the offer down.

One day, while he was demonstrating the new exhaust system of his project to touring engineers, the white canvas glove he was wearing got caught in the rotating gears, severing a finger. After bandaging the hand, he continued the tour. Once the ship was commissioned, Nimitz was named the executive officer and chief engineer of the *Maumee*, which put to sea for a shakedown cruise. It was during that voyage that he and Commander Henry Dinger drew up the first plans for refueling while underway. In April 1917 they successfully refueled two destroyers simultaneously, something that would be of critical importance in maintaining the far-flung U.S. Fleet in the Pacific during the next war.

Promoted lieutenant commander in August 1917, Nimitz was asked to serve as engineering aide to Captain Samuel Robinson, Commander, Submarine Force, Atlantic Fleet, and then was made chief of staff in 1918 as they toured British naval bases and shipyards. They went on to wartime France and to the Mediterranean, later returning to the American battle squadron at Scapa Flow in northern Scotland, where Chester Nimitz was introduced to Admiral Sir David Beatty. Unlike

King, Nimitz got on very well with the British, and indeed with just about everyone, apart from the Germans.

With the signing of the armistice that November, Nimitz was called to the office of the CNO to serve on the Board of Submarine Design, followed by a tour of duty as executive officer aboard the battleship *South Carolina*.

Promoted commander in 1920, Chester Nimitz was transferred to the Pacific to build the submarine base at Pearl Harbor and in December was put in command of that new base, as well as of Submarine Division 14. Because of the heavy toll on British shipping during the war, submarines had taken on much more importance in the eyes of the U.S. Navy. Throughout his career Nimitz was accompanied whenever possible by Catherine and their brood, and they all found this Honolulu assignment especially satisfying.

Posted to the Naval War College at Newport, Rhode Island, two years later, the Nimitzes rented a large house for their three small children and dog (Nimitz always had a dog). During the many war games conducted at the War College, Japan was always the enemy, "and the courses were so thorough," Nimitz later recalled, "that after the start of World War II, nothing that happened in the Pacific was strange or unexpected." Rear Admiral William Sims, president of the college, introduced the first aircraft carriers into naval war games, a move that was much resented by some old hands. Although not an aviator, Nimitz was curious, open-minded and objective, and as a result profited from this experience.

Assigned as assistant chief of staff and tactical officer to Admiral Robinson (now Commander in Chief, Battle Fleet), the ever innovative Nimitz introduced the new "circular" fleet formation, in which the flagship was always surrounded and protected by the other ships. In this way the fleet could easily be re-formed into the traditional battle lines when required. Nimitz met much resistance to this idea and other new concepts, but it should be kept in mind that as late as 1924 pilots were still communicating with their carriers by homing pigeon. Nimitz also insisted that a carrier, the newly commissioned *Langley*, participate in maneuvers with the main fleet, another first in U.S. naval history. Nimitz, though never destined to be a pilot himself, was adamant about the important new role of the carrier in naval warfare. When

Admiral Robinson was appointed Commander in Chief, U.S. Fleet (CINCUS), he brought Chester Nimitz along as his aide.

In this capacity Nimitz stressed the necessity to create reserve officer corps throughout the country. The navy may still have been small, as a result of its very limited budget, but it could at least plan for the future by creating a pool of reserve officers. He introduced this program at six universities, and in 1926 he and his family went off to the University of California, Berkeley, to initiate the first such Naval Reserve Officer Training Corps (NROTC). At Berkeley, Nimitz took the title of professor of naval science and tactics.

Nimitz was popular with Berkeley students and he himself very much enjoyed teaching. Always a great walker, he would walk or hike with cane in hand for miles every day, sometimes to the chagrin of his young daughters who occasionally accompanied him—for frequently, when spying the overhanging branch of an apple or pear tree, he would reach up with his cane and bring the fruit down. He was only caught once, by an elderly lady. Passing through the garden gate, he approached the stern woman and complimented her on the fine quality of her harvest. Chester Nimitz could charm anyone.

He later reflected: "I have enjoyed every one of my assignments and I believe it has been so because of my making it a point to become as deeply immersed and as interested in each activity as it was possible. . . . My life in the Navy has been very happy and I know of no other profession for which I would forsake my present one. . . . My wife, my children, my profession as a naval officer, and good health, combined to make me a happy man."

Throughout his long career Nimitz was also famous for his "Texas tall tales"; indeed they became legendary, such as his creation about a marine recruit about to make his first parachute jump. The marine sergeant told him not to worry as he opened the door of the aircraft. "Just pull the rip cord there," he said, and showed it to him. "And if it doesn't work?" the young man asked. "Then pull this second rip cord on the emergency chute, and when you land, a station wagon will be waiting for you to bring you back to camp." The marine did not seem convinced, muttering, "I can see it now: the first rip cord won't work, and the second won't work, and I'll bet that damned station wagon won't be there either!" It was pure Nimitz, and every week there was a new one.

In 1927, Nimitz was fleeted up to the rank of captain and given command of thirty-five destroyers. Two years later he assumed command of the new heavy cruiser *Augusta*, the flagship of the Asiatic Fleet, at Shanghai under the general command of Admiral Frank Upham. Nimitz was as thorough as he'd always been. He insisted on constant gunnery practice, night and day. He also gave a series of lectures on China, to better educate and prepare the officers for their forthcoming task. *Augusta*'s arrival in Japan coincided with the death and funeral of Admiral Tōgō, which Nimitz insisted on attending. The cruise took them through the South Pacific and Far East, including the Dutch East Indies and the Philippines—the same areas concerned in the War College's war games. In this assignment and others, Captain Nimitz was much admired not only by his men but by superiors as well, resulting in model fitness reports.

In the spring of 1935 he was ordered to a new posting in Washington, D.C., to serve as assistant to the chief of the Bureau of Navigation (naval personnel). Although he applied for flight training, there were no openings at Pensacola at that time. Instead, three years later, the by-now Rear Admiral Nimitz was given command of Cruiser Division Two at San Diego; after an unexpected hernia operation, he lost his cruisers and was given command of Battleship Division One.

In September 1938, the fifty-three-year-old Nimitz boarded his flagship *Arizona* while his wife and family rented another house in San Diego. Commanding Task Force 7, Nimitz carried out difficult operations designed to prepare his ships and men for the growing Japanese menace. These included complicated fueling at sea with all classes of ships under all weather conditions and executing amphibious landings with the marines. The results were poor, and Nimitz knew that in the future much more had to be done to improve them. It was also obvious that new designs for landing craft were badly needed, but congressional allocations were still pitifully small, and very little research and development was done.

When he returned to Washington yet again in the spring of 1939, it was as chief of the Bureau of Navigation, which meant another move for his wife and family. Nimitz's new job required the urgent task of finding additional officers and men for the new warships approved by the naval appropriations bill of 1938 (the second Vinson Act), granting

$1 billion a year. Roosevelt had been pushing Congress hard and was getting results, aided by the navy's best friend in Congress, Carl Vinson, chairman of the House Naval Affairs Committee. For his part, Nimitz enlarged naval training stations across the country while extending NROTC courses to twenty-seven universities, permitting the newly commissioned officers to transfer to the regular navy. The numbers at the Naval Academy were also increased.

And thus it was while at the Bureau of Navigation in December 1941 that Frank Knox conferred with Roosevelt about Kimmel's replacement following the debacle of December 7. "Tell Nimitz to get the hell out to Pearl and stay there till the war is over," the president ordered the navy secretary. That same morning, December 16, Knox called Chester Nimitz to his office in the Navy Building and handed him his orders, which included cleaning up the mess in every sense of the word: repairing the fleet and assuming command of the entire U.S. Fleet in the Pacific. This time his wife would remain behind, for the next four years.

With his capital ships sunk or damaged, on December 31, Chester Nimitz relieved his classmate of '05, Husband Kimmel, at a brief ceremony on the deck of the submarine *Grayling*. Wearing his well-earned dolphins (a warfare device worn by submariners), Admiral Nimitz thought it only fitting to raise his new four-star flag on its mast, surrounded by the oil-choked waters of Pearl Harbor and across from Ford Island's naval graveyard, which held the remains of many of his friends. "We have taken a tremendous wallop," he told the men present, "[and] we're going to be here for a long time." They would have to start working very hard if they were to win the war, and they "had better get used to it," he declared as he left for his new office atop Makalapa Hill, overlooking the harbor and the submerged ruins of his former flagship, USS *Arizona*.[22] Thousands of miles away in the Philippines, the commander of the U.S. Army in the southwest Pacific was facing an even gloomier scene.

CHAPTER IX

. . . and a General

"The history of failure in war can be summed up in two words: Too Late. Too late in comprehending the deadly purpose of a potential enemy; too late in realizing the mortal danger; too late in preparedness; too late in uniting all possible forces for resistance; too late in standing with one's friends."

—*General Douglas MacArthur, 1964*[1]

In November 1903 a second lieutenant was leading a party of engineering troops through the jungles of Guimaras Island, in the Philippines off the harbor of Iloilo, when the crack of a rifle was followed by a bullet tearing through his campaign hat, missing the lieutenant's head by a quarter of an inch. Automatically pulling out his holstered .38-caliber pistol, he quickly fired at two assailants before him, dropping them in their tracks. He had come here to collect timber for a wharf he was building at Iloilo.[2] Stepping over the bodies, Lieutenant Douglas MacArthur and his men set to their task.

MacArthur had fallen in love with these islands the moment his ship first steamed into Manila Bay the previous month. He was fulfilling his destiny, he felt, and was at peace with himself even when he came under fire for the first time in his life. But, more important, he was fulfilling a personal agenda: to avenge the humiliation his father had suffered when he was relieved of his post as military governor of the Philippines in 1901.

As for this attack, it was just one of dozens by rebel Filipinos against American troops since their arrival in 1898, after the departure of the defeated Spanish. Washington had ordered the "liberation" of the country, but instead the American liberators had found themselves under siege by large bands of rebel groups who apparently had not appreciated their generous gesture. Most of the nationalist patriots had by now surrendered to the U.S. Army and were working alongside them, including a nineteen-year-old officer by the name of Manuel L. Quezon who had surrendered in 1900 to Major General Arthur MacArthur, the commanding general.[3]

It was that general's son, Douglas MacArthur, who was now continuing in his footsteps and who would one day, decades later, return here as the commander of all American and Philippine forces.

Lieutenant MacArthur was born on January 26, 1880, at the army post in what is now Little Rock, Arkansas. His father, a career officer and distinguished veteran of the Civil War (for which he had earned the Congressional Medal of Honor), was serving there as a captain with the 13th Infantry at the time. An older brother, Arthur, had preceded young Douglas by three and a half years; a sister died in childhood.

The MacArthurs had emigrated from Glasgow in 1825 and settled in Milwaukee, Wisconsin, where Douglas MacArthur's grandfather became a distinguished judge, lieutenant governor of the state, and eventually a U.S. Supreme Court justice. Douglas's father met his wife-to-be, Mary Pinkney Hardy (known as "Pinky"), at a ball in New Orleans late in 1874. As Pinky's family was part of the landed "aristocracy" of Virginia—four of her brothers had fought for the Confederacy—her choice of a Yankee soldier did not go down at all well. They were married in May 1875, without the presence or blessing of Pinky's brothers.[4]

Captain MacArthur's career had been typical of post–Civil War America, moving him from one "western" fort to another as the last of the Indian uprisings were suppressed and their land seized—including Fort Bridger, Fort Sanders, Fort Kearney, Fort Leavenworth, Fort Wingate, Fort Sam Houston, and Fort Selden, among others. Living conditions at most of these wilderness outposts were usually primitive, with virtually no cultural life, apart from what the officers and wives could themselves provide. For a young, impressionable American boy such as Douglas MacArthur, on the other hand, nothing could have been more wonderful. Real soldiers were fighting real Indians, and Douglas learned to ride and shoot at an early age. Boys grow up, however, and this one soon had to prepare for West Point. He completed his preparatory studies at the West Texas Military Academy in 1897, the same year his brother Arthur was receiving his commission at the U.S. Naval Academy. As Arthur advanced his own career, married, and started a family, Douglas would remain intensely jealous of his older sibling.

Douglas returned to Milwaukee for further study prior to taking the entrance exams for the Military Academy. At the same time he also underwent intensive medical treatment for a year and a half to correct a bad curvature of the spine.

On June 13, 1899, at the age of nineteen, he entered West Point for what he was later to call some of the happiest years of his life. But he was not alone, for his mother had arrived with him. Intent on keeping an eye on her son (and apparently abandoning her husband in the process), she installed herself at Craney's Hotel just below the Academy for the next four years.[5]

MacArthur the cadet looked taller than his five feet eleven inches owing to his slender, erect frame, and his fellow cadets could not help but notice the handsome young man with the well-brushed dark brown hair, meticulous uniform, unusual poise, self-confidence, and seriousness. Above all he stood out for his superb academic record, as he was first in his class from the outset. But the whole while, his mother ruled his life when she could. Douglas was expected to take tea with her every afternoon and he could not accept an invitation elsewhere without her approval; indeed, she was rarely to leave his side, apart from army assignments that later took him abroad. Mother and son were literally to share the same roof until the time of her death thirty-five years later.

Having been raised in army forts all his life, MacArthur found that military life and all aspects of it—the drilling, the discipline—came to him naturally, and even the professional officers on the staff compared him with his glorious predecessors such as Robert E. Lee and John Pershing. About the only sphere in which he failed was team sports: although he remained passionately fond of baseball and football all his life, he never excelled in any sport except polo. He did, however, possess a strong unruly streak, and when on rare occasions he was allowed to go to New York for a special event, he took great pride in escaping to a saloon or a burlesque show. MacArthur was also reputedly involved in the disappearance of the Academy's reveille gun, which was found mounted mysteriously upon the roof of the West Academic Building one morning. He graduated with the highest honors at the top of his class on June 11, 1903.[6]

Second Lieutenant Douglas MacArthur's posting to the Philippines later that year concluded prematurely as a result of a severe case of malaria, and he was sent back to the States in October 1904. In the autumn of 1905, after having spent several months with the engineers at San Francisco, he was ordered to Tokyo to serve as his father's aide-de-camp, which gave the young man a unique opportunity to visit the Far East in some depth over the ensuing months. The tour took them to Japan, Singapore, Hong Kong, Malaya, Java, Burma, a considerable portion of India, French Indochina, and much of China, including Shanghai and Peking. In all the countries they visited, the MacArthurs inspected public and military facilities and met the countries' leaders. When the mission was completed in July 1906, the entire family sailed from Yokohama for California, with the young lieutenant concluding that as a result of this fascinating trip, "it was crystal clear to me that the future and, indeed, the very existence of America, were irrevocably entwined with Asia and its island outposts"—as indeed was his own life.[7]

Although not particularly interested in engineering, Lieutenant MacArthur was one of eleven students enrolled in the Army's Engineer School in Washington, D.C., from 1906 to 1907, while the new Army War College was being built next door. His lack of interest at the school led to his first negative annual report, in which his commanding officer criticized him for showing "little professional zeal," even though MacArthur was concurrently working at the White House for Theodore Roosevelt's senior military aide. President Roosevelt even asked him for his views on the Far East, and the young lieutenant took it all in stride as if advising the president were the most natural thing in the world.[8] His next posting, a stint at the district office of engineers in Milwaukee, Wisconsin, that began in August 1907, brought more rebukes from his new commanding officer for his absences—often for weeks at a time—from his assigned project.

Lieutenant MacArthur was happier to leave for his next assignment with the 3rd Engineer Battalion at Fort Leavenworth, Kansas, in 1908, where he was given his first command of troops as a company commander. Nevertheless, once again the final fitness report was less than glowing, indicating that he had not performed his duties "in a satisfactory manner" while acknowledging his strong potential. Douglas MacArthur deeply resented criticism of any kind and in this case was mortified at "the ineradicable blemish" placed on his military record.[9] Yet the comments did not prevent him from being promoted adjutant of his battalion, and he received praise in his next annual report as "an exceptionally excellent officer in every respect."

In February 1911, MacArthur was promoted to captain and then appointed head of the department of military engineering of the Field Engineer School in Fort Leavenworth. Clearly he was beginning to do something right, although he had still not found the niche he was seeking. Annual maneuvers held near San Antonio, Texas, in the summer of 1911 proved a fiasco, and the chief of staff, Major General Leonard Wood, conceded that the U.S. Army was not prepared "to meet with a trained enemy" if there were a sudden foreign emergency.

Detached briefly from Fort Leavenworth, Captain MacArthur toured the great engineering marvel of the century, the Panama Canal, which was scheduled to open in 1914. His father, whom he had always greatly admired, died in September 1912. At the end of that year MacArthur was ordered back to the War Department in Washington to serve as assistant to the chief of staff, General Wood.[10] Less than a year later, in September 1913, he was appointed to the General Staff itself, declining President Woodrow Wilson's invitation to serve as a military aide. (Wilson was a Democrat, MacArthur a Republican.) He continued to live with his mother.

Events in Mexico would soon pull MacArthur out of Washington. After Mexico's new dictator, Victoriano Huerta, had had a few run-ins with the U.S. government—insulting the U.S. flag, arresting American officers, and accepting arms from Germany—Wilson ordered the navy to occupy Veracruz. General Leonard Wood was to prepare an expeditionary force to seize Mexico City, and in May 1914 he dispatched Captain MacArthur to assess the situation. There MacArthur got into more than one skirmish with armed Mexicans who fired upon him; ultimately he killed at least two. When MacArthur reported back to Washington that August, he was highly praised by General Wood, who recommended him for the Medal of Honor—a recommendation that the army rejected. Frustrated, MacArthur condemned the decision of the board as "rigid narrow-mindedness and lack of imagination."[11] His response was not appreciated by the assistant secretary of war, Henry Breckinridge. The events in Europe that August 1914, however, soon eclipsed such matters.

If Washington initially avoided military participation in World War I, it could not ignore the raid by the Mexican bandit Pancho Villa on Columbus, New Mexico, in December 1915. Immediately President Wilson ordered Brigadier General John Pershing into Mexico with five thousand men. That same month Douglas MacArthur was promoted to major, and in the spring of 1916 both MacArthur and Major Palmer Pierce were appointed, as a committee of the Army General Staff, to study motor transportation. The presence of Pershing's forces in Mexico made this particular issue one of pressing importance; and it was while working closely with a similar naval committee to coordinate requirements (trucks, cars, and engines) that Douglas MacArthur first met the assistant secretary of the navy, Franklin D. Roosevelt.[12]

Next the new secretary of war, Newton Baker, assigned MacArthur to his Bureau of Information, where he chiefly handled press interviews and the release of information to national newspapers. MacArthur's campaign was apparently largely responsible for convincing Congress to create the Selective Service Act of May 18, 1917, permitting further enlargement of the U.S. armed forces. (The president had already asked Congress for a declaration of war on April 2.) MacArthur's work at this bureau also brought him into contact with many influential journalists, including one Stephen Early, who would later become Franklin Roosevelt's press secretary.

With the declaration of war against Germany, the army had to formulate its war plan, and the recently promoted Major General "Black Jack" Pershing worked feverishly to create an American Expeditionary Force. Secretary of War Baker, assisted by Major MacArthur, met with Woodrow Wilson to explore the best means of enlarging the army quickly. It was during these talks that Douglas MacArthur suggested the creation of one division out of the surplus national guard units from several states, which would "stretch over the whole country like a rainbow"—hence the creation of the 42nd, or Rainbow Division. MacArthur now received a jump promotion to full colonel.[13]

Created in August 1917, the Rainbow Division was to draw men from twenty-six states and divide them into three brigades: 27,114 men now had to be assembled, trained, and fully equipped, and Colonel MacArthur was appointed the new division's chief of staff. Although it usually took a year to fully prepare a division for war, Congress had left it until too late, and the 42nd was given only a few weeks of training before the first units embarked for Europe in October 1917. MacArthur sailed with the men from Hoboken, New Jersey, on a seized Hamburg-America liner, the *Covington*. Escorted by a cruiser and two destroyers, they safely reached St. Nazaire, France, on November 1. (The *Covington* was sunk by a U-boat on its return voyage to America, adding to the 8 million tons of Allied shipping already destroyed.)[14]

By December 1917 the United States still had only four divisions in France, and only one of those was trained. That year General Robert Nivelle's much-vaunted offensive was smashed by the Hindenburg Line, resulting in a great slaughter. Major General Charles Menoher, new commander of the Rainbow Division, ordered MacArthur to work closely with Pershing's staff at Chaumont in northeastern France, but the young colonel did not always get along with his new colleagues—among them Colonel George Marshall and Pershing himself (who had served as a rebellious young officer under MacArthur's father in the Philippines). Other officers associated with the 42nd and MacArthur at one time or another were Brigadier General Charles Summerall, Colonel Robert Wood, "Wild Bill" Donovan (who later commanded the OSS in World War II), one Captain Harry Truman, Eddie Rickenbacker, and George Kenney. The U.S. Army was still a small world in those days.

It was here in France, 1917–18, that MacArthur for the first time began to distinguish himself from his fellow officers. Not only was his unorthodox "uniform" unique and his bearing unusually calm even under the most trying of circumstances, but he was to lead his men in one successful mission after another until practically the entire American Expeditionary Force, along with British and French headquarters, was made aware of his presence. When reprimanded for not following orders—he refused to carry a gas mask (despite numerous mustard gas attacks), wear a steel helmet most of the time, or even carry a pistol, preferring instead a riding crop, jodhpurs, and a turtleneck sweater—MacArthur quipped, "It's the orders you disobey that make you famous," and fame was what he sought and lived for.[15]

Before entering battle, Pershing ordered the 42nd to an area between Lunéville and Baccarat in Lorraine, southwest of Nancy. His men were to undergo intensive training just a few miles from the German frontier of 1871, which had incorporated much of Lorraine and Alsace. Pershing's headquarters at Chaumont were located on the Marne, well to the southwest.

From the very beginning his superiors encountered a new, hitherto unknown MacArthur, despite his having only limited activities as chief of staff. He went on raids through heavy barbed-wire defenses and intense German gunfire, sometimes without authorization from Menoher; and he brought back German prisoners and documents starting in February 1918. The still powerful German force was determined not only to hold the main Hindenburg Line but also to drive through the Allied forces—British, French, and American—and seize Paris. It was to come very close to achieving that goal. For eighty-two days the Rainbow Division was under almost constant fire and threat from across no-man's-land, including major gas attacks, to which the Americans reciprocated in kind between February and June 1918. Local villagers who remained in their homes lived in fear of bombardment from both sides.[16]

After nearly three months at the front, the 42nd was ordered to withdraw to another sector. Under new orders from General Gouraud's Fourth Army, MacArthur was in the town of Charmes overseeing the loading of his weary troops (they had suffered some two thousand casualties) onto trains for the Champagne region, east of Rheims, when General Pershing arrived unexpectedly to inspect MacArthur's ragged, mud-splattered men. The general began to chew out their chief of staff: "This division is a disgrace . . . you are not properly trained. The whole outfit is just about the worst I have seen. MacArthur," he barked before his officers and men, "I'm going to hold you personally responsible for getting discipline and order into this division. . . . I won't stand for this. It's a disgrace." For once, the exhausted MacArthur, who had been absorbed in his work when this tirade had hit him, turned red as a beet and got out a "Yes, sir!" Black Jack Pershing then disappeared as quickly as he had arrived. MacArthur had been humiliated before his own men and stung to the quick, and he afterward developed the theory that Pershing and his "Chaumont faction" were out to destroy his career.[17]

Nonetheless, Pershing still only had four sufficiently trained divisions for front-line duty and lacked enough good senior officers; so in spite of the opinions of "Black Jack," Washington promoted MacArthur to brigadier general on June 26, 1918. (His mother had been bombarding Pershing and the secretary of war for this promotion.)

The overall operation on the Allied side to halt a major German drive on Paris was run by the superb French general Henri Gouraud, destined to absorb German chief of staff Erich von Ludendorff's Champagne-Marne offensive and stop it in its tracks. Of all the French field commanders he ultimately knew, including Foch and Pétain, Douglas MacArthur thought the brilliant and courageous Gouraud—who had lost one arm and part of a leg in previous campaigns—the most impressive. "He was the greatest of them all," MacArthur, who rarely praised anyone, insisted. And Gouraud reciprocated, declaring MacArthur "to be one of the finest and bravest officers I have ever served with,"[18] quite a compliment for a Frenchman to pay an American.

General Gouraud laid a careful trap for the advancing Germans, and during the night of July 14, 1918, some 5,500 big French and German guns clashed in yet another vast slaughter. "The whole sky seemed to be torn apart with sound," recalled Father Duffy, the divisional chaplain.[19] The main enemy thrust was hurled directly at the Rainbow Division between St-Hilaire-le-Grand and Perthes-les-Hurlus. "A boiling bank of dirty smoke hides the flower of the Prussian Guard," in one soldier's words. Or as MacArthur put it, the Allied artillery barrage "descended like an avalanche."

"The German has clearly broken his sword on our lines," a victorious Gouraud announced. "Whatever he may do in the future, he shall not pass." Nor did he. "The German's last great attack of the war had failed, and Paris could breathe again," Brigadier MacArthur later wrote.[20] This had been the first major, large-scale combat of his career;

and he had not only prepared meticulous plans (successful, as it turned out) but had also left HQ during the battle, advancing to the front line to encourage his men in the heart of the worst fighting. General Menoher described his chief of staff as "the bloodiest fighting man in this army . . . there's no risk of battle that any soldier is called upon to take that he is not liable to look up and see MacArthur at his side." MacArthur himself was not as exalted by the great victory after so many months of fighting, despite winning a second Silver Star. He would explain, "I found something missing. It may have been the visions of those writhing bodies hanging from the barbed wire. . . . Perhaps I was just getting . . . "[21] For the first time in his life he could not finish a sentence. He passed his entire tour in France without taking a single day's leave. He was always with his men or in a field hospital.

Marshal Foch, who was in supreme command, now ordered his forces, including Pershing's troops, up to a position just northeast of Château-Thierry, where he launched the Aisne-Marne offensive (July 18 to August 6, 1918) in the big drive to the Vesle River. In the midst of this intense fighting, on July 31, General Menoher replaced the unsatisfactory commander of the 84th Brigade with MacArthur. This was Douglas MacArthur's first battle command of his own,[22] and he took one German position after another, though paying a very high price in American casualties. Of his many field messages sent to Menoher, that of August 2 was typical:

> Have personally assumed command of the line. Have broken the enemy's resistance on the right. Immediately threw forward my left and broke his front. Am advancing my whole line with utmost speed. The enemy is immediately in front but am maneuvering my battalions so that he cannot get set in position. . . . I intend to throw him into the Vesle. I am using small patrols acting with great speed and continually flanking him so that he can not form a line of resistance. I am handling the columns myself. . . .[23]

The cost of nine days' heavy fighting in the Ourcq sector was prohibitive. MacArthur's brigade, which had entered the battle with 5,155 soldiers, suffered 2,689 casualties—a loss of more than half.[24] The Germans had been well entrenched and had retained complete control of the air, their planes decimating the Americans below. The lack of superior airpower made a deep impression on MacArthur. For his actions he was awarded his second *Croix de Guerre* and made a Commander of France's Legion of Honor. On August 18, Menoher made him permanent commander of the 84th; he had earned it.

The Rainbow Division was next ordered to take the St. Mihiel Salient, which critically straddled key rail links and had been held by the Germans for the past four years. This was to be the first American operation independent of other Allied forces and of direct central control, although Foch remained in strategic command. The salient encompassed some two hundred square miles in some of the worst terrain in the country: wet clay and vast pools of water covered the landscape for months on end. Behind it lay the massive medieval fortress of Metz, a German stronghold since 1871. To Foch's astonishment, the Americans knocked out the well-entrenched Germans in just four days, between September 12 and 16.

In fact, MacArthur's 84th advanced so swiftly that he inadvertently set off one of the biggest controversies of the war. While reconnoitering deep behind German lines once more, he had discovered that Metz was in a state of chaos. Many of its troops had been transferred or killed, and the city-fortress was so weakened that MacArthur believed the Americans could take it if they drove hard and fast. Returning to HQ, he requested permission to do just that. Foch and Pershing refused this request—many believed because the French wished to be the first to enter the city—and the result was that later, when the French were finally ready, so too were the Germans. Only after a bloody siege and heavy loss of life was Metz at last taken.[25]

The Meuse-Argonne offensive was launched against the Germans on the night of September 25–26, with Brigadier General MacArthur's command of the raiders resulting in success and another Silver Star. Yet 200,000 Americans were still unable to break through this sector of the sweeping Hindenburg Line. All attempts by MacArthur to take Châtillon Hill, for instance, met with failure, and then General Summerall personally gave him the order to "Give me Châtillon, or a list of five thousand casualties!"[26] He was tired of excuses. MacArthur tried and failed again, and Summerall began to relieve some brigade commanders. Then, on October 16, MacArthur at long last took Châtillon

Hill, sustaining heavy casualties once again. As usual he had been in the front line leading the assault, for which he was recommended for another Congressional Medal of Honor and promotion to major general—both of which were overruled by General Pershing. Instead, MacArthur received a second Distinguished Service Cross (Oak Leaf Cluster) for having "personally led his men [and] displayed indomitable resolution and great courage . . . thereby making victory possible. On a field where courage was the rule, his courage was the dominant factor," according to the official citation.[27] But Douglas MacArthur never forgot Pershing's actions against him, seemingly just another example of that general's wish to destroy his career. Years later, MacArthur would seek his revenge on the Chaumont clique when he was chief of staff of the U.S. Army.

In battle MacArthur had proved himself both a fearless leader much respected by his men and a first-class commanding officer. Nevertheless, he was also an egotist of the first order, fond of parading before others to attract attention. For instance, he continued to refuse to wear a regulation uniform, preferring his old Academy sweater with its big black "A"; he also tended to sport a long cigarette holder and wrap himself in a four-foot-long scarf woven by his mother. If his men had been out of uniform or had failed to wear their heavy steel helmets or gas masks, he would have punished them. But Douglas MacArthur—"the Dude," as they had called him at West Point—was the worst transgressor of all.

After the battles of September 12–16, MacArthur added a new element to his command, one that would be repeated on occasion throughout his career. For the first time, he deliberately exaggerated his accomplishments in his official report, indeed lying outright:

> We turned in 10,000 prisoners and, although my brigade had pierced further than any other unit, and had been the spear point of the American advance, it suffered fewer casualties than any other.[28]

This was very much in the style of Napoleon's celebrated half-fabricated "Bulletins" of the Grande Armée that were drawn up on the battlefield. MacArthur was a great fan of Napoleon and had studied the man, his campaigns, and his Bulletins. The distortions in MacArthur's summary of his achievements and those of the 84th—"my brigade"—

included his claim of prisoners captured, the real figure being closer to five hundred than the ten thousand he claimed. Nor did MacArthur's brigade spearhead the advance, those laurels belonging instead to the 26th Division. As for casualties, the 83rd had lost far fewer men—317—than had the 84th, with 528. During World War II, MacArthur was again to exaggerate the "fewer casualties" suffered by army troops under his command than by those in the marines. The summary of these early September battles was just the beginning of the distorted and self-congratulatory reports that were to follow hereafter.

The war in France continued, but Ludendorff's last great offensive had collapsed. Despite Crown Prince Wilhelm's order of October 19 demanding that his armies take a decisive stand, morale in the German ranks, already bled white by outrageous casualties, was plummeting, resulting in desertions and mutinies. Conversely, the spirits of the Rainbow Division remained remarkably high in spite of high casualty figures—some four thousand killed and wounded—a resilience due in large part to the superb leadership of General Menoher. Unlike MacArthur, Menoher was a most modest man, who gave his brigade commanders all the credit for the division's success. And MacArthur's leadership of the 84th certainly contributed to the troops' good morale. But by the end of October the 42nd Division was in a bad way, depleted of over 100 officers and some 7,100 enlisted men. The division had won battle after battle but had paid too great a price, and now even Pershing acknowledged that it lacked the manpower to continue. The 42nd was relieved from its position on the front line on October 31.[29]

With the renewal of the Meuse-Argonne offensive on November 1, and the subsequent routing of the German army, every man was needed; and even the much-battered Rainbow Division had to be recalled by November 5. Its new objective was to capture the bridgehead at Sedan in order to prevent the Germans from regrouping. Although German troops succeeded in blowing up the bridges across the Meuse, the weary 42nd continued to advance in that direction. French and American forces were again vying to be first to recapture another famous French city, Sedan, which had been in Prussian hands since Napoleon III's surrender there in 1870. But in the rush Pershing gave contradictory orders, urging the 1st Division to seize the city while Menoher, uninformed of Pershing's orders, was pressing the 42nd to do precisely the same thing. This confusion resulted in the 1st Division's passing directly before the 42nd, and only MacArthur's personal reconnaissance narrowly saved the two American divisions from attacking one another.

MacArthur was in fact taken prisoner by the 16th infantry of the 1st Division during this reconnaissance, having been mistaken for a "Boche" because of his non-regulation hat, sweater, and scarf. He was quickly released, but the two divisions were mixed and in an "intolerable" state of confusion, according to Menoher. What is more, the French were now angry because the American mix-up completely barred the advance of their own 40th Division, which was also determined to be the first to enter Sedan. Indeed, American troops came under French artillery fire. General Hunter Liggett finally ordered the 1st Division out of the sector, and Jack Pershing acceded to let the French pass Menoher's 42nd and seize the city.[30] French history books later failed to mention this generous American gesture. In any event, as soon as patrols of the Rainbow Division reached the Meuse opposite Sedan on the night of November 9–10, they were relieved by the fresh 77th Division and sent to the V Corps' reserves.

When the armistice then went into effect on November 11, 1918, Menoher was promoted to corps commander and the thirty-eight-year-old Douglas MacArthur designated to succeed him as major general and commander of the 42nd. But with the signing of the armistice, all promotions were frozen. MacArthur served as divisional commander only until November 22, when he was relieved by a major general; after that, he returned to command the 84th Brigade.

Brigadier MacArthur's troops entered Germany on December 1, their commander cursing Pershing's betrayal of him yet again. On March 16, 1919, Pershing himself reviewed the Rainbow Division near Bonn and personally pinned the Distinguished Service Medal on Douglas MacArthur, which was added to his seven Silver Medals, two Purple Hearts, and the nineteen foreign honors awarded him by various governments.[31]

The 42nd then embarked for home, reaching New York City on April 25 to find the docks empty. Not a soul was there to greet the brigadier, who now sported a natty raccoon fur coat for the photographers who failed to materialize. "Amid a silence that hurt—with no one, not even the children, to see us—we marched off the dock, to be scattered to the four winds—a sad, gloomy end to the Rainbow," MacArthur later reminisced. "There was no welcome for fighting men. . . ."

That evening a splendid ball was given in MacArthur's honor at the Waldorf-Astoria. He appeared in dress uniform with a beautiful young woman on his arm. MacArthur was dancing with his guest when the maître d'hôtel interrupted, informing him he must remove his spurs. "Do you know who I am?" MacArthur asked. "Yes, General." "And I took my lady and we walked off the dance floor, and I never set foot in that place again."[32] It was a bitter ending.

But great was his joy when in May 1919 he was ordered to assume the superintendency of the Military Academy at West Point, with strict instructions to shake it up by modernizing the curriculum and some of the customs of the Academy. Naturally, his mother moved into the Superintendent's residence with him.

On Valentine's Day 1922, a great change came to MacArthur's life when he married Louise Henriette Cromwell Brooks, much against the wishes of his horrified mother, who moved out when Louise moved in. The bride was a beautiful divorcée in her thirties with two children from her previous marriage. The daughter of two distinguished families and the product of East Coast finishing schools, she was a child of the Jazz Age, a first-class flapper who lived for pleasure and society. Unfortunately for MacArthur, she had been Black Jack Pershing's mistress when they first met, and Pershing was now army chief of staff. An angry Pershing's wedding gift arrived in June 1922: orders for MacArthur to interrupt his tour at West Point and to proceed forthwith to the Philippines, where he was to assume command of the Military District of Manila and the Philippine Scout Brigade. He wanted MacArthur out of the country.

Quartered in No. 1 Calle Victoria, known as "the House on the Wall," MacArthur and Louise were greeted by Manuel Quezon. After Quezon had been captured by MacArthur's father back in 1900, he had studied law and was now president of the Philippine Senate. The Quezons and MacArthurs became good friends, and the new commanding general was introduced to the principal families of the capital. Pershing, still not content with having removed MacArthur from a posting he had very much liked, now intervened again, this time ordering

Brigadier MacArthur to survey personally the whole of the Bataan Peninsula—a task ordinarily assigned to a very junior officer. MacArthur said nothing and got on with it. He ultimately mapped forty square miles of the jungle headland while continuing to oversee the training of the troops.

Despite the remoteness of the location and tedium of the job, MacArthur enjoyed some happy times here, compounded by the arrival of his old friend from Milwaukee, Billy Mitchell, and his bride. MacArthur also took great joy in his two stepchildren. Louise, on the other hand, was growing increasingly bored with Manila and army life.

In 1923, MacArthur's mother, Pinky, asked her son to come home immediately, as she was gravely ill. MacArthur, Louise, and the children returned to the States on the next steamer. But on reaching the Wardman Park Hotel in Washington where Pinky lived, they found her making a miraculous recovery. (This was neither the first nor the last time she would do so.) The MacArthurs spent two months in the capital while Louise and Pinky pulled all the strings they could to obtain a promotion and better posting for MacArthur, though in reality he was quite content with life in Manila.

It was not until January 17, 1925, that MacArthur was promoted major general, in one of Pershing's last acts before he stepped down as chief of staff of the U.S. Army and retired.[33] MacArthur was ordered back to the States to take command of III Corps, at Baltimore. His wife owned a large estate near Corps HQ, and their new life included hunting to hounds and an unceasing whirl of social rounds and fashionable balls, all of which Douglas MacArthur detested. Louise coaxed him to resign his commission and to take up a position on Wall Street, but he resisted; his marriage to the army was stronger than that with his wife.

During his three years at Baltimore, MacArthur was given the most disagreeable order of his career: to serve on the board of officers for the court-martial of General Billy Mitchell. The army aviator was charged and convicted of "conduct prejudicial to good order and military discipline," which cast "discredit upon the military service." The court-martial ended his military career. Earlier, Mitchell had also ridiculed Hawaii's air defenses, which he found grossly wanting, and then blamed the army for the crash of one of its dirigibles while not forgetting the army's

General Staff, which he claimed was guilty of negligence by failing to approve adequate allocations for the army's air arm. In addition, Mitchell had gotten just about everyone's hackles up by demanding the creation of a large new consolidated air force, comprising all the services—army and naval—as one unit, similar to England's RAF. This whole affair greatly upset Douglas MacArthur, and it is believed that the sole dissenting vote cast against Mitchell's conviction was his, although he would never admit to it.[34]

Within two years of the trial, Louise abandoned her husband and moved into an apartment of her own in New York, leading a wild life, much to the delight of the city's scandal sheet editors. At about the same time, in September 1927, MacArthur was asked to assume the presidency of the American Olympic Committee, which he did with surprising zest, preparing for the 1928 Olympics, to be held in Amsterdam. That was followed by another stint in the Philippines at No. 1 Calle Victoria, but now as commander of all forces in the Philippines. It was after his arrival there that he was informed that his wife had filed for divorce. The end of his marriage came as a relief to MacArthur, although he would miss the children.

Now on his third tour of duty in the Philippines, MacArthur was responsible both for the training of Philippine troops and for the defense of the country against what was perceived to be an ever-growing Japanese threat. He was astonished and dismayed by the increased number of Japanese immigrants he found in the islands, the ramifications of which he discussed with Filipino political leaders. Quezon, on the other hand, maddeningly failed to grasp any possible danger, and indeed even went so far as to encourage still further Japanese immigration, and with it the badly needed skills and capital this would attract. He and MacArthur had some strong words on the subject. Although Quezon pooh-poohed the suggestion of Japanese subversion, two of his own servants later turned out to be fairly high-ranking Japanese army spies. MacArthur was particularly concerned about the situation on the island of Mindanao, where forty-one Japanese corporations controlled some 372,000 arable acres, without counting other substantial interests held elsewhere in the country by Filipino-fronted Japanese businesses, a clear indication of Tokyo's long-term plans for a future occupation of that land.[35] The governor of the Philippines,

Colonel Henry Stimson, a high-powered Wall Street lawyer, shared MacArthur's anxiety, however.

Before MacArthur had left Baltimore, a joint Army-Navy Committee had convened to discuss War Plan Orange (WPO) and the defense of the Philippines. According to the Five-Power Naval Treaty, the committee was not permitted to construct new fortifications and naval bases in the Philippines. Nevertheless, that committee did now call for the buttressing of the defenses of Bataan, the strengthening of the rocky island fortress of Corregidor at the entrance to Manila Bay, and the deployment of more U.S. troops and aircraft there. As things stood, with a mere 18 U.S. warplanes to defend the 17,000 islands that made up the Philippines, the Japanese could land at least 100,000 men and easily conquer the country. The previous governor, Cameron Forbes, had argued that the Philippines "are indefensible and from a military point of view are not worth defending."[36] Both MacArthur and Stimson vociferously disagreed with this point of view, but they were in a small minority. The following year, 1929, President Herbert Hoover recalled Stimson to serve as his new secretary of state. It was hoped that in his new position, Stimson could wield more influence and win others to his way of thinking.

In 1930, General Charles Summerall, one of MacArthur's former commanders in France and now Hoover's army chief of staff, notified Douglas MacArthur that President Hoover wished to appoint him chief of the Army Corps of Engineers. MacArthur declined the post out of hand, considering it to be a dead-end appointment.

Growing more and more depressed by Quezon's resistance to the idea of self-defense, a dejected MacArthur applied to the chief of staff to be reassigned to the United States. On August 6, 1930, much to his astonishment, MacArthur was not only recalled to Washington but named Summerall's successor as army chief of staff. This was an appointment MacArthur was later to regret in some respects because of the deepening national depression and the heavy toll it was taking in army reductions.

On November 24, 1930, MacArthur was sworn in and moved into his new Washington office in the Munitions Building. He had brought with him a mistress, Isabel Rosario Cooper, a woman of mixed European-Asian background, who soon became something of a headache for MacArthur. Her demands for a chauffeur-driven car and thousands of dollars for clothes—not to mention her growing collection of jewels . . . and lovers (who kept her company during MacArthur's frequent absences)—reached the gossip columns, and in September 1934 MacArthur sent her a one-way ticket back to Manila, intending to sever all relations. Instead, she moved into a flat closer to his office on Constitution Avenue.[37] MacArthur continued to share his mother's apartment. But the issue of his mistress would reemerge in 1944, causing considerable, if unnecessary, scandal.

A more direct, overtly vain MacArthur was beginning to emerge in the 1930s. He spoke of himself in the third person ("MacArthur will do this now; MacArthur thinks that . . . "), wore a Japanese ceremonial kimono in his office, and insisted upon his own private railway carriage. As chief of staff, he observed French army maneuvers, and War Minister General André Maginot awarded him the Grand Cross of the Legion of Honor after personally guiding him through the miles of elaborate cement bunkers, complete with underground trains, that he was building halfway across northern France. Douglas MacArthur found the so-called Maginot Line depressing indeed, representing a defensive attitude on the part of the French instead of robustly condemning various German violations of the Versailles Treaty. The French were still thinking in terms of trench warfare where a gain of one hundred yards was considered a great success; worse, they were spending most of their feeble military budget on this concept. Like Churchill in England, however, Douglas MacArthur was rightly warning Washington that "the next war is certain to be one of maneuver and movement," not the trench warfare of the past. To begin with, the next war would require command of the air: MacArthur recalled the many months of fighting he and his brigade had endured with little or no air cover for protection. His strategy followed the maxim that he who is defenseless in the skies will lose the war; and therefore, he believed, the army budget should be spent on arms, planes, and men, not on cement.

MacArthur was still traveling in Europe in 1931 when he received news of the Japanese invasion of Manchuria. Rushing back to Washington, he, along with Secretary of State Stimson, called for economic sanctions against Japan. Hoover refused. When the president then ordered MacArthur to attend the 1932 Geneva Disarmament Conference sponsored by the League of Nations, MacArthur likewise refused. One does not end wars by disarming, leaving oneself defenseless, he insisted—or, as Duff Cooper put it, one does not prevent wars by throwing away one's rifles.

When MacArthur did return to Europe, it was not to Switzerland, but to tour military installations in Poland and Austria. Unlike Charles Lindbergh, he declined an invitation to observe Nazi army maneuvers. With only a $284 million annual budget and by now only the sixteenth largest army in the world—a mere 132,069 men, smaller even than that of Portugal—Chief of Staff MacArthur was not sanguine about his work or the country's future,[38] even as Congress continued to cut army appropriations.

Although there was already talk in Republican circles of MacArthur becoming a presidential candidate, the events of the summer of 1932 soon undermined that. First, he denounced the 19,372 Protestant clergymen who supported pacifism and refused to defend their country. In his criticism, MacArthur declared his belief "that a red-blooded and virile humanity which loves peace devotedly, but is willing to die in defense of that right, is Christian from center to circumference."[39]

Also in that summer of 1932, penniless, unemployed veterans by the thousands, along with their families, congregated in the nation's capital to protest their situation to Herbert Hoover. Ragged, encamped in tents and shacks for months, their numbers swelled to approximately 25,000. They demanded a government cash bonus to help them get through the period of unemployment that had struck when much of the country's industry had closed down. Hoover scorned them, adamantly refusing to meet with them or help them financially or in any other manner. Disbelieving their claims, Hoover and MacArthur referred to them in newspapers and on radio as Communist hoodlums, thugs, and the scum of the country. In reality, as a Veterans Administration survey later demonstrated, 94 percent of the protesters were bona fide veterans, the vast majority of them having served overseas, some with MacArthur's own Rainbow Division.

For the most part they were orderly, and even marched everywhere in military formation, but as the blistering hot Washington weeks passed, the patience of vets and their families—there were many babies and young children among them—wore thin. When the Washington police tried to eject them from abandoned buildings some of them had occupied, bricks were thrown, and two veterans were shot by the police. Hoover ordered MacArthur to bring in the troops to put down and eject the Bonus Expeditionary Force (BEF), as they called themselves, once and for all. But there were strict provisions, as the secretary of war instructed MacArthur:

> You will have United States troops proceed immediately to the scene of disorder. Cooperate fully with the District of Columbia police force which is now in charge. Surround the affected area and clear it without delay.
>
> Turn over all prisoners to the civil authorities.
>
> In your orders insist that any women and children who may be in the affected area be accorded every consideration. Use all humanity consistent with due execution of this order.[40]

At the end of July, when several thousand protesters left the city and moved across the Anacostia River, Hoover sent a message to MacArthur instructing him *not to cross that bridge and follow them*. MacArthur arrogantly refused to receive the White House messengers who twice attempted to hand him the president's additional instructions. Before his own staff, he deliberately disobeyed the orders of the president of the United States.

Chief of Staff MacArthur called up the 2nd Squadron of the 3rd Cavalry—in those days, literally saber-bearing troops on horseback—the 3rd Battalion of the 12th Infantry, the Headquarters Company of Washington, five tanks of the 1st Tank Regiment, and the 29th Motor Transportation Company. The troops soon poured in from Forts Myer, Meade, Washington, and Howard, totaling nearly eight hundred well-armed men wielding machine guns and artillery.

"I accompanied the troops in person," MacArthur reported to War Secretary Patrick Hurley, "anticipating the possibilities of such a serious situation arising. . . ."[41] Indeed, MacArthur appeared in full dress uniform, wearing every medal and ribbon he had ever earned. His deputy, Major Dwight Eisenhower, implored him not to go, but Douglas MacArthur was Douglas MacArthur, and he ignored this good advice. Arriving with the troops, he threatened to arrest one man as he and his family were forced out at bayonet point. The angry veteran called out: "The American flag means nothing to me after this!"

"That mob down there was a bad-looking mob," MacArthur told reporters afterward. "It was animated by the essence of revolution. . . . [T]hey were about to take over in some arbitrary way either the direct control of the Government or else to control it by indirect methods. . . . [I]f there was one man in ten in that group today who is a veteran, it would surprise me." He insisted that "absolutely no instructions have been issued from the War Department . . . dealing with any riot troubles," whereas, of course, he had personally received such instructions from Secretary Hurley. "So far as I know there is no man on either side who has been seriously injured."[42]

In fact, MacArthur's troops had charged with bayonets and glistening cavalry sabers, some of them firing several hundred defective tear gas canisters that exploded into flames, burning men and women. MacArthur then ordered his troops across the 11th Street bridge, over the Anacostia River—in defiance of the presidential order—burning thousands of tents and shacks set up on the Anacostia Flats. In addition to the two men shot earlier, one seven-year-old boy was now bayoneted in the leg because he was attempting to save his pet rabbit from the flames of his family's tent. One veteran's ear was hacked off by a saber after his head was nearly split in two, and two babies inhaling the burning tear gas were killed. Hundreds of others suffered tear gas burns. Over twenty thousand homeless people left the Washington "riots" with even less than they had possessed upon their arrival.

Once again the MacArthur version of events painted him in the most favorable light. The assistant secretary of war, Trubee Davison, was pleased to learn that this "polyglot mob of tramps and hoodlums" had been dispersed.[43] Herbert Hoover complimented MacArthur in person on a job well done.

When Franklin Delano Roosevelt replaced Hoover in the White House, the Roosevelt who had denounced the brutal treatment of the war veterans astonishingly asked MacArthur to remain as army chief of staff in 1933. No one was more surprised than Douglas MacArthur, and Roosevelt quipped, "Douglas, I think you are our best general, but I believe you would be our worst politician."[44] Indeed, MacArthur would prove a great liability for FDR; but instead of thanking the president, the chief of staff made derogatory comments about him behind his back. Secretary of the Interior Harold Ickes, for one, could see that the general was a dangerous man: "MacArthur is the type of man who thinks that when he gets to heaven, God will step down . . . and bow him into His vacated seat."[45] MacArthur, the self-righteous Bible-quoting Christian, drew much criticism from the national press, including searing articles by Drew Pearson and by Robert S. Allen, who called him a fraud.

MacArthur's relationship with the president was a curious one. He never felt comfortable in the presence of Franklin Roosevelt, the only man who not only was not intimidated by him but could also usually get the best of him. One day MacArthur inquired why the president would frequently ask his opinion about social reforms "but pay little attention to my views on the military?" A beaming FDR put down his long cigarette holder, replying: "Douglas, I don't bring these questions up for your advice but for your reactions. To me, you are the symbol of the conscience of the American people."[46] MacArthur almost stormed out of the room.

Nevertheless, MacArthur's criticisms on the deteriorating state of the U.S. military had some validity, and when Roosevelt announced that he was slashing the budget for army reserves and national guard units, MacArthur blasted, "When we lose the next war, and an American boy with an enemy bayonet through his belly . . . spits his last curse, I want the name not to be MacArthur, but Roosevelt!" No one had ever addressed the president like that, and MacArthur later apologized.[47]

It was painful for the chief of staff to see the army whittled down year after year, first under Hoover and then under Roosevelt.[48] At least FDR was using the funds saved in order to fight back at the all-devouring national depression, shoring up the economy and creating vast employment programs for the millions out of work. One of these, the Civilian Conservation Corps (CCC), was in fact organized by MacArthur himself, for he realized that these men would make fine soldiers when national conscription was reintroduced.

Ever since the Chaumont days in France, Douglas MacArthur had thought there were jealous soldiers and politicians trying to ruin his career. "My worst enemy has always been behind me," as he put it. But when the long-retired General Pershing, who had once denied

MacArthur promotion and the Congressional Medal of Honor, now wrote asking for a personal favor—to promote his old Chaumont chief of staff, Colonel George Marshall, to brigadier general—MacArthur could at last strike back. Refusing this request out of hand, he had Colonel Marshall transferred to the prairies of the Midwest, to a National Guard Armory in Chicago.[49]

Roosevelt, in turn, avenged himself on MacArthur when he finally discovered some of the defamatory things the army chief of staff had been saying about the president of the United States. In 1935, instead of sending MacArthur to the Philippines as its high commissioner with an enticing salary, as he had earlier considered in September, Roosevelt changed his mind and sent MacArthur in a far lesser role as "military adviser" to President Quezon.[50] It was all part of the Chaumont plot, MacArthur insisted.

MacArthur's first years with President Quezon were a success. The two men worked closely together, and Quezon promised MacArthur a substantial increase in military expenditures of up to $8 million annually over the next ten years. (By 1941, that would be cut to a mere $1 million a year.) With these promised funds, MacArthur was authorized to conscript and train a large new army while preparing the country's defenses on the land, in the air, on the sea. But ever since March 1934, the entire situation of American relations with the Philippines had become confused and complicated; the passage of the Tydings-McDuffie Independence Act of 1934 had conferred "Commonwealth" status on the Philippines, and had committed the United States to giving the country its independence in 1946. Thereafter the extent to which Washington would invest in that country's defense wavered in a sort of limbo, with congressmen muttering about throwing "good money after bad," to no certain purpose.

For his part, Douglas MacArthur, whose reputation had suffered severely since his crushing of the BEF in 1932, was having personal problems with Congress and the U.S. Army, and the government forced him to resign his commission on December 31, 1937. Although MacArthur was no longer the official "military adviser" to the Philippine government, Quezon named him commander in chief of his country's army, giving him the title of field marshal and an impressive increase in salary.[51]

Over the years President Quezon again began to waver, however, fearful of a Japanese attack and wary of encouraging such an attack by enhancing the Philippines' defenses—even though MacArthur confidentially assured him that Tokyo would never dare attack Manila. Finally Quezon backtracked, calling for Philippine neutrality and demanding immediate independence, which, he argued, would put the Japanese at ease and prevent military intervention on their part. Chamberlain was acting similarly with the Germans, he reasoned; why would it not work here? Washington, already in a quandary as to its military commitment to the Philippines, was upset with Quezon's unpredictable ups-and-downs—as was MacArthur himself when Quezon then reneged, slashing the military budget.

The result was that MacArthur, newly married to Jean Marie Faircloth of Tennessee, slacked in his effort to prepare the defense of the country. He spent far more time in his luxurious penthouse atop the Manila Hotel, where his balconies overlooked the spacious bay, Corregidor, and the jungles of Bataan, some twenty-five miles away through the tropical haze. Morale was plummeting, and annual conscription—155,100 men in 1936—dropped to 90,700 by 1940. Worse yet, never more than 36,600 of those officially drafted completed their five-and-a-half-month basic training. Indeed, by 1940, the new Philippine Army of career soldiers, of which "Field Marshal" MacArthur had so boasted a couple of years earlier, comprised a mere 468 officers and 3,697 men. The pivotal 1st Infantry Division had only one regiment of more than 300 men. On paper, Douglas MacArthur reported to the Philippine government that their spanking new army comprised some 6,000 officers and up to 135,000 enlisted men when including the reserves, organized into ten infantry divisions. In reality, MacArthur did not have one tenth of those forces.[52]

As for the Philippine air force, its first squadron had twenty-one attack and observation planes when it was finally organized in 1939. By New Year's Eve of 1941, it had been increased by only nineteen more warplanes, with a total of one hundred pilots available for all types of aircraft.[53]

MacArthur was living in a dream world. When he had attempted to call up his reserves, tens of thousands of men had never reported for duty and that year's maneuvers had been a fiasco. Many of those men who did report often lacked discipline, and did not even know the manual of arms. They came from different regions speaking a variety of languages, and thus most orders were not even understood. Nor was MacArthur helped by the defeatist President Quezon who, when addressing thousands of Filipinos in Rizal Stadium, declared that the "islands could not be defended even if every last Filipino were armed with modern weapons,"[54] while earlier, MacArthur had assured the readers of the *Christian Science Monitor* that Luzon had "only two coastal regions in which a hostile army of any size could land. Each of these is broken by strong defensive positions, which, if properly manned and prepared *would present to an attacking force a practically impossible problem of penetration.*"[55] He added that "a Japanese blockade would be practically unfeasible without the tacit agreement of the other nations surrounding the Pacific,"[56] and he further insisted that the Philippine government could "achieve a respectable defense and enjoy a reasonable safety if it is prepared and determined to repel attacks." What was more, there was a "lack of plausible reason for attack" by the Japanese here, he added by way of conclusion, and therefore there was nothing more to discuss.[57] Simultaneously President Quezon was telling his countrymen that the nation was indefensible, regardless of what they did.

Chapter X

The Philippines: "A Limit to Human Endurance"[1]

"There has been a constant effort on the part of the [U.S.] press, inspired no doubt, by imperialists, to deprecate the potential ability of the Filipinos along all lines, but especially in the arts of war."

—*Douglas MacArthur, February 1941*[2]

"The Philippines Army Units with the North Luzon Force were doomed even before they started to fight. . . . They never had a chance to win."

—*Jonathan Wainwright,*
General Wainwright's Story *(1946)*[3]

On December 13, 1939, three months after the German invasion of Poland, Field Marshal Douglas MacArthur and his young wife Jean were at the pier in Manila to see off MacArthur's former chief of staff, Dwight David Eisenhower, and his wife Mamie. It was quite an occasion, and the quayside was crowded as the last of the passengers boarded the luxury liner, filled chiefly with American wives and the families of servicemen. "Ike" had served under MacArthur ever since he was chief of staff in Washington, and had been offered various commands of his own by the War Department time and again, all resisted by MacArthur until now. Despite President Quezon's recent award of the Philippine Distinguished Service Star, Eisenhower could not wait to get away from the overbearing MacArthur. Nevertheless, alleged "hostility between us has been exaggerated," Ike insisted; "after all, there must be a strong tie for two men to work so closely for seven years. . . . We [now] talked of the gloominess of world prospects, but our foreboding turned toward Europe—not Asia."[4] MacArthur was a master at avoiding realities, and Ike did not wish his farewell voyage to end on a sour note. Jean and Mamie embraced one another as they said good-bye, tears in their eyes. The MacArthurs then watched the big Grace Line cruise ship slip its moorings and disappear into the tranquil haze of Manila Bay—bound for California via Honolulu and a very different world.

The guns were "not yet roaring," in the Philippines, Ike later wrote MacArthur from Washington, "but . . . once they really open up, I'll expect to see you in the thick of it." MacArthur did not agree. Eisenhower later said that Quezon had told him that "when the Japanese attacked Pearl Harbor, MacArthur was convinced for some strange reason that the Philippines would remain neutral and would not be attacked.[5] MacArthur's attitude of denial was hardly new. During World War I in France, he had rarely worn a helmet, gas mask, or pistol, even when leading troops into the thick of battle. Although he was subsequently gassed twice as a result of his own arrogance, he firmly believed that the German bullet or shell had not been made that would kill him. The finger of God was on him, as the Duke of Wellington had been wont to say after Waterloo, and would now protect MacArthur as well. And since he was untouchable, the Philippines were equally so: he believed his prestige to be so immense that the Japanese would not dare attack. Or at least he thought this at times. His views and estimation of events altered considerably, often depending upon his mood or the audience he was addressing. And then there was his famous "ten-year plan" to build Philippine defenses, which, he declared, would clearly defy any enemy attack.

Reality was quite another matter, as the American Philippine resident commissioner to Washington, Joaquin "Mike" Elizalde, acknowledged in April 1941, saying, "I don't want to appear pessimistic, but at this point I can hardly see how this country will avoid war in 60 to 90 days from now."[6] And in his memoirs Elizalde wrote of knowing that war as a whole would ultimately have to be fought by "attrition against Japan itself." The Philippines were completely surrounded by the Japanese, but, he wrote, "We knew all along that . . . we [with the United States] could outbuild Japan and ultimately overwhelm her on sea, on land and in the air." President Quezon disagreed in every respect with both Roosevelt and Elizalde, instead recommending that by signs of friendship with Japan —i.e., appeasement—the Philippines could remain neutral in any war, particularly if the United States granted his country independence before hostilities broke out. MacArthur agreed in part, causing a national furor in the process. Quezon's ploy "might offer the best possible solution for what is about to become a disastrous débâcle," MacArthur was to comment a few weeks after Quezon's request, inviting the wrath of Franklin Roosevelt. "We can't do this at all!" FDR severely reproached him, much to the relief of his chief of staff, George Marshall. "I immediately discredited anything in my mind I had held to his [Roosevelt's] discredit," Marshall later said, "and I decided he was [after all] a great man." MacArthur, too, eventually gave in, claiming that he had never intended to suggest neutrality and that of course he had been "misunderstood." Yet MacArthur's initial acquiescence to Quezon's plan may have had its roots elsewhere. He had secretly coerced Quezon to oblige the Philippine Treasury to slip him $500,000 for his support, money never reported to the U.S. Treasury but probably meant as an insurance fund for his wife and son in the event of his death.[7] He was, at the time, still receiving a full salary from the Philippine government and his pension as a retired U.S. major general.

At other times Quezon supported fully MacArthur's efforts to build a large Philippine army and air force of well-trained reservists. He would then swing wildly in the opposite direction, slashing the military budget he had solemnly promised after MacArthur had resigned from the American army—under duress, after refusing to report for duty in the United States—to take up the position of field marshal in Quezon's new army.

That there was considerable doubt expressed by foreign correspondents about just how capable the Filipinos were of defending themselves greatly offended Douglas MacArthur, as did Quezon's own deep-seated anxiety. "There has been a constant effort on the part of the [U.S.] press, inspired no doubt, by imperialists, to deprecate the potential ability of the Filipinos along all lines, but especially in the arts of war," an angry MacArthur remonstrated with Commissioner Elizalde in February 1941.[8] There was a group, the general insisted, that "contends that the Philippine Nation cannot afford to build up a defense establishment. . . . The answer to this contention is that self-defense is the first law of nations as well as of individuals and to say that the new nation cannot defend itself is simply to say that the Philippines cannot become an independent nation. Still other opponents of the defense system are simply ignorant of the factors and of the lessons of history," he concluded, referring to the evidence of the enthusiastic manner in which Filipinos of all walks of life had responded to every call the government made upon them to carry out the provisions of the Philippine Defense Plan.[9]

The head of the U.S. Army War Plans Division in Washington, Leonard Gerow, strongly disputed MacArthur's assertions. The latter's so-called well-trained Philippine army "is of doubtful combat efficiency," he officially advised George Marshall in June 1941.[10] Gerow recommended against the establishment of any U.S. Army command in the Far East, for it was in no position to defend the region. War Plan Orange had already conclusively established this policy and called for the sacrifice of the Philippines. Nevertheless, George Marshall was still taken in by the MacArthur rhetoric, mystique, and uncanny self-confidence. This included MacArthur's misleading assessment of both the situation in the Far East and the quality of a Philippine army that he had been personally responsible for training since his arrival in Manila late in 1935. Nevertheless Roosevelt, in turn, firmly believed both in Chief of Staff Marshall and in his old sparring partner, Douglas MacArthur, and went out of his way to emphasize that "whatever differences arose between us [MacArthur and FDR], it never sullied in [the] slightest degree the warmth of my personal friendship for him."[11]

Whatever talk there was to the contrary, MacArthur for his part saw no reason to worry about the Philippines and a Japanese threat. As he ebulliently informed journalist John Hersey in mid-1941, "The Philippine situation looks sound: twelve Filipino divisions are already trained." In reality, except for the famous Philippine Scouts, which were not a part of the Philippine army proper but trained by the U.S. Army and directly under its control, twelve trained Filipino divisions did not exist. On paper there were only ten divisions, and not a single one of those was fully trained, manned, or equipped, even five years after MacArthur's arrival in the Philippines. MacArthur also assured Hersey that "the Germans have told Japan not to stir up any trouble in the Pacific" because Germany was already holding down a large portion of the U.S. Navy there—ships that would otherwise align with British and Dutch forces against the German navy in the Atlantic and Mediterranean. This, too, was palpably absurd, and MacArthur never provided proof for such an assertion. Relations between Tokyo and Berlin were at best formal, undermined by mutual racial suspicion. Berlin adamantly refused to cooperate on most of the major campaigns or the war effort. Indeed, Hirohito had gone on record as stating that he personally did not trust the Axis powers.

Pacing back and forth across the long sitting room of his Manila Hotel penthouse, MacArthur told Hersey that in the remote event that Japan eventually did enter the war, "the Americans and the British and Dutch could handle her with about half the forces they now have deployed in the Far East." Here was another reflection of his inability to comprehend basic naval matters and, in this instance, the situation of the forces available in the Pacific compared with those of the Imperial Japanese Navy. The United States was short of ships—even before Pearl Harbor—and then worse off after sending several of its principal ships, including battleships and a carrier, to the Atlantic to help the British. This left the U.S. Pacific Fleet with battleships, a few cruisers, and only three carriers, as opposed to Japan's seven big veteran carriers and four smaller ones. Moreover, the combined Japanese army and navy air force comprised several thousand modern high-performance bombers and fighters, manned by pilots with years of wartime experience gained in China. The U.S. bomber and fighter production, on the other hand, was only just beginning. And it did not have nearly enough warplanes or veteran pilots even to defend Hawaii, the Panama Canal, or the Philippines, let alone the continental United States.

Yet MacArthur dismissed this stark reality, choosing instead to portray Japanese forces as vulnerable and informing John Hersey that the Japanese army itself "has been reduced in effectiveness [in China] from a first-class to a third-class standing." In fact, Japan had well over 2 million crack troops just in China. Furthermore, MacArthur went so far as to assure Hersey that Japan would not dare push farther in Southeast Asia because of the "bristling united front" presented by the British, Dutch, and Americans. Quite the contrary: Tokyo's plans had already been long prepared, and Japan was about to invade southern Indochina, Malaya, Thailand, Borneo, Java, Sumatra, Hong Kong, Singapore, and the Philippines, and to embark on an eastward thrust against Wake, Guam, Midway, and Pearl Harbor.

"The general is emphatic . . . and seems very sure of what he says. . . . You go out feeling a little more confident about things," Hersey assured his readers back home.[12] It is clear that MacArthur's version of reality—his judgment and ability to offer Washington an accurate assessment of events of the Far East, of which he modestly considered himself the greatest expert—was skewed at best. The fact is that every one of his predictions and assessments made to John Hersey was soon proven to be totally wrong. Once again, MacArthur's "facts" were reminiscent of Napoleon's creative war "Bulletins of the Grand Army." (It is hardly surprising to learn that MacArthur literally dictated many of his own important "news releases" through his command's Public Relations Office, much to the chagrin of the officers in charge.)

Until this point War Plan Orange-3 (WPO-3)—or revised Rainbow 5, as it was now called—had advocated the abandonment of the Far East, including the Philippines, in the event of a Japanese attack, at least until reinforcements could be brought in months later. This would require all U.S.-Filipino forces to withdraw to the Bataan Peninsula, Cavite Naval Base, and the recently completed maze beneath Corregidor—the large, rocky fortress seen from the country's capital which guarded the entrance to Manila Bay. While many American journalists dispatched to report on the Philippines failed to grasp the complexities of the region's parlous state of affairs, the U.S. Navy did have experts au courant of the actual situation in the Far East. These included Kelly Turner, who met daily with Leonard Gerow, filling him in on the naval side of events; Gerow, in turn, continued to confirm certain harsh realities to George Marshall, the army's chief of staff.

"Both the Secretary of War [Henry Stimson] and I are much concerned about the situation in the Far East," Marshall confided in a secret message to MacArthur on June 20, 1941.[13] At this stage MacArthur was still on the retired list, and Marshall now notified him that because of the quickly deteriorating situation there, he would soon be recalled to the colors as "Army Commander in the Far East."

•

The capitulation of southern Indochina to the Japanese in July 1941 proved the catalyst required to jolt Roosevelt into action. On July 26,

FDR officially joined MacArthur's Philippine Commonwealth Army with that of the United States, while General Marshall radioed MacArthur independently that "effective this day . . . you are hereby designated as Commanding General, United States Army Forces in the Far East," or USAFFE. The sixty-one-year-old MacArthur replied, "I can but do my best."[14]

One look at Douglas MacArthur's World War I record alone established him as the most dynamic, brilliant, original, and aggressive general in the U.S. Army, a factor acknowledged even by the French. But many decades had since passed, and what Washington failed to take into account was that the MacArthur of 1918 was no longer the same man. The youthful general who had spent every day of that first war at the front with his men, personifying drive, extraordinary leadership, and sound split-second judgment, all based on meticulous staff planning, seemed no longer capable of any of these things.

Since 1935 he had been extraordinarily lax in executing his duties of preparing a new Filipino army, as the mobilization orders of November 1941 were to demonstrate only too painfully. Described now as "extremely aloof," he rarely met with many of his officers any more, even men in key positions. Instead, he bastioned himself in an office, no longer in a trench or field headquarters, and was protected always by a relatively new staff headed by Richard Sutherland, a frequently unsound, secretive chief of staff, full of his own personal superiority. What is more, MacArthur came into social contact with more Filipinos than Americans, whom he seemed deliberately to shun. It was Manuel Quezon, not a fellow American officer, whom MacArthur asked to act as the godfather of his much-spoiled son, Arthur MacArthur IV.

Japan's invasion of southern Indochina suddenly altered the political climate in Washington, where a great sea change was taking place across the usually languid waters of the Potomac. "Due to the situation in the Far East," Secretary of War Stimson wrote FDR on July 25, "all practical steps should be taken *to increase the defensive strength of the Philippine Islands*." Quite an about-face, even for Stimson, who had always been a supreme hawk. Leonard Gerow, head of Army War Plans, was shocked. It takes years to prepare any army for war, to call up men, train them, provide supplies, armament, and munitions, and arrange the logistics to get them to their theater of operations. It also takes years to prepare fortresses, modern defensive facilities, depots, and ports, and to develop new types of equipment. When even the hardheaded Sutherland admitted that this sudden new call for the defense of the islands amounted to "an almost insurmountable task," MacArthur ignored him just as Stimson had. "These islands must be defended," MacArthur insisted, as usual full of the contradictions that left everyone mystified if not confused.[15]

The pessimism of Gerow and Sutherland did nothing to dampen George Marshall's newly aroused ardor, however, and on October 18, 1941, he informed the Joint Chiefs of Staff that they were about to abandon the old War Plan Orange, or Rainbow 5, in favor of MacArthur's "brilliant" new aggressive plans to protect the archipelago from Japanese attack.[16] Marshall therefore immediately promised MacArthur and his air force chief dozens of B-17 Flying Fortresses and P-40 fighters. Artillery, munitions, and men would also soon be on their way.

But orders had to be placed with industry, and ships had to be found to transport the crated P-40s, artillery, matériel, and men. Marshall suddenly realized that Kelly Turner's complaints about a lack of shipping had in fact been only too true. Indeed, even when some ships (including large luxury liners) could be found or seized, it took weeks to get them from the East Coast of the United States to the Far East. Even then there was not enough time to prepare and deploy them as "combat-loaded transports."* Doing so, Marshall discovered, would have caused a delay of an additional fortnight. As a result, all cargoes would have to be unloaded and completely repacked in New Zealand and Australia, and then loaded onto the vessels that would take them to the battle zone. Added to the transport problem was the inevitable manpower shortage facing the army and navy. Millions of men would have to volunteer or be conscripted within the next twelve months, and crash training programs would have to be inaugurated for officers, pilots, and soldiers.

In spite of the freezing of Japanese assets in America and the closing

*"Combat-loaded" meant that all related matériel of war—e.g., aircraft wth their spare parts, propellors, engines, tires, and so forth—were to be kept on the same ship (preferably in the same hold) and not dispersed among several different vessels, some of which might have arrived weeks later, thereby rendering them, in this instance, immobile. The same applied to tanks, trucks, artillery, etc.

of the Panama Canal to Japanese shipping, MacArthur himself still was not fully convinced that the Japanese would indeed attack the Philippines, and was only to modify that outlook over time. He certainly did not believe there would be an attack before April 1, 1942, as he told Sutherland, Wainwright, and Marshall, among others. The Japanese, vividly aware of their precarious position, would have to move immediately to establish new sources of nickel, rubber, aviation fuel, oil, and aluminum. The Philippines had the nickel Japan needed. Borneo and Java could provide all the gasoline and oil required, Malaya the rubber, and Indochina the rice; Indochina also possessed valuable strategically situated military camps, ports, and airfields that could serve future operations.

Meanwhile, the stubborn Gerow persisted in attempting to present these unpleasant realities to a George Marshall just as determined to ignore them. MacArthur assured Washington that he would soon have 200,000 well-trained men in the field. Nonsense, said Gerow, who more realistically estimated that MacArthur could only mobilize 76,000 Filipino reservists. In fact these reservists had not only not yet been called up, but in most cases had never received even the five-and-a-half-month basic training theoretically required for each new group inducted into the reserves. Too many enlistees, as it turned out, had never even fired a rifle. Gerow told Marshall that, including U.S. forces, MacArthur could count on only 101,550 men by August 1, 1941—just one half the number claimed by Douglas MacArthur.[17]

After MacArthur finally, if reluctantly, conceded the "wide scope of enemy operations" in the Far East, "especially in aviation," he nevertheless continued to assure Marshall that "the strength and composition of the defense forces here are believed to be sufficient" to carry out their mission of protecting the entire Philippine Archipelago. MacArthur even dismissed George Marshall's offer of an additional American division now, reporting instead that his Philippine defense plans were "progressing by leaps and bounds," and would certainly be ready by April 1, 1942.[18]

What he did need from Washington, MacArthur stressed, were arms, munitions, modern antiaircraft guns, radar, communications equipment, and above all, warplanes with which to attack potential Japanese landing fleets as well as crucial air bases, located chiefly on Formosa (now Taiwan).

In fact Major General Lewis Brereton, who had just arrived at Manila on November 3 to head the U.S. Air Force there at MacArthur's express request, already had 74 heavy and medium bombers and 175 pursuit planes (including 107 Curtiss P-40Es), which should have been able to discourage any Japanese landings. Yet when the day came for those very landings, MacArthur would tell President Quezon that he had been doubtful about the entire beach defense scheme, even though it was MacArthur who had devised and promulgated the plan accepted by Washington.[19]

As usual, Douglas MacArthur gave so many contradictory explanations of his actions and plans that he managed to cover himself under any eventuality. For instance, he later commented, "My orders were explicit not to initiate hostilities against the Japanese. . . . While I personally had not the slightest doubt we would be attacked, great local hopes existed that that would not be the case. . . . [A]s a matter of fact, I had for safety reasons ordered the bombers to withdraw from Luzon." Conversely, Brereton requested authorization from MacArthur's GHQ that in the event of war, his bombers could strike at Formosa. MacArthur denied that Brereton ever made such a request. "Had such a suggestion been made to me, I would have unequivocally disapproved," he asserted firmly after the war.[20]

When blistering defeat came, MacArthur praised Brereton but viciously attacked the U.S. Navy. The whole debacle was the fault, he claimed, of Hart and CNO King. "Admiral Thomas C. Hart . . . was certain that the islands were doomed and made no effort to keep open our lines of supply" and later "withdrew the bulk of his forces to the Dutch East Indies."[21]

In reality, on October 27 Admiral Tom Hart had specifically requested that Washington permit him to allow his miniature Asiatic Fleet to remain in Manila Bay to protect the country and MacArthur's forces, a request that was rejected by Frank Knox on November 20, when he ordered Hart to depart.[22] The "bulk of his forces" comprising only one heavy cruiser (*Houston*) and two light cruisers escorted by thirteen vintage destroyers and twenty-seven submarines of all classes, Hart's "Asiatic Fleet" was simply considered too vulnerable. It was certainly incapable of either preventing a major Japanese naval and air force from approaching Philippine shores or even of protecting itself, since carrier air cover was nonexistent. On the other hand, it was hoped that a large number of operational submarines, widely dispersed, could prove of some use. MacArthur would lament in his memoirs that under the provisions of Rainbow 5, which was still in effect, the navy was to have ensured "that our supply lines—the sea lanes, should be kept open. . . . The Pacific Fleet would then move in with massive force, escorting relieving ground troops. The Navy, being unable to maintain our supply lines, deprived us of the maintenance, the munitions, the bombs and fuel and other necessities to operate our air arm." MacArthur's criticisms did not end there. "Although Admiral King felt that the fleet did not have sufficient resources to proceed to Manila, it was my impression that our Navy deprecated its own strength and might well have cut through to relieve our hard-pressed forces. The Japanese blockade of the Philippines was to some extent a paper blockade. . . . There was a great reservoir of allied naval power in the Atlantic Ocean and the Mediterranean Sea," he persisted. "*A serious naval effort might well have saved the Philippines, and stopped the Japanese drive to the south and east.*"[23] And MacArthur was not yet finished. "With only a minor threat from the fleet of Germany and Italy, the American and British navies can assemble without serious jeopardy to make this thrust." For, as he put it, "the lines of weakness from time immemorial have been the lines of communication," and since the Japanese naval line "is not defended by enemy bombers," and what was more was held only "by scattered naval elements," then a major American naval attack would "immediately relieve the pressure on the south and is the only way that pressure can be relieved." But in the final analysis, MacArthur conceded, the United States could not win in the Far East without "the building up of air supremacy," a factor that outweighed the naval element.[24]

First it was the fault of the navy and its lack of presence; then, in the final analysis, it was not the navy upon which victory depended but "air supremacy." What emerges most from these conflicting comments by Douglas MacArthur is that he disagreed with the Combined Chiefs of Staff (British and American) and the priorities of the war established back in August 1941 between Roosevelt and Churchill. These priorities were reiterated in the Arcadia, or First Washington Conference, which began in late December 1941 and stipulated the defeat of Germany as the number-one goal of the war, leaving the campaign in the

Pacific as, at best, an early holding campaign. At this stage, there simply were neither men nor matériel to conduct two major military campaigns simultaneously in both Europe and the Pacific.

George Marshall went out of his way to apologize for General MacArthur's miscomprehension of the situation to Field Marshal Sir John Dill. "The measures General MacArthur advocates would be highly desirable if we were at war with Japan only. In our opinion the Pacific should not be made the principal theatre."[25] In fact, MacArthur's earlier remark about the German and Italian navies providing only a "minor threat" to the British and Americans in the Atlantic and Mediterranean revealed appalling judgment and an astonishing inability to grasp the war's major issues on a global scale. For example, in the Mediterranean alone, the Royal Navy was fighting for its life on a daily basis, as it attempted to escort convoys of supplies to Malta, Alexandria, and the Eighth Army.[26] The toll that Germany's U-boats exacted on the British merchant marine was frightening, with some 568 ships totaling 3,116,703 gross tons lost just during the first six months of 1942.[27] This figure excluded warships sunk by the Germans. (From the Japanese attack on the Philippines until May, German U-boats sank some 206 ships just off the East Coast alone.)[28] MacArthur's version of events revealed a grave, indeed frightening distortion of facts, one not expected of a competent, unusually well-read military commander of his rank. Even his usual protector, fellow soldier George Marshall—who never particularly liked the arrogant MacArthur—was disturbed and embarrassed by MacArthur's lamentable mistakes, assertions, and fabrications. Marshall was to feel even more bitter when MacArthur's claim that he was prepared "for any eventuality" proved a painful fraud, one that was to cost many Filipino and American lives. And when later the Philippines had fallen and the Allies were fighting in New Guinea, MacArthur was to do it again, boasting to the press that he was personally leading the troops at Buna and Gona, whereas in reality he refused to leave the governor's comfortable residence at Port Moresby even once to witness a near disaster that was saved only at the last minute by the intervention of Major General Bob Eichelberger. Then, to rub salt in the wound, MacArthur ordered that a photo be taken of him and Eichelberger "at the front" in New Guinea, a photo actually shot at Eichelberger's training camp in Australia. These fabrications were all the more pathetic given the fact that Douglas MacArthur had been a superb commanding officer who feared absolutely nothing and had personally led his men into battle time and again in France during World War I. To a superb war record, the envy of any veteran, he had heaped lie upon lie, thereby defiling his own good name.

•

Nor for the most part was the staff with which MacArthur now surrounded himself any more reassuring. Dick Sutherland, who had replaced Dwight D. Eisenhower as MacArthur's chief aide in 1939, had good enough paper credentials. Of an old, distinguished family, he had graduated from Yale University, gained an army commission, and served in the AEF in France. He later attended Infantry School, and Command and General Staff School, but only met MacArthur for the first time while taking a course at the Army War College from 1932 to 1933. In 1938, MacArthur had selected Sutherland as Eisenhower's deputy chief of staff.

Initially MacArthur was pleased with his choice, describing Sutherland as "a real find. Concise, energetic and able, he has been invaluable in helping me clarify and crystallize the situation." But ultimately, MacArthur was the only person to appreciate Sutherland's difficult and arrogant qualities. By the time he reached the rank of major general, Sutherland had shown himself to be a power-hungry manipulator who prided himself on keeping senior army, naval, and air force officers waiting for long periods before permitting them to see him. MacArthur's future air force chief, George Kenney—who, more than any other individual on his staff apart from General Eichelberger, really won the army's war in the Far East—recalled an evening at Port Moresby with Sutherland and MacArthur when Sutherland talked "about the shortcomings of a democracy in time of war." There was, he said, "too much debating by Congress," and he felt that the president himself should settle the main issues. Kenney recalled, "In time of war he thought it might even be advisable to stop having elections," to which Douglas MacArthur blandly replied, "The trouble with you Dick, I am afraid, is you are a natural-born autocrat."[29] (This was something, coming from the greatest natural-born autocrat of them all.) Sutherland's wish to suppress Congress altogether and instead have one-man rule did not appear to disturb MacArthur. Any other senior commander would no doubt have been deeply troubled by such a mentality. General Robert Eichelberger, MacArthur's finest field commander, who was handed only the most difficult of assignments, had known Sutherland back at Fort Leavenworth and as a general staff officer in Washington. Now obliged to work closely with him under MacArthur, Eichelberger concluded privately to his wife, "Miss Em" (after whom he would entitle his memoirs), that Sutherland "is one person out here . . . that I will never trust until the day he dies." Eichelberger went on to say that Sutherland treated him "more like a lieutenant than a lieutenant-general," and that he went out of his way to render life for Eichelberger as disagreeable as possible. "He is the type that will cheerfully cut our throats if it will present him any advantages," Eichelberger concluded. "A fly may not know when its wings are being pulled off, but I did."[30]

Sutherland continued to cast a long, gloomy shadow over MacArthur's general headquarters throughout the war. He was responsible for intimidating Brereton during the critical first days in the Philippines after Clark and Iba air fields were destroyed. But when Sutherland later tried the same thing on Brereton's successor, the much tougher, thicker-skinned George Kenney, sparks flew. Kenney later observed that Sutherland "always rubbed people the wrong way . . . an unfortunate bit of arrogance combined with his egotism had made him almost universally disliked."[31]

With one or two exceptions, such as his affable and diligent (but somewhat subservient) supply officer, Colonel Jim Collier, MacArthur surrounded himself with very difficult staff members. General Charles Willoughby, a local lawyer who was in charge of G-2, Army Intelligence, was described as "a handsome man with a Roman profile." Close to MacArthur and a hard worker, he was nevertheless limited by "a difficult temper . . ." and a "brittle . . . personality"—in brief "an aloof, 'hard man' " who in combination with the equally brittle Sutherland gradually sowed seeds of discord among MacArthur's staff. This resulted in an ambiance hardly conducive to victory. As Bob Eichelberger put it, "One could see the play of personalities and the lack of broad vision," a crippling deficiency attributable largely to Sutherland.[32]

It is hardly surprising that given this background there were divided feelings at MacArthur's GHQ as to how to proceed in the Far East. Initially, MacArthur's forces were to have followed WPO-3 (Rainbow 5) and withdrawn back into a well-fortified and prepared Bataan Peninsula, and later to Corregidor. But by mid-November 1941 the old Plan Orange had been discarded by MacArthur in favor of a forceful "offensive" attack on the beaches and at enemy air bases—an idea strongly opposed by Sutherland. Any change of plan naturally affected logistics and supplies in particular, and MacArthur's G-3, Jim Collier, was to suffer agonies as a result, as he tried valiantly to follow the changing objectives when a clash did occur. With George Marshall's blessing, however, MacArthur would be able to put his own new plan into effect: to stop an enemy invasion on the beaches. But when the prudent Collier protested that it might be a good idea to maintain some substantial defenses and reserves of provisions on Bataan, just in case, MacArthur replied with a curt, "Oh, no!" And that was that, because Collier, like most others, was afraid of what Bob Eichelberger called "the big chief." Therefore there were to be no major depots of food and munitions on Bataan, nor were there any fortifications there.[33]

Ironically, later, on December 23, 1941, Douglas MacArthur was to decide to change horses yet again in midstream and to revert to WPO-3 after all. But by then it was too late—far too late.

●

During the last weeks of peace in the Philippines, there were obvious signs that senior leaders were ill at ease. The ailing President Quezon, suffering from an advanced case of tuberculosis, was vacillating once again, now warning students at the University of the Philippines that Japanese "bombs may be falling on this campus soon."[34] If many of the students sniggered at such an idea, their attitude reflected the times. The frustrated U.S. High Commissioner to Manila, Francis B. Sayre, found "uncertainty and considerable confusion on the part of the general public" when he requested the elementary step of taking civil defense measures, and he received little cooperation even among educated Filipinos.[35] Curiously, much of the public, Americans in particular—whether civilian or military—lacked real concern over the impending war; the most important event for many seemed to be the latest film or the next party. The MacArthurs themselves were keen cinema aficionados.

On the other hand, American and British pilots over a wide area reported much increased Japanese naval air and sea activity in the South China Sea, heading south and west, and on December 2, 1941, a brazen Japanese reconnaissance plane was even spotted directly over Clark Field in Luzon. Major General Brereton was anxious enough to call for nightly fighter patrols over northern Luzon, effective December 4. They in turn reported even more Japanese aircraft over the coast that night, and the next two as well, but these fled when challenged by U.S. warplanes, and nothing further was done about them. Clearly they did not signify.

Back on November 27, MacArthur had received George Marshall's "war warning," and of course had access as well to the Purple intercepts regarding the deteriorating diplomatic situation between Tokyo and Washington. He was to do nothing, however, until December 6, when he increased the twenty-four-hour guard around all airfields. According to Charles Willoughby, MacArthur's chief of intelligence, "There was no sense of urgency in preparing for a Japanese air attack." Japanese bombers, he insisted, lacked the range to reach Luzon from their large air bases on Formosa, less than six hundred miles away. And yet where, then, did these recent sightings off the Philippine coast come from? Furthermore, it was well known that the Japanese had been using with devastating effectiveness their Mitsubishi twin-engine, 230mph G3M (type 96 "Nell") land-based bomber, capable of carrying an 800-kilo bombload (or single torpedo) and protected by three machine guns. The bomber was designed to operate over a distance of 2,300 miles, which meant, Mitsubishi assured the high command, that it could reach Manila on two round trips without refueling. That same company's G4M (type 1, "Betty") was almost equally effective for long-range land-based bombing. In addition, by 1938 the Japanese navy had put into service the four-engine land-based Kawanishi H6K (type 92, "Mavis") bomber, which had a range of 2,200 miles. "By the eve of the Pacific War," as Clayton James puts it, "these aircraft constituted as a group some of the most advanced aviation technology in the world."[36] But intelligence chief Charles Willoughby seemed unaware of their existence, thereby giving MacArthur inaccurate information about the true threat from the skies. And yet the ruthless effectiveness of attacks by various types of Japanese land-based bombers over China had been thoroughly documented for some years now. Why were the well-read MacArthur and his G-2 staff so ignorant of these basic factors, reported commonly enough in the world press?

MacArthur had boasted to John Hersey of his military strength in the Philippines, asserting that there was little to worry about and that American, British, and Dutch forces were handily prepared to subdue Japan in the Pacific. (This was of course before the attack on Pearl Harbor.) Furthermore, MacArthur had assured Quezon, "we pose no threat to them," and even FDR, a seasoned politician and military realist, firmly believed that Tokyo would not be so foolish as to attack the United States or Great Britain. Japan already had more than enough with which to cope on two major fronts: in Manchuria, facing the unpredictable Russians, and in China. Japan lacked American gasoline, raw materials, and, above all, the large-scale technical industry required to wage a long, victorious war. Thus Roosevelt reasoned that the Japanese would avoid hitting the Philippines; on the other hand, he realized that because of the large-scale military move into southern Indochina, Tokyo would have the ideal springboard from which to strike at the Netherlands East Indies, where it could acquire essential sources of gasoline and oil in Borneo, Java, and Sumatra, enough to replace the loss of its American source. As the United States and Britain were allies of the Dutch, they then would inevitably be drawn into the conflict, and the war would begin for them in the Far East. Roosevelt always thought as a professional sailor would, and he knew that without an assured source of fuel the Japanese navy was powerless. Logic seemed to dictate that Tokyo *would* begin the war in the Far East, for in that respect at least the Japanese were a very practical people. But like the Soviets, they were not always predictable: on this almost all the American and British experts agreed.

●

By November 1941, even the dubious MacArthur had come around to the possibility of fresh Japanese attacks in the western Pacific, which could include the Philippines. Japan continued to build new airfields on nearby Formosa and other islands, threatening Manila more and more. But MacArthur insisted that if any attack were to occur, it could not possibly come before the following April, given the rains and foul weather. Although he did not have the forces to hold even Luzon and Mindanao, MacArthur stressed America's obligation to protect the entire archipelago of thousands of islands. That would require a large navy of carriers, battleships, and cruisers, artillery, and trained troops, all of which he lacked, public bravado and private assurances to Washington to the contrary. With the Philippines secured, the Japanese could easily control the whole of the South China Sea, Malaya, British and Dutch Borneo, the Celebes, Singapore, Burma, and Hong Kong. The list seemed endless, and indeed it was.[37]

MacArthur waited until the end of November before finally deciding to divide the Philippines into "a number of major commands." Jonathan Wainwright would be given the toughest job, commanding the North Luzon Force, including Lingayen Gulf where the largest invasion forces would be expected to land; Brigadier General Albert Jones was to head the South Luzon Force, from Batangas to Legaspi; General Bradford Chynoweth was responsible for the Visayan Force, including the central island group; William Sharpe was given command of the important island of Mindanao. George Moore was placed in charge of Corregidor; Major General Ed King would command the artillery; and Major General Lewis Brereton the air force. "My staff," boasted MacArthur, "was unsurpassed in excellence," pointing to the "outstanding" Sutherland as chief of staff, Charles Willoughby in charge of intelligence, Dick Marshall heading supplies, Spencer Aikin in communications, and Fred Marquat overseeing the rest of the artillery. "No command was ever better served," MacArthur later declared.[38]

●

Prior to taking his new command over the North Luzon Force at Fort Stotsenburg on December 3, 1941, the fifty-eight-year-old cavalry officer Jonathan "Skinny" Wainwright had instructed General Ed King to set up a staff for him and have everything ready so that operations could begin immediately. "I discovered on my arrival at Fort Stotsenburg that afternoon that . . . the headquarters of the North Luzon Force was [in reality] just about nil. All I had to start with were King's post adjutant . . . a supply man, and a surgeon." King had not only failed to follow orders and set up Wainwright's staff, but "we got practically no transportation for any purposes; hardly a truck, hardly a car," he recalled.[39] Nor was there much in the way of "artillery," especially antiaircraft guns. All 108 tanks in the Philippines serving on Luzon were kept out of Wainwright's hands and left instead directly under the supervision of MacArthur himself, which, like "his" air force, could not be deployed without his approval. Later on, when Wainwright desperately needed dozens of those tanks, MacArthur agreed to send him five. But it was his officers and the troops of the Philippine army that General Wainwright was really depending upon, and what he further discovered now shocked him as nothing else had so far.

In theory, the 31st Division's Engineer Battalion had been mobilized on October 1, its 2nd Infantry Regiment on November 1, its 3rd Infantry Regiment only on November 25. "The majority of its artillery . . . was mobilized after December 8," reported Wainwright. What little artillery was available consisted of British 75mm's and 2.95-inch mountain howitzers—all decades obsolete, as was their by now defective ammunition.

The position of the 71st and 91st divisions was hardly better: both of them were grossly undermanned, with a large portion of the reservists called up never appearing. Moreover, according to Wainwright, "American Army officers were completely frustrated in their desperate efforts to make combat troops overnight out of recently mobilized Filipinos. . . ." None of Wainwright's divisions had an antitank battalion, transportation, or even the most elementary signals communication equipment, such as radios. Men in the field were unable to communicate or coordinate their efforts. In consequence, "the only means of communication with the various divisions was through means of the public telephone lines." In addition, ammunition was in short supply, with low numbers of infantry mortar shells, .50-caliber machine-gun ammo, and even hand grenades.[40] Few men had completed their five-and-a-half-month basic training course (later reduced to three), and most were led by "extremely inexperienced Filipino officers. What I am saying is this," Wainwright summed up: "The Philippine Army Units with the North Luzon force were doomed before they started to fight. That they lasted as long as they did is a stirring and touching tribute to their gallantry and fortitude. They never had a chance to win." Even as late as December 9, 1941, "all five of my divisions were still mobilizing."[41]

On November 21, "upon the recommendation of General Brereton," according to MacArthur, the B-17 Bombardment Group was to be moved from the vulnerable Clark Field, just sixty-five miles from Manila, to the nearly completed Delmonte Field on the southern island of Mindanao. But only half the bombers went there. "I never learned why these orders were not promptly implemented," MacArthur later commented. His statement—"my orders from Washington were not to initiate hostilities against the Japanese under any circumstances"—was in fact a deliberate distortion of the orders he had received. "There was apparently some hope that the somewhat indeterminate international position of the [Philippine] commonwealth might eliminate it from attack," MacArthur insisted, clinging to straws. George Marshall, on the other hand, made no such pretense that the islands were not high on the Tokyo hit list, given past and recent Japanese military action in the region.

By the night of December 4, American night air patrols began encountering numerous Japanese reconnaissance planes "from 20 to 90 miles" off the Philippine coast. "Whatever might come, we were as ready as we possibly would be in our inadequate defences" on the night of December 7, MacArthur would backtrack many years later. "Every disposition had been made, every man, gun and plane was on the alert"; but as the historical record and the general's own commanders later testified, this was utter nonsense.[42]

●

"The sparkle went out of Manila in the spring of 1941. War was coming and we knew it," Wainwright recalled.[43] On December 6 (in Manila), 1941, that general was still attempting to bring a semblance of order to the forces he had just inherited at Stotsenburg. That day, MacArthur's GHQ rang him, ordering him to have his troops ready to move promptly to their beach defenses. Wainwright said that he would move right out. "Oh, that much rush isn't necessary," MacArthur told him.[44]

After meeting with the two air corps squadron commanders who had recently arrived with a flight of thirty-five B-17s, Wainwright held an inspection of the troops MacArthur had assigned him at Stotsenburg, whose mission was to protect adjacent Clark Air Field. These included the 26th Cavalry (838 officers and men on horseback), a battery of the 23rd Field Artillery, and one pack train. This was the extent of the units available, despite orders to be on the alert also against possible sabotage. With this Wainwright was expected to protect the largest and most important airfield in the Philippines. In fact, Wainwright was further given only four Filipino divisions, 28,000 men in all (far below effective numbers) with which to cover the whole of northern Luzon, from its northernmost headland and airfield to its beaches—hundreds of square miles.

And yet MacArthur had earlier declined the offer of an additional U.S. division by Washington. MacArthur's imaginary eleven or twelve divisions and "200,000 men" were numbers on paper only. "The strength and composition of the defense forces projected here, are believed to be sufficient to accomplish such a mission," MacArthur had assured Marshall. In light of these assurances, by October 18 the chief of staff had agreed to drop the WPO-3 in favor of a strong offensive force promised by MacArthur. The mighty force he had promised was nowhere in sight even by December 9.

MacArthur also had the 91st American Division, or U.S. Harbor Defense Division (a part of his own private strategic reserve), which included a few hundred marines just transferred from Shanghai to Manila in the first week of December. This gave him a total of 16,634 American troops in the Philippines, including 4,940 air corps personnel and 3,452 service departments (quartermaster, medical, and financial units); in addition he had 11,957 American-trained and -equipped Philippine Scouts.[45]

General Wainwright went to bed on Sunday, December 7, at 2300, just as a big party given at the Manila Hotel in honor of the new air force chief, Lew Brereton, was getting underway. If the loud voices and blaring band disturbed the unflappable Douglas MacArthur and his young family in the penthouse above, nothing was said. Sixty-five miles away at Fort Stotsenburg, all was quiet; as Wainwright put it, "it was the last decent sleep I was to have for three years and eight months."[46] At 0140 Monday, December 8 (Manila time, still December 7 at Pearl Harbor), Japanese naval and air forces struck at Kota Bharu in British Malaya; at 0305 they hit Singo in nearby Singora, Thailand; at 0600 they attacked Hong Kong by air. Ten minutes later they attacked Singapore at the southern tip of Malaya, and at 0900 Hong Kong was hit again in a wave that included Wake Island and the Philippines.[47]

Lieutenant Colonel William Clement, the duty officer at the U.S. Asiatic Fleet headquarters in the Marsman Building in Manila, received a radio message from Pearl Harbor at 0230 stating that the base was under attack. After confirming this, Clement rang Admiral Tom Hart at 0300: "Admiral, put some cold water on your face. I am coming over with a message: 'Air Raid on Pearl Harbor. This is no drill.'" Hart immediately radioed the fleet: "Japan started hostilities. Govern yourselves accordingly," and at the same time sent Captain Bill Purnell over to inform Dick Sutherland.[48]

At 0435 December 8 (0735, Sunday the 7th at Pearl Harbor), Colonel Peter Irwin, MacArthur's assistant chief of staff for operations, told MacArthur that Admiral Hart had informed him of Japan's having initiated hostilities in Hawaii.[49] At 0500 General Brereton rushed over to MacArthur's GHQ in Manila, but was denied access to him by Sutherland.* Sutherland also denied Brereton authorization to launch an early morning strike against Japanese air bases in Formosa in retaliation. At 0540 MacArthur was finally notified officially by Washington that hostilities had begun and that he was to execute Rainbow 5.[50] At 0714, a by now most anxious Lewis Brereton again returned to MacArthur's headquarters, only to be turned away again by a brusque Sutherland. MacArthur was too busy to see him, he said. "I know nothing of any interview with Sutherland, and Brereton never at any time recommended or suggested an attack to me," Douglas MacArthur said after the war—yet another falsehood.[51] In fact it was incumbent upon Commanding General Douglas MacArthur—who was previously so emphatic about the key role of the air defense—to have called the earliest possible meeting with Brereton to give him the necessary orders required when under attack. MacArthur made no such attempt. What is more, he knew that Brereton could not attack Formosa or even the Japanese over the Philippines without his, MacArthur's, express authorization. MacArthur had already made it clear that no one acted without his approval.

At 0730, General Hap Arnold rang Brereton from California and tried, in Arnold's words, "to give him some idea of what had happened

*MacArthur's exact whereabouts are unknown; his wife claimed he was at home reading his father's Bible.

at Pearl Harbor, so that he would not be caught the same way and his entire air force destroyed. He explained to me what he was trying to do. . . ."[52] Brereton's B-17s, already fueled, took off by 0800—without bombs—in order to avoid repeating the Hawaii disaster. Tokyo had in fact scheduled the bombing of the Philippines hours earlier, but dense fog had prevented their bombers and fighters on Formosa from taking off.[53]

At 0855, MacArthur's Manila headquarters informed Wainwright of a potential attack at Baguio, just ninety-five miles from Stotsenburg, and alerted him to the possibility of enemy paratroopers landing to attempt to seize Clark Air Field. Unfortunately, as General Wainwright reminded headquarters, "I had no infantry available"—MacArthur had failed to provide him with any. Instead, he called upon the only force available, Colonel Clinton Pierce's 26th horse-mounted, saber-bearing cavalry, to guard the perimeter of the adjacent airfield. Not much had changed since the American Civil War.[54] Japanese parachutists with machine guns blazing could have liquidated Pierce's horses and troops before they even touched ground. Five minutes after the call from Manila, Japanese warplanes sighted over Lingayen Gulf altered direction, swinging abruptly eastward to bomb and strafe Tuguegarao and Baguio at 0930. They encountered no American opposition in the air. Far out over the Pacific, another squadron of Japanese bombers was simultaneously striking Wake Island.[55]

While Brereton's bombless bombers* were circling high above Clark, Brereton, still having received no reply from MacArthur, made a third attempt to reach him. At 1000, he "personally called Sutherland and informed him . . . that if Clark Field was attacked successfully, we would be unable to operate offensively." The need for action was imperative. But he was informed that MacArthur, still unavailable, was again denying Brereton permission to bomb Japanese airfields at Formosa. Ten minutes later, Colonel Burbank rang from Sutherland's office authorizing the bombers instead to conduct a photographic reconnaissance mission over southern Formosa.[56] Japanese planes were bombing Pearl Harbor, Hong Kong, Singapore, Malaya, the Philippines, and Wake Island, and MacArthur's chief of staff was authorizing a

*MacArthur refused to authorize the loading of bombs.

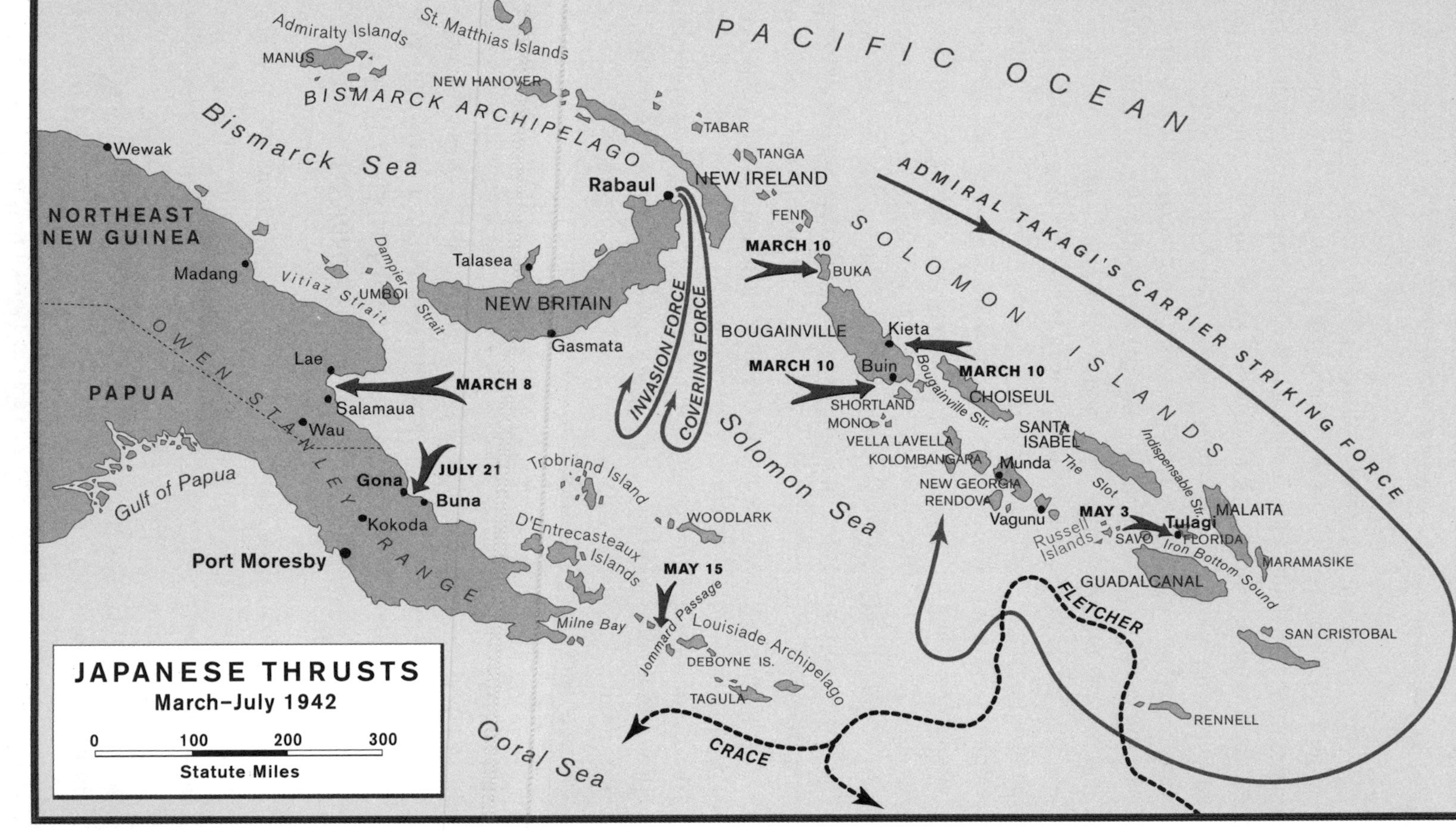
JAPANESE THRUSTS
March–July 1942
0
100
200
300
Statute Miles
PACIFIC OCEAN
Admiralty Islands
MANUS
St. Matthias Islands
NEW HANOVER
BISMARCK ARCHIPELAGO
Bismarck Sea
Wewak
NORTHEAST NEW GUINEA
Madang
Vitiaz Strait
UMBOI
Dampier Strait
Talasea
NEW BRITAIN
Gasmata
Rabaul
TABAR
TANGA
NEW IRELAND
FENI
MARCH 10
BUKA
SOLOMON ISLANDS
ADMIRAL TAKAGI'S CARRIER STRIKING FORCE
INVASION FORCE
COVERING FORCE
BOUGAINVILLE
Kieta
MARCH 10
Buin
MARCH 10
CHOISEUL
Bougainville Str.
SHORTLAND
MONO
VELLA LAVELLA
KOLOMBANGARA
NEW GEORGIA
RENDOVA
Munda
Vagunu
SANTA ISABEL
The Slot
Indispensable Str.
MALAITA
MAY 3
Tulagi
FLORIDA
SAVO
Russell Islands
Iron Bottom Sound
MARAMASIKE
GUADALCANAL
FLETCHER
SAN CRISTOBAL
RENNELL
PAPUA
OWEN STANLEY RANGE
Lae
Salamaua
MARCH 8
Wau
Gona
JULY 21
Buna
Kokoda
Port Moresby
Gulf of Papua
Trobriand Island
D'Entrecasteaux Islands
WOODLARK
Solomon Sea
MAY 15
Milne Bay
Jommard Passage
Louisiade Archipelago
DEBOYNE IS.
TAGULA
Coral Sea
CRACE

now frantic Brereton to take photos of the enemy instead of attacking them. But for over eight hours after receiving news of the attack on Hawaii, Brereton did not hear one word from MacArthur himself.

By 1015 the fog was beginning to clear enough over Formosa to permit Japan's first major squadrons—108 twin-engine bombers escorted by 84 Zeroes—to take off for the Philippines' more important targets. The planes were sighted over Nielson Field at 1130 while most of Brereton's bombers and fighters were landing to refuel at Clark, leaving the airfield completely without air cover. At 1045 Sutherland phoned Brereton, finally authorizing the bombing of Formosa with two heavy bomber squadrons "at the latest daylight hour today that visibility will permit." Several hours earlier, Brereton had requested just such a maneuver, but had wanted it started *before dawn* on December 8. Sutherland, the soldier, was instructing the chief of the air force how to run his operation. To confuse matters further, MacArthur radioed George Marshall in Washington that same day, saying: "I am launching a heavy bombardment [to] counterattack *tomorrow morning* on enemy airdromes in south Formosa."[57] No doubt Brereton was beginning to think he was living in the world of the Mad Hatter. (The next day MacArthur again radioed Washington, informing George Marshall that he had changed his mind and was canceling his air attack over Formosa after all.)[58] What was happening at MacArthur's headquarters, and why did he refuse to see and consult with his air force chief in the first place? Indeed, why did he refuse to permit the air force to arm and defend the Philippines?

But it was now too late . . . many hours too late. At 1145 Colonel Alexander Campbell, the air raid officer, sent a teletype to Clark Field warning Brereton of imminent attack. That message was never received. When Campbell made another attempt, he failed again. The radio operator had apparently left his post unattended to go out for an early lunch. Campbell did not try to telephone, despite the gravity of the situation.

Meanwhile Brereton had taken the necessary measures to provide what fighter protection he could. Colonel Harold George at Nielson Field was ordered to send up the 34th Squadron to cover Clark Field and the 17th to protect the Bataan Peninsula, while the 21st covered Manila. The 3rd Squadron at Iba was dispatched over the South China

Sea to meet a reported enemy formation—in vain, as it turned out, for it was a false report, of which there was no shortage.[59] At Clark, the squadron of new B-17s and the 20th Pursuit Squadron were being refueled, unaware of any impending danger. At about 1145, pilots were ordered to go aloft once their planes had been serviced. This had been completed by 1215, just as the first air-raid sirens sounded and the first formation of Japanese bombers droned overhead, dropping their lethal loads on the parked B-17s, P-40s, and the buildings below. Although pilots rushed out to their planes, only three P-40 fighters managed to get off the ground. It is unclear why Brereton had not staggered the fueling—which would have permitted him to keep a squadron of air cover constantly over his field—instead of bringing all the planes down at the same time. The squadron of P-35s at Del Carmen Field, grounded until now by a heavy dust storm, finally took off; but they were also too late.

Fighters on the ground at Iba Air Field were likewise caught off guard, with all but two of the 3rd Squadron's pursuit planes destroyed where they were parked. Iba, like Clark, lacked all but the most elementary antiaircraft batteries, while General King's 200th Coast Artillery was also proving next to useless against the incoming waves of enemy planes. Five out of every six shells of his ancient 3-inch guns failed to explode due to rotten fuses. Thus Japanese bombers and fighters swept in, practically unchallenged, destroying fuel dumps, communications towers, hangars, repair shops, and even more planes.[60]

At the end of just the first day of the war in the Philippines, the disappearance of Douglas MacArthur—which has yet to be explained to this day—and his refusal to meet with his air chief led to the destruction of seventeen of Brereton's thirty-five B-17s, the remainder of which were sent south to the new field at Del Monte. Fifty-three of his P-40s and three P-35s had also been destroyed—most of them, like the bombers, on the ground—along with another 25 miscellaneous planes and 250 lighter aircraft. Both Clark and Iba fields lay in ruins, their planes wrecked and burning or damaged beyond repair, the airfields pitted with craters. Most of their ground facilities were put out of commission. The Japanese lost a mere seven fighters that day.

Admiral Hart's Asiatic Fleet (or Task Force 5), too, would have been destroyed for lack of air cover and sufficient firepower had he not earlier been ordered by Washington to dispatch his flagship, the heavy cruiser *Houston*, to Iloilo, the light cruiser *Boise* to Cebu, and another light cruiser, *Marblehead*, to Balikpapan along with five destroyers and a tender[61] His only ship to come under fire, the tender *Preston* at Davao, successfully escaped and put to sea that night. Admiral Ernie King then ordered Hart's "fleet" to Dutch Borneo to refuel and combine forces with the Dutch and British, where Admiral Karel Doorman was preparing to challenge the Japanese navy.

Of what remained of the American fleet in the Manila area, three destroyers were on patrol and two others under repair at Cavite, as were three of the twenty-seven American submarines. Naval Patrol Wing 10, comprising twenty-eight twin-engine patrol bombers (PBYs) and five smaller planes, was stationed at Sangley Point, Cavite, Panay, and Olongapo. Despite a long series of unpleasant arguments with MacArthur, Hart, whom the historian Samuel Eliot Morison described as a "small, taut, wiry and irascible . . . strict disciplinarian," refused to abandon MacArthur or leave his Naval Headquarters in the Marsman Building, in Manila, until the very last minute. He remained loyal to the end in spite of MacArthur's string of abusive taunts about his "useless navy." When he did at last put to sea, he left Rear Admiral Frank Rockwell, of the 16th Naval District, in command with the remaining half-dozen PT-boats, three gunboats, and some submarines that were deployed in those waters . . . after having first mined both Manila and Subic bays.[62]

The heavy Japanese naval air attacks of December 8 continued unabated on the 9th. These, which included the bombing of Nichols Field near Manila, forced MacArthur to inform Chief of Staff Marshall that due to the destruction of his B-17s at Clark and most of his P-40s at various bases, he was canceling his plans to raid Formosa.

This bewildering news from Manila, given the early warning MacArthur had received from Pearl Harbor, left George Marshall in a state of dismay and disbelief. While still publicly lauding Douglas MacArthur, saying that "the resolute and effective fight of your men, air and ground has made a tremendous impression on the American people and confirms our confidence in your leadership," privately Marshall confided to General John Pershing, "I just don't know how MacArthur happened to let his planes get caught on the ground."[63] General Claire Chennault of the Flying Tigers and Air Force Chief Hap Arnold were equally shocked and dismayed. And yet even more astonishingly, MacArthur later was to deny this entire sequence of events in his *Reminiscences*, in spite of the fact that solid documentation proved he had refused even to speak to Brereton for many hours but then had sent orders to Marshall informing him of his intention to bombard Formosa.

For a figure such as Douglas MacArthur, renowned for his decisiveness and the clarity of his prose, almost all of his actions on the 8th and the days to follow—including his muddled orders concerning Brereton's B-17s—remain mystifying and contradictory. Air attacks originating from Formosa, Palau, and elsewhere continued to intensify, unhindered for the most part by U.S. forces. Japanese planes destroyed all the air bases on Luzon, as well as many of the PBYs across the bay at Cavite, which did not stand a chance against the highly maneuverable Zeroes and dive-bombers that struck again in full force on December 10.

But the attack on the Philippines remained only one small part of a very complicated set of plans. On December 8 and 9, Japanese forces totaling nearly 150,000 men made amphibious landings on the Malay Peninsula, and at the same time another force occupied Bangkok, Thailand, and still another Arawa and Makin islands in the Gilberts. On the 10th, the Japanese military kept up the pressure, sinking two powerful British capital ships, the *Prince of Wales* and the *Repulse*; 840 officers and men were lost, including Admiral Sir Tom Phillips and Captain John Leach, who had courageously sailed around Africa and thence to the Far East without air protection[64] on the express orders of Winston Churchill (over the vigorous protests of the First Sea Lord).[65] Other Japanese bomber squadrons leveled the Cavite Naval Yard just south of Manila, and the adjacent airfield, rendering them an inferno that burned for days.

In northern Luzon, the Japanese navy began amphibious landings at Appari on December 10, followed the next day by further assaults at nearby Vigan. The 12th saw even more amphibious operations at Legaspi in southern Luzon. On the 14th, they began coming ashore at Tuguegarao. By the 18th, the Japanese army was also advancing on Hong Kong, where the British and Commonwealth forces were outnumbered and overwhelmed. On December 20, another Japanese amphibious force hit the port of Davao, on Mindanao, and then the nearby island of Jolo. But the major invasion of the Philippines began in earnest on December 22 at Lingayen, followed by a coordinated enemy army landing at Lamon Bay on the 24th, precisely as Kelly Turner had predicted back in 1929.

On the 23rd, Wake had fallen after a valiant fight, and by Christmas Eve, even as the supercilious Douglas MacArthur was abandoning Manila, Japanese bombers were continuing to blister Rangoon and elsewhere in Burma, and then Hong Kong finally surrendered on Christmas Day. On December 30, 1941, Japanese planes bombed Corregidor without respite. By January 10, 1942, enemy troops were already in control of several oil fields and refineries in Dutch Borneo, and the following day they at long last declared war on Holland. By January 15, General Homma Masaharu's 14th Army had forced General Wainwright's beleaguered and starving army to fall back to the undefended, unprovisioned wilderness of the Bataan Peninsula. Before the month of January was out, the Japanese were attacking Australian Rabaul and landing in the Solomons at Bougainville, in the Dutch Celebes, in New Guinea at Lae, and on Russell Island. In less than two months' time they had carried out a spectacular blitzkrieg that had made Germany's seizure of Western Europe look like a minor operation in comparison.

●

With the initial Japanese invasion of the Philippines at Appari and Legaspi, "the rat was in the house," as Jonathan Wainwright grimly put it, "and it was no comfort. I drove back [from Lingayen] to half wrecked Stotsenburg that night of December 12 to find that it had been rebombed during the day." On the 13th, "the Japs truly began to hit us [at Vigan] with a task force of warships and began unloading eighty-four jammed transports. That was the day I realized, for all time, the futility of trying to fight a war without an Air Force. . . . My orders from MacArthur were simple and to the point: 'In the event of a landing, attack and destroy the landing force,' but with what?" Wainwright asked.[66] Soon Homma Masaharu would have not only his initial 14th Army ashore (over 43,000 men) but ultimately a force of 250,000 men. (MacArthur had predicted that the Japanese would find it impossible to land even 100,000.)

The situation had indeed grown desperate by December 23, when

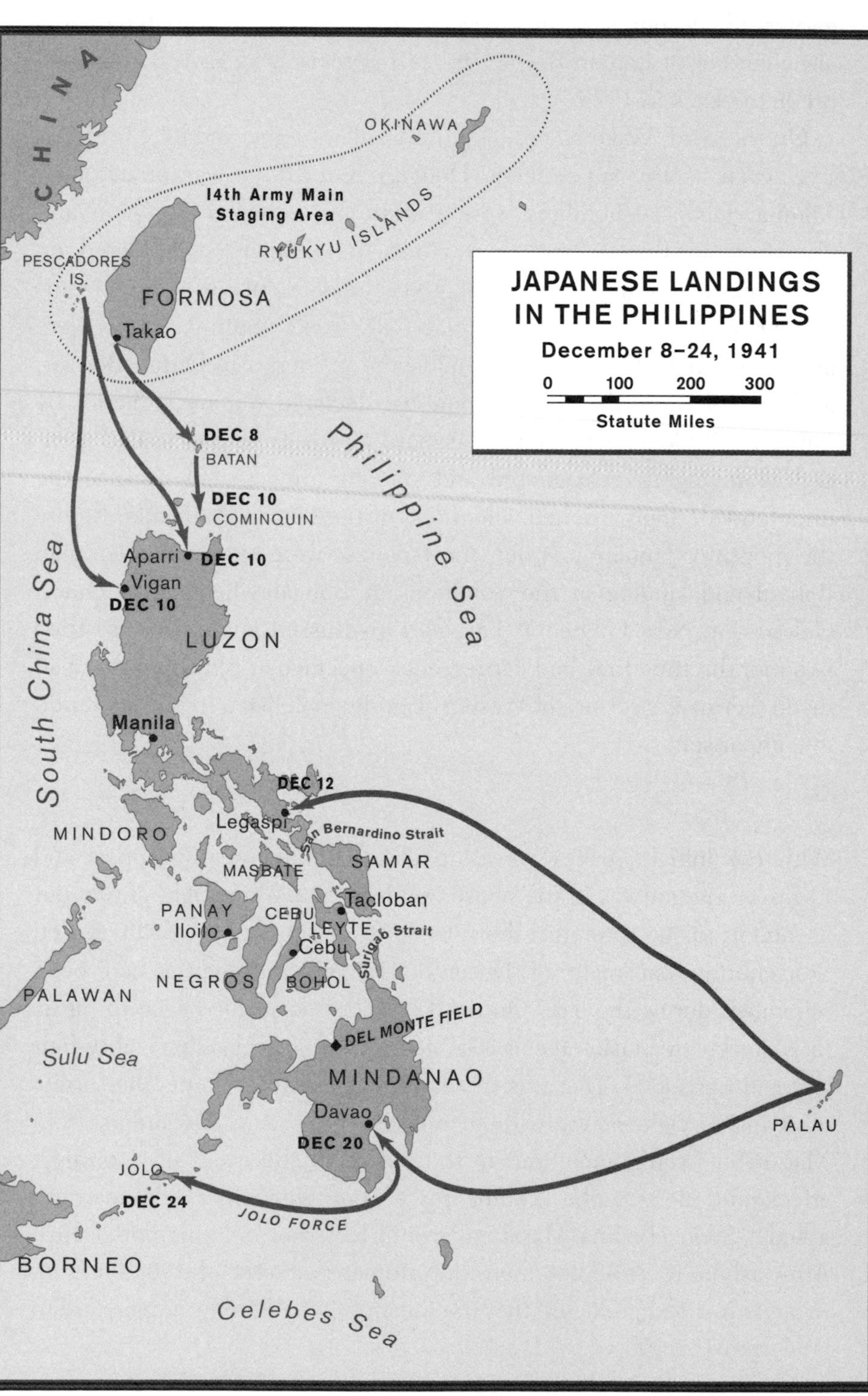
JAPANESE LANDINGS
IN THE PHILIPPINES
December 8–24, 1941
0 100 200 300
Statute Miles
CHINA
OKINAWA
14th Army Main
Staging Area
RYUKYU ISLANDS
PESCADORES
IS.
FORMOSA
Takao
DEC 8
BATAN
Philippine Sea
DEC 10
COMINQUIN
Aparri
DEC 10
Vigan
DEC 10
South China Sea
LUZON
Manila
DEC 12
Legaspi
San Bernardino Strait
MINDORO
SAMAR
MASBATE
Tacloban
PANAY
CEBU
Iloilo
LEYTE
Surigao Strait
Cebu
NEGROS
BOHOL
PALAWAN
DEL MONTE FIELD
Sulu Sea
MINDANAO
Davao
DEC 20
PALAU
JOLO
DEC 24
JOLO FORCE
BORNEO
Celebes Sea

Wainwright received a telephone call from MacArthur's headquarters. "It was Pete Irwin calling. 'WPO-3 is in effect,' Pete said. It was a bitter pill to swallow for War Plan Orange No. 3 meant the last ditch; the long-ago planned desperation withdrawal to Bataan."[67] He was ordered to hold off the major part of a well-equipped advancing Japanese army.

Upon reaching Bataan in the first week of January 1942, a shocked Colonel Glen Townsend discovered to his dismay that "no work was ever done on these positions," and the troops found themselves instead "in the raw jungle." Not only were fortifications, artillery, and munitions stores not in place, but there were also no medical facilities and no food depots. Because Douglas MacArthur had earlier refused to accept that WPO-3 would be implemented, no preparations had been made. The result was that as early as January 1942, MacArthur had to order Wainwright's army at Bataan on "half-ration," which meant 3.7 ounces of rice, 1.8 ounces of sugar, 1.2 ounces of tinned milk, and 2.44 ounces of tinned fish daily for each fighting man.[68] "Our food situation was growing rapidly worse," Squadron Leader Bill Dyess, a tall, quiet Texan, noted. "We are eating lizards, monkeys, and anything else that comes under our guns." The USAFFE surgeon officially reported that only 55 percent of the Bataan troops were "combat efficient" by February as a result of "debilities due to malaria, dysentery and general malnutrition," leaving even the few remaining pilots too weak to fly the two remaining P-40s.[69] Worse was to come. On March 2, over Wainwright's most vigorous protests, MacArthur would be ordering an even more drastic cut in rations for the men defending Bataan, down to three eighths of a regular ration. But in MacArthur's memoirs written after the war, he claimed: "Bataan itself was quickly organized for a protracted defense by the construction of depot areas." Furthermore, he insisted that he sent the men there enormous quantities of supplies: "Day and night, endless columns of motor transportation moved goods, ammunition, equipment, and medical supplies from Manila to Bataan." Alas, not a single survivor of Bataan ever saw any of those phantom depots or shipments.[70]

•

Yet ironically there was no shortage of food. For instance, "all the piers [at Manila] from 1 to 6 and the vacant lots there . . . were piled high with a conglomeration of cargo," Robert Levering, a civilian engineer working for USAFFE, later attested. Thousands of tons of supplies of all types were just waiting to be transported by some three hundred boats and barges across Manila Bay. Sutherland, however, refused to provide sufficient manpower to move them. And most of those supplies and munitions were never forwarded to Bataan, where the combined U.S.-Filipino army was making its last stand in delaying the advancing Japanese. Instead, MacArthur ordered these provisions to Corregidor, although the vast majority remained, untouched, ashore. Vacant lots at the Manila docks were left piled high with everything from "100-lb bags of wheat flour, to canned cherries," as a disbelieving Levering recalled. Because MacArthur in the final analysis refused to release these supplies, Wainwright and his men would soon be down to half-"Filipino" rations (less than those of the U.S. Army's definition of half-rations). The goods on the wharf of Manila were "now being looted right and left, and nobody seemed to care. Beggars and priests, children and wrinkled old men preyed on the heaps like flies on a dung hill."[71] Even after the war, MacArthur would provide no explanation for his puzzling actions, but the facts speak for themselves: men died of starvation on Bataan.

Another principal supply of food on Luzon, some 50 million bushels of rice, was stored in large sprawling warehouses at Cabanatuan, along with tons of sugar and tinned food. But Quezon, MacArthur, and General Sutherland adamantly forbade the distribution or confiscation of any of these provisions. As tank battalion commander Colonel Ernest Miller confirmed, there was enough food just at Cabanatuan "to have fed the troops on Bataan for almost a year." What was more, "a vast number of commercial trucks were available," not to mention military vehicles with which to transport this food to the troops in Bataan. But Quezon insisted that all this food be left for the sole use of the local Filipinos. MacArthur further ordered American supply officers not to break into the large Japanese-owned food warehouses there, and Sutherland went so far as to threaten one American colonel with a court-martial if he dared confiscate the tinned fish and corned beef Wainwright so desperately needed. In consequence, as a disgusted Colonel Miller summed up, "not one grain of the rice at Cabanatuan" was touched.[72] Thus, nothing reached the starving men on Bataan. As for the warehouses at Cabanatuan, they were all bombed and completely destroyed by the Japanese. The local Filipinos got nothing.

The Manila Railroad from the capital north to Tarlac (due west of Cabanatuan) and up to Lingayen had been intended to be used to transport huge food stocks north, but the Filipino railway crews fled when the first Japanese warplanes attacked on December 9. They were in turn replaced by the Philippine Constabulary. But these troops were then ordered to form the 2nd Division to protect Manila. Thus the Manila Railroad lay totally abandoned a second time, and no supplies ever reached Bataan from Tarlac. All troops were later ordered out of the capital when it was declared an open city.

Further to the south, Brigadier General Bradford Chynoweth found still another large source of badly needed supplies and munitions at the port of Cebu, where "everything was on the docks . . . [including] ten million rounds of ammunition held for the quartermaster in Manila." But the American officers at the port distributed none of it to the local troops, who were down to a few rounds each. "It was a nightmare," the tough Chynoweth lamented.[73]

Similarly there was no shortage of gasoline: nearly 10 million gallons were stored at Manila alone, without counting the storage depots at various forts, ports, and airfields. But instead of distributing it, MacArthur, caught totally unprepared by the Japanese advance, ordered the entire gasoline storage depot at the capital *to be blown up by American troops* while U.S. Army vehicles, including most of the 108 tanks there, lacked enough fuel to be deployed.[74] As Colonel Lloyd Mielens summed up, "many supplies could have been saved [everywhere] and the troops finally retreating into Bataan, for example, would have been much more adequately provided for" if General Douglas MacArthur had not persuaded Marshall to drop WPO-3, leaving operations in a state of utter chaos.[75]

The fact emerges that Douglas MacArthur, the much-touted chief of staff and famed planner of World War I's Rainbow Division, had not done his elementary homework and was apparently incapable of making the competent decisions required of a senior commanding officer. Through his arrogance and his failure to do his job, he contributed to one of the greatest fiascos in U.S. military history, far outweighing the tragedy of Pearl Harbor in long-term importance, according to the historian D. Clayton James.[76] In the final analysis, MacArthur, as senior commanding officer, was fully responsible for the debacle in the Philippines. When the Japanese attack came after the destruction of the U.S. Air Force, the befuddled MacArthur insisted for the first forty hours that his unprotected beaches be held. He was no longer living in the world of reality, and in consequence men had to die by the thousands.

As a result of his refusal to provide depots of food and munitions, Douglas MacArthur dared not show his face on the peninsula. He couldn't face the men. He couldn't visit the wounded. Indeed, the only two times he came over briefly, literally for a couple of hours, was to speak to commanding officers before returning to Corregidor the same day. Ballads about "Dugout Doug" soon began to circulate across Bataan, including one entitled "USAFFE Cry of Freedom":

> Dugout Doug MacArthur lies ashaking on the Rock [Corregidor]
> Safe from all the bombers and from any sudden shock
> Dugout Doug is eating of the best food on Bataan
> And his troops go starving on.
>
> . . .
>
> Dugout Doug, come out from hiding
> Dugout Doug, come out from hiding
> Send to Franklin the glad tidings
> That his troops go starving on![77]

On Christmas Day, Army Chief of Staff George Marshall sent a top-secret "Memorandum for the President" informing Roosevelt that, thus far, the United States had only seventy pursuit planes and dive-bombers available in the whole of Australia, but that ships carrying more fighters and ammunition would begin leaving U.S. ports from the East and West coasts beginning January 8. He admitted that "the situation in the Philippines apparently has changed to an extent that makes it improbable that pursuit plane reinforcements [required, among other things, to escort B-17s] can be forwarded to General MacArthur," while Admiral Ernie King was ordering Admiral Hart to "take extreme means to deliver ammunition" to Manila by submarine.[78] In the meantime, for reasons that remain unclear, Marshall continued to congratulate MacArthur privately, in spite of the utter fiasco he had brought about. "Your splendid resistance has contributed materially to the general situation in Malaya."[79]

A few weeks later, in a secret memorandum to Admiral King dated January 20, Marshall acknowledged that "sufficient shipping is not available on the Atlantic Coast to provide for unit loading of the organizations which are to go to [New] Caledonia, much less combat loading." They were, however, doing their best to find ships with which to transport U.S. troops and equipment to Australia as soon as possible. This would mean another several weeks' delay, but Marshall closed by assuring King that 996,036 troops were being dispatched in the period between December 7 and January 31, 1942.[80]

The Philippines were quite another matter. Marshall's various memos to Franklin Roosevelt became gloomier by the day, especially when it came down to the means of getting heavy bombers to the Philippines in order to attack the Japanese. "If it becomes impracticable to land B-17's on Borneo or at the Del Monte Field in Mindanao [because of the Japanese air force in occupation there], it would be impracticable to service such a project." In other words, neither MacArthur nor his senior commander in the field, Wainwright, could expect future air help or cover—despite Marshall's earlier message to MacArthur that the American people "confirm our confidence in your leadership. We are making every effort to reach you with air replacements and reinforcements as well as other troops and supplies." Even before January 1942 had ended, the situation looked beyond remedy. Nevertheless, Marshall informed CNO King that they were "making strenuous efforts to organize blockade running on an extensive scale from Australia to both Mindanao and Luzon. Vessels are now under way for this purpose and others are being secured as rapidly as possible." Shipments of food and munitions would also be sent to the Philippines by submarine.[81] Although MacArthur was authorized by Washington to pay exorbitant prices to private merchantmen to bring these provisions to the Philippines, in fact only three small vessels ever succeeded in reaching the archipelago. But King at least ordered Tom Hart to send in converted submarine transports to ferry over gasoline, food, medicine, and munitions, which reflected just how grave the situation was. Of the ten submarines dispatched, seven did eventually reach Corregidor, then collecting nurses, ailing senior officers, and key personnel, took them back to the safety of Australia.

"Ours was a sorry procession into [southern] Bataan," Wainwright recalled, his original force of 28,000 already down to 16,000, including hundreds of planeless pilots, ground crews, and shipless sailors all converted into makeshift infantrymen.[82] The troops continued to scavenge for whatever food they could find to supplement their slender rations —rice, roots, wild fowl, and animals. Those in Wainwright's 26th Cavalry were forced to kill and eat their own horses and mules until not one was left. MacArthur's "construction of food depots" was nothing but a figment of his overwrought imagination.

On January 10, 1942, MacArthur made an unannounced visit to Bataan, "congratulating" General Wainwright. "The creation of your withdrawal and your mission . . . were as fine as anything in history," he told the commander (who was ill with malaria), and again promised him a promotion. Just out of sight, several hundred troops were dropping daily from disease and malnutrition.[83] The resourceful doctors and nurses hurriedly created tented field hospitals in the jungles, coping as best they could while morale plummeted and the death rate rose. The canvas beds were filled, but the medicine cabinets were as empty as the patients' stomachs.

War correspondent Frank Hewlett, witnessing the condition of Wainwright's men, wrote a tune that soon became famous across the Pacific and then America:

> We're the battling bastards of Bataan:
> No momma, no poppa, no Uncle Sam.
> . . .
> No aunts, no uncles, no nephews, no nieces,
> No rifles, no guns or artillery pieces,
> And nobody gives a damn.[84]

Very late on March 9, General Wainwright was summoned to Corregidor by MacArthur. The next day he crossed the two miles of sea separating the port of Mariveles, Bataan, from the tadpole-shaped rocky island known as Corregidor. Upon reaching the tunneled office of Commander MacArthur, Wainwright was as usual first intercepted by Sutherland, who according to Wainwright said, "General MacArthur is going to leave here and go to Australia. . . . You will be placed in command of all troops on Luzon." And then he was greeted by MacArthur, who offered him a cigar. In Wainwright's recollection, MacArthur told him, "Jonathan. . . . I want you to understand my position very plainly. I'm leaving for Australia pursuant to repeated orders of the President. . . . I want you to make it known throughout all elements of your command that I'm leaving over my repeated protests." This, in fact, was true enough. "Of course I will, Douglas," Wainwright answered. The conversation went on, with MacArthur's command: "In the meantime you've got to hold." Wainwright thought of "the little ammunition we had left, and of the malaria and dysentery, the one-half rations, the wounded in their vulnerable hospital tents, my Air Force of two P-40s, and of many other things," but he remained silent. " 'Good-bye, Jonathan,' he [MacArthur] said shaking hands. 'When I get back, if you're still on Bataan I'll make you a lieutenant general.' " It was the usual rhetoric, the same old promises of glory. Wainwright, who had not eaten in over twenty-four hours, would have preferred a good meal, even a bad one, in exchange for that cigar and an additional star.[85]

When back in December MacArthur had sent Brereton away to Darwin with what remained of his bomber force, his final words had not been "good luck," but "I hope you will . . . protect my reputation as a fighter."[86] Privately, MacArthur had told his staff that he would resign his commission before obeying FDR's orders to leave Corregidor. Instead, he said, he would join the guerrilla movement in the hills, apparently with his wife and son; but of course he never did so. It was the usual MacArthur bravado. No one could forget that day back in December when his house on Corregidor had been bombed. Jean had grabbed their four-year-old son and run outside to the air-raid shelter, totally ignored by MacArthur. Any other husband would surely have attempted to protect his wife and child, but not Douglas MacArthur. He seemed oblivious of their presence as he stood there glaring at the enemy bombers that had dared defy him and were once again plastering the Rock, nearly killing his own family in the process. Time and again one returns to the question, who was Douglas MacArthur?

Finally on February 24, 1942, he had replied to Washington that he would follow the president's orders and leave for Australia. On the evening of March 11, the MacArthurs, along within Sutherland, Marshall, Willoughby, Marquat, Aikin, and other members of his staff, boarded four of the remaining six PT-boats under the command of Lieutenant John Bulkeley, on whose "flagship," PT-41, the MacArthur family and amah were secured. They carried one suitcase each. Shortly before eight o'clock that evening they cast off, heading for the entrance of a Manila Bay infested with Japanese subs, warships, and planes.[87] Their destination was Mindanao, where B-17s had been sent expressly from Australia to collect them. Two of the planes had had to turn back because of mechanical failure. The two remaining planes took off from Del Monte Field on March 16 and 17 and landed at Batchelor Air Field forty miles from Darwin, Australia, at 9:30 A.M. on March 17.* MacArthur and his party then went by train to Melbourne and eventually to Brisbane, where MacArthur was ordered to execute the next phase of the war.[88]

On the morning of March 21, Wainwright was informed by Washington that "you are assigned to command all United States Forces in the Philippines (including the Navy)." When MacArthur, who had not yet been informed that he had been relieved, later got the news, he sent Wainwright an outraged rebuke.

Wainwright, now back on Corregidor, was left with the task of salvaging the situation at Bataan, which was hopelessly out of control. "At the start of the twenty-seventh day of the Battle of Corregidor we had in the neighborhood of 11,000 men, opposed to a force of 250,000."[89] On April 9, he ordered Major General Edward King on Bataan to launch a fresh counterattack. Two subs had just arrived with enough food for the men on that peninsula, enough, that is, for one more day's supply.

"But the men on Bataan, who had prayed for that food, never tasted it," Wainwright recorded, for without notifying his commanding officer, Ed King had offered to surrender to the Japanese. "I was shocked," Wainwright admitted. " 'Go back and tell him not to do it,' I shouted. But he did it anyway."[90]

The situation was desperate, and that very night barges and boats

*The passengers intended for the other two planes—men and women—had to be left behind and were captured and held as POWs.

brought about two thousand men and women from Bataan to Corregidor. The "hospital wards" in Malinta Tunnel would soon be filled with some fifteen thousand people suffering from wounds, malaria, dysentery, or famine.

●

For Wainwright and his men, the reality of attempting to defend themselves was fraught with obstacles. Although Eisenhower, as MacArthur's previous chief of staff, had been able to persuade the War Department to sell the Philippine government many thousands of outdated .30-caliber machine guns, it was now discovered that the majority did not work. They either jammed or broke down, or the barrels literally melted away because they were not water-cooled. The standard rifle, the old World War I Enfield, proved equally defective, with extractors frequently breaking, and the guns unusable until makeshift parts could be made by hand. Thousands of Filipino reservists replaced these guns with the traditional *bolos* (machetes) instead, as wave after wave of Japanese planes, and artillery, pounded them. But there was no longer any viable defense. Brigadier General Clyde Selleck, commanding the 71st Division, lamented that "the divisions were never organised . . . never adequately equipped and the training was so meager that when attacked by veteran troops and bombed and confronted by tanks, they had a minimum of stability." General Homma, the Japanese commander and scourge of the Philippines, described the defenders in the jungles as nothing but "a mob."[91]

Enemy warplanes and artillery bombarded Corregidor daily. But according to Wainwright, the shelling from the powerful 105mm Japanese guns at Cavite was even worse than the uncontested aerial attacks: and "their 240-mm. howitzers firing from Bataan [were] something else. They made our lives hell."[92] Ears ached and heads throbbed hour after hour and there was a constant pall of dust during every big shelling; water pipes broke and the water supply dwindled. The electrical system was knocked out time and again. The pumps bringing the main source of fresh air into the hundreds of meters of the Malinta Tunnel network faltered daily, rendering breathing difficult for these underground residents, nowhere more so than for the fifteen thousand patients of the two hospital wards. And the food supply, already rationed, was gravely reduced again, with no means of replenishing it.

Wainwright, who had replaced MacArthur here at Corregidor on March 11, had by May 1 found the pounding his troops were taking inhuman and untenable. On the 6th of that month he received a final message from President Roosevelt, even as Japanese bayonets were closing in for the kill.

> During recent weeks we have been following with growing admiration the day-by-day accounts of your heroic stand against the mounting intensity of bombardment by enemy planes and heavy siege guns. . . . [You have proven] a shining example of patriotic fortitude and self-sacrifice. The American people ask no finer example of tenacity, resourcefulness, and steadfast courage. . . . You and your devoted followers have become the living symbols of our war aims and the guarantee of [ultimate] victory.[93]

Japanese infantry and tanks were now moving to the entrance of the Malinta complex itself. It would be a veritable slaughter in those tunnels of horror. Wainwright had not answered Homma's first order to surrender. "I had to make up my mind—a mind reeling with the task of trying to find ways and means of averting the inevitable. . . . I thought of the havoc that even one of these [tanks] could wreak if it nosed into the tunnel, where lay our helpless wounded and their brave nurses." Yet they could not hold out another day. His arsenal by now reduced to a prayer, he finally made the inevitable decision to surrender. "It was 10:15 A.M. on the black day of May 6, 1942." Jonathan Wainwright then radioed a last message to Franklin Roosevelt:

> With broken heart and head bowed in sadness but not in shame I report to Your Excellency that today I must arrange terms for the surrender of the fortified islands of Manila Bay. . . . May God bless and preserve you and guide you and the nation in the effort to ultimate victory.
>
> With profound regret and with continued pride in my gallant troops I go to meet the Japanese commander. . . . There is a limit of human endurance and that limit has long since been past. . . . Good-bye, Mr. President.[94]

When the Japanese then blackmailed Wainwright with the daily exe-

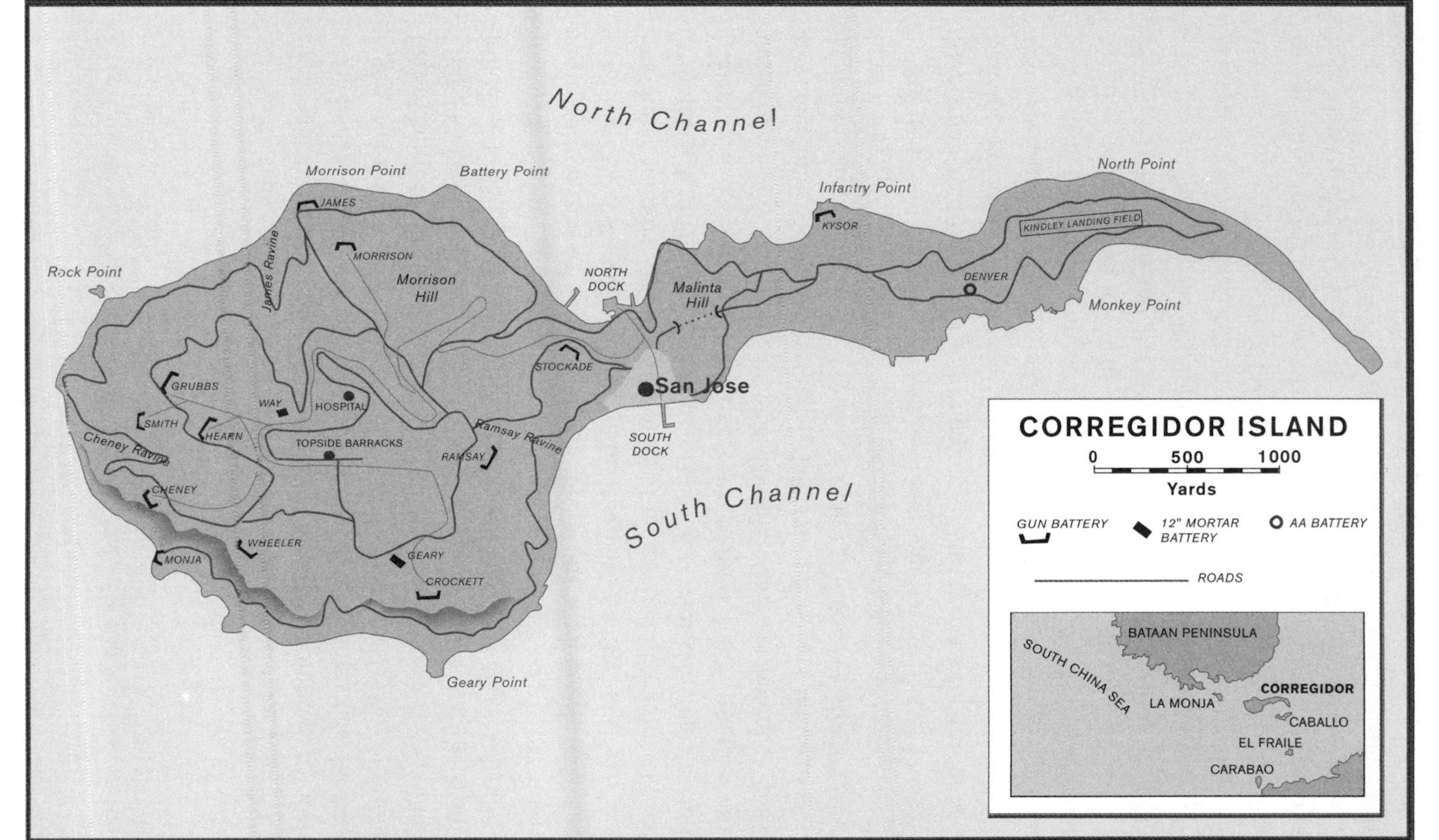
CORREGIDOR ISLAND
0
500
1000
Yards
GUN BATTERY
12" MORTAR BATTERY
AA BATTERY
ROADS
North Channel
South Channel
Rock Point
Morrison Point
Battery Point
Infantry Point
North Point
Monkey Point
Geary Point
JAMES
MORRISON
Morrison Hill
James Ravine
NORTH DOCK
SOUTH DOCK
Malinta Hill
KYSOR
KINDLEY LANDING FIELD
DENVER
STOCKADE
San Jose
GRUBBS
WAY
HOSPITAL
SMITH
HEARN
TOPSIDE BARRACKS
Cheney Ravine
RAMSAY
Ramsay Ravine
CHENEY
WHEELER
MONJA
GEARY
CROCKETT
BATAAN PENINSULA
SOUTH CHINA SEA
CORREGIDOR
LA MONJA
CABALLO
EL FRAILE
CARABAO

cution of American officers until the whole of the Philippines had surrendered on May 7, 1942, General Wainwright officially notified all forces to surrender as prisoners of war.[95] He had seen too much suffering, too much blood spilt. The Philippines had fallen.

•

As Wainwright attested, the American and Filipino troops defending the Philippine Archipelago were doomed from the beginning. Enough men had not been adequately trained by MacArthur since he had taken over those responsibilities six years before; the U.S. government had planned to abandon the country for decades as part of War Plan Orange-3 because in the 1930s Congress had promised that the Commonwealth would gain its independence in 1946. Therefore, Washington had refused to send the modern arms and American personnel required to give the Philippine army the means to defend itself—not even the fifty dollars a year per soldier required for the most elementary basic training. President Quezon himself had dithered, at first demanding strong training for his people and then denying the very budget he had assured MacArthur for that purpose. He further complicated matters by welcoming many tens of thousands of Japanese "businessmen" to his country to establish themselves (many of them, in fact, Japanese career officers in disguise, as Hap Arnold and others would later testify).

But in the final analysis it was the much-altered psyche of Douglas MacArthur that doomed the Philippines. "The reasons for the unpreparedness of the Philippine Army when it was mobilized are manifold and largely predate 1941," as D. Clayton James acknowledges, emphasizing that "MacArthur himself must bear a large share of the blame for the pitiful situation which would lead to military disaster."[96] MacArthur had convinced George Marshall in the autumn of 1941 that the defenses of the Philippines were strong, bolstered by a well-trained reserve army. Encouraged by this positive report, Marshall agreed to drop old War Plan Orange, or Rainbow 5, in favor of rushing troops, equipment, and modern warplanes to the Philippines to support MacArthur at the last minute. But it was all too late—one does not build an army in two or three months' time. The logistics were complicated, and the United States itself was not prepared for war, mentally or physically. That Marshall should have been so taken in by MacArthur, with his pattern of extraordinarily poor judgment and lies, seems astonishing, and the error of this misplaced trust was to be borne out by the rapid, successful Japanese conquest of the islands. Marshall and Roosevelt went on to fight more battles, while Stark, Kimmel, and Strong did not.

Neither MacArthur, Sutherland, nor any of the rest of MacArthur's high command was ever brought to account or even reprimanded for the errors and incompetence of the MacArthur 1941–42 Philippine regime. "The lightness with which the cardinal military sin was excused by the American high command . . . has always seemed to me one of the most shocking defects of the war," commented Lieutenant General Claire Chennault. "Our general and leaders committed one of the greatest errors possible to military men—that of letting themselves be taken by surprise."[97]

"We supposed that an official investigation would follow," wrote Philippine high commissioner Francis Sayre, but none did. D. Clayton James reported: "Although the Pearl Harbor attack was the subject of several lengthy investigations resulting in the removal of the top commanders in Hawaii, the Clark-Iba fiasco did not produce even one official inquiry."[98] In conclusion, one cannot but wonder how it came about that Douglas MacArthur happened to forget his own admonition: "The history of failure in war can be summed up in two words: Too Late. Too late in comprehending the deadly purpose of a potential enemy; too late in realizing the mortal danger. . . ."[99] It is the greatest irony in military history that MacArthur was condemned by his own words.

After the war, all the commanders of the Philippines during the 1941–42 campaign were invited by the Army Center for Military History to provide full accounts of what had occurred. Wainwright, despite a severely weakened condition brought on by malaria and the almost daily torture suffered during his captivity, prepared one of the longest accounts, entitled *Report of Operations of USAFFE and USFIP in the Philippine Islands, 1941–1942*. Replete with fourteen exhaustive Annexes, it covered every aspect of the operations during Wainwright's command. But as the official army historian Louis Morton noted in his *Fall of the Philippines*, "Still to be heard from are General MacArthur and his principal staff officers," whose lips remained sealed.[100] Instead,

MacArthur came out with the grossly distorted memoirs he called his *Reminiscences*. The commander in chief of all Philippine operations in 1941–42, who bore the elementary responsibility of disclosing the truth, instead suppressed it. The old-boy network closed ranks almost to a man, with the full support and blessing of George Marshall. General Bob Eichelberger was one of the few brave enough to publish the truth about the real MacArthur in his memoirs, *Dear Miss Em*.

●

One more aspect of this tragic saga remains to be told: that of the fate of the American and Filipino POWs taken by the conquering Japanese.

Perhaps the most poignant account of all comes from a reluctant, withdrawn twenty-seven-year-old army pilot, Lieutenant Colonel Bill Dyess, who, while recuperating in a military hospital for months after escaping General Homma's seventy-two-mile Bataan Death March, finally agreed to tell his story.[101] A journalist patiently recorded what were, for young Dyess, the most painful memories of his life.

He began where the Death March began, at Mariveles on the southern tip of Bataan in early April 1942. One of the American captains had been searched, and planted yen had been found in his pocket. Dyess related:

> The big Jap [officer] looked at the money. Without a word he grabbed the captain by the shoulder and shoved him to his knees! He pulled the sword out of the scabbard and raised it high over his head with two hands. Before we could grasp what was happening . . . [he] had swung his sword: I remember the sun flashed on it. There was a swish and a kind of chopping thud, like a cleaver going through beef. The captain's head seemed to jump off his shoulders. It hit the ground in front of him and went rolling crazily from side to side between the line of prisoners. . . . This was the first murder. In the year to come there would be enough killing of American and Filipino soldier prisoners to rear a mount of dead. . . . The thing . . . almost drove me crazy. They were slugged and beaten. . . . The Japs made no move to feed us.

Dyess himself was interrogated time and again, and chiefly asked where the Americans had hidden their money. (MacArthur had burned everything in the Philippine Treasury and had buried the silver in Manila Bay.) When his interrogators did not like his answers, the Japanese officer "seized my shoulder and whirled me around with a quick twist that sent me staggering toward the line. I expected a bullet to follow the push. . . ." Weakened American officers were beaten and fell. "Those who fell were kicked aside by the Japs. The Japs forbade us to help these men. Those who tried it, were kicked, slugged, or jabbed with bayonets. . . ." When an elderly American colonel begged for food, "a squat Jap officer grinned at him and picked up a can of salmon. Then he smashed it against the colonel's head, opening the American's cheek, from eye to jawbone." The captors were no longer content with mauling stragglers or pricking them with bayonet points, as Major Burt Bank, another survivor, has corroborated.

"The thrusts were [now] intended to kill," Dyess continued. Walking for hours in the midday heat,

> I stumbled over a man writhing in the hot dust of the road. He was a Filipino soldier who had been bayoneted through the stomach. Within a quarter of a mile I walked past another. This soldier prisoner had been rolled into the path of the trucks and crushed beneath the heavy wheels. . . . Now and again we passed the huddled forms of men who had collapsed from fatigue or who had been bayoneted. . . . The bloodthirsty devils now were killing us for diversion. . . . I heard a cry, followed by thudding blows. . . . An American soldier so tortured by thirst that he could not sleep had asked a Jap guard for water. The Jap fell on him with his fist then slugged him into insensibility with a rifle butt.

They were then forced to drink and eat carabao (water buffalo) urine and excrement mixed with seawater. "We held our noses to shut out the nauseating reek, but we drank all the water we could get." When the prisoners fell, "there was a sharp crack of pistols and rifle fire behind us," and they dared not turn around. "The bodies were left where they lay, that other prisoners coming behind us might see them. . . . The executioners were on the job [following us] to kill or wound mortally every prisoner who fell out of the marching line. All through the night there were occasional shots. I didn't count them. I couldn't." When six Filipinos ran to a pool of stagnant water, they were shot. "Two of them, desperately wounded, kept inching to the water, their hands outstretched." They were shot a final time. Passing one barbed-wire fence, Dyess saw a Filipino soldier. "The victim had been bayoneted, his abdomen was open. The bowels had been wrenched loose and were hanging like great grayish purple ropes. . . ." Upon reaching Camp O'Donnell, the prisoners were addressed by a captain's interpreter. " 'Captain, he say you are not prisoners of war. You are sworn enemies of Japan. He say you will be treated like captives. He said you do not act like soldiers.' . . .

"When we had been at O'Donnell about a week, the daily death rate among the Americans was twenty a day. Filipinos were dying at a rate of 150 a day. In two weeks fifty Americans were dying each day . . . [and] 350 Filipinos each twenty-four hours. . . . The Japs provided no medicine. American doctors who were prisoners in the camps were given no instruments, medicines, or dressings. They were not allowed sufficient water to wash the human waste from the sick and dying men. . . . Starvation was everywhere. . . . On seeing a man lying asleep it was difficult to say whether he was alive or dead." Corpses were stuffed beneath buildings. "The most common causes of death at O'Donnell were malaria, dysentery and Beriberi." The Japanese also tortured the prisoners by forcing them to stand at attention in the tropical midday sun for hours at a time. It was called the "sun cure." "Most of these inspections never came off. . . . In the two months we spent at O'Donnell more than 2,200 American war prisoners died. The Filipino death toll was many times this."

They were later sent to Cabanatuan. There, "it was not uncommon that twenty per cent of each [work] detail would die on the job in a day or in the barracks that night. On one occasion nine men of a detail of twelve were left dead where they had fallen. . . . Soldiers were stripped of their shirts and flogged until their backs were raw. After the beatings, an American doctor, also a prisoner, applied dressings. When he had . . . gone, they were tied up again and flogged until the dressings were beaten into the open wounds." Bill Dyess witnessed it all.

"When I left the camp in October 26, 1942, there were 2,500 Americans sick in their barracks, or in the hospital . . . and there they died. One middle-aged colonel, adjutant of American headquarters, had to bring a report to Japanese headquarters. There was a slight error and the Jap adjutant went into a rage. . . . [T]he interpreter sprang after him and beat him insensible with a blackjack." When the Japanese caught American sailors trying to escape, "at sunrise they were stripped of their clothing, tied up in the glaring sunlight and flogged. When the sun was directly overhead, the six were flogged again." When one man did finally escape, he was caught immediately, tied up "to the whipping post, trussed up, and all six [of the other] prisoners were flogged again. . . . I had come to hate the Japs through every waking hour and to dream of it when I slept. Two lieutenant colonels and the naval lieutenant who had almost escaped were flogged daily in the face with two-by-fours, day after day. They were finally all shot."

On another occasion Bill Dyess saw a Japanese officer on horseback at the head of a procession of two hundred soldiers, and behind them "marched two soldiers carrying a pole upon which was stuck the head of a Filipino." Dyess with other prisoners was next put on a 7,000-ton vessel crowded with POWs. On November 7, 1942, the ship landed near Davos, and the prisoners were sent to yet another camp. Finally, in spring 1943, Dyess, Steve Mellnik (a former coast artillery officer at Corregidor), and others escaped. By that time, some 27,000 Americans and Filipinos of the original Death March had been shot, bayoneted, beheaded, tortured, bludgeoned, or starved to death by the Japanese.[102]

●

When General Wainwright became a prisoner of war from May 1942 through August 1945, he witnessed just as many acts of inhumanity. Chaplain John Borenman told Wainwright later that "he had to witness twelve murders of United States Army officers at Cabanatuan, twelve murders which followed sadistic beatings lasting twenty-four hours." Another chaplain, Colonel Alfred Oliver, "was beaten pitilessly for days." Eventually they broke his neck. "Three Filipino envoys—a Colonel Valariana and his two aides—were murdered . . . as they advanced under a flag of truce," Wainwright recalled.[103]

Over the next three years Jonathan Wainwright was moved many times: from Tarlac to Formosa; to Kyushu, Japan; to Fusan, Korea; to three different camps in Manchuria; to Chungking, China; and then back to the Philippines. What the Japanese did to captured American nurses and wives is unrepeatable. All the officers, regardless of rank, were treated rudely on a routine basis, beaten by Japanese privates, and forced to do manual labor (considered a humiliation by the Japanese). Famished American officers were forced to eat their own feces at bayonet point. Red Cross packages that eventually arrived were mostly taken by the Japanese and eaten by them as the desperate prisoners looked on. At Karenko, in Formosa, Wainwright, who was living on a starvation diet like the others, was bayoneted in the left wrist for dropping a dish he was too weak to carry. He was then kept standing at attention for an hour, as his wound bled. "Our beatings never stopped at Karenko. Some of the enlisted men were slugged as many as three times every day, and it became a rare sight to find one whose eyes were not blackened, nose mashed, or head and body full of lumps." Then there was the case of Lieutenant General Sir L. M. Heath, "a grand and decent man," who had lost three inches of bone from his arm during World War I, leaving him incapable of saluting. When he failed to salute a Japanese private, "the Jap raised his gun and beat General Heath unmercifully over the face with the barrel of the weapon. Then he beat the butt of the gun into the boneless portion of the British general's back and arm and left him lying there in the dirt hardly conscious. . . . For weeks after that Heath's eyes were like twin pools of blood, and his arm had to be put in a sling."[104]

When Colonel Charles Lawrence sent a letter of protest to the commander of Karenko over how badly his men were treated, the Japanese officer, according to Wainwright, "gave him a dreadful beating all over the kitchen—while our enlisted men who had been turned into kitchen slaves, had to stand by and watch." Lawrence then protested to the senior American officer. The Japanese ordered Lawrence back again, "and he took another terrible whipping. . . . His face was hardly recognizable for days after that." Many other men and officers by the hundreds starved to death, or died for want of needed drugs, including Colonel Bunker, who had commanded the seawall defense on Corregidor. "He was starved to death, coming down with moist beriberi. His legs, feet, arms and hands had swollen incredibly from the water with which he tried to assuage his hunger." He died in front of Wainwright, no longer able to recognize him. Having witnessed the bayoneting and beheading of dozens of officers and enlisted men, Wainwright bitterly concluded: "By this time I was convinced that, with the possibility of one exception, no Jap was even a reasonable facsimile of a human being."[105] Wainwright was released from a POW camp just before the signing of the Japanese surrender aboard USS *Missouri*, a ceremony he attended.

The Australians and the British, too, were tortured and murdered by the thousands. Martin Gilbert relates that of 809 Australians who surrendered on Dutch Timor, for instance, "426 of them were bayoneted to death by their Japanese captors, or died of torture and starvation. . . . On February 4, 1942, a further thirty Australian prisoners-of-war were bayoneted to death, or decapitated." Their executioner, Lieutenant Nakagawa, testified after the war: "They were taken one by one to the spot where they were to die and made to kneel down with a bandage over their eyes." Each one of Nakagawa's men then "stepped out of the ranks, one by one as his turn came, behind a prisoner-of-war with a sword, or to stab him through the breast with a bayonet."[106]

Gilbert recorded: "In Hong Kong . . . on Christmas Eve . . . a further fifty-three British and Canadian soldiers were roped together after being captured, and then shot or bayoneted to death. On Christmas Day, the wounded Canadians of a platoon which had surrendered were also murdered, as were two doctors and seven nurses—four of them Chinese—who had been attending wounded soldiers at the St Stephen's College Emergency Hospital. The wounded, more than fifty in all, were killed in their beds."[107]

•

Meanwhile, in Washington, D.C., a grateful George Marshall, Henry Stimson, and Franklin Delano Roosevelt in March 1942 were rewarding Douglas MacArthur for his most extraordinary services, Marshall stating, "I am certain that this will meet with the popular approval, both within and without the armed forces. . . ."[108] Douglas MacArthur received his nation's highest honor, nothing less than the Congressional Medal of Honor. The citation praised him for "conspicuous leadership in preparing the Philippine Islands to resist conquest . . . [and for] his calm judgement in each crisis [which] inspired his troops. . . ."[109] It failed to mention that his loss of the Philippines led to the worst disaster in U.S. military history . . . and the surrender of 78,000 American and Filipino prisoners of war to the Japanese.[110]

CHAPTER XI

First Washington Conference

"I have so many battles to fight, I am never quite sure whether I am fighting you [the British], or the President or the [U.S.] Navy!"

—General George Marshall to Field Marshal Sir John Dill[1]

"This country has not—repeat not—the sightest conception of what the war means. . . ."

—Field Marshal Sir John Dill to General Sir Alan Brooke, December 28, 1941[2]

On the eight day of her voyage from Scotland, the *Duke of York* sailed up the Chesapeake to Hampton Roads. There, on December 22, 1941, the British prime minister and his very large staff left the battleship and boarded a special train that was waiting to whisk them off to Washington, D.C. After so many months of a harsh one-sided struggle to save his country from the pounding it had been taking by the German and Italian military, Winston Churchill was most anxious to be underway. He and Roosevelt were about to meet as full wartime Allies at last, and Churchill was bursting with all the plans he had prepared long before. He was now "like a child in his impatience to meet the President," remarked his physician, Sir Charles Wilson. "He spoke as if every minute counted. It was absurd to waste time; he must fly."[3] An airplane magically appeared and the prime minister, Air Chief Sir Charles Portal, Averell Harriman (in charge of expediting Lend-Lease in London), and

Churchill's exhausted and aging production chief, Max Lord Beaverbrook ("living on his nerves," according to Wilson), along with the physician, were soon on their way. "Our Lockheed was over the lights of Washington in three-quarters of an hour. It gave me a sense of security; we were a long way from the war and the London blackout," Wilson recalled. And Churchill recounted, "There was the President waiting in his car. I clasped his strong hand with comfort and pleasure."[4]

Lord Halifax, the British ambassador to Washington, led the rest of the staff to the Mayflower Hotel, which was to serve as unofficial headquarters for dozens of senior officers and officials. Max Beaverbrook and Churchill would stay at the White House, where they were to live and work for the next few weeks. Churchill was installed in a bedroom directly across the wide hall from Hopkins's, and in addition was given an adjacent room to serve as his "war room," for his maps and charts. They had arrived at last.

•

At four o'clock on Wednesday, December 24, the White House guards opened the southwestern gate and some thirty thousand people entered the grounds to watch the president light the traditional fifty-foot spruce Christmas tree. Roosevelt's personal guests gathered about the South Portico of the White House, where he appeared nearly two hours later as the sunset gun was fired across the Potomac at Fort Myer. To the south, high up in the Washington Monument, a red lamp shone. All eyes were on the South Portico now, where FDR and Churchill stood silhouetted against the lights behind them. Seated around them were Eleanor Roosevelt, Crown Prince Olav and Crown Princess Martha of Norway and their children, Supreme Court Justices Stanley Reed and Robert Jackson, and Attorney General Anthony Biddle.

The president was the first to speak as the last rays of the wintry sun slipped behind the Virginia hills. He reminded those gathered below that "our strongest weapon in this war is that conviction of the dignity and brotherhood of man which Christmas Day signifies—more than any other day or any other symbol. Against the enemies who preach the principles of hate and advertise them, we set our faith in human love and in God's care for us and all men everywhere."

Following the applause there seemed a tense excitement in the extraordinary silence, for apparently it was Churchill whom most of them especially had come to see and hear.

"I spend this anniversary and festival far from my country," Churchill began,

> but . . . I cannot feel myself a stranger here in the center of the summit of these United States. I feel a sense of unity and fraternal association which, through all your kindness convinces me that I have a right to sit at your fireside and share your Christmas joys.
>
> This is a strange Christmas Eve. Almost the whole world is locked in deadly struggle. Armed with the most terrible weapons which science can devise. . . . [But let us] cast aside, for this night at least, the care and dangers which beset us, and make the children happy in a world of storm. Here then for one night only, each home throughout the English-speaking world should be a brightly lighted island of happiness and peace. Let the children have their night of fun and laughter; let the gifts of Father Christmas delight their thoughts; let us share to the full in their unstinted pleasure, before we turn again to the stern tasks in the year that lies before us. But now, by our sacrifice and daring, these same children shall not be robbed of their inheritance, or denied the right to live in a free and decent world. And so, in God's mercy, a Happy Christmas to you all.

The applause was deafening in the chill December air as the president pushed the button lighting the multicolored Christmas tree. The Marine Corps Band down below in the garden played "God Save the King" and "The Star-Spangled Banner," followed by a series of Christmas carols beginning with "Joy to the World"; choristers joined them in "Silent Night," "O Little Town of Bethlehem" (which Churchill had never heard before), and "God Rest Ye Merry Gentlemen."[5]

But the mood was not as merry as usual with the Roosevelt children and grandchildren absent. Stockings had been hung for Hopkins's daughter Diana and Roosevelt's Scottish terrier, Fala, but the president's four sons were all in uniform elsewhere and his daughter was in Seattle with her family. Churchill was promised the traditional American Christmas dinner, including turkey, yams, cranberry sauce, and of course, Christmas pudding.

The next day, they all attended services at the Foundry Methodist Church, where Churchill and Roosevelt joined in the hymns. "I am glad I went," Churchill told Charles Wilson. "It's the first time my mind has been at rest for a long time." That was no exaggeration, as Wilson, for one, well realized. The enormous weight of all the bad news reaching Churchill had thrown him at times into a state of depression bordering on despair, and it was shortly to become even worse.

Americans were beginning to comprehend just how real war was, as the first American soldiers were buried in Arlington National Cemetery and the mournful sound of the bugle carried across the tombs of fallen warriors. And now they were informed that they could no longer buy new automobiles or even tires for their old cars. Indeed, even the clothing industry was affected, with 50 percent of all wool going to the military. This did not, however, prevent the steel welders in the San Francisco area from going on strike, refusing to build the ships the navy was waiting for.[6]

●

It was the unique informality concerning the activities on the second floor of the White House that now hastened many decisions, and even disputes. Roosevelt, for example, made constant jibes about the concept of "empire," insisting for some impish reason that India be given its independence forthwith. Churchill was courteous enough not to remind the president of America's own budding empire, which included Puerto Rico, Alaska, Hawaii, and the Philippines. FDR went on to tease Churchill that when the president was an undergraduate at Harvard, he, as a good Dutchman, had supported the Boers against Britain during that long and bloody war.

There were frequent visits between Churchill and Hopkins accomplished merely by walking across the hall, and of course between Churchill and Roosevelt, with the British prime minister dropping in on the president at his second-floor office or pushing his wheelchair for him. On one occasion, rumor had it that FDR wheeled into Churchill's bedroom just after the prime minister had taken a bath; Churchill was stark naked, puffing away on a big, black Havana cigar. Roosevelt was embarrassed, but Churchill just smiled and parried, "The Prime Minister of Great Britain has nothing to conceal from the President of the United States." They both laughed.[7]

The ambience surrounding each of these two national leaders was very different. While the Secret Service men were rigid and omnipresent, intent on protecting the president, the British paid little heed to the possibility of a threat to Churchill. Their personal habits and interests were also very different. Roosevelt, if not a teetotaler, rarely took wine even with dinner—although at the end of each long business day, surrounded by his colleagues, he personally prepared his own home-brewed cocktail of which he was very proud but which made some of his guests wince. Churchill, on the other hand, was an alcoholic. He was, however, on his best behavior at the White House, beginning before breakfast with a decanter of sherry (instead of his usual two whiskeys), followed by some watered-down whiskeys before lunch, plenty of champagne at the table, and so on during the day until he went to bed anywhere between two and four o'clock in the morning. And yet curiously enough, he was almost never drunk.

●

One of the first acts taken upon the arrival of the British mission was to create a Combined Chiefs of Staff of the United States and Britain. It was also decided to make Washington, D.C., the headquarters for the direction of the war. Each of the British chiefs would leave a deputy permanently in the American capital.

The first meeting had been held at the White House on the very evening of the British delegation's arrival on the 22nd; present were Franklin Roosevelt, Secretary of State Cordell Hull and his assistant Sumner Welles, and the ubiquitous Harry Hopkins, who bore no official title but was always in attendance. On the British side were Churchill, Lord Beaverbrook, and Lord Halifax. They set to work immediately, the diplomatic protocols and niceties of yesteryear discarded. That night they talked about Hitler's next likely move in the event the German army was held in Russia. There was always the very real possibility of an invasion of Great Britain, but the general consensus now was that the Germans would probably drive through Spain and Portugal to seize Gibraltar and French Morocco. This would then permit them to join up with their Panzer divisions, currently fighting General

Sir Claude Auchinleck's forces in Libya. Once this was achieved, the Germans could literally close the Mediterranean. On the other hand, Anglo-American strategy was to attempt to "join hands" with the French forces in the Maghreb (Morocco, Algeria, and Tunisia), *if* somehow the French, at present "allied" with Germany, could be won over to cooperate with them instead in the fight against the Axis powers.[8] As it turned out, that was to prove one of the biggest "ifs" of the war.

Christmas Eve, which had thus far passed so well with the lighting of the Christmas tree and the playing and singing of Christmas carols, was suddenly interrupted when FDR was informed that General Charles de Gaulle's Free French resistance forces had seized the two small French islands of St. Pierre and Miquelon, just off the southwestern coast of Newfoundland. Roosevelt was furious; he had been betrayed, because de Gaulle had promised not to do this. Cordell Hull, who had been advocating acceptance of Pétain's Vichy government, was equally outraged.

This had all begun earlier in December when de Gaulle had approached the British foreign secretary, Anthony Eden, to see if Britain would have any objection to the Free French's occupying these two Vichy-run islands. The powerful radio antenna there would be a valuable prize; in addition, it was feared that the Vichy government was tapping the Western Union cable that crossed the islands. Finally, Vichy might allow German ships and U-boats to use its facilities there as a base from which to attack the United States or Canada. Eden gave his government's approval, and de Gaulle sent Admiral Emile Muselier to Ottawa, Canada, to obtain permission from Prime Minister Mackenzie King on December 16. The latter opposed the scheme, however. Admiral Muselier next turned to the American minister to Canada, J. Pierrepont Moffat, for American consent. Hull gave Moffat a very rapid thumbs down on the project, as he was still pushing Roosevelt to try to work with Pétain and Vichy in order to win them over to the Allies. But Pétain, for all his friendly remarks to U.S. ambassador Admiral William Leahy, remained in fact unwooable.

It was de Gaulle's turn to become outraged, and he took matters into his own hands by ordering his people "to carry out the rallying of St Pierre and Miquelon by your own means and without telling any foreigners about this. I take complete responsibility for the operation."[9] Muselier, ever the patriot, followed these orders and flew to Halifax, where he found three Free French corvettes and a submarine. He ordered them to sail to St. Pierre and Miquelon. With Muselier aboard, they set off for their objective, reaching the islands late on December 23. A small commando unit landed and quickly seized the central telephone system, the big radio transmitter, and the cable, customs, and gendarmerie offices—all without a shot being fired, for the islanders, mostly fishermen, were anti-Vichy. In fact, over 98 percent of the five thousand islanders officially voted then and there to accept de Gaulle and the Free French, and on the afternoon of the 24th, the three corvettes—*Mimosa*, *Alysse*, and *Aconit*—followed by the submarine *Surcouf*, entered the harbor, the tricolor flying from their masts, a cheering crowd giving them a warm welcome.[10]

Hence Roosevelt's fury late on Christmas Eve upon receiving word of de Gaulle's devious actions. Relations with Vichy were already severely strained, and in fact Ambassador Leahy would shortly be recalled to Washington. On the other hand, the American press universally cheered de Gaulle's act as a fait accompli, and FDR and Hull came under attack even by newspapers and radio stations owned by Democrats. De Gaulle had outwitted the American president.

●

Meanwhile, Winston Churchill was going through his own personal ordeal on the 25th, as he wrote and rewrote the speech he was to give the next day before the U.S. Congress. The 26th came faster than he might have wished, and Roosevelt's orders for delivering Churchill safely to Capitol Hill did not help the tension within, as Sir Charles Wilson relates. "We set off from the back entrance of the White House, dashing through the streets with the siren wailing and two G-men on each of the running boards, their pockets bulging with revolvers, ready to jump off in a second if anything happened."[11]

In any event, the "G-men" duly delivered Churchill, and at about twelve-thirty on Friday, December 26, he addressed the combined houses of the U.S. Congress in the Senate chambers.

"I cannot help reflecting," he began, "that if my father had been American and my mother British instead of the other way around, I might have got here on my own," which brought applause and laughter. But then more somberly he reminded the audience of senators and congressmen that

> Twice in a single generation the catastrophe of world war has fallen upon us. . . . If we had kept together after the last war . . . this renewal of the curse [of war] need never have fallen upon us. . . . Five or six years ago, it would have been easy, without shedding a drop of blood, for the United States and Great Britain to have insisted on the fulfillment of the disarmament clauses of the treaties which Germany signed after the Great War, and that also would have been the opportunity for assuring to the Germans those materials, those raw materials, which we declared in the Atlantic Charter, should not be denied to any nation, victor or vanquished. The occasion has departed; it is gone. Prodigious hammer strokes have been needed to bring us together. . . . I avow my hope and faith, sure and inviolate, that in the days to come the British and American peoples will for their own safety and for the good of all walk together side by side in majesty, in justice, and in peace.

And as he closed his speech, he held up his hand high, forming a "V" for victory. One journalist reported, "The effect was instantaneous, electric. The cheers swelled into a roar."[12]

There had rarely been a moment like this on Capitol Hill, and it was a good omen for the close cooperation now required to execute the war. But late that night, Churchill paid for all the anxiety that had accumulated prior to the delivery of that speech. He was hit with a mild heart attack, although he didn't know what the pain meant at the time. The next morning, he told his doctor about the dull pain over the heart and down his left arm. Sir Charles was in a quandary as to what to tell the prime minister. "The textbook treatment for this is at least six weeks in bed. That would mean publishing to the world . . . that the P.M. was an invalid with a crippled heart and a doubtful future. . . . I felt that the effect of announcing that the P.M. had had a heart attack could only be disastrous." So much of what was happening in the world depended on Churchill and Roosevelt. Wilson made up his mind. "I did not like it, but I determined to tell no one." Thus when Churchill asked him what it was, he replied that the prime minister's "circulation was a bit sluggish." It was not serious, he told him, but he had to slow down and relax more, for as Wilson pointed out, "the pace here is prodigious."[13]

●

Meanwhile, the British and American chiefs of staff were meeting daily at their newly created Combined Chiefs of Staff offices in the Federal Reserve Building. Talks were being carried out simultaneously at several different levels: between the president and prime minister, between representatives of the American secretary of state and the British foreign minister, and at a lower level, among "technicians" from the various military missions who were working on planning and operations at the Mayflower Hotel. As Foreign Secretary Eden and Commander of the Imperial General Staff (CIGS) Field Marshal Sir Alan Brooke could not leave London, they had sent their deputies. Most of Churchill's entourage was in military uniform, in contrast with Roosevelt's team, who were dressed in civilian attire. A constant flow of British officers carrying red leather dispatch boxes came in and out of Churchill's bedroom.

The president and prime minister dined together on a daily basis, permitting two strangers to get to know each other almost as if they had been close friends of long standing. And Harry Hopkins, who was present at most of their meetings and dinners, acted at times as a catalyst and at other times as a mediator. During these dinners they would make the main decisions for that day's official meeting, which usually followed. These informal meals streamlined the whole process, saving much time.

Arcadia, as the First Washington Conference was code-named, accomplished a great deal. To begin with, the newly created Combined Chiefs of Staff, or CCS, of the two nations were to convene on a regular basis—directly or via their lieutenants—to establish policy, objectives, and priorities, war matériel, and other matters. This would eliminate duplication and prevent one side's neglecting to inform the other about a specific subject; in particular, it would establish overall strategy for the war, by determining, for example, which cities or regions were to be bombed next, or which islands were to be occupied.

The creation of the Combined Chiefs meant changes, especially for the Americans, who were almost always outranked by their British counterparts. The British, including the head of the Royal Air Force, were all the equivalent of field marshals. The United States did not have a combined air force, and Henry "Hap" Arnold had to be promoted to command the U.S. Army Air Force, with George Marshall remaining his boss. Ernie King was named "Admiral of the Fleet," which caused a considerable amount of printers' ink to flow, one major newspaper referring to him as "one tough hombre."[14] Due to his dislike of anything British or British-sounding, King immediately changed his own title to "Fleet Admiral."

King began a drastic reorganization of the entire naval administration, but Roosevelt put his foot down and would not authorize it. Nevertheless, when FDR's back was turned, King initiated the first of his changes anyway. When the president heard of this, he was furious that an admiral had defied an order of the president, commander in chief of the U.S. armed forces. King was ordered to appear at the White House, where the president read the Riot Act to this insubordinate sailor. King had always gotten away with things like this throughout his career, but this time he was caught red-handed. It was a foolish move. After that, Roosevelt and Secretary of the Navy Knox began to look for a way to relieve King of his command, but apparently they were unable to come up with a suitable replacement without removing someone valued—Admiral Chester Nimitz, for example—from an important position where he would be sorely missed. Knox disliked King, and King reciprocated by telling Knox as little as possible about what he was doing. This wrangling with King took much out of the president, who on the contrary could have used his limited reserves of energy in a more useful manner.

On George Marshall's recommendation, FDR recalled Admiral William Leahy from Vichy and named him chief of staff to the commander in chief of the army and navy. Leahy, the son of Irish immigrants, was now the most senior officer of any of the services. In his new position he would be invited to direct and convene the CCS, and would work closely with both George Marshall and Field Marshal Sir John Dill.

Although Dill officially possessed no real title or power—he had stepped down as the chief of the Imperial General Staff, and was now referred to simply as head of the British Mission—he was for all intents and purposes acting as deputy minister of war. (Churchill held the portfolio of the War Ministry for himself.) Dill was responsible for liaising between his own team and that of the Americans, and thanks to an especially close social and professional relationship between himself and George Marshall, several very delicate misunderstandings or obstacles were amicably resolved. A gentleman of the old school (Cheltenham College and the Royal Military College, Sandhurst), Dill could charm anyone and was well known for his integrity, thus trusted and respected by the Americans (even by the "tough hombre") and the British alike. Dill's only enemies were Churchill and Beaverbrook, who had always fought with Dill over questions of strategy when he was the chief of the Imperial General Staff. (Dill had vetoed the disastrous Greek expedition, but was overruled by Churchill. Churchill never forgave him for having been right.)[15]

Other British chiefs of staff included Admiral of the Fleet Sir Dudley Pound, First Sea Lord, who directly commanded the entire Royal Navy and was the equivalent of CNO Admiral King. Pound had led a distinguished career and was remembered for having taken part in the battle of Jutland in World War I. But Pound was neither young nor well, and would not live to see the war through. Sir Charles Portal, chief of the Air Staff, commanded the entire Royal Air Force; he was another aging gentleman of the old school, and he, too, had severe health problems. Sir Alan Brooke (later Lord Alanbrooke) had replaced Dill as chief of the Imperial General Staff, or CIGS. Like the other chiefs, he had a permanent deputy representing him in Washington. He was Dill's protégé and thought Churchill's earlier dismissal of Dill as CIGS was dreadful.

All the Combined Chiefs, including Dill, would meet a couple of times a year during scheduled summit meetings—now at Washington, later at Casablanca, Quebec, and Teheran. At these summits they would jointly establish whatever was the next development in their strategy, to be adopted by both sides and by all branches of the military. Their number-one priority was to defeat the Axis powers. Thus, the European theater was for the first year or so to receive about 85 percent of the *matériel de guerre*, from ships to planes and tanks to manpower. But a considerable part of that production included what they were sending the Soviets and other Allies. It was the CCS that established the precise quota of ships, aircraft, and tanks that were to be produced and allocated each year.

Once the Joint Chiefs in Washington had laid out their military requirements that Christmas, the British were staggered both by how few planes, ships, and tanks the Americans actually had on hand and by the timorous tenor of American public opinion vis-à-vis the war. As Dill confided to Field Marshal Brooke on December 28, "This country is the most highly organised for peace you can imagine. . . . Never have I seen a country so utterly unprepared for war and so soft. [T]his country has not—repeat not—the slightest conception of what the war means, and their armed forces are more unready for a war than it is possible to imagine."[16] And what he did not point out was that the vast majority of American newspaper headlines in bold print were not about the European war, but rather, the war in the Far East. This was typical in every state of the Union, for example: "GOVERNMENT AND U.S. FORCES MAY LEAVE MANILA," "200,000 JAPANESE ESTIMATED LANDED ON LUZON," "BATTERED WAKE ISLE FALLS DESPITE VALIANT 400," "HARD FIGHTING AT DAVAO," "NEW ENEMY FORCE 175 MILES ABOVE SINGAPORE."

•

After some pretty frank talking on Friday, January 2, 1942, Roosevelt and Churchill personally presided over a meeting on the war matériel required, now and in the future. Beaverbrook made an impressive presentation at two other meetings the next day, and the Joint Chiefs agreed to increase production of combat aircraft from 12,750 to 45,000 per year by the end of 1942, tanks from 15,450 to 45,000, and machine guns from the 262,000 already planned to 500,000. As for shipping, the problem seemed more insurmountable, given the number of merchant and warships that were being sunk each month, especially by U-boats. Roosevelt promised 6 million tons of new shipping by the end of 1942, and 10 million for 1943. FDR also demanded that combat aircraft production be increased to 100,000 units per year by the end of 1943, tank production to 75,000 units, and production of airplane bombs to 720,000 long tons. If Dill, who really was fond of Americans, had once criticized their initial war preparations, he changed his mind when he went over these new estimates. Now he was seeing America go into high gear.[17]

On January 12, Roosevelt and Churchill concluded the final meeting of this first war summit, and summed up their accomplishments: They had agreed that defeating Germany and Italy was their number-one priority in every respect, both in manpower and matériel; U.S. bombers were to start operating from England as soon as possible. American troops would replace British soldiers in Ulster, to release the British for combat in North Africa. The Allies were to combine their resources in the Far East in an organization referred to as ABDA (American, British, Dutch, and Australian) under a united command, to be headed by Lieutenant General Sir Archibald Wavell; the United States would be solely responsible for the entire Pacific Ocean east of the Philippines and Australia. They discussed the necessity of opening a new front against the Germans in North Africa later in 1942. The CCS would establish a Combined Raw Materials Board. They would pool their entire munitions resources, while doing the same thing with all their shipping through the Anglo-American Shipping Adjustment Board. They would greatly increase production of planes, tanks, guns, munitions, and ships. No single meeting in the future was to accomplish so many sweeping achievements for the direction of the rest of the war.[18]

In addition, the United States and Britain reconfirmed their policy of not signing separate peace agreements. This was formalized in a Declaration by United Nations, drafted largely by Roosevelt and signed by twenty-eight countries. The document summed up the above achievements and the statements made earlier in the Atlantic Charter; among the signatories were the USSR, the United States, Great Britain and Northern Ireland, China, Canada, Belgium, Poland, India, and South Africa.

While Arcadia, or the Washington Conference, was certainly a success, it was nevertheless overshadowed by the loss of Wake, Guam, Tarawa, Makin (in the Gilberts), the Dutch East Indies, Malaya, and Hong Kong. In addition, Singapore was under threat, and a quarter of a million Japanese troops were fighting 78,000 Americans and Filipinos in the Philippines. The Americans had seen eight of their battleships sunk or severely damaged. The British had lost the battleship *Prince of Wales* and the cruiser *Repulse*; in the Mediterranean they'd lost another cruiser, *Neptune*; and two more British battleships, the *Queen Elizabeth* and *Valiant*, had been severely damaged by the Italians.

Perhaps Churchill's New Year's toast best summed up the situation on that January 12:

> "Here's to 1942,
> A year of toil,
> A year of struggle,
> A year of peril,
> But a long step forward to victory."[19]

CHAPTER XII

Yamamoto's Great Offensive: Coral Sea and Midway

"With the cooperation of the South Seas Army Department and the Navy, we will occupy Port Moresby and important positions on Tulagi and in southeastern New Guinea. We will establish air bases and strengthen our air operations in the Australian area."

—*Admiral Yamamoto: Operation MO*[1]

The choice of Admiral Chester Nimitz for the command at Pearl Harbor brought with it the rare combination of wisdom, inspiration, leadership, and sense of aggressive determination that was required to offset the demoralization and losses suffered in Hawaii and the Philippines. A variety of American counterattacks were carried out, including the sinking of at least five freighters off the coast of Japan by the Pacific Fleet submarines. William Halsey's *Enterprise* force escorted several marine transports past Samoa, joined by Rear Admiral Frank Jack Fletcher's *Yorktown*, newly arrived via the Panama Canal to strengthen the fleet. Losses were to be expected, of course; the carrier *Saratoga* was so badly damaged by a Japanese submarine on January 11, 1942, that she had to be brought all the way back to Bremerton, Washington, for major repairs and the modernization of her armament.[2]

As a result of a decision by the Combined Chiefs of Staff (CCS) in Washington, the Australia–New Zealand Command (ANZAC) was formed, comprising those two nations' cruisers and destroyers, reinforced by the USS *Chicago*. Meanwhile, Halsey's *Enterprise* now launched a series of carrier plane strikes and bombardments of Wotje, Maloelap, and Kwajalein in the Marshall Islands as Fletcher's *York-*

town, supported by a small cruiser force, struck Makin, Mili, and Jaluit, destroying warplanes and sinking a few Japanese transports and auxiliaries.

But it was the major Japanese advances into the Malay Barrier area and south toward New Guinea that worried Allied headquarters. The American-British-Dutch-Australian Command (ABDA) was formed on January 15, 1942, under Field Marshal Sir Archibald Wavell, with U.S. Lieutenant General George H. Brett serving as his deputy. They were strongly encouraged in the Dutch East Indies by the very aggressive Dutch officers Rear Admiral Karel Doorman, Vice Admiral C. E. L. Helfrich, General Hein Ter Poorton, and General van Oyen. The Dutch navy in those waters may have been small—with its three light cruisers (*Java*, *De Ruyter*, and *Tromp*), seven destroyers, and sixteen submarines—but was far from undaunted. Those vessels were reinforced now by Vice Admiral Tom Hart's Asiatic Fleet of three cruisers (*Houston*, *Boise*, and *Marblehead*), thirteen destroyers (under the command of Rear Admiral W. A. Glassford), and three naval tenders. To this Britain added three more cruisers, *Exeter*, *Hobart*, and *Perth*, and three destroyers.[3] If this Allied naval force was hardly impressive, given the overwhelming strength of the Imperial Japanese Navy it was facing, it made up in part with strong leadership and sheer determination, in particular from the Dutch, ever mindful of the German occupation of Holland. Considering the five Japanese carriers and numerous heavy cruisers in Vice Admiral Ozawa Jisaburo's Western Force, not to mention battleships and a variety of additional aircraft carriers elsewhere, the Allied task seemed almost suicidal, as a grim Admiral Ernie King pointed out.

The oil fields and refineries of the Dutch East Indies were certainly primary Japanese objectives, as the Allies well knew. A series of surface battles ensued as they attempted to prevent enemy warships from escorting large numbers of troop transports via Davao, on Mindanao, and elsewhere to these Dutch-held isles, beginning with the major port of Balikpapan, Borneo, on the night of January 23–24, 1942. Japanese possession of the Philippine ports for these advances reflected to what degree General MacArthur had failed to grasp just how essential the ports and airfields were for the success of this imposing Japanese operation. Four Japanese *marus* were sunk, however, and Balikpapan's enormous oil depots and refineries destroyed by the Dutch before the Japanese landings began.

The Allies were of course forced to retreat. This being Dutch territory, a Dutch officer (Vice Admiral Helfrich, RNN) replaced Tom Hart, while Wavell, who had failed, was ordered back to India and General Brereton to the United States. Unlike the ubiquitous Japanese, the unprepared Allies could not be everywhere.

The resourceful and courageous Rear Admiral Karel Doorman, RNN, was placed in command of the Allied Striking Force units, consisting of the three remaining navies based at Surabaya: two heavy cruisers, *Houston* and HMS *Exeter*; three light cruisers, HMAS *Perth*, HMNS *De Ruyter*, and *Java*; and six destroyers. If the situation seemed discouraging, in Doorman the Allies had found an extraordinary leader, full of daring and intrepidity.

By February 19, in addition to Ozawa Jisaburo's Western Force, they were also facing another powerful Japanese attack group—Vice Admiral Takahashi Ibō's Eastern Group. Timor was soon occupied by the Japanese, and on February 20 Port Darwin, Australia, was very heavily bombed by many dozens of warplanes. The situation was complicated by the fact that the four Allied forces, having been only recently brought together for the first time, had never previously worked together as a team. Ozawa's fifty-six transports headed west while Rear Admiral Nishimura Shoji led another forty-one transports to the east with air cover. The number of Japanese naval ships of all classes and aircraft was indeed overwhelming.

Doorman was determined to attack Nishimura's forty-one transports, despite the formidable odds posed by Rear Admiral Takagi Takeo's task force. On the afternoon of February 17, Takagi's strike force pressed ahead against Doorman's squadron between the north coast of Java and Bawean Island (already in Japanese hands). The Dutch commander had no time to form a battle plan, signaling simply, "FOLLOW ME," as Takagi pushed forward to clear the way for an invasion of Java. Determined to foil enemy plans, Doorman led in *De Ruyter*, followed by *Exeter*, *Houston*, *Perth*, and *Java*, and flanked by the half-dozen destroyers.

The Japanese made the first attack at 1631, but despite a strong spread of forty-three torpedoes, made no hits. At 1700 another remark-

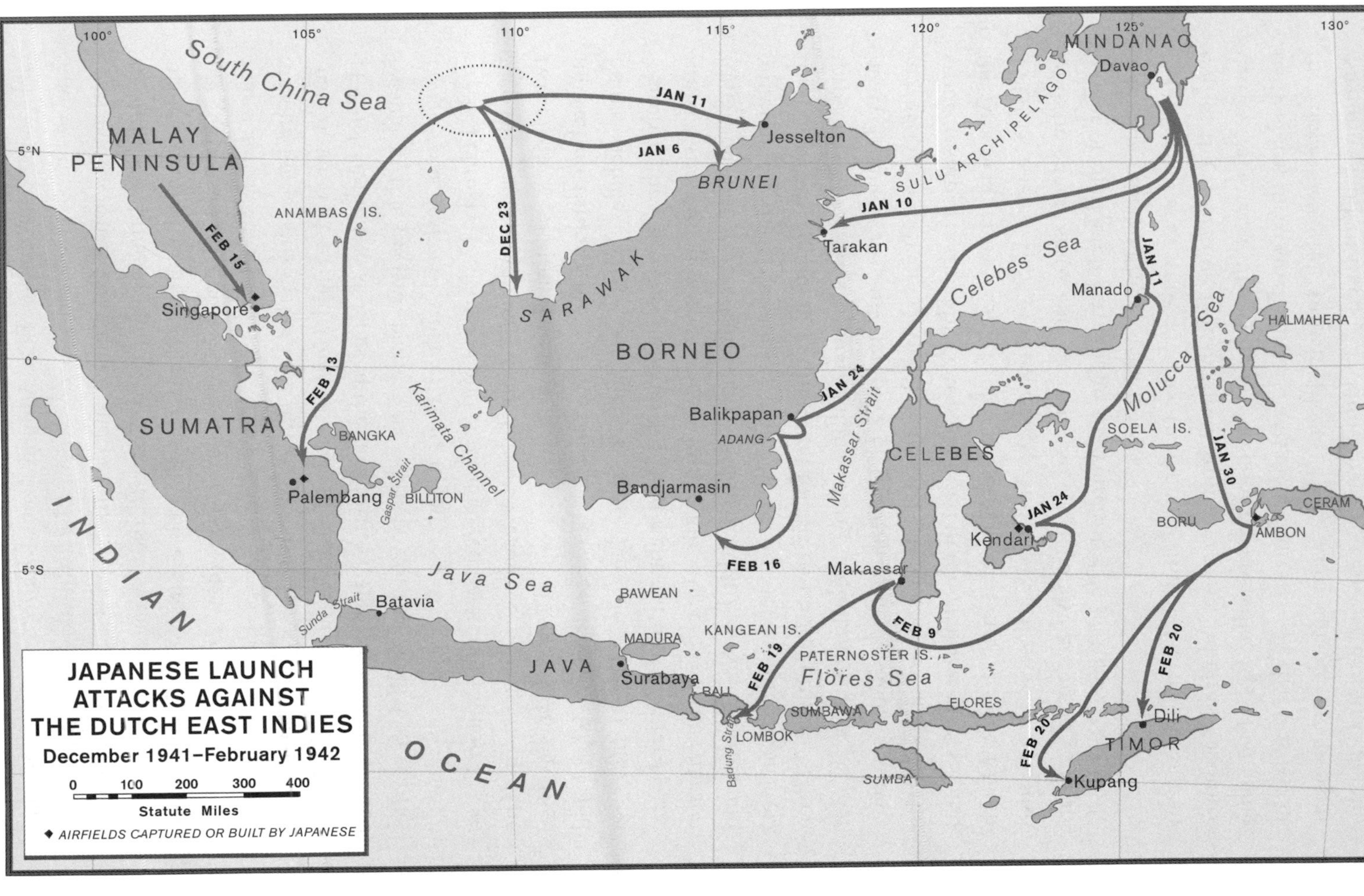

JAPANESE LAUNCH ATTACKS AGAINST THE DUTCH EAST INDIES
December 1941–February 1942
0 100 200 300 400
Statute Miles
◆ AIRFIELDS CAPTURED OR BUILT BY JAPANESE
100°
105°
110°
115°
120°
125°
130°
5°N
0°
5°S
South China Sea
MALAY PENINSULA
Singapore
FEB 15
ANAMBAS IS.
SUMATRA
Palembang
FEB 13
BANGKA
Gaspar Strait
BILLITON
Karimata Channel
DEC 23
JAN 11
JAN 6
Jesselton
BRUNEI
SARAWAK
BORNEO
Balikpapan
ADANG
Bandjarmasin
FEB 16
JAN 10
Tarakan
SULU ARCHIPELAGO
MINDANAO
Davao
Celebes Sea
JAN 24
Makassar Strait
CELEBES
Manado
JAN 11
Molucca Sea
HALMAHERA
SOELA IS.
JAN 30
CERAM
AMBON
BORU
Kendari
JAN 24
Makassar
FEB 9
Java Sea
BAWEAN
MADURA
KANGEAN IS.
PATERNOSTER IS.
Flores Sea
FEB 19
Sunda Strait
Batavia
JAVA
Surabaya
BALI
Badung Strait
LOMBOK
SUMBAWA
FLORES
SUMBA
FEB 20
FEB 20
Dili
TIMOR
Kupang
INDIAN
OCEAN

able naval commander, Rear Admiral Tanaka Raizo, crossed Doorman's line and made a second torpedo sweep, which the skillful Doorman also managed to avoid. Outgunned and outnumbered, Doorman was forced to withdraw, bringing him even closer to the Javanese coast. Japanese planes followed, dropping flares, revealing his entire force. Finally reversing course, Takagi, only 8,000 yards away now, drew up parallel to Doorman's force, launching more "Long Lance" torpedoes and this time striking home, sinking both *De Ruyter* and *Java*. For safety's sake, Doorman ordered *Perth* and *Houston* back to Batavia, where they notified Helfrich of the two sinkings in the Java Sea that had reduced their force by half in this decisive battle. On February 26, the small U.S. carrier *Langley* was next sunk while en route to Java.

On February 27, *Houston* and *Perth* charged back into Bantan Bay to face the might of Admiral Kurita Takeo's Western Covering Group. The two cruisers put four Japanese transports out of commission as they plowed on through the narrow channel between Panjang Island and Saint Nicholas, where the Japanese were lying in wait. At 0005 on March 1, the *Perth* was torpedoed. Lifted right out of the water by the impact, she went down with heavy loss of life. The crew of the *Houston* fought on, but were outnumbered; one shell hit her No. 2 turret and ammunition hoist, forcing Captain Rooks to flood both magazines, thereby depriving him of ammunition for his two 8-inch turrets. Three torpedoes then hit *Houston*, killing many, including Rooks. Under heavy Japanese machine-gunning of the quarterdeck, Rooks's surviving executive officer, David Roberts, gave the order to abandon the stricken ship. The final bugle was sounded in the *Houston* at 0033, and the American cruiser sank twelve minutes later. On that same March 1, HMS *Exeter*, U.S. destroyer *Pope*, and HMS *Encounter* were also sunk by enemy ships and aircraft, and the Japanese accepted the surrender of the Dutch East Indies on March 9, 1942.[4] Tokyo completely dominated the Southwest Pacific area.

Japanese forces were now free to roam the Indian Ocean and put an end to the remaining British threat from the west. Admiral Nagumo's carrier force went after Admiral Sir James Somerville, RN's five aging battleships, three small carriers, and eight cruisers—all that was left of the once powerful British Fleet. They were unable to prevent Nagumo's modern force from launching two heavy strikes at Colombo and at Trincomalee, in Ceylon (now Sri Lanka), between March 25 and April 8, in the process sinking the carrier *Hermes*, two heavy cruisers, and a considerable number of merchantmen. "The Malay Barrier was now shattered," as Paul Dull remarks.[5] And Admiral Yamamoto, the commander of the Imperial Japanese fleet, emerged an even greater hero than before.

•

But who was this much-vaunted Admiral Yamamoto Isoruko, the man who had drafted and executed the daring plan to strike at Pearl Harbor and then thoroughly disrupted and destroyed the combined Asiatic naval fleets of America, Great Britain, and the Netherlands?

His beginnings were modest enough. Born Takano Sadakichi on April 4, 1884, he was the seventh child of an impovershed village schoolmaster. (He would later change his name to Yamamoto.)[6] Attracted by the sea, Takano applied to and entered the Imperial Naval College at Etajima at the age of fifteen.

The vigorous four-year course involved much physical endurance. On one occasion the young Sadakichi was required to swim along the coast for thirteen consecutive hours; despite the ice-cold waters and attacks by jellyfish, he survived the ordeal. A diligent student, Takano Sadakichi graduated seventh in his class. During the Russo-Japanese War, he was posted to the cruiser *Nisshin* and participated in the destruction of the Russian Fleet in the Straits of Tsushima on May 27, 1904. "When the shells began to fall above me I found that I was not afraid," he later recalled, although he was badly wounded in the right leg and lost two fingers of his left hand.

While recovering in the hospital, he practiced his English by reading the Bible regularly. This, added to his lifelong abstention of alcoholic beverages, further singled him out from most of his peers. Upon the death of his parents, he was adopted, in accordance with Japanese custom, by a locally prominent family and changed his name to Yamamoto Isoroku. (The name itself was odd: *Isoroku* meant "fifty-six," his father's age at the time of his son's birth.) When it came time for him to marry, he had many possible brides from which to choose but again did the unexpected, selecting Mihashi Reiko, the daughter of a local dairy farmer. She was unusually tall and not particularly

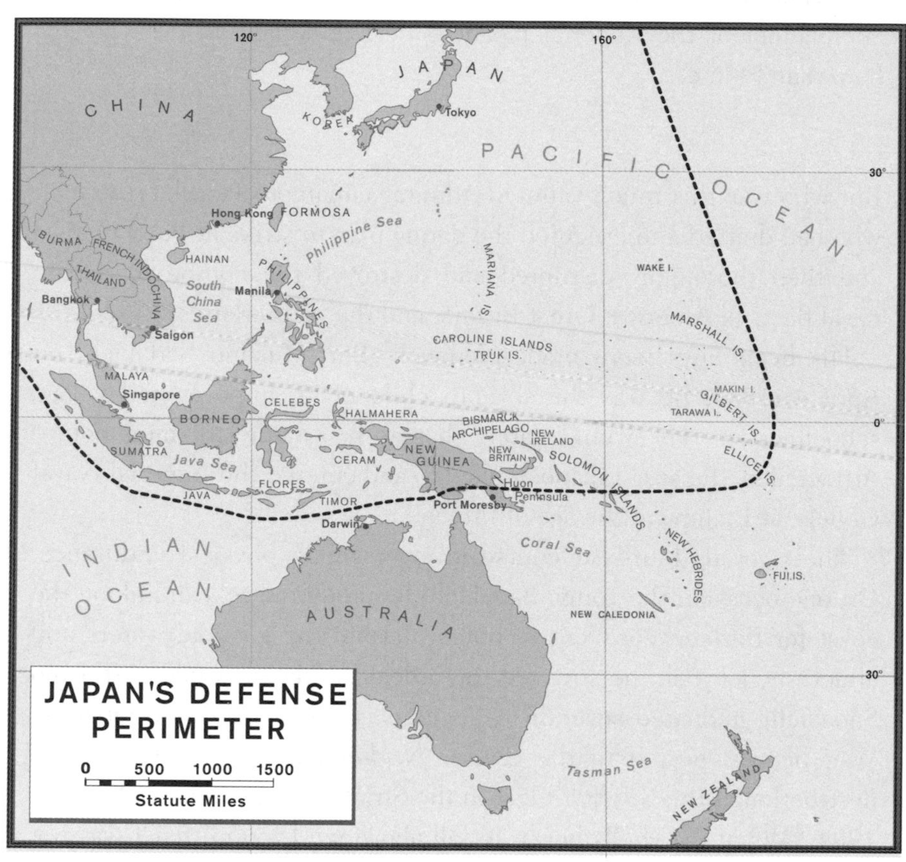

JAPAN'S DEFENSE PERIMETER
0
500
1000
1500
Statute Miles
120°
160°
30°
0°
30°
CHINA
JAPAN
Tokyo
KOREA
PACIFIC OCEAN
Hong Kong
FORMOSA
Philippine Sea
BURMA
FRENCH INDOCHINA
THAILAND
HAINAN
South China Sea
Bangkok
Saigon
Manila
PHILIPPINES
MARIANA IS.
WAKE I.
MARSHALL IS.
CAROLINE ISLANDS
TRUK IS.
MALAYA
Singapore
BORNEO
CELEBES
HALMAHERA
MAKIN I.
TARAWA I.
GILBERT IS.
ELLICE IS.
BISMARCK ARCHIPELAGO
NEW IRELAND
NEW BRITAIN
SOLOMON ISLANDS
SUMATRA
Java Sea
CERAM
NEW GUINEA
JAVA
FLORES
TIMOR
Huon Peninsula
Port Moresby
Darwin
Coral Sea
NEW HEBRIDES
FIJI IS.
INDIAN OCEAN
AUSTRALIA
NEW CALEDONIA
Tasman Sea
NEW ZEALAND

attractive. The couple then settled down in a furnitureless house.

Yamamoto Isoroku was now ordered to Harvard University in 1919 for a special two-year course, leaving his wife at home. He enjoyed entertaining friends and delighted the American postgraduates there, sometimes standing on his head or spinning dishes at dinner parties. He liked to play chess and baseball and became a poker fanatic, once playing for twenty-six hours nonstop.

He also did a lot of sightseeing, from Boston to Washington, D.C. Later he hitchhiked down to Mexico, where he studied the oil fields. During World War I, he became fascinated by the introduction of aviation in warfare and visited American aircraft factories and fields, buying all the books he could find on the subject. When the first American plane was flown off the USS *Birmingham*, and later the *Pennsylvania*, his thoughts dwelt more and more on the future of aircraft as a weapon as opposed to the traditional battleship in war. He was enthralled when at the end of the war the Royal Navy had launched its first carrier, HMS *Furious*, followed by the keel laying of Japan's first carrier, the 7,470-ton *Hōshō*.

Back in Japan in 1923, having made excellent use of his time abroad, Captain Yamamoto was appointed executive officer of the new naval air-training center at Kasumigaura. It was only now that he finally learned to fly, curiously enough. His great aim was to create a powerful new Naval Aviation Unit for his country.

In 1925, Yamamoto was sent back to the United States for two years to serve as naval attaché at the Japanese Embassy. He mingled easily with American officers and learned a new card game that was to captivate him—bridge—and became an avid follower of major league baseball. During this period the Washington Arms Limitation Conference had in 1921–22 reduced Japanese naval power to a third place, reducing its armaments to a 5:5:3 ratio. At the same time, the Versailles Conference had awarded Japan possession of the "Mandates," former German colonies in the Pacific including the Carolines and Marianas, the significance of which did not escape Yamamoto's notice. Nor did he fail to follow the main stories in American newspapers on Billy Mitchell's pronouncements about a possible war with Japan.[7]

Upon returning to his country in 1928, Yamamoto was given command of the carrier *Akagi* and then served as chief of the Technical

Bureau of Naval Aviation Department from 1930 to 1933. In 1933, he was rewarded with the command of Carrier Division One, and was promoted vice admiral the following year.

That same year he attended the London Naval Conference, where he announced at a startled press conference, in fluent English, that "Japan can no longer submit to the ratio system. There is no possibility of compromise by my Government on that point." Japan, he concluded, was simply withdrawing from this unobliging naval treaty, which is precisely what he repeated later to Prime Minister Ramsay MacDonald. Yamamoto also presented the conference with a shocking proposal: a declaration to abolish all capital ships and aircraft carriers in 1935. He added that if given a free hand throughout Asia, Japan might agree to a world program of disarmament. "We consider the aircraft carrier the most offensive of all weapons," he asserted—and thus it would have to be included in any such disarmament agreement. It did not seem to have occurred to Yamamoto that asking the Western powers to allow Japan to occupy the whole of Asia might appear a rather bizarre proposal, one fraught wih contradiction.

But even as the disarmement talks were taking place, Japan was in the midst of a secret major new warship construction program that, amongst other "items," included four giant battleships of the *Yamato* class: 73,700 tons each with 18.1-inch guns and 16 inches of hull armor. Two would be completed; the third, the *Shinano*, ultimately begun in 1940, would be converted into the world's largest aircraft carrier, and the fourth abandoned altogether.

In 1936, Yamamoto was named vice minister of the Imperial Japanese Navy and would also serve as chief of the Naval Aviation Department,[8] providing him with the power and position to accelerate aircraft production. Japan already had two big carriers, *Akagi* and *Kaga*, and despite much opposition from the old "Gun Club" the new vice minister prepared for the construction of two more, the 30,000-ton, 34-knot *Shokaku* and *Zuikaku*. Yamamoto also demanded long-range flying boats, and had them by the late 1930s. These were capable of flying a total distance of 1,600 miles; the land-based navy bombers being developed had ranges of up to 2,300 miles. Another Yamamoto project, the new Zero, also went ahead, as the United States painfully discovered after Pearl Harbor. A hard and dedicated line officer, Yamamoto

Crown Prince Hirohito bowing before the Cenotaph War Memorial, London, 1921.
(Permission of the British Library, from *Illustrated London News*, May 14, 1921)

FDR
(U.S. Naval Historical Center photograph)

Prime Minister Winston Churchill; First Sea Lord Admiral Sir Dudley Pound; and Captain John C. Leach (DSO, MVO), in command of the *Prince of Wales*, which brought the British Prime Minister to Newfoundland for this top-secret meeting with President Roosevelt in August 1941. Later Churchill ordered Leach to take the battleship *Prince of Wales* and the cruiser *Repulse* without any air cover to the Far East. Both ships were sunk by Japanese bombers off the Malay coast, Captain Leach and most of his men going down with their ship. (Permission of Admiral leach, photographer unknown)

Roosevelt convenes his new war cabinet. *Left to right, starting with the man in the gray suit in the foreground*: Harry Hopkins, Lend-Lease administrator; Frances Perkins, secretary of labor; Colonel P. B. Flemming, Federal Works administrator; Vice President Harry A. Wallace; Mayor Fiorello H. La Guardia, Civilian Defense chief; Paul V. McVatt, Federal Security administrator; Jesse Jones, secretary of commerce and Federal Loan administrator; Harold Ickes, secretary of the interior; Frank C. Walker, postmaster general; Harry L. Stimson, secretary of war; Cordell Hull, secretary of state; President Roosevelt; Henry Morgenthau, Secretary of the Treasury; Francis Biddle, attorney general, Frank Knox, secretary of the navy, and Claude W. Wickard, secretary of agriculture. (Library of Congress)

World War II: Atlantic Charter, August 10–12, 1941. *Left to right (standing):* General George C. Marshall (leaning over, talking to FDR), Admiral Ernest J. King, Admiral Harold R. Stark; *(sitting):* President Franklin D. Roosevelt and Prime Minister Winston Churchill. Photo taken at the conclusion of church services aboard HMS *Prince of Wales*, off Newfoundland, August 10, 1941.
(U.S. Naval Historical Center photograph)

World War II: Atlantic Charter, August 10–12, 1941. *Left to right:* Ensign Franklin D. Roosevelt, Jr.; Prime Minister Winston Churchill; President Franklin D. Roosevelt; and Captain Elliot Roosevelt, aboard USS *Augusta* (CA 31), off Newfoundland, August 1941.
(U.S. Naval Historical Center photograph)

The inimitable Harry Hopkins when he was still in fairly good health. (Courtesy of Time Life Magazine Archives)

The proud USS *West Virginia* (BB-48), one of the eight U.S. battleships bombed and torpedoed during the sneak Japanese attack, December 7, 1941. (U.S. Naval Historical Center photograph)

Admiral Nagumo Chuichi, who successfully attacked Pearl Harbor, December 7, 1941, was then defeated at Midway, June 1942, and later committed suicide.
(U.S. Naval Historical Center photograph)

Admiral of the Fleet, Commander of the Combined Fleet, Yamamoto Isoroku.
(U.S. Naval Historical Center photograph)

Fleet Admiral, Commander in Chief (COMINCH), and CNO Ernest J. King, who commanded the entire U.S. Navy throughout the war. (U.S. Naval Historical Center photograph)

Admiral Sir Dudley Pound, First Sea Lord, and Admiral Harold Stark, following Stark's dismissal as CNO and just prior to Pound's death; he was succeeded as Britain's First Sea Lord by Admiral of the Fleet Sir Andrew Cunningham. (U.S. Naval Historical Center photograph, courtesy of the Stark Collection)

USS *Dauntless*, Fleet Admiral and COMINCH U.S. Fleet Ernest King's flagship and quarters in the Washington Naval Yard, where on August 12, 1942, he received news of the defeat at the battle of Savo Island.
(U.S. Naval Historical Center photograph)

Fleet Admiral Ernest J. King and General of the Army George C. Marshall secretly asking FDR to make the Pacific theater the first priority (over Germany).

(U.S. Naval Historical Center photograph)

Admiral William Leahy, White House chief of staff.

(U.S. Naval Historical Center photograph)

Secretary of the Navy Frank Knox, (*right*) confers with Admiral Thomas Hart about the grave situation in the Philippines, March 1942.
(U.S. Naval Historical Center photograph, from the collection of Admiral Thomas C. Hart)

Triumphant Japanese troops and tanks advance on Corregidor, May 1942.
(U.S. Naval Historical Center photograph, courtesy of Dr. Diosdado M. Yap, editor-publisher, *Bataan* magazine, Washington, DC)

Japanese burn Luzon.
(U.S. Naval Historical Center photograph, courtesy of Dr. Diosdado M. Yap, editor-publisher, *Bataan* magazine, Washington, DC)

Ruins of Battery Crockett, Corregidor, May 1942.
(U.S. Naval Historical Center photograph, courtesy of Dr. Diosdado M. Yap, editor-publisher, *Bataan* magazine, Washington, DC)

Lieutenant General Jonathan Wainwright, who was given command of all U.S. and Philippine forces when MacArthur was ordered to Australia. The courageous Wainwright fought until the end and was then placed in a series of Japanese concentration camps and constantly tortured, until he was released in August 1945. (U.S. Army photograph from the National Archives)

The Japanese lower the U.S. flag on Corregidor after its capture on May 6, 1942.
(U.S. Naval Historical Center photograph, courtesy of Dr. Diosdado M. Yap, editor-publisher, *Bataan* magazine, Washington, DC)

Philippine invasion, 1941–42: American prisoners of war, who surrendered at the end of the Bataan campaign, April 1942. (U.S. Naval Historical Center photograph, courtesy of Dr. Diosdado M. Yap, editor-publisher, *Bataan* magazine, Washington, DC)

American POWs beginning Bataan "Death March," April 1942. (Marine Corps photograph from the National Archives)

The unsung hero, Joseph John Rochefort, USN, chief of Nimitz's HYPO (intelligence gathering and analysis) station at Pearl Harbor, who was responsible, with his team, for cracking the Japanese naval code warning of the enemy's intention to attack Midway in June 1942. This permitted Admiral Chester Nimitz to send his entire fleet to Midway, ultimately defeating Yamamoto, including the sinking of four big Japanese carriers. Rochefort's reward: to be drummed out of Naval Intelligence by members of a plot including the Redman brothers, who were jealous of his spectacular achievements, his fate then sealed by Admiral King himself.
(U.S. Naval Historical Center photograph, courtesy of Captain R. Pineau)

Autographed photo of General MacArthur to Admiral Chester Nimitz, with the inscription: "To Admiral Nimitz with regards and admiration, Douglas MacArthur," which Nimitz referred to as the "Jovian Bolt." (US. Navy Historical Center photograph, courtesy of Fleet Admiral Nimitz)

Admiral Raymond A. Spruance, USN, commander at Midway in June 1942.
(U.S. Naval Historical Center photograph)

Japanese cruiser *Mogami* after being bombed by U.S. carrier planes, Midway, June 1942.
(Library of Congress)

U.S. naval warplanes in action over Midway, June 1942.
(Library of Congress)

U.S. antiaircraft guns splash another Japanese warplane over Midway.
(Library of Congress)

Vice Admiral Frank Jack Fletcher, USN, who abandoned Rear Admiral Turner, his transports, and Major General A. A. Vandegrift and his marines on Guadalcanal on August 8, 1942, resulting in his removal from carrier command.
(U.S. Naval Historical Center photograph)

Lieutenant General Robert Eichelberger, probably MacArthur's finest field commander, who helped save MacArthur's reputation when he was sent in several times at the last minute to lead troops in the course of being defeated. Eichelberger transformed these actions into U.S. victories with the aid of the most able Australian forces.
(U.S. Army photograph from the National Archives)

Lieutenant General George C. Kenney, USAAF, the superb commander of MacArthur's air force.
(U.S. Air Force photograph from the National Archives)

Vice Admiral Robert L. Ghormley, commander of the U.S. Navy in the South Pacific, based at Nouméa, New Caledonia, 1942. He was relieved of his command by Vice Admiral Bill Halsey after failing to support Admiral Turner's amphibious landings at Guadalcanal and Tulagi and General A. A. Vandegrift's marines thereafter on those southern Solomon Islands.
(U.S. Naval Historical Center photograph)

The difficult Generalissimo Chiang Kai-shek, head of the pro-American government, who was fighting both the Japanese and Chinese Communist armies.
(U.S. Naval Historical Center photograph)

Admiral Kelly "Terrible" Turner—the architect and commander of the U.S. naval amphibious forces throughout the war in the Pacific. (U.S. Naval Historical Center photograph)

Lieutenant General Alexander A. Vandegrift, USMC, who commanded the U.S. marines on Guadalcanal, and who later succeeded to the post of head of the U.S. Marine Corps. (U.S. Naval Historical Center photograph)

Battle of Savo Island, August 9, 1942, sinking U.S. and Allied ships following Japanese naval attack.
(U.S. Naval Historical Center photograph, courtesy of Dr. Diosdado M. Yap, editor-publisher, *Bataan* magazine, Washington, DC)

U.S. Army unit advancing toward the front on Guadalcanal, January 20, 1943.
(U.S. Naval Historical Center photograph)

The versatile amphtracs deployed for amphibious landings throughout the Pacific.
(Library of Congress)

The stench of death at the Tenaru River, Guadalcanal, after Vandegrift's marines annihilated a Japanese attack on August 21, 1942.
(Library of Congress)

Rear Admiral John S. McCain (*left*) shaking hands with Rear Admiral Aubrey Fitch as Fitch relieved McCain as commander of aircraft, South Pacific Force, September 21, 1942, at which time McCain became chief of the Bureau of Aeronautics, Washington, D.C.
(U.S. Naval Historical Center photograph)

Exhausted U.S. marines taking a brief rest prior to a new attack against the Japanese on Guadalcanal, 1942.
(U.S. Naval Historical Center photograph)

The undauntable Rear Admiral Tanaka Raizo, Imperial Japanese Navy, the brilliant commander of the "Tokyo Express" to Guadalcanal.
(U.S. Naval Historical Center photograph, courtesy of Dr. Diosdado M. Yap, editor-publisher, *Bataan* magazine, Washington, DC)

Admiral John H. Towers, USN, architect of the U.S. naval air and carrier force, who later served as Admiral Nimitz's second in command.
(U.S. Naval Historical Center photograph, A. A. Burke Collection)

The battleship *Yamato*, along with her twin, the *Musashi*, was the world's largest battleship and, equipped with 18.1-inch guns, the most powerful afloat.
(U.S. Navy photograph from the National Archives)

General A. M. Patch, who relieved Marine General A. A. Vandegrift at Guadalcanal, January 1942, receiving the DSM from Vice Admiral Aubrey Fitch, after Patch had mopped up Guadalcanal. Behind Patch are Brigadier General R. L. Spragins, corps chief of staff, and Brigadier General William R. Woodwart, artillery commander.
(U.S. Naval Historical Center photograph)

Emperor Hirohito, who secretly personally directed Japanese military strategy throughout World War II, and who had given Yamamoto authorization to attack the United States in 1941, and later to use biological and chemical warfare.
(U.S. Naval Historical Center photograph)

Wounded Americans at Buna, New Guinea, ignored by MacArthur, who refused to tour the front during the battles for Buna and Gona, battles won by Lieutenant General Robert Eichelberger.
(Library of Congress)

Admiral Chester Nimitz, CINCPAC, whose audacity resulted in the U.S. naval victory at Midway in 1942 and the successful invasion of Guadalcanal in August. These two events checked the Japanese offensive, thereby marking the turning point in the war in the Pacific.
(U.S. Naval Historical Center photograph)

was greatly respected by his men and in the highest military circles. And thus his promotion to the supreme post of commander in chief of the Combined Fleet in 1933 came as no surprise.[9] But when Prime Minister Konoe asked later what chance there was of Japan's defeating the United States and Britain, a wary Yamamoto replied, "I can raise havoc with them for one year or at most eighteen months. After that I can give no one any guarantees." By January 1940 Yamamoto's navy already had 3,500 veteran pilots.

Although the admiral had hoped to retire in November 1940 at the age of fifty-six, his unique qualities could be found in no other man, and the empire's needs came first. Addressing some schoolchildren that same year, he warned that they should never underestimate the enemy:

> It is a mistake to regard the Americans as luxury-loving and weak. I can tell you Americans are full of the spirit of justice, fight and adventure. Also their thinking is very advanced and scientific. . . . Do not forget, American industry is much more developed than ours—and unlike us they have all the oil they want. Japan cannot beat America. Therefore we should not fight America.[10]

And yet, ironically, in the last analysis, it was this very Admiral Yamamoto who had convinced his country to attack Pearl Harbor; but he, like most of his fellow countrymen, was controlled by an all-pervasive fatalism. Events occurred because they were so fated, and no one, not even the emperor himself, could defy fate.

•

By March 1942, "fate" had cast its long shadow over the Far East, bringing with it a world of confusion, fear, and brutality. The Asiatic fleets of the United States, Great Britain, and the Netherlands had been practically annihilated, from the Philippines to India and the Dutch East Indies. The Imperial Army and Navy commanders were debating with and among one another as to the next step. The Imperial Japanese Army staff were more united. Disturbed by American air and naval attacks in the Marshalls and at Wake, New Guinea, and Marcus Island, the Japanese army wanted to drive farther south through the southwest Pacific to occupy New Guinea, part of the Solomons, and perhaps Australia and New Caledonia. But as the empire's greates naval hero and commander of the navy, Admiral Yamamoto argued against the army's plans to expand operations, for they could not be achieved without the strong support of the Japanese navy and its large air force, both at sea and on land. Instead, by March 30, Combined Fleet Headquarters presented its own, very different objective: to seze Midway and force Nimitz's Pacific Fleet to come out to meet them, coercing the U.S. into one colossal battle of annihilation.[11]

Although several naval staff members, including Vice Admiral Inouye Shigeyoshi, opposed the Midway plan—and Vice Admirals Kondo of the Second Fleet and Nagumo of the First Air Fleet were not even consulted—the plan was accepted. There had to be a compromise, however, for even Yamamoto could not outvote the Imperial Japanese Army, whose senior staff included several members of Hirohito's own family. Therefore Yamamoto agreed to provide a part of his Combined Fleet for the invasion of New Guinea, including Port Moresby in particular, and also, across the sea, the small island of Tulagi in the southern Solomons, from which the Imperial Navy could sweep the sea of any Allied forces—American, Australian, or New Zealand—that might attempt to come to the rescue. This was designated Operation "MO." When it was successfully completed through the use of overwhelming army and naval force, Yamamoto could then withdraw his naval task forces there and recombine them with the Combined Fleet for the attack on Midway.

The Doolittle Raid over Japan on April 18 merely hardened Tokyo's resolve. But what senior army chiefs, in pushing through their plans for Operation MO, took for a victory over the Imperial Navy, would in fact only hasten the downfall of both the army aand navy by overextending their logistics and fighting abilities, sapping their strength instead of tightening their imperial defense perimeter. Once again, dissenting voices were muted, resulting in a Japanese failure to anticipate any and all consequences of a radical new operation. The army chiefs' cockiness would prove their own undoing. And thus was cast the proverbial die, blood-red, as in the imperial flag.

> "I am firmly convinced that the Pacific war was started by men who did not understand the sea, and fought by men who did not understand the air. Had there been better understanding of the sea and air, Japan would have pondered more carefully the wisdom of going to war."
>
> —*Commander Okumiya Masatake, February 1951*[12]

> "Had we lacked early information of the Japanese movements, and had we been caught with carrier forces dispersed . . . the Battle of Midway would have ended differently."
>
> —*Admiral Chester Nimitz, June 28, 1942*[13]

The U.S. Navy had learned much since Pearl Harbor through Commander Joe Rochefort's Fleet Radio Unit Pacific (FRUPac), the Naval Intelligence station code-named "HYPO." situated in the windowless basement of the new cement, bombproof administrative annex on Makalapa Hill, which now continued to intercept Japanese naval messages, aided by the former intelligence unit at Corregidor that had since been moved to the southwest Pacific. As the Japanese had changed their naval code just before Pearl Harbor, "only one in ten intercepted messages," HYPO's Lieutenant Jaspar Holmes attested, "could be forced to yield information." The man who tried to crack this "bucked a large element of chance."[14] At Pearl Harbor, Rochefort's best man for just that sort of work was cryptanalyst Joseph Finnegan, who kept coming up with strange material almost out of the blue. He and other officers were working throughout March and early April 1942 when Finnegan first came across the phrase "MO Covering Force." The volume of radio traffic emanating from Japanese GHQ at Rabaul—the New Britain port, off the northeast coast of New Guinea, that Japan had captured in January—began to increase greatly, indicating to HYPO new, large-scale activity in that area. The commander of the

Japanese Fourth Fleet at Rabaul kept referring to a ship called *Ryukaku*, previously unknown to HYPO. (Only months later were they to learn that *Ryukaku* was in fact the light carrier *Shoho*.) The Naval Intelligence officers at Pearl "translated bits of messages, collated with traffic analysis" and after much work pieced together "a reasonable estimate" of what sort of ship it was, one capable of supporting flight operations. HYPO also discovered that four heavy cruisers that had arrived at Truk, in the Caroline Islands, had next sailed southward in the direction of the Coral Sea. Curiously enough, many of their messages also somehow seemed to be linked with *Ryukaku*. Finnegan began to associate "MO Covering Force" with the Cruiser Division Six, which included the *Aoba*. Next, the unrelenting Finnegan came across another new phrase, "MO Occupation Force," and a second one that appeared to be related, referring to an unidentified location in the Solomon Islands.

Slowly the pieces were coming together. Rochefort had for some time suspected a major naval attack against New Guinea, but had previously found little hard evidence to substantiate it. As a fluent Japanese linguist, having learned the language in Tokyo, he knew—better than most—the Japanese military psyche, and that was something a mere language could never instill. HYPO analysts also learned now that the seaplane tender carrier, *Kamikawa Maru*, in another task group, was currently operating in the Louisiades, an archipelago of small islands trailing off the southern tip of New Guinea. Rochefort came to the conclusion that a complex Japanese operation was about to take place. He determined that a strike force would thrust around the east coast of the Solomons and into the Coral Sea in support of the seizure of Port Moresby, while another one would seize and occupy an advanced base somewhere in the Solomons. At least four heavy cruisers and the *Ryukaku* would cover this campaign, Rochefort thought. It was imperative to learn the dates of these combined attacks, for part of the Japanese Fleet was already at sea. According to Holmes, the best estimate was the first week of May. Acting upon this assessment, on May 1 Admiral Nimitz dispatched an Allied naval force of two carriers (*Lexington* and *Yorktown*), eight American and Australian cruisers, and eleven destroyers to the eastern end of the Coral Sea to meet the fresh threat[15] Chester

Nimitz, for one, took Commander Joe Rochefort very seriously.

Even as the American navy deployed, Rochefort's team linked the commander of the Fourth Fleet at Rabaul with two large carriers, *Shokaku* and *Zuikaku* (Carrier Division Five). The Japanese carriers had evidently given up looking for Halsey's carriers, *Hornet* and *Enterprise*, which had participated in the Doolittle Raid and which were on the return voyage back to Pearl Harbor. Japan's carrier strike force, *Kido Butai*, began to detach ships, ordering Cruiser Division Five and the *Myoko* and *Naguro* to the island fortress of Truk. The Americans obviously lacked the strength to attack six or seven carriers at once, but they could take on two at a time.

Meanwhile, at HYPO offices overlooking Ford Island, the pressure was mounting by the minute. "The chart desk was strewn with charts of New Britain, New Guinea, and the Solomon Islands," Lieutenant Holmes recalled. "The air was thick with conversations about the *Kamikawa Maru*, the Port Moresby Occupation Force, and Rabaul. Each incoming message was quickly scanned for reference to the Fourth Fleet or Carrier Division Five. We lived and breathed and schemed in the atmosphere of the Coral Sea. . . . I wanted Rochefort to go over to CincPac Headquarters and suggest to Admiral Nimitz that Halsey take that cutoff, bypassing Pearl Harbor [altogether], and make a high-speed run to join up with the *Lexington* and *Yorktown*." Rochefort disagreed. It was his job to provide Nimitz with the intelligence and his analysis, he informed Holmes, not to tell him how to run operations.

Rochefort was quite right, of course, for Holmes, who was not a pilot, had overlooked one major fact. In addition to having to reprovision and refuel, the *Hornet*, which had carried Doolittle's sixteen B-25s, their crews and equipment, would also have to take on new flight crews and dozens of new naval bombers, torpedo planes, and fighter aircraft. Reaching Pearl Harbor on 25 April, Halsey received orders from Nimitz to proceed to the Coral Sea—a voyage of 3,500 miles—as soon as the *Enterprise* and *Hornet* were ready. That carrier task force hauled out of Pearl Harbor five days later. Time was of the essence and the distance great. Nimitz and Rochefort's team had done all that they could do for the moment, except pray.

•

It seemed as though nothing could slow down, much less stop, the Japanese invasion of New Guinea now. "When I reflect how I have longed and prayed for the entry of the United States into the war," Churchill confided to Roosevelt when news came through of the recent losses incurred in the Java Sea, "I find it difficult to realise how gravely our British affairs have deteriorated since December 7."[17] So far everything in the Pacific had been failing, and FDR was at times almost as despondent as the British prime minister himself. Roosevelt's response had been totally unexpected, however: the Doolittle Raid on the capital of Japan itself, which only hardened a humiliated Yamamoto's resolve to seize Port Moresby and Tulagi and especially to destroy the U.S. Fleet.

Thanks to their success in the Philippines, Japanese troops had already landed at Lae and Salamaua, New Guinea, with strong reinforcements en route. Yamamoto hoped that if Tokyo took Port Moresby, it would force the Americans to come to the Australians' aid in that region, although the scaled-down size of his carrier force there indicates that he knew in advance that this would not be the great final battle with the U.S. Navy required for its destruction. On May 1, Yamamoto ordered one light and two heavy carriers, two heavy cruisers, and six destroyers, under the command of Vice Admiral Takagi Takeo, to the Coral Sea. If successful in the Port Moresby operation, they could then occupy New Caledonia, among other islands. Hence the necessity for also including Tulagi, in the Solomons, as part of the Port Moresby campaign to ensure the severing of American naval communications in the Coral Sea area.[18] Twelve transports under Rear Admiral Abe Koso sailed for Port Morseby via the Solomon Sea on May 4. Swinging around the east coast of the Solomons, Takagi's Carrier Strike Force—the *Zuikaku*, *Shokaku*, and *Shoho*—would soon be in position, along with the Support Force Main Body, including six more heavy cruisers, one light cruiser, and twelve destroyers.[19] To meet this threat Nimitz had sent out the two heavy, or fast, carriers, *Yorktown* (under Frank Jack Fletcher) and *Lexington* (commanded by Rear Admiral Aubrey Fitch), six heavy American cruisers, one Australian cruiser, and a dozen destroyers.

Early on May 7, Takagi found the first two American ships—an oiler and a destroyer—but nothing else. As noted, on May 5, U.S. Task Force 17 joined the two other carriers near the easternmost part of the Louisiades, at the southeast end of New Guinea. Fletcher ordered Rear Admiral J. G. Crace's three cruisers and two destroyers to somehow prevent the Port Moresby Japanese force from advancing around the Louisiades. Although coming under heavy enemy attack (not to mention a few bombs dropped in error by the U.S. Air Force), Crace succeeded in his mission, and the Japanese turned back.[20] Meanwhile, the second Japanese force was still on its way to Tulagi as planned.

As planes from *Zuikaku* and *Shokaku* were attacking the only two American ships they saw—the oiler *Neosho* and destroyer *Sims*—they at last discovered the presence of two American carriers. In turn, at 0815 a *Yorktown* surveillance plane pilot reported sighting the two fast enemy carriers and four cruisers only 225 miles northwest of the Allied task force. Shortly before 0900, Frank Jack Fletcher ordered a large-scale attack of ninety-three war planes from the *Lexington* and *Yorktown*. But it was only when his planes were en route that Fletcher discovered he had not found the main carriers after all, but rather the smaller part of the MO Force heading for Tulagi under Rear Admiral Gotō Aritomo. Instead of two large carriers, his pilots found only the light carrier, *Shoho*, which they then sank, while forcing Gotō's cruisers to retire.

Takagi's two big carriers now had a fix on Fletcher's ships, but Fletcher was still unaware of his opponent's position. At 2200, *Zuikaku* and *Shokaku* were in fact arming in preparation for the attack against Fletcher's carriers, at this point just one hundred miles away.

It was only at 0722 the following morning, May 8, that Fletcher finally spotted Takagi's big carriers and at 0738 launched thirty-nine planes from the *Yorktown* and forty-three from "*Lady Lex*." At 1000 *Yorktown*'s squadrons swept down to attack *Shokaku*, which was in the course of launching her own aircraft. The torpedo-bombers dropped down to sea level but launched their torperdoes from too great a distance and failed to hit her. The American dive-bombers were a little more successful as two bombs damaged part of the flight deck, but not yet seriously enough to prevent her planes from landing. As for *Lexington*'s planes, due to rain squalls they were unable to locate *Zuikaku*, while only one of their bombs hit the already damaged *Shokaku*, whose deck was still on fire. But apparently the final hit on the flight deck was enough for the captain of the *Shokaku*, as he withdrew from the battle and shaped a new course that would take him back to port, along with 223 casualties. Because of her by now substantial flight deck damage, forty-six of her planes had to make emergency landings on the *Zuikaku*.[21]

Meanwhile, sixty-nine of Takagi's planes were attacking both the *Lexington* and the *Yorktown*, which Fletcher had failed to provide with adequate air cover, or combat air patrol (CAP). Fletcher was not a pilot and had never learned to think like one. As a result of his alarming oversight, a bomb struck the starboard side of the *Lexington* at about 1020; a second strike followed. Another bomb hit the port side of *Lex*'s bow, destroying a ready-ammunition box there, and a fourth bomb exploded in her funnel. The *Yorktown* for her part was hit by a bomb on her flight deck, although she was still able to launch and recover aircraft. Then at 1247 a mass of gaseous fumes exploded in the *Lady Lex*, followed by a series of fires from ruptured fuel tanks. At 1707 the captain of the *Lexington* gave the order to abandon ship; and she was then sunk by the American destroyer *Phelps*. The badly gutted *Yorktown* withdrew to Nouméa, New Caledonia, and limped on to Pearl Harbor for serious repairs.

Both task forces retreated, although Takagi's remaining planes did return to finish off the *Yorktown*, but failed to find her. *Zuikaku* sailed back to Truk, while the *Shokaku*'s return voyage resulted in even greater damage, apparently caused by severe storms. Although the *Zuikaku* suffered no serious damage, she had lost many planes and pilots, as had *Shokaku*. The fact that the *Zuikaku*, lacking sufficient planes and pilots, was unable to put to sea again until June 12 was apparently not fully appreciated at the time. In reality it indicated that even at this early stage of the war the Japanese were already having considerable trouble in replacing qualified men and *matériel de guerre*. Thus even the sinking of a small carrier like *Shoho* was a blow. It is indeed ironic under the circumstances that the American fleet suffered far more serious losses in men and ships—the *Lexington* sunk and the *Yorktown* left a floating mass of twisted steel. But the latter nevertheless had succeeded in turning back the Japanese carrier strike force, resulting in the aborting of their plans to attack and invade both Port Moresby and Tulagi.

The battle for the conquest of New Guinea, however, was just beginning, and would involve much bloody fighting in the days ahead. The battle of the Coral Sea, May 7–8, marked the first of several entirely carrrier-to-carrier engagements in the Pacific. Fletcher had proven his inability to grasp carrier command, while his green air crews were still not a match for Japan's veteran pilots. *Enterprise* and *Hornet*, although failing to arrive in time, would get their chance when a very stubborn Admiral Yamamoto sprung his next, even greater surprise. The battle of the Coral Sea was in fact but "a prelude," as Admiral King put it.

●

Following the events in the Coral Sea, with Operation MO in shambles, Yamamoto immediately began preparing his new enormous Combined Fleet for the attack on Midway and the annihilation of Admiral Nimitz's entire Pacific Fleet . . . with or without the *Shokaku* and *Zuikaku*.

Back at Pearl Harbor, Joe Rochefort's cryptanalysts at HYPO were continuing to work overtime. There would be no weekends off. According to Lieutenant Jaspar Holmes, Commander Rochefort, who seemed to possess an extraordinarily accurate strategic sense, was convinced that Midway would be the next major operation carried out by Yamamoto, just as he had earlier predicted the attack against Port Moresby. Unusual things were beginning to happen once again, and Rochefort started assembling a dossier, a sort of jigsaw puzzle with many blank spaces to fill in. On March 10, 1942, a Japanese spy plane had been shot down over Midway. Nothing further happened—there were no further flights for the moment—and that fact was filed along with thousands of other seemingly unimportant items. But Rochefort now recalled the incident in the critical month of May when a considerable increase in naval radio traffic from air operations in the Marshall Islands (to the south and approximately halfway between Midway and New Guinea) was noted. This was accompanied by strong Japanese reinforcements arriving at Kwajalein, in the Marshalls, and then by additional radio traffic with Air Squadron 24 at Kwajalein, almost a replay of what had preceded the surprise attack on Pearl Harbor. All this pointed to the formation of another new fleet, new naval stations, and the buildup of forces around Saipan, in the Marianas (between the

Marshalls and Japan). The Fourth Fleet, also in the Mandates, and the position of the Second Fleet, now indicated to Rochefort the assembly of another *Kido Butai*. All appeared to be interrelated.

Many of the messages intercepted were between commanding officers of these units. Then something else cropped up: a completely new two-letter area designator, "AF," two letters that, as it turned out, would change the direction of the war. Previously, "AFG" had referred to the French Frigate Shoal, off Hawaii. Therefore, perhaps "AF" was somewhere in the long Hawaiian chain. Suddenly the alarm bells began to ring in Rochefort's department when analysts decrypted a message referring to AF Occupation Force." Rochefort presented this information to CINCPAC's fleet intelligence officer, Edwin Layton: First the formation of the largest Japanese fleet thus far and now the introduction of an occupation force associated with this new *Kido Butai*.

Soon afterward, some good news reached CINCPAC. Bill Halsey's two carriers, which had failed to reach the Coral Sea in time, were returning to Hawaii. As the Japanese had incorrectly reported the sinking of the *Yorktown* in the Coral Sea, they now assumed that Halsey's two carriers, the *Enterprise* and *Hornet*, were the only two remaining U.S. carriers in the Pacific. Moreover, Tokyo thought that Halsey's ships were still thousands of miles away from the area of the forthcoming operation, and thus could not possible interfere with the Japanese attack against Midway.

Rochefort persisted, now asking his staff to report any and all references to the new, but badly damaged carrier *Shokaku*. Then, shortly after Admiral Nagumo issued Order No. 18 authorizing the Midway operation to proceed, on May 5, HYPO began to intercept messages referring to Attu, Kiska, and Dutch Harbor—all in the Aleutians. Did this indicate another separate operation, or was it all part of the Midway strategy? To be sure, the Aleutians were a part of Alaska, and hence American territory, but of little strategic value given the foul weather and lack of sufficient safe anchorages in a region known for its unfriendly seas. Midway, on the other hand, would provide the Japanese with a good submarine base—the Americans had one there already—airfields, and hence an excellent springboard from which to attack Oahu again. Moreover,

Pearl Harbor was only 1,150 miles away from Midway.

Dismissing the Aleutians attack as merely a diversionary strategy intended to draw Nimitz's fleet to the north and therefore far from the central Pacific, Rochefort and his team continued to concentrate on the meaning of "AF." As Holmes points out, "From the beginning, Combat Intelligence [HYPO] and CINCPAC Intelligence [Ed Layton] concurred on the premise that AF was Midway." Naval Intelligence OP-20-G in Washington, however, strongly disagreed. Nimitz therefore was required to establish absolute proof that "AF" did indeed refer to Midway. Finnegan discovered that Japanese-occupied Wake Island was now definitely running long-range air searches over "AF," and Admiral Nimitz had reports of such aircraft over Midway again. Japanese intercepts also referred to the submarine base at "AF." But Nimitz required concrete evidence to make his case. Then, on May 20, Yamamoto issued the total Japanese battle order for the assault on "AF" *and* the Aleutians, thereby confirming that "AF" was certainly not the Aleutians.[22]

Yet a very stubborn Admiral King was still not convinced, again demanding absolute confirmation of Midway as "AF" before he would authorize Nimitz to commit the entire Pacific Fleet. It was Lieutenant Holmes, an engineer and mathematician, who came up with the solution. He suggested that CINCPAC telephone Midway on the underwater cable, ordering the officials there to announce by radio to Pearl Harbor the next day that they were having problems with the water filtration plant, and required spare parts to repair it. This was done and Japanese intelligence then promptly radioed Tokyo that same report, almost verbatim, but referring to "AF" as having water filtration problems. Thus "AF" was confirmed.[23]

Nimitz presented this information to Washington, D.C., and Ernie King reluctantly conceded. But one important factor remained: when would the assault on "AF" take place? Admiral Nimitz would have to assemble a carrier task force and get it to Midway in advance to await the arrival of Yamamoto's Combined Fleet. Meanwhile, he sent additional patrol planes and Marine Corps fighters to Midway, as well as Marine land reinforcements. Nimitz believed so firmly in HYPO that he was going to commit *everything* he had in Hawaii to prevent the Japanese assault at Midway. Admiral King, however, reminded Nimitz that if he was wrong, Hawaii would remain undefended, as would the West

Coast of the United States—leaving them vulnerable should Yamamoto strike there instead. Yet HYPO continued to make progress; Joseph Finnegan worked out that the launching point of the first air attack of Midway would come out of the northwest, and concluded that the Japanese military already had an important operation underway seven hundred miles due west of Midway.

On May 26, Halsey's Task Force 16 returned to Pearl Harbor from the Coral Sea. The much-battered *Yorktown* was brought into drydock where 1,400 repairmen of every category immediately began work on her. They would need three months to rebuild the ship, but Nimitz gave them only a few days before the *Yorktown* would have to be ready to put to sea again. It seemed impossible even to the greatest optimist. Meanwhile, Halsey had come down with a serious skin disease and had to be hospitalized, which meant that a replacement for him was needed overnight. Frank Jack Fletcher was given overall command of the Carrier Strike Force, comprising Task Force 16 (Captain George Murray's *Enterprise* and Marc "Pete" Mitscher's *Hornet*) and Task force 17 (Captain Elliott Buckmaster's *Yorktown*). But Nimitz's choice of his chief of staff, Ray Spruance—a man with no aviation experience—as Halsey's replacement to command TF 16 surprised many.

Raymond Ames Spruance was born into an upper-middle-class family from Baltimore on July 3, 1886, later moving to Indianapolis, where his father had a comfortable estate. Alexander Spruance came from five generations of a distinguished Delaware family; his wife, Annie Ames Hiss, disliked parenting and preferred to spend her time in social activities. Raymond, the firstborn, had two younger brothers, Billy and Philip. More attached to Philip, Annie relinquished Raymond to the care of her parents and sisters in Baltimore, while she and Raymond's father returned to Indianapolis with the other siblings.

Spruance was brought up in a cultivated home of considerable ease, and proved an excellent scholar in his studies. But he was by nature shy and withdrawn and remained so essentially throughout his life. When he was a teenager, his grandfather Hiss went bankrupt, altering Raymond Spruance's life permanently. He was forced to return to Indianapolis, where the family was living under much-reduced circumstances.

A brilliant student, Spruance completed high school in 1902. As the family had no money, his mother arranged for him to take the entrance examination for the Naval Academy, which he easily passed. Spruance was sworn in as a midshipman on July 2, 1903. A tall, slender, quiet student, he went almost unnoticed, leaving the Academy with high honors as a "passed midshipman" in 1907. Thereafter he served on a variety of ships and was gradually promoted (avoiding aviation when it was offered), beginning his career with Teddy Roosevelt's voyage of the Great White Fleet to Japan.

As he was ever the recluse, Spruance's marriage to Margaret Dean in 1914 took everyone by surprise. The marriage never appeared to be either warm or close, with Spruance frequently away at sea. The couple did have one son, who eventually went into the navy as well.

Spruance was renowned for his integrity, but he tended to take a closed-minded view of things. He was always uncompromising. And although he seemed mild enough, he was a man of very strong likes and dislikes. The dislikes included Ernie King and all aviators, especially Jack Towers, now Nimitz's naval air chief.

Yet in other areas Spruance seemed somewhat less resolute. He was an avid reader, but never collected a private library, nor did this reading appear to broaden his horizons. He was an agnostic, holding no religious convictions. Neither ambitious nor a hard worker, he openly avoided working more than the equivalent of a nine-to-five day. And when he could delegate work, he gladly did so, never taking work home with him—except now, in 1942, working on Nimitz's staff and sharing a house with him.[24]

•

Back in the basement of the Administrative Annex at Makalapa Hill, Rochefort's team was struggling with the inflow of Japanese naval intercepts, trying to establish the date of the attack, and even the hour if possible. Finnegan, Ham Wright, Tom Dyer, and Joe Rochefort joined in this final, concerted attack, working three straight days and nights. They finally came up with the answer.

On May 24, Admiral Nimitz set an appointment with Commander Rochefort for the following morning. Nimitz and his entire staff sat inside Nimitz's office waiting in vain, looking more and more annoyed as the appointed time came and passed. Finally, half an hour late, according to Jaspar Holmes, "Rochefort, looking a bit rumpled and distraught, was admitted." He apologized, explaining that the entire team had been up all night attempting to pinpoint the dates of arrival of the enemy fleet. Frowns turned to beams when he gave them the precise dates: June 4 for the attack on Midway and June 3 for Dutch Harbor in the Aleutians. Nimitz, himself under agonizing pressure, could not have acted without this data; if he were to make a mistake, a jealous King, who was looking for an excuse to get rid of him, would relieve him of his command. Layton fully supported Rochefort's conclusions, despite strong opposition from Op-20-G in Washington. Indeed, that same day, King informed Nimitz that he and his Naval Intelligence officer, Arthur McCollum (who was head of the Far East Section), still disagreed with HYPO, instead giving contradictory "estimates" that the Japanese Fleet was too dispersed to attack Midway and was instead set to attack Australia, or perhaps had the West Coast of the United States as its real objective. But Rochefort, HYPO, Nimitz, and Layton stuck to their guns, and it was Layton who was later able to establish both the precise bearing and the hour at which the Japanese would arrive off Midway.[25]

As for the exhausted HYPO team, it was time to relax a little, as the analysts emerged from their basement prison into the fresh air. Holmes was out for the first time in days when he ran into an old friend who was unaware of the plans underfoot. "Just then [Thomas] Dyer [the chief cryptanalyst] came out of the basement on his way home . . . after the . . . cipher blitz," carrying an old lunch box under his arm, Holmes remembered. His uniform "looked as though he had slept in it for three days. He had." He was unshaven, his hair unkempt. Holmes's friend looked up at him, saying, "Now there goes a bird who should be sent to sea to get straightened out." Holmes was furious, yet he could hardly reveal that Dyer was one of the brilliant analysts who had just helped crack the code that was going to save Midway.[26]

Nimitz still faced a long bout with King over the telephone, but he stood up to King and won. On May 28, Admiral Spruance sortied from Pearl Harbor with the *Enterprise* and the *Hornet*, escorted by six cruisers and ten destroyers. This was Task Force 17. Fletcher's *Yorktown*, flooded with lights as workmen continued laboring through the night, would follow two days later, attended by two cruisers, six destroyers, and hundreds of workmen finishing their repairs en route. Her complement of planes was soon flown aboard. Spruance would be able to arrive at Midway with three big aircraft carriers after all.

Spruance's staff, which he had inherited from Halsey, was another problem. Not only had Spruance no knowledge of aviation, but his chief of staff, Miles Browning, also had as disagreeable a reputation as any man in the navy, including John Hoover and Ernie King. He was considered to be a mentally unsound man, a misfit who was denounced by Admiral King himself: "Browning was no good at all. . . . He had no brains, no understanding."[27] Samuel Morison, the historian, who knew him personally, agreed, describing him as intelligent yet "erratic and unreliable." Spruance, the most even-tempered of men, found Miles Browning "unstable and evil-tempered," his "hawk-like face" one to be avoided—especially when he was on one of his heavy drinking binges, during which he attacked anyone in sight.[28]

Despite this background, Spruance announced upon taking command, "Gentlemen, I want you to know that I do not have the slightest concern about any of you. If you were not good, Bill Halsey would not have chosen you." These were words he was soon going to regret, as he would find that he headed a very unhappy, ill-at-ease and ill-coordinated staff during the great battle that lay before him.

What is more, the selection of Frank Jack Fletcher as carrier commander raised more than one eyebrow. King in particular strongly objected to this man who had lost one carrier, and nearly a second, in the Coral Sea. King forced Nimitz to interrogate Fletcher for a full three days before Nimitz assured him that Fletcher could be counted on. Fortunately, the captain of Nimitz's flagship, Elliott Buckmaster, was considered first rate, as were Captain Murray of the *Enterprise* and the still relatively unknown, soft-spoken Captain "Pete" Mitscher, who was commanding the *Hornet* and was known as a superb aviator in his own right. As for Nimitz, he had earlier flown out to Midway to inspect the island's defenses for himself. He was satisfied that everything possible had been made ready, including the reinforcement of the 6th Marine Defense Battalion, Fleet Marine Force commanded by Colonel Hal Shannon.

•

Yamamoto's Combined Fleet, part of which was assigned to the Aleutians, sortied from Ominato Harbor on May 26 and was soon lost in a dense fog: Nagumo's force sailed on the 27th from Hashirajima anchorage via Bungo Strait into the Pacific. On May 28, the rest of the Aleutian Northern Force Main Body cleared Ominato, while far to the south, the Midway Landing Force, escorted by Rear Admiral Tanaka, sailed from Saipan. The last to put to sea was the Main Body of the Midway Invasion Force under Vice Admiral Kondo, including the supreme commander, Admiral Yamamoto himself, his flag hoisted high above the world's largest battleship, *Yamato*.[29] Nimitz knew he was facing an imposing armada, but not even he knew that the Combined Fleet was the largest ever to be assembled by Japan. It included four heavy carriers—*Akagi*, *Kaga*, *Soryu*, and *Hiryu*; two light carriers—*Hosho* and *Zuiho*; five seaplane tenders; seven battleships—*Yamato*, *Nagato*, *Mutsu*, *Haruna*, *Kirishima*, *Hiei*, and *Kongo*; ten heavy and light cruisers; forty-three destroyers; and thirteen tankers, as well as a variety of auxiliary ships. The table of organization for the diversionary Aleutians comprised two more light carriers—*Ryujo* and *Junyo*—five heavy and light cruisers, a seaplane tender, and twelve destroyers. The Combined Fleet of over 200 vessels included 234 combat aircraft, a surprisingly low figure given the number of carriers, but previous clashes and Allied air raids were already beginning to cripple the Imperial Japanese Navy.[30]

En route, the Japanese occasionally encountered American submarines and scout planes, but insisting on the integrity of the Japanese naval code, Yamamoto arrogantly dismissed the danger they portended. The Americans, he repeated, had no idea what his forces were up to. Bad weather soon engulfed much of the Combined Fleet, further assuring concealment. As Fuchida put it, the admiral was "as a whole feeling very snug and secure behind the 18.1-inch guns of *Yamato*,"[31] a curious sentiment coming from the founder of Japanese naval aviation.

●

Once underway, Spruance announced to the U.S. Fleet the purpose of their rush to put to sea: "An attack for the purpose of capturing Midway is expected. The attacking force may be composed of all combatant types including four or five carriers, transports and trains vessels." He further stated that the intention of his Task Forces 16 and 17 was to be able "to make surprise flank attacks on the enemy carriers from a position northeast of Midway." Spruance's fleet equaled the enemy in only one field, warplanes, with 233 to Yamamoto's 234. Aside from that, Spruance had no battleships and eight heavy and light cruisers, screened by twenty destroyers.

Spruance was a strange choice for the role now. It was in fact a most disturbing picture for competent carrier commanders like Marc Mitscher, aboard the *Hornet*, who rarely left the bridge.[32] Nor did Spruance know or bother to find out what Fletcher expected of the carrier formations. "Have you any instructions for further operations?" an anxious Fletcher, hoping for specific orders, signaled Spruance. "Negative," the laconic Spruance replied. "Will conform to your movements." There were other disturbing aspects of this command. While both Halsey and Mitscher lived on the bridge, Spruance was rarely to be found there. "Come sit with me for a while," Spruance beckoned one officer while he was having breakfast. "They don't need us up there." "What kind of man is Spruance?" one bewildered officer, Robert Oliver, later asked. On another occasion, Spruance was awakened because of a radar contact of some importance, but he refused to get out of bed.[33] And when Miles Browning drew up plans one day for sending planes, including Clarence Wade McClusky's squadrons, out on search missions, the plans were so overextended that the pilots would not have had enough fuel to return. McClusky and others complained angrily, and a mildly surprised Spruance overruled Browning. Later, during a combat launch, the *Enterprise* soon cleared her decks, but Spruance forgot to give clearance to a fuming Mitscher aboard *Hornet*. It had slipped his mind to notify one of his own carriers to launch.

●

Beginning on May 30, twenty-two Catalinas flew from their base at Midway, searching as far out as seven hundred miles for the approaching enemy while submarines probed the waters around the six-mile-long island. Midway's own air force was of course small, consisting of eighteen Dauntless dive-bombers, seven TBF torpedo planes, seven Wildcat fighters, nineteen army bombers, seventeen obsolete Vindicator dive-bombers, and twenty-one ancient "Buffalo" fighters ("flying coffins," as their pilots dubbed them).

The following days were very tense ones both at Pearl and Midway, as Spruance's battle fleet took up its position joining Fletcher's on June 2, about 325 miles northeast of Midway. The three carriers, now at sea and separated, were on their own. Nevertheless, Spruance had the great advantage over Yamamoto, knowing as he did the precise date of the opposition's arrival and the direction from which he was coming. Yamamoto had no similar information.

Just before 1900 on June 3, an American plane first spotted the Japanese Fleet some seven hundred miles from Midway.[34] Nine U.S. Army bombers from Midway were sent out to attack the enemy transports, but they released their bombs too high, missing all the Japanese ships that afternoon. The second attack hit an enemy oiler, missing all the capital ships.

Fletcher's *Yorktown*, however, continued to close on the enemy, reaching a point two hundred miles from the transports on June 4. At 0430 Fletcher launched ten SBDs (navy Dauntless dive-bombers) on a search mission. At the same time, Nagumo was independently dispatching his first air strike against Midway. (Rochefort's analysis had proven very precise indeed.) At 0534 on that June 4, the *Enterprise* received a message from a PBY reporting "ENEMY CARRIERS." Fourteen minutes later, the same surveillance plane elaborated: "MANY ENEMY PLANES HEADING MIDWAY BEARING 320° DISTANCE 150." At 0603 two Japanese carriers and their battleships on the same bearing were sighted just 180 miles from Midway. Fletcher recalled his search planes and waited. At 0607 he ordered the *Enterprise* and *Hornet* to "PROCEED SOUTHWESTERLY AND ATTACK ENEMY CARRIERS WHEN DEFINITELY LOCATED."[35]

At 0559 Midway radar had first picked up "bogies" that were heading directly for them, apparently from the carrier *Hiryu*. Only ninety-three miles away, 108 Kates (torpedo), Vals (dive-bombers), and Zekes (Zeroes) would soon be upon them, and a Marine Corps fighter squadron scrambled to greet their approach. The planes first clashed a couple of dozen miles from shore. The Marine Corps fighters fell on their attackers from an altitude of 17,000 feet, but they were greatly outnumbered, and Midway soon suffered its first bombardment. The marines sustained heavy damage on the ground when the command post, mess hall, and power station on Eastern Island were hit, as were a hospital, warehouses, oil tanks, and other facilities on nearby Sand Island. This was the first and only attack directly over Midway and lasted some twenty minutes.[36] The U.S. Marines had lost seventeen pilots and planes. A few of the land-based aircraft, including half a dozen Avenger torpedo planes and four army marauders, did reach the enemy carriers, but most of the American planes were destroyed in the air, one deliberately crashing into *Akagi*'s flight deck.

Nagumo, who had reserved another ninety-three planes with bombs and torpedoes intended for American warships, now gave the order to change armament for another surface attack against Midway, instead. His surveillance planes had still found no ships—that is, until 0728, when one of them spotted "ten enemy surface ships on a course of 150." There was no mention of any American carriers. At 0745, Nagumo again changed the planes' arming order, instructing that torpedoes and bombs be left on the planes after all. The first news of a carrier sighting reached Nagumo's bridge at 0820. As he was rearming, Nagumo ordered the flight deck to be cleared for the first attack group due to be returning from Midway.

Land-based planes attacked the Japanese carriers in driblets. Sixteen marine dive-bombers with inexperienced pilots started to descend on *Hiryu* at 0755 but were mauled by the large Zeke combat air patrol. Only eight returned to Midway, most of them heavily damaged. Fifteen B-17s from Midway attempted to bomb the carrier at 0810 from as high as 20,000 feet, all bombs missing the large carrier. Then, ten minutes later, eleven marine Vindicators attacked the enemy carriers and a battleship, but again missed as they themselves were attacked by Zekes. Altogether over half the land-based American planes on Midway had been destroyed at this point.

Just after 0600, carriers *Enterprise* and *Hornet* had changed to a course of 240 degrees. Spruance finally made the decision to launch, and by 0702 the first aircraft were taking off: twenty Wildcat fighters, sixty-seven Dauntless dive-bombers, and twenty-nine Devastator torpedo bombers.[37] The Americans decided to make an all-out attack against the Japanese carriers, whose planes Spruance and Browning calculated they could catch just as they were returning from battle.

A more cautious Fletcher, on the other hand, had postponed launchings for over two hours in the event he came across more

Japanese carriers. He gave the order now, and by 0906 *Yorktown*'s seventeen SBDs, twelve TBDs, and six F4F-3s were in the air. Weather conditions were clear and cool, and the pilots had excellent vision in all directions right to the horizon. Simultaneously, Nagumo's own Striking Force of planes and ships was closing the distance with the Americans, continuing on a course that would take them to Midway within an hour. The four big carriers formed a square in the center of their formation protected by two battleships, three cruisers, and eleven destroyers.

These heavy carriers began recovering their planes sooner than Spruance's staff had calculated, beginning at 0837. But even before all the planes had returned, an impatient Nagumo altered course by 90 degrees in order to attack and destroy the enemy task force. At 0917, the decks of all four Japanese carriers were packed with freshly fueled and armed bombers ready to take off; this was a perfect time for the Americans to strike, if they could only get there on time.

Hornet's thirty-five SBDs with fighter cover were unable to locate the enemy carriers because of the change of course. Short of fuel, they were forced to land on Midway, some even having to ditch before that. Everyone was trying his hardest, but that was not yet good enough.

Lieutenant Commander John Waldron, leading the carrier's torpedo squadron, went up to the bridge to talk to Marc Mitscher before taking off, determined to get at the carriers. "If there is only one plane left to make a final run-in, I want that man to go in and get a hit," he told a most sympathetic Mitscher, who realized that he would probably never see the fatalistic Waldron again. "May God be with us all," Waldron said as he left.[38] Going over to the bridge's microphone, Mitscher informed Jack Waldron's squadron that "we intend to launch planes to attack the enemy while their planes are still returning from Midway." Waldron's squadron took off, but soon lost its air fighter cover in the clouds even as all four enemy carriers came into view. The torpedo planes swept down to just above the sea to go in for the attack, but were all destroyed by Zeroes and antiaircraft fire. Mitscher sat on the bridge, listening to the combat chatter, until suddenly the speaker was utterly silent. Everyone in Waldron's squadron had died, except for one lucky pilot, Ensign George Gay, who hid in the water to witness the terrible scene.[39]

The *Enterprise*'s torpedo squadron arrived shortly after 0930. Ten of these fourteen planes were shot down, and no hits were made. It was starting to prove a pretty bleak beginning for Admiral Spruance, who was informed at 1000 when *Yorktown*'s torpedo squadron, under Lieutenant Commander Lance Massey, came in to attack. His six Wildcat escorts were overwhelmed by swarms of Zekes. Seven Devastators, including Massey's, were destroyed, while all five of the torpedoes launched once again missed. Only six of the torpedo planes returned that morning out of the forty-one launched.

But the fortunes of war were finally about to turn. At 0745 Lieutenant Commander Clarence Wade McClusky's dive-bombers took off without fighter protection. When they failed to find the enemy carriers where they were supposed to be, the bombers altered course to the southwest, finding a couple of Japanese ships and following them at 0955. Meanwhile, American fighters broke radio silence at this time to say they had found half the missing Strike Force. This was the first that Fletcher, Spruance, or Mitscher had heard of this, and Miles Browning shouted: "ATTACK!" Below them, the four big Japanese carriers were maneuvering to avoid the American torpedo planes.

McClusky went in for the kill with his two squadrons of Dauntless dive-bombers, thirty-seven in all. He ordered one squadron to follow him in attacking the carrier *Kaga*, and another to take the flagship *Akagi*. Some of the latter's planes mistakenly attacked the *Kaga* with their heavier, 1,000-pound torpedoes. The Japanese had very little protective air cover or antiaircraft fire for once, as the Zekes were too far below to reach them in time. Spruance and Browning had calculated it correctly, finding the decks of the *Akagi* jammed with forty fueled and loaded planes. At 1026, McClusky's team struck. Three bombers hit the *Akagi* from an altitude of only five hundred meters, destroying the critical elevator amidships and the flight deck on the port side. The third bomb landed in the midst of the lines of the refueled planes, causing a roaring inferno and a series of explosions. Another bomb hit the hangar below, igniting a store of torpedoes. The *Akagi* reverberated with detonations and was engulfed in fire from stem to stern. The stubborn Nagumo, refusing to abandon ship, literally had to be dragged from his burning carrier and transferred to the cruiser *Nagara*. By this time both the *Soryu* and *Kaga* were also completely wrapped in flame

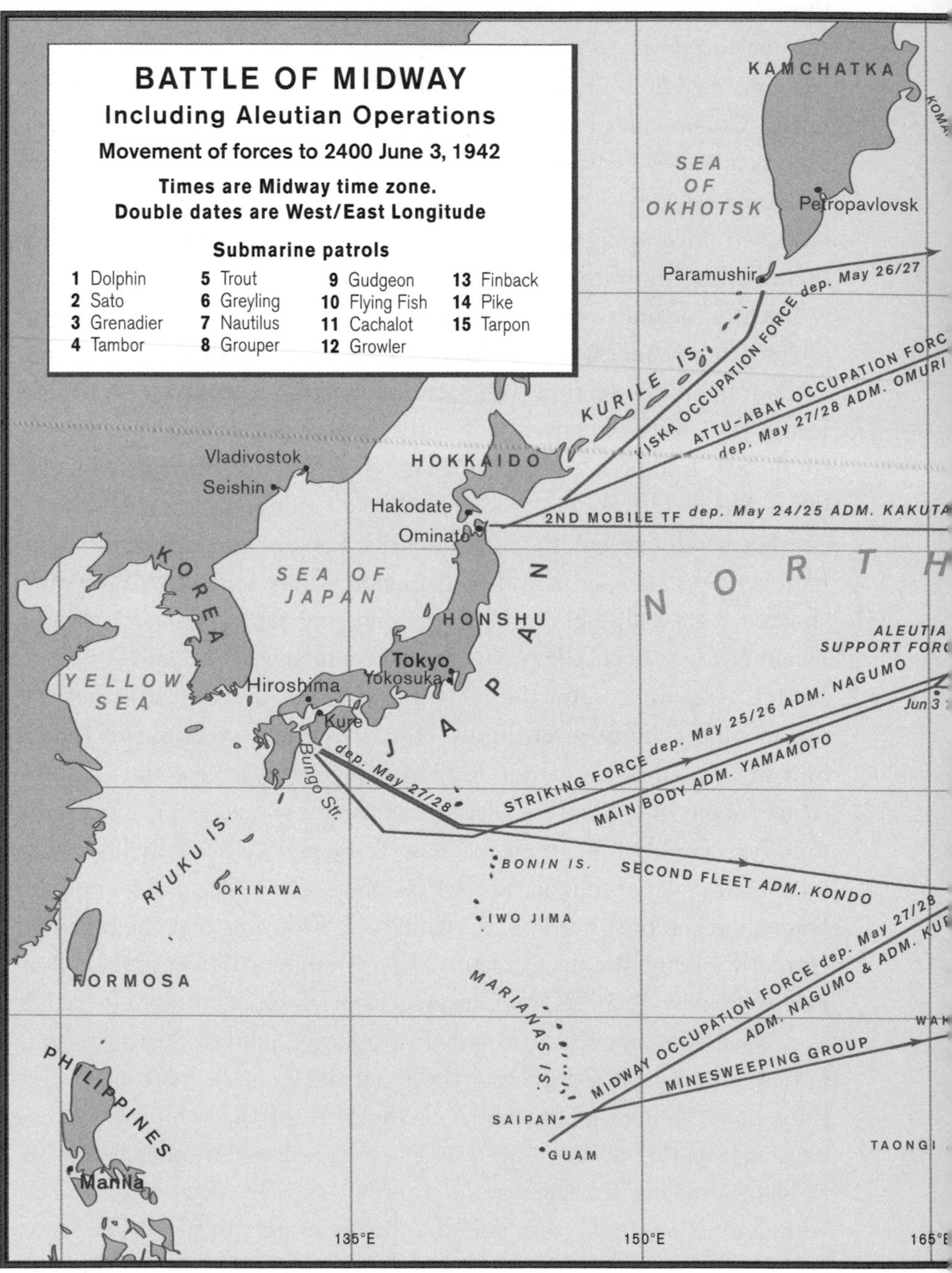
BATTLE OF MIDWAY
Including Aleutian Operations
Movement of forces to 2400 June 3, 1942
Times are Midway time zone.
Double dates are West/East Longitude
Submarine patrols
1 Dolphin
2 Sato
3 Grenadier
4 Tambor
5 Trout
6 Greyling
7 Nautilus
8 Grouper
9 Gudgeon
10 Flying Fish
11 Cachalot
12 Growler
13 Finback
14 Pike
15 Tarpon
KAMCHATKA
SEA OF OKHOTSK
Petropavlovsk
Paramushir
KISKA OCCUPATION FORCE dep. May 26/27
KURILE IS.
ATTU-ABAK OCCUPATION FORC
dep. May 27/28 ADM. OMURI
Vladivostok
Seishin
HOKKAIDO
Hakodate
Ominato
2ND MOBILE TF dep. May 24/25 ADM. KAKUTA
SEA OF JAPAN
KOREA
HONSHU
JAPAN
NORTH
ALEUTIA
SUPPORT FOR
YELLOW SEA
Tokyo
Yokosuka
Hiroshima
Kure
Bungo Str.
dep. May 27/28
STRIKING FORCE dep. May 25/26 ADM. NAGUMO
MAIN BODY ADM. YAMAMOTO
RYUKU IS.
OKINAWA
BONIN IS.
SECOND FLEET ADM. KONDO
IWO JIMA
MIDWAY OCCUPATION FORCE dep. May 27/28
ADM. NAGUMO & ADM. KU
MINESWEEPING GROUP
MARIANAS IS.
FORMOSA
PHILIPPINES
Manila
SAIPAN
GUAM
TAONGI
135°E
150°E

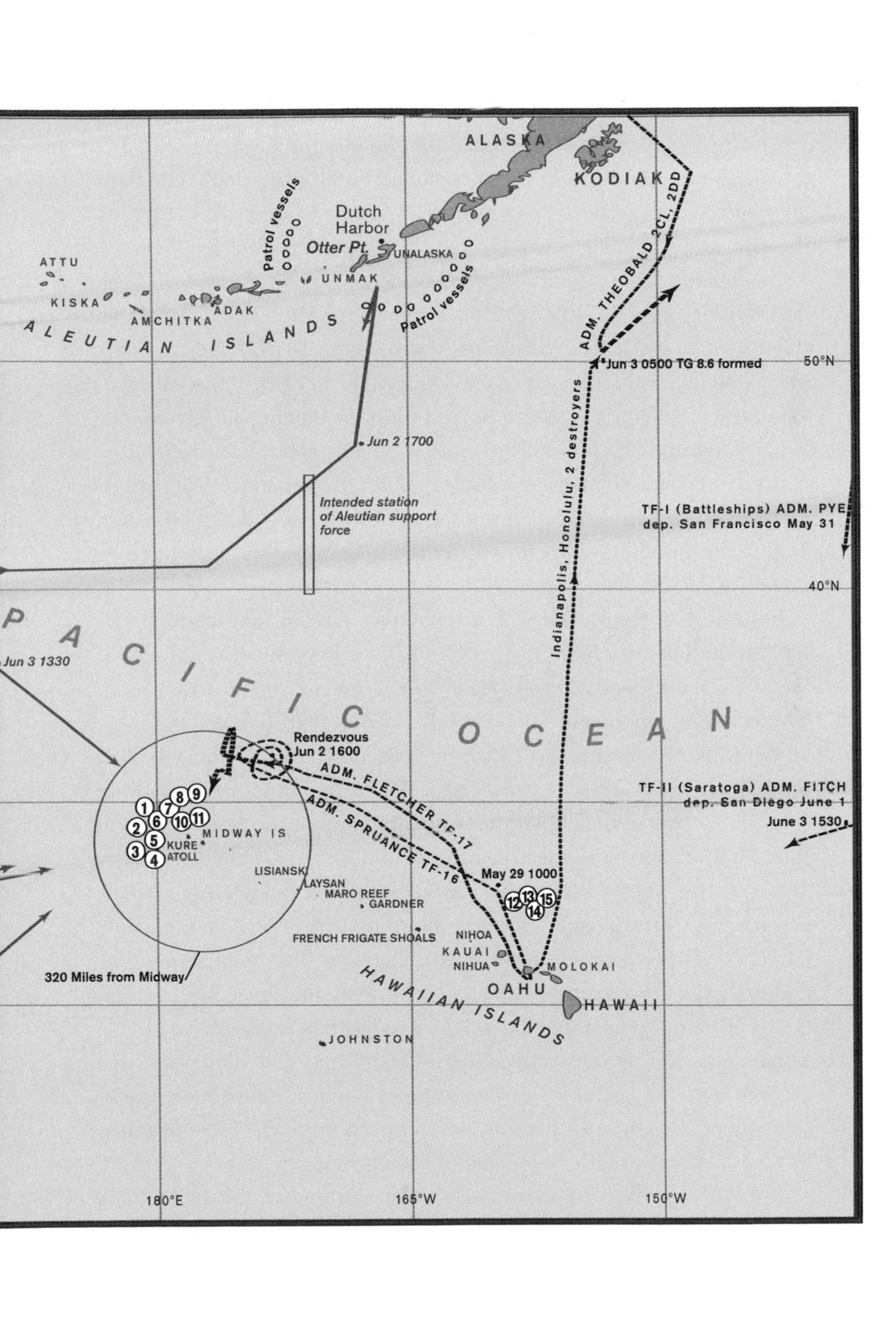

ALASKA
KODIAK
Dutch Harbor
Otter Pt.
UNALASKA
UNMAK
Patrol vessels
Patrol vessels
ATTU
KISKA
AMCHITKA
ADAK
ALEUTIAN ISLANDS
ADM. THEOBALD 2CL, 2DD
Jun 3 0500 TG 8.6 formed
50°N
Jun 2 1700
Indianapolis, Honolulu, 2 destroyers
Intended station of Aleutian support force
TF-I (Battleships) ADM. PYE dep. San Francisco May 31
40°N
PACIFIC OCEAN
Jun 3 1330
Rendezvous Jun 2 1600
ADM. FLETCHER TF-17
ADM. SPRUANCE TF-16
TF-II (Saratoga) ADM. FITCH dep. San Diego June 1
June 3 1530
1
2
3
4
5
6
7
8
9
10
11
MIDWAY IS
KURE ATOLL
LISIANSKI
LAYSAN
MARO REEF
GARDNER
May 29 1000
12
13
14
15
FRENCH FRIGATE SHOALS
NIHOA
KAUAI
NIHUA
MOLOKAI
OAHU
HAWAII
HAWAIIAN ISLANDS
320 Miles from Midway
JOHNSTON
180°E
165°W
150°W

as a result of direct hits by American bombs and torpedoes. (*Akagi* was finally sunk by a Japanese torpedo on June 5.)

McClusky's team scored a total of four hits on the *Kaga* as flames following the fuel lines down below exploded bomb magazines. The *Kaga* later suffered an anguishing explosion—sending a huge ball of fire into the air—and was sunk by two Japanese destroyers at 1800.[40]

Lieutenant Commander Maxwell Leslie's squadron of seventeen ABDs from *Yorktown* struck the *Soryu* right after McClusky's attacks on the other two carriers. Sweeping down from 14,500 feet, Leslie's planes attacked the carrier's plane-laden flight deck in three consecutive groups, leaving the entire deck a mass of flames and explosions. What was more, Leslie did not lose a single plane. They were then assisted by U.S. submarine *Nautilus* under Commander William H. Brockman, which slammed three torpedoes into the already tortured *Soryu*. The gasoline storage area aft erupted, breaking the vessel in two. It sank at 1910.

Returning to the *Yorktown*, Leslie's planes circled, waiting for Lieutenant Commander John S. Thach's nearly empty Wildcat fighters to land. Back on board, Thach began to debrief his pilots when radar warned of an imminent attack. Leslie's SBDs had to clear the area, landing instead aboard the *Enterprise*, although two of them had to ditch with their crews because of lack of space. At 1050 an irate Nagumo, who had transferred tactical command of the Strike Force to Rear Admiral Abe, nevertheless ordered Admiral Yamaguchi on *Hiryu* to "ATTACK THE ENEMY CARRIER" (i.e., *Yorktown*), even though three Japanese carriers were already afire or about to sink. *Hiryu* immediately launched all her planes, and by 1100, eighteen dive-bombers and six fighters—the first group dispatched—were in the area. The second group of ten torpedo bombers and six fighters took off at 1331. Yamamoto, by now desperate, ordered the *Ryujo* and *Junyo*, the two carriers that had been sent earlier to the Aleutians, to abandon operations there and come to their rescue, although given the great distance involved, there was little likelihood of their arriving in time.[41]

When the *Yorktown* received the radar warning of the first attack from *Hiryu*, she had a combat air patrol of a dozen Wildcats circling in the air, with another patrol just beginning to refuel. *Yorktown*'s speed jumped to 30.5 knots and Fletcher prepared to receive the first few dozen bogies headed for him. His patrol Wildcats shot down over half of the eighteen Vals, but eight got through, two of which were downed by antiaircraft fire. The remaining six Vals made three hits, one bomb striking beneath the American carrier's flight deck and starting numerous fires and explosions, killing many hands. A second bomb destroyed the port side of the smokestack, causing more fires and rupturing three boilers. A third exploded deep on the fourth deck, igniting a major fire forward of the gasoline tanks and magazines. The fire in the *Yorktown*'s "island" also destroyed the ship's communications, and Admiral Fletcher was obliged to shift his flag to the cruiser *Astoria*. The cruiser *Portland* tried to take the raging *Yorktown* under tow, but then the crew got four of the boilers working again—and to everyone's amazement, she was soon churning out 18 knots.

When *Hiryu*'s second attack arrived, it was fought ferociously by the last eight Wildcats, which were launched hurriedly with just 23 gallons in each tank. They joined the other four fighters already in the air. Sixteen Japanese warplanes, under antiaircraft fire from the *Portland* and *Astoria* and accompanying destroyers, swept in from four different directions. Just after 1442, two torpedoes exploded against *Yorktown*'s port side fuel tank and jammed the rudder. She was soon listing at 26 degrees and lost all power. A few minutes before 1500, Captain Elliott Buckmaster, his ship having never been fully repaired since her last ordeal in the Coral Sea, faced the inevitable and ordered all hands to abandon ship. Fortunately, the sea was smooth, and four escorting destroyers collected the entire crew. No one drowned.[42]

The planes that Fletcher had initially kept back later undertook a search mission commanded by Lieutenant Wallace Shot. They found the carrier *Hiryu*, two battleships, three cruisers, and four destroyers steaming northwest some 110 miles ahead of them.

At 1530 a desperate Spruance ordered *Enterprise* to launch twenty-four SBDs, but without fighter escort. The ten navy planes hit *Hiryu* four times, starting a mass of fires and smashing the forward elevator platform. The *Hiryu* had earlier been strafed by a number of Flying Fortresses from Molokai and Midway. All their bombs had missed the target, apart from knocking out some AA guns, which constituted "the only damage inflicted by B-17s on the enemy in the Battle of Midway." Captain Kaku Tomeo gave the order to abandon Admiral Yamaguchi

Tamon's flagship, *Hiryu*, at 0315 on June 5. Yamaguchi then gave the order to torpedo his devastated vessel, and it would go down with 416 men aboard—including Yamaguchi and Kaku, who had first committed *seppuku*, or suicide.[43]

Vice Admiral Mitscher, who was later to prove the greatest carrier commander in the Pacific, waited anxiously in the dark for the return of his planes which were, he knew, short on fuel. They would be unable to see the blacked-out *Hornet* in the darkness and all would soon be ditching miles from the carrier. He ordered the truck lights on the mast and the deck lights turned on to guide them in, but was warned about enemy submarines. Mitscher, who loved his fellow pilots as if they were his own sons, said, "The hell with the subs," and the truck lights and deck lights lit up the flight deck. This action saved the lives of most of his pilots, whom, on arrival, the flight surgeon found "a little shaky." "Give them each a bottle [of whiskey] and see to it that they get to bed," Mitscher quietly ordered. No carrier commander was ever closer to his fellow aviators than was "Pete" Mitscher, and the feeling was fully reciprocated.[44]

●

A frustrated Yamamoto had never before been so disastrously defeated. Right there and then he ordered Kondo to relieve the disgraced Nagumo of his command, and the much-battered Combined Fleet altered course for friendlier waters to the northwest.

Spruance, instead of pursuing him as some had wanted, sailed in the opposite direction, ready to reverse course again the next day. "I did not feel justified in risking a night encounter," he wrote in his report, wary of the next clash with possibly superior enemy forces. "But on the other hand I did not want to be too far away from Midway the next morning." He duly reversed course at midnight.

But the story was not quite over, for in their feverish attempt to flee, two Japanese cruisers, *Mogami* and *Mikuma*, collided, causing severe damage to each other. *Mogami* burst into flames, her bow severely smashed. *Mikuma* was trailing oil. Six SBDs along with six Vindicators were dispatched to find them, but were repulsed by fierce, accurate AA fire. Their bombs missed both ships and one of the navy's planes crashed on the after-turret of *Mikuma*.

While Yamamoto was collecting four of his by now scattered groups, the *Enterprise* launched more planes with orders to sink the two cruisers. They attacked, joined by Mitscher's planes. The *Mogami* received several bomb hits, but nevertheless somehow managed to limp back to Truk. As for the *Mikuma*, Mitscher's final dive-bomber attack from *Hornet* successfully hit the target, exploding *Mikuma*'s store of torpedoes. The resulting explosion proved to be the *coup de grâce*: *Mikuma* sank that night along with 648 of her 888-man crew.[45] The battle of Midway was over, while in the Aleutians the Japanese were forced to abandon the island of Attu, holding on to Kiska for a while longer before withdrawing.

For the United States, the final cost of Midway—the second entirely carrier-launched air battle of the Pacific—was the loss of one carrier, a destroyer, 147 aircraft, and 307 men. The Japanese, for their part, had lost their great naval superiority with the sinking of four of their largest carriers and a battle cruiser, not to mention 234 naval aircraft and some 2,000 men.[46]

Although Hap Arnold's Air Corps PR men had called in the nation's media to claim the four carriers for the high-altitude B-17s, the obvious fraud was soon revealed when documentary proof established that they had not sunk a single vessel. In any event, for Nimitz this was a "momentous victory. . . . Pearl Harbor has now been partially avenged." Admiral King, initially cautious, finally described this battle as "the first decisive defeat suffered by the Japanese Navy in 350 years."[47] The navy was very generous in its distribution of medals and promotions, with the exception of Joe Rochefort, whom an angry Ernie King fired, thereby removing his most talented cryptanalyst at this, the most critical time in U.S. history since the American Civil War.[48]

From the Japanese viewpoint, "The catastrophe of Midway definitely marked the turning of the tide in the Pacific War," remarked Fuchida and Okumiya, two of its participants, "and henceforth that tide bore Japan inexorably on toward final capitulation."[49] The wounded were secreted ashore, and any public mention of the battle was silenced. The wounded Fuchida Mitsuo found himself in an isolation ward. "No nurses or corpsmen were allowed entry, and I could not communicate with the outside. . . . I sometimes had the feeling of being a prisoner of war." After the war, the Japanese government ordered studies on the defeat at Midway burnt.[50] In Japan, if the results were not favorable and patriotic, they were suppressed, as if they had never existed. It is a policy that continues to the present day regarding the 200,000 foreign women forced into prostitution for the Japanese military, the atrocities that the military committed, and the extensive use of Korean slave labor, all omitted from or played down in even the most recent Japanese history schoolbooks.

As Fuchida and Okumiya concluded:

> In the final analysis, the root cause of Japan's defeat not only in the Battle of Midway but in the entire war, lies deep in the Japanese national character. There is an irrationality and impulsiveness about our people which results in actions that are haphazard and often contradictory. A tradition of provincialism makes us narrow-minded and dogmatic, reluctant to discard prejudices and slow to adopt even necessary improvements if they require a new concept. Indecisive and vacillating, we succumb readily to conceit, which in turn makes us disdainful of others. Opportunistic but lacking a spirit of daring and independence, we are wont to place reliance on others and to truckle to superiors. Our want of rationality often leads us to confuse desire and reality, and thus to do things without careful planning. . . . In short, as a nation, we lack maturity of mind and the necessary conditioning to enable us to know when and what to sacrifice for the sake of our main goal.
>
> Such are the weaknesses of the Japanese national character. These weaknesses were reflected in the defeat we suffered in the Battle of Midway, which rendered fruitless all the valiant deeds and precious sacrifices of the men who fought there. In these weaknesses lies the cause of Japan's misfortune.[51]

CHAPTER XIII

Australia–New Guinea

"'It was close,' I remarked to Dick Sutherland when we landed, 'but that's the way it is in war. You win or lose, live or die—and the difference is just an eyelash.'"

—*MacArthur to Sutherland, March 17, 1942, after narrowly avoiding a Japanese air attack against their plane immediately upon reaching Australia from the Philippines*[1]

"Australia, like the Philippines, is expendable in terms of global strategy."

—*Anonymous high-ranking Australian officer*[2]

When Douglas MacArthur lost the Philippines to the Japanese, he opened the floodgates, thereby permitting Tokyo to advance quickly southward and precipitating the threat to New Guinea and Australia. This in turn exacerbated the already tense, at times almost hostile relations between Great Britain and the Antipodes, reflecting a most undiplomatic, nay acrimonious correspondence between Prime Minister Churchill and Australia's anti-British, imperialistic premier, John Curtin. Although they were Allies in World War I and II, the Australians greatly resented the considerable military contributions they had had to make across the globe to support the empire. Now Japanese troops would soon be upon them, Curtin maintained, and as early as

December 27, 1941, he opened a public attack against Churchill and Britain in the Australian press. Curtin began:

> We refuse to accept the dictum that the Pacific struggle must be treated as a subordinate segment of the general conflict. . . . By that it is not meant that any one of the theatres of war is of less importance than the Pacific, but that Australia asks for a concerted plan evoking the greatest strength at the Democracies' disposal, determined upon hurling Japan back.
>
> The Australian Government therefore regards the Pacific struggle as primarily one in which the United States and Australia must have the fullest say in the direction of the Democracies' fighting plan.
>
> Without any inhibitions of any kind, I am making it quite clear that Australia looks to America, free of any pangs as to our traditional links with the United Kingdom. We know the problem that the United Kingdom faces. We know the constant threat of invasion. We know the dangers of dispersal of strength [by the British military]. We know too that Australia can go, and Britain can still hold on.
>
> We are therefore determined that Australia shall not go, and we shall exert all our energies towards the shaping of a plan, with the United States as its keystone, which will give to our country some confidence of being able to hold out until the tide of battle swings. . . .[3]

In other words, the British could no longer count on Australia's war contributions in the Middle East, Malaya, and the Netherlands East Indies when the homeland was at risk. Australia had a handful of warships, planes, and troops, and it wanted them at home. And yet Churchill still demanded compliance in providing contributions in the defense of other parts of the empire. He insisted that they were vital to the protection of the Far East. "Our men have fought and will fight valiantly," Churchill declared. "But they must be adequately supported. . . . Should the Government of the United States desire, we would gladly accept an American commander in the Pacific area." On January 14, 1942, Churchill told Curtin, "I do not see how anyone could expect Malaya to be defended once the Japanese obtained the command of the area and while we are fighting for our lives against Germany and Italy." Thus, "it is clearly our duty to give our support to the Supreme Commander," meaning the high command in London,

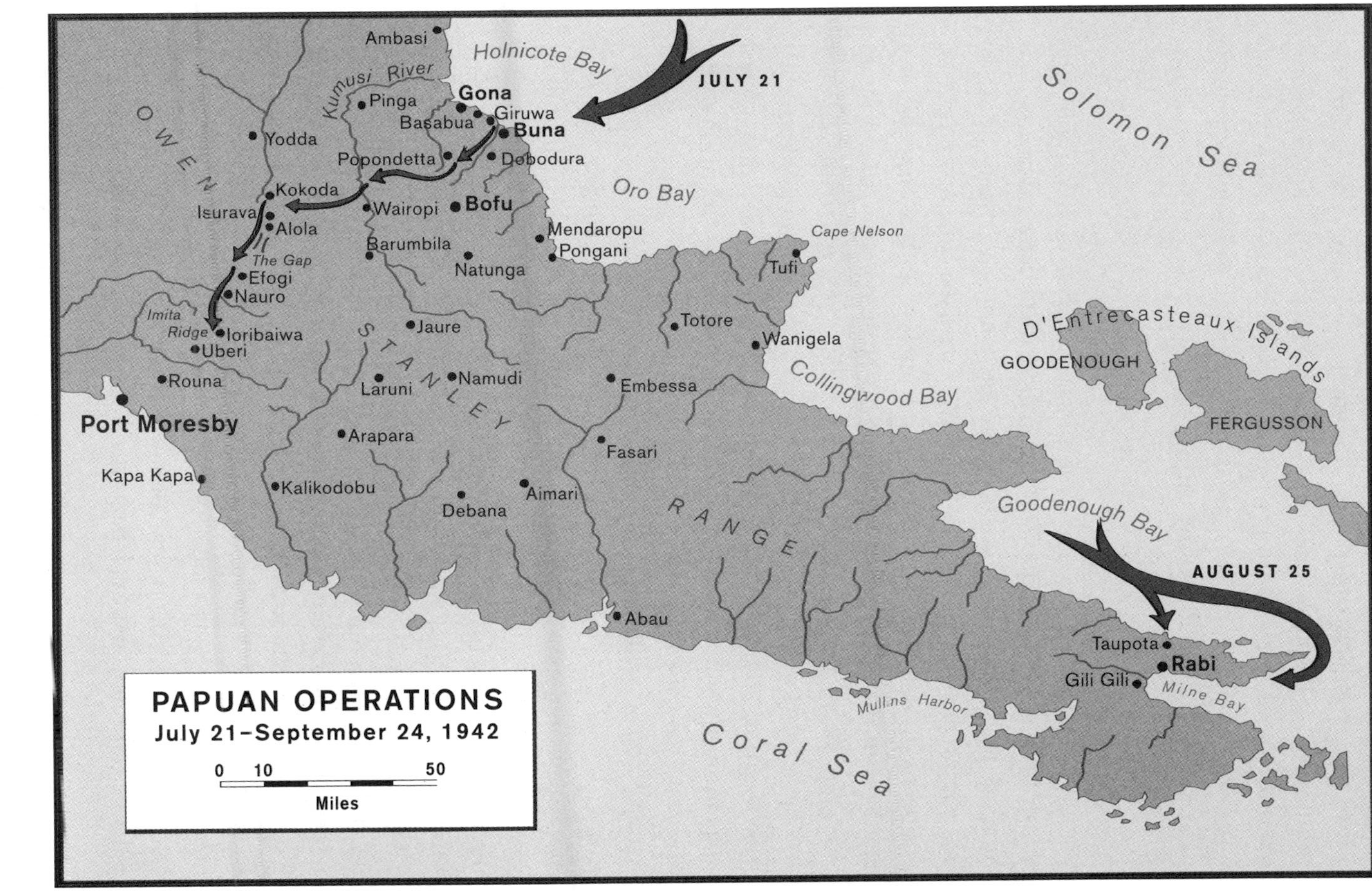

PAPUAN OPERATIONS
July 21–September 24, 1942
0 10 50
Miles
JULY 21
AUGUST 25
Solomon Sea
Coral Sea
Holnicote Bay
Oro Bay
Cape Nelson
Collingwood Bay
Goodenough Bay
Milne Bay
Mullins Harbor
D'Entrecasteaux Islands
GOODENOUGH
FERGUSSON
OWEN STANLEY RANGE
Kumusi River
Ambasi
Gona
Pinga
Giruwa
Basabua
Buna
Yodda
Popondetta
Dobodura
Kokoda
Isurava
Wairopi
Bofu
Alola
Mendaropu
Barumbila
Pongani
The Gap
Natunga
Efogi
Nauro
Tufi
Imita Ridge
Ioribaiwa
Uberi
Jaure
Totore
Wanigela
Rouna
Laruni
Namudi
Embessa
Port Moresby
Arapara
Fasari
Kapa Kapa
Kalikodobu
Debana
Aimari
Abau
Taupota
Rabi
Gili Gili

"with a larger view of things." New Zealand's prime minister, Peter Fraser, however, also opposed Britain's unilateral demands for his forces.[4]

Curtin's reply to Churchill was steadfast. "We have contributed what we could in land and air forces," he wrote on January 18, referring in part to Australia's doomed defense of Malaya and Pacific outposts. But he noted that he was troubled by the "speedy progress" of Japanese forces and emphasized that he found the situation "disturbing. . . . No one has a greater admiration for the magnificent efforts of the people of the United Kingdom than their kinsfolk in Australia. Nevertheless, we make no apologies for our effort, or even for what you argue we are not doing." Churchill had made promises to send munitions to Russia, and Curtin voiced a plea for similar help: "No one could tell what Japan would do, but I was sure that if she [Japan] attacked us, you and the United States would enter the war . . . the safety of Australia and ultimate victory would be assured."[5]

Curtin was stating the stark reality that Australia's very existence depended upon the return of the Australian divisions currently deployed in the Middle East and the Far East. Churchill ultimately gave in and began releasing the troops, while remaining in full accord with the proposed new role of the United States in the Pacific. "In our view the American Navy should assume the responsibility for the communications [i.e., defense], including the islands right up to Australia and New Zealand. . . . Night and day I am labouring here to make the best arrangements possible in your interests and for your safety," he assured Curtin. "We must not be dismayed," he closed, "or get into recrimination, but remain united in true friendship."[6] After all, in the long run they both sought the same goal: victory over Japan.

●

And well might Prime Minister Curtin worry, for enemy forces were advancing quicky during that January of 1942. Japan had secured the Java Sea down to Timor, and by January 28 Imperial Army troops were landing at Lae and Salamaua, more than halfway down New Guinea's east coast. Next to fall was Buna. By July 21 the Japanese army, under the command of General Horii Tomitaro, had landed some twenty thousand men, and by July 29 his men had taken the head of the crucial

Kokoda Trail, which led over the 7,500-foot pass across the Owen Stanley Mountains, and thence down to Port Moresby. With the loss of the Australian airfield at the end of that trail, the Japanese could now bomb Port Moresby at will. The Australians, however, were just as determined to hold that port, the administrative center of New Guinea.[7]

Australia had two veteran divisions returning from the Mediterranean theater and were organizing and training an additional seven divisions. Morale in some instances was, understandably, pretty low, even among some high-ranking Australian officers like the one who admitted to a reporter that, from a strategic standpoint, Australia and the Philippines were ultimately "expendable." This paraphrased almost exactly Eisenhower's own assessment in Washington now.

America's entry into the war combined with MacArthur's arrival did indeed give the Australian military and government the great boost in morale they badly needed. On March 26, 1942, Prime Minister Curtin gave a splendid reception for MacArthur at Government House in Canberra, where the American general addressed the government and the Australian Advisory War Council: "I have come as a soldier in a great crusade of personal liberty as opposed to perpetual slavery. My faith in our ultimate victory is invincible, and I bring you tonight the unbreakable spirit of the free man's military code in support of our joint cause." The applause was tumultuous, and the confident MacArthur closed: "There can be no compromise. We shall win or we shall die."[8]

After MacArthur and his family arrived at their spacious suite at the Lennox Hotel, which had been placed at the disposal of the U.S. military for its personnel, he moved into his new GHQ on the eighth floor of the nine-story AMC Building in downtown Brisbane. The first green American troops were soon arriving, and MacArthur set up a vast training camp for them at Rockhampton, Queensland, under the command of Major General Robert Eichelberger, probably the finest American field commander in the Far East. This was a man who was to save MacArthur's army and reputation on more than one occasion in the near future. But Eichelberger never really trusted a certain ruthlessness in MacArthur, as he related in the letters he sent to his wife after coming to Australia in July 1942. He was wary from the very beginning. Eichelberger, personally, liked the Australians, but immediately upon his arrival there he received a dictum from MacArthur:

"General MacArthur ordered me to pay my respects to the Australians, and then to have nothing further to do with them."[9] MacArthur's paranoia, unfortunately, often led him to extremes even at a time when he required the closest cooperation possible with his new allies.

Eichelberger already had an impressive military reputation behind him. Born on March 9, 1886, in Urbana, Ohio, he was one of five surviving children of a well-known local lawyer and a young southern woman from Mississippi.[10] He was the typical hometown boy. Upon graduating from Urbana High School, he went directly to West Point in 1905 (Class of '09) and graduated 68th out of 103 students—hardly a propitious start. Among his fellow classmates, George Patton, William Simpson, Edwin Forrest Harding, and Horace Fuller would all attain the rank of general.

As a lieutenant, Eichelberger served with the Tenth Infantry at Fort Benjamin in Harrison, Indiana, and in 1911 was sent to San Antonio during the Mexican troubles with Pancho Villa. Later that year he was posted to the Panama Canal where he met his future wife, Emma Gudger, daughter of the Chief Justice of the Canal Zone. It was a whirlwind courtship, and the two were married on April 3, 1913. They would remain a very close couple.

Eichelberger served as professor of military science and tactics at Kemper Military School in Boonville, Missouri, for a year. In 1917 he joined the 20th Infantry at Fort Douglas, Utah, and was then promoted captain, commanding in the 43rd Infantry. His next job took him to the War Department General Staff, Washington, D.C., where he served as executive assistant to the army chief of staff, General William Graves. When in July 1918 Graves was named commander of the 8th Division at Camp Fremont, California, Eichelberger followed as his G-3 (Operations). Then came a shock as Graves and Eichelberger were posted to Siberia that same year to join the international forces there, ostensibly to help save the seventy thousand Czech soldiers who were former Russian POWs of the Bolshevik Revolution. He served as Graves's assistant chief of staff and then as chief intelligence officer at Vladivostok, Siberia, where he got to meet his Japanese allies, who were loath to end their occupation of that region.

With the arrival of his wife in 1920, Eichelberger moved to Japan, serving as assistant chief of staff for Military Intelligence in the Philippine Department. He was sent on to Tientsin with other U.S. troops to help keep order. Afterwards he returned to the old War Department in Washington, dealing with China, the Philippines, and Siberia. It was in this capacity that he attended the Arms Limitation Conference held in Washington, 1921–22.

He was next transferred to the Adjutant General's Department. In 1926, he attended the Command and General Staff School at Fort Leavenworth, where Eisenhower was also a class member. This was followed by a stint at the Army War College in Washington. In August 1931 he was named adjutant and secretary of the academic board at West Point, and in 1935 Lieutenant Colonel Eichelberger became secretary to the War Department, serving as MacArthur's chief of staff. (He had first met the general back in San Antonio in 1911.) At this early stage, Eichelberger enjoyed working with MacArthur, describing him as "very friendly, extremely courteous. His mind was scintillating." MacArthur, in turn, praised Eichelberger's "tact, loyalty, intelligence and initiative."[11] Eichelberger continued in his position when General Malin Craig succeeded MacArthur as chief of staff.

In 1936, with the coming of war now looking inevitable, Eichelberger requested to be transferred to the infantry. He attended the Infantry School at Fort Benning, and was then named commander of the 30th Infantry at the Presidio in San Francisco.

In October 1940, Eichelberger was promoted brigadier general and appointed Superintendent of West Point, which pleased him greatly. But two years later, in January 1942, he was named commander of the 77th Division at Fort Jackson in South Carolina—considered one of the best in the army. Activated in March, the division staged an elaborate demonstration for Prime Minister Churchill and his staff, mainly to prove to the British that American troops were ready to enter the war.

In June 1942, Marshall issued orders to take I Corps GHQ to Australia. During the campaigns to follow, first in New Guinea and later in the Philippines, Eichelberger was destined, as he put it, to "pull MacArthur's chestnuts out of the fire"[12] on more than one occasion in his role as head of the Eighth Army in the liberation of the Philippines. The first opportunity was to occur a few months hence at the sieges of Buna and Gona.

•

Long before Bob Eichelberger arrived in the Antipodes in 1942, the Japanese had continued to advance southward, threatening Australia proper. Having already established airfields at Lae, Salamaua, and Buna, Tokyo had further plans to seize Tulagi in the southern Solomons as part of the attack against Port Moresby. The Allies, intent on preventing Japanese transports from reaching Moresby and Tulagi, were to end up in a big carrier duel in the Coral Sea on May 7–8, 1942, after which the Japanese had canceled plans for the naval invasion of Port Moresby while still holding firmly on the east coast of New Guinea.

Earlier in the year, on April 18, MacArthur, with Curtin's blessing, established the Allied Land Forces under General Sir Thomas Blamey, the Air Forces under George Brett,[13] and the Allied Naval Force under Vice Admiral Herbert Leary. After the Allies had consolidated their forces, MacArthur replaced both Leary and Brett.

The result was the arrival on July 28, 1942, of a five-foot-six, scarred, swarthy air force chief by the name of George Kenney, who hardly looked the imposing, inventive, and aggressive officer he would turn out to be. Ultimately he was largely responsible for MacArthur's "leapfrog" victories that were to follow.

•

Born into a middle-class family from Brookline, Massachusetts, on August 6, 1889,[14] George Kenney entered the Massachusetts Institute of Technology to study civil engineering. In 1917 he enlisted as a private in the U.S. Signal Corps, quickly winning his wings and flying a total of seventy-five missions; he downed two German planes and was himself shot down once. George Kenney ended World War I as a captain, having earned the Distinguished Service Cross and Silver Star. By 1939 the extrovert Kenney was a lieutenant colonel, and between then and 1942 he served brief tours as Air Corps observer with the navy in the Caribbean, assistant attaché for Air at the American Embassy in Paris, and commanding officer of the Air Corps Experimental Division and Engineering School at Wright Field, Ohio. His next promotion brought him to California, as commander of the Fourth Air Force.

By July 1942, Kenney was posted to Australia to replace George Brett as commander of the Allied Forces in the Southwest Pacific. "He [MacArthur] wanted to know what my recommendations were for the use of the Air Force. I told him that I didn't have any as I didn't know what there was to work with, but I intended to fly to New Guinea that night, look the show over there, and visit the airdromes in the Townsville area on the way back to Brisbane about the 2nd of August."[15]

What Kenney found was more than discouraging. It was a shambles. "One thing was certain. No matter what I accomplished," he remarked, "it would be an improvement. It couldn't be much worse." For instance, he found that eighteen of the thirty B-17s of the 19th Bombardment Group at Mareeba were out of commission. Altogether the United States in Australia had 245 fighters, 53 light bombers, 70 medium bombers, 62 heavy bombers, 36 transports, and 51 miscellaneous aircraft—a total of 517 planes in all.[16] Of the 245 so-called fighters, 170 "were awaiting salvage or being overhauled." Kenney also noted that "None of the light bombers were ready for combat" and only thirty-seven of the medium bombers. For the sixty-two heavy bombers, the situation was a little better; only nineteen were out of service. As for the Australian air force, although it boasted twenty-two squadrons, most were filled with light, unarmed training planes. The two Australian squadrons in New Guinea had a total of thirty aircraft. And this was only part of the report a dismayed Kenney had to give MacArthur upon his return to Brisbane.

He also brought with him notebooks filled with required changes and suggestions for improvements. The air force high-level bombing was failing to hit any of the shipping it attacked. Kenney's team therefore developed a low-level "skip-bombing" technique that was to prove very effective in the future. With this method, a bomber would come down to water level, then release bombs that bounced over the water into an enemy ship. Most bombers still did not even have bombsights; a formation always followed the leader, with its sole bombsight. Of course, if the leading plane was shot down, the others in the formation could not find the target. Kenney continued to demand further improvements.

Kenney also got his new air force officially recognized to include the 5th Fighter Command. He wisely reorganized it under the able Lieutenant Colonel Paul Wurtsmith and then deployed the 29th Fighter

Group from Darwin to New Guinea to help the 35th Fighter Group at Seven Mile Field. But the loss of the Kokoda airdrome by the Australians had made Port Moresby a much easier target, resulting in many daily raids. Kenney immediately installed two new radar stations no more than fifty miles from Moresby for earlier warning of attack. He had the fighter cockpits armored to better protect his men—a fact unknown to Japanese fighters—and added heavy 50-caliber machine guns to a variety of aircraft, from fighters to B-25s. And he introduced the use of parachute fragment bombs (parafrags) with which to bomb both enemy planes on the ground and their airstrips.[17]

Even before he had been there a week, Kenney had begun to strike at New Guinea's Gona, Buna, Lae, and Salamaua, destroying many airplanes and Japanese troop transports coming from the base at Rabaul. What is remarkable about Kenney's incessant offensive was that he frequently had only eight to twelve bombers available for his missions. But Kenney was not easily intimidated by numbers. His aim was to keep bombing all the Japanese bases, their supporting buildings, and fields to prevent Japan from building new fields. First he would slow them down, and then he would push them back.

But in addition to the bombing, it took troops on the ground to win the war. The American soldiers of the 32nd Division, who had been thrown into the fighting before they had been properly trained—over Eichelberger's adamant protests at his base camp in Rockhampton, Australia—had not only been fighting badly but were defeatist and poorly led. "Stories of [improper] actions," as George Kenney put it, "and even cowardice of our troops were filtering back. The officers didn't know their jobs." That included the most senior ones. "We were bringing back planeloads of shellshocked and sick boys every day." When Douglas MacArthur offered General Sir Thomas Blamey (a veteran of distinction, newly returned from the Mideast fighting and now serving as Allied Ground Forces commander in New Guinea) the U.S. 41st Division from Australia, "Blamey frankly said he would rather put in more Australians," who were better fighters. "I think it was a bitter pill for General MacArthur to swallow," Kenney acknowledged, "but he agreed."[18]

By the end of November, the situation was to become so desperate around the Buna Mission area that Lieutenant General Bob Eichelberger was ordered from Rockhampton to Government House at Port Moresby on the afternoon of November 30. "In order to break the existing deadlock, I sent in General Eichelberger with the last reserves," MacArthur recalled. Eichelberger recounted their discussion in slightly more detail. "When I saw General MacArthur in Moresby," he informed his wife, "he told me I was to capture Buna or lose my life [i.e., not come back alive], but that if I succeeded . . . I would be a very prominent figure in theUnited States." Eichelberger, a remarkable leader of men, did indeed turn the situation around amidst very fierce fighting. The Australian commander there, General George Vasey, would capture Gona on December 9; by January 2, 1943, Eichelberger's Americans would have captured Buna Mission as well.[19] The troops continued up the coast to secure Sananada after even tougher fighting, but Douglas MacArthur never once came to the front at Buna, despite later stories issued by him to the contrary.

Kenney continued to create new airfields on New Guinea as the Allies moved forward. He built the first at Waingela Field, near Buna, another at Dobodura, a third at Wewak, and a secret base at Wau. These were to put his fighters and bombers closer and closer to the last Japanese outposts on New Guinea, providing platforms from which to launch raids against Japanese convoys and island outposts. This required moving up air supplies, including new engines and spares, which were badly in demand. Accordingly he took the highly controversial step of closing down the main Australian Air Supply, Repair and Storage Depot, hidden well to the south of the country at Tocumwal, and moving it over a thousand miles further north near Townsville. It would prove a wise and efficacious decision.

Kenney's bombing raids now intensified. He targeted the Lae airfield and its main fuel supply center for Japan's Rabaul air force, as well as another nearby coastal field, Salamaua, due west of Rabaul. On August 26, 1942, Allied planes attacked Japanese transports landing at Milne Bay and destroyed transports, barges, light tanks, and huge supplies already on the beach as part of the planned attack against Port Moresby. As noted, the Japanese were forced to evacuate Milne Bay and turn back.

The raids on Lae were to continue nonstop, and by the end of the month of August they had "left the place a mess," according to Kenney.

One mission after another was dispatched by the American and Australian air forces. On September 13, they dropped more parafrag bombs on Buna Field, destroying most of the enemy planes on the ground.[20] Kenney also hit hard on the Kokoda Trail, which crossed the Owen Stanley Mountains between Buna and Port Moresby. On September 13, the Japanese reached Ioribaiway Ridge, and the Australians finally stopped their advance at Imita Ridge, a mere twenty-six miles from Port Moresby. Allied troops strafed and bombed, forcing General Horii's quickly disintegrating army back down the mountain to the sea. As Kenney recalled, "For nine successive days we pounded the Japs along the trail with every airplane we could put in the air."[21]

Kenney, who had first flown MacArthur to Port Moresby in September to "show him the town," also made an enormous effort to redress MacArthur's "Corregidor" image, which had rendered him so unpopular with American GIs and airmen. A fresh squadron of P-38s had just arrived at the newly constructed Laloki Air Field near Port Moresby, and Kenney suggested a visit. "I introduced the P-38 pilots. General MacArthur was glad to meet and talk with them, and they to listen to him. After fifteen minutes they were sold on Douglas MacArthur."[22] Kenney did this time and again. He was one of the very few senior American commanders who genuinely liked and admired MacArthur and got on well with him.

Although George Kenney's air force was still limited in size and rarely had more than two dozen bombers available per raid, he gradually built up his arsenal with additions of his favorite fighter, the P-38; his B-17s, B-25s, and B-26s; and the Catalinas that were also used by Australians. His warplanes were soon seen everywhere and in all weathers, totally reshaping and making possible MacArthur's successful campaign in New Guinea.

Kenney became MacArthur's golden boy, without whose extraordinary abilities and energies the fighting in the southwest Pacific—and later in the Philippines—might have turned out very differently indeed. In the Army Air Force's official history of World War II, Kenney was simply summed up as "brilliant."[23]

CHAPTER XIV

"Sock 'Em in the Solomons"

"The catastrophe of Midway definitely marked the turning of the tide in the Pacific War. . . ."

—*Fuchida Mitsuo and Masatake Okumiya,* Midway: The Battle That Doomed Japan *(1955)*[1]

"As you know, it has been my conviction that the Japanese will not stand still in the South Pacific and will not let us stand still. Either they will press us with an extension of their offensives, seeking weak points in order to break our lines of communications, or we will have to be pressing them."

—*Admiral Ernest King to General George Marshall, June 25, 1942*[2]

Ever since Arcadia, the First Washington Conference with the British in December 1941 and January 1942, Admiral Ernest King had resented the priority given the war against the Axis powers. To him, the bombing of London was clearly not as important as was the attack against Pearl Harbor. "I have found it necessary," he confided to a colleague, "to find time to point out to some 'amateur strategists' in high places [Churchill and Roosevelt] that unity of command is not a panacea for all military difficulties—and I shall continue to do so."[3] Now, with the triumphant naval victory at Midway in the first week of June and the attendant sinking of four Japanese aircraft carriers, Fleet

Admiral King was bent on blood and on the beginning of a real American naval offensive against Japan.

Little did he realize, of course, that the Japanese army and navy themselves were at odds with one another, each having a totally different objective. The Imperial Japanese Army wanted to concentrate its forces on China, Manchuria, and the Soviet threat. Its strategists were not interested in going deep into the "Bismarck Barrier" (New Guinea, Australia, or beyond). The Japanese navy, on the other hand, had a southern objective: the breaking of the 7,500-mile line of communications running from eastern Australia to the Panama Canal, the line so essential for Australia, New Zealand, Hawaii, and the United States. Admiral King was of course intent on keeping those air and sea lanes open. In the U.S. Army, however, Brigadier General Eisenhower, for one, openly disputed the importance of defending these very lines of communication between Australia and the United States. As he put it, the United States's "maintaining contact with Australia and . . . preventing further Japanese expansion to the southwestward . . . are not immediately vital to the successful outcome of the war."[4] This statement outraged Ernie King, who was going to do everything within his considerable power as chief of all U.S. naval forces not only to keep those lines of communication open but also to widen and strengthen them. Such a strategy would serve the dual advantage of giving America ports, fuel depots, and airfields scattered over a series of islands between Hawaii and Australia while providing sites from which to launch attacks against the Japanese military in the future. Tokyo had already made deep inroads into the western and southern Pacific thanks to the fall of the Philippines, permitting its troops to begin landings in New Guinea and threatening Port Moresby, the capital itself. MacArthur's failure had also allowed Japan to take Rabaul and Bougainville, to bomb Darwin in Australia, and to threaten New Caledonia. Meanwhile, Japanese forces continued to move eastward toward Hawaii, with the intention of occupying it.

But even the persistent, hard-driving Admiral King had formidable opponents against the attempt to launch an early offensive in the Pacific. The Allies, having already made the European theater their number-one priority, were agreeing upon their first offensive, a great attack against French North Africa that would occur later in 1942.

However, George Marshall, in unusually forceful language for him, *demanded* a direct Channel crossing to Europe by 1943—if not in 1942 itself—rather than an invasion of Morocco, Algeria, and Tunisia. U.S. naval chief King, on the other hand, insisted that most shipping currently situated in the Atlantic be sent to the Pacific.

For several reasons, Churchill's government pressed for a major North African landing, instead of crossing the Channel in the face of heavily defended northern France. Churchill, for one, did not want to revisit the needless slaughter of hundreds of thousands of men that he had witnessed during World War I (when he personally commanded a front-line battalion); nor did the American army, which was just beginning to mobilize on a large scale, have anywhere near the sufficient training required for such a challenge, as would soon be proven in New Guinea and North Africa. The combined British and American air forces also lacked many hundreds of planes and experienced pilots and crews to cover such an operation. Finally, they simply did not possess the enormous naval and shipping strength required to transport and land even a small portion of such a major cross-Channel expedition as they were envisioning, let alone to withstand the still-growing U-boat menace in those waters. These were elementary facts that George Marshall, on the American side, refused to face.

The result was one of the most bizarre moments of the war. In July 1942, George Marshall and Ernie King decided to foil the entire European idea, sending a joint memorandum to Franklin Roosevelt stating that "we are definitely of the opinion that we should turn to the Pacific and strike decisively against Japan," rather than against Germany.[5] To which Churchill responded to Ambassador Lord Halifax, "Just because the Americans can't have a massacre in France this year, they want to sulk and bathe in the Pacific!"[6] A flabbergasted, infuriated Roosevelt in turn immediately demanded to see detailed strategic plans for the Pacific. These were quickly drafted and signed by Arnold, King, and Marshall, and then handed over to FDR, who read the proposal and turned it down flat, strongly chastising the American Chiefs of Staff. "My first impression is that is exactly what Germany hoped the United States would do following Pearl Harbor," the president riposted. American troops intended for England and Europe would instead be shifted to dozens of scattered islands across the Pacific, where they would accomplish nothing and indeed would only harm the war effort while half the cities of Great Britain were literally burning night after night as a result of nonstop German bombing. "*Therefore, it is disapproved* as of the present," signed: "ROOSEVELT C IN C."[7]

It may be recalled that back on March 31, 1942, Roosevelt and the American Joint Chiefs of Staff had agreed to create a demarcation line dividing, if not the world, at least the Pacific into two different theaters. Admiral Chester Nimitz, as Commander in Chief, Pacific Ocean Area (CINCPOA), was to command the navy, air force, and army throughout the Pacific, except in the new South West Pacific Operational Command, which was given to Douglas MacArthur. The latter's jurisdiction included the Philippines, Australia, New Zealand, the New Hebrides, New Guinea, and the Solomons.

On June 8, 1942, MacArthur had seriously proposed the invasion of the Japanese bastion of Rabaul, with the U.S. Navy serving under his command. King quickly rejected this idea, as did Roosevelt.[8] Where was MacArthur to obtain the troops, ships, and aircraft for such an operation? Retaliating, in part, against MacArthur's earlier Rabaul concept, Ernie King announced his intention of invading the Solomons, still theoretically within MacArthur's area of command. Since MacArthur lacked the troops, transport, and will to execute this operation himself, Nimitz's South Pacific Area was extended a few dozen miles to the west to encompass the eastern Solomons, including Tulagi and Guadalcanal. Vice Admiral Ghormley would command the eastern Solomons under Nimitz's name and orders. Marshall and King agreed to this on July 2, on condition that once the navy and marines had taken these areas, they would revert to MacArthur's command.

•

Although they had not yet received approval for a further advance in the Pacific, on July 4, 1942, Admirals King, Nimitz, and Turner met at the 12th Naval District Headquarters in San Francisco to work out their next objectives—to be ready to act when that authorization came. They were planning "Operation Pestilence," of which "Operation Watchtower" (code name for the Solomons and Rabaul) was a part. They were even thinking well ahead to the time when they would also be attacking Truk, Saipan, and Guam. To this end, King had already begun further development of naval installations, airstrips, and fuel depots on Johnston Island, Palmyra, Christmas Island, Canton (in the Phoenix group), Bora-Bora, American Samoa, Tongatabu, Funafuti, Fiji, Pago-Pago, Efate, and Espíritu Santo, among others. And in fact, as far back as January 12, 1942, the final day of the First Washington Conference, Marshall—supported by Hopkins and Roosevelt—agreed with the newly formed Combined Joint Chiefs of Staff to send some ten thousand U.S. troops to French New Caledonia as a first step (before the Japanese took over that colony for themselves).

As for the operations against the Solomons, after the great victory at Midway, on June 4, 1942, these would be the first of a series of amphibious landings in the Pacific, and King ordered Rear Admiral Kelly Turner to organize and command all such operations for the navy throughout the Pacific. No mean undertaking, that. As King was wont to say, "The best defense is offense . . . an offensive which will keep the enemy engaged and occupied to such an extent that he cannot gather the means to make any serious threat to the continental U.S."[9]

The decision to hasten Turner's amphibious organization came as a result of more Japanese naval intercepts made by HYPO, following Joe Rochefort's great coup in uncovering Yamamoto's intended sneak attack on Midway in June. Further intercepts by the army's SIS helped complete the picture. In the first days of July 1942, while King, Nimitz, and Turner were meeting in San Francisco, Rochefort's unit intercepted a Japanese radio message stating that "Guadalcanal landing was designated Operation 'AN,' " with July 4 as "X" (D)-Day.

"I first knew definitely of the Operation [destined for the Solomons] on June thirtieth," Turner recalled. He was ordered to draw up an assault plan, which he then submitted to King and Nimitz on July 3. It was accepted the next day. For such a hastily devised plan, its sweep was great, if not a little fantastic, given the very limited resources and personnel available, not to mention the brief time allotted. "Operation Pestilence" included the occupation of Ndeni Island (in the Santa Cruz Islands); the capture of Tulagi and neighboring Florida Islands in the lower Solomons (560 miles northwest of Espíritu Santo in the New Hebrides) and the airfield on the adjacent coast of Guadalcanal; the establishment of an elaborate aircraft warning system throughout the outer Solomons; the occupation of Funafuti (in the Ellice Islands); and reinforcement of the Espíritu Santo army garrison and the construction of an airfield there, some four hundred miles north of Nouméa, New Caledonia, whose U.S. Army garrison was to be beefed up to twenty-two thousand men.[10]

The team Turner was given that July was lamentably small—nine captains and ten commanders—comprising three divisions of transports and cargo ships (APs and AKs). "Amphibious Force South Pacific" was officially organized on July 18, less than three weeks prior to Turner's putting his entire new amphibious force to sea.

Obviously there were too many objectives to be accomplished with such limited resources, and thus the Santa Cruz project was postponed. The U.S. military still had no hard information as to the importance of Tulagi, the best deep-water port in the Solomons. Why did Tokyo want it at this time? The answer was that it would help close American air and sea communications, and in particular would be needed for attacks on New Guinea and the seizure of Port Moresby. In any event, the Americans did learn on June 26 that a pre-landing group of Japanese engineers were burning vegetation on Guadalcanal "for an airdrome," and some tents could be seen. Finally, on July 10, the first confirmed report was received of actual construction on the airfield.[11] Turner was not given an assignment; he was handed what would prove to be the biggest nightmare of his life.

•

The essential key to success or failure of the U.S.'s planned amphibious landings and assaults was the landing craft, whose necessity had been pointed out by Admiral Robert Coontz back in 1925 and then promptly forgotten. In 1935, the navy was given only $40,000 with which to create, develop, and produce the first landing craft, and the first testing of the vehicles in a fleet exercise occurred in 1939. By 1940, the budget for their production had risen to a heady $400,000.[12]

It was only in the spring of 1941, when President Roosevelt informed the marines that they would need such craft for operations in the Azores *by July 1 of that same year*, that the navy finally got cracking. An enterprising Captain Roswell Daggett was acquainted with a man named Andy Higgins, who was building such boats in New Orleans for some South American companies. Daggett rang him up and, as he later recounted, "I flew down that night. . . . We designed a ramp for the bow and Higgins proceeded to alter the lighter."* As he lacked sufficient space, Higgins began work in "the middle of a roped off New Orleans street next to his shop." And thus the U.S. Navy got its first new landing craft in 1941, and many hundreds thereafter.[13] Ironically, earlier, when Higgins had gone to Washington to suggest the building of such craft, Ernie King had shown him the door.

In turn, large transports would be required to carry these landing craft all around the world. As late as October 1941, the U.S. Navy had only 30 large transports (capable of carrying 816 landing craft, a number it did not possess), with 11 AKs (amphibious cargo ships that could hold another 80 landing boats) either in commission or under construction. By that October, the navy still had only two large AKs in the entire Pacific Ocean. By the spring of 1942, Admiral King, as CNO and commander in chief, U.S. Fleet (COMINCH), got that number up to six APs, two AKs, and three APDs (destroyer transports) in the Pacific.[14]

It is only after recognizing the extreme limitations confronting Kelly Turner that one can begin to appreciate fully the seemingly almost impossible pressure placed on him for the execution of his first amphibious operations. Scheduled for August 1942, this would all have to be accomplished within a matter of weeks.

•

That the inimitable, ever arrogant Fleet Admiral Ernie King, commander in chief of the nation's entire fleet, had selected Turner for this operation was in itself an extraordinary tribute. What is more, Turner, like King, had been experiencing marital troubles, and his personal life was in turmoil. Although it was a happy marriage at the beginning, the Turners had both wanted a large family and instead remained childless. This childless state aggravated problems of a pronounced nature: Turner's wife had developed into a serious manic-depressive, and he at times was called from work after news of an emergency or suicide attempt. Or, on very rare occasions, she would go on a buying spree

*The lighter was the barge used to ferry men and equipment from the boats to the land.

and Turner would suddenly receive enormous bills that put him in debt to the point that he could not afford to buy new uniforms for years—a failure duly noted in his fitness reports.

Marital woes aside, King knew perfectly well that Kelly Turner had not participated in any of the latest fleet problems involving amphibious landings, which had taken place when Turner was still at the Naval War College in Newport. Furthermore, King was aware that Turner knew practically nothing whatsoever about the actual machinery of landing craft. But such confidence did King have in Turner that he expected him to be fully capable of mastering every aspect of this newly created naval organization, and of drafting the basic manual for amphibious operations, which he then submitted to the commandant of the U.S. Marine Corps for his suggestions and approval. The protocols were duly approved, although they also gave Turner considerable authority over the marines during amphibious landings and immediately thereafter—something that Archie Vandegrift, the marine commander, later failed to comprehend.[15] And all preparations had to be accomplished in just a few weeks' time. In fact, it was only in June that Turner was apprised of his new command; by the first week of August, he would have to find competent commanding officers, ships, and repair crews, and have his new officers training members of an organization that would one day number three quarters of a million men. Few flag officers envied Kelly Turner.

Moreover, Turner now discovered that he would not have the immediate support or assistance of his commanding officer in the South Pacific, Robert Ghormley, who was getting ready to sail from New Zealand to his new station at Nouméa, New Caledonia, at the end of July 1942. The two men, truth be known, did not understand one another—Ghormley was not at the same level of competence as Turner. To be sure, Ghormley, a pleasant man, was nearing the end of his career and already mentally and physically tired even before operations began. He was not used to working under great pressure.

By contrast, Ernie King was a veritable steamroller, a man who expected action and full compliance with his orders. King had put himself out on a limb. This offensive in the South Pacific was the riskiest operation of his career, and he had not yet done the most basic planning. Only a man of his extraordinary self-confidence would have even considered a project as ambitious as this series of amphibious assaults on the southern Solomons, set for the end of the first week of August.

As already noted, the Japanese were landing at several points on the east coast of New Guinea. Their transports brought thousands of veteran troops, including those who were attempting to round Milne Bay (at the southernmost point of New Guinea) in order to seize that country's capital, Port Moresby, the residence of the Australian governor and located just across the Coral Sea from the exposed coast of Australia itself.*

This unexpectedly desperate situation had arisen as a result of the loss of the Philippines, which had served as a shield against Japanese operations in the South Pacific. The Philippine "barrier" was responsible for protecting the Allies' Malay Barrier, extending from Malaya to New Guinea, which once in Japanese hands would give Tokyo access to all the oil, refined gasoline, rubber, tin, copper, nickel, and other materials needed for its expanding war machine. It is surprising that Marshall and his advisers had not earlier appreciated the real strategic importance of the Philippines as a barrier in the event Japan lost access to American markets. It was precisely this Philippine barrier that had been largely responsible for keeping Borneo, Sumatra, Java, Singapore, Hong Kong, Thailand, Indochina, Malaya, New Guinea, and Australia from falling into enemy hands.

Hence Admiral King's determination now to aid MacArthur—his frequent sparring partner—in preventing the Japanese invasion of New Guinea and Port Moresby by directing Turner and Vandegrift's landing and seizure of the southern Solomons, islands which just a few months earlier were barely known even to senior U.S. military personnel.

As the Solomons had originally fallen within MacArthur's sector of the South West Pacific Command, he had strongly recommended his own army troops taking them until his discovery that he lacked both troops and shipping for such an expedition. Bob Ghormley, for his part, was entirely against the Solomons operations, which he was convinced were doomed to failure. As he confided to Archie Vandegrift, "I don't see how we can land at all."[16] In a vote against the Solomons venture,

*New Guinea had been an Australian territory since the end of World War I, when it was mandated to Australia by the League of Nations.

Ghormley and MacArthur warned King: "The two commanders [i.e., MacArthur and Ghormley] are of the opinion, arrived at independently . . . that the initiation of the operation at this time . . . would be attended with the gravest risk. It is recommended that this operation be deferrred."[17]

They were right, in part. The navy was certainly not ready for such an undertaking; but on the other hand, Nimitz had no other choice if he were to check the Japanese advance. Some would call it brinkmanship. After Ghormley and MacArthur voted their opposition, the Joint Chiefs of Staff made the decision to support King and Nimitz and to give a small portion of the southwestern section of the Solomons temporary priority for invasion and occupation.

Since there were insufficient amphibious forces in the South Pacific with which to invade and conquer all the islands, the U.S. military concentrated on the most immediate threat from Tulagi and Guadalcanal, pressed by the Japanese construction of an airfield and seaport there. On July 16, King and Nimitz set D-Day for the invasion of the Solomons for August 7, 1942.[18]

On July 16, Kelly Turner's Amphibious Task Force 62, as it would come to be known, was hastily thrown together at Wellington, New Zealand. Turner's flagship, the 13,000-ton *McCawley*, or AP-10 (later designated APA-4), was capable of 17 knots and was commanded by Captain Charles McFeaters, with Lieutenant Commander George Reilly serving as Turner's new executive officer. Time was short, but King was determined to push on with the assault on Tulagi and Guadalcanal as quickly as possible.[19]

•

Another major participant in Operation Watchtower was the navy's largely land-based air force in this region. Task Force 63 was headed by Rear Admiral John McCain, Commander, Air Fleet, South Pacific (COMAIRSOPAC), who reported directly to Ghormley.[20] The objective of these land-based aircraft was to support and cover the Solomons Expeditionary Force and to carry out prior scouting missions for it. This team, too, was hurriedly arranged as bombers and fighters were shipped from Hawaii and elsewhere in the United States to islands across the Pacific. Nimitz dispatched thirty-one navy PBY patrol bombers to New Caledonia and the Fijis. Ninety-three naval fighters were soon based at Efate, New Caledonia, the Fijis, Tongatabu, and Samoa; the bases were reinforced by a variety of other planes, including thirty-five army B-17s at New Caledonia and the Fijis. By August 1, 1942, McCain's TF 63 comprised some 291 aircraft of all types, including units of the Royal New Zealand Air Force.[21]

Dividing this force into seven groups, McCain issued his first orders on July 25, barely a fortnight before D-Day. In effect, these divisions were like seven slices of a big pie, each responsible for covering up to 650- and 700-mile-wide sectors over and round the approaches to Guadalcanal and Tulagi. They in turn were supported by MacArthur's Southwest Pacific air force, which included both American and Australian units responsible for a sector as far as longitude 158° fifteen minutes east and latitude 15° south. But as McCain had no aircraft actually at Guadalcanal, the slices of this pie did not begin from its center but from the outlying island or seaplane bases, including those at Nandi in the Fijis, Koumac (New Caledonia), Espíritu Santo, Efate, Ndeni (Santa Cruz Islands), and so on. They included PBY squadrons, a Marine fighter squadron, scouting squadrons, and even a heavy bombardment group. Most of the slices of this pie carried out their reconnaissance hundreds of miles directly to the north of Espíritu Santo and then well to the west, forming an enormous arc well over fifteen hundred miles wide. In theory, if all the pieces were in place, all sectors leading to the approach of the southern Solomons should have been covered. If, on the other hand, even one air group failed to sweep its allotted sector, a gap would be left through which enemy ships or aircraft could arrive unnoticed. Furthermore, once Turner and Vandegrift's assault on Guadalcanal and Tulagi began, MacArthur was to withdraw his aircraft, unless Ghormley should call them in during an emergency. Thus any enemy force heading for Guadalcanal could be spotted while still hundreds of miles away, barring weather or atmospheric problems. Turner and his task force, aided by Fletcher's three carriers, could then prepare an adequate defense.[22]

●

Supply ships from the United States and Australia continued to reach Wellington in New Zealand, but the workforce and port facilities there proved inadequate to handle such a large expedition on such short notice. Furthermore, the stevedores worked very limited union hours, which included long "tea-breaks," and ships were backing up, although New Zealanders' very safety from Japanese attacks depended upon their cooperation with the Americans now. "This was my first introduction to practical socialism," commented Vandegrift.[23] Upon his arrival, a frustrated Vandegrift met urgently with Prime Minister Peter Fraser in the face of hostility from the local unions. Fraser gave his full backing, and soon teams of three hundred U.S. marines at a time, working twenty-four hours a day at the small Aotea Quay (which could accommodate only five ships at once), were unloading.

All vessels arriving with supplies and equipment from the United States had to be completely unloaded. They were then "combat-loaded,"* their original contents completely rearranged and reloaded on ships destined for the war zone. The ship transports of Task Force 62 were divided into eight groups (including the Support and Screen groups), each one assigned to a special island or task; in all, 19 large transport and cargo vessels carried some 472 landing craft and thousands of tons of weapons, munitions, vehicles, food, and medical supplies. Altogether the expedition under Turner's command would comprise some seventy-six ships.[24]

Originally, the marines were to be left with enough supplies to hold them over for between two and three months, and they were greatly aided in the loading process by the use of eighteen U.S. ten-wheel trucks and some thirty flatbed trucks provided by the New Zealand army. Even so, Turner found himself short of dozens of big transport ships and was forced to leave much behind, including 75 percent of his heavy trucks.[25] Vandegrift's 19,500 marines were obliged to reduce still further what they could carry in their kits, limiting contents to what they could "fight with and live on."

Like everyone else, General Vandegrift, who had been sent to New Zealand to oversee several months of training for his men, had only

* Most ships were loaded in the United States helter-skelter, e.g., 50-caliber machine-gun ammunition with howitzers or rifles instead of on the same ships (and preferably in the same hold) as the appropriate guns. The same applied to vehicles such as fighter aircraft, which were often loaded into ships without spare tires, engines, and other necessary parts.

been informed of Operation Watchtower at the last minute. On July 20, two days after Turner hoisted his flag in his *McCawley*, Vandegrift gave his tactical orders to the commanders who would be leading the 1st Marine Division (less one regiment), which was to be reinforced by the 2nd Marines, the 1st Raider Battalion, and the 3rd Defense Battalion. King had not given much notice, and because conferences and long travel distances were necessary to bring everyone together, when all parties involved finally arrived in New Zealand, "There was no time for a deliberate planning phase," Archie Vandegrift explained. (The last of the task force finally cleared Wellington Harbour on July 22, a logistical miracle, and probably the fastest operational preparations made in U.S. Navy history.) The marines' next destination: the Fijis, for landing rehearsals. They were to be given air cover there by three carriers under the overall command of Vice Admiral Frank Jack Fletcher: his flagship, the *Saratoga*; Rear Admiral Kinkaid's flagship, the *Enterprise*; and Rear Admiral Leigh Noyes's flagship, the USS *Wasp*. All three admirals had one thing in common, in that there was not a single aviator among them to command these three aircraft battlegroups. In addition to the carriers, a hastily thrown together Screening Group including eight cruisers—American and Australian—a Fire Support Group, and seventeen destroyers was assembling, with Rear Admiral V. A. C. Crutchley, RN, in charge. Crutchley, having just reached the region, was a stranger to just about everyone, as indeed were most of the ships' captains.

The first meeting, July 26 on board the *Saratoga* off Koro, Fiji, was hardly a success; nor were the rehearsals to follow. Owing to the deep water, the transports could not anchor, and most of the marines never had an opportunity to land.[26] But at least the carrier planes and Crutchley's ships had a chance to get in some bombing and shelling practice, while Turner practiced lowering and raising his fragile, largely wood-hulled Higgins boats, greatly reducing the time required for this procedure at Guadalcanal.

At the end of July, adding to the various obstacles impeding the brief landing practices, which were due to conclude in just a few days, the most unexpected, indeed shattering, news came from the overall task force commander, Vice Admiral Fletcher. During a conference of seventeen senior commanding officers held aboard the *Saratoga*, Fletcher announced bluntly that his three carriers would remain with them for only two days upon their arrival at Guadalcanal, thereafter leaving Turner's TF 62—including all his ships, men, and marines—stranded *without any air protection whatsoever* after Sunday morning, August 9. One officer described the meeting as "stormy," Fletcher's bombshell stunning everyone, including a shocked and betrayed Turner. "The conference was one long bitter argument between Vice Admiral Fletcher and my new boss," as Thomas Peyton, Turner's new chief of staff, described it. Fletcher, a close friend of Ghormley, was jeopardizing the whole operation with a move that would have disastrous long-term results. Turner reminded Fletcher that the decision had been made at the highest levels and was to be executed as planned.[27] Fletcher responded, "Now Kelly, you are making plans to take that island from the Japs and the Japs may turn on you and wallop the hell out of you." Fletcher, it may be remembered, had recently lost one carrier and nearly lost a second one in the battle of the Coral Sea. "What are you going to do then?" A bitter Turner looked at the embarrassed admiral and replied, "I am just going to stay there and take my licking."

"Kelly was tough, a brain, and a son-of-a-bitch," Fletcher later recalled. For his part, Fletcher, though he may have been called a son-of-a-bitch and later even a traitor, was never referred to as "tough" or "brainy," not when it came to a real battle.[28]

But Turner was not the only person to protest Fletcher's unilateral decision. Vandegrift also voiced his opposition. "My Dutch blood was beginning to boil," he recalled, "but I forced myself to remain calm while explaining to Fletcher that the days 'of landing a small force and leaving' were over. This operation was supposed to take and hold Guadalcanal and Tulagi. To accomplish this I commanded a heavily reinforced division which I was to land on enemy-held territory, which means a fight. I could hardly expect to land this massive force *without air cover*—even the five days mentioned by Turner involved a tremendous risk [for the marines]." But Fletcher was adamant.[29]

One cannot help but surmise that Frank Jack Fletcher was anxious about two things: his carriers and his own hide, and not the thousands of sailors and marines involved in an operation of which he totally disapproved. Fletcher seemed to forget that his number-one objective now was to provide air protection for the otherwise helpless, anchored landing craft as they were slowly being unloaded[30]—and this included many tons of food, equipment, artillery, munitions, tanks, trucks, and fuel, as well as Vandegrift's 19,500 men (11,000 of them destined for Guadalcanal alone). They would be nearly one thousand miles away from MacArthur's nearest bombers. Furthermore, although Nimitz had ordered Ghormley to "exercise strategic command in person," Ghormley had even failed to show up for the exercises and meetings at Fiji, preferring the safety of Auckland, which he was now about to leave for his new station off Nouméa.[31]

Such was the unhappy background to the landings on Guadalcanal. Turner had just about everything against him: he was short on officers, transports, and cargo ships, and now his only immediate source of air cover was set upon disappearing over the horizon two days after the shooting had begun. Nor did Ghormley ever give a reason for failing to appear at Fiji, where he was to have issued the final orders. Even more troubling, most of the ships' commanders and crews, of both the Amphibious Force and the Screening and Fire Support groups, had never worked together before. Fletcher then further stumbled at the conclusion of the Fiji exercises: "No general conference was held after the rehearsal, a *sine qua non*" for all such operations, noted Turner's friend and biographer, Vice Admiral George Carroll Dyer.[32] Instead, Fletcher merely complained about the lack of fuel and of the task force's possible discovery by the Japanese (who in fact had no knowledge either of its present location or of its destination).

As the exercises broke up and the ships left Fiji for their objective, morale could not have been lower. To make this tragic farce complete, Vice Admiral Robert Ghormley had the gall to send the combined Task Forces 61, 62, and 63 the rousing message: "We look to you to electrify the world with news of a real offensive. . . . Sock 'em in the Solomons."[33]

Leaving Fiji on July 31, the seventy-six ships set sail for the Solomons, and on August 5, Turner's Task Force 62 altered course to the north at 13 knots, heading for the Russell Islands. Turner navigated through haze and squalls, giving the dangerous shoals of the Russells a clearance of seven miles and reducing the front of his task force to 3,500 yards in the narrowing channel between the Russells and Guadalcanal, amid the notoriously tricky currents of the Coral Sea. In the late afternoon of August 6, Fletcher's carrier group of twenty-six ships broke off contact and disappeared to the south, as Turner's transports, still concealed by heavy rain squalls, formed into columns of squadrons and reduced speed to 12 knots.

As August 6 gave way to August 7, the destroyers *Henley* and *Bagley* led the task force into the shark-infested waters between Guadalcanal and Tulagi, which was later dubbed as "Ironbottom Sound." At 0050 visibility suddenly cleared, revealing a sky full of stars. Task Force 62 split into two groups off Cape Espérance on the northwest tip of Guadalcanal. The lead transports heading the Tulagi Group passed north of Savo Island, while Captain L. F. Reifsnider's division, bound for Lunga Point on Guadalcanal, took the channel to the south of Savo Island. Sunrise was due to occur at about 0633. Although one marine correspondent described Guadalcanal as "an island of striking beauty," with "blue-green mountains towering into a brilliant tropical sky," Kelly Turner, with all his worries, had no time for such poetic enthusiasm.

At 0600 they spied the first traces of Japanese forces: the lights of two planes were seen taking off near Lunga Point, and red flares were dropped over HMAS *Australia* nine minutes later. At 0613 three heavy American cruisers, joined by four destroyers, opened fire on the beaches of Guadalcanal. The ships on the Tulagi side also commenced firing, while minesweepers both at Guadalcanal and at Tulagi swept the waters between the two islands.

The Japanese at Tulagi were taken completely by surprise, and, not sure of what was happening, waited until 0652 to warn air command at Rabaul: "ENEMY TASK FORCE SIGHTED." At 0715 they sent a final message: "ENEMY HAS COMMENCED LANDING." The battle for Guadalcanal was about to begin.[34]

CHAPTER XV

Guadalcanal

"[E]nemy air attacks and reduction of fighters in our forces due to losses, together with critical fuel situation, has caused CTF 61 [Fletcher] to recommend to COMSOPAC [Ghormley] that carriers be withdrawn."

—*Rear Admiral Thomas Kinkaid, Task Force 61*[1]

"My despatch didn't say anything about needing to withdraw to fuel. . . ."

—*Vice Admiral Frank Jack Fletcher, Task Force 61*[2]

"We took one hell of a beating."

—*Rear Admiral Richmond Kelly Turner, Task Force 62*[3]

"On August seven this force will recapture Tulagi and Guadalcanal Islands which are now in the hands of the enemy," Rear Admiral Kelly Turner announced to his task force. At 0614 hours on August 7, 1942—D-Day—the heavy cruiser *Quincy*'s big guns, joined by those of two other American cruisers and four destroyers, suddenly roared to life, pounding Japanese shore installations and announcing the onset of the first major American amphibious landings since the Spanish-American War.[4] Turner and Vandegrift were expecting an opposition of upward of 7,000 Japanese men, but in fact there were only 2,230, most of them construction workers.

"Land the landing force," the transport *Hunter Liggett* signaled the other fourteen members of the flotilla off Guadalcanal at 0650. Thousands of U.S. marines in full battle gear clambered down the nets into the dozens of landing craft still nine thousand yards from the beach. The sea was calm and ideal for this operation. By 0913 the first marines were fanning out over the mile-long, black volcanic sand designated "Beach Red," but apart from numerous snipers from coastal palm trees, they encountered very little fire, even as forty-four planes from the *Saratoga* and *Enterprise* struck the island and another forty-one hit Tulagi. But to the consternation of a keyed-up Archie Vandegrift, many of his marines were either lounging on the beach or advancing through the jungle very slowly. "The 1st Battalion, 5th Marines," he said, was "moving as if it were about to encounter the entire imperial army. I gave the battalion commander hell."[5]

A much more serious problem was arising along the beaches, however. Approximately one hundred landing barges were jammed side by side, barely able to land material, while Turner reported that "a considerable number of landing boats, chiefly ramp lighters, were stranded on the beach . . . because these ramps had been loaded too heavily by the head" and were now being swamped by the waves. Also, in the words of Turner, there was a "vast amount of unnecessary impediments" to be unloaded but not enough sailors to unload them. The marines did little or nothing to help, delaying the landing of supplies by many hours and then blaming it all on Turner. Turner complained about this to one marine officer,[6] and his displeasure was echoed by other transport commanders as well. The Boat Group commander of USS *Barnett* found only fifteen to twenty men unloading the boats while fifty others swam in the lagoon. "While looking for the Beachmaster, I saw about one hundred men lounging around under the palm trees eating coconuts. . . . All of these men were Marines that should have been unloading boats." The captain of the *Hunter Liggett* similarly disparaged the marines' lack of cooperation, which resulted in a massive backlog of boats along the shore; behind them still others waited, unable to unload landing craft "due to the great congestion on the beach." The captain of the Ak-22 ship *Formalhaut* succinctly described the mayhem as a "very slow procedure." And although George Rowan, the beachmaster, pointed out the problem to Vandegrift, the marine commander said he could not spare a man, calling such a move "a levy patently impossible at this critical time."[7] Finally the meticulous Turner, upon whom so many thousands of lives now depended, took matters in hand and ordered a halt to the unloading of any more boats for the next several hours until the clogged beaches could be cleared.

Meanwhile, Vandegrift was encountering problems of his own. Although Douglas MacArthur had promised him detailed aerial photographs of Tulagi, the Florida Islands, and Guadalcanal, the general had failed to deliver these. The few maps Vandegrift now had were hand-drawn sketches by Australians who "knew" the islands. These, alas, were largely inaccurate. For instance, the marines' first objectives were to secure the beaches, cross the river, seize the airfield, and take Mt. Austen, which the map indicated was nine miles away. In reality, the mountain proved closer to ninety miles away through virgin jungle. That goal thus had to be postponed, which was a delay that would cost the operation dearly.

Aboard the *McCawley*, the Air Support director was having difficulties communicating with and coordinating attacks by Fletcher's planes. By comparison, Japan's planes—dispatched by Rabaul with orders to retaliate—were quick off the mark, with at least two major air strikes hitting Tulagi and Guadalcanal the first day. The Fighter Director Group, aboard the U.S. heavy cruiser *Chicago*, had the most modern radar, but although the group had effectively warned Turner an hour in advance of the first two attacks by Japanese bombers, for some reason its radar began to malfunction and the task force was caught completely unawares.

When dozens of Japanese twin-engine bombers did appear, all landing operations had to stop, and the United States's precious big transports—the only ones in the Pacific—had to weigh anchor and disperse, which they did effectively the first day. The initial enemy wave of twenty-five bombers from Rabaul attacked the task force early in the afternoon of the 7th, and several were shot down. An hour later, a second wave arrived, harmlessly bombing the Americans, but greatly disrupting the landing schedule.[8] The next day a third wave of forty more bombers flew over the Florida Islands around noon. One plane crashed into the *George F. Elliott*, setting it aflame; the nearby destroyer *Jarvis* was badly damaged and had to put to sea.

If Vandegrift's men on Guadalcanal encountered only sniper fire and received no casualties, the navy forces on Tulagi and adjacent islets met with heavy resistance after landing on Blue Beach. The 1st Raider Battalion's attacks on caves and well-entrenched dugouts on the three-mile-long Tulagi and nearby Tanabogo and Gavute resulted in more than 140 American casualties. Hard fighting continued into the next day, and the islands were finally secured on August 8 and 9.[9]

Vandegrift was still having trouble with inexperienced, slow-moving marines who were now engaged in their first real fighting. They did reach Lunga Point and the airfield, from which some 1,130 Japanese sailors and laborers had fled westward. The marine command, in its first operation in the Pacific, was surprised by the elaborate preparations already made by the Japanese, including machine shops, ice plants, two large electric power plants, an air compressor plant for torpedoes, hangars, and two powerful radio stations—not to mention large stores of weapons and ammunition at Kukum (.25-caliber rifles, .303-caliber machine guns, two 70mm and two 75mm guns, with ammunition), plenty of gasoline, thirty-five trucks, and most surprisingly, two radar units. In addition they found large stores of food—rice, tea, noodles, tinned food, beer, and sake.[10] None of this would go to waste.

The unloading continued along the beaches continued until more Japanese bombers appeared, when everything stopped again, often for hours at a time. Yet only 490 men of the Pioneer battalions were left on the beach to handle the supplies and get them ashore to the marines.

Turner and Crutchley protected the sea entrances leading to Tulagi and Guadalcanal by posting two radar-equipped destroyers, the *Ralph Talbot* and the *Blue*, northwest of Savo Island. Because of the risk offered by two separate entrances to the island, the American-Australian forces were divided into two groups: the cruisers *Australia*, *Canberra*, and *Chicago*, along with two destroyers, *Bagley* and *Patterson*, screened the southern entrance between Cape Espérance and Savo, while three more cruisers—*Quincy*, *Astoria* (Turner's former flagship), and *Vincennes*—and two more destroyers—*Helm* and *Wilson*—patrolled the entrance between Savo and Florida-Tulagi.[11]

On Guadalcanal, the marines' airfield was being readied to receive its first American squadrons of B-17s and the slow-moving P-40 fighters. Eleven dive-bombers were sent from the *Enterprise*, and fourteen P-40s were added by the army when fuel depots were constructed later in August. But while work on the airfield went on and Vandegrift's men established the first tentative perimeter around it, unexpected tragedy was about to strike by sea. Meanwhile, Nimitz and King were closely monitoring the situation, with Pearl Harbor informing Washington, "At last we have started."[12]

•

The hitherto unchecked Japanese high command was left in a state of utter bewilderment when news of the American landings on Guadalcanal and Tulagi reached it on August 7. From Admiral Yamamoto on down, the Imperial Japanese naval command, in particular, was stunned—but not for long. Following an emergency war council, Hirohito's men went into action.

Admiral Yamamoto ordered his five airfields on Rabaul to launch a series of extensive bombing raids, while Vice Admiral Mikawa Gunichi hurriedly issued instructions to his Eighth Fleet to fuel and arm. On such short notice, there were two options available to him, and he acted on both. On his orders, a convoy of trucks appeared before Rabaul's main army barracks to collect 519 troops. They were soon lumbering down to the docks, where the only two transports there were busily fueling and taking on supplies and munitions. The skippers of those vessels would set sail later that same evening.

Mikawa's second decision was to assemble as many cruisers as possible, diverting four of them already en route for Buna, New Guinea, to a rendezvous with him instead. Later that same morning of August 7, a grim Admiral Mikawa hoisted his flag in the powerful cruiser *Chokai* and, accompanied by the light cruisers *Tenryu* and *Yubari* and the sole remaining destroyer in port, shortly set sail from Rabaul for a position east of the island of Bougainville. There, at 1400 hours, they duly made their rendezvous with the other four cruisers—a mere seven hours and fifteen minutes after receiving the SOS from Tulagi.

Addressing his captains, Mikawa disclosed their destination and objective as they charted a fresh course that would take them down the east coast of Bougainville, between the islands of Shortland and Choiseul to the entrance of the "Slot" (the large channel beginning at the southern tip of Bougainville), then between Choiseul and the New Georgia Group. On entering the Slot, the cruiser force was to steam straight down on a southeasterly bearing. Mikawa's battle plans called for the commencement of hostilities at Guadalcanal by nightfall on August 8.

The two slower troop transports that had set sail at 2200 on the 7th received a change of orders just before 0100 the following morning. Due to an inability to assemble at Rabaul a large force of transports from other islands, and also because of a disturbingly revised upward estimate of U.S. marine strength on Guadalcanal—which had been greatly underrated—the pair of Japanese transports was ordered back to Rabaul. At 2125 hours that evening off Cape St. George, Lieutenant Commander H. G. Munson's submarine, S-38, one of several deployed in Operation Watchtower, fired a spread of torpedoes, sinking one of the transports, with a loss of 373 men.[13] Earlier, at 2000 on the 7th, Munson had reported the sighting of Mikawa's cruisers as they left the St. George Channel on a southeasterly course at high speed.[14] U.S. B-17s flying at high altitude over that area, however, reported nothing.

At 1026 on August 8, the pilot of a Royal Australian Air Force bomber did spot Mikawa's cruisers north of the strait between the islands of Bougainville and Choiseul; the ships were reportedly on a southeasterly bearing that would take them right down the Slot to Guadalcanal. In reality they were farther away, some forty miles off the central eastern coast of Bougainville, and not yet on a course that would take them down the Slot. The same pilot likewise incorrectly identified them as "3 cruisers 3 destroyers 2 seaplane tenders or gunboats," a few minutes later adding "2 subs" on the same course.[15] At 1101 another RAAF Hudson confirmed the sighting, but listed four cruisers. There was no further mention of any "seaplane tender."

Surprisingly, neither of these two pilots immediately radioed in these most urgent reports, and in fact they waited many hours until their return to base to do so. Nor did they observe standing orders to maintain surveillance of enemy vessels.[16] Thus Admirals Turner and Fletcher and everyone else remained totally ignorant of the approaching enemy threat. Indeed, the second Australian pilot did not hand in his report for another nine hours and forty-six minutes.[17]

A more alert Mikawa, after discovering that he had been seen, catapulted five float planes from his cruisers to scout his objective well in advance. Two of them returned reporting an American battleship, half a dozen cruisers, nineteen destroyers, and eighteen transports between Tulagi and Guadalcanal. They were unable to find the American carriers, however.

Coming down the Slot at 24 knots in a single battle column with flagship *Chokai* leading the pack, Mikawa issued his battle plan. Maintaining their present order—*Chokai*, *Aoba*, *Kako*, *Kinugasa*, *Furutaka*, *Tenryu*, *Yubari*, and the destroyer *Yunagi*—they were to launch a lightning torpedo attack against the warships, first at Guadalcanal and then at Tulagi, and then would presumably return to destroy the eighteen large AP transports and the men and supplies aboard them.[18] (Chester Nimitz, himself both a former submariner and destroyerman, afterward described the principal Japanese weapon—the oxygen-driven, 61-centimeter (24-inch), 9-meter-long Type 93,or Long Lance torpedo, with a warhead of 500 kilos (1,102.5 pounds) of explosives, capable of traveling at a top speed of 49 knots for eleven miles, and nearly twice that distance at a slower speed—as "the most lethal torpedo in the world.")[19] Because of the unknown U.S. carrier factor, Mikawa intended to strike hard and fast at night, as American fighters and bombers rarely flew after dusk.

Since the two Australian planes had failed to report promptly their sightings of the enemy warships, this most vital of information was only broadcast by the Australian military transmitter at Canberra to Pearl Harbor, and passed on to the Australian forces many hours later. Admiral Crutchley's flagship was the first to learn of the sightings at 1837 the evening of the 8th, and he then failed to apprise Admiral Turner, who was listening to a separate U.S. military radio channel at the time and only received the information at about 1900, some *nine and a half hours* after the first sighting.[20] Had the first pilot radioed his report immediately, carriers only 350 miles away from the American invasion force could have launched preemptive air strikes earlier that morning, and Crutchley could have prepared his defenses instead of leaving his ships widely dispersed, as his cruisers and destroyers now were. Instead, partly as a result of a divided command in that theater—the Australian pilots were now under Douglas MacArthur's command—the two critical messages were not even sent directly to the military authorities most immediately concerned with, and indeed directly in the line of fire of, the situation at Guadalcanal. This double delay was to result in tragic consequences for the U.S. Navy in particular, ultimately completely altering the Allied plans for the conquest of Guadalcanal.

As already noted, General MacArthur and the navy shared the responsibility for long-distance air surveillance covering the whole of the Solomons and up to the northwest including Bougainville and as far west as New Britain. Admiral John McCain, as commanding officer of TF 63's land-based air force, which was under Bob Ghormley's overall command, had aircraft available on Efate, New Caledonia, Espíritu Santo, Fiji, Tongatabu, Samoa, and other scattered islands. In theory, the sectors assigned to General Kenney (MacArthur's air chief) and Admiral McCain had been closely coordinated so that all sea lanes to the northwest were covered. In reality, because of poor visibility and weather, some of McCain's long-range search planes either were not sent out at all, or their missions were severely curtailed. What was more, no long-range flights were dispatched late in the afternoon of the 8th, when an approaching enemy force would have been spotted. *Turner had in fact specifically requested that these extra flights be made.* Having heard nothing to the contrary from McCain, he assumed that all surveillance sectors had been duly covered as ordered[21] and that there were no enemy ships entering or well within the Slot heading directly for his task force. McCain in particular was responsible for the very area in the Slot where Mikawa's cruisers were proceeding.[22] Nor did Turner, Crutchley, or Vandegrift realize that Fletcher's carriers were no longer on station to protect the ships and men in and around Guadalcanal but had prematurely "Bonaparted" hours before and were now sailing further and further away.[23]

Yet intuition and anxiety about the first Australian air sightings, news of which reached the bridge of the *McCawley* at about 1900, led Kelly Turner to call for a war council with Crutchley and Vandegrift aboard his ship at 2032. For at 1807 that evening, Turner's radio operators had intercepted an astonishing message[24] from Admiral Fletcher to Admiral Ghormley, requesting authorization for "the immediate withdrawal of my carriers." The message was sent just *thirty-six hours* into Operation Watchtower, instead of the minimum of forty-eight hours Fletcher had personally promised Turner in the presence of several senior officers.

Assuming that Fletcher, merely impatient, was still on station awaiting Ghormley's reply and that the Slot was clear of Japanese warships,

Turner, Crutchley, and Vandegrift made their arrangements based on the first Australian report of the only immediate enemy danger: namely, the possibility that the enemy was bringing in seaplanes on two tenders that would be capable of launching torpedoes from Rekata Bay. When the meeting broke up, Crutchley returned to his flagship, the cruiser *Australia*, and Vandegrift to Guadalcanal. Turner called in heavy air raids on Rekata Bay and the supposed Japanese seaplanes there early the next morning,[25] which would at once destroy the only possible threat known to him.

"Late on August 8th . . . I was still waiting for Ghormley's reply to Fletcher," Turner later testified. "I was hoping against hope that Ghormley would say 'No' to Fletcher and tell him to stay around for another 24 hours. I had no idea that Fletcher had been heading southeast all late afternoon and evening and was well south of San Cristobal by 2300. That information would have been most valuable to me and to all the Screening Group," he stated, barely concealing his anger.[26] The second Australian pilot's report, received at 2230, did not worry Turner. "I didn't think 3 Jap cruisers and 3 destroyers would come to Guadalcanal and attack our 7 cruisers and 25 destroyers. . . . My error was one of judgment, putting faith in the [Australian pilot's] contact report."[27]

Fletcher's carriers had, of course, also received the various reports of Yamamoto's buildup around Rabaul and Truk, of the S-38 sightings of enemy warships, and of the first Australian pilot's sighting of more Japanese warships, which was finally broadcast just after 2030 on August 8. Despite the air raids against Guadalcanal on the 7th and 8th, Fletcher's own carriers had not been attacked, nor indeed even been detected by the enemy. Nevertheless, they had literally abandoned the men and ships in and around Guadalcanal, leaving them under the mistaken impression that they were still being protected. Fletcher had left AWOL, without Ghormley's authorization. "[E]nemy air attacks and the reduction of fighters in our forces [down from ninety-nine to seventy-eight], together with critical fuel situation, has caused CTF 61 [Fletcher's task force] to recommend to COMSOPAC [Ghormley] that carriers be withdrawn," On Fletcher's orders, Rear Admiral Tom Kinkaid, a TF 61 carrier group commander, reported at 2330 on August 8, hours after the big carriers had put to sea.[28] In his cowardice—for which he would be court-martialed and then relieved of his command—Fletcher had not even had the elementary courtesy to inform task force commander Turner of his flight. An anxious Kelly Turner had to signal Ghormley to ask if he was going to approve the request, which would require abandoning the entire operation. It took Ghormley *five and a half hours* to reply to Fletcher's original message. In fact he did authorize Fletcher's departure, and it was not until 0330 on August 9 that Ghormley, not Fletcher, first informed Admiral Turner that Fletcher had flown the coop and that Turner would therefore have to halt in mid-operation.[29] Kelly Turner had at last received his answer, the one he so dreaded; but by that time it was not only too late, it was totally irrelevant. Ghormley simply presented Fletcher's flight as a fait accompli to Admiral Nimitz at Pearl Harbor at 0834 the following morning: "Carriers short of fuel proceeding to fuelling rendezvous."[30]

"My despatch didn't say anything about needing to withdraw to fuel," Fletcher later protested before official hearings. And "I didn't know anything about Savo Island happening until about five to six the next morning."[31] Both statements were proven to be false. At any rate, as Admiral Dyer and Samuel Morison have subsequently established, all of Fletcher's carriers and big ships had plenty of fuel; the one or two destroyers that were running low could have been topped up by one of the cruisers or even a flattop, as was frequently done at sea.[32] As for shortage of aircraft, Fletcher had more Wildcat fighters now than the U.S. carriers had had on the eve of the battle of Midway. The fact is that Fletcher was fleeing at the dawn of battle. The only item he was short of was courage.*

Upon learning of Fletcher's treachery, a furious Kelly Turner exploded that Fletcher had left him "bare arse!" "He ran away!" Admiral Jack Towers declared when he was told.[34] In fact, Captain Forrest Sherman, in command of Fletcher's third carrier, the *Wasp*, had argued vehemently with Rear Admiral Noyes, demanding the release of his carrier, whose pilots had been trained in night operation, and begging to fly to Guadal-

*On another hot August day 144 years earlier, Admiral Lord Nelson, approaching a superior enemy force in Egypt, had announced: "I will bring the French Fleet to action the moment I can lay hands upon them." If in a battle there is any doubt as to what to do, he added at Trafalgar, "no captain can do very wrong if he places his ship alongside that of the enemy."[33] Frank Jack Fletcher was clearly no Horatio Nelson. He was, as Napoleon once put it when referring to one of his fleet commanders, "seeing double," or twice as many dangers as existed.

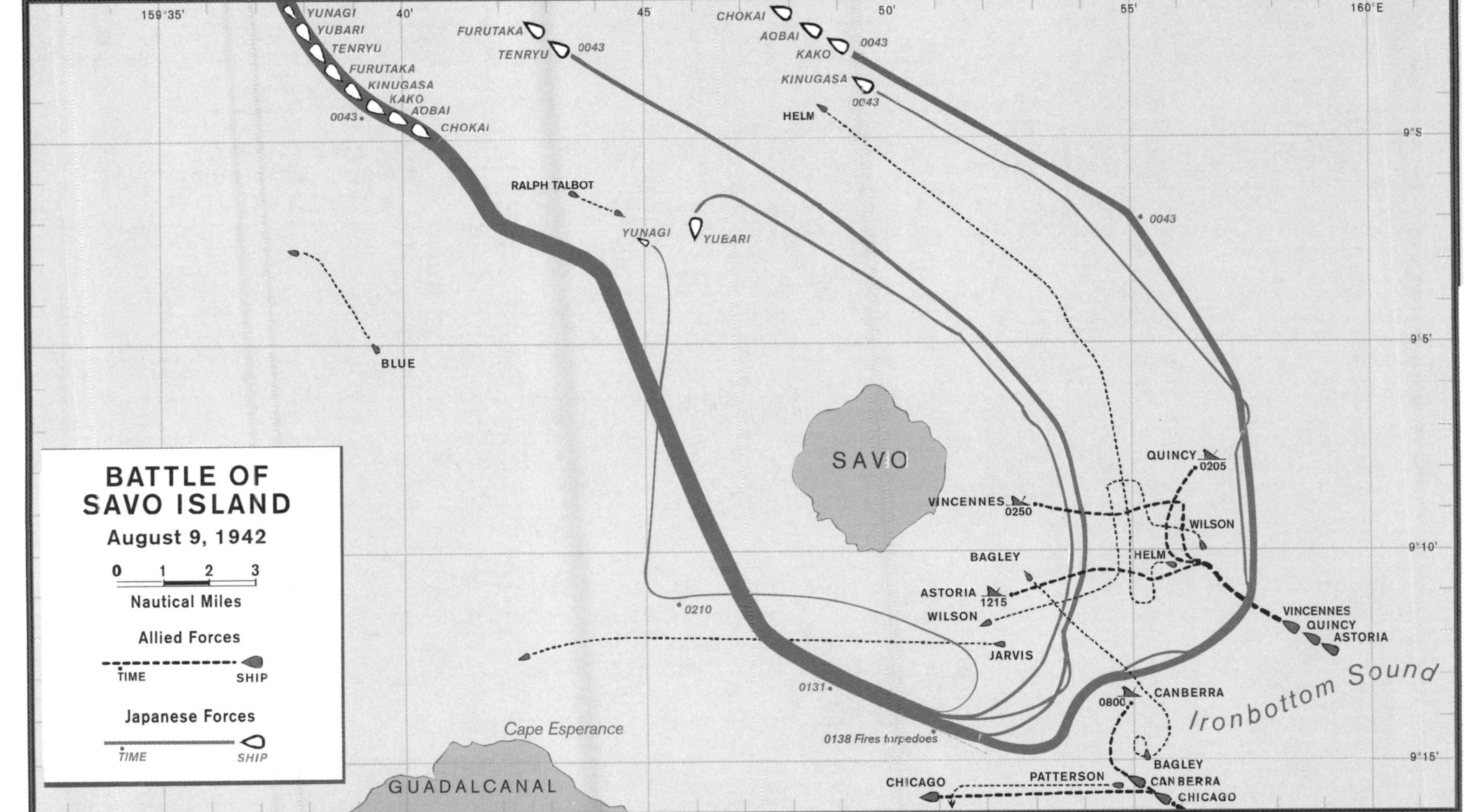
BATTLE OF
SAVO ISLAND
August 9, 1942
0 1 2 3
Nautical Miles
Allied Forces
TIME
SHIP
Japanese Forces
TIME
SHIP
159°35'
40'
45'
50'
55'
160°E
9°S
9°5'
9°10'
9°15'
YUNAGI
YUBARI
TENRYU
FURUTAKA
KINUGASA
KAKO
AOBAI
CHOKAI
0043
FURUTAKA
TENRYU
0043
CHOKAI
AOBAI
KAKO
0043
KINUGASA
0043
HELM
RALPH TALBOT
YUNAGI
YUEARI
0043
BLUE
SAVO
QUINCY
0205
VINCENNES
0250
WILSON
BAGLEY
HELM
ASTORIA
1215
WILSON
0210
JARVIS
VINCENNES
QUINCY
ASTORIA
0131
CANBERRA
0800
Ironbottom Sound
Cape Esperance
0138 Fires torpedoes
BAGLEY
PATTERSON
CANBERRA
CHICAGO
CHICAGO
GUADALCANAL

GUADALCANAL
and Adjacent Islands
August 7, 1942
0 5 10 15 20
Nautical Miles
DEBARKATION AREA
REEFS
NOTE On August 7, 1942 the only airstrip was the partially completed Henderson Field.
159°20'
159°40'
160°20'
160°40'
9°20'
9°40'
RUSSELL ISLANDS
BUENA VISTA
NGGELA GROUP
OLEVUGA
Sandfly Passage
FLORIDA
TULAGI
MALAITA
SAVO
TRANSPORT GP Y
0637
Ironbottom Sound
TRANSPORT GP X
0650
ROUTE OF AMPHIBIOUS FORCE
Kamimbo Bay
Visale
Cape Esperance
Marovovo
Verahue
Doma
Doma Cove
Cape Nagle
Tassafaronga
Pt. Cruz
Lunga Roads
Lunga Pt.
Koli Pt.
Tasimboko Bay
Sealark Channel
Lengo Channel
Indispensable Strait
Bonegi R.
Kokumbona
Kukum
Matanikau
HENDERSON FIELD
Metapo
Teter
Tasimboko
Taivu Point
Taivu
Poma R.
Matanikau R.
MT. AUSTEN
Lunga R.
Tenaru R.
Nalimbiu R.
Metapona R.
Gurabusu R.
Aola R.
Aola Bay
Aola
Susu Pt.
West Cape
Beaufort Bay
Cape Beaufort
Wanderer Bay
MT. POPOMANASEU
Kaukau Bay
Marau Sound
GUADALCANAL
Cape Hunter
Lanvie Pt.
Cape Henslow

canal. Noyes adamantly refused to let Sherman come to Turner's aid, and furthermore, declined even to pass on this urgent request by a carrier commander to Fletcher.[35] Treachery begat treachery.

Crutchley had been as anxious as Turner about the situation in Ironbottom Sound that day, and as early as nine o'clock on the morning of the 8th had requested a "rough outline of present situation and future intentions."[36] Crutchley and Turner had discussed those plans at some length later that evening, and had considered the possibility of canceling the operation altogether once it was learned that Fletcher wished to abandon them.[37]

Crutchley had correctly divided his naval force in order to cover Savo Island's two entrances into the sound—the twelve-mile-wide northern opening and the seven-and-a-half-mile southern approach—especially as he had not received any news of an imminent enemy threat. The British commander was further restricted upon his arrival because his force comprised American and Australian vessels thrown together for the first time. Battle tactics and the crews' training were different. Moreover, neither *Australia* nor *Canberra* was fitted with TBS, or voice radio, which was a definite drawback, especially in a rapidly developing situation. Crutchley's ships had done some night training with *Chicago* and Desron 4 (Destroyer Division 4), but none with the other cruisers, and thus Crutchley was determined to avoid handling a mixed, untrained force at night.[38] As Turner himself admitted, they did not have enough advance pickets on station to warn them in event of attack.[39]

•

Admiral Crutchley's cruiser, *Australia*, now lay just a few miles off Lunga Point, and *Canberra* and *Chicago* were alone patrolling the southern entrance of the sound, screened by three destroyers on either side, while the northern entrance between Savo and Florida Island was being covered by cruisers *Vincennes*, *Astoria*, and *Quincy*, with three destroyers off either side of their "battle column." *San Juan* and *Hobart*, with six more destroyers, were screening the transports anchored off Florida, to the southeast of Tulagi. Just after 2300 on August 8, U.S. destroyer *Ralph Talbot*, on picket duty north of the *Vincennes* column, radioed: "WARNING–WARNING: PLANE OVER SAVO HEADED EAST." The other picket destroyer patrolling the southern channel, *Blue*, picked up another bogey on its radar. A black, torpid night engulfed the Slot as heavy rain squalls veiled Savo Island's rugged volcanic mountain. Radio reception was exceptionally poor, and Admiral Turner's flagship, only twenty miles away, was one of many failing to pick up *Talbot*'s critical message. The other vessels, including the cruiser *Quincy*, received the message but simply disregarded it: *Vincennes*'s captain, for some curious reason, assumed the planes were "friendly," although everyone knew perfectly well that American planes almost never flew after dark. As Turner had sounded no warning, the others thought that he, too, had heard *Ralph Talbot* and dismissed it; and for the next *ninety minutes* Japanese spotter planes flew over the entire American flotilla with impunity, carefully pinpointing most of the ships for Admiral Mikawa[40] even though dark clouds, lightning, and rain gradually closed across the tropical horizon. Meanwhile, the gutted transport, *George F. Elliott*, continued to burn to the northeast, a perfect beacon for the still undetected approaching Japanese warships.

Although completely lacking radar, Mikawa's vessels conned a clear, determined course. After receiving a final confirmation by his planes of the Allies' naval disposition, at 1840 Mikawa signaled his force: "LET US ATTACK IN THE TRADITIONAL NIGHT ASSAULT AND WITH THE CERTAINTY OF VICTORY," as they plowed on.[41] At 2300, float planes were now launched to drop flares before their strike.

"Battle Stations Alerted," Mikawa informed his ships at 0025 hours on August 9. At 0044, *Chokai* spotted *Blue* on picket duty to her starboard, but remained undetected by an inattentive American crew, despite *Blue*'s advanced radar and lookouts. A column of eight Japanese warships passed directly astern of *Blue* at a smart 26 knots, still invisible to American eyes and ears. At 0108 Mikawa ordered the column to enter the sound through the southern channel of Savo Island. Seventeen minutes later, with the island now behind the column to its left and Cape Espérance to the right, Mikawa gave the order his men were tensely awaiting: "INDEPENDENT COMMAND." Each ship executed this well-rehearsed battle instruction at 0131 as Mikawa ordered, "ALL SHIPS ATTACK!" The ships passed the badly damaged destroyer *Jarvis* well off to the west, and the *Ralph Talbot* eight miles off their port beam. Destroyers *Patterson* and *Bagley* were next spotted ahead, coming straight at them. A pattern of torpedoes was launched against the *Jarvis*, but missed, as the two approaching U.S. destroyers suddenly peeled off to the right and left, revealing the cruisers *Chicago* and *Canberra* in column behind them heading toward the *Chokai*. At 0138 *Chokai* launched four torpedoes at the two lead Allied cruisers some five thousand yards away, the rest of the Japanese ships joining in on the general attack.[42]

It was only at 0143 that the laggard *Patterson* finally saw the enemy. "WARNING–WARNING: STRANGE SHIPS ENTERING HARBOR!" she alerted. Enemy planes now dropped flares over the transports at Lunga Point, brilliantly silhouetting *Chicago* and *Canberra*. Japanese 8-inch guns opened fire. At 0143 the *Canberra*'s guns were unmanned, the general alarm still sounding, as two Long Lance torpedoes tore through her starboard side and 8-inch shells smashed her hull. Nearly everyone this morning of August 9 was to pay dearly for his lassitude and for the incompetence of the two Australian crews. After firing torpedoes, *Canberra* was dead in the water.[43] Her two screening destroyers, the *Patterson* and *Bagley*, were caught daydreaming, unprepared for action, and thus failed to get away a single torpedo at the quickly disappearing Japanese ships.[44]

Awakened from a deep sleep, Captain Howard Bode had barely reached the bridge of USS *Chicago* when a lookout spotted the first torpedo, coming at her to starboard. Ordering a hard right rudder, however, did not save Bode as another Long Lance torpedo on the port exploded against the bow one minute later, at 0147. At long last his gun crews fired defective starshell and failed to illuminate the swiftly passing enemy, whom in fact they never saw or found, although a Japanese shell hit the *Chicago*'s foremast. Sighting a ship through the darkness, Bode fired on *Yunagi*—the sole Japanese destroyer that had been left behind to guard the southwestern entrance to the sound—and damaged it somewhat. But in the confusion of the moment he forgot to alert the northern *Vincennes* group of cruisers.[45]

At 0144, having severely crippled both the *Canberra* and *Chicago* in a mere six minutes, Mikawa altered course abruptly to seek out the northern group, which included *Vincennes* patrolling in a northeasterly direction. But in the midst of that maneuver, Mikawa lost the last three cruisers of his column—the *Furutaka*, *Tenryu*, and *Yubari*—when he sheered off in a more northerly direction. The *Patterson*, trying to keep up with Mikawa as he turned north, was now hit and set afire. Mikawa's four remaining cruisers continued separately to the east, turned their searchlights on three cruisers less than four miles away, and at 0147 opened fire with guns and torpedoes on the still-unsuspecting American heavy cruiser column, which was steaming at a leisurely 10 knots in a northwesterly direction on the other side of the sound, to the south of Savo Island.[46]

Although they had seen and heard gunfire from the direction of Tulagi at 0143, and had even felt the tremor of a torpedo exploding nearby (the one fired earlier at the *Chicago*), thanks to Bode's failure to warn them the officers on the bridge of the *Astoria* still had no idea that they were under attack. Captain William Greenman was grabbing a few minutes of sleep, fully dressed, in the emergency cabin. Incredibly, the officers on the bridge apparently had not seen the brilliant Japanese flares or heard the *Patterson*'s warning. There had also been an earlier submarine warning, and they thought the tremor they felt had probably been a distant depth charge. Lieutenant Commander J. R. Topper, the damage-control officer, was acting as supervisor of the bridge watch when another series of starshell and flares erupted far to the west over Guadalcanal. The more alert Lieutenant Commander W. H. Truesdell ordered General Quarters, just as Japanese searchlights stretched out toward them at 0150, followed seconds later by the explosion of 8-inch shells fired at them by the *Chokai*.

Captain Greenman darted onto the bridge when he heard the alarm sounding, demanding to know who had ordered it even as the *Astoria*'s guns were beginning to return fire. Still groggy, Greenman thought they were firing on their own ships and ordered them to cease fire, despite *Astoria*'s having already been hit *four times*. "Sir, for God's sake, give the word to Commence Firing!" an astonished Lieutenant Commander Truesdell shouted above the din; and at 0154 the *Astoria* recommenced firing.[47] Moments later, 8-inch Japanese shells exploded amidships, setting the big cruiser afire as dozens of shells came raining down. Joined by the guns of the *Quincy*, just ahead, Greenman was able to get off eleven salvoes, one of which exploded in Admiral Mikawa's chart room on the *Chokai*. But Japanese shells continued to tear the *Astoria* apart. By now, with communications knocked out, Greenman found his ship yawing into the field of fire between the *Quincy* and the enemy cruisers. Shells in and around the bridge had killed the chief quartermaster, the navigator, and the signals officers. Although badly wounded, the assistant helmsman, Boatswain's Mate J. Young, somehow managed to crawl back to the wheel. Below decks, just about everyone had been forced out by the intense heat and smoke, but a few of *Astoria*'s guns were still firing. Lieutenant Commander W. B. Davidson, the ship's communications officer, climbed into turret No. 2 and turned the guns on *Chokai*, which was blasting away from her forward turret. But that was the end of the shooting. *Astoria* was now barely moving in the water.

Mikawa's swiftly advancing four cruisers were not through, however, and they now trained their guns on the cruiser ahead of *Astoria*, the *Quincy*. "Fire at the ships with the searchlights on!" Captain Samuel Moore ordered from the bridge, but after firing a couple of nine-gun salvoes from a range of four and a half miles, he ordered all guns to cease fire. He, too, feared that the distant ships might be friendly, so great was the confusion by now. Then while Quincy was turning to starboard in order to avoid ramming the *Vincennes* directly ahead, a shell struck the scout plane on the catapult: it exploded into a ball of fire. Now the *Quincy* found herself hemmed in a crossfire between the *Furutaka* group, of three cruisers coming from the southwest directly at *Quincy*'s beam, and *Chokai*'s column, which was passing well to the starboard of the American cruiser column. "We're going down between them. Give them hell!" Moore shouted as another shell destroyed the No. 2 turret and yet another the bridge, killing just about everyone and mortally wounding Captain Moore himself. A Long Lance torpedo struck the ship's port side, demolishing the No. 4 boiler room.

All communications were by now knocked out as fires and explosions erupted throughout the stricken vessel, sealing off the men trapped in the engine room. The sick bay was gone, and the big guns and their crews fell further victims to this fierce onslaught. When gunnery officer Lieutenant Commander H. B. Heneberger reached the bridge level to request instructions, he "found it a shambles of dead bodies . . . [and] in the pilothouse itself the only person standing was the signalman at the wheel. . . . The Captain, who was at that time lying near the wheel, had instructed him to beach the ship . . . I stepped to the port side of the pilothouse, looked out to find the island

[Savo] and noted that the ship was heeling rapidly to the port, sinking by the bow." Heneberger ordered those still alive to abandon ship, and none too soon. The *Quincy* capsized, twisted completely around with her stern in the air, and then, at 0235, disappeared forever into the funereal waters of Ironbottom Sound.[48]

Having received *Talbot*'s earlier warning of an enemy plane sighting at 0145, Captain Frederik Riefkohl of the *Vincennes* had ordered extreme vigilance; and yet it was only when the first Japanese flares were spotted off her port quarter that Riefkohl was called from his nap while General Quarters sounded throughout his ship. Neither he nor his executive officer, Commander W. E. A. Mullan, understood what was happening and what the explosions and gunfire in the distance meant, assuming that *Chicago* and other cruisers on the other side of the sound were firing at aircraft. But scarcely had Captain Riefkohl increased the ship's speed to 15 knots when searchlights from three ships far off the port beam focused on him. Thinking they were friendly vessels, he radioed them at 0152 to shut the lights off, just as a salvo from *Kako* exploded short of his ship. At 0153 the *Vincennes*'s 8-inch guns responded in kind, hitting the cruiser *Kinugasa*. But that was the only good news, as a rain of Japanese shells smashed into the *Vincennes* amidships, exploding planes on the catapults and setting the ship afire. As Riefkohl conned the ship to port, one shell exploded on the port side of the bridge and others destroyed much of the superstructure, including some big guns and the ship's communications system.

Riefkohl now tried to escape the veritable avalanche of Japanese shells at 0155 by throwing the ship a hard starboard just as a couple of *Chokai*'s torpedoes struck the port side, leveling the No. 4 fireroom. This was followed at 0203 by another torpedo smashing through the hull and taking out the No. 1 fireroom. The captain still had not learned his lesson, however, for when more searchlights lit up the *Vincennes* from the other side, he, again thinking them to be friendly, ordered a set of colors raised to identify himself. The Japanese, to the contrary, taking it for an admiral's flag, concentrated their gunfire even more intently. "Guns" (the gunnery officer) informed Riefkohl that all his batteries had been destroyed. The *Vincennes*, her guns drooping, was a mass of twisted metal wrapped around corpses or the dying and was everywhere aflame, a situation only intensified by exploding American ammunition. But at 0215, just as suddenly, the Japanese ceased firing, shut off their searchlights, and disappeared into the blackness to the east of Savo Island as abruptly and mysteriously as they had arrived.[49]

Admiral Mikawa, who had put each of the five heavy American and Australian cruisers out of commission in a matter of minutes without even slowing down, had expended his entire supply of torpedoes, and, fearful of an American air attack, he retreated at 30 knots into the tropical murk. As for Rear Admiral Crutchley, he was still cruising off the coast of Guadalcanal with seven destroyers, too far distant to do anything but watch the destruction of his squadron.

Mikawa now had to make a snap decision: either return to the shores of Guadalcanal in order to destroy the valuable American transports per his written orders, which would mean facing a likely attack by the planes of the American carriers encountered earlier that day; or turn north, regroup his by now scattered forces, and sail back up the Slot. Ignorant of the fact that Fletcher was in flight in the opposite direction, putting as many sea miles as possible between him and the battle at Guadalcanal, Admiral Mikawa decided to break off action and steam north. Picket destroyer *Ralph Talbot* suddenly found herself in the path of a quickly retreating enemy whose searchlights now lit her up like a Christmas tree, and she faced the full blast of Japanese guns. A confused Lieutenant Commander Joe Callaghan *turned on his recognition lights* before finally returning the fire and launching four torpedoes. Badly hit and listing, the *Talbot* escaped in a rain squall, and at 0223 Mikawa broke off and continued on a northerly course. As Fletcher had by now found safer water, there were no aircraft left with which to pursue Mikawa, despite the pleas of Forrest Sherman aboard the *Wasp* to return. Mikawa returned safely to Rabaul, a great hero.[50]

Admiral Mikawa's lightning attack had lasted exactly thirty-three minutes and had resulted in the eventual sinking of four heavy cruisers—*Canberra*, *Vincennes*, *Quincy*, and *Astoria*—with the crippled *Jarvis* following their fate later on the 9th. The USS *Chicago* was badly damaged, as were the destroyers *Patterson* and *Ralph Talbot*. All of the Japanese ships but one returned to port: the cruiser *Kako* was sunk on August 10 by U.S. submarine S-44. Two Japanese cruisers were damaged, but there were fewer than 100 Japanese casualties, as opposed to

1,347 U.S. and Australian dead (including the crew of the *Jarvis*) and another 709 wounded, some of whom were then attacked by sharks, even when on a raft.[51]

Task Force Commander Kelly Turner's transports and what remained of his landing craft—rightly anticipating a follow-up Japanese air raid, deserted by Fletcher, and with neither air nor cruiser protection—had no choice but to sail prematurely from Guadalcanal at 1330 that same August 9, their cargo holds still half-full.[52] Archie Vandegrift's marines were on their own.

The battle of Savo Island, as it is known, was not only the worst naval defeat in U.S. history, but also proved a turning point in Operation Watchtower. The conquest of Guadalcanal could have been achieved in perhaps a matter of days, with very few American casualties to show for it; yet now it was in fact to take many months of very tough fighting resulting in thousands of American casualties and many more ships ultimately going down in Iron Bottom Sound. Asked years later what he thought was the principal reason for this unique naval disaster, Admiral Kelly Turner replied: "Inadequate and faulty air reconnaissance, and more faulty than inadequate."[53] Despite Turner's tireless efforts on behalf of the marines, they held him responsible for the whole debacle—and still do.

•

Early on the morning of August 12, 1942, far away on the Potomac River in USS *Dauntless*, a grim duty officer, Commander George Russell, reluctantly knocked on Fleet Admiral Ernest King's bedroom door. It was a courageous, if not foolhardy, act that under ordinary circumstances would have resulted in a tongue-lashing of which there was no equal in the U.S. Navy. But this was different, and a groggy King ordered him in. "Admiral, you've got to see this. It isn't good," Russell said, handing the commander in chief of the U.S. Navy the just-received dispatch on the Savo Island disaster. The eyes of the notoriously unflappable King widened in disbelief as he read and then reread it. "They must have decoded the dispatch wrong. Tell them to decode it again." But he knew that it was true, and as King himself later commented, "That, as far as I am concerned, was the blackest day of the war. The whole future then became unpredictable."[54]

CHAPTER XVI

Operation KA

"You will be governed by the principle of calculated risks which you shall interpret to mean the avoidance of your force without good prospect of inflicting as a result of such exposure, greater damage to the enemy."

—*Admiral Chester Nimitz, May 28, 1942*[1]

"My estimate, upon leaving Admiral Ghormley's headquarters was this: So far, the Navy had taken one hell of a beating and at that time was hanging on by a shoestring."

—*Lieutenant General Hap Arnold,*
Global Mission *(1949)*[2]

Because over half of their guns, munitions, and provisions had not yet been unloaded, the marines were now expected to survive for the next two months on a four-weeks' supply of tinned B and C rations and whatever could be scavenged from the surrounding jungle. In the midst of Fletcher's precipitous abandonment of the U.S. marines on Guadalcanal, Turner was forced to take back with him the powerful coastal guns and even some of their antiaircraft artillery, leaving a furious General Archie Vandegrift and his men defenseless against both enemy naval bombardment and bombers over the next several months. Fortunately, the steel-willed determination of Admiral "Terrible" Turner, who was in charge of all subsequent supply convoys as well, did get a few 90mm antiaircraft batteries landed, which prevented enemy planes from coming in too low. But in the long term there was absolutely nothing to deter enemy warships and bombers and their inevitable daily raids.

On August 15, 1942, Turner somehow managed to slip past four small supply vessels carrying badly needed ammunition, aviation gas, and bombs for "Henderson Field," as the marines' muddy airstrip was now named. But what the marines needed most desperately of all were naval ships to patrol and protect the approaches to, and the waters around, Guadalcanal (or 'Canal), and of course fighters and bombers to cover their skies. Savage, unchallenged attacks by the enemy continued undiminished while Frank Jack Fletcher's carriers cautiously guarded the sea lanes between the Solomons and Espíritu Santo, well to the south of Guadalcanal and the main battle zone. Nor did his old Academy friend, Admiral Robert Ghormley, do anything to correct the situation. He protected his warships (far from Guadalcanal); it was up to Vandegrift to protect the marines.

Living in mildewed canvas tents pegged into primordial ooze, constantly infested with clouds of deadly malaria-bearing mosquitoes and inundated by daily squalls, the marines now had to defeat the remaining fifteen hundred or so Japanese on Guadalcanal. But with only about ten thousand men available for field operations on Tulagi and the whole of Guadalcanal—including the island's long, roadless, forested coastline—General Vandegrift was restricted, by and large, to the securing of his immediate defense perimeter around the airfield. Without aircraft, the marines' only real lifeline for the moment, they were doomed.

Nevertheless, limited offensive operations were mounted against the Japanese troops based to the west, beyond the Matanikau River, and on August 19 three companies of the 4th Marine Regiment attacked and briefly seized the villages of Kokimbona and Matanikau, killing sixty-five of the enemy. At this painful rate it would take weeks to mop up the island, as the daily and nightly air and naval bombardments that Vandegrift had most dreaded were severely hampering his actions.

And then a new dimension was added to his problems as the Japanese began landing fresh reinforcements on remote beaches, something Vandegrift was incapable of preventing. Indeed, Tokyo was beginning to pay more attention to the implications of the freshly evolving situation in the southern Solomons, where strategically situated air bases were needed if Japan was to conquer Port Moresby and to cut U.S. naval lines. The Japanese navy was the key to the solution, and Admiral Yamamoto assembled his Combined Fleet and some seventeen thousand troops at Truk. Since the Philippines had gone largely unprotected during the first fortnight of the enemy assault there, the Japanese forces were free to move south much more quickly than even they had anticipated. They could now concentrate on Port Moresby, and in consequence, Guadalcanal. Had events in the Philippines worked out differently, the situation facing Vandegrift and the Australian army in New Guinea would not have deteriorated so rapidly.

Rear Admiral Tanaka Raizo, certainly one of the most aggressive and competent flag officers in the Japanese navy, now brought Yamamoto's first emergency convoy of reinforcements to Guadalcanal on August 17, landing them secretly at Tassafaronga, to the west of Henderson Field—well beyond the effective range of the marines' guns. He repeated the operation the next day, ferrying supplies aboard half a dozen submarine transports. Although the Japanese high command still greatly underestimated American troop strength on the island—putting it at a mere two thousand—its own six thousand additional fresh troops were soon to play havoc with the marines, while Tanaka's destroyers continued to bombard them with complete impunity.[3] As the first thirty-one U.S. planes were not to reach the island for another two days, on August 20 Vandegrift radioed an SOS to Espíritu Santo for long-range help. Although some army B-17s did arrive hours later, only one of their hundreds of bombs struck a destroyer, and it caused no serious damage. As a result, Tanaka would return unhindered the following night, and the next and the next, and still a paralyzed Robert Ghormley did nothing but bemoan this futile situation.

At the same time, Prime Minister Tōjō relieved the Japanese navy of ground operations as the army assumed command on Guadalcanal, which they expected to reconquer in short order. General Tōjō and the Supreme War Council had already misjudged other situations that were to have far-reaching consequences for Japanese land, sea, and air forces. The military was, for instance, already greatly overextended, lacking the logistical support to maintain these operations despite the Combined Fleet's impressive show of strength at Truk. That naval strength, however, would gradually be whittled away, and Tokyo was already incapable of either augmenting or replacing it. The Japanese were not only very short of transport vessels—hence their growing dependence, instead, on destroyers and submarines for transport duty—but of supplies, guns, and troops, with most of their armies committed in China, Taiwan (Formosa), the Philippines, and New Guinea. Their air force, too, was beginning to suffer, losing many of its veteran pilots now and over the next dozen months once Marc Mitscher took charge at Guadalcanal.

On the other hand, Vandegrift still had no idea about Tokyo's decision to reinforce Guadalcanal. His first inkling of an important change occurred only on August 20, when Japanese troops ambushed a Marine Special Weapons Battalion in strength along the Ilu, or Tenaru, River to the east of Henderson. In the resulting fierce, hand-to-hand battle, the marines finally killed most of their attackers thanks to a platoon of light tanks. By nightfall, 777 of Colonel Ichiki Kiyonao's 900 freshly arrived soldiers had been wiped out. In astonishment and despair, the hitherto undefeated colonel wrapped himself in his national flag and fell on his sword. The U.S. marines suffered 100 killed or wounded.[4] Apart from the original landings here, this had been their first face-to-face combat with the purportedly "invincible" Japanese army that had so easily and successfully overrun so much of the Far East—and the marines had annihilated them.

Port Moresby and Australia remained Tokyo's number-one priority at this stage, but before that conquest could be achieved, the last two phases of the high command's master plan had to be realized. This included the establishment of a couple of major airfields on Guadalcanal and the seizure of Milne Bay, at the southern tip of New Guinea. Yet time was not on Tokyo's side in this war. The Eighth Japanese Fleet, comprising fifty-five warships and three fast carriers, was ordered to seek out and destroy the American navy and sweep the seas clear of its ships once and for all. At the same time, Japan's Eleventh Air Fleet bombed Guadalcanal literally night and day while troops of the Seventeenth Army continued to land with orders to seize Henderson Field in a mere three days. That, at least, was the plan. The first contingent of those troops having been annihilated by the marines, the freshly revised plans for the reconquest of Guadalcanal, or "Operation KA," called for the use of overwhelming force. The Japanese had already been hitting the hard-pressed American marines with daily air attacks, sometimes twice daily, since their landings. General Tōjō now insisted that the Americans be crushed once and for all. D-Day for Operation KA, employing the combined forces of Rabaul and Truk, was set for August 24. Not another moment could be lost.

The initial squadrons of marine Dauntless dive-bombers and F4F Wildcat fighters that landed at Henderson Field on August 20, even including those anticipated to arrive over the ensuing weeks, would obviously be insufficient for the defense of either the land or the naval vessels in the waters around Guadalcanal. So far, the combined Allied army, marine, and naval aircraft here had been deployed so ineffectively that they had not even appreciably slowed down Japanese air or sea attacks. Just from a technological point of view, American aircraft had problems. The army's P-40s were slow and limited to low-altitude flying, unlike the lighter Japanese "Zekes," with their greater maneuverability and far more powerful engines. And all U.S. warplanes lacked even the bare minimum of spare parts necessitated by battles, frequent accidents, and daily wear and tear. This problem was to plague the navy for many, many months, until Admiral Towers came to grips with it. Furthermore, ammunition and gasoline were so severely rationed—to a large degree owing to the daily air raids and naval bombardments—that on some days American planes were simply grounded, even when well forewarned of imminent attack. Yet despite these woes, help was on its way.

On September 1, 1942, the first of the newly organized Seabee Naval Construction Battalions, comprising 392 officers and men and directed by Commander Joseph Blundon, USNR, would land on Guadalcanal with heavy equipment (and six 5-inch guns) to improve the airfield and build roads, wharves, and bridges. Professional engineers and construction workers, these older men—who had been inducted as marines and given combat training—were to meet successfully the previously unknown challenges of the malarial swamps. Ultimately they would add a couple more airfields, as well.

●

Admiral Ghormley rarely left his headquarters ship at Nouméa, and it was there that he had been informed of the unusual military preparations at Rabaul and Truk and had alerted Admiral Fletcher and his three carriers—*Enterprise*, *Saratoga*, and *Wasp*—which were still stationed well south of the Solomons. Fletcher was expecting reinforcements in the form of the carrier *Hornet*, the new battleships *Washington* and *South Dakota*, the special antiaircraft cruiser *Juneau*, and more destroyers, all then en route from the East Coast and Pearl Harbor. And yet Ghormley and Fletcher continued to avoid the Slot and the predicament of the marines. Thus the Japanese navy sailed back and forth several times a week, and on such a regular schedule that the marines grimly now referred to these enemy convoys as the "Tokyo Express."

Bob Ghormley, the arch pessimist, was past his prime in every sense of the word, and his staff, lacking leadership, was demoralized and paralyzed, incapable of making the decisions or taking the actions so desperately needed. The navy lacked carriers, cruisers, bombers, and fighters, Ghormley informed Nimitz, despite the obvious presence of four big carriers with several hundred planes. But his hands were tied, Ghormley insisted, and in consequence marines needlessly died on Guadalcanal because Bob Ghormley and Frank Jack Fletcher failed to step in and provide the air and artillery protection they required. This apathetic attitude was enervating and, unfortunately, highly contagious. Clearly something had to be done to shake up the American command, but nothing was done . . . yet. It would take fresh losses of American ships, planes, and lives before a much-troubled Nimitz would act.

On August 23, Operation KA was right on schedule. The Japanese Combined Fleet, under the strategic command of Yamamoto Isoroku aboard the super-battleship *Yamato*, proceeded on a southeasterly course to destroy the U.S. Pacific Fleet and dislodge the marines from Guadalcanal. The admiral's force comprised Vice Admiral Nagumo's two large carriers, *Zuikaku* and *Shokaku*, the light carrier *Ryujo*, the small escort carrier *Junyo*—for a total of 177 aircraft—four battleships, sixteen cruisers, thirty destroyers, a seaplane tender, transport units, and a couple dozen submarines. Against this impressive-looking armada, Fletcher, who had not yet been relieved of his command, had three carriers—with 259 planes—one battleship, seven cruisers, and eighteen destroyers.[5] In addition, land-based fighters and bombers were to support his Task Force 61.

Yamamoto's Combined Fleet dwarfed anything Nimitz and Ghormley could have put together, but not when it came down to the essentials: airpower. Warplanes were the "biggest guns" of any fleet. Only 101 Japanese sorties were to be launched against the U.S. Fleet.

Fletcher had the clear advantage in the air, but as a traditional surface battle line officer, he was intimidated by Yamamoto's superior surface hardware. Fletcher simply could not grasp the elementary fact that Yamamoto's mighty battleships and cruiser force would be unable to get close to the American ships if Admiral Fletcher were to act vigorously and launch his air force first, in well-coordinated attacks. Instead, that American admiral looked at the size and number of enemy vessels and flinched.

Vice Admiral Kondo's Second Fleet, Support Force, formed the vanguard of Yamamoto's sprawling fleet: the battleships *Hiei* and *Krishima* and two heavy and light cruisers under destroyer escort, but only one carrier for the moment—*Junyo*, the slowest in the fleet. Nagumo, in tactical command, was, like Fletcher, a "black shoe"* who disliked carriers and did not know how to make the best use of them. If he had deployed his fast carriers closer, things might have turned out very differently.

The Eighth Fleet, or Outer South Seas Force, commanded by Admiral Mikawa, comprised six heavy and light cruisers, some destroyers, and no carrier. Admiral Tanaka's Convoy Escort Force—the light cruiser *Jintsu*, eight destroyers, and three troop transports—was not there to fight, but to land men and equipment.

The real might of Yamamoto's fleet lay in the hands of Admiral Nagumo and his Third Fleet, which held the key to any possible victory with the three fast carriers *Zuikaku*, *Shokaku*, and *Ryujo*. The Japanese victory at Pearl Harbor had proven that it was the warplanes that counted, but on this day they and the Third Fleet were held too far behind. Fortunately for the Japanese, Frank Jack Fletcher had learned even less from the air attacks on December 7, 1941.

As the two opposing fleets closed in on one another, half a dozen submarines, sailing abreast, swept the seas before Kondo's van. In an

*Naval ship officers wore regulation black shoes and were hence given the title "black shoes." Naval aviators, on the other hand, were dubbed "brown shoes" after their own footwear, adopted in defiance of tradition and to emphasize intership rivalry.

unusual move for the Japanese, who normally deployed their subs well off the scene, another division of submarines cruised southwest of the Santa Cruz Islands to intercept any American ships coming from that direction, while four more divisions were deployed to the south of the Solomons. A determined Admiral Yamamoto was casting a very wide net indeed; he did not want another Midway.

Meanwhile, Admiral Tanaka's separate convoy was right on course for Guadalcanal, where his three transports were ordered to land their 1,500-man reinforcement group during the naval bombardment of the island. Their carrier warplanes were simultaneously bombing Henderson Field. It was a big, complex operation, the sort of thing that so appealed to Yamamoto and Hirohito. If the operation was successful, Guadalcanal would soon be in Japan's hands again, and the U.S. carriers at the bottom of the sea.

This time around, however, the Americans were not taken completely by surprise, thanks to the alert Australian coastwatchers in their isolated jungle outposts and the U.S. reconnaissance planes that at 0950 apprised Ghormley's HQ of the Combined Fleet's movements. A PBY seaplane first sighted part of the fleet—Japanese transports and destroyers—far to the west of the main body on course for Guadalcanal. Fletcher's three carriers were now south of San Cristobal Island and approximately 180 miles from Henderson Field, within easy striking distance.

Once again Fletcher dithered, letting valuable time pass before launching a powerful search force of thirty-seven dive- and torpedo bombers at 1445—*nearly five hours after the Japanese Fleet had been sighted*. At 1515, Fletcher's squadron were joined by twenty-three additional planes from Henderson Field. But Fletcher (and the U.S. Navy) paid a heavy price for his procrastination, for by now the clear morning skies were overcast with thick cloud cover, and all planes returned to Henderson Field that evening without having seen anything. Five more twin-engine PBYs sent out later that night were equally unsuccessful.

Admiral Tanaka had reacted immediately, however, upon seeing the first scout plane, reversing course and heading in the direction of Santa Isabel Island. Admiral Kondo's group, well over a hundred miles to the east of Tanaka's transports, also took the precaution of reversing course to the northwest at 1800. Why it had taken Fletcher so long to react to the initial sighting is not clear even today, but his failure to act promptly was once again to have deadly consequences for the men under his command. The result was that even as late as midnight on August 23, Pacific Fleet Intelligence no longer knew where the main part of the Japanese battle fleet was, including its carriers. Fletcher suggested it was probably north of Truk, but could find no logical reason for its being in such an unlikely position.

In a sense, Fletcher was facing a similar situation to that preceding the devastating cruiser battle off Savo Island a fortnight earlier. Coastwatchers then, too, had seen the enemy fleet leave Truk only to disappear for several hours and then suddenly reappear before Savo Island. Now a far larger Japanese force had totally vanished. But its destination was obvious to almost anyone—except Frank Jack Fletcher. Indeed, only two targets were possible, thought Chester Nimitz: New Guinea or Guadalcanal. Since the Japanese knew about the major new American effort to secure and develop Guadalcanal, and also that the U.S. Fleet was in that area in strength with the carrier planes with which they had already tangled at Midway, then Guadalcanal was thought to be the more likely destination.

To compound his earlier failure of judgment, Fletcher now did it again, detaching Admiral Leigh Noyes's *Wasp* carrier group and ordering it hundreds of miles to the south—away from Guadalcanal and the anticipated battle—"to refuel" the destroyers. It was later established that Fletcher's destroyers were *not* low on fuel, each having been carrying an average of 84,824 gallons, enough for several days' sailing.[6] The result was, of course, that Fletcher was left with only two carriers, reducing his airpower—his "big guns"—by one third even though he had been notified that part of a powerful Japanese fleet had been spotted at sea earlier that same day. Yamamoto himself could not have asked for a better ally. The same leaden skies continued throughout the night and next morning, and once again *Saratoga*'s search planes had to be recalled that August 24 because of negative results.[7] But the complete disappearance of the Japanese Second, Third, and Eighth fleets—three carriers, four battleships, and sixteen cruisers—did not seem to worry Admiral Fletcher, nor even to arouse his suspicions.

At 0905 on August 24, American naval reconnaissance planes at last began to report sightings of the approaching enemy fleet, beginning with the carrier *Ryujo*, the cruiser *Tone*, and a brace of destroyers. They were not to the north of Truk as Fletcher had predicted, but heading *south*, in fact only 260 miles northwest of Fletcher's Task Force 61. By 1100 that morning Fletcher knew that he, too, had been spotted, even as the enemy position was reconfirmed twenty-eight minutes later as being only 245 miles from him and closing. But instead of alerting his pilots and having the planes armed, Fletcher did nothing. It was only at 1229—sixty-one minutes after that reconfirmation—that he authorized Tom Kinkaid to launch the *Enterprise*'s planes. Yamamoto's two big carriers were then also located, although Fletcher initially failed to give credence to the reports of his own pilots because of course that would have proven that his earlier prediction of their being north of Truk had been incorrect.

Unlike Fletcher, a decisive Rear Admiral Hara Chuichi, now a mere 190 miles northeast of Guadalcanal, launched his first dozen fighters and bombers from the deck of *Ryujo* at 1420; these were joined by twin-engine Japanese bombers from Rabaul. Their objective: to bomb Henderson Field. Twenty-eight minutes later, when the *Ryujo* was one hundred miles from Fletcher's TF 61, it launched nine more fighters and was finally captured on Fletcher's radar for the first time.[8] Marine Fighter Squadron 223 was scrambled at Henderson in time to engage them, and although a few bombs did hit the airfield, U.S. fighters blasted twenty-one Japanese planes out of the sky and scattered the rest.

It was not until two hours and thirteen minutes after the 1128 sighting that Admiral Fletcher finally acted, dispatching thirty-eight bombers and torpedo planes against the *Ryujo*, but not against the big carriers. This was *four hours and forty-five minutes* after that light carrier had been first spotted. The first report on the remainder of Yamamoto's Combined Fleet came through at 1400, with definite confirmation of the heavy carriers. Half an hour later, the carriers *Shokaku* and *Zuikaku* were only 198 miles from Fletcher's fleet and still closing. Radio communication between the American planes and Fletcher's flight director was erratic owing to tropical storms, and he was unable to divert the initial thirty-eight planes to the more important targets. With more Japanese scout planes near Fletcher's fleet, the American admiral increased the strength of the combat air patrol protecting his carriers.

But part of the radio message apparently got through to some of *Enterprise*'s planes, for five Avengers launched earlier attacked both *Shokaku* and *Ryujo* with no results. Another pair of Avengers preparing to attack the big cruiser *Tone* were set upon by Japanese fighters, and only one of the American planes escaped. Meanwhile, at 1557, the first of *Saratoga*'s group had reached *Ryujo*. The engines of the thirty U.S. dive-bombers screamed as the planes hurtled downward from an altitude of fourteen thousand feet, their 1,000-pound bombs exploding around the light carrier. Six more Avengers joined in the attack, dropping their torpedoes at the *Ryujo* from a height of two hundred feet amidst heavy Japanese antiaircraft and fighter fire. At least one torpedo hit *Ryujo*'s port side, jamming her rudder as the carrier burst into flames. The shattered *Ryujo* was abandoned and went down at 2000 with 624 of her 924-man crew; fourteen of her planes returning from Guadalcanal later ditched in the sea.[9] All but one of the American planes returned safely. The pilots were jubilant, but of course they had missed the primary target, the two big Japanese flattops.

Admiral Nagumo, who had lost four carriers at Midway in June, now avenged himself, launching two attacks against Fletcher's carriers at 1455—twenty-two planes from *Shokaku* and another fifteen from *Zuikaku*, followed by a second wave at 1600.[10] By this time even Fletcher was ready, although the two American carriers were operating independently and located far from one another, each encircled by cruisers, a single battleship, and destroyers. Towers had implored his carrier commanders to work closely together in order to provide a greater concentration of antiaircraft fire, but Fletcher ignored Towers's advice.

At 1602, the ships' radars picked up the first "bogies" only eighty-eight miles away and more F4F Wildcats took off, bringing the air patrol over the carrier to fifty-three planes. *Enterprise* then cleared her decks, her last eighteen bombers and torpedo planes soaring off against Kondo's carriers well over an hour after Kondo had launched his aircraft, which were at that very moment diving on the U.S. carriers. But even now Fletcher was so dazed and unprepared that the crews of *Saratoga*'s last seven planes did not have time to put on their flight suits or grab their flight or navigational gear before taking off. Jack Towers's grave misgivings about Fletcher's competence for a carrier command were now borne out.

At 1638, some three dozen enemy bombers, protected by bevies of fighters, appeared over the U.S. Fleet, and the Wildcats fell upon them in a series of lethal dogfights, with Warrant Officer Don Runyan downing four planes in a matter of minutes. Confusion reigned as Japanese bombers, torpedo planes, and fighters mixed with U.S. Wildcats. A group of ten American carrier bombers returning from the *Ryujo* excursion suddenly discovered four "Val" dive-bombers beneath them and happily joined in the melee, sending three enemy planes down in flames.

The fighting was not yet over. At 1641, *Saratoga* warned *Enterprise* of approaching "Kates" and "Vals"* only ten miles away.[11] Two dozen Vals dropped from eighteen thousand feet and were met by a barrage of 5-inch, 1.1-inch, and 20mm antiaircraft fire from the *Enterprise*. The big carrier awkwardly turned and turned again to evade the bombs released by the shrieking dive-bombers. Down the enemy planes swooped to flight deck level, and after one very near miss, the first strike hit: a delayed-fuse, armor-piercing bomb crashed through the after flight deck elevator of the American carrier and through the hangar, exploding on the third deck below, killing some three dozen sailors, setting off a series of fires, and rupturing the ship's hull well below the waterline. A second bomb followed, detonating amid 5-inch guns and killing another thirty-nine men. A third bomb hit the flight deck just abaft the island but was partially defective, causing only a muted explosion.[12] Damage-control officers and crews were in action throughout the ship, putting out fires, staunching the flow of seawater, and saving the wounded. High in the skies above the burning carrier, American planes were fighting another battle against the Vals and Kates. U.S. Wildcats brought down more bombers while intense antiaircraft fire from the battleship *North Carolina*, just astern of the carrier, and the circling cruisers and destroyers brought down many more. The Vals diving against the *North Carolina* missed their target completely thanks to intercepting navy Wildcat fighters. Many miles over the horizon, the *Saratoga* had not been touched.[13]

Badly wounded or no, the *Enterprise* still had planes in the air and by 1749 had increased speed to 24 knots to recover them. Barely had they touched down than the carrier's steering engine was knocked out of action as an aftereffect of the bombs; the rudder was locked at 20

* "Kates" = Nakajima 97-2 naval high-level or torpedo bombers; "Vals" = Aichi 99-1 navel torpedo bombers; "Zekes" = Mitsubishi Zero = 3 navy fighters.

degrees, rendering Captain Arthur Davis's huge circling ship a sitting target should Nagumo's second wave of planes now arrive. Forty minutes later, the engineering officers had an auxiliary motor connected to rejuvenate the massive rudder, permitting the *Enterprise* to resume her course. Nagumo's second launch of thirty planes came within fifty miles of the smoking carrier but missed her, and the planes returned to their own ships with their full load of bombs and torpedoes.

American pilots were no more successful in attacking Nagumo, the *Enterprise*'s last wave of twenty-five torpedo and dive-bombers jettisoning its unspent loads before landing at 2000. *Saratoga*'s seven planes, having missed their rendezvous with a squadron of planes from the *Enterprise*, nevertheless did at least find Kondo's Advance Force at 1735, at a position just north of the Steward Islands and still on a southeasterly heading. Enemy antiaircraft fire was dense, causing five of the U.S. torpedo planes to miss Kondo's big ships. The remaining two *Saratoga* dive-bombers found what the pilots thought was a battleship and approached rapidly in a steep dive, releasing their bombs and hitting *Chitose*—not a battleship but in fact a seaplane tender. The hull of that ship was severely pierced and imploded, sucking in water while, on deck, damaged seaplanes exploded, spreading fires quickly across the rapidly listing ship.

Although *Saratoga* was not touched in battle, she had lost most of her planes, with only seven returning and a few more reaching Guadalcanal and San Cristobal. Captain DeWitt Ramsey and Air Group Commander Harry Felt remained on the bridge for hours, scanning the skies for planes and pilots that would never return. On board the listing *Enterprise*, Captain Davis and Air Group Commander Maxwell Leslie were more fortunate in this respect, retrieving seventy of their eighty-seven planes.[13] Far away to the south and steaming north at top speed, Captain Forrest Sherman, in the carrier *Wasp*, was praying that he would arrive in time, cursing the admiral who had detached him just before a major battle.[14]

Admiral Kondo, despite his second launch's having failed to find the American carriers, had received erroneous reports from his pilots that two U.S. flattops and one battleship had been badly damaged. He now continued to pursue Admiral Fletcher's task force with the intention of finishing off those damaged ships in a final night surface battle. Joining his vanguard group again at 1630 that afternoon, he set out at full speed for a point just southeast of the Stewart Islands where his pilots had earlier spotted Fletcher. But by 2330 the persistent but dismayed Kondo had found nothing and ordered his two battleships, ten cruisers, and accompanying destroyers to head north again, reaching Truk on August 28.[15] Fletcher's fears about immense battleship and cruiser superiority proved groundless; only TF 61's "biggest guns," its airplanes, had come into contact with enemy warships. Fletcher's apparent misjudgment of the situation resulted in hundreds of unnecessary American casualties.

That was not the end of the Japanese operation, however, for Admiral Tanaka's separate, and as yet undetected, Transport Group was still on course for Guadalcanal. At 0223 on August 25, its luck ran out when it was discovered by a PBY. Then, as Tanaka's flagship *Jintsu* was approaching Taivu Point on Guadalcanal in broad daylight at 0740, where she was to have been joined by a powerful bombardment force (which would never arrive), four marine SBDs, or navy dive-bombers, from Henderson Field spotted her and attacked. One direct hit exploded between *Jintsu*'s A and B turrets, causing extensive damage to the vessel and destroying its communications. With *Jintsu* out of action, Tanaka transferred his flag to the destroyer *Kagero*, and the damaged cruiser limped back to Truk.

For once, the Americans were unrelenting. At 0807 more warplanes arrived, bombing and strafing the 9,300-ton troop transport *Kinryu Maru* and destroying it as its separate cargo of ammunition blew up. As Vandegrift had radioed the position of Tanaka's convoy when it was first sighted, three B-17 Flying Fortresses arrived from Espíritu Santo at 1027, critically damaging destroyer *Mutsuki* while she was helping survivors from the sinking *Kinryu Maru*. After scuttling that destroyer, Tanaka received fresh orders to withdraw to the Shortlands because Operation KA had been called off. He transferred most of the remaining men to his destroyers, putting several hundred troops ashore before heading north once again.

It is not clear why Yamamoto canceled the cruiser bombardment of Henderson scheduled for the early hours of August 25, since U.S. planes and ships rarely flew, sailed, or fought at night. In any event, he did instead dispatch twenty-two bombers with fighter escorts to bomb

Henderson Field. Although they caused very little damage, they successfully distracted U.S. Navy and marine pilots, allowing Tanaka to escape and thereby bringing to a close the battle of the Eastern Solomons (or the Second Battle of the Solomon Sea, as it is sometimes called).

•

Some 175 miles southeast of San Cristobal, Admiral Fletcher was once again refueling his task force in his usual leisurely manner, now attaching both the *North Carolina* and *Atlanta* to protect *Saratoga* as the much-battered *Enterprise* slowly made her way back to the drydocks of Pearl Harbor for substantial repairs (which cost several million dollars, even then). Admiral Fletcher's indecision and failure to act hours earlier in the battle of the Eastern Solomons had allowed Tanaka to land reinforcements, and the Japanese air force to hit Henderson. During the actual battle, he had permitted Japan's two biggest carriers, *Shokaku* and *Zuikako*, all of their battleships, and their heavy cruisers to escape more or less unscathed. Air Group commanders Harry Felt and Max Leslie, of the *Saratoga* and *Enterprise*, respectively, had sunk the light carrier *Ryujo* and the tender *Chitose*, and of course had damaged *Jintsu* and sunk a destroyer. Had Ghormley and Nimitz put a Mitscher in charge of TF 61—someone who would never have detached *Wasp* with a major battle brewing, and who knew something about carrier tactics—the battle of the Eastern Solomons could well have turned out to be a great American victory. As it was, under the command of Ghormley, the Slot remained open, and Japanese ships and aircraft continued to ply those lanes nightly; to bomb and bombard Henderson Field; and to bring continuous reinforcements, guns, and supplies to Guadalcanal while American ships and planes obligingly retired from the scene after dusk. The situation can only be described as grotesque. There was absolutely nothing to prevent Ghormley and Fletcher from cruising up and down the Slot and the sound, just as the Japanese did, or from stationing submarines at the chokepoints on either side of Savo Island. If nothing else, they could have easily closed the north and south channels of Savo Island with coastal artillery and destroyers around the clock, and with the aid of PT boats that arrived later. In other words, the basic *matériel de guerre* was already in the

South Pacific, but Admiral Bob Ghormley refused to deploy it. And thus the Japanese were permitted to reinforce Guadalcanal with ultimately over thirty thousand men and tons of munitions, tanks, and big guns. On the other hand, the Japanese master plan KA, calling for the total destruction of the U.S. Pacific Fleet and the immediate reconquest of Guadalcanal by Yamamoto's imposing Combined Fleet on August 24–25, was dead. Yet there was nothing to prevent Tokyo from trying again, for the Slot remained wide open.

On August 31, 1942, the by now exasperated Japanese high command convened and officially gave the recapture of Guadalcanal top priority. The Imperial Army and Navy could have whatever it took to achieve this objective. The campaign in New Guinea would continue, of course, but now even more ships, planes, and manpower would be first allocated to Guadalcanal and its reconquest, whatever the price. That same day, General Hyakutake Harukichi, who from his headquarters on Rabaul was in charge of all troops on Guadalcanal, received the joyous news that the *Saratoga* had been torpedoed and badly damaged while on routine patrol some 260 miles southwest of Henderson Field.[16] Frank Jack Fletcher requested sick leave immediately. He never returned. With both *Lexington* and *Yorktown* already put out of action, and *Enterprise* in drydock for extensive repairs for the next several months, there were now only two U.S. flattops, *Wasp* and *Hornet*, left to protect the entire Pacific. No admiral in U.S. naval history had ever suffered such major losses at sea. Both Ghormley and MacArthur told Chester Nimitz that Guadalcanal could not hold out and recommended the evacuation of the U.S. marines. Admiral Nimitz strongly disagreed with them, however, and it was he who made the final decisions here in the Pacific.[17]

CHAPTER XVII

The Open Slot

"I have never heard or read of this kind of fighting. These people refuse to surrender. The wounded will wait until the men come up to examine them and blow themselves and the other follow to pieces with a hand grenade."

—*Major General Archie Vandegrift to Marine Corps Commandant Thomas Holcomb, Guadalcanal, October 1942*[1]

Between August 28 and 30, 1942, three thousand Japanese troops and tons of supplies were landed on Guadalcanal by night, while every day at noon, Japanese bombers laid waste to that island and Tulagi. After nightfall on the 31st, another flotilla of enemy destroyers arrived undetected, landing an additional 650 troops made up of engineers, gunners, and antitank units, as well as the island's new commanding officer, Major General Kawaguchi Kiyotake, who promised headquarters he would take Henderson Field by the revised date of September 10.[2]

From August to November, the "Tokyo Express" was transporting troops and supplies *to the same beaches* with predictable regularity every few days; and toward the middle of each month, this pace intensified for several days scarcely hindered by U.S. naval warships. Japanese resistance on land continued, aided by the usual daily lunchtime bombing raids carried out by an average of two dozen twin-engined bombers. Most American aircraft on Guadalcanal were inadequate or limited in performance (underpowered and not as maneuverable) P-40s or the

SBD-3s, the navy's Dauntless dive-bombers, which had a flying radius of a mere two hundred miles, compared to similar Japanese planes with a flying radius of three hundred miles or more. Even these two American types were in short supply, as were aviation fuel and ammunition. Yet Japan was paying dearly for these attacks, losing four to eight planes daily over Henderson Field, compared with the loss of one U.S. aircraft for every ten of Japan.[3]

Some help was on the way for the Americans, however, with the arrival of the first contingent of Seabees on September 1. One hundred Seabees could fill and repair a 500-pound bomb crater at Henderson Field in forty minutes, a job that included the laying of Marston mat perforated sheets of metal over the runway foundation.

But even a buffer distance of 260 miles from Guadalcanal had not bought protection for Frank Jack Fletcher and the *Saratoga* on August 31. Because he and Ghormley had failed to take effective steps even to slow the schedule of the Tokyo Express, the Japanese force on Guadalcanal—which had been reduced to fewer than a thousand men by General Vandegrift during the first weeks—exceeded five thousand by September 10, thanks to nightly reinforcements, and was growing steadily.[4] General Kawaguchi's offensive to take Henderson Field was now rescheduled for September 12.

Kawaguchi, who had never failed on the battlefield before, was going to take no chances now. Bent on annihilating the U.S. marines, he drew up a thorough if complicated all-out, three-dimensional, multiple-pincer attack, involving land forces on three sides and a naval assault on the fourth. Simultaneously, for good measure, air raids would pelt the American position with antipersonnel bombs. So completely enveloped would the U.S. force be that it would be literally impossible for it to escape total destruction—or so Kawaguchi assured his commanders. Once success was achieved, the Imperial Navy would attack and sink the U.S. carriers in a final, great battle. Fortunately for Vandegrift's men, the indigenous people of the islands, who had been maltreated by the Japanese, cooperated with the Americans in reporting the positions of large new numbers of enemy troops. Vandegrift decided to hit the enemy immediately before they could attack him. This action was to have most unexpected results, providing far-ranging help for the marines.

Lieutenant Colonel Merritt A. Edson's Raider Battalion, six hundred men strong, landed east of Taivu Point at dawn on September 8. When Kawaguchi saw them pouring ashore, attended by the two destroyer transports that had brought them from Tulagi and another pair of passing transports unrelated to this operation, he assumed that a major landing was taking place involving thousands of men. In a panic, he hastily evacuated his main headquarters and supply depot at Tasimboko village, abandoning everything. Edson's marines, in turn, quickly seized the village, where they discovered large stores of artillery, munitions, medical supplies, and food. As they were unable to take most of this with them on their transports back to Tulagi, much of it had to be dropped into the sound so as to be kept out of enemy hands. More important, Edson also came upon documents on Kawaguchi's desk outlining the forthcoming attack. The Raiders embarked for Tulagi later that afternoon, their mission a complete success at the cost of only eight casualties. The information they sent to General Vandegrift about a much larger Japanese force than had been known, and one now involved in the proposed attack, came as an unpleasant shock. Although it would be folly for Kawaguchi to continue now knowing the Americans had his plans, Vandegrift was nonetheless going to be ready for him, come what may.

Vandegrift's men, well dug in behind barbed-wire barriers on three sides of Henderson Field, did not have to wait long. Skirmishing began on the 12th as Japanese patrols probed to find weak points in the marines' perimeter, one group of infiltrators temporarily cutting off an entire company of marines. Clearly Kawaguchi felt that, despite losing the element of surprise, his men well outnumbered the Americans and had every reason for success. Even the air raids were on schedule as intensive bombing began doing considerable damage to Henderson Field, although fourteen Japanese fighters and bombers were shot down by marine Wildcats and antiaircraft fire. Other raids were to continue over the next two days. During the daylight hours, Vandegrift could put up some sort of air defense, but when a Japanese cruiser and three destroyers arrived in Ironbottom Sound on the night of September 12—U.S. planes were grounded as usual, and lacking sufficient heavy coastal artillery—he could do nothing but continue to plead fruitlessly with Ghormley to send the navy. Meanwhile, per his original plans, Kawaguchi launched a series of small, quick night attacks along the marines' perimeter, complete with Japanese war cries and insults hurled in broken English. Neither side was to get much sleep that night.

Colonel Edson had placed his combined Raider-Paratroop Battalion on "the Ridge," some high land overlooking Henderson Field, a mere quarter of a mile ahead of Vandegrift's own headquarters. As it turned out, he was correct in expecting the brunt of the Japanese attack here, and skirmishing, including bayonet charges, continued during the night, developing into more serious attacks throughout the 13th. But Vandegrift's ten thousand men were spread too thinly over several miles to allow them to take the offensive. The airfield had to be held at all costs, for if they lost it, they lost 'Canal.

The main assault finally came from two thousand of Kawaguchi's men at 2230 hours on September 13. A red rocket suddenly shot above the dense jungle, and the Japanese unleashed a barrage of intense mortar fire at the Ridge. They were clearly intent on seizing Vandegrift and his headquarters. But because they had had their heavy artillery taken out by Edson during the earlier raid of September 10, Kawaguchi and his men were at a distinct disadvantage, as Brigadier General Pedro del Valle's much more powerful 105mm howitzers zeroed in on the Japanese positions on the other side of the Ridge.[5]

Under cover of a heavy smoke screen, Kawaguchi's troops hit Edson's men hard, dislodging the marines and exposing their flank, including their center company, as hundreds of bayonet-wielding Japanese infantry lunged forward. So fierce was this attack that Edson finally had to withdraw his entire battalion to the last hillock of the Ridge standing between the enemy and Henderson Field, less than a mile away. At least here he could better concentrate his firepower and tighten his defenses. Greatly outnumbered, the exhausted but determined marines fought on. Some Japanese soldiers did get through the line, actually reaching marine GHQ, where they were killed at the last minute, only a few feet away from Vandegrift, by some of the staff officers.

Both eastern and western perimeters also came under assault, these by smaller enemy units. Lieutenant Colonel William McKelvy's 3rd Battalion of the 1st Marine Regiment fought on a two-mile stretch of the Tenaru (or Ilu) River, while Lieutenant Colonel F. C. Biebush's troops, on the western perimeter extending to the sea well over on the other side of the Lunga River, also managed to beat off attacks.[6]

It was the marines' superior artillery that made up for their inferior numbers in depth, with Brigadier General del Valle's guns taking their relentless toll, repelling one Japanese attack after another. Time and again the Japanese charged under withering fire with a ferocity that was nothing short of amazing, the entire scene dramatically lit up by powerful calcium flares. But in the long run they were no match for the marines' well-coordinated and concentrated rifle and machine-gun fire, grenades, and mortars, which decimated the Japanese in waves.

As dawn broke on the 14th, the remnants of Kawaguchi's bloodied troops at last withdrew into the jungle as marine fighter planes strafed them from above, pushing them farther and farther into the already simmering tropical morass known as Guadalcanal.

Beaten and no doubt astonished, Kawaguchi, a soldier unaccustomed to defeat, returned to his base at Kokumbona having suffered 1,138 casualties to the marines' 143. There were now only 2,313 Japanese troops left on the island . . . for the time being.[7] Colonel Edson's men had held, if only just. This news did not go down at all well in Tokyo, where on September 17–18 the Supreme War Council met again with the emperor and decided to divert troops from elsewhere to aid this effort. Aircraft and warships, including a division of the Seventeenth Army, were reassigned to the capture of Guadalcanal. That island would now have top military priority until the Americans were defeated. This move was to release pressure on MacArthur's men in New Guinea.[8] Additional Japanese warplanes were lined up at Rabaul, fueled and armed, ready to fly to Henderson Field even as the Imperial Navy was preparing to bring in more reinforcements.

●

Archie Vandegrift was awaiting reinforcements of his own. On September 18, six troop transports under the command of Admiral Kelly Turner were en route from Espíritu Santo, ferrying the 7th Marine Regiment (some four thousand men). Rear Admiral Leigh Noyes commanded their escort, made up of the last two available carriers in the Pacific, *Hornet* and *Wasp*, which were screened in turn by the new battleship *North Carolina*, three cruisers, and seven destroyers. Following a westerly course, they were one hundred miles from the southern Solomons. There had been many reports of Japanese activity, in the air and at sea, on September 14; but by two o'clock on the 15th, a splendidly clear, sunny day—ideal submarine weather—the convoy was still only about halfway between Espíritu Santo and San Cristobal.

Kelly Turner was under enormous pressure as his bevy of wallowing transports slowly plied its way across the treacherous waters known as "Torpedo Junction." Thus far, at least one Japanese scout plane had been shot down. But had it first reported the convoy's position?

At 1430 the *Wasp* turned into the wind to launch twenty-six dive-bombers and Wildcats, destined to reinforce Henderson Field. Just as Captain Forrest Sherman was bringing the carrier around to a northwesterly heading again, a lookout spotted a spread of torpedoes coming fast at the awkward ship's starboard beam. Sherman ordered a right full rudder, but steaming at a mere 16 knots, the ship did not answer quickly enough. Japanese submarine 1-19 had patiently awaited this moment, and two of the torpedoes struck forward, one amidships ahead of the bridge.[9] The force of the torpedo's 1,000-pound warhead rocked the American carrier, ripping huge gaps along her starboard side and causing tons of seawater to pour in. Fire and explosions above and below decks soon engulfed one section of the ship, and the remaining airplanes on deck, all fueled, armed, and ready to take off, exploded into flames as well. Fire quickly spread through the fuel system, bursting the forward water mains used for firefighting, and the immense flight deck began to list heavily to starboard. But Sherman, a first-rate ship handler, had trained his officers and men well, and the damage-control center was acting as quickly as was humanly possible. Sherman had ordered a left rudder in order to get the wind to starboard to blow the flames away from the undamaged portion of the vessel, and with a final maneuver he brought the carrier round again with another full right rudder to complete the action. The *Wasp* was entirely engulfed in flames. Below decks, the officers continued to shift thousands of gallons of fuel from starboard to port, which greatly reduced the list and the amount of inflowing seawater almost immediately. Captain Sherman thought he could still save his ship as it struggled on at 10 knots.

At 1452 another Japanese sub, 1-15, torpedoed the battleship *North*

Carolina, despite that big battleship's attempt to evade it.[10] The explosion caused a geyser of water and oil to shoot high into the air and then fall in a vast downpour, drenching the vessel. Some twenty feet below the waterline, the powerful torpedo had ripped a jagged, thirty-two-foot-long hole into the hull on the port side. And yet she maintained her course at 25 knots, while below decks the undaunted damage-control teams were containing a slight list. Two minutes later, another torpedo hit the destroyer *O'Brien*, tearing off the bow down to the keel itself and leaving in its place a huge blunt-nosed gap. Although the ship was momentarily saved, her keel had received a mortal shock, and the destroyer was to break up a few weeks later while en route to the West Coast for repairs.

The *Wasp* was in even greater agony. Fire raged out of control, intensified by an enormous explosion at three o'clock that engulfed the command bridge, killing several men and lifting Admiral Noyes off that bridge and onto the signal bridge, his uniform aflame and his face singed. Miraculously, he suffered only minor wounds. With the bridge gone, Captain Sherman then moved back to "Battle II," or the after station, designed for emergency steering. Another explosion ripped open the hangar deck below, hurling the massive steel flight deck elevator and dozens of men through the air. The fore area of the mangled carrier that had taken the first two torpedoes was in the most critical condition, for the seawater that continued to pour rapidly into the ship spread oil- and gasoline-fed flames amidst exploding machine-gun ammunition. With vast sheets of fire engulfing the superstructure and mountainous black smoke belching upward high above the ship, the *Wasp* looked almost like a floating volcanic island in eruption. The damage reports came in from every deck—the situation was utterly hopeless. At 1720 on that strangely beautiful South Seas day, Sherman had to issue the one order every skipper dreads: "Abandon Ship!"

Superhuman effort was made to get the wounded through walls of flame and to release those trapped below. Life rafts and floating mattresses were used to support the severely injured, particularly those badly burnt. At four o'clock that afternoon of the 15th, Captain Sherman was the last to leave the stricken vessel . . . apart from the dozens of men caught below decks, locked behind sealed bulkheads, impenetrable fire, and hot twisted metal, their pleas for help lost in the fury of destruction.

Sherman and some members of the crew were picked up by the destroyer *Farenholt*, with more destroyers moving in quickly to save hundreds of others despite the paralyzing jolts of depth-charge explosions far beneath them. Aboard the cruiser *San Francisco*, Rear Admiral Norman Scott ordered destroyer *Lansdowne* to sink the anguished *Wasp*, and she went down at 2100 hours that evening. Torpedo Junction had lived up to its name. The final count was a shock for everyone: 559 dead and wounded. Yet 1,688 men had survived, thanks to the superb skills and actions of the ship's captain, officers, men, and the unsung heroes, the damage-control teams. Admiral Nimitz's official statement on the loss concluded simply that "no persons should be blamed or censured for the loss of the *Wasp*." The *North Carolina* was escorted back to Pearl Harbor for repairs.[11]

Without the protection of *North Carolina*'s big guns and the *Wasp*'s air cover, Kelly Turner might well have turned back, but knowing how desperately Vandegrift needed his reinforcements, he bravely pushed on. Reaching "Cactus" (the code name for Guadalcanal) on September 18, he began unloading Colonel Sims's 7th Marine Regiment and many tons of very badly needed food, medicine, ammunition, vehicles, and even light tanks, while the destroyers *Monssen* and *MacDonough* kept General Kawaguchi's troops distracted with a steady coastal bombardment.

If the Tokyo Express was still managing to land thousands of men, the Japanese air force was not doing as well. By September 27, General Vandegrift announced that over two hundred Japanese planes had been destroyed since the beginning of the campaign, against the loss of thirty-two U.S. aircraft. "How's that for a record!"[12] he proudly informed headquarters at Nouméa.

Alas, the marine general's positive report was soon effaced by growing signs of yet another Japanese buildup. Enemy destroyers were continuing to land between 750 and 900 men nightly, with little or no interference from Ghormley's navy. General Kawaguchi was clearly getting ready to launch another offensive before the month of September was out. To forestall that, Vandegrift decided to send units of the freshly arrived 7th Marines around the position occupied by Kawaguchi, in the vicinity of the Matanikau River to the west of Henderson Field.

Beginning on September 23, Lieutenant Colonel Lewis Puller's 1st Battalion was ordered there and encountered strong resistance in rough terrain while crossing the foothills of Mt. Austen. They reached the mouth of the Matanikau on the 26th, reinforced by Lieutenant Colonel Samuel Griffith's 1st Raider Battalion and Lieutenant Colonel D. S. McDougal's 2nd Battalion of the 5th Marine Regiment. In the ferocious fighting that followed, Griffith was severely wounded and his men pulled back to the mouth of the river at Ironbottom Sound. At one stage, two companies of marines found themselves completely encircled by far superior numbers of Japanese and were only saved when the destroyer *Monssen* moved in, covering their retreat along the jungle-clad coastline with a powerful barrage of gunfire and then ferrying the marines to her decks in the face of persistent Japanese fire. Four days of "skirmishing" had resulted in 160 marine casualties. It was becoming clear that it took an awful lot to be able to survive on Guadalcanal.

On October 8, six marine battalions were ordered back to the Matanikau, unaware that General Hyakutake Harukichi's latest battle plan to retake Guadalcanal was to be launched that same day. Hyakutake had promised Tokyo that Vandegrift and Henderson Field would be in his hands by the 15th. The operation was to commence with the arrival of Lieutenant General Maruyama Masao's 2nd Division, which would add 22,500 additional troops over the next few days. Addressing his division as it set sail from Shortland Island, Maruyama declared the forthcoming operation on Guadalcanal to be "the decisive battle between Japan and the United States," one in which the rise or fall of the Japanese Empire would be decided.[13] And he concluded that in the event they failed, "no one should expect to return to Japan alive." This was precisely what Douglas MacArthur told General Eichelberger before dispatching him to the front at Buna: Succeed or die in the attempt.[14]

Once again, two very determined forces were about to face one another on opposite banks of the Matanikau. The 8th Marines advanced through the jungle to the east bank for a surprise attack against Colonel Nakaguma Tadamasu's 4th Infantry Regiment on the opposite shore. Simultaneously, two of Colonel Edson's Raider battalions of the 5th Regiment sloshed painfully upstream through leech-infested waters while torrential day-long rains obligingly provided them with the element of cover and complete surprise, allowing them to fall upon the unsuspecting Japanese troops at Nippon Bridge. The Japanese retaliated forcefully. Breaking from the west bank, they mauled the marines with far superior numbers in hand-to-hand fighting. But the marines stood their ground, and by the end of the day had turned the situation around, using automatic weapons to exterminate their opponents. The following day, Colonel William Whaling's 3rd Battalion, Lieutenant Colonel Herman H. Hanneken's 2nd Battalion of the 7th Marines, and Colonel Lewis Puller's 1st Battalion successfully crossed the Nippon Bridge and the much-bloodied waters of the Matanikau, marching now unopposed along the previously intractable Japanese-held west bank.

Continuing westward, it was Puller's battalion that unexpectedly came upon Colonel Nakaguma's main force, concealed below in two large ravines. Again, sheer guts, automatic weapons, and General Pedro del Valle's murderous artillery enabled the marines, though still greatly outnumbered, to defeat the Japanese in an intense firefight. The results: 700 Japanese dead versus Puller's 195 dead and wounded. It was a battle fought and won the hard, old-fashioned way. There were no shortcuts. Puller's victorious but exhausted battalion returned to the east bank of the lower Matanikau late that same day with its mission accomplished. Lieutenant Colonel R. Hill led a separate, smaller operation around Aola Bay, where he destroyed the only base threatening Henderson Field from the east.

Late that night of October 9, unknown to Vandegrift, yet another Tokyo Express—comprising a light cruiser and nine destroyers—was disgorging the first contingent of the crack 2nd Division along with its commanding officer, Lieutenant General Hyakutake.[15] Vandegrift was astounded when he eventually learned the extent of these reinforcements, not to mention the fact that their leader was a foremost three-star Pacific veteran, a man who had never lost a battle. Clearly, something had to be done. Thousands of American lives were at stake, and the navy in particular could not continue to abandon the Slot and sound every night.

●

On that same momentous October 9, the U.S. Navy was indeed actively preparing for a night action off the shores of Guadalcanal as

Kelly Turner's latest convoy of urgently needed troops—the 164th U.S. Army Infantry Regiment of 2,817 men—was arriving from Nouméa. The naval escort included Rear Admiral George D. Murray's flagship, *Hornet*, screened by eight destroyers (this was the last U.S. carrier group available in the Pacific); Rear Admiral Norman Scott's cruiser flotilla, TF 64; and Rear Admiral Willis Lee's powerful new battleship and flagship, the USS *Washington*.[16]

This unusual show of strength was based on intelligence indicating that Mikawa was still assembling an impressive task force with which to attack, among other objectives, Turner's convoy. What Naval Intelligence did not know, however, was that the Japanese were bringing a very special convoy of their own—one that included the bulk of Hyakutake's 2nd Division—down the Slot on October 10, to be supported by three heavy cruisers and a couple of destroyers. As the troops were landing, three heavy cruisers were to shell Henderson Field, preventing U.S. air strikes (using planes coming from as far north as Bougainville) while landing its own troops. On the other hand, the Japanese were equally ignorant about the presence of Admiral Scott's TF 64, which would be waiting for them in the sound that night.

With Mikawa now at sea again, Robert Ghormley, after learning of the threat to Guadalcanal, and then only after enormous pressure from both CINCPAC (Nimitz) and Admiral King, had in fact ordered the creation of this task force. Even as *Hornet* was taking its station to the east of the island of Malaita, some 180 miles from Guadalcanal itself, Admiral Norman Scott's task force, having completed three intensive weeks of night operations, was detached and ordered to Savo Island to "search for and destroy enemy ships." For the first time during the Pacific Campaign, American warships were at long last going on the offensive in a night operation. Given the regularity of Japanese shipping traffic in these waters, the outcome would not be long in coming. Archie Vandegrift, for one, had repeatedly and adamantly called for the necessity of stopping the Tokyo Express; finally, after many deaths, and weeks of arguments and excuses by the indecisive Ghormley, something was being done.

"You are hereby ordered and directed to seize and destroy": the instructions Admiral Horatio Nelson had received prior to the battle of

Trafalgar in October 1805 had not changed much, in wording or intent. Now, in October 1942, Admiral Scott seemed the very man to carry on in the best Nelson tradition. The fifty-three-year-old native of Indianapolis and member of the Academy Class of 1911 was one of the few remaining American naval officers to have experienced battle conditions. During World War I, he had served aboard the destroyer *Jacob Jones* when she was torpedoed and sunk by a German U-boat in 1917. He subsequently served as aide-de-camp to President Woodrow Wilson and as a gunnery instructor at the Naval Academy. After taking the Naval War College course at Newport, he was given command of the *Pensacola*, and later served under the CNO. Promoted to rear admiral, he had been commanding task forces in the South Pacific for the past four months.

Admiral Scott wanted nothing better than to sink and destroy Japan's ships, and he was one of the first naval commanders here to prepare a carefully devised battle plan for TF 64, which comprised his flagship, the heavy cruiser *San Francisco*, the heavy cruiser *Salt Lake City*, and two light cruisers, *Boise* and *Helena*, screened by five destroyers: *Farenholt*, *Buchanan*, *Laffey*, *Duncan*, and *McCalla*. They were to enter the sound and the Slot in battle column, with orders to open fire independently—that is, without the task force commander's authorization—whenever they saw a viable target. In theory, at least, that is how the orders read.

During his previous approaches to Cape Espérance on October 9 and 10, Scott had had to turn back when scout planes and radar reported no sightings of Japanese warships. Admiral Mikawa, who was in fact landing troops off the northwestern cape of Guadalcanal on a nightly basis, had been foiled on the 8th when American bombers from Henderson stopped the Tokyo Express, although General Hyakutake and his troops got through successfully the following day when they landed at Tassafaronga. Clearly American warships were still not being properly deployed in sufficient numbers or in the right places to prevent the Express from reaching its objective. Scott was now determined to put a halt to that by destroying the next powerful flotilla Mikawa sent down the Slot.

With American air strikes against land and port targets beginning to take their toll on the Japanese, on October 11, when Mikawa was due to send in another Express, Vice Admiral Kusaka Ryunosuke, commanding the Eleventh Air Fleet at Rabaul, promised a heavy raid of some sixty-five bombers and fighters intended to neutralize Henderson Field. The raid was not a complete success—the Japanese lost twelve planes—but at least it did permit Mikawa's force to enter the Slot once again. This time, however, an American B 17 spotted two cruisers and six destroyers moving rapidly southward, a sighting confirmed again at 1910 that evening at a position less than four hours' sailing time north of Savo Island. Admiral Scott was informed and acted promptly, dashing to Savo Island at 1600 at a full 29 knots. The Tokyo Express had to be derailed.[17]

Admiral Mikawa's plan involved sending a cruiser division under the command of Rear Admiral Gotō Aritomo to escort Rear Admiral Joshima Takaji's Reinforcement Group, made up of seaplane carriers *Chitose* and *Nisshin* carrying not planes but 728 army personnel, a variety of heavy artillery and ammunition, medical supplies, tractors, and landing craft. These were screened by half a dozen destroyers. Separating from Gotō's escort while still in the Slot, Joshima's reinforcements set out on a new course that would take his flotilla to the west of Savo Island, headed for the northwestern shore of Guadalcanal as usual while Gotō's cruisers continued down the Slot in the direction of Savo Island. No reports had yet reached Gotō of the welcoming party awaiting him.

"All hands, man your battle stations!" the voice rang out in speakers throughout TF 64. On every deck of every vessel, the traditional summoning cry of the bugle and the boatswain's pipe rent the calm of another balmy tropical evening as thousands of men scrambled to their stations. The senior officer of each department then reported:

"Bridge! Bat[tery] Two, manned and ready for General Quarters." "Bridge! Gunnery Department, manned and ready for General Quarters." This was repeated by Damage Control, Engineers, and other groups down the line.[18]

It was still early, and there were hours before any unexpected confrontation with the Japanese, but Norman Scott, with the eyes of the entire South Pacific Fleet on him, was determined not to repeat the performance of another cruiser task force in these very waters off Savo Island just two months earlier. Scott had plenty of time in which to prepare now—perhaps too much. He could not keep his sailors at their battle stations, at General Quarters, for hours before engaging the enemy. The officers and men would lose their edge. In the age of sail, when ships of the battle line proceeded ever so slowly compared with the fast warships of today, this problem was perhaps more acute, but there was always plenty of manual work on those leviathans to keep sailors occupied. Nelson, for one, would pipe all hands below to a hot meal and a special tot of rum. In those days, ships' crews needed a good deal of physical strength for the frequently long hours of fighting. Things were, of course, very different now. Battles could begin and finish in thirty minutes, as in the case of Savo Island. Keeping all hands physically and mentally alert, tense and ready for anything, was an art. And lookouts thus far had sighted no one.

At 2200, Scott's TF 64 left Cape Espérance behind on a fresh bearing, taking them close to Savo Island and the southwestern channel opening into the Slot. Scott had already given the order for his cruisers' four Kingfisher float planes to be launched on a search mission for Admiral Gotō's cruiser division. But mishaps had occurred, and only two planes were now in the air—a third having caught fire while still aboard *Salt Lake City* (serving as a splendid signal to an enemy force), while on the fourth ship, the captain misunderstood Scott's instruction and had instead jettisoned the fueled plane overboard rather than risk an explosion and fire in battle. All those weeks of preparation were now at risk because of the plane burning on the catapult. It was dark enough for it to be seen for miles, and Scott no doubt cursed his luck, fearing he would lose the great advantage of surprise.

More than fifty miles away, Gotō did indeed see the pinprick of light represented by the burning plane, but assumed it to be a Japanese signal from the beach and flashed back a reply with his signal lamps. There was no reply, of course, but ignoring that as well as an earlier report by a search plane, Gotō pounded on at an even 26 knots.

Scott and his captains remained on the alert for anything unusual, and at 2250 the spotter plane radioed the position of three small vessels off the coast of Guadalcanal. As two of them were "small," Scott chose to ignore them. In fact, these were some of Joshima's ships preparing to disembark, and the purpose of this entire operation was, after all, to prevent these very reinforcements from landing. But Scott, following battle procedure, wanted to concentrate his force on the big ships, and he knew they were out there somewhere.

Then, at 2308, *Helena*'s new SG search radar finally made contact with three of Gotō's ships less than sixteen miles to the northwest. But again there was a problem in naval communications, and *Helena*'s captain waited *a full quarter of an hour* before informing Admiral Scott, whose older flagship had not yet picked up anything. Then, just to complicate matters, Scott had earlier ordered his ships not to use the SG radar gun units for, although none of Admiral Gotō's ships had radar, they did have radar receivers, which could possibly alert them to the American presence, but not their precise position. *San Francisco*'s weaker radar still detected nothing whatsoever.

Even after receiving the report from *Helena*, Scott did not act, instead demanding confirmation, which he hoped the spotter planes would provide. But one of the two remaining float planes then went down with engine trouble, and the sole plane left merely repeated the sighting of Joshima's ships landing men and munitions along the coast.

Instead of attacking, a cautious Scott pressed on with his plan to patrol the passage between Cape Espérance and Savo Island, through which Japanese ships would first have to pass in order to enter or leave the sound. At 2332 he ordered his task force to form a single battle column again. This turned out to be a mistake, as it was a complicated maneuver performed in pitch dark which required the three destroyers in the van to separate from the cruisers and come about to port, swinging well away from the rest of the column but then passing the reversing columns to reattach themselves at the head of the column once the other ships had completed this move. As for the crews of TF 64, they had long since been piped to battle stations and had definitely lost their battle "edge."

Helena's SG radar continued to track the enemy throughout. At last that ship's captain, Gilbert Hoover, positive of the enemy ships, which were now only six miles away, finally informed Scott, giving them a bearing of 285 degrees and closing fast. Scott's flagship still detected nothing. At 2338 the *Boise*, in the midst of swinging round to re-form the van, now added to the confusion by reporting five "bogies," a term usually referring to planes. Scott thought *Boise* actually meant ships, but could not be sure. Furthermore, part of the report was garbled, including the bearing of the "bogies." From which direction would they be attacked, and in which should they fire? American naval officers had not been trained thoroughly enough in these reporting procedures and were to suffer as a result, here and in the future.

Indeed, at this stage Scott was not even sure where Captain Robert Tobin's destroyer, *Farenholt*, was, and all ships were blacked out, with visibility zero in the thick, overcast tropical night. The second destroyer in the lead, *Duncan*, also spotted something on its radar and went after it, leaving the re-forming van without informing either Tobin or Scott. According to the action report, *Duncan* simply "assumed" that *Farenholt* had picked up the same thing on her own fire-control radar. That was an error compounded and repeated in many naval operations throughout the war, one ship "assuming" that the other ships had seen the same thing, or were taking similar action, without signaling the others. Now breaking away from Scott's task force, the lone *Duncan* charged straight at the incoming Japanese cruisers at a full 30 knots.

It was only at 2345 that the *San Francisco* finally made her first clear radar contact, a full thirty-seven minutes after the first warning and now only three miles away to the west-northwest. But Scott was not sure whether the ship spotted was the enemy or one of his own screening destroyers. What would it take to wake up the admiral? *Helena* impatiently requested permission to open fire, although technically permission was not needed. Then there were other communications misunderstandings regarding the term "Roger" between the *Helena* and Scott. Finally, the exasperated captain of the *Helena* turned on her searchlights and gave the order to open fire with both her 6- and 5-inch guns at 2346, thereby commencing the battle of Cape Espérance.

Gotō's force had had no idea whatsoever that there were even any American warships out there, that is, until they suddenly opened fire. *Laffey*, still out of column between Japanese and friendly fire, had to reverse at full speed, but not before her starshell illuminated the cruiser *Aoba*, which she quickly fired on, hitting the bridge and mortally wounding Admiral Gotō. *Duncan* was in an even worse position, receiving not only friendly fire but coming even closer to the Japanese, now less than a mile away. Lieutenant Commander E. B. Taylor attempted hastily to correct *Duncan*'s error by pressing on at full speed straight toward the heavy cruiser *Furutaka*, his guns raking her decks. At 2347, before she could fire on her next target, the destroyer *Hatsuyuki*, *Duncan* was badly damaged—but by whom? Admiral Scott was caught in a predicament. If he continued to fire, he might be hitting American destroyers, which had silhouettes similar to those of the Japanese. If he ceased firing, the Japanese, though reversing course, could still fire with impunity. In a controversial decision, Scott ordered his entire squadron to cease fire immediately at 2347, one minute after the action had begun.[19]

Ironically, the gravely wounded Gotō thought *he* was being fired on by his own ships and ordered his column to reverse course. It did so, bringing it in a position perpendicular to Scott's approaching cruisers.

Some American ships' captains had not followed Scott's orders, and with the aid of their searchlights and those of the *San Francisco*, they continued to fire at *Aoba* and *Furutaka*, hitting them many times and causing them to burst into flames. Scott repeatedly ordered his ships to cease firing, but some either failed to get the message or refused to heed it as Scott's own flagship came under heavy fire by *Kinugasa*, among others. Finally, at 2351, Scott gave the order to resume firing after distinguishing the recognition lights of his destroyers in the van. It was the *Duncan* that took the brunt of the concentrated Japanese barrage, although she did manage to launch one torpedo at the *Furutaka*. But Captain Tobin was putting on *Duncan*'s identification lights and in consequence was hit repeatedly in lethal crossfire from both sides. *Farenholt*, in the same situation, was badly hit as well, by both enemy and friendly fire. If American searchlights permitted their gunners to sink the destroyer *Fubuki* in a few moments' time, they also obligingly pinpointed their own position for the remarkably fast and accurate Japanese gunners, whose ships were now under the orders of Gotō's second in command, Captain Kijima Kikunori. Meanwhile, the stern chase continued, with *Furutaka* taking another torpedo.

At midnight, Admiral Scott attempted to reorganize his battle column and for that purpose once again ordered the ships to cease firing, an order not universally respected. Once again he ordered the ships to switch on their recognition lights: two green lamps vertically over a white. As midnight of the 11th yielded to Monday, October 12, the

Japanese continued to flee as best they could. *Aoba* was hit over forty times by 8- and 6-inch shells as Gotō lay dying aboard the flame-wrapped cruiser, which was still maintaining steam. The much-battered heavy cruiser *Furutaka*, with a shattered No. 3 turret and a torpedo tube and both engine rooms in flames and then flooded, was in a very bad way to the northwest of Savo Island. She would be abandoned there at 0238 before sinking and joining the destroyer *Fubuki*, both having suffered heavy casualties.[20]

Scott now ordered the resumption of the stern chase, which did not prevent the Japanese from making excellent use of their guns. Scarcely scratched throughout the melee, the heavy cruiser *Kinugasa* trained her 8-inch guns on the searchlights of Captain Edward Morgan's *Boise*, peppering her from bow to stern. She was saved only by the swift maneuver of *Salt Lake City*, which came up smartly to shield the now-burning ship, permitting her to slip away. Far above the battle, *San Francisco*'s lone float plane dropped flares over the Japanese ships as U.S. guns fired away. Although *Salt Lake City* received some minor damage, the unfortunate *Boise* seemed to serve as a veritable magnet for the big 8-inch Japanese guns. One blast smashed through her No. 1 turret and another pierced the armored hull well below the waterline, detonating one magazine and then all the forward magazines right up to the forward turrets, literally tearing men and gun crews apart when not incinerating them. The ship's damage-control team having fallen victim to the destruction, the flaming *Boise* was saved only by a wall of seawater gushing through her gashed hull, effectively extinguishing the raging flames by 0020 on the 12th.

Admiral Scott's column no longer existed, as his ships took evasive action to avoid lethal enemy fire and torpedoes. Fearing that the coming mayhem might cause his vessels in the rear to mistake their own destroyers for the enemy's, Scott ordered all ships to break off at 0028 and began to take count. Three—*Boise*, *Farenholt*, and *Duncan*—failed to answer *San Francisco*'s order to flash their recognition lamps. Having altered his course from NW to SSW for the second time, Scott considered pursuing the enemy after reassembling his column, but at one o'clock the admiral broke off the action definitively, and destroyer *McCalla* escorted the three damaged ships. Somehow the *Boise* was able to maintain 20 knots, quite a feat for such a battered vessel, one that had suffered 142 dead and wounded. Her captain would have many a letter to write to the bereaved. *Farenholt*, too, managed to retreat under her own steam.

At morning's first light, Henderson Field finally launched planes that had done nothing during the night. As they passed over the blackened mass of twisted steel known as the *Duncan*—her bridge smashed, charthouse gone, and all communications destroyed—Lieutenant Commander Taylor ordered the wounded down to the life rafts even as some of her gunners continued to fire. Taylor and his officers, now completely cut off by the fire and gnarled steel occupying what was left of the bridge, themselves barely escaped by diving into the sea. Lieutenant Herbert Kabat, at Battle II, took over command and attempted to beach the *Duncan* on Savo Island, for the guts of the ship were now a mass of flame. But he and the remaining few men aboard were at last forced to abandon the valiant little ship. Although the executive officer tried to reboard her an hour later, the attempt was in vain, and he joined the other officers and men in the sea fighting floating sheets of oil-fed flames and swarming sharks that were beginning to take further victims. The *Duncan* finally sank off Savo Island just before noon that same day. She had lost 48 men, but 195 were saved.[21]

The Japanese warships, among their number the wounded *Aoba* and *Kinugasa*, had by now sailed north through the New Georgia Sound for their base at Shortland Island. The convoy had successfully landed its reinforcements; but while sailing back to Shortland the following day, it was attacked by dozens of U.S. warplanes, which sank the destroyer *Natsuguma* and so badly damaged another, the *Murakumo*, that she had to be scuttled. Captain Kijima was relieved of his temporary command.

In the end, Scott had lost the *Duncan* while the *Boise* and *Salt Lake City* headed for drydocks in safer waters. He had suffered fairly high casualties and made many mistakes, but it was not for want of courage in battle, often in the face of inevitable death. Moreover, for the first time in the war, the Japanese had been met at night by the U.S. Navy and forced to retreat. The battle of Cape Espérance was a clear American victory in that sense and in the tonnage of ships sunk. On the other hand, Admiral Mikawa had achieved most of his objectives, with another seven hundred reinforcements successfully landed at Tassafaronga along with some powerful artillery pieces and a large supply of munitions.[22] Amid the perils and confusion, Kelly Turner, for his part, had safely landed the 164th Regiment of the Americal Division on Guadalcanal on the 13th.

The Japanese were relentless, however, their places again bombing Henderson Field heavily on the 14th. And they could fly at night, while American pilots still crouched in foxholes. Something was very wrong indeed, both at Henderson Air Field and at Admiral Ghormley's headquarters. As for Admiral Mikawa, he simply ordered another task force to sea, including the battleships *Kongo* and *Karuna*, each of whose sixteen 14-inch guns spewed flames and death into Vandegrift's camp late that same October 14. Archie Vandegrift and his much-battered marines remained more discouraged than ever, and at dawn on October 15, five more enemy transports landed on "Cactus." Ghormley did nothing.[23]

CHAPTER XVIII

"A Goddam Mess"

"All the Amphibious Force ships, all my staff, and I myself are working our hearts out to keep you going. . . . Your situation as regards food, fuel, and ammunition as you well know, gives me the greatest anxiety. This is still a hand-to-mouth existence. . . ."

—*Admiral Kelly Turner to*
General Archie Vandegrift,
November 7 and 16, 1942[1]

"My anxiety about the Southwest Pacific is to make sure that every possible weapon gets into the area to hold Guadalcanal, and that having held in this crisis, munitions, planes and crews are on the way to take advantage of our subsequent success."

—*Franklin D. Roosevelt,*
Memorandum to Joint Chiefs of Staff,
October 24, 1942[2]

After landing the 164th Infantry Regiment of the Americal Division and many tons of badly needed supplies and aircraft on October 13, 1942, Kelly Turner dispatched the battle-weary Marine 1st Raider Battalion for a much-needed rest at Nouméa, even as Rear Admiral Scott's battered task force limped across the Pacific for repairs.

The next day, enemy bombers destroyed or damaged half of the ninety newly arrived warplanes, not to mention the remaining fuel storage tanks and many of the munitions Turner had just delivered. Once again the question was asked: how was such a large enemy force, with accompanying fighter cover, permitted to fly hundreds of miles down the Slot without being reported to Henderson? And to add to the general gloom on 'Canal, a new element of terror was introduced as heavy field artillery, landed by Japanese destroyers just days earlier, now began the regular shelling of Henderson Field, day after day, night after night, for the next several weeks.

The Seabees were working round the clock to repair the pockmarked airfield while transports, barges, and converted submarines brought in supplies, which included that very precious commodity, aviation fuel—that is, when enemy planes and subs did not get them first. Even before Turner had weighed anchor, another powerful Japanese task force, under the command of Vice Admiral Kurita Takeo, was steaming down Ironbottom Sound, escorting yet another convoy of reinforcements. Secure in the knowledge that four of the five U.S. aircraft carriers lay at the bottom of the sea, Tokyo, maintaining the momentum, was determined to throw the Americans out. Obviously this was the time to strike, and remorselessly so.

Convoy after convoy had come down the Slot, and still Ghormley failed to take sufficient measures either to detect or deter them, in spite of Admiral Nimitz's recent personal admonition at the Nouméa meeting. And Admiral Kurita's force of two battleships, a light cruiser, and five destroyers went once again undetected not only in the Slot but even as it sailed right past the unguarded choke points of Savo Island. Where were the U.S. picket destroyers and submarines allegedly patrolling these waters, if only during daylight hours, Vandegrift angrily asked Nouméa. And where were McCain's and MacArthur's dozens of reconnaissance planes, available at army and navy airfields and responsible for this surveillance? Where, for that matter, was the badly needed coastal artillery for Savo and Guadalcanal? Turner put his finger on part of the problem in a private letter to Captain William Greenman, as he explained, "One of our troubles is to get decisions [i.e., by Ghormley] on matters I do not have under my control, and to get material to you which is available, but for which we have no transportation."

Thus, once again U.S. forces were taken completely unawares when at one o'clock in the morning of October 14, the 14-inch fragmentary shells of the battleships *Kongo* and *Karuna* exploded over Guadalcanal, their sixteen big guns wreaking havoc on Henderson and the American camp. The battleships continued to fire almost with impunity, the marines possessing only 5-inch coastal guns that could not even reach those big ships. American planes that should have been in the air before the enemy arrived were now instead being methodically shattered on the ground, the field so thoroughly cut up that it was too late to get them launched.

Indeed, the only effective action was taken by the young skippers of four newly arrived PT, or motor-torpedo boats, at Tulagi. Their men roused and at General Quarters, the light craft tore across the open waters of Ironbottom Sound* within minutes, soon weaving in and about the startled Japanese destroyers, with whom they exchanged torpedoes and machine-gun fire. These four small boats may have done little damage, but their unexpected and erratic action was enough to unsettle Admiral Kurita, who, having expended most of his ammunition, at 0220 ordered his task force to hastily withdraw. These wooden-hulled PT boats were most vulnerable, to be sure, but they were also very small and fast, proving difficult targets for the enemy. And at least they and their high-spirited crews were doing something. Kurita's ships escaped without further ado or interference from the Americans.

That morning, as Seabees continued to repair the runways at Henderson, the toll was taken yet again: forty-one dead this time and a great many wounded. As for the newly arrived warplanes, of the original ninety, only forty-two remained, with enough fuel for just one mission for eleven of them. Back at Pearl Harbor, the reports coming through left Chester Nimitz a very worried man.

Even as Kurita was steaming northwest back up the Slot on October 14, he passed the next Tokyo Express going in the opposite direction: six transports escorted by destroyers. By the time the eleven planes from Henderson finally arrived, their big quarry, including the battleships, had already disappeared from sight. Instead, the Americans continued to be caught off guard and checked by Japanese fighters flying protective cover for the equally unexpected fresh transports. U.S. planes managed to damage only one of the destroyers slightly. As usual,

* So named after the sinking of so many vessels in those waters.

all the transports successfully reached Tassafaronga on October 14–15, as Mikawa's cruisers *Chokai* and *Kinugasa* simultaneously gave Vandegrift's men a good drubbing for the second night running. This time there were no PT boats available to run interference.

The next morning, the Japanese could be seen calmly disembarking 4,500 more troops on the beach near Tassafaronga in broad daylight.[3] There was not a single U.S. Navy vessel in sight. Meanwhile, just enough gasoline was being ferried to Henderson by transport planes all the way from Espíritu Santo, permitting the quick launching of a mélange of pilots from the three U.S. services—army, navy, and marines—to strafe and bomb the transports. At the same time, they were fighting off the highly maneuverable Zeroes, downing seven of them. Three large, partially unloaded transports were badly damaged and had to be beached, with the others sailing for the Shortlands before four o'clock that afternoon. But once again there were no American carrier planes in sight, and taking advantage of that, two more Japanese cruisers, *Myoko* and *Maya*, approached the island and for the third consecutive night bombarded Henderson Field. Nor had Ghormley dispatched a single warship there, claiming that all available vessels had gone to the Atlantic for the landings in French North Africa, which was false. Far below the ocean surface, Admiral Lockwood's U.S. submarines did sink three enemy freighters; but other than that the only immediate help coming was a ship en route with a few more U.S. planes. By now the situation was quite desperate. Something had to change.

●

Enough was enough, even for the long-suffering Admiral Chester Nimitz, who flew into Nouméa for an emergency conference on October 15 with his old friend from the Academy days, Bob Ghormley, and Archie Vandegrift. "We are unable to control the sea," Nimitz declared abruptly. "The situation is not hopeless, but it is certainly critical."[4]

The Japanese now had some 22,000 troops on Guadalcanal—20,000 more than they had had on August 9, when the marines had landed. U.S. forces, including support personnel, stood at 23,000. By November 12, the Japanese figure would reach a maximum of just over 30,000 men. Nimitz promised to have 50,000 U.S. troops in place by the end of the year. Morale was low on Guadalcanal, and Nimitz found it far worse now aboard Ghormley's sweltering headquarters ship, *Argonne* (the French Gaullist officials still having refused to allow U.S. commanders and staff to land and use offices on New Caledonia). Indeed, Nimitz was deeply shocked by the atmosphere of all-pervasive despair here. Moreover, with temperatures aboard the steel-plated warships above 120 degrees (up to 150 degrees below decks in the engine room), and portholes closed much of the time because of the constant infestation of hundreds of thousands of flying insects, life was barely tolerable at best. About the only positive news was the anticipated arrival of Vice Admiral Bill Halsey from California, who was coming to hoist his flag in the one remaining U.S. carrier.

By now the usually mild-mannered Nimitz had had enough and ordered Ghormley to pull himself together, to assemble his scattered men on various islands, ships, and planes, and, instead of whining, to move in and protect Guadalcanal and the marines. Why had he not been using idle warships, so ineffectually deployed elsewhere, to help halt the Tokyo Express?[5] Never in his career had Nimitz been forced to give a senior flag officer such a dressing down, but men were dying daily because of Ghormley's incompetence and failure to act.

The fact is that both Ghormley and MacArthur had continued to be against the Guadalcanal campaign since the beginning, albeit for different reasons, and both of them now stated that the United States would be forced to evacuate that island. This rank pessimism—defeatism would be more accurate—could be seen on the faces of Ghormley's staff, as Nimitz immediately noticed during his visit. For his part, Chester Nimitz promised to rush all of the central Pacific American airfields' warplanes out to Guadalcanal while ordering the army's 25th Division, presently in Hawaii, to embark immediately to reinforce Vandegrift. Before flying back to Pearl Harbor, Nimitz left a message to be given to Admiral Halsey upon his arrival. Once back at his GHQ on Makalapa Hill, Nimitz summoned an emergency staff conference concerning the situation.

•

After spending a few days of consultations in Hawaii, Bill Halsey flew out to the South Pacific to take up his new carrier command off

Guadalcanal. Charles de Gaulle's Free French refusing to allow him to land at the Nouméa airport, his seaplane set down in the harbor at 1515 on the afternoon of October 18, 1942. As he stepped down onto the barge Ghormley had sent for him, Ghormley's flag lieutenant handed him a sealed envelope, which he tore open and read as the boat headed for the USS *Argonne*. Halsey's big, bushy eyebrows suddenly shot up. "Jesus Christ and General Jackson!" he exclaimed before a startled lieutenant, as he read the brief note:

> Immediately upon your arrival at Nouméa, you will relieve Admiral Robert L. Ghormley of the duties of Command of South Pacific and South Pacific Forces.
>
> NIMITZ

"This is the hottest potato they ever handed me!" he marveled.[6] At this time, Admiral Halsey was perhaps the most popular officer in the U.S. Navy, and staff headquarters became a different place literally the day he came aboard. He was a dynamic leader, at times almost reckless, and a real fighter regardless of the odds. Nothing was impossible for him.

Nimitz had given him carte blanche, and Halsey began to act immediately. First, he called in General Vandegrift for a report on Guadalcanal. With no ships guarding the Slot and "Cactus," and with no fresh reinforcements for his battered battalions, Archie Vandegrift was most grateful for this change of command. "I held nothing personally against Ghormley, whom I liked," he commented later. "I simply felt that our drastic, imperiled situation called for the most positive form of aggressive leadership at the top. From what I knew of Bill Halsey, he would supply this like few other naval officers."[7]

After explaining the situation in some detail to Halsey, the new commander of the South Pacific asked Vandegrift, "Can you hold?" "Yes," the exhausted marine replied, "I can hold, but I have to have more active support than I've been getting." "You go on back there Vandegrift," Halsey assured him. "I promise you everything I've got."[8] The marine commander gave a sigh of relief and smiled for the first time in two and a half months.

Next, Halsey unilaterally canceled the operation already in progress for the seizure of the Santa Cruz Islands, intended to provide a badly needed airfield at Ndeni. Instead, he ordered that troop convoy, already at sea, to set a fresh course for Guadalcanal. Meanwhile, Nimitz was also sending troop reinforcements and fifty warplanes immediately, as promised, not to mention an additional twenty-four submarines to defend the waters around the Solomons and those between the islands and New Caledonia.[9] This was bolstered by the unexpected good news that a second carrier, the *Enterprise*, was on its way, fully repaired and accompanied by a new battleship, *South Dakota*, to create TF 16. These ships would in turn rendezvous with TF 17 and the *Hornet* on October 24. Halsey, himself a part-time aviator, unfortunately named Tom Kinkaid, a non-aviator, to command the two carriers,[10] a decision that Jack Towers and other senior officers in naval aviation strongly opposed.

The situation in the southern Solomons was "a goddam mess," Halsey told his old friend Kinkaid. "Look around and see what's to be done, and do it." Halsey ordered Kincaid to drive his ships aggressively, establishing a station to the north of the Santa Cruz Islands.[11] The carriers would now be closer to any enemy forces heading for Guadalcanal, permitting them to locate ships and intervene well in advance. October 1942 was not yet over, however, and was subsequently to be long remembered by old sailors for the extreme setbacks that still lay ahead, setbacks that would try the likes of even a tough Vandegrift and an equally determined Bill Halsey.

•

In a less dramatic, indeed almost unnoticed, move, Jack Towers, the first naval aviator to be promoted to the rank of vice admiral, was being transferred to deal with all naval aviation in the Pacific. In his new capacity he would serve directly under the command of Chester Nimitz in Hawaii. Towers, as the dynamic head of the Bureau of Aeronautics in Washington, D.C., and therefore air chief of the U.S. Navy, had accomplished a great deal, preparing the pivotal actions that would see their development and startling transformation over the remaining years of the war. Secretary of the Navy Frank Knox, a loud, egotistical newspaperman but dedicated navy advocate, had never liked the unassuming but grimly determined Towers, who was anything but a sycophant.

The officers who had served with or under Towers over the years knew him far better than any politician. They realized what extraordinary work he had quietly achieved over the past three decades and were greatly appreciative of his equally extraordinary prescience in matters where naval aviation and carrier development and tactics were concerned. He was "the kind of man who wouldn't take any credit for anything he did, and I never noticed that he got particular credit anyway for a lot of things that he did [achieve]," commented his lifelong friend and fellow naval aviator William "Gus" Read.[12] Towers's contribution to the ultimate victory over Japan was, Read said, "incalculable." Yet there were some, like Read, who while fully cognizant of Towers's achievements, nevertheless criticized King and Frank Knox for his transfer now. The *New York Times* complained that this move left "no airman in a position to participate in the strategic thinking of the Navy."[13]

This seasoned line officer would gradually earn the respect and trust of Nimitz by correcting and modifying carrier tactics, decisions that would win great battles and even influence and help create the critical island-hopping strategy required to advance to Japan itself. It was a strategy whose origins are sometimes erroneously attributed to Douglas MacArthur alone, but MacArthur in fact was to reject several of those major proposals in order to provide himself and the army with a greater role in the Pacific and its conquest.

On October 14, Vice Admiral Jack Towers, as Commander of the Air Fleet, Pacific (COMAIRSOPAC), arrived at his new headquarters on Ford Island, just across the sound from Nimitz on Makalapa Hill. Although the relationship between Towers and Admiral King was tense—as it was between King and every one of his colleagues and subordinates—others who had worked closely with Towers over the years continued to praise him, including future Supreme Court Justice Carl Vinson and Treasury Secretary Henry Morgenthau, the latter assuring Towers that the nation was indeed fortunate in "having a man of your caliber" in this new important post in the Pacific.[14] And since Captain Forrest Sherman—himself a brilliant aviator—was now free after the sinking of the *Wasp*, Towers quickly snapped him up as his new chief of staff.

In his capacity as COMAIRSOPAC, Towers was given a formidable task little understood by the general public. One of his duties was to supervise three new fleet commands—at Seattle, Alameda (near Oakland, California), and San Diego—which were responsible for providing the Pacific with the planes and pilots needed throughout the war. Towers was also in charge of all aircraft repairs and maintenance, as well as training, tactical doctrine, and the state of combat readiness of every plane flown by the navy and marines in the Pacific. This of course encompassed those on all carriers, which ultimately meant thousands of aircraft.[15] As noted earlier, over the preceding years Towers had helped to develop, design, order, and produce every type of fighter, bomber, and seaplane employed by the U.S. Navy throughout the war. Now he was going to see those planes in action.

Some navy veterans perhaps remembered Fleet Problem VIII of June 1928, when a certain Captain Jack Towers, as skipper of the carrier *Langley*, had prepared the plans for and the execution of the first successful simulated surprise air attack against Pearl Harbor, at a time when everyone had said it was quite impossible. On March 29, 1938, Admiral King, then in command of the fleet, and Flag Captain Towers in command of the carrier *Saratoga* from a point northwest of Oahu, had launched another successful predawn air attack exercise against Pearl Harbor, yet again catching both the army and navy there off guard. Facilities everywhere would have been destroyed had this been the real thing. Admiral Yamamoto, for one, had carefully studied the reports of this exercise and then with equal but more destructive success followed Towers's plan three years later in December 1941, launching real bombs and torpedoes, sinking real ships, burning real planes, and killing real Americans, some of whom had received him as a guest in their homes many years earlier. U.S. naval and army commanders had learned nothing since Towers's first warning back in 1928, fourteen years before.[16] But Admiral Ernie King was now commander in chief of the U.S. Navy, and he had sent the best airman in the navy, Admiral Towers, to Hawaii to serve under Admiral Nimitz to see that this time, the carriers and their planes were put to their best use . . . at long last, and after so many tragic losses.

To be sure, Admiral Towers's aloof, almost formal manner did not smooth the way for him with Nimitz and his team, and in particular with Nimitz's chief of staff. Vice Admiral Raymond Spruance, himself a block of human ice, had never liked Towers or, for that matter, naval aviation. Alas, neither Nimitz nor Spruance were pilots, and indeed were both traditional "black shoes," career officers steeped in the mystique of battleships as the key to, and principal vessels of, any fleet. Although Spruance remained closed and even hostile to the role of aviation in the new navy, Chester Nimitz fortunately was at least open-minded, capable of accepting new ideas even if there still was not yet a single aviator on his staff.[17] The two felt—as did many career officers—that a line officer who spent most of his career in naval aviation was incapable of commanding warships and fleets, despite the fact that every aviator, including Towers, wanted to, and in many cases did, assume such command during his career. At this stage, Nimitz still believed in, and relied strongly upon, the judgment of Ray Spruance, deliberately keeping Towers at a distance, even though Towers was his air chief for the entire Pacific. It would take many months and campaigns before Nimitz gradually came to see and appreciate Towers's true worth and the wisdom of his advice and analyses; in turn, Towers would begin to pull away from Spruance's judgments and decisions in future battles and operations. Eventually it was Jack Towers who would be raised to the position as deputy CINCPAC, given license virtually to run Pearl Harbor during the final months of the war when Nimitz moved his advance headquarters to Guam. Given the tragedies now about to waylay the American navy in the Pacific, Jack Towers's presence was sorely needed.

•

"KILL JAPS, KILL JAPS, KILL MORE JAPS!" read the large, hand-painted sign over the fleet landing at Tulagi, practically an exact quotation from Admiral Bill Halsey himself. An exasperated Franklin Roosevelt still was not satisfied with the slow assistance being given Vandegrift and his marines in the Solomons. On the 24th of that eventful October, the president ordered the Joint Chiefs of Staff "to make sure that every possible weapon gets into that area to hold Guadalcanal. And that having held it in this crisis that munitions, planes and crews are on the way to take advantage of our [subsequent] success."[18] More artillery, planes, and an additional six thousand marines were soon en route to the beleaguered island of Guadalcanal, even as the Allies received the grim news of the sinking of eighty-eight British and American merchant ships that same month by the German and Italian navies in the Gulf of Mexico, the Atlantic, and the Mediterranean.[19]

In the Pacific, the Japanese continued to push on relentlessly, moving one hundred warplanes from Rabaul up to the newly completed airfield at Buin, on the southern tip of Bougainville. This was a superb strategic ploy that now gave Japan an air base at the northern end of the Slot, saving hours of flying time while permitting even its fighters to attack Guadalcanal and American warships at their leisure. It was just one of the steps taken as the Japanese high command prepared its next offensive.

> After reinforcement of Army forces has been completed [a Japanese imperial directive now stated], Army and Navy forces will combine and in one action attack and retake Guadalcanal Island airfield . . . the Navy will take whatever action is required to stop the efforts of the enemy from augmenting his forces in the Solomons Area.[20]

Both Admirals King and Nimitz were more determined than ever to foil those plans, but they still lacked the means with which to check the regular arrival of the Tokyo Express with further reinforcements. Nor did Nimitz and King realize that General Maruyama's troops were ordered to be in possession of Henderson Field by October 22.[21]

On Guadalcanal itself, nightly Japanese naval bombardment continued, now introducing the more deadly antipersonnel, high-explosive (APHE) shells. These were followed by almost daily air raids as well. Sleep, along with just about everything else, was in short supply for the marines and soldiers on "Cactus." But despite the recent reinforcement provided by the 164th Army Infantry Regiment, the U.S. forces were barely equal in number to those of General Hyakutake, who now confined most of the marines to the perimeter of Henderson Field as Japan prepared to unleash its next concerted attack. A major air assault would coordinate with Admiral Yamamoto's Combined Fleet, which sortied from Truk for that purpose on October 11.[22]

The attack came from the west of the airfield on October 20, with Major General Sumiyoshi Tadashi's Seventh Army artillery pounding

Lieutenant Colonel William McKelvy's battalion near the mouth of the Matanikau River. The next day an enemy tank attempted to cross that river, but was thwarted by marine artillery.[23] On the 22nd, the destroyer *Nicholas* also fired on enemy positions; this proved only a symbolic gesture compared with the tremendous artillery barrage General Sumiyoshi hurled at the marines late on the 23rd, which was followed just before midnight by a major attack of Japanese tanks and infantry. Colonel McKelvy's men held their ground, slaughtering hundreds of Japanese while the 11th Marines' howitzers destroyed a dozen tanks, halting that advance as well. But Maruyama's 2nd Division struck from the west with even greater force on the 24th against the marines' 3rd Battalion of the 7th Regiment, which was reinforced higher up the Matanikau by the 2nd Battalion, brought up from Henderson. Maruyama pushed forward, although Major General Kawaguchi was delayed in his southern attack on the central sector of the Henderson perimeter, near "Bloody Ridge." On the eastern sector, Major General Nasu Yumio was attacking along the Tenaru (Ilu) River, which was held by two army battalions of the 164th Infantry. It was Colonel Puller's weakened 1st Battalion that took the brunt of the attack there on the 24th.[24] The enemy was now on the verge of breaking through the American line.

Nasu's forces first overran a marine outpost at 2130, but the main attack came at 0030 on October 25, in the midst of a heavy tropical rain storm, as Japanese troops crossed a field of seven-foot-high, razor-like Kunai grass. Supported by a reserve army battalion, both the 164th and the marines continued to hold. They threw everything they had at the seemingly endless waves of Japanese, slaughtering them in large numbers, including their commander, General Nasu. But still the enemy did not withdraw, and that night Nasu's troops, supported by units of Kawaguchi's brigade, attacked one final time, adding to the piles of the dead at "coffin corner," as the marines now referred to it.[25]

Along the western flank near the Matanikau, Colonel Hanneken's 2nd Marine Battalion came under withering fire from Colonel Oka Akinosuka's troops and heavy artillery. As a unit, the marines had lost almost an entire company and were about to collapse; so hardpressed were they that Major Odell Conoley even distributed rifles to clerks, cooks, and messboys in an effort to knock out the devastating Japanese machine-gun fire on the ridge. He succeeded in doing so with a final hand grenade assault.

By daybreak on the 25th, all three Japanese attacks against Henderson Field had failed, and the defeated enemy, its ranks much thinned by thousands of casualties, retreated through the jungles whence it had come. The 7th Marines lost 182 men, the 164th Regiment 166 men.[26] It took a great deal of American blood and courage to hold that airfield.

On October 25, while the Americans were putting down the last of the Japanese, the three destroyers *Akatsuki*, *Izkazuchi*, and *Shiratsuyu*, then supported by the light cruiser *Yura* and five more destroyers, arrived in Ironbottom Sound for a daylight bombardment of Henderson, fully expecting that airfield to be in Maruyama's hands by nightfall, as promised by the Japanese army's chief of staff.[27]

The destroyers were the first to appear, at midmorning. Sighting two U.S. destroyer minesweepers (armed with only 3-inch guns), they gave chase, but the Americans were saved at the last minute by the chance passing of some B-17 Flying Fortresses overhead. Breaking off this engagement, the enemy ships then came upon two boats at anchor in the process of landing U.S. troops, arms, munitions, and fuel. Spying the Japanese warships, the American supply boats packed up and tried to get underway, but were hardly a match for them. By 1120 both American transports, unable to move quickly enough, had been sunk with their entire crews on board. Kelly Turner was cursing the enemy and his own inability to get more troops and supplies to Guadalcanal. That he himself was never killed during so many of these landings was a miracle. "This is still a hand-to-mouth existence. . . . The enemy has held up our deliveries so continuously that our cash-in-bank is very low," he lamented to Archie Vandegrift.[28] But he was happy to learn that the *Akatsuki* had been hit by returning coastal fire while shelling Lunga Point, leaving a trail of oil behind as she steamed away.

The light cruiser *Yura* and her five destroyers were the last to arrive, reaching the sound at 1255 to continue this brazen daylight bombardment. They were fiercely attacked by hastily scrambled aircraft from Henderson, whose bombs hit both the *Yura* and one destroyer, forcing them all to withdraw. The *Yura* had been badly damaged, and her captain was preparing to beach her at 1700 when six B-17s caught up with her, leaving that ship engulfed in flames. Abandoned off Ramos Island, she was sunk by Japanese destroyers. Back at Henderson, American fighters tangled with still another large raid by enemy bombers and fighters, shooting down 22 and bringing to 103 the number of Japanese planes destroyed over the previous nine days.[29]

•

Hundreds of miles away at Truk, an impatient Admiral Yamamoto aboard his flagship, *Yamato*, awaited confirmation from Lieutenant General Hyakutake that Henderson Field had been taken.[30] The admiral's fleet orders were straightforward: "to apprehend and annihilate any powerful forces in the Solomons area." Given the imposing size of his fleet, there seemed to be no reason why he could not achieve those ends, for in addition to his flagship, Yamamoto commanded the battleships *Kongo*, *Haruna*, *Hiei*, and *Kirishima*; the three big carriers *Shokaku*, *Zuikaku*, and *Zuiho*; and the smaller carrier, *Junyo*, all screened by fourteen cruisers, forty-four destroyers, and a half-dozen submarines.

Bill Halsey first learned that this formidable enemy force had put to sea on October 23, when a PBY reported sighting one flattop and its escorts some 650 miles to the north of Espíritu Santo. Only one of the planes sent out to attack it found anything—a large cruiser—and its torpedo completely missed the target. Nothing more was sent out that day by aircraft commander Aubrey Fitch. Why? When additional planes were dispatched the following day, they found nothing whatsoever. Yet the Japanese had only two possible objectives at this time, namely, the conquests of New Guinea and Guadalcanal, as Halsey well knew.

The carrier *Enterprise*, fresh out of drydock and attended by the new battleship *South Dakota*, returned to these waters just in time, rendezvousing with the *Hornet* on the 23rd. Their orders were to steam north of the as yet unoccupied Santa Cruz Islands and then down to the Solomons, the goal being to intercept and destroy Yamamoto's fleet while it was still approaching Guadalcanal.

On October 24, Rear Admiral Thomas Kinkaid, commanding TF 16 aboard the *Enterprise*, and Rear Admiral George Murray, an experienced naval pilot directing TF 17 aboard the *Hornet*, were searching for the enemy fleet, still unaware of its vastly superior force. On the other hand, Japanese pilots had been no more successful in finding "the" American carrier. Both forces were in for a surprise.[31]

At noon on the 25th, a long-awaited and crucial intelligence report reached Kinkaid. Two enemy carriers had been seen 360 miles to the northwest of the Santa Cruz Islands on a south-southeasterly course, heading in their general direction. Kinkaid launched a dozen search planes and twenty-nine fighters and bombers. But hours passed and nothing more was reported, and to complete the failure, seven of the returning planes crashed as they attempted to make night landings.

In fact, when Yamamoto had been spotted by the PBY, he had reversed his Strike Force to the north while allowing his vanguard force to continue south.[32] For once, Admiral Aubrey Fitch's planes from Espíritu Santo got lucky, locating Kondo's ships. An attempt to bomb the battleships, however, failed. That evening the "Cats," black PBYs specially equipped for night operations, flew out again on a search mission, locating the heavy carrier *Zuikaku* in the early hours of the morning; but their torpedoes, too, missed the big ship. The still undetected American flattops were rounding Santa Cruz when they were at last given a fresh fix on the first two Japanese carriers.

Fitch's land-based Catalinas and B-17s again attacked the enemy, again missing the battleship *Kirishima*. The army's bombing of ships in the war, by the Flying Fortresses in particular, had thus far been negligible at best despite the vast budget accorded Hap Arnold, which led Ernie King to complain about the wildly extravagant claims made by the Army Air Corps in the American press. (The four Japanese carriers eliminated at the battle of Midway, having at first escaped unscathed from army B-17s, had all been sunk by navy planes and a submarine.) And if enemy planes were not yet attacking the American carriers now, it was simply because they still had been unable to find them.

Task Forces 16 and 17 were steaming on a northwesterly heading when, at 0011 on October 26, another PBY found Nagumo's Strike Force only three hundred miles ahead of them. This report was confirmed three hours later, when the enemy was now one hundred miles closer and therefore within easy striking distance. Unfortunately, Aubrey Fitch did not relay this vital information to Kinkaid and Murray until 0512 that day—two hours after the second sighting. To be sure, Tom Kinkaid, a little more alert now, had already dispatched sixteen SBDs on a search mission from the *Enterprise* at 0500, making contact with Nagumo's vanguard at 0630 but failing to discover the enemy carriers for another twenty minutes. Even then, however, Kinkaid waited *another fifty minutes* before ordering the first *Enterprise* launch against the light carrier *Zuiho* at 0740. That attack was successful, leaving a gaping fifty-foot crater in the flight deck of *Zuiho*, although not preventing her from launching her aircraft. Another navy attack against the cruiser *Tone*, however, proved fruitless.

Nagumo, too, had sent out scout planes, the first of which broke through the heavy cumulus layer and discovered Kinkaid's carriers at 0650, the very moment American planes were bombing *Zuiho*. Fortunately for Kinkaid, Nagumo was slow in arming his planes: the initial sixty-two from the carriers *Shokaku*, *Zuikaku*, and the wounded *Zuiho* were not dispatched until just before eight o'clock that morning. By 0845 Nagumo had launched an additional forty-nine bombers, including planes from the carrier *Junyo*.[33]

Hornet got off her first fifty-three planes between 0730 and 0815, those joined by another nineteen from *Enterprise*. But both Kinkaid and Murray were slow off the mark. A more alert commander such as "Pete" Mitscher would certainly have attacked much sooner, as Mitscher's later actions would soon bear out.

At 0910 the first Japanese squadrons, numbering 135 planes, plunged through the heavy cloud cover from an altitude of 17,000 feet, swooping down upon and through *Hornet*'s low-flying 38-plane combat air patrol, which was caught napping far too close to the carrier. One bomb exploded on the *Hornet*'s flight deck, followed by a flaming plane smashing through the *Hornet*'s deck. Two torpedoes immediately struck the carrier's hull, crippling the engine rooms, while three more bombs struck deep into the bowels of the vessel, the performance concluding with another enemy plane's colliding with the bow. Within a mere ten minutes the USS *Hornet* was a smoldering, motionless hulk, hundreds of her men lying dead and wounded.

The stricken carrier, almost totally concealed by a pall of black smoke caused by burning oil, listed heavily to starboard. The punishment she took was extraordinary. Two minutes later, all the Japanese planes were gone as suddenly as they had reappeared—or to be more precise, the only two enemy planes out of the original twenty-seven that had survived the attack abruptly retreated.[34] Japan, too, had paid a heavy price, but had achieved its objective, leaving the *Hornet* a mass of twisted steel from the bridge down to the fourth deck. Commander Henry Moran, in charge of damage control, had an utterly impossible task, even with the aid of accompanying destroyers *Morris* and *Russell*, whose powerful water hoses showered the beleaguered carrier. Astonishingly, most of the bad fires were under control within fifty minutes. Alas, what the ship's captain, C. P. Mason, did not yet know was that this had been but the first of three separate air strikes by Admiral Kondo. The ship was still listing as engineers attempted to work up enough steam to get underway again. The heavy cruiser *Northampton* prepared to take *Hornet* under tow, successfully evading an isolated bomber attack as the rest of the ships escorting TF 17 circled to protect the carrier.[35]

At 0925, while the *Hornet* still lay burning, fifty-two of her aircraft led by Lieutenant Commander "Gus" Widhelm were reaching their target, Admiral Kondo's fleet. Widhelm's fighter escort of American Wildcats tangled in fierce dogfights with Kondo's combat air patrol; Widhelm's SBDs reached carriers *Shokaku* and *Zuiho* five minutes later, but were set upon by more Zekes. Widhelm was one of the first to be hit, but he ditched safely into the sea. Another navy bomber was destroyed, and two more damaged badly. Lieutenant James Vose, who had assumed command, directed the remaining eleven navy divebombers to attack *Shokaku*, and at least three 1,000-ton bombs exploded on that carrier's flight deck, also destroying the hangars below.[36] Meanwhile, six navy Avengers (torpedo bombers) that had been separated earlier from Widhelm's original squadron, having failed to find either the carriers or any lesser ships, instead attacked one of Vice Admiral Abe Hirokai's cruisers, without results. *Hornet*'s second launch was no more successful in finding the enemy carriers. Further American air strikes, however, seriously damaged the heavy cruiser *Chikuma* and carriers *Shokaku* and *Zuiho*, putting all three ships out of the battle and back to drydock for the next several months. Total Japanese casualties were not known, but *Chikuma* alone suffered 344 dead and wounded.[37]

Admiral Kinkaid's TF 16 and the *Enterprise*, some twenty miles to the east of the *Hornet*, were in turn hit by a second wave of forty-four Japanese carrier planes, launched earlier (at 0822) from *Zuikaku* and

Shokaku. It was Captain Thomas Gatch's *South Dakota* radar that first detected the approaching dive-bombers and torpedo planes when they were fifty miles from the fleet. Unlike Murray, Kinkaid had failed to provide any protective air cover, and the enemy went straight for the huge *South Dakota*, coming under a powerful barrage of flak from the battleship's new, 40mm antiaircraft guns. Gatch conned his fast-moving ship with great agility, escaping the first two dozen bombs dropped, and downing several enemy bombers in the process.

The *Enterprise*, a half-mile astern of *South Dakota*, was much more unwieldy and not as fortunate during this first attack. One armor-piercing bomb plowed through the wooden flight deck and forecastle, its delayed fuse exploding against the hull itself as the sea poured in. Another bomb struck just abaft the forward elevator, part of it destroying the hangar deck below and shearing away heavy steel to the next deck.

A second wave of Kates (Nakajima 97-2 torpedo bombers) followed, but was pounced upon by a division of Wildcats just returning from battle over the *Hornet*. Low on fuel and ammunition, the Wildcats could stay only for a few moments, "splashing" (downing into the sea) nine of the enemy. Another fourteen Kates reached the exposed *Enterprise*, nine of them surviving intensive flak to drop their torpedoes on either side of the carrier. Captain Osborne Hardison adroitly conned the *Enterprise* past three torpedoes off the starboard beam, then threw the rudder abruptly, narrowly missing a fourth. Although other Kates were brought down by antiaircraft fire, three torpedoes did hit the cruiser *Portland*, detonating but failing to explode. The escorting destroyer *Smith* fell victim to a wounded pilot, his torpedo still in place as the plane crashed into her forecastle, exploding into a ball of flame. This did not prevent *Smith*'s guns from continuing to fire against planes attacking the *Enterprise*. Extraordinary courage, determination, and heroism won the day for the *Smith*, whose fires were soon extinguished. American damage-control teams were superb.

The clear skies and calm seas of earlier in the day were now giving way to darkening cumulus. *Enterprise* attempted to clear her shattered and cluttered flight deck, pushing damaged planes overboard and turning into the wind for her returning planes as well as for those of the ruined *Hornet*. If dozens of planes low on fuel were not to be landed soon, they would all crash into the sea. As late as 1120, the *Enterprise* still reported no more "bogies" in sight when sixty seconds later *Junyo*'s launch suddenly burst through the lowering clouds, diving straight for the carrier, its prime target. Eight Japanese planes were shot down, and only one bomb landed even near the American ship. Five minutes later, the next group of that squadron followed, falling upon the escort vessels and also blasting away some of *South Dakota*'s big guns in the No. 1 starboard turret, but failing to pierce the thick armored roof protecting the gun crew. The bridge was also badly damaged, and a painful hot shell fragment lodged in Captain Gatch's neck; yet somehow he managed to order the executive officer's station to take over the steering of the ship. For several minutes the huge vessel ran out of control until the damaged telephone system was restored.

Enterprise, directly astern, had to maneuver adroitly to avoid a collision. The cruiser *San Juan* was damaged much more seriously when a bomb went through one deck after another, the bomb's delayed fuse finally igniting as it reached the hull and the ensuing explosion at once flooding the ship and jamming the rudder. At least ten enemy planes were shot down by antiaircraft fire.[38] With the *Enterprise*'s forward elevator destroyed and the hangars directly below inaccessible, all depended now on the two remaining elevators aft, resulting in long delays in accommodating the returning planes "stacked" above the carrier. Freshly arrived planes were stowed below while others, badly shot up and out of fuel, ditched into the sea, with destroyers rushing in to collect all the crews still alive. Even so, the flight deck was still too congested with *Hornet*'s planes as well, and some that had safely landed on *Enterprise* simply had to be shoved overboard. Another dozen or so planes with sufficient fuel were dispatched to Espíritu Santo, as there was still no airstrip on the nearby Santa Cruz Islands. At 1400, *Enterprise*, no longer operational or able to launch or receive more planes, had no choice but to withdraw from the battle zone.

Back at Admiral George Murray's TF 17, the *Northampton*'s first attempt to tow the crippled, burning *Hornet* had failed. It was only at 1330 on the afternoon of the 26th that a 2-inch wire cable was successfully secured, and they at last got underway . . . at 3 knots. Murray transferred his flag from the *Hornet* to the *Pensacola*, and by 1440 some

875 wounded and non-essential personnel had been evacuated to two destroyers.

But the Japanese were not through yet. At 1230 Admiral Kondo had ordered the carrier *Zuikaku* and her destroyer screen—which, along with most of the rest of his fleet, had still been steaming on a northerly heading, away from the Americans—to reverse course, launching planes to pursue the U.S. carriers. Unable to find them, however, they were recalled early that evening, and Kondo once again withdrew to the north.

Junyo, too, had resumed her original southeasterly course at 1100, and at 1315 Rear Admiral Kakuta Kakuji launched his remaining fifteen planes at about the same time that the *Hornet* was coming under tow by *Northampton*.[39] Two hours later the planes suddenly appeared over the carrier, which had been left completely unprotected by any air cover. Murray's radar had detected the planes' approach but was unable to launch a counterattack to meet the Nakajima 97-2 torpedo bombers. *Northampton* hurriedly severed her towing cable with a blowtorch and turned the ship, narrowly missing torpedoes heading directly at her. *Hornet*, on the other hand, lay dead in the water as a torpedo slammed into her. Commander E. P. Creehan, on the *Hornet*'s third deck port side, saw

> a sickly green flash . . . [that] seemed to run both forward, toward Repair Station 5, and aft. . . . This was preceded by a thud. . . . Immediately following the flashing a hissing sound as if escaping air was heard, followed by a dull rumbling noise. The deck on the port side seemed to crack open and a geyser of fuel oil which quickly reached a depth of two feet swept all personnel at Repair Station 5 off their feet and flung them headlong down the sloping decks . . . to the starboard side.

The men then formed a human chain, reaching an escape ladder that led them to the upper decks.[40]

If the Vals (dive-bombers) following the torpedo planes at 1740 failed to locate the flaming *Hornet*, not so the next wave of bombers arriving ten minutes later, one of whose torpedoes exploded on the starboard flight deck of the already ruthlessly mauled ship. With the *Hornet* listing badly and beyond repair, Captain Mason had no choice but to order all hands to abandon ship. Admiral Abe Hirokai's Vanguard force finally sank the valiant *Hornet* with a brace of destroyers at 0135, off the Santa Cruz Islands on Tuesday, October 27.[41] Kondo had intended to return again, but after two navy "Black Cat" PBYs attacked the *Zuikaku* and one of his destroyers was crippled, at 0200 on the 27th he finally ordered all remaining ships, including *Junyo*, to break off action and return to Truk, thus ending the battle of the Santa Cruz Islands.[42]

Kondo's powerful Striking Force and Advance Expeditionary Force, whose intent was to seal the fate of the marines and GIs on Guadalcanal, failed to execute their orders and meet their appointment there. This was probably the deciding factor in saving the American position on Guadalcanal that critical October 1942. General Vandegrift had pleaded with Nimitz and Halsey for help from the U.S. Navy, and they had sent it, but there had been a very high price to pay for this ill-coordinated effort. The *Hornet*, with a casualty list of 219 men—most of them killed outright—had gone down, and many men were lost aboard other ships. The *Enterprise* had suffered severe structural damage and more casualties, in part because TF 16 and 17 were not given precise enough air surveillance information in advance. On the other hand, Admiral Yamamoto's plans to land on Guadalcanal personally to receive Archie Vandegrift's surrender were foiled yet again, despite his deployment of a vastly superior force. What is more, he had lost another one hundred veteran pilots and their planes, pilots whom Japan was already having difficulty replacing.

Nevertheless, the American fleet disposition had been poor, and there was not even a single submarine screening Kinkaid's thin Task Force. Time and again Kinkaid himself had failed to launch planes, even to protect the vulnerable carriers and ships with a proper combat air patrol. With their excellent new search radar, why were fighters not sent out in advance to intercept attacking enemy warplanes well before reaching the fleet? Indeed, why were the Japanese carriers themselves not attacked *before they had the opportunity to launch their first strike against the* Hornet? As Admirals Turner, Towers, and Nimitz constantly repeated, *strike at the source*, instead of simply waiting for the enemy to come to you.

Many strange things had been happening within the U.S. Navy since the battle of Savo Island, and many tough questions had to be confronted by those in authority after this fourth carrier battle. One of the few men with some of the answers was Vice Admiral Jack Towers, but no one was listening sufficiently yet, not even the normally open-minded Chester Nimitz. Apparently there would have to be more deaths before Nimitz and King would be willing to act to make the sweeping decisions required. But at least Nimitz did relieve Ghormley, Fletcher, and Noyes, among others. As Admiral Nimitz had soberly acknowledged to his staff even before this disastrous battle of the Santa Cruz Islands, the U.S. Navy was still "unable to control the sea."[43] Or in the words of the more plainspoken Bill Halsey, the situation in the Pacific remained "a goddam mess."

CHAPTER XIX

"Friday the Bloody Thirteenth"*

"I don't want to hear or see such pessimism. Remember the enemy is hurt too."

—*Nimitz to staff, November 15, 1942*[1]

"The men of Guadalcanal lift their battered helmets in deepest admiration."

—*General Archie Vandegrift to CINCPAC, November 1942*[2]

The outcome of the battle of the Santa Cruz Islands, October 26–27, 1942, had a most sobering effect on the American naval high command, nowhere more so than at Nimitz's headquarters in Pearl Harbor.

On November 9, Admiral Towers, as naval air chief of the Pacific, made several suggestions to Admiral Nimitz, beginning with the urgent necessity of removing Tom Kinkaid as a carrier commander and replacing him with Rear Admiral "Pete" Mitscher, a highly skilled pilot who truly understood carriers. It would take yet another battle, however, before a reluctant Chester Nimitz would begin to appreciate the wisdom of this advice. In fact, Mitscher, Towers, and even young Forrest Sherman were probably the best carrier commanders available. But for now, Nimitz and his chief of staff, Spruance, rejected Towers's advice.

*An expression of Samuel E. Morison's—Morison, *The Struggle for Guadalcanal*, p. 258.

Nimitz's staff, all non-aviator "black shoes" known as the "Gun Club," preferred battleships to carriers, referring disparagingly to Towers and the other pilots as "brown shoes." So endemic was this prejudice against naval aviators that Nimitz did not even invite his air chief, Jack Towers, to his nine o'clock morning staff conferences.

In an earlier memo to Nimitz of October 28, Towers had revealed that unlike the non-aviators on Nimitz's staff, he had a much wider, more balanced perspective on the position in the Pacific. As a result of the Japanese loss of four carriers at Midway, he said, "the present situation in [the] Pacific indicates to me [the] probability of more extensive use by the Japanese of heavy surface forces [battleships and cruisers]. Because of the attack on Pearl Harbor our [own] position is weak. Temporary disablement of one of our BBs [i.e., battleships, in Halsey's fleet] by torpedo might render it critical."[3] Japan's recent losses of planes and pilots and damage to its carriers considerably reduced the threat from that quarter for the moment, he pointed out. He also agreed with Halsey that when not on an offensive operation, American carriers should take advantage of their great strategic mobility and keep well out of range of land-based aircraft.[4] Nevertheless, Towers indicated that there remained enough old battleships at Hawaii, for instance, that some could be spared for active front-line duty in the South Pacific. Admiral Towers's prescience and analysis regarding the need for heavy surface ships at this particular time, so unexpected from an airman, was to be fully borne out soon enough that November. Towers, no air fanatic, could always remain objective, and when another class of ship besides carriers was called for, he would support its use. Nimitz would soon begin to respect this unusual judgment, so rare among his own fellow black shoes.

Having struck a powerful blow at the U.S. Navy on October 26, Tokyo was bent on yet another major attempt to take Guadalcanal. Between November 2 and 10, sixty-five destroyers and two cruisers serving as troop transports landed 13,400 men on Guadalcanal, bringing Japan's effective field force up to 30,000 men against the marines' and army's 29,000. Admiral Yamamoto was also in the process of assembling a large number of warships at Rabaul, Truk, and Shortland Island (just south of Bougainville). In consequence, Admiral Halsey, who had been intending to send the ships damaged on the 26th and

27th to Pearl for repairs, instead reluctantly ordered them to remain and have temporary repairs made there at Nouméa. At the same time he immediately ordered Kelly Turner to escort another six thousand troops from his own garrisons in New Caledonia to Vandegrift. It was a marked difference from the situation under Ghormley.[5]

There was no holding Bill Halsey back. On November 8, he flew in a Flying Fortress to Henderson Field to see the situation there for himself, something Bob Ghormley had never taken the trouble to do. What a morale booster this proved to be. A grateful Archie Vandegrift acknowledged that the visit was "like a wonderful breath of fresh air."[6] Halsey, Vandegrift, and members of their staffs climbed into Jeeps for a tour of the entire defense perimeter. Halsey being who he was, he insisted, despite occasional sniper gunfire, on stopping several times "to talk to the men," which had a rocketlike effect on their spirits. His very name was a tonic for these gaunt, weary marines, many of whom were suffering from wounds, dysentery, and malaria.

Meeting with war correspondents at Vandegrift's headquarters afterward and asked to explain his strategy, he gave a reply that was pure Halsey: "To kill Japs, kill Japs, and keep on killing Japs." When asked how long he thought the Japanese could hold out, he snapped, "How long do you think they can take it?"[7] That night, once again, a Japanese ship arrived offshore without opposition and bombarded the marines and Henderson Field. Halsey, joining the men in a dugout, began to get a very good idea of what life was like for them during these unrelenting nightly visits.

He left 'Canal the next morning, stopping en route at Efate to visit the naval base and hospital there—again, something Ghormley had never taken the trouble to do. Morale kept soaring as word got around that "Halsey is back."

●

Nouvelle Calédonie, or New Caledonia, was a strategically situated island to the southeast of Townsville, Australia, halfway between that country and the Fiji Islands to the northeast. A lovely, mountainous green island with an average temperature in the lower 80s, much like Madeira, the French territory was a favorite of Europeans. American naval strategists realized that the Japanese would soon attempt to take this country as part of their overall plan in order to cut their own naval and air routes between Australia and Hawaii.

Back on January 23, 1942, the U.S. State Department had requested the creation of American army camps and airfields on New Caledonia, and after some discussions with de Gaulle's Free French, a partial agreement had been reached. On March 9, General Alexander M. Patch had arrived at the capital and part of Nouméa with the first contingent of troops, which would soon reach a figure of over twenty thousand men.[8] Patch was not always the most diplomatic of soldiers, but he was soon popular with much of the local French population and their cooperative governor, Henri Sautot. Alas, Sautot was not de Gaulle's man, and he was ordered out over everyone's protests, including Patch's.

De Gaulle had appointed a new governor by the name of Montchamp to replace Sautot, and more important also introduced a new, anti-American Haut Commissaire for the entire Pacific region, Thierry d'Argenlieu. Politics thereafter at Nouméa were complicated, for there were also important Pétainists in support of the Vichy government of the southern half of unoccupied France who did not want the Americans at Nouméa, fearing their presence would cause the Japanese to attack. (This was the same argument Quezon had used in the Philippines earlier on. No one seemed to learn even from recent history.) It was not until May 7, 1942, that d'Argenlieu finally succeeded in putting Sautot aboard a ship bound for Europe, after which the subtle de Gaulle immediately ordered High Commissioner d'Argenlieu to "tell General Patch that neither I nor the Comité National Français will accept any interference by him in 'une affaire française.' "[9] Hence the later hostility to Ghormley's request to bring his headquarters ashore.

One of the first things Halsey did upon his arrival at Nouméa in October 1942 was to request permission to move ashore. On learning the outcome of Ghormley's earlier attempt to do the same, he dispatched Colonel Julian Brown, who was not only a fluent French speaker but had also served previously with French troops and been awarded the prestigious *Croix de Guerre*.

The meeting at Government House was duly arranged, and after the usual civilities, Colonel Brown explained the nature of his visit and Admiral Halsey's needs. "What do we get in return?" Montchamp asked. "We will continue to protect you as we have always done." Although the French had neither army nor naval units of their own with which to provide local security, that, apparently, was not what Son Excellence was hoping to hear, and he merely replied that he would give the matter due consideration.

Days passed, and no response. Then weeks. Brown returned again and again; after all, there were already American army camps and airfields on the island. Finally, an exasperated Brown had a showdown with Montchamp. "We've got a war on our hands, and we can't continue to devote valuable time to these petty concerns. I venture to remind Your Excellency that if we Americans had not arrived here, the Japanese would have." The little Frenchman simply threw his hands feebly in the air and, with a disdainful gallic shrug of his shoulders, turned his back on the official representative of the U.S. Commander of the South Pacific.

Governor Montchamp, a man with small power but a golden title, merely reflected de Gaulle's anti-American attitude. The man with real power in this region was the high commissioner, Rear Admiral Georges Thierry d'Argenlieu. D'Argenlieu, as anti-American as de Gaulle himself, had earlier threatened to throw out the Australians who were also building airfields on New Caledonia. Upon his arrival with fifteen thousand troops, the irritable Brigadier General Alex Patch had informed the Haut Commissaire that the Australians would stay, and that the airfields would be built. Ironically, Patch had found the haughty d'Argenlieu actually held prisoner by the local Pétainiste population, and it was only due to the intervention of that American general that d'Argenlieu was freed. This was too much for the Frenchman, who was more humiliated and embittered by the Americans than ever before. To him, everything was the Americans' fault (and furthermore he did not know how to say "thank you").

All this was too much for the short-fused Bill Halsey, who had the patience of a polecat. He had had quite enough of such nonsense. Calling for his barge and an impressive marine guard, Vice Admiral Halsey landed at Nouméa, marched up to the offices of the absent reactionary French high commissioner, and surrounded the building with armed marines who immediately hoisted the American flag as Halsey installed himself in his new offices. He next had the house that had formerly served as the Japanese Consulate seized for his own personal quarters, and teams of marines transferred his belongings—not to mention some good, thick American steaks—ashore to his new palm tree-enshrouded brick home on a cool hill overlooking the sea. The marines raised the Stars and Stripes and posted a guard. "The hell with it," was Halsey's only comment. An old French house was next commandeered by the admiral for more office space, to which a couple of Quonset huts were added, soon to be known as "Havoc Hall" and "Wicky-Wacky Lodge." Also, recreational facilities—hitherto forbidden to U.S. marines and troops on New Caledonia by the French governor—were now set up. The confining of R-and-R to warships in 120-degree heat after battle on Guadalcanal had not been particularly popular. All of that was changed overnight. Bill Halsey had arrived. Neither Montchamp nor d'Argenlieu lodged any complaints, and in London the penniless Brigadier General de Gaulle continued to be housed, clothed, fed, armed, and paid, courtesy of His Britannic Majesty's Government. De Gaulle could mumble, but he, too, could not complain.[10]

●

Following the tour of Guadalcanal and return to Nouméa on November 10, Miles Browning, Halsey's irascible new chief of staff, informed the admiral that urgent enemy intercepts had just revealed Japan's plans to launch its next big attack by mid-November, meaning at any time over the next five days.

At this moment Admiral Turner's latest two convoys of reinforcements, escorted by emergency cruiser-destroyer forces commanded by Rear Admirals Norman Scott and Daniel Callaghan, were approaching the beaches of Guadalcanal. Halsey radioed Turner, informing him of the critical situation and advising him that under the circumstances he would now have to have everyone landed by the 12th of the month and be underway again before the anticipated enemy attack on Guadalcanal. Halsey next ordered Admiral Kinkaid, in the *Enterprise*, to put to sea as soon as the most basic repairs to that carrier were completed. In addition to *Enterprise*, Kinkaid's new command—Task Force 67—would include two new battleships, *South Dakota* and *Washington*, a couple of cruisers, and eight destroyers, all taken from various scattered units of the region and most of which had never before worked together as a team. It was certainly not much with which to meet the usual floating Japanese arsenal Admiral Yamamoto was undoubtedly assembling. The *South Dakota*'s battered 16-inch forward turret had not been repaired, and much of the *Enterprise* was still gutted below decks. As for watertight integrity, it was thus far nonexistent. Eighty-five men were aboard the *Enterprise* day and night, acetylene torches glowing against the night sky, but no one was sure whether the forward elevator would even work. (It would not.) At least the two after elevators, however, were fully operational. Aircraft could be brought up to the flight deck and lowered to the hangars below, but much more slowly than usual. Meanwhile, Turner's transports were unloading on November 11 despite several waves of Japanese dive-bomber attacks intended to discourage them. One transport was badly mauled. But the enemy did not know the tenacity of "Terrible" Turner, despite Halsey's inability to protect him and his men on the beaches of Guadalcanal at this stage, for want of warships and aircraft.

Even as the second convoy was landing and unloading on November 12, search planes reported Yamamoto's armada at sea, 335 miles north of Guadalcanal and heading for the Slot at full speed. Nevertheless, Kelly Turner continued operations on the 12th until temporarily stopped when a Japanese plane crashed into Rear Admiral Callaghan's flagship, *San Francisco*, damaging her radar and antiaircraft-gun director. Damaged or not, every available ship would now be needed. Unprotected, Kelly Turner's transports sailed at dusk that evening, their mission accomplished.[11]

While "Operation Torch" in North Africa was unrolling in a great Anglo-American confrontation involving the armies of Germany, Italy, and Vichy France, Admiral Bill Halsey's South Pacific Force was deploying in and around the Solomons. The sole exception was the *Enterprise*, which, in spite of every effort, would be unable to arrive in time to prevent a heavy bombardment of Henderson Field and key supply depots there.

The naval strength Yamamoto had mustered for the creation of his armada reflected the urgency and importance given this vast operation by Tokyo. It was a risk to go to sea without the usual carriers and their air cover, apart from the small converted carrier *Junyo*. This was in fact the great surface fleet of yore, its tactical command in hands of the fifty-six-year-old Vice Admiral Kondo Nobutake, a gentleman with most impressive credentials.

A graduate of the Japanese Naval Academy and the Naval Staff College (of which he was later president), Kondo had served as vice chief, and then as chief of staff, of the Combined Fleet. Between 1941 and 1945 he commanded the Second Fleet during the successful invasion of the Philippines, Malaya, and Java and the failed attempt to seize Midway. He played a major role in the battles of the Eastern Solomons and the Santa Cruz Islands.[12] In brief, he was a traditional career officer who had displayed a high degree of competence in every command he held, and Yamamoto had rightly selected him to execute this major new operation with its triple objective of destroying the American Pacific Fleet and bombarding Henderson in conjunction with the Japanese land attack on Guadalcanal, while Admiral Tanaka escorted some ten thousand troops of the 38th Army Division to that island. All the units in this armada had worked closely together and under most of the same officers for years. Unlike their U.S. counterparts, they formed a highly experienced team.

Kondo's fleet was preceded first by thirteen submarines sweeping the Slot and the waters around Guadalcanal, then by the Third Fleet's Advance Raiding Force, commanded by Vice Admiral Abe Hirokai* and comprising two battleships, a light cruiser, and fourteen destroyers. This group would make the initial contact with the American forces in its role as a Bombardment Force. Next came Admiral Nishimura's Outer South Seas Bombardment Force of five cruisers and eight destroyers. Kondo himself commanded the Main Attack Force and principal Bombardment Force intended for Henderson Field, with four battleships, five cruisers, twenty-four destroyers, and the carrier *Junyo* (accompanied by Admiral Tanaka's Destroyer Escort Force). Kondo's task force was divided into five subcommands,[13] and as there was insufficient air coverage, he was to rely on long-distance air support from Vice Admiral Kusaka Janichi's Eleventh Air Fleet (some 215 warplanes) stationed at Rabaul.[14] Nothing had been left to chance. Admiral Towers's anxiety

*Not to be confused with Vice Admiral Abe Koso, who was not present.

about the need for battleships and cruisers was now fully confirmed.

Yamamoto was absolutely determined to have his "final" showdown, but Admiral Halsey was equally so, though with far fewer resources at his disposal. Task Force 67 in fact represented the totality of U.S. ships in the South Pacific available for what portended to be quite a battle. Halsey's task force included only two battleships, commanded by Admiral Willis Lee (plus, he hoped, the *Enterprise*); six cruisers, directed by Admirals Dan Callaghan and Norman Scott; and fourteen destroyers, dispersed in three task groups.[15]

For once there was no shortage of sightings of the advancing enemy armada on Thursday, November 12, 1942. After the morning sighting of surface ships 335 miles to the north, five destroyers in another group were later seen less than 200 miles to the northwest. Then two carriers were incorrectly reported to the west, whereas the carrier *Junyo*, now joined by the *Hiyo*, was in fact far to the north.

Kondo's fleet was running slightly late due to the necessity of having to reverse course a couple of times after being sighted by American scout planes. This also applied to Admiral Abe's Advance Raiding Force, which was sailing in three columns: a central one led by the light cruiser *Nagara*, the battleships *Hiei* and *Kirishima*, and a destroyer escort on each side.[16] This Bombardment Force was now using flashless gunpowder—a luxury the Americans did not yet have—which would permit the ships to conceal their positions during night action; in addition, their big guns had been armed with APHE shells. Abe was surely not anticipating an encounter with an American force at sea,[17] at least not this night, as the U.S. Navy—with only a couple of exceptions—had obligingly continued to abandon the Slot nightly. Just before midnight on the 12th, Abe was again forced to reverse course, this time because of a heavy squall northwest of Savo Island. Forty minutes later he returned to a course that would take him to Lunga Point, where his bombardment was scheduled to commence at 0130 on Friday, November 13.

Intent on avoiding another disaster like Crutchley's in this same Ironbottom Sound, Rear Admiral Callaghan had his task group in place well before the Japanese warships appeared. The crucial element of surprise was certainly on his side, confirmed at 0124 when the light cruiser *Helena*'s radar picked up Abe's first ships some fifteen miles away.[18] Callaghan did not have Abe's two battleships, but he did at least have considerable firepower behind him, his battle column led by four destroyers and followed by five cruisers—*Atlanta*, *San Francisco*, *Portland*, *Helena,* and *Juneau*—and then five more destroyers (two having been attached when entering the sound). As a result, Callaghan ordered his column to modify course slightly to starboard, bringing the ships up on a northerly bearing that would permit them to block the approaching force. They were still completing this maneuver at 0140 when destroyer *Cushing* spotted the Japanese force visually as two of their van destroyers passed between Savo Island and Cape Espérance.[19]

Abe's leading destroyer, *Yudachi*, saw Callaghan's force at 0142, alerting the other ships. Although he had the Japanese task group right before him, Callaghan froze and refused to allow his ships' captains to open fire—their very purpose for being there now—despite their advantage and their frustrated pleas to do so. His captains were bewildered, especially as no shot had yet been fired by the Japanese. What was Callaghan thinking? Admiral Abe, for his part, made a split-second decision and ordered his ships to take all their antipersonnel shells down to the magazines and exchange them for the heavier, armor-piercing ones, including those for his battleships'14-inch guns.[20] Eight minutes of feverish activity took place, leaving a paralyzed Callaghan no doubt puzzled by this long period of silence from enemy guns as the two sides approached one another at 20 knots. At 0145 the cautious Callaghan finally ordered his ships to "STAND BY TO OPEN FIRE."

But by 0150 Admiral Abe was ready and, taking the initiative from Callaghan, suddenly blinded the American ships with his powerful searchlights, as the battleship *Hiei* and the destroyer *Akatsuki* opened fire on the *Atlanta* and launched a spread of torpedoes.[21] Although American 5-inch guns quickly shot out the searchlights, the damage had been done, their position revealed. *Hiei*'s precise 14-inch salvos lashed at the *Atlanta*, concentrating on the bridge and killing Rear Admiral Norman Scott and most of his staff, while at least one of the Long Lance torpedoes struck with such impact as to knock out *Atlanta*'s engines and literally lift the heavy cruiser right out of the water. Directly behind her, on board *San Francisco*, Callaghan finally gave the order: "ODD SHIPS COMMENCE FIRE TO STARBOARD, EVEN SHIPS TO PORT."[22]

Unlike *Atlanta* and *San Francisco*, all four U.S. van destroyers had fired immediately at battleship *Hiei*. But *Cushing* had been ordered by Callaghan to withhold fire and now paid the price in full as she was pelted by 14-inch shells. Massive explosions on board caused many fires, and she quickly took on water. *Laffey*, directly astern of *Cushing* and almost colliding with the towering *Hiei* as she passed, got off a sweep of torpedoes but failed to arm owing to the short distance between the ships, the torpedoes merely bouncing off *Hiei*'s armored steel hull. *Hiei* in turn fired two 14-inch shells directly into *Laffey*, which was also hit by a torpedo, sending that valiant little ship and her crew to the bottom of the sea. As the remaining rear destroyers continued to fire at *Hiei*, one of her salvos shattered *Sterett*'s steering gear and radar mast, which did not prevent *Sterett* from reposting with four torpedoes. *O'Bannon*, next in the column, almost crashed into *Sterett* while managing to get off two torpedoes that failed to detonate. Alas, in the utter confusion of battle, too much American fire had been hitting American ships, and Callaghan had to order, "CEASE FIRING OWN SHIPS!" Although Abe ordered his ships to reverse course, he nevertheless kept up a barrage of lethal fire. *Akatsuki*, however, had been critically damaged and *Hiei*'s superstructure badly shot up.[23]

The guns of *San Francisco* now silenced, she received a heavy pounding from her port side by the other battleship, *Kirishima*. Destroyers *Inazuma* and *Izkazuchi* struck the defenseless ship from her starboard, knocking out both her steering and engines, blistering her bridge and killing Captain Cassin Young and Rear Admiral Dan Callaghan—the latter a victim of his own mistakes. Captain Sam Jenkins assumed command of the burning cruiser.

The next ship in column, the cruiser *Portland*, attempted to protect the wounded *San Francisco* when she, too, came under attack from a torpedo fired by *Yudachi*, which blasted off a part of her stern. Her steering out of control, the big ship looped in circles, although her forward turrets continued to train their guns on *Hiei*.

The light cruiser *Helena*, also coming to the defense of the battered *San Francisco*, was all the while firing her 5- and 6-inch guns, severely damaging *Amatsukaze* before having to confront a concerted attack by three of Abe's destroyers. In all the mayhem, *Juneau* had considerable difficulty identifying enemy ships, especially Japanese destroyers, whose silhouettes were so similar to those of the Americans. At 0203 *Juneau* took a deep running torpedo which convulsed her in an enormous explosion, destroyed her forward boiler room, and gravely damaged the keel, leaving a gaping hole through which the sea poured in. She, too, was knocked out of action.

The destroyer squadron astern of the cruisers was under the command of Captain Robert Tobin, aboard *Aaron Ward*. Not only had Callaghan neglected to give him any orders, but his ship had defective radar, which made it difficult for Tobin to select targets amidst the distant flashes of explosion, periods of blackness, and more explosions of the intermingling vessels. When *Aaron Ward* finally opened fire, she was immediately forced to cease because friendly cruisers more than once crossed her field of fire. Adding to the turmoil was the constant threat of collision. To avoid hitting the now badly damaged *Helena*, directly ahead, *Aaron Ward* had to go full astern, taking a direct hit in the automatic-gun director as she did so. Behind her, the seven-month-old destroyer *Barton* launched four torpedoes, only to be forced to stop her engines to avoid hitting a ship as a torpedo struck her in the forward boiler room, followed by a second torpedo. She broke in two and sank with almost her entire crew.[24]

Nor was Tobin's third destroyer, the previously damaged *Monssen*, any more fortunate. After launching five torpedoes and barely missing one herself, she fired another spread. But when suddenly lit up by an exploding starshell, *Monssen* came under intensive Japanese fire. Her captain, thinking he was under friendly fire, turned on her recognition lamps, thereby better defining her position for two Japanese searchlights and more shells. Hit time and time again, *Monssen* was reduced to a burning wreck within minutes—another American ship out of action. Callaghan's death toll continued to mount. The Americans seemed to be doing nothing right.

The captain of the last destroyer in the column, *Fletcher*, had taken advantage of her superior search radar, selecting targets with the aid of searchlights and setting another Japanese ship ablaze. With *Barton* gone, *Monssen* under heavy fire, and the situation in chaos, *Fletcher* wisely left the congested area to get her bearings. Returning to the location of the by now nonexistent American column several minutes later, she launched the last of her torpedoes and, still untouched herself, left the scene for good at a full 35 knots, weaving through a maze of crippled or burning ships and avoiding enemy fire and torpedoes all the while. High above her, the night sky was convulsed with tracer rounds, flares, and exploding shells, a setting intensified by the oil-fed flames below.

After fifteen intense minutes of battle, most of the fighting ended; at around 0200, Admiral Abe's ships, led by *Nagara*, withdrew, leaving behind *Hiei* and the badly damaged *Amatsukaze*. The battleship *Hiei* would be sunk by U.S. planes later that day, as would the *Yudachi* by *Portland*. *Akatsuki* had already gone down.[25]

Although most of the fighting had ceased, battles of another sort were taking place aboard many a wounded vessel. *Atlanta* was somehow still afloat in spite of the more than four dozen pockholes from large-caliber shells that riddled her superstructure and the water that continued to flow in from a torpedo explosion. Bodies, barely visible through the pall of smoke, littered every deck as oil and water sloshed through the compartments below and bucket-brigades attempted to quench the expanding fires that were threatening magazines. Captain Sam Jenkins, in defiance of the complete devastation around him, remained at his post, directing the damage-control crews attacking the flames. Amazingly, he managed to keep *Atlanta* from sinking.

Despite almost equally appalling damage—twisted metal jutting up, guns drooping down—the gutted heavy cruiser *San Francisco*, too, defied the laws of probability, remaining afloat, if only just. Both Admiral Callaghan and the ship's captain, Cassin Young, were dead, as were the executive and other officers on the navigation bridge. Communications officer Lieutenant Commander Bruce McCandless was left to con the ship and direct her course through the debris-cluttered sound, while back at the central station, Lieutenant Commander H. E. Schonland took overall actual command of the vessel. Schonland, an expert in damage control, personally directed the efforts to extinguish some two dozen fires eating through the steel bowels of the ship.

Portland, with her smashed stern, continued circling for the next several hours; *Helena* was completely out of action. The *Aaron Ward*, badly damaged and dead in the water, was finally towed to the haven of Tulagi along with the *Portland*. The exploding *Monssen* had to be abandoned by those still left alive and in condition to do so, and they paddled away from the flaming ship in life rafts as sharks moved in for the kill. At 0315 the *Cushing* also had to be abandoned just before she, too, went down.

Callaghan's Task Group 67 had taken a most horrible beating, one that moreover could have been avoided if the admiral had attacked expeditiously at the outset of the confrontation, while the Japanese were still incapable of fighting back. All five cruisers were badly mauled, with many dead and injured. Destroyers *Barton* and *Laffey* were sunk early on, joined in a few hours by *Cushing* and *Monssen*. Ironbottom Sound had indeed earned its name. *Helena*, *San Francisco*, *Portland*, *Atlanta*, and *Juneau*, attended by destroyers *O'Bannon*, *Sterett*, and *Fletcher*, ultimately limped away through Indispensable Strait to apparent safety. Admirals Callaghan and Norman Scott, and many hundreds of other men had also died in this part of the Naval Battle of Guadalcanal. But the list was not yet complete, for *Juneau* was sunk by submarine I-26 at 1101 that same Friday the 13th, with a loss of an additional 690 of her complement of 700 officers and men. *Atlanta*, too weak to cross the Pacific for repairs on the West Coast, had to be sunk a few days later.

Even though Abe had put Callaghan's entire task group out of commission, neither Admiral Yamamoto nor Vice Admiral Kondo was very pleased with Vice Admiral Abe Hirokai and his "shameful" withdrawal under fire. Abe had not only lost the celebrated battleship *Hiei* but had also failed to execute his orders and primary mission, to bombard Henderson Field.

The situation had to be corrected, as Yamamoto made clear. Kondo was to go down the Slot, remove Abe from his command, and add the remnants of Abe's Advance Raiding Force (the battleship *Kirishima*, cruiser *Nagara*, and four destroyers) to his own Attack Force of heavy cruisers *Atago* and *Takao* and several destroyers. His objective: to bombard Henderson Field on November 14–15 as Admiral Tanaka was unloading his eleven transports. Meanwhile, Admiral Mikawa Gunichi's Outer South Seas Support Force, which included heavy cruisers *Chokai*, *Kinugasa*, *Mayo*, and *Suzuyu* escorted by a destroyer screen, was to proceed separately to Guadalcanal by a circuitous route: well to the north of the Solomons, then straight down longitude 160 degrees between the islands of Santa Isabel and Florida, and finally past Savo Island to Guadalcanal where Mikawa was to hit Henderson the night of November 13–14, preparatory to Kondo's follow-up bombardment the next night.

Admiral Bill Halsey was still equally determined to hold "Cactus" and to prevent Yamamoto from executing his plans. With nearly a hundred workmen still aboard the *Enterprise* carrying out final repairs, Halsey had dispatched her and the rest of Kinkaid's TF 16—including the two battleships *Washington* and *South Dakota* (the latter's big forward guns still out of commission), the cruiser *Pensacola*, and two more destroyers—to halt and destroy Kondo, Tanaka, and Mikawa.

Unfortunately, the voyage of Kinkaid's TF 16 took longer than anticipated due to the sighting of enemy submarines, Kinkaid then ordering Rear Admiral Willis Lee to proceed separately to Ironbottom Sound with his two battleships and destroyers in order to prevent an attack on the night of November 13–14. The unanticipated delays at sea, however, had made that quite impossible, and in consequence the sound remained unguarded on the evening of the 13th. Admiral Mikawa's Bombardment Force was undetected as it slipped past Savo Island just after midnight, as Friday the 13th gave way to Saturday the 14th. There was not an American warship in sight, and unlike Kinkaid, the Japanese were right on schedule. Mikawa and his tactical commander, Rear Admiral Nishimura Shoji, had achieved complete surprise.[26]

Leaving Mikawa well offshore with the screen, Nishimura entered the sound with three heavy cruisers, *Chokai*, *Maya*, and *Suzuyu*, and two destroyers. Taking his station off Lunga Point and aided by a Japanese aerial spotter dropping flares over Henderson, Nishimura opened fire on Henderson Field at 0128, catching the Americans completely unawares yet again. The pilot circling the field then radioed corrections to the cruisers' gunners, who fired unimpeded until they had exhausted their ammunition at 0245 and then steamed away, encouraged by a couple of annoying PT boats from Tulagi. Following their rendezvous with the rest of Mikawa's ships at 0800 that Saturday morning, the cruisers made their exit, sailing north of Russell Island and continuing on a northwesterly course well to the west of the New Georgia Group.[27]

When American marines and GIs awoke at dawn that grim morning, they found the airfield well dug up like a lunar landscape, eighteen planes destroyed and another dozen belonging to the 67th Fighter

Squadron damaged.[28] But Kinkaid was sending an additional fifteen bombers and fighters, and by seven o'clock on Saturday the 14th, enough of the runway was filled in to permit some planes to take off in search of Mikawa. These were joined by bombers from Espíritu Santo arriving after a 600-mile flight.

They found Mikawa's cruisers off the west coast of the New Georgia Group just after 0830 that morning. The fifteen-year-old heavy cruiser *Kinugasa* took the brunt of the American attack as direct hits set her afire, destroying her forward guns and then stopping her engines altogether. She was finally abandoned and sunk off Rendova Island at 1122. Meanwhile *Chokai*, too, had been damaged by near misses and strafing, while an American plane that had been shot down crashed into the *Maya*, damaging the upper deck, guns, and torpedo tubes. Two destroyers were also damaged and one had to be towed while Mikawa himself escaped to the Shortlands.[29] The Americans had partly avenged themselves for Mikawa's bombardment, but the battle was not over yet, for Kondo's fresh force and Tanaka's convoy were still coming down the Slot for a final round in the attempt to seize this very troublesome island.

In the meantime, off Savo Island, American efforts to sink the battleship *Hiei*, badly damaged the day before, were proving to be more embarrassing by the hour. U.S. bombers, torpedo planes, and fighters attacked the ship time and time again without sinking her, *Hiei*'s crew only abandoning her at 1800 on the evening of November 14, just before the battleship slipped beneath the waves.[30]

The final phase of the battle of Guadalcanal was about to be played out. Search planes from Henderson had first sighted Tanaka's convoy in the Slot, still north of the New Georgias, at 0700 on the 14th. At 0900 Kondo's attack force and convoy were spotted by two SBD pilots from the *Enterprise*, who found the Japanese ships much closer now, between Santa Isabel and New Georgia. The two SBDs plunged down, scoring perhaps one hit, only to find themselves set upon by seven Zeroes (Zekes) from the carrier *Hiyo*. One of the SBDs was shot down while his partner escaped, safely landing on the *Enterprise*.[31]

By now the Seabees and mechanics had sufficiently repaired the field and planes to permit a much larger force to be launched from Henderson, one that would include twenty-five Marine Corps and navy torpedo and dive-bombers, escorted by a dozen Wildcats. They found Tanaka's convoy at 1150, scoring hits on several transports. No sooner had they left than another seventeen U.S. dive-bombers descended upon the convoy at 1245, sinking at least one more precious transport. Henderson dispatched even more waves of bombers. Undeterred, the remarkably cool-headed Tanaka continued to steam straight down the Slot, only to be rewarded with yet another aerial attack at 1430 by B-17s from Espíritu Santo. As usual, however, they dropped their 30,000 pounds of bombs from an altitude of over 15,000 feet, resulting in only one hit and some near misses; a final dogfight with fighters saw six Japanese planes shot down.[32] *Enterprise*'s planes, too, partook of the operation, and at 1530 her fighters found the transports when a mere sixty miles northwest of Savo, where Tanaka was attempting to re-form his convoy. Four more of his transports were hit, set afire, and abandoned. *Enterprise*'s fighters and SBDs continued to sweep down, strafing the decks of the crowded troopships without any loss of American lives. In the turmoil, Tanaka managed to transfer between six hundred and one thousand men from each of the abandoned transports to his destroyers. More squadrons followed from Henderson. By now Tanaka was down to only four of his original eleven transports at a loss of thousands of men and tons of food and munitions meant for Guadalcanal.

Having now been spotted by the enemy, Halsey intervened, ordering *Enterprise* and escorts back to Espíritu Santo and Nouméa after transferring all but eighteen of the carrier's planes to Henderson.[33] The air war diminished somewhat, and the focus shifted to the surface operations of the two navies as Kondo closed on the sound.

Influential in the action to come would be Rear Admiral Willis Lee, certainly one of the brightest of the aspiring senior officers in the U.S. Navy. Like so many career officers, he was a southerner, born in Natlee, Kentucky, in 1888, and was quite well educated before entering the Naval Academy, from which he graduated in 1908. His active career began with duty off Veracruz in 1914, followed by destroyer duty in the Atlantic during World War I, which was to prove very good preparation for what was to come. After commanding several different destroyers, he was nominated as a student to the Naval War College. His subsequent roles as executive officer of the battleship *Pennsylvania* and, later, captain of the cruiser *Concord*, lent variety to his experience in sea duty. Lee next served as a staff officer to the commander of Cruisers Battle Force and director of fleet training before being appointed assistant chief of staff to the commander in chief of the U.S. Navy. Clearly he was being groomed for superior command. In August 1942, at the age of fifty-four, Rear Admiral Lee was transferred to the Pacific as commander of Combat Division 6, his first command of battleships. He was one of the few flag officers with a detailed knowledge of the various newly introduced radar systems, possessing the rare ability to "read the screen" and draw correct conclusions. He was also known as a good ship handler, and someone who could make rapid decisions when under pressure. The Japanese navy was shortly to put him to the test.

•

Admiral Kondo's Emergency Bombardment Group next set out from Ontong, Java, at 0100 on November 14 with the battleship *Kirishima*, heavy cruisers *Atago* and *Takao* and their escorting destroyer squadron, as well as the light cruiser *Sendai* and her three destroyers. A third section, the light cruiser *Nagara* with her six destroyers, was attached en route.[34] Admiral Tanaka and his convoy proceeded down the Slot separately.

Willis Lee had by now moved his small force to within nine miles of the western shoreline of Guadalcanal. His four-destroyer screen of *Walker*, *Benham*, *Preston*, and *Gwin* was followed by his flagship, *Washington*—her powerful 16-inch guns commanded by Captain Glen Davis—and by the newly repaired *South Dakota*, under Captain Tom Gatch. Lee was new to the South Pacific and his ships new to each other, in addition to having been thrown together at the last minute by Halsey to meet this emergency. Not only had the battleships and destroyers never worked together before, but Lee also did not know his new subordinate commanders. And in his great haste, Halsey had even forgotten to assign a radio code recognition sign to the ships, yet none of his staff caught this error. Admiral Callaghan had been in a similar position with his hastily assembled force, as had Crutchley even earlier. What was more, the battleships were now restricted to the confining waters around Guadalcanal—a dangerous thing, especially under battle conditions, for big ships requiring a lot of sea room in which to maneuver. But the situation was desperate, and one had to make do as best one could.

At 2100 on the 14th, Admiral Lee's Task Force 64 entered Ironbottom Sound itself, his aim being to catch Kondo's Bombardment Group first and then to take on the screen covering the landing of Tanaka's transports. Events were to prove otherwise. As Lee steered south-southeast, the seas were calm, and for once, heavy electrical storms were not playing havoc with radio communications. At 2148, with radar still detecting nothing, Lee tried to contact "Cactus" at Henderson Field. But as Halsey had neglected to give Lee a "call sign," Henderson simply replied: "We do not acknowledge you." Lee himself finally came to the radio room and addressed Henderson personally. "Cactus, this is Lee. Tell your big boss Ching Lee is here and wants the latest information." Archie Vandegrift was an old classmate from Annapolis, and had known Lee by his nickname, "Ching." Meanwhile, Lee overheard radio transmissions among three PT boats off Savo talking about "two big ones," and fearing their mistaking him for an unfriendly force, Lee quickly added, "Call off your boys." Vandegrift came on the air to acknowledge "Ching" Lee now, informing him that the "two big boys" they were referring to were not his ships. Apart from that, there was, he said, no new information.

At 2210 on the 14th, one hour after Lee's arrival, Kondo's screen of a light cruiser and three destroyers, commanded by Rear Admiral Hashimoto, appeared off the north coast of Savo Island. Reporting the sighting of "two enemy cruisers and four destroyers,"[35] Kondo immediately dispatched reinforcements to the cruiser *Sendai* in the form of the cruiser *Nagara* and another four destroyers under the command of Rear Admiral Kimura, which arrived just as two of *Sendai*'s destroyers were sneaking around the western shore of Savo to lay an ambush. Lee, like Callaghan and Scott before him, had lost the initiative.[36] In fact it was only at 2300 hours, just after changing course in column, that *Washington*'s radar finally detected *Sendai* moving in rapidly. For some inexplicable reason, *Washington* waited *another seventeen minutes*, until 2317, before her 16-inch guns opened fire on *Sendai*, missing their target as the enemy cruiser and her destroyers quickly retreated.[37]

In the meantime, at 2322, destroyers *Walker*, *Benham*, and *Preston* spotted *Ayanami* and *Uranami* coming around the southern shore of

Savo and opened fire, after which *Gwin* fired starshell high above the sound and her guns at the larger target, *Nagara,* just north of those two destroyers. As usual, Japanese gunners responded with rapid, precise fire, hitting *Gwin* twice as *Washington* moved up to protect her. Several of *Kondo*'s destroyers next launched torpedoes, and *Walker,* already badly hit by gunfire, now took a torpedo that blew off her forecastle, leaving the fragile ship to sink. *Nagara* next battered *Preston,* destroying her funnel and both firerooms, and eventually leveling her entire superstructure. *Benham,* too, came under heavy fire, followed by a torpedo that blew her bow right off. And yet, astonishingly, none of the U.S. destroyers had yet launched a single torpedo in return.

American gunnery continued to be very poor, and when *Washington* trained her guns on *Nagara,* she missed again. As if things were not already complicated enough, at 2333 *South Dakota*'s circuit breakers tripped, and the ship lost all power for her lights, radar, turrets, and steering for three tense minutes until the breakers were repaired. In the confusion, she and *Washington* were inadvertently separated as they made their way through the maze of burning, exploding, and sinking ships. *Nagara*'s searchlight now caught *South Dakota,* and Admiral Kimura's ships launched thirty-four torpedoes at the battleship, which miraculously evaded them all. But *Nagara*'s guns, joined by those of *Kirishima,* were all too accurate in pounding *South Dakota. Washington,* in turn, trained her 16-inch guns on *Kirishima,* badly crippling that battleship. Elsewhere in the battle, *Preston* was abandoned at 2336, sinking stern first, followed by *Walker* at 2342 as *Benham* escaped clear of the area. Hashimoto's *Sendai* and *Shikinami* were now coming up to strike from the rear, and although *Ayanami* was badly damaged,* *Uranami* came to her aid. American ships were being attacked from three different directions. *Gwin,* though heavily shot up, bravely continued to fire.

At 2348, Admiral Kondo's battle column was on a westerly heading just eight miles north of Cape Espérance and ready to commence its bombardment of Henderson, only to be distracted at the last moment by Lee's big ships *South Dakota* and *Washington.* First he would deal with the American battleships, Kondo decided, swinging abruptly to

*She later sank.

attack from the southeast. Within minutes, his ships' guns had laid a heavy barrage across *South Dakota*, mottling her superstructure with shells. Meanwhile, Lee's *Washington* continued to pound *Kirishima* with her 16-inch guns, knocking her out of the fight in a mere seven minutes as flames swept the Japanese battleship. Her steering was also destroyed, and to complete this devastation, one of her own gun blasts set fire to planes on the catapults.[38] She would sink from these wounds early on November 15.

South Dakota and *Washington* also struck Kondo's heavy cruisers *Atago* and *Takao*, forcing them to withdraw from the battle. Yet *South Dakota* was already badly damaged herself, her radar knocked out along with her radio communications, and with one damaged main battery turret and the superstructure holed everywhere by large- and small-caliber shells alike. Many gunnery casualties further reduced the ship's ability to defend herself, and Captain Gatch withdrew at full speed on a heading of 235 degrees while damage control tried to cope with a series of fires raging throughout the vessel.

Unable to locate her sister ship, Lee's *Washington* altered course to 340 degrees at 0020 on Sunday, November 15, to draw fire away from the other vessels, and was immediately pursued by both the bombardment unit and Kimura's force. Five minutes later, however, Admiral Kondo ordered a halt to the chase. At 0030 he reluctantly canceled the planned bombardment of Henderson, laying a concealing screen of smoke and retreating back up the Slot with 333 casualties aboard.[39]

Having skillfully evaded a fierce last-minute launch of torpedoes by the retreating enemy, Admiral Lee's *Washington* retired from the Naval Battle of Guadalcanal at 0033 on a heading of 210 degrees for a prearranged rendezvous with *South Dakota*. After saving the entire crew of the scuttled *Gwin*, *Benham*, the last destroyer, also set out across "Torpedo Junction" for Espíritu Santo.[40]

If ever there were a dauntless sailor, it was Rear Admiral Tanaka Raizo, who, in spite of the unfavorable outcome of this three-day battle and his late arrival, was still absolutely determined to follow his orders and land the four remaining transports, which would now inevitably come under American air attack early the next morning. Tanaka was fully aware that he had been abandoned by Mikawa, Kondo, and Yamamoto, who earlier on had failed to provide him with air support either from carriers *Junyo* and *Hiyo* or from Admiral Kusaka's Eleventh Air Fleet at Rabaul. Left at this point with only a small portion of the troops originally entrusted to him and even fewer of their precious supplies, Tanaka nevertheless forged doggedly ahead.[41]

Reaching the beaches of Tassafaronga by 0215 on November 15, Tanaka began unloading his remaining four transports, for the first time coming under heavy nighttime artillery fire from the marines at Lunga Point. The change in American policy reaped immediate dividends. All of Tanaka's transports were eventually hit, and of the initial ten thousand troops of the 38th Division, only two thousand were landed, along with enough food for only four days and some munitions. The remaining troops and supplies on his destroyers never reached the shore before Tanaka finally withdrew at dawn, hauling out of Ironbottom Sound for Shortland.[42] With the coming of first light, waves of U.S. Army, Navy, and marine warplanes arrived, strafing and bombing the beached transports, destroying the complete supply of valuable howitzer ammunition just landed, and raking the newly arrived troops in the nearby jungle. Aided by the destroyer *Meade*, they ensured that all four of the mangled transports, smoke belching from their holds, would never again serve the Tokyo Express.[43]

●

The two American battleships made their rendezvous at 0900 on Sunday, November 15, after which the severely damaged *South Dakota* and the practically unscratched *Washington* sailed on to Espíritu Santo. Ultimately Admiral Lee, with the aid of air attacks from Henderson, had helped prevent most of Tanaka's troops and supplies from being landed. What was more, in the Naval Battle of Guadalcanal, which involved some of the bloodiest surface fighting of the war, Gatch and Lee had succeeded entirely in forcing Admirals Kondo and Mikawa to withdraw under heavy fire, aborting plans for the bombardment of Henderson Field while sinking both the battleships *Hiei* and *Kirishima*.[44]

The Naval Battle of Guadalcanal (or, as it is sometimes called, the Third Battle of the Solomon Sea) proved to be decisive not only in the struggle for that island but also in the eventual outcome of the war. Messages of praise and enormous relief reached the U.S. Navy. Nimitz, who had earlier chastised his own staff—"I don't want to hear or see such pessimism. Remember the enemy is hurt too"—was the first to send congratulations to Halsey as he lauded the admiral's "military audacity" at a press conference.[45] One of the most moving messages came from Henderson Field and a grateful Archie Vandegrift. "The men of Guadalcanal," he said, "lift their battered helmets in deepest admiration." Halsey, too, praised his victorious fleet: "You have written your names in golden letters in the pages of history . . . magnificently done." "We can lick them," a buoyant Navy Secretary Knox sincerely told the press. "I don't qualify that, we can lick them."[46]

The United States now began to control more of the air space over the southern Solomons and the sea around it—at least much of the time—and fewer Tokyo Expresses would come down the Slot hereafter. But American naval casualties, which numbered in the thousands, had been far higher than those suffered by Yamamoto's navy. American seamanship and gunnery, too, still left much to be desired. Nevertheless, these largely surface battles of Guadalcanal had altered the equilibrium of the war in the Pacific and put the Americans definitely on the offensive, although they did not yet realize it. As a result, MacArthur, too, was permitted to advance at long last, and his troops and those of the Australians were finally ferried around the end of New Guinea several miles south of Buna, clearing the Japanese out of that area after much fighting and a lot of help from Kenney's superb new air force. The Japanese high command had thrown practically its entire navy at Guadalcanal—except, for some reason, its available carriers—and had failed to take the island, while the Americans grew stronger week by week throughout November and December. As U.S. troop strength on Guadalcanal continued to build from 29,000 men to an eventual 50,000, the Japanese force would dwindle by two thirds before total evacuation. And for the first time in history, the invincible Imperial Japanese Navy had lost two battleships, which was symbolic in itself and a further retribution of sorts for the events of December 7, 1941. Such a triumph was thanks in large measure to two very determined sailors: Chester Nimitz and Bill Halsey.

Although the Japanese had not yet given up—and dramatic battles and defeats for both navies still lay in the future—for the first time the sons of Nippon had been forced to retreat ignominiously after their finest commanders had failed to achieve their objectives. The moment that Yamamoto himself had long ago predicted and feared had arrived. The Combined Fleet would never again attempt to take Guadalcanal. Or as one of Japan's officers put it, the fleet had come to "the fork in the road." Upon learning the outcome of the Naval Battle of Guadalcanal, a most anxious Franklin Roosevelt agreed. " . . . It would seem," he sighed with relief, "that the turning point in this war has at last been reached." Fresh reinforcements were crossing the Pacific, and American and British troops on the far side of the world were sweeping across North Africa.[47] But Tokyo's high command and emperor were not yet finished, concocting even now another unpleasant surprise for the U.S. Navy.

●

Roosevelt's optimism was, as it turned out, somewhat premature. To be sure, the *Saratoga* would soon be joined by the partially repaired *Enterprise* and several battleships, including the *Washington,* the patched-up *North Carolina,* the *Indiana,* and the *Colorado*. Perhaps even more important was the arrival of badly needed cruisers, including three heavy cruisers, *Minneapolis*, *New Orleans*, and *Pensacola* and the light cruisers, *Northampton, Helena,* and *Honolulu*. Nor were the submarine-infested waters of Torpedo Junction, bordered by the Solomons, Espíritu Santo, and New Caledonia, overlooked, where eight more destroyers were ordered to deal with that problem. PT boat strength was brought up to fifteen at Tulagi, with the addition of their tender *Jamestown*. On Guadalcanal, the Seabees were extending Henderson's 2,000-foot runway another 3,000 feet, to accommodate bigger bombers, and adding two additional airstrips for fighters. By the end of November 1942, despite all its previous losses, Guadalcanal boasted 124 warplanes of all categories. Roosevelt was keeping his word about reinforcing the Solomons.

The 1st Marine Division, having borne the brunt of most of the fighting for eleven bloody weeks, was relieved on November 4 by the 8th Marine Regiment, to be joined shortly thereafter by the marines' 6th Regiment and then by the army's 182nd Infantry Americal Division. An exhausted General Archie Vandegrift would soon be replaced by Major General Alexander Patch.[48] With the arrival of the army's 101st Medical Regiment on November 13, the medical and sanitation situation was quickly to improve, on an island infamous for its dysentery and deadly malaria. But no one could solve the problem of keeping dry on Cactus, with temperatures in the 90s and matching humidity abetted by daily tropical downpours. Dry tents and floors, like dry clothes and boots, were rare luxuries indeed.

Nimitz had by now fortunately realized the wisdom of Jack Towers's assessment of Rear Admiral Thomas Kinkaid, who was relieved of his final carrier command once and for all and instead assigned on the 24th to head the new cruiser force at Espíritu Santo, only to be reassigned on the 29th of the same month to the North Pacific and the Aleutians. Yet another new man, Rear Admiral Carleton Wright, was brought in to replace him. But before leaving, Kinkaid had prepared a careful analysis of the mistakes made in the past and had handed it over to Wright. Communications were to be simplified, searchlights were no longer to be used in night engagements; "recognition lights" were to be used sparingly and radar more effectively, as were float planes and the flares they used to identify the enemy. Destroyers were encouraged to become more independent and aggressive in battle, and after spearheading an attack and firing their torpedoes, they were to peel off to clear the way for the big ships' field of fire. There was much to be learned from the Japanese.[49] But old problems remained. The constant replacement of ships, crews, and commanding officers meant that ships had no time to practice working together as a team, let alone to know one another.

On the evening of November 29, 1942, scarcely had Carleton Wright hoisted his flag over his new cruiser command when he received urgent orders from Halsey to sail immediately for the Solomons. Several hours later, Wright was still at Espíritu Santo, and an angry Halsey radioed him a second time to remind him that "immediately" meant immediately. A lack of alertness still plagued the American command. The ships had already had steam up for several hours and were fully armed and provisioned, but Wright, who was new to the area, was a methodical ordnance man and not in the habit of receiving such orders. The emergency at hand was news of another convoy of six Japanese transports and their escorts, due to reach Guadalcanal the night of November 30. Wright was certainly put in an awkward position, a virtual stranger to his men as his Task Force 67 set off across

Torpedo Junction that night without a battle plan or even a briefing of his commanders.

On the Japanese side, Rear Admiral Tanaka Raizo, en route to Tassafaronga, had made some changes, having replaced his slow, diminishing, and poorly armed transports with destroyer convoys which beginning on November 30 would run every four days, landing men, fuel, food, and munitions. Upon reaching his destination, he would jettison rafts of troops and a couple hundred rubber-coated steel drums containing supplies and munitions while his ships were still several hundred yards from the beach—and they would scarcely slow down to do even that. He could not afford to lose more ships.

Late on the 29th, Tanaka set out through Bougainville Strait, apparently unnoticed by an American scout plane overhead. An alert Australian coastwatcher at Buin did, however, see and report Tanaka's movements. On the evening of the 30th, Wright's task force nearly collided with some eastbound American ships as they were about to enter Lengo channel, at which time Halsey ordered two more destroyers, *Lamson* and *Lardner*, to join TF 67. They received no instructions from Wright, who also failed to follow standard procedure of sending his picket destroyers ahead a full ten miles to give him enough notice of an approaching enemy. Meanwhile, the choke points on either side of Savo Island remained open and unmanned.

Carleton Wright's TF 67 entered Ironbottom Sound at 2225 on the 30th, the four destroyers in the immediate van being followed in column by cruisers *Minneapolis*, *New Orleans*, *Pensacola*, *Honolulu*, and *Northampton*, and they by the two new destroyers. Altering their course 280 degrees, they proceeded at 20 knots across the calm, black waters. Unlike Wright's ships, Tanaka's still lacked radar, but they were a long experienced team, and experts in gunnery and torpedoes.

Wright's radar first picked up the Japanese convoy at 2306, when it was only six miles distant.[50] At 2316, leading destroyer *Fletcher*, only four miles from the enemy, requested permission to launch torpedoes, but Wright hesitated, just as Callaghan had, with the same results. Wright's plans calling for independent firing were completely ignored, as were his instructions to peel away after firing. There was no response from Wright's flagship *Minneapolis* as the precious seconds ticked away, bringing the ships closer to Tanaka's force. After four very long minutes, Wright gave the "Affirmative," but it was already too late; he had lost the initiative. Closing in at 2320, *Fletcher* launched a first spread of five torpedoes, accompanied by the 6- and 8-inch guns of *Minneapolis* and *New Orleans*.

Wright had caught Tanaka at his most vulnerable moment, just as he was transferring troops and rolling the drums over the side; but the well-experienced Tanaka was a fast worker, and the *Kuroshi* was the first to launch her torpedoes at 2329. Peeling off, she was followed by *Oyashio* a minute later, which launched eight "fish," claiming two hits. Next came *Kagero*'s two spreads, then *Makinami*'s as Tanaka's ships cut away to the northwest as planned. *Kawakaze* fired nine torpedoes, but *Susukaze*, disobeying orders, fired at the American column with her largest guns. The last destroyer, *Naganami*, launched her torpedoes and was slightly damaged by an American shell. All six of Tanaka's destroyers and the cruiser *Jintsu* then withdrew to the northwest at full speed.[51]

The first two of the four dozen or so enemy torpedoes reached the American battle column at 2327, hitting Captain Charles Rosendahl's *Minneapolis*; one exploded through the hull forward of her No. 1 turret, and the other destroyed the No. 2 fireroom, creating two gigantic geysers of oil, fuel, and water on the port side that reached as high as the ship's mast. So great was the force of the two explosions that the big cruiser rolled groggily as the huge columns of water came crashing down, knocking two men overboard who were never to be seen again. At the same time, the flooding water extinguished a sheet of flames. On the bridge, Rosendahl, though momentarily stunned by the impact like everyone else, took the situation in hand, cutting power to the two forward turrets. He had always run an efficient ship, and his damage-control team, in place almost instantly, got all engines working for a time. But the ship was taking on tons of water, settling lower and lower. Every heavy object was thrown overboard to help keep her afloat, including a magazine of 8-inch shells and heavy powder charges.[52]

Captain Cliff Roper, directly astern in *New Orleans*, narrowly avoided colliding with *Minneapolis* when the latter ship suddenly lost way. But in so doing, he himself ran into a torpedo that shattered the hull and two main magazines. The explosion, even more colossal than that which shook *Minneapolis*, killed the captain and everyone else on the bridge. It literally sheared the heavy cruiser in two. The exec, Commander W. Riggs, took over the conning of the ship from the watertight after-control station in "Bat. II" as he watched the blackened bow, with its dead crew, float eerily away. A superb executive officer, Riggs kept everything under control despite the chaos around him, and his guns even continued to fire. But the situation was of course grave, with combinations of serious flooding below and spreading fires on the upper deck around No. 2 turret. Poisonous gases now formed, and several officers in the damage-control station succumbed for want of gas masks. Flooding continued unabated such that the mighty cruiser, which usually drew twenty feet of water, was now down by forty feet. But somehow the engine room worked up 5 knots, permitting *New Orleans* to pull away.[53]

In the midst of this disaster, Admiral Wright's "flare planes," catapulted hours earlier and sent on to Tulagi, finally arrived, having been delayed by the lack of enough wind to permit liftoff. They had orders to await Wright's instructions but received none, and instead of dropping their flares over the Japanese ships, merely continued to circle uselessly overhead.

Next in column after *New Orleans*, *Pensacola*, too, had to alter course abruptly to avoid a collision when the preceding cruiser was hit. At 2338, while she was turning again to clear the southern shore of Savo Island, a torpedo hit her squarely amidships on the port side, followed by another as water engulfed the after engine room. At the same time the explosions knocked out three gun turrets and the ship's electrical system, including communications and gyros, while rupturing the tanks that held tens of thousands of gallons of fuel oil now flowing to the upper deck. Sloshing around the main deck at the base of the mainmast, the fuel ignited into walls of searing flame, roasting sailors and officers alive. As in most of the other ships, the fire mains were destroyed as well, limiting firefighting to bucket-brigades and hand pumps. But at least the 13-degree list was being corrected by the jettisoning of other fuel. Despite the hellish conditions, the cool-headed Captain Frank Lowe was somehow able to maintain a few knots and turn his battered vessel away from the fighting.[54]

Directly astern of *Pensacola* came the cruiser *Honolulu*, which swung smartly to starboard to avoid collision, keeping to the lee of the two gnarled cruisers and thus shielding herself from the wash of torpedoes and enemy gunfire. These she returned in kind while increasing speed to a full 30 knots.

The final cruiser, *Northampton*, which left the column and turned to starboard while maintaining a steady shelling of the Japanese with her big 8-inch guns. Returning to a westerly course at 2348, Captain Willard Kitts saw the two torpedoes (fired by destroyer *Oyashio*) closing rapidly on his port bow and turned hard aport, but the maneuver was not fast enough: 1,320 pounds of high explosive tore through the hull, inundating the engine room as the ship began to list to port. Separately, thousands of gallons of black diesel oil gushed upward, covering the main deck aft and igniting into a devastating fire that spread across the entire length of the embattled cruiser.[55] Following the textbook procedure for a severe list, damage control jettisoned thousands of gallons of fuel and water from the lower port side. Other crews attempted to deal with the floating walls of flame, and Captain Kitts hove to in order to better cope with this nightmare. It was impossible to close the gaping holes in the hull, which had disintegrated during the first seconds of the twin explosions, and by 0015 on December 1, *Northampton* was listing dangerously at 23 degrees. Such battles were not for the fainthearted, and the captain with a salvage crew remained on board while ordering the rest of the hands to abandon ship, to be picked up later by *Fletcher* and *Drayton*.

The two undamaged destroyers following the cruisers also attempted to screen the *Honolulu*. Unfortunately, among other things, Wright had neglected to issue instructions about the recognition lamps to be used that night. Unable to produce the lamps when challenged by other ships now, *Lamson* and *Lardner* were fired upon by their own ships, and thus instead of attacking the enemy were forced to pull out of range.

By 0130 on December 1 all the Japanese ships were gone, apart from the doomed and abandoned *Takanami*. Wright asked Rear Admiral Mahlon Tisdale, aboard the only undamaged American cruiser, *Honolulu*, to assume tactical command. The destroyers were to guard the sound and pick up all survivors possible before the sharks got to them. The crippled task force, so painstakingly assembled by Nimitz and Halsey, gradually limped back to Tulagi, some eighteen miles away. The *Minneapolis* made the trip under tow, the others under their own steam, including the extraordinary cruiser *New Orleans*, which had 120 feet of bow missing. Fires continued to rage for hours on the *Pensacola*, *Minneapolis*, and *New Orleans* as the shouts of men and occasional explosion of ships' munitions filled the tropical night. The *Northampton*, with her growing list, finally sank off the south of Savo Island at 0304 that morning, 773 members of her 831-man crew having been saved. So ended another debacle, the battle of Tassafaronga.

CHAPTER XX

A Troubled Hirohito

"The Emperor is troubled by the great difficulties we are currently experiencing in the war [in New Guinea and Guadalcanal]. The present darkness is indeed profound, but dawn is about to break over the Eastern Sky."

—*Emperor Hirohito, message to the people on December 26, 1942, the Japanese New Year*[1]

By the beginning of December 1942, Japanese army, air, and naval commanders were taking even more energetic action than usual to cope with the disturbing developments in the southwest Pacific. The situation at Port Moresby and in southern New Guinea had altered dramatically since September, when American and Australian troops, General Kenney's air strikes, and Halsey's fleet had forced General Horii Tomitaro's army to withdraw over the Owen Stanley Mountains, with mortal consequences for Horii and most of his army. This victory at Papua, attributable largely to General Robert Eichelberger's leadership (MacArthur had repeatedly refused to leave the comfort of the governor's residence at Port Moresby to visit the front lines), aggressive Australian troops, and Kenney's air force, was to free Australia from any further direct Japanese threat, although the bitter fighting between Buna and Gona would not actually end until the guns at Sanananda Point were finally silenced by the third week of January 1943.[2]

Kenney's unrelenting lethal air attacks had been particularly effective, in addition to the new tactics and equipment he had quickly developed.

During the first week of August he was not only carrying out bombing missions in New Guinea but, at Ghormley's request, bombing runs against Tulagi and Guadalcanal just prior to the landing of the U.S. marines there. His attack against Rabaul, the major Japanese fortress of the region and site of a good harbor and two airfields, destroyed dozens of bombers and fighters, most of them on the ground, thereby preventing many of those aircraft from being used against Guadalcanal and U.S. shipping. He completed his task by striking new Japanese airfields at Buin on the island of Bougainville. Kenney too was creating new airfields on New Guinea as the Allies moved forward. He built one at Wanigela, near Buna, another at Dobodura, a third at Wewak, and a secret base at Wau. These put his fighters and bombers closer to the last Japanese outposts on New Guinea, providing platforms from which to launch deeper raids against Japanese convoys and island outposts. He also targeted the Lae airfield and its main fuel supply center for Japan's Rabaul air force, as well as another nearby coastal field, Salamaua, due west of Rabaul, which of course also took pressure off Guadalcanal.

On August 26, 1942, Kenney's planes and Rear Admiral Glace's task force attacked Japanese transports landing at Milne Bay and destroyed transports, barges, light tanks, and large new supply depots on the beach, all intended for the Japanese attack on Port Moresby. These raids stopped the Japanese in their tracks, forcing them to evacuate Milne Bay and turn back. By the end of August, Kenney had also plastered Lae. On September 13, his planes dropped more parafrag bombs on Buna Field, destroying most of the enemy planes on the ground.[3] And Kenney hit hard along the crucial Kokoda Trail, which crossed the Owen Stanley Mountains between Buna and Port Moresby, forcing the Japanese to halt their advance on that port and to turn back to Buna. But they had come within twenty-six miles of Port Moresby, MacArthur's main GHQ at this stage of the fighting. "For nine successive days we pounded the Japs along the trail with every airplane we could put in the air," George Kenney recalled. He was also responsible for personally flying MacArthur up to Port Moresby in order "to show him the town," as that air force commander put it.[4]

At an important meeting on Ghormley's flagship at Nouméa, the *Argonne*, attended by Ghormley, Nimitz, Turner, air force chief Hap Arnold, and MacArthur's representatives, it was agreed on September

28 that a reluctant MacArthur would help more in the fight for Guadalcanal. That meant lending more airpower.

Kenney was not one to let the grass grow under his feet. Beginning on September 19 he hit Rabaul Harbor with Major Bill Benn's 63rd Bombardment Squadron, repeating this again on October 2. On October 9 and 10 his flyers fire-bombed Rabaul. On October 17 they bombed Buka, Buin, shipping in Faisi anchorage, and the Vunakanau airfield for the second time, and then repeated this the following day, hammering at the enemy relentlessly. Having developed the technique of "skip-bombing," his pilots would drop down to an altitude of only one hundred feet above sea level and release their bombs, which skipped over the water into the hulls of Japanese ships. Rabaul too was repeatedly hit in this manner, and on October 31 Buin was hit in broad daylight, bombs striking airfields, fuel dumps, munition depots, and ships in harbor.[5] The result was soon felt at Guadalcanal, which would have suffered far more severely had not Kenney made this contribution.

Nevertheless, in spite of a good showing, the U.S. Air Force and Navy remained the weak links around Guadalcanal at this stage. Most of their combined arsenal had of necessity been concentrated in North Africa for the November landings, and both General Imamura and Admiral Yamamoto were determined to take full advantage of that situation, with Imamura Hitoshi's Eighth Army amassing some fifty thousand troops at Rabaul—a figure that would soon nearly treble—with which to reinforce Guadalcanal and New Guinea. "We must . . . rouse our officers and men to a fighting rage . . . [and] deal the enemy annihilating blows," Imamura instructed his commanders,[6] promising them two more divisions by February 1, 1943. Soon, it was hoped, there would not be a single American alive on that irksome island which, along with Papua New Guinea, the Japanese could not afford to lose. Yet the naval high command was already beginning to have grave doubts about this operation. And on Guadalcanal, the swelling numbers of Japanese troops continued to fail to defeat those of the Americans. One operation after another ended in disaster and staggering losses, stopping Imamura in his tracks. Hyakutake's men also suffered from scant supplies of medicine and food and from disease raging through their ranks. Nevertheless, living on a daily diet of a handful of rice and roots from the jungle, enfevered troops had continued to launch astonishingly ferocious assaults before being stopped and pushed back. If Hyakutake's men were to continue, however, they would need help, and that help was now en route.

While Imamura was gathering his Eighth Army, Yamamoto was assembling his navy around Rabaul and Truk, vowing to get reinforcements, guns, and provisions to Guadalcanal, regardless of the cost. Rear Admiral Tanaka, as tenacious as any officer in the navy, was absolutely determined to ensure that this promise was kept. And Tanaka was as good as his word, running his convoys almost every four days with nearly the precision of a Swiss railway timetable.

On December 3, 1942, Tanaka drove down the Slot again at high speed, accompanied by air cover. There was not a single U.S. warship to challenge him, so thoroughly smashed and discouraged had Admiral Wright's force been by the 1st of the month. Ten destroyers again successfully discharged supplies in steel drums sealed by Malayan rubber. But Henderson Field could still scramble bombers, torpedo planes, and fighters, which kept Tanaka on his toes. Nevertheless, apart from damage to one destroyer, all ten of Tanaka's ships drove right back up the Slot during the 4th, again unopposed by the navy.

On December 7, a cocksure Admiral Tanaka, emboldened by the fairly smooth success of the previous run, charged down the Slot with hundreds of drums of supplies lashed to the decks of eleven more destroyers. This time, however, U.S. warplanes swarmed over his convoy while it was still in the Slot, dropping bombs and torpedoes and strafing the Express, seriously damaging one destroyer. Eight newly arrived PT boats patrolling Ironbottom Sound then gave Tanaka another unexpected welcome, off Cape Espérance, while four more lay in wait off Savo Island. The Americans had learned how useful these small but powerful craft could be in the confined waters here, and for once they stopped even the unflappable Tanaka (who upon his return was to recommend the introduction of similar boats for his own navy). Twice he attempted to enter the sound and deliver the supplies, only to be harassed and repulsed by these speeding boats as their flashing twin 50mm machine guns sprayed the decks of the enemy destroyers. Tanaka was forced to return to Bougainville with all drums still on his decks.[7]

A humiliated Tanaka did not have to be reminded by Yamamoto that he had a schedule to meet, and on December 11 he made another predictable dash down the Slot with the same supplies. Although the destroyers were attacked by American planes off the northern Georgia Isles, all ten escaped unscathed. The situation at Guadalcanal was another matter. The PT boats were still there when Tanaka arrived between Cape Espérance and Tassafaronga, and they darted around erratically at up to 45 knots (52 mph), attacking from every direction and torpedoing the destroyer *Teruzuki*, which sank off Savo Island in the early morning hours of the 12th with heavy loss of life. One PT boat was destroyed with nine of its eleven-man crew. This new element thrown in by the Americans was proving more and more effective, inflicting as much damage as did their naval cruisers and army B-17s. And even if Tanaka was still managing to deliver enough men and provisions, he was also losing irreplaceable destroyers, which finally forced him to remain safely in port for the rest of December. For the first time in his career, the dauntless Tanaka had been stopped, resulting in some serious quarrels with his superiors.[8]

●

But the Japanese situation could be remedied by the new airfields they were building in the New Georgia group, whose shores formed the western side of the Slot. With strong air reinforcements placed there, Tanaka would have closer fighter support, and heavy bombers could more readily lay waste Henderson Field, now only 173 miles away. This would save hundreds of miles for bombers now having to come from Rabaul or Truk. In addition, Japan now had a major seaplane base and barge-staging point across the Slot at Rekata Bay on Santa Isabel Island in the Solomons, just as Kelly Turner had anticipated, back in August.

Construction of the first and most important new airstrip had begun the last week of November 1942 at Munda, ten miles north of Kula Gulf, which had previously been noted only for its Australian-owned coconut plantations. The Japanese did everything conceivable to conceal this heavy construction by felling only adjacent trees, afterwards adding camouflage by erecting a series of wires to keep the tops of the trees still in place.

By November, however, American aerial reconnaissance operations were becoming more accurate, and daily photos were gradually revealing the emergence of the airstrip despite the Japanese efforts. On

December 3, Admiral Halsey was handed a report confirming the existence of this new threat. A pilot himself, he at once saw the ramifications. Fighters and bombers launched from there, a mere hour's flying time from the already much-harassed Henderson, would have disastrous results, not only for Guadalcanal but also for the naval ships protecting it and those bringing in supplies. He acted that same day, ordering preparations to be made for the destruction of Munda Air Field before it became fully operational.

The initial U.S. air attack against Munda—four days after its completion—was launched from Henderson on December 6, followed by a far more substantial strike with eighteen B-17s carrying bigger bombs on the 9th. Thereafter the daytime bombing of Munda was carried out several times a week on a regular basis. No sooner would the Japanese have repaired the previous damage than a fresh raid would leave all in shambles again, cutting up the landing strip, destroying planes on the ground, preventing others from taking off, and blowing up fuel storage tanks and ammunition dumps. American bombing was also continued almost nightly by PBYs. The Japanese were beginning to learn what it had felt like on Guadalcanal when their positions had been reversed. A particularly powerful air raid on the morning of December 24, for instance, destroyed twenty-six planes on the ground and in the air, planes Japan by now could ill afford to lose. A second air raid that same day destroyed barges in the Kula Gulf that were intended for the landing of troops and supplies.

On Nimitz's insistence, American submarines were also becoming much more active in the Solomon Sea during the months of December and January. *Wahoo*, *Grouper*, *Albacore*, *Sea Dragon*, and *Grayback* sank at least one barge, four valuable troop transports, the light cruiser *Tenryu*, and two submarines, while damaging the light carrier *Ryujo* and other vessels.[9]

Tokyo was finally beginning to realize just how vulnerable its far-flung, overly extended forces had become. Before attacking Pearl Harbor in 1941, Admiral Yamamoto had already advised against bringing the United States into the war, arguing that if Tokyo persisted in doing so, it would have to defeat its new adversary at the outset, before the Americans could arm. If not, all would be lost. Perhaps the Japanese high command recalled these words now as the war of attrition severely depleted its military resources. In addition to sixteen destroyers, Japan had already lost six cruisers, two battleships, six of its fast carriers, and dozens of transports. Emperor Hirohito's New Year's message at the end of December 1942 reflected a new, deep-seated preoccupation with this change of fortune.

On the other hand, Nimitz and Halsey were themselves most anxious about the impressive assembly of nearly eighty enemy warships in Simpson Harbour, Rabaul, by December 31. They feared yet another powerful naval offensive against the fleet and Guadalcanal, and in the days and weeks to come, U.S. Naval Intelligence, now without Rochefort, was unable to provide any explanation. Halsey simply had to keep hitting the enemy's ports and airfields, as MacArthur's most able new air chief, George Kenney, was continuing to do from Australia and New Guinea.

On January 4, 1943, Task Force 67, escorting Turner's convoy of U.S. infantry reinforcements from Espíritu Santo, reached Luna Roads at Guadalcanal without incident. This task force was now under the command of yet another naval officer new to the South Pacific, the fifty-six-year-old Rear Admiral Walden "Pug" Ainsworth, a native of Minneapolis, destined to carry out many future missions. Graduating from Annapolis in 1910, Ainsworth went on to an impressive and varied career, and had served on three different ships by 1917 while a junior officer. During World War I he served as gunnery officer on troop transports, then on ordnance duty ashore, which was followed by his appointment as executive officer first of the *Hancock* and then of the *Birmingham*. After commanding *Marcus* with the Asiatic Fleet, he returned to the Naval Academy as an instructor for the next three years. At sea once more, he served as navigator aboard *Idaho* and then *Pensacola*; a stint in the Panama Canal Zone preceded his return stateside for the senior War College Course at Newport, Rhode Island. He later served as executive officer of the USS *Mississippi*, as head of the Naval ROTC Department at Tulane University, and then as commander of Destroyer Squadron 2, before finally returning to the *Mississippi* as its new captain. He came strongly recommended—an ideal candidate with plenty of sea experience behind him—for this post in the South Pacific, with its reputation for breaking the careers of more than one seemingly promising flag officer.

The new year had also brought the return of the redoubtable Tanaka on January 2 with his first Tokyo Express since mid-December, ten destroyer transports that, significantly, were now without air cover. Clearly the constant American raids on Rabaul, Munda, Rekata, and Buin were taking their toll. Tanaka's transports, however, were coming through bombing runs by U.S. B-17s completely unscathed. As usual, planes flying between fifteen and twenty thousand feet rarely did any damage to moving surface vessels, although George Kenney, at least, was learning this and attempting to correct it with his low "skip-bombing" technique. It is not clear why General Arnold continued to waste time, money, and men on those futile high-altitude attacks. In any event, Tanaka reached Savo Island as dusk was setting in, when suddenly the drone of low-flying navy Dauntless dive-bombers was heard overheard, their bombs quickly putting the destroyer *Susukaze* out of commission and forcing it to retire under destroyer escort. Reaching Cape Espérance and preparing to drop their drums off Tassafaronga as usual, the remaining eight destroyers were set upon by a pack of eleven American PT boats—or "Green Dragons," as Tanaka called them—their 12,150 horsepower motors screaming out of the sound as they launched eighteen torpedoes.[10] But the wily Tanaka, even with his heavily laden destroyers, somehow dodged them all and delivered his cargo before steaming away at full speed, retracing his northerly course up the Slot.[11] If ever there was a naval magician, it was the intrepid Tanaka Raizo.

On January 4, having escorted the 6th Regiment of the 2nd Marine Division and various supplies to Guadalcanal, Pug Ainsworth was ordered to execute a night bombardment of the new Munda air base and its squadrons of deadly Zeroes. He was to be accompanied by light cruisers *Helena*, *Nashville*, and *St. Louis*, which would be screened by destroyers *Fletcher* and *O'Bannon*. Admiral Mahlon Tisdale's squadron, comprising the heavy cruiser *Louisville* and light cruisers *Achilles*, *Columbia*, and *Honolulu* escorted by three destroyers, remained far to the southeast of New Georgia as a distant support group. Submarine *Grayback* was already on station just off Rendova Island, to the west of Georgia Island, to act as a navigational beacon for Ainsworth. Far overhead, concealed in the rain-swollen night skies, twin-engine "Black Cat" PBY Catalinas of Squadron V-12 out of Henderson were preparing to serve as gunfire spotters for Ainsworth's task force. This was a more serious and far better planned and coordinated operation than any before. For the first time, thanks to Bill Halsey, the Japanese were going to learn what it felt like to be on the receiving end of a night bombardment.

By 0100 on January 5, 1943, Ainsworth's ships were in place and began to pound Munda with the aid of fire-control radar. The PBYs overhead confirmed that they were dead on target, and the big guns methodically decimated munition dumps and gasoline storage tanks, encountering very little returning fire of any kind. Fifty minutes later, having expended his ammunition, Ainsworth withdrew at a full 28 knots, reaching the coast of Guadalcanal at midmorning on the 6th, where he was joined by Tisdale's support force. Suddenly, four Japanese dive-bombers swept down upon the ships apparently without any radar warning, three bombs barely missing *Honolulu*, while another knocked out one of the gun turrets of the New Zealand light cruiser *Achilles*.[12]

●

Back on January 4, as Admiral Ainsworth had been steaming up the Slot, a special top-secret meeting of the Japanese Supreme War Council, equivalent to the U.S. Joint Chiefs of Staff, was convening in Tokyo. Present were Hirohito; General Tōjō Hideki, the war minister; Sugiyama Hajime, chief of the Army General Staff; and Admiral Nagano Osami, chief of the navy's General Staff. After several very grim hours of heated discussion, they concluded that it was necessary to evacuate Guadalcanal as well as Buna and Gona, New Guinea, thereby admitting the failure of their plan for the control of Australia. The emperor was not the only person in Tokyo who was troubled. This proposed operation, code-named "KE," was to be executed within a month's time. Admiral Nimitz's "gamble" of invading the Solomons had worked. The first American land offensive in the Pacific had been a success, although even four weeks later, no one in Pearl Harbor or Washington had an inkling of this. Quite the contrary, American top brass were still interpreting the large-scale buildup of ships and troops at Rabaul as a sign of a very stubborn Japanese determination to dig in. In reality, of course, facilities at Buin, Bougainville, and Rekata Bay and bases in the New

Georgias, the Russells, and at Rendova were now preparing to help *evacuate* General Hyakutake's army from Guadalcanal . . . but that was to occur only after the last major battle on that island.

On December 9, Major General Alexander Patch had finally relieved an exhausted General Vandegrift and four regiments of the 1st Marine Division—the 1st, 5th, 7th, and 11th—who began sailing away on December 22 for some badly needed R-and-R after months of the most intensive fighting in the history of the Marine Corps to date.[13] The departing marines were replaced by fresh reinforcements convoyed by Kelly Turner: 7,737 men of the 25th Infantry Division from Hawaii and the 6th Marine Regiment of the 2nd Marine Division, which was now at full strength.

Almost from the outset of the campaign, Japan had taken advantage of its continued possession of Mt. Austen, which overlooked all shipping off Lunga Point, and Henderson Field, just three miles away. It had been one of the great tragedies of the Guadalcanal campaign that because of poor maps and Fletcher's premature flight, Vandegrift had been unable to reach Mt. Austen that first week of his arrival. The Japanese, to be sure, had been quick to take advantage of this, digging in and gradually building powerful gun emplacements. Since their arrival at Henderson, the marines had been launching attacks around Mt. Austen and Matanikau, but the military situation there only became critical in December.

Colonel Oka Akinosuka, in command of that mountain, launched a series of raids against the American airfield, actually reaching it once or twice and destroying some planes. American reconnaissance patrols, for their part, penetrated Mt. Austen briefly. By mid-December, two of Colonel Oka's well-entrenched, battle-proven battalions staunchly held Mt. Austen—or Gifu, as they called it. From these heights big mountain guns landed earlier by Tanaka now daily tore up Henderson Field when Japanese naval bombardment did not do so. In addition, Oka had constructed a superb, impregnable, mile-long line of pillboxes concealing forty machine guns that no American aerial or ground bombardment had yet been able to take out of action.

Having had enough, General Patch ordered a large-scale attack to take that obdurate mountain once and for all. Beginning December 17, Colonel John Arthur's 3rd Marine Battalion launched a series of concerted attacks. By the 20th, action had diminished to sporadic fighting, culminating on Christmas Eve with the seizure of a Japanese observation post on Gifu's highest point.[14] The Americans celebrated New Year's Day 1943 with an even bigger combined attack by the 1st, 2nd, and 3rd Battalions of the 132nd Regiment, two companies breaking through to the summit itself before noon on the 2nd. The Japanese artillerymen occupying it were killed or driven out. An outraged Oka counterattacked half a dozen times with a ferocity hitherto unknown, only to be utterly crushed and beaten by American machine guns and artillery.

On January 9, the 25th Army Division finally relieved the exhausted marines.[15] But their occupation was still limited, and on the 10th they began the assault on Colonel Oka's lethal ridge of forty pillboxes, only to be beaten back. The next day they launched another bloody attack, which was also repulsed. A third attempt was made by the GIs on the 12th, resulting in heavy casualties and failure again. On the 15th, American troops gained a mere one hundred yards, until the constant pounding of U.S. 105mm and 150mm howitzers from Henderson finally began to take their toll. On the 21st, infantry, protected by a marine tank, moved up the hill one final time and silenced the last deadly machine guns. During the night they repulsed a fierce enemy suicide counterattack, killing every one of the Japanese; with fifty thousand American troops, marines, airmen, and sailors on Guadalcanal and Tulagi, ultimately the Japanese did not stand a chance. Finally, on January 22, 1943, Lieutenant Colonel S. R. Larsen, leading a battalion of the 35th Infantry Regiment, overran the last of the Japanese positions, placing the Americans in complete control of Mt. Austen. It had been four weeks of some of the bloodiest fighting yet seen on Cactus, despite Japanese orders to withdraw and prepare to evacuate the island. Henderson Field would never again be shelled from bloody Mt. Austen.[16]

●

While lesser assaults were being launched by both sides elsewhere on Guadalcanal beginning on January 10, Rear Admiral Tanaka was arriving in the sound with another eight destroyers, which were met by four young, zestful American PT boat skippers who badly damaged two of the destroyers between Cape Espérance and Doma Cove at a cost of two of the small American craft. Nevertheless, these 77-foot boats were rendering Tanaka's job pretty harrowing, and he retreated up the Slot as the two remaining PT boats moved in and seized or destroyed the 250 drums of food and munitions that had been fruitlessly dropped.

The undauntable Tanaka reappeared again on the 14th, this time with nine destroyer transports whose cargo included six hundred fresh troops to be landed as a rearguard to hold the beach during the evacuation. Having sailed all the way down the Slot without the slightest hitch, they were discovered only late that evening, and, of course, most American warplanes still did not fly at night. Thirteen PT boats, based at their tender at Tulagi, had no such reservations as they raced across Ironbottom Sound at top speed. This time, however, Tanaka had brought air cover to deal with these agile boats while the admiral got on with his deliveries. Bombed and strafed, the PT boats were kept fully occupied until Tanaka's departure, when they finally attacked five destroyers off Cape Espérance but achieved nothing. The following morning, fifteen Dauntless dive-bombers found and attacked the retreating destroyers, damaging two, although once again the wily Tanaka managed to escape.

This admiral's seemingly unstoppable Express continued to land both supplies and troops fairly regularly. On the other hand, Marine Fighter Squadron 121 was more successful now, bringing down some thirty enemy planes; their air ace, Major J. J. Foss, personally shooting down twenty-six. His squadron alone would ultimately account for the downing of 164 Japanese planes by the end of January.

On the ground, General Hyakutake's troops were not putting up the same resistance everywhere now, and the U.S. 35th Infantry Regiment moved in on January 10 to take the heavily wooded "Seahorse Sector" well to the west of Henderson. It was fully secured by the 11th. A final sector, known by its shape in aerial photographs as "Galloping Horse," was taken by the 27th Regiment on the 13th, thereby clearing much of General Patch's western front.

To the northwest, three miles from Point Cruz, there remained a large Japanese base at Kokumbona, facing the sound, from which Hyakutake retreated to Cape Espérance on January 22. By the time Brigadier General A. DeCarre's combined army-marine force entered Kokumbona on the 23rd, the place was empty, apart from some four hundred dead rearguard troops. Continuing his pursuit, DeCarre pushed up the coast where, just below Tassafaronga at the Bonegi River, his men met up with the fleeing soldiers, including the six hundred troops newly landed by Tanaka. Only 10,652 enemy troops remained. The ensuing clash with the rearguard proved to be a suicide mission for the Japanese, fighting literally to the last man. It was a slaughter.[17]

•

Stopping Tanaka's Express in the Slot or the sound, however, was quite another matter. Complete success would be ensured only if his transports and destroyers were prevented from ever reaching Ironbottom Sound in the first place. This meant hitting them at their source: in particular Faisi, on Shortland Island off the southern tip of Bougainville, which was also supplying Munda Air Field. Moreover, by the third week of January, the indefatigable Japanese were completing yet another airstrip, this time a 6,000-foot runway near Vila on the southern coast of the volcanic island of Kolombangara, off Kula Gulf and just north of Rennell Island. The very long runway was obviously being prepared for Japan's largest bombers. Upon receiving this intelligence, Halsey, who was meeting with the touring Admiral Nimitz on Espíritu Santo on January 21, again ordered "Pug" Ainsworth to sail north, this time to cut the supply line to and from Shortland.

Setting out from the New Hebrides via the Russells two days later, Rear Admiral Ainsworth's Task Force 67 was soon shadowed by Japanese scout planes which Ainsworth, with no air cover of his own, could not deter. Upon reaching the Solomons, he pushed up the Slot toward Vila with two cruisers, *Nashville* and *Helena*, and their four-destroyer escort. Far to the south, his reserve support group, including the cruisers *Honolulu* and *St. Louis* and their three destroyers, took up their new station.

Reaching Kula Gulf just off Vila at 0200 on January 24, right on schedule, Ainsworth commenced his bombardment of the new airstrip under a full moon. Like the Americans on Guadalcanal, the Japanese had very little coastal artillery and were in no position to protect themselves. Pounding that field for nearly an hour, Ainsworth then turned south. Half an hour later, TF 67 came under attack by Mitsubishi medium bombers which they beat off with their new radar-controlled antiaircraft guns and secret Mark-32 fuse shells, bringing down one of the planes before the enemy broke off its attack. The next day, Henderson dispatched fifty-nine bombers and fighters to pulverize that new field on Kolombangara yet again. On the 25th, a powerful Japanese force of eighty-six fighters and bombers attempted to retaliate against Guadalcanal, only to be turned back by American fighters.[18]

Still much preoccupied with Yamamoto's growing navy at Rabaul, Buin, and off the coast of Ontong, Java—a force that now included four aircraft carriers and four battleships—Halsey and Nimitz decided to order all American warships in the South Pacific to form six separate task forces to rendezvous at the Solomons. Among these was Rear Admiral Robert "Ike" Giffen's Task Force 18, comprising the escort carriers *Chenango* and *Suwannee* (which had just arrived following the November "Casablanca" landings in North Africa), heavy cruisers *Chicago*, *Louisville*, and *Wichita*, light cruisers *Cleveland*, *Columbia*, and *Montpelier*, and a couple of destroyer divisions.[19]

Giffen's TF 18 set out from Efate on January 27 but two days later detached the two escort carriers, whose slow speed was holding everyone else, thereby losing Giffen his air cover. *Chenango* and *Suwannee* would have to join him later. In fact, Giffen's failure to dispatch the carriers in advance of his task force, so as to have them in place near Guadalcanal when he arrived, was to be of vital importance. This was the first of several serious errors that would prevent the successful execution of Halsey's orders. While en route to Cactus, Giffen's task force and the other parts of the fleet were to escort Kelly Turner's large transports of men and matériel to Guadalcanal, after which Giffen alone would sail up the Slot to meet the enemy. Before doing so, he was to rendezvous with the last of his destroyers on the 30th. That was a meeting he was destined never to make. In order to avoid being spotted by the Japanese, Giffen had ordered strict radio silence at sea, which was to prove his undoing. Japanese submarines had already been following him and reporting the position and composition of his task force; at the airfields north of the Solomons, twin-engine bombers were now awaiting his arrival. Various unidentified aircraft far to the north were detected on *Chicago*'s radar, but Giffen did not call Guadalcanal for assistance, more wary was he of submarines than warplanes. Nor did he allow his fighter-director to signal his carriers for air cover, even to investigate these ominous "bogies." And thus Giffen steamed ahead, determined, regardless of the consequences, to make the rendezvous with his destroyers southwest of Guadalcanal planned for the next day, the 30th. At the end of the day, just before 1900 on the 29th, his combat air patrol left him and returned to the two trailing escort carriers still far to the south, leaving Giffen now completely unprotected by air.

Just before sunset, when TF 18 was some fifty miles north of Rennell Island, more bogies were detected by radar only sixty miles away, but for some reason Giffen failed to alert his other ships. Nor did he order a change of course or require his six screening destroyers to tighten formation in order to provide a more effective antiaircraft shield, as Samuel Morison so aptly points out. Indeed, some ships were not even at General Quarters when two groups of "Bettys" attacked the task force from out of the northeast, coming straight in on the starboard beam. Giffen and his task force were completely unprepared for battle, many guns not even manned, as the planes swept down to attack. The first torpedoes came at *Waller* and *Louisville*, both of which barely avoided being hit. Belated antiaircraft flak finally filled the sky, mainly from the destroyers, bringing down one Mitsubishi torpedo bomber just astern of *Chicago*. And then, just as suddenly as they had appeared, the planes disappeared.

Apparently thinking that the attack was over, Rear Admiral Giffen then maintained *the same course* to the northwest and ceased zigzagging at 1930. After all, he did not want to be late for his rendezvous with his destroyers. One minute later, as darkness began to settle, the Japanese planes reappeared, this time dropping yellow, red, and green flares, each color meant to indicate either the ship's location, course, or class of vessel.[20] More torpedoes were launched from the air: one, a dud, missed *Chicago*'s bow before hitting *Louisville*. The ships' antiaircraft batteries replied in full tenor this time, firing their new, top-secret shells to great effect. Despite suffering heavy losses, the Japanese planes continued to attack. One exploded astern of the destroyer *Waller*, off *Wichita*'s port bow; another flaming bomber barely missed *Chicago*'s deck. At 1945 that cruiser took its first torpedo, flooding the starboard engine rooms and stopping three of the four drive shafts while knocking out the ship's steering gear. The explosion of a second torpedo flooded even more of the vessel.

Directly astern of the wounded ship, *Louisville* put her wheel hard over to avoid colliding with *Chicago* and the debris of two downed Japanese bombers. Taking up her new position astern of *Wichita*, she was hit by another dud. But while the Japanese pilots had held the upper hand initially, they were surprised by the unusual accuracy of American guns in the cloud-covered night sky, little realizing that radar gun control combined with the new type of ammunition could follow their every move. And then the second wave of planes was gone.

This time Giffen had learned his lesson and altered course at long last to the southeast—and just in time, for when the Japanese torpedo bombers returned in a third wave a few minutes later to finish off what they had begun, they were unable to locate TF 18. Although the fires aboard *Chicago* had been put out, she was still soaking up the sea and beginning to list badly as *Louisville* prepared the slow process of taking her in tow once *Chicago*'s jammed steering was released. After midnight, the two ships set out for Espíritu Santo at all of 4 knots. In Nouméa, Halsey sent a tugboat to the scene and ordered the escort carriers to launch fighter protection at dawn's first light, something Giffen had failed to take into account. At 1300 on the afternoon of the 30th, Giffen and the remainder of TF 18 were ordered to abandon *Chicago* and to alter course for Efate. Admiral Giffen would neither make his rendezvous nor complete his mission.

Meanwhile, the heavily listing *Chicago*, now under tow by the navy tug *Navajo* (which had replaced *Louisville*) and escorted by half a dozen destroyers, was notified at 1505 by Henderson Field that still more "bogies" were heading her way. Expecting the planes by 1600, *Enterprise*, some forty miles to the southeast of *Chicago*, launched ten fighters to provide air cover for that cruiser. Among other things, Admiral Giffen seemed to have forgotten all about the two escort carriers under his command and had neglected to inform them that he was sailing back to Efate without *Chicago*.[21]

Although an earlier enemy scout plane had been shot down by *Enterprise* fighters, the carrier's radar failed to pick up the first dozen attacking enemy planes until 1554, when a second group of fighters was hurriedly scrambled. Enemy bombers were apparently coming straight for the *Enterprise* when they were intercepted by half a dozen Grumman Wildcats just seventeen miles from the big carrier. Dissuaded by this reception, the bombers altered course for their secondary objective, *Chicago*, losing three planes even before reaching it. Seven more were shot down by the Wildcats and antiaircraft fire, and the remaining planes released their torpedoes. Four of them, launched at 1624, struck the already damaged cruiser on her starboard side, causing enormous damage and increasing the ship's list as tons of seawater poured in unabated. The holing was now too huge and the vessel beyond help. Captain Ralph Davis ordered all hands to abandon her, and the tug severed its steel towing hawser. The destroyer *La Vallette*, screening the big cruiser, was the last to be torpedoed, the hit flooding part of the vessel and killing twenty-one men outright. Her skipper kept her afloat, however, and she was still moving slowly, later to be taken in tow by *Navajo*. Twenty minutes after being struck, *Chicago* went down off the coast of Rennell Island, with four of the other ships moving in to save 1,049 of her crew. Thus ended the lamentable battle of Rennell Island.[22]

So, too, ended the final naval battle involved in the conquest of Guadalcanal—and just as it had begun, in yet another American defeat brought about by flag officers who lacked battle experience or an understanding of the situation and what was required of them. Many paid with their lives. It would appear that few senior naval officers had learned much since the battle of Savo Island, nearly five months earlier.

Ironically, neither CINCPAC Headquarters at Pearl Harbor nor Halsey's team at Nouméa yet had any idea as to Japanese plans for the total evacuation of Guadalcanal. Fresh American reinforcements escorted by *Saratoga* and *Enterprise* were still disembarking there, and another five troop transports were en route as well. As it turned out, the Japanese were pulling out just in time, but not before bringing down the curtain in grand fashion.

●

On February 2, 1943, General Alexander Patch, as commanding officer on Cactus, was continuing with his plans to crush the Japanese forces there. This involved an amphibious operation that would ferry the 2nd Battalion of the 132nd Infantry, its vehicles, and artillery by LCTs (landing craft, tanks) and destroyer transports around the northern cape of Espérance to Verahue beach, on the southwestern coast of

Guadalcanal. Unknown to Patch, Admiral Kondo's "Operation KE" to evacuate the island was also in motion that day, sending the first of three super Tokyo Expresses—this one of twenty destroyers and a light cruiser, under the usual command of the fearless Tanaka—steaming down the Slot, preceded by a protective Japanese air attack.[23]

Just before 1500 on the 2nd, fourteen Vals suddenly lunged from the skies over Savo Island as two U.S. destroyers and three LCTs were returning from Verahue beach to Ironbottom Sound. For some reason, Commander Charles Tolman delayed the order for his destroyer, *DeHaven*, to open fire. He was not allowed a second chance, for three Japanese bombs dealt fatal blows to his fragile vessel. Holman and 166 members of his crew went down with the sinking warship in a mere two minutes. The skippers of the LCTs, a little more alert than the destroyermen, immediately fired on the low-flying planes even as they moved in to collect survivors. Another bomb damaged the steering gear of the remaining destroyer, *Nicholas*, before the enemy planes scurried off.

That same day Guadalcanal was simultaneously receiving reports of the sighting of the big Express shooting down the Slot at full speed. Forty-one SBDs, TBFs, and F4Fs rose into the muggy tropical skies above Henderson and were soon on their way north, reaching Tanaka's ships near Vangunu Island at 1820. The American pilots were met by a powerful air patrol of thirty Zeroes, resulting in a brief but fierce battle that sent four U.S. planes down in flames. Only one destroyer, *Makinami*, was damaged, and now left behind.

GHQ at Guadalcanal was dismayed to learn that up to nineteen destroyers and a cruiser were still steaming pellmell straight toward them, and for the first time the coastal waters between Cape Espérance and Doma Reef were hastily mined. Captain R. P. Briscoe's remaining three destroyers in that area were ordered to lie in wait for Tanaka's arrival in the sound. Having already intercepted the American destroyers, preventing them from attacking Tanaka, Japanese planes left the island; and since American fighter pilots did not yet fly at night, there was no pursuit. A second enemy destroyer, *Makigumo*, damaged earlier, finally sank, leaving Tanaka with eighteen ships.

Just after 2300, eleven American PT boats out of Tulagi went into action again, two of them spotting the first Japanese destroyers and unsuccessfully launching torpedoes before dashing back to safety. Fast as they were, these small, unarmored craft were not fast enough for destroyer *Kawakaze*'s sharp gunners, who slammed a shell into the wooden hull of PT-111, setting the splintered boat ablaze as the crew leaped into the dark waters of the sound. Two of the men fell victim to sharks, as had many others in previous battles, and PT-48 was forced to beach on Savo Island amidst a rain of enemy shells. PT-37, off Cape Espérance, was blown up next, with the loss of its entire crew, while PT-123 was destroyed by aircraft. Only PT-124 claimed to have hit a destroyer before escaping the wrath of the Japanese and disappearing in a hovering rain squall.

As for Tanaka, despite losing on of his destroyers, he nevertheless managed to evacuate all 4,935 Japanese troops from barges off Cape Espérance and Kamimbo Bay. He ignored a dawn aircraft attack from Henderson Field and sailed smartly north, collecting the previously damaged *Makinami* en route to the Shortlands.[24] Following the escape of this latest Tokyo Express, American pilots found thirty abandoned barges off Cape Espérance, adding to General Patch's puzzlement. But another alert now reached Guadalcanal, this time concerning four battleships, six cruisers, and their screen some one hundred miles north of Choiseul.

On February 4, Tanaka slipped his moorings at Faisi to execute part two of Operation KE, steaming down the Slot once more now with a light cruiser and twenty-two destroyer-transports, protected by a strong combat air patrol. Tanaka would need all the planes he could get when-sixty-four bombers and fighters arrived from Henderson, their guns blazing. Although seventeen Japanese planes were "splashed"—to ten of the Americans'—and two of his destroyers damaged, Tanaka somehow successfully evacuated the 3,921 exhausted troops awaiting him.[25]

Japanese twin-engine bombers coming down the Slot that night were more successful, enlisting the aid of flare planes to bomb Henderson for long periods with complete impunity. Not a single U.S. plane rose to the field's defense. This time, the usually persistent PT boats made no contact, and a belated air strike launched against Tanaka's destroyers on the morning of the 5th failed even to locate them. Nothing seemed to be going right for the U.S. military. The thirty abandoned barges found drifting west of Cape Espérance should have told headquarters everything, but those in charge still failed to comprehend fully what Yamamoto was about.

On February 7, the third and last part of Operation KE again went off right on schedule, as Admiral Tanaka led the final convoy of eighteen destroyers down the Slot under heavy rain cover while two other destroyers went on to evacuate Russell Island. The fifteen U.S. dive-bombers attacking the main force in mid-Slot slightly damaged one destroyer, but otherwise failed even to slow the convoy down. Upon reaching Cape Espérance and the Russells, Tanaka found the remaining group of 1,796 troops awaiting him in barges off shore. Neither U.S. surface ships, submarines, nor aircraft attempted to hinder the boarding of his final Express, leaving Tanaka—surely the most highly skilled tactician in the Imperial Japanese Navy—to complete the successful evacuation of a total of 10,652 men from Guadalcanal during the first week of February. They were all that remained of the Seventeenth Army's 36,000 men who had fought there.

The following morning, February 8, abandoned boats, barges, and supplies were once again found. General Patch finally realized what had happened, and after sending out reconnaissance teams, he radioed Admiral Halsey the next day: "Total and complete defeat of Japanese forces on Guadalcanal effected 1652 today. . . . 'Tokyo Express' no longer has terminus on Guadalcanal." Halsey's reply: "When I sent a Patch to act as a tailor for Guadalcanal, I did not expect him to remove the enemy's pants and sew it on so quickly. . . . Thanks and congratulations."[26] Admiral Turner, however, received not a word of thanks—even from the marines—for his constant flow of convoys of supplies and reinforcements to Guadalcanal, frequently under the most harrowing of conditions.

In the end, fewer than one third of the Japanese troops had survived battles and disease. But Tanaka's execution of a seemingly impossible evacuation operation was a remarkable tour de force that remains, even today, almost impossible to explain.

•

On the other hand, never before had the U.S. marines encountered such an inexhaustible foe, composed of slight men who fought like the very devil, men whom the U.S. military quickly came to respect and would never again underestimate. In the face of the worst odds, the Japanese had kept charging, day after day, week after week, month after month.

But if the enemy had found it very hard going, then it was no more so for them than for the valiant defenders. The marines and GIs fought, held, and won some of the most difficult terrain imaginable: dense, snake-infested jungles intermeshed with rugged volcanic hills and mountains, and fields of razor-sharp, seven-foot-high Kunai grass. The men were beset by tropical heat and daily deluges. Equally trying was the prevalence of disease, including dysentery and a malaria so powerful that it frequently defied the most modern medicines. The U.S. soldiers and marines lived in quagmires, their tents, even at base camp, often planted in vast pools of leech-infested water. Existing on reduced rations for the first several weeks, with no heavy artillery and very limited supplies of munitions, the marines had been expected to attack the Japanese and defend themselves on Guadalcanal while the enemy was being reinforced regularly by the Tokyo Express.[27] As if this were not enough, they had been bombed, strafed, and bombarded twice daily—once at noon and once during the night—by Japanese warplanes and ships at a time when Vice Admiral Robert Ghormley had continued to provide them with little or no protection by air or sea. That those marines survived and ultimately overcame conditions no human being should have had to endure remains their ultimate testimonial.

General MacArthur, with his great sense of drama, later falsely accused the Marine Corps of incurring "unnecessarily high casualties" while boasting of the conquest of Buna and Gona, achieved through "so low an expenditure of life and resources"—whereas in reality, his army casualty figures there were twice those of the marines and soldiers who died on Guadalcanal.[28] Nor did MacArthur seem to remember the many thousands of civilians and soldiers who had suffered in the Philippines because of his thoroughly bungled defense of those islands, which resulted in the loss of 27,000 of General Wainwright's men after their surrender, exclusive of his battle casualties. General, and future presidential candidate, Douglas MacArthur had a most curious sort of memory.[29] Admiral Nimitz, for his part, was too much of a gentleman to reciprocate in kind.

In the final analysis it was in fact thanks to the careful preparations and professional skill of General Archie Vandegrift, and later Alexander Patch, that of the 50,000 or so marines, GIs, airmen, and sailors actually serving on Guadalcanal and Tulagi, the United States lost about

1,600 men, or 3.2 percent of its force. By comparison, 20,706 Japanese—over 60 percent of the Japanese force—were buried on the islands. (MacArthur, for his part, had already lost 3,300 men with an additional 5,500 wounded at Buna and Gona, and this was just at the beginning of the fighting in New Guinea.)[30]

•

On the other hand, the various naval battles around Guadalcanal had resulted in shocking losses to the U.S. Navy that left Admiral Nimitz greatly astonished and dismayed, as one task force after another suffered heavy losses in men and ships.* The names of Scott, Callaghan, Wright, and Giffen, among others, are not easily forgotten, primarily for their slow reactions and tactical blunders. But Congress had refused to provide the navy with adequate funding over the preceding decades, and the navy now paid the price in the lack of men, ships, and aircraft required to meet the inevitable war. With some notable exceptions, American naval officers were not properly trained for "the real thing," and their lack of decisiveness in battle too frequently meant death and destruction for thousands. When summing up the previous six months, Chester Nimitz stressed one factor over and over again: "Training, *Training*, and MORE TRAINING."[31] And this applied to naval aviators as well, who were still largely incapable of defending themselves during night fighting.

Nevertheless, far more important, the United States had stopped further Japanese expansion, and this fact proved a turning point in the war, gradually forcing Japan to withdraw planes and men from New Guinea and Guadalcanal. From now on, it was the Japanese who were on the defensive, and would remain so. A troubled Hirohito asked, "I wonder if this is not the start of the American-British counteroffensive?"[32] Indeed it was.

*According to Samuel Morison's figures, the U.S. Navy, like that of the Japanese navy, lost twenty-four warships throughout the campaign, including eight U.S. cruisers; a large number of other ships were heavily damaged. Auxiliaries and PT boats were not included—Morison, *The Struggle for Guadalcanal*, p. 372.

Special Terms and Abbreviations

JAPANESE AIRCRAFT

"Betty"—Mitsubishi Zero-1, navy (2) medium bomber
"Emily"—Kawanishi Zero-2, navy (4) patrol bomber (flying boat)
"Helen"—Nakajima, navy (2) medium bomber
"Judy"—Aichi, navy (1) torpedo bomber
"Kate"—Nakajima 97-2, navy (1) high-level or torpedo bomber
"Pete"—Sasebo, Zero-0, navy (1) float plane
"Sally"—Mitsubishi 97, army (2) medium bomber
"Tojo"—Nakajima, army (1) fighter
"Val"—Aichi 99-1, navy (1) dive-bomber
"Zeke"—Mitsubishi Zero-3, navy (1) fighter (referred to as "Zero" in 1942–43)

AMERICAN AIRCRAFT

A-20—Boston, army (2) light bomber
A-29—Hudson, army (2) light bomber
B-17—Flying Fortress, army (4) heavy bomber
B-24—Liberator, army (4) heavy bomber (called PB4 by navy)
B-25—Mitchell, army (2) medium bomber
B-26—Marauder, army (2) medium bomber
Black Cat—PBY specially equipped for night work
C-47—Skytrain, army (2) transport
Dumbo—PBY equipped for rescue work
F4F—Wildcat, navy fighter
F4U—Corsair, navy fighter
F6F—Hellcat, navy fighter
P-38—Lightning, army (2) fighter

P-39—Aircobra, army fighter
P-40—Warhawk, army (1) fighter
PBY—Catalina, navy (2) seaplane
PBY-5A—amphibian, navy
PV-1—Ventura, navy (1) torpedo bomber
SB_2C—Helldiver, navy (1) dive-bomber
SBD—Dauntless, navy (1) dive-bomber
TBF—Avenger, navy (1) torpedo bomber

NAVAL LANDING CRAFT

LCI—Landing Craft, Infantry
LCM—Landing Craft, Mechanized
LCT—Landing Craft, Tank
LCVP—Landing Craft, Vehicles and Personnel
LSD—Landing Ship, Dock
LST—Landing Ship, Tank
LVT—Landing Vehicle tracked (Amphtrac)
LVT(A)—Landing Vehicle tracked (Armored)

NAVAL SHIPS

APC—Small Coastal Transport
APD—Destroyer-Transport
ADA—Attack Cargo Ship
APA—Attack Transport
BB—Battleship
CA—Heavy Cruiser
CL—Light Cruiser
CV—Aircraft Carrier
CVE—Escort Carrier
CVL—Light Carrier
DD—Destroyer
DE—Destroyer Escort
DMS—Destroyer Minesweeper
PC—Patrol Craft
PT—Motor Torpedo Boat

TITLES AND CODE NAMES

Cactus—Code name for Guadalcanal
CIC—Combat Information Center
CINCPAC—Commander in Chief, U.S. Fleet, Pacific
CINCPOA—Commander in Chief, Pacific Ocean Area
CINCUS—Commander in Chief, U.S. Fleet
CNO—Chief of Naval Operations
CO—Commanding Officer
COMAIRSOPAC—Commander, Air Fleet, South Pacific
COMINCH—Commander in Chief, U.S. Fleet
COMPHIBFORSOPAC—Commander, Amphibious Force, South Pacific
COMSOPAC—Commander, South Pacific
CTF—Commander, Task Force
CTG—Commander, Task Group
FlinkLock—Operation to the Marshall Islands to take Kwajalein
FRUpac—Fleet Radio Unit, Pacific, at Pearl Harbor
Galvanic—Operation to the Gilbert Islands (Tarawa & Makin)
HYPO—Code name for Naval Intelligence unit at Pearl Harbor
JICPOA—Joint Intelligence Center, Pacific Ocean Area
Kido Butai—Japanese Strike Force
OP-20-G—Naval Communication Center, Washington, D.C.
Ringbolt—Code Name for Tulagi
SIS—Signal Intelligence Service, U.S. Army, Washington, D.C.
SOPAC—South Pacific Area, South Pacific Force
SOWESPAC—South West Pacific Area
USAAF—U.S. Army Air Force
USAFFE—U.S. Army Air Forces in the Far East
USSBS—U.S. Strategic Bombing Survey
Watchtower—Code name for operations in the Solomons

Notes

Prelude

1. George Carroll Dyer, *The Amphibians Came to Conquer: The Story of Admiral Richmond Kelly Turner*, vol. 1 (Washington, DC: U.S. Government Printing Office, 1972), p 145.
2. For coverage of the funeral and Saitō's obituaries, see the *Washington Post*, the *New York Times*, and London's *Daily Telegraph*, February 27, 1939, and March 18–20, 1939.
3. For the role of Kelly Turner in the various ceremonies in Tokyo in April 1939, see Dyer, *Amphibians*, pp. 140–49.

Chapter 1: A Distinguished Visitor

1. Harvey quoted in the *Daily Telegraph*, Monday, May 9, 1921.
2. *The Times* (London), Tuesday, May 10, 1921.
3. Detailed coverage in *The Times* and especially the *Daily Telegraph* of Tuesday, May 10, 1921. For general coverage of the Crown Prince's visit, see the above newspapers, May 9–20, 1921.
4. *The Times* and *Daily Telegraph*, Tuesday, May 10, 1921.
5. *The Times*, Wednesday, May 11, 1921.
6. *Daily Telegraph*, Monday, May 9, 1921
7. Lawrence James, *The Rise and Fall of the British Empire* (London: Abacus/Little Brown, 1994), p. 367. That casualty figure included 76,000 men killed in action. The Canadian recruitment slogan is quoted on p. 368.
8. *The Times*, Thursday, May 12, 1921.
9. Martin Gilbert, *Churchill, A Life* (London: Minerva/Heinemann, 1992), p. 436.
10. Sterling and Peggy Seagrave, *The Yamato Dynasty: The Secret History of Japan's Imperial Family* (London: Bantam Books, 1970), p. 104.
11. Gilbert, *Churchill*, p. 468.
12. Robert G. Albion, ed. Rowanna Reed, *The Making of Naval Policy, 1878–1947* (Annapolis: Naval Institute Press, 1984), p. 233.
13. *Ibid.*, pp. 226–34.
14. Herbert Bix, *Hirohito and the Making of Modern Japan* (New York: HarperCollins, 2000), pp. 36–43. Nogi was an army hero of the Russo-Japanese War, while Tōgō's fleet had defeated Nicholas's navy.
15. *Ibid.*, 42, 46.
16. *Ibid.*, 21–30.

17. Seagrave and Seagrave give much more background on Chichibu, *The Yamato Dynasty*, pp. 122–28. See also Ruth Benedict, *The Chrysanthemum and the Sword* (Tokyo: Kodansha International, 1990); Kawahara Toshiaki, *Hirohito and His Times. A Japanese Perspective* (Tokyo: Kodansha International, 1990); Irokawa Daichi, *The Age of Hirohito: In Search of Modern Japan* (New York: Free Press, 1995); Stephen Large, *The Emperor Hirohito and Shōwa Japan: A Political Biography* (London: Routledge, 1992); Stephen Large, *Emperors of the Rising Sun: Three Biographies* (Tokyo: Kodansha Ltd., 1997); Princess Chichibu Setsuko, *The Silver Drum. A Japanese Imperial Memoir* (Folkestone, UK: Global Oriental, 1996); and Ben-Ami Shillony, *Politics and Culture in Pre-War Japan* (Oxford: Oxford University Press, 1982).
18. *New York Times*, April 11, 1931.
19. *Ibid.*
20. *Japan Times and Mail*, December 2–7, 1928; Nakajima Michio, *Tennō no daigawari to kokumin* (Tokyo: Aoki Shoten, 1990), pp. 79–80; Bix, *Hirohito*, p. 195; James Dunningan and Albert Nofi, *Victory at Sea: World War II in the Pacific* (New York: Quill/Morrow, 1995), p. 83.
21. David C. Evans and Mark R. Peattie, *Kaigun: Strategy, Tactics, and Technology in the Imperial Japanese Navy, 1887–1941* (Annapolis: Naval Institute Press, 1997), p. 362. Their naval factories and yards included those at Yokosuka, Kure, Sasebo, Maizuru, Mitsubishi's yards at Nagasaki, Kobe, and Yokahama, with smaller yards at Kawasaki, Ishikawajima, Uraga, Fujinagata, and Mitsui.
22. *Japan Times and Mail*, December 2–7, 1928.
23. Senda Kakō, *Tennō to chokugo to Shōwa-shi* (Kyoto: Sekibunsha, 1990), p. 77; Nezu Masahi, *Tennō to Shōwashi, jō* (Tokyo: San Ichi Shobō, 1976), pp. 46–47; *Tokushū Bungei Shunjū: Tennō hakusho* (October 1956), p. 77; Okada Seiji and Hikuma Takenori, "Sokui no rei, daijōsai no rekishiteki kentō," in *Bunka hyōron*, 357 (October 1990), pp. 62–87.
24. Composition by Hirohito, 1920, translated by Bix, *Hirohito*, p. 92.
25. Prince Konoe, translated by Bix, *ibid.*, p. 267.
26. Shibuno Junichi, "Taishō junen Kawasaki, Mitsubishi dai sōgi no bunken to kenkyū," *Rekishi to Kobe* (August 1967), p. 11; Bix, *Hirohito*, p. 52.
27. See Jean Strouse, *Morgan, American Financier* (New York: Random House, 1999), pp. 547–49. "Commodore" Morgan entertained high Japanese officials on his latest yacht on the Hudson, negotiating deals, though for the moment largely favoring Chinese investments—Ron Chernow, *Titan: The Life of John D. Rockefeller, Sr.* (New York: Little, Brown/Random House, 1998), p. 373. The presence of Jewish bankers raising government bonds and loans for Japan at the turn of the twentieth century stemmed from their opposition to Tsar Nicholas's long-term state policy of pogroms against hundreds of thousands of Jews in Russia.
28. Bix, *Hirohito*, p. 52.
29. The Matsukata family, recipient of enormous "loans," was typical—Noriō Tamaki, *Japanese Banking: A History, 1859–1959* (Cambridge: Cambridge University Press, 1995), p. 158.
30. Daichi, *The Age of Hirohito*, p. 8.
31. Itō Hirobumi, *Commentary on the Constitution of the Empire of Japan* (London: Greenwood Press, 1978 [1906]), p. 7.
32. Article 3—Minobe Tatsukichi, *Chikijō kempō seigi* (Tokyo: Yūhikaku, 1927), p. 512.
33. Shinohara Hatsue, "An Intellectual Foundation for the Road to Pearl Harbor:

Quincy Wright and Tachi Sakutarō." Paper given at Conference on the USA and Japan in World War II, Hofstra University, December 1991, p. 3. Tachi Sakutarō's study on international law is discussed by Bix, *Hirohito*, p. 134; Takahashi Hiroshi, et al., eds., *Shōwa shoki no tennō to kyuchu: Jijūjicho Kawai Yahachi nikki* (Tokyo: Iwanami Shoten, 1993–94): Diary of Kawai Yahachi—*dai ikkan*, pp. 31, 36, and *dai gokan*, p. 16 (January 29, 1931).

Chapter II: The World in Flux

1. Frank B. Freidel, *Franklin D. Roosevelt: Launching the New Deal* (Boston: Little Brown, 1973), p. 120.
2. George Carroll Dyer, *The Amphibians Came to Conquer: The Story of Admiral Richmond Kelly Turner*, vol. 1 (Washington, DC: U.S. Government Printing Office, 1972), p. 150.
3. *Ibid.*
4. *Ibid.*, p. 154—Dyer's interview with Stark, February 16, 1962. Turner assumed this rank by special intervention of President Roosevelt in January 1941.
5. *Ibid.*, p. 155.
6. Edward S. Miller, *War Plan Orange: The U.S. Strategy to Defeat Japan, 1897–1945* (Annapolis: Naval Institute Press, 1991), pp. 2, 7.
7. Clark G. Reynolds, *Admiral John H. Towers. The Struggle for Naval Air Supremacy* (Annapolis: Naval Institute Press, 1991), pp. 211–18, 203–04, 217–18.
8. Towers was told this by a Japanese officer in 1950—Reynolds, *Admiral John H. Towers*, pp. 237–39.
9. *Ibid.*, pp. 185–87.
10. Dyer, *Amphibians*, p. 3. See Dyer for family history.
11. *Ibid.*, p. 26.
12. Turner to his mother, November 28, 1909, *ibid.*, 35–36.
13. Carter's letter to Dyer, February 25, 1964, *ibid.*, p. 59.
14. Dyer, *Amphibians*, p. 66.
15. *Ibid.*, p. 77.
16. Nathan Miller, *Theodore Roosevelt, A Life* (New York: Quill/Morrow, 1992), pp. 481–82; James Reckner, *Teddy Roosevelt's Great White Fleet* (Annapolis: Naval Institute Press, 1957), for a general coverage.
17. H. H. Arnold, *Global Mission* (New York: Harper & Bros., 1949), pp. 11–12.
18. *Asiatic Annual Report, 1928*, p. 33, and *Asiatic Annual Report, 1929*, pp. 6, 11.
19. The firing of Prince Minister General Tanaka Giichi cited by Herbert Bix, *Hirohito and the Making of Modern Japan* (New York: HarperCollins, 2000), pp. 207–08; *The Cambridge History of Japan*, vol. 6: *The Twentieth Century* (Cambridge: Cambridge University Press, 1988), pp. 100ff.
20. COMAIRONS (Commander, Air Operations), *Annual Report*, 1928, p. 9; COMAIRONS, *Annual Report*, 1929, p. 19.
21. COMAIRONS, *Annual Report*, 1929, p. 31; Dyer, *Amphibians*, pp. 89ff.
22. COMAIRONS, *Annual Report*, 1929, p. 28; see also Dyer, *Amphibians*, p. 99.
23. Dyer, *Amphibians*, p. 99. MacArthur remained hostile to the navy all his life, which may have stemmed from sibling jealousy of his brother, Captain Arthur MacArthur III, USN, who had died of appendicitis in December 1923. Arthur of course was MacArthur's father's name.
24. Captain Crutchfield Adair, USN, to Admiral Dyer, April 23, 1962, and Commodore Russell Ihrig to Admiral Dyer, February 1962—Dyer, *Amphibians*, pp. 105–07.

25. On the naval buildup, see Winston Churchill, *The Second World War*, vol. I: *The Gathering Storm* (London: Cassell, 1948), pp. 123–28.
26. *Ibid.*, pp. 84, 123–27.

Chapter III: "Spreading Imperial Virtue"

1. Konoe's essay, *Reform of the World's Status Quo* (*Sekai no genjō kaisō seyo*), trans. Herbert Bix, *Hirohito and the Making of Modern Japan* (New York: HarperCollins, 2000), p. 266.
2. Lord Moran (Sir Charles Wilson), *Churchill: The Struggle for Survival, 1940–1965, Taken from the Diaries of Lord Morau* (Boston: Houghton Mifflin, 1966), p. 12.
3. Bix, *Hirohito*, pp. 235–36, 243. The imperial Japanese family owned a controlling interest in this railway. See Eguchi Keiichi, *Jūgonen sensō shōshi shinpan* (Tokyo: Aoki Shoten, 1991), pp. 36–37. See also Seki Hiroharu, "The Manchurian Incident 1931," in James W. Morley, ed., *Japan Erupts: The London Naval Conference and the Manchurian Incident, 1928–1932* (New York: Columbia University Press, 1984); Hatano Sumio, "Manchū jihin to Kyūchū seiryoku," *Tochigi shigaku*, 5 (1991), p. 110; Harada Kumao, *Harada nikki, dai nikan* (Tokyo: Iwanami Shoten, 1956), p. 64; Fujiwara Akira, *Shōwa tennō no jūgonen sensō* (Tokyo: Aoki Shoten, 1991), pp. 68, 46; Louise Young, *Japan's Total Empire: Manchuria and the Culture of Wartime Imperialism* (Berkeley: University of California Press, 1998), several chapters: Otabe Yūji, "Nii ten niiroku jiken, shubosha wa dare ka," in Fujiwara Akira, et al., eds., *Nihon kindaishi no kyozō to jitsuzō 3, Manshū jiben—haisen* (Tokyo: Osuki Shoten, 1989), pp. 81, 206; and Kisaka Junichirō, "Ajia-Taiheiyō sensō no rekishiteki seikaku o megutte," in *Nenpo: Nihon gendaishi, sōkan, sengo gojūnen no rekishiteki kenshō* (Tokyo: Azuma Shuppan, 1995), pp. 29–30—no ed. but contains an important article on Muchukuo war deaths.
4. "Nara Takeji jijūbukanchō nikki (shō)," in *Chūō koron* (Septemer 1990), pp. 340–41, 342, 344; Eguchi, *Jūgonon sensō shōshi shinpan*, p. 41; Bix, *Hirohito*, p. 239.
5. Herbert Bix, "The Shōwa Emperor's 'Monologue' and the Problem of War Responsibility," *Journal of Japanese Studies*, vol. IV, no. 2 (1992), p. 344.
6. The Japanese killed 41,688 Chinese and pro-Chinese forces in the conquest of Manchuria—Bix, *Hirohito*, p. 719, note 102.
7. *Ibid.*, p. 245.
8. Takahashi Hiroshi, et al., eds., *Shōwa shoki no tennō to kyūchū: Jijūjicho Kawai Yahachi nikki* (Tokyo: Iwanami Shoten, 1993–94): Diary of Kawai Yahachi, pp. 219–27; Bix, *Hirohito*, pp. 246–47.
9. Toshihiko, "The Extension of Hostilities, 1931–1932," pp. 287ff.; Gary B. Ostrower, *Collective Insecurity: The United States and the League of Nations During the Early Thirties* (London: Associated University Press, 1993), pp. 94–96.
10. Ostrower, *Collective Insecurity*, pp. 94–96. Hirohito did of course resume hostilities a few years later.
11. Bix, *Hirohito*, p. 252.
12. Young, *Japan's Total Empire*, and Winston Churchill, *The Second World War*, vol. I: *The Gathering Storm* (London: Cassell, 1948), pp. 84, 123–27.
13. Bix, *Hirohito*, pp. 256–57.
14. Herbert Bix, "Japanese Imperialism and the Manchurian Economy, 1900–1931, *China Quarterly*, 51 (1972), pp. 425–43; Dan Kurzman, *Kishi and Japan: The Search for the Sun* (New York: Ivan Obolensky, 1960), p. 126 and chap. 12.

15. Bix translates, *Hirohito*, p. 258; Ito Takashi and Hirose Junkou, eds., *Makino Nobaki nikki* (Tokyo: Chūō Koronsha, 1990): Diary of Makino Nobaki, pp. 534–35.
16. *Makino Nobaki nikki*, p. 546.
17. Takamatsu, *Takamatsu no miya, dai nikan* (Tokyo: Chuo Koronsha, 1997), pp. 89–91. Takamatsu's diary.
18. Captain Ernie King, Moffett's previous second in command, had made an attempt to take over the bureau and oust Moffett. This was a familiar pattern to be found throughout King's aggressive scramble to the top, no holds barred—Thomas Buell, *Master of Sea Power. A Biography of Fleet Admiral Ernest J. King* (Boston: Little, Brown, 1980), p. 79.
19. Bix, *Hirohito*, pp. 250–51, gives this figure; Terasaki Hidenari and Marika Teresaki Miller, eds., *Shōwa tenno dokuhakuroku, Terasaki Hidenari, goyōgakari nikki* (Tokyo: Bungei Shunjūsha, 1991), p. 28; Walter LaFeber, *The Clash: U.S.-Japan Relations Throughout History* (New York: W. W. Norton, 1997), pp. 172ff.
20. Yu Shinju, *Manshū jihenki no Chu-Nichi gai koshi: kenkyū*, (Tokyo: Tohō Shōten, 1986), p. 381.
21. Kenneth S. Davis, *FDR: The New York Years, 1928–1933* (New York: Random House, 1994), p. 411. Stimson announced this on January 7, 1932.
22. Winston Churchill, *The Second World War*, vol. IV: *The Hinge of Fate* (London: Cassell, 1951), p. 60. Although made later, Churchill's statement applies in the full sense here as well.
23. Archibald Turnbull and Clifford Lord, *History of United States Naval Aviation* (New Haven: Yale University Press, 1949), p. 276.
24. The secretary of the navy's *Annual Report, 1930*, pp. 8, 567. These figures were effective as of June 30, 1931, total 79,991 naval personnel including 5,451 line officers. The hard reality of the budgetary cutbacks meant that the navy had only 520 aviators with a total of 928 aircraft of all kinds. Five hundred of these planes were assigned outside the United States. At the same time, the navy's air arm, the Bureau of Aeronautics, lost $20 million of the funds available for its experimental aircraft program and for the purchase of planes and engines which would be needed in the event of a new war or conflict. The navy's governing General Board, as well as the secretary of the navy, described these reductions as "unsafe and inadvisable," while counseling at Geneva now that the United States should support "a worldwide system of armaments stabilized at the lowest level obtainable without undue friction or misunderstanding." General Board letter of October 1931, in George Caroll Dyer, *The Amphibians Came to Conquer: The Story of Admiral Richmond Kelly Turner*, vol. 1 (Washington, DC: U.S. Government Printing Office, 1972), pp. 108, 111.
25. On the *Ranger*, etc., see Turnbull and Lord, *History of United States Naval Aviation*, p. 285. *Yorktown* was laid down on May 21, 1934, and the *Enterprise* on July 16, 1934.
26. In 1927, the navy's General Board recommended more than 1,000 planes for the navy and the construction of five 13,800-ton carriers over the next five years, but was overruled by a Congress that allotted funds for one carrier only: the *Ranger*, which arrived many years too late—Turnbull and Lord, *History of United States Naval Aviation*, p. 261.
27. D. Clayton James, *The Years of MacArthur*, vol. I: *1880–1941* (Boston: Houghton Mifflin, 1970), p. 378.
28. February 1933—Bix, *Hirohito*, p. 266.

29. Ibid., pp. 271–72, translated by Bix. The province can also be spelled Hepei.
30. Youli Sun, *China and the Origins of the Pacific War, 1931–1945* (London: St. Martin's Press, 1993), chap. 12 (italics added). See also Young, *Japan's Total Empire*, for various sections on ideology, etc.; James B. Crowley, *Japan's Quest for Autonomy: National Security and Foreign Policy, 1930–1938* (Princeton: Princeton University Press, 1966), p. xv; for documentary film, Minzo in GS40, pp. 242–52.
31. Hijoi Kokumin, *Essays on the Time of Emergency Confronting the Nation*, cited in Bix, *Hirohito*, pp. 277–78.
32. Chiang Kai-shek was removed in June 1935 by the signing of the Ho Ying-ch'in-Umezu Yoshijirō Agreement. For Chiang's participation throughout this period, see Keiji Furuya, *Chiang Kai-Shek: His Life and Times*, trans. Chun-ming Chang (New York: St. John's University, 1981), beginning with Parts IV and V.
33. This doctrine of "no surrender" was officially printed in the army's Field Service Code (*senjikun*), issued during World War II: "Do not shame yourself by being taken prisoner alive; die so as not to leave behind a soiled name."
34. Bix, *Hirohito*, p. 295.
35. *Ibid.*, p. 297. The officer in question was Aizawa Saburō.
36. See Bix, *Hirohito*, pp. 295–301, for the best coverage of these events.
37. *Ibid.*
38. Hiranuma was also a senior Justice Ministry official—Bix, *Hirohito*, p. 227. Bix translates Masuda Tomoko, "Saitō Makoto kyokoku itchi naikakuron," p. 247.
39. Bix, *Hirohito*, pp. 65, 308, 723; Gaimushō Hikota, ed., *Nihon gaikō nenryō narabi ni shuyō bunsho, ge* (Tokyo: Hara Shohō, 1969), pp. 344–45, 347.
40. Bix, *Hirohito*, p. 302, gives Japanese army figures for this year. David C. Evans and Mark R. Peattie, *Kaigun: Strategy, Tactics, and Technology in the Imperial Japanese Navy, 1887–1941* (Annapolis: Naval Institute Press, 1997), provides naval personnel figures for the period 1928–42 at p. 402. On foreign policy objectives, see Antony Best, *Britain, Japan and Pearl Harbor: Avoiding War in East Asia, 1936–41* (London: Routledge, 1995), pp. 17–28; Kohayashi Motohiro, "Hirota Koki ni sensō sekinin wa nakatta ka," in Fujiwara Akira et al., eds., *Niho kindaishi no kyozo to Jitsuzō*, 3 (Autumn 1991), pp. 105–07; and Gaimushō, ed., *Nihon gaiko nenryō narabi ni shuyō bunsho, ge*, pp. 344–45, 347—paraphrased by Bix, *Hirohito*, p. 308.
41. T. A. Bisson, *Japan in China* (New York: Macmillan, 1938; Greenwood Press, 1973), pp. 222–35; Moriyana Atsushi, *Nichi Bei kaisen no seiji katei* (Tokyo: Yoshikawa Kobunkan, 1998).
42. Yamada Akira, ed., "Kokusaku no kijun," August 7, 1936, in *Gaikō shiryō: Kindai Nihon no bochō to shinryaku* (Tokyo: Shin Nihon Shuppansha, 1997), p. 270; Bix, *Hirohito*, pp. 309, 311.
43. Evans and Peattie, *Kaigun*, p. 404, charting the years 1934–41. Japan's absurd shortsightedness regarding the manpower and logistics needed for the seizure, conquest, and consolidation of many millions of peoples in dozens of scattered lands would mirror Gemany's own overreaching of its capabilities in its aims of conquest over the whole of Europe. See also Jonathan Marshall, *To Have and Have Not: Southeast Asian Raw Materials and the Origins of the Pacific War* (Berkeley: University of California Press, 1995), pp. 7–32, 36–53.
44. Evans and Peattie, *Kaigun*, p. 408.
45. *Ibid.*, p. 406.
46. Including isoctane for use as an additive.

47. Evans and Peattie, *Kaigun*, p. 410.
48. On oil, see *ibid.*, pp. 406–11. In December 1941, Japan's total oil reserves from all sources were 10.39 million kiloliters. Reserves by the second year of the war, in 1942, had fallen to 2.14 million kiloliters, and by 1943 to a negative reserve capacity of –1.29 million kiloliters, despite the optimistic and fictive reserves of 2.74 million kiloliters claimed by the Japanese navy. See Evans and Peattie, *Kaigun*, chart 11-3, p. 412.
49. Bix, *Hirohito*, pp. 313–35, quoting *Kokutai no Bongi*.
50. The comparisons to Napoleon are inevitable. He too made catastrophic decisions in defiance of all logic, indeed often based merely on capricious or egotistical whim. These would include the campaigns against Egypt, Britain, Spain, and Russia, to name four of the most obvious ones, all of which ended in unmitigated disaster. Napoleon, like the Japanese military leaders in the 1930s and 1940s, failed to draw up lists of his real capabilities and compare them with those of his enemies.

Chapter IV: "The Eight Corners of the World"

1. Herbert Bix, *Hirohito and the Making of Modern Japan* (New York: HarperCollins, 2000), p. 383.
2. *Ibid.*
3. *Ibid.*, pp. 317–18; Kobayashi Hideo, "Ryūjōkō jiken o megutte: Ryūjōkō jiken rokujussūnen ni yosete," in *Rekishigaku kenkyū*, 699 (July 1997), pp. 30–35; Jonathan Haslam, *The Soviet Union and the Threat from the East, 1933–41: Moscow, Tokyo and the Prelude to the Pacific War* (Pittsburgh: University of Pittsburgh Press, 1992), pp. 89–90; Clark W. Tinch, "Quasi-War Between Japan and the USSR, 1937–1939," *World Politics*, vol. 3, no. 2 (July 1951), pp. 177–78.
4. Kobayashi, "Ryūjōkō jiken o megutte," pp. 30–35.
5. *Ibid.*
6. Bix, *Hirohito*, pp. 321 and 322.
7. David C. Evans and Mark R. Peattie, *Kaigun: Strategy, Tactics, and Technology in the Imperial Japanese Navy, 1887–1941* (Annapolis: Naval Institute Press, 1997), pp. 305, 308–10. These new models were commissioned in 1935 and 1936, respectively.
8. Bix, *Hirohito*, p. 324; Usui Katsumi, *Nitchū sensō: Wahei ka sensen kakudai ka* (Tokyo: Chūō Shinsho, 1967), p. 46; and *Sensi shōha: Shina jihen rikugun sakusen (1): Shōwa jūsannen ichigatsu made* (1975), pp. 283–85, 290–91, 297–99.
9. Bix, *Hirohito*, p. 325, Bix's translation; Fujiwara Akira, "Nitchū sensō ni okeru horyo gyakusatsu," in *Kikan sensō sekinin kenyū*, 9 (Autumn 1995), p. 23.
10. Kenneth S. Davis, *FDR: Into the Storm, 1937–1940* (New York: Random House, 1993), pp. 130ff., 250ff.; Robert Sherwood, *Roosevelt and Hopkins, An Intimate History* (New York: Harper & Bros., 1948), p. 125; Henry L. Stimson and McGeorge Bundy, *On Active Service in Peace and War* (New York: Harper & Bros., 1948), p. 142; Ed Cray, *General of the Army. George C. Marshall, Soldier and Statesman* (New York: W. W. Norton, 1990), pp. 123–24; and for FDR's Quarantine Speech, Samuel I. Rosenman, ed., *The Public Papers and Addresses of Franklin D. Roosevelt* (New York: Macmillan, 1938), vol. 6, pp. 407–11.
11. Statistics provided by Bix, *Hirohito*, pp. 333–34.
12. On Japanese looting, see Herbert Bix, "Japanese Imperialism and the Manchurian Economy, 1900–1931," *China Quarterly*, 51 (1972), pp. 425–43; W. G. Beasley,

Japanese Imperialism, 1894–1945 (Oxford: Oxford University Press, 1987); Meirion and Susan Harries, *Soldiers of the Sun: The Rise and Fall of the Imperial Japanese Army* (New York: Random House, 1991); Sterling and Peggy Seagrave, *The Yamato Dynasty: The Secret History of Japan's Imperial Family* (London: Bantam Books, 1999), chap. 8; John Toland, *Rising Sun: The Decline and Fall of the Japanese Empire, 1936–1945* (New York: Random House, 1970), chap. 10 and p. 168; and Haruko Taya and Theodore F. Cook, *Japan at War: An Oral History* (New York: Free Press, 1992).

13. The figure of 200,000 women kidnapped as slaves for Japanese army brothels in the 1930s and 1940s is given in the *International Herald Tribune*, Thursday, December 7, 2000. See also Iris Chan, *The Rape of Nanking: The Forgotten Holocaust of World War II* (New York: Basic Books, 1997), pp. 222ff.; Taya and Cook, *Japan at War*; Toland, *Rising Sun*; Cambridge University Press's *History of Japan*, vol. V; Bix, *Hirohito*, pp. 334–35; *The Tokyo War Crimes Trial: The Complete Transcripts of the Proceedings of the International Military Tribunal for the Far East*, ed. John Pritchard and Sonia Maganua Zaide (New York and London: Garland, 1981).
14. "Records of the US Dept. of State, Political Relation Between the US and Japan, 1930–1939," reel no. 3, file no. 711.94/1184, Nat. Arch.
15. Bix, *Hirohito*, p. 340; George Carroll Dyer, *The Amphibians Came to Conquer: The Story of Admiral Richmond Kelly Turner*, vol. 1 (Washington, DC: U.S. Government Printing Office, 1972), p. 168; *Washington Post*, December 14, 1937; *New York Times*, December 14–17, 1941; *The Times* (London), December 14 and 16, 1941.
16. Bix, *Hirohito*, pp. 343–44, 361–62, 617; Kasahara Tokushi, *Nitchū zenmen sensō to Kaigun* (Tokyo: Iwanami Shinso, 1995), pp. 304–05.
17. Alvin Cox, *Nomonhan: Japan Against Russia, 1939* (Stanford: Stanford University Press, 1985), vol. 1, pp. 255ff, vol. 2, p. 919; Watanabe Toshihiko, "Nanajū ichi butain to Nagata Tetsuzan," in *Chūō Daigaku* (Tokyo: Chūō Daiku Shuppanhu, 1993), pp. 275–76, 296, 303, note 68.
18. Bix, *Hirohito*, pp. 364, 617. See also Hal Gold, *Unit 731: Testimony* (Tokyo: Yenbooks, 1996), pp. 65–66; Robert Harris and Jeremy Paxman, *A Higher Form of Killing: The Secret Story of Chemical and Biological Warfare, 1932–45* (New York: Hill & Wang, 1982); Sheldon Harris, *Factories of Death: Japanese Biological Warfare 1932–45* (London: Routledge, 1994); B. V. A. Röling and Antonio Cassesse, *The Tokyo Trial and Beyond* (Cambridge: Polity Press, 1993); Arnold Brackman, *The Other Nuremberg: The Untold Story of the Tokyo War Crimes Trials* (New York: Morrow, 1987); Robert Gomer, John Powell, and B.V. A. Röling, "Japan's Biological Weapons, 1930–1945," *Bulletin of the Atomic Scientists* (October 1981), pp. 45–53; and *The Times*, July 7, 1994. Biological weapons were used in China until 1942, when forbidden by Hirohito. See Awaya Kentarō and Fujiwara Akira, "Kaisetsu," in Kin Gakujn, ed., *Nihongun no kagakusen: Chōgoku senjō ni okeru dokugasu sa kusen* (Tokyo: ōtsuki Shoten, 1996), p. 376; Stephen Endicott and Edward Hagerman, *The United States and Biological Warfare: Secrets from the Early Cold War and Korea* (Bloomington: Indiana University Press, 1998); Yoshimi Yoshiaki and Matsumo Seiya, "Dokugasusen kankei shiryō II, Kaisetsu," in *Fugonen sensō Gōkuhi Shiryōshū bokan*, 2 (Kyoto: Funi Shuppananankan, 1997), p. 27; *Gendai shishiryō*, 9, *Nitschū sensō* 2; Usui Katsumi (Tokyo: *Misuzo shohō*, 1964), pp. 211–12; Tanaka Nobumasa, *Dokyumento Shōwa tennō 2, kaisen* (Tokyo: Ryokufu Shuppan, 1985), p. 96; and Hoshimi Matsuno, *Dokugasusen kankei shiryō II: Kaisetsu* (Tokyo: Fuji Shuppan, 1997), pp. 25, 29. According to Dr. Oiu Min-

gauan's testimony before a Japanese court in January 2001, "cholera, typhoid, anthrax and bubonic plague"–doused fleas killed 50,000 Chinese in the province of Zhejiang. "Japan's germ warfare has left behind problems that still threaten our lives," he testified—*International Herald Tribune*, June 25, 2001, p. 4. See also John Dower, *Embracing Defeat: Japan in the Wake of World War II* (New York: W. W. Norton, 1999), pp. 444ff.

19. Sterling and Peggy Seagrave, *The Yamata Dynasty* (London: Bantam Books, 1999), pp. 172–74. See especially Gold, *Unit 731*, which covers all aspects of Hirohito's biological warfare.
20. Bix, *Hirohito*, pp. 360–61, Bix's translation.
21. *Ibid.*, pp. 364–65; Peter Calvocoressi, Guy Wint, and John Pritchard, *Total War: The Causes and Courses of the Second World War*, 2nd rev. ed. (Harmondsworth, UK: Penguin, 1995).
22. Bix, *Hirohito*, p. 353, Bix's translation.
23. *Ibid.*, p. 354.
24. Bix analyzes this relationship—*ibid.*, pp. 370–71.
25. *Zokugendaishi shiryō 4: Rikugun, Hata Shunroyku nisshi* (Tokyo: Misuzu Shohō, 1983), p. 258: Diary of Hata Shunroku. Hirohito to Kido, June 20, 1940, Bix's translation, *Hirohito*, pp. 371–72.
26. Bix's translation, *Hirohito*, p. 372.
27. The new Konoe government was created on July 17, 1940. Matsuoka's interview *New York Herald Tribune (Sunday)*, July 21, 1940.
28. Marshall, *To Have and Have Not*, chap. 5; Moriyama, *Nichi-bei kaisen no seiji katei*, p. 54.
29. Bix's translation, *Hirohito*, pp. 376–77; Sawada Shigeru, *Sambō jicho Sawada Shigeru kaisōruku* (Tokyo: Fuyō Shohō, 1982), pp. 72–74.
30. Bix, *Hirohito*, p. 377.
31. French colonial interest in the Pacific and Far East dated from Louis Philippe's July Monarchy, 1830–48, and resulted in the later annexation of Tahiti as a colony under the Third Republic in 1880. Cambodia and Cochin-China (South Indochina) were occupied by Napoleon III's Second Empire in the late 1860s, and under the Third Republic in 1870s. The Treat of Hué, signed in 1883, gave France a protectorate over Annam and Tonkin, an expansion sponsored by Jules Ferry and confirmed by the Treaty of Tsientsin with China in June 1885. "Pacification" of these regions continued for many decades thereafter and was never fully achieved, hence the large French army presence there as late as the eve of World War II.
32. Roosevelt was of course attempting to buy time and to rearm. Even a year and a half later, when Japan attacked Pearl Harbor, American armed forces were hardly able to hold their own.
33. J.-B. Duroselle, *L'Abîme, 1939–1944* (Paris: Imprimérie Nationale, 1986), p. 251.
34. *Ibid.*, pp. 251, 253.
35. Accord signed by Ambassador Arsène Henry and Foreign Minister Matsuoka at Tokyo, September 22, 1940, Archives, Ministre des Affaires Etrangères (Paris: MAE, 1940), Baudouin, carton no. 14, T. 201–203, September 20, 1940, T. 703–708, and T. 709–714, Arsène Henry, September 22, 1940; and Duroselle, *L'Abîme, 1939–1944*, pp. 255–56. The MAE 1940 Baudouin Papers, carton no. 14, are the essential ones for the original documentation.
36. Bix, *Hirohito*, p. 380.
37. Harada diaries—Harada Kumao, *Harada nikki, Saionji kō to seikyoku*, vol. I (Tokyo: Iwanami Shoten, 1950), p. 347.

38. Bix, *Hirohito*, p. 276 (italics added).
39. Bix's translation, *Hirohito*, p. 383, of Senda's *Tennō to Chokugo to Shōwashi*, pp. 311–13.
40. Churchill to Lord Moran, December 23, 1941: Lord Moran, *Churchill: The Struggle for Survival, 1940–1965, Taken from the Diaries of Lord Moran* (Boston: Houghton Mifflin, 1966), p. 12.
41. Konoe international press conference in Kyoto, October 4, 1940, *New York Times*, October 7, 1940 (italics added).
42. Article in *The Oriental Economist*, vol. 7, no. 11 (November 1940), p. 640.

Chapter V: Unlimited National Emergency

1. Winston Churchill, *History of the Second World War*, vol. III: *The Grand Alliance* (London: Cassell, 1950), p. 21.
2. George Carroll Dyer, *The Amphibians Came to Conquer: The Story of Admiral Richmond Kelly Turner*, vol. 1 (Washington, DC: U.S. Government Printing Office, 1972), p. 181.
3. Dyer, *Amphibians*, p. 133.
4. R. K. Turner to CNO Stark, "Report of conversation with Japanese Ambassador," March 13, 1941, in Dyer, *Amphibians*, p. 166. U.S. Congress, Joint Committee on the Investigation of the Pearl Harbor Attack, *Hearings: Pearl Harbor Attack* (Washington, DC: U.S. Government Printing Office, 1946), Part 12, pp. 45, 68, 72–73. See also DWP (Turner) to CNO (Stark), OP-12-CTB, memorandum, July 11, 1941, in Dyer, *Amphibians*, pp. 167–68.
5. Japanese Soviet Neutrality Pact, signed April 13, 1941.
6. Herbert Bix, *Hirohito and the Making of Modern Japan* (New York: HarperCollins, 2000), p. 396.
7. *Ibid.*, p. 397 (italics added); Nobutake Ike, ed. and trans., *Japan's Decision for War: Records of the 1941 Peace Conference* (Palo Alto, CA: Stanford University Press, 1967), pp. 78–79.
8. Dyer, *Amphibians*, p.167. Admiral Nomura informed Turner on July 20, 1941, of Japanese plans to invade Indochina, but the CNO had learned of this on July 19 after decoding a Japanese diplomatic message dated July 14.
9. Treaty of May 9, 1940, Thailand-Indochina, following a heavy French naval bombardment, but resulting in the French having to return the Laotian provinces claimed by Thailand—J.-B. Duroselle, *L'Abîme, 1939–1944* (Paris: Imprimérie Nationale, 1986), p. 295.
10. *Ibid.*, pp. 295–96.
11. Turner report to CNO, July 20, 1941, in Dyer, *Amphibians*, pp. 167–68.
12. Sherwood, *Roosevelt and Hopkins*, pp. 41ff.
13. Ibid., pp. 31, 41ff. On Hopkins's earlier days and social work, see June Hopkins, *Harry Hopkins, Sudden Hero, Brash Reformer* (New York: St. Martin's Press, 1999). On pp. 144–45, she discusses his three sons and Hopkins's abandonment of his wife, Ethel Gross, for Barbara Duncan.
14. Dr. Jack Goldberg, quoted in Sherwood, *Roosevelt and Hopkins*, pp. 29, 49.
15. *Ibid.*, p. 33.
16. *Ibid*, p. 52.
17. Hopkins remarried a third time, to Louise Macy, July 1942. On his illness, see *ibid.*, p. 113.
18. *Ibid.*, pp. 202–04, 8–9.

19. *Ibid.*, pp. 8–9.
20. Turner to Hopkins, White House, April 29, 1921, quoted in Dyer, *Amphibians*, p. 170.
21. The Declaration of a Limited National Emergency was made by FDR on September 8, 1939.
22. Dyer, *Amphibians*, pp. 170–72. See also Sherwood.
23. Sherwood, *Roosevelt and Hopkins*, p. 233.
24. Lord Moran, *Churchill: The Struggle for Survival, 1940–1965, Taken from the Diaries of Lord Moran* (Boston: Houghton Mifflin, 1966), p. 13.
25. Churchill, *Grand Alliance*, p. 21.
26. Sherwood, *Roosevelt and Hopkins*, pp. 256–57.
27. *Ibid*, pp. 242–43. On merchant ship sinkings just by U-boats: from April 10, 1940, until March 17, 1941, 1,677,000 gross tons had gone down in the Atlantic; from March 18, 1941, to December 6, 1941, Britain lost another 1,130,000 gross tons of merchant shipping in that sea. Churchill, *Grand Alliance*, pp. 136–37. Cf. p. 130 for shipping lost due to warplanes. For U-boat sinkings in 1942, see Churchill, *The Second World War*, vol. IV: *The Hinge of Fate* (London: Cassell, 1951), pp. 109, 112, 116–17.
28. See Kenneth S. Davis, *FDR: The War President, 1940–1943* (New York: Random House, 2000), for details on these torturous negotiations, pp. 103ff. It was known as HR (House of Representatives Bill) 1776. Davis gives the best coverage of the agonizing procedure over several months.
29. See Churchill, *Hinge of Fate*, pp. 60 and 14, for the Curtin correspondence.
30. PM Churchill's Personal Telegram, T. 871, no. 7472, to FDR, November 26, 1941, Churchill Papers, quoted in Martin Gilbert, *Winston S. Churchill, 1939–1941*, vol. VI: *Finest Hour* (London: Minerva/Heinemann, 1983), pp. 1260–61.
31. Sherwood, *Roosevelt and Hopkins*, pp. 272–73.
32. Martin Gilbert, *The Second World War. A Complete History* (New York: Henry Holt, 1989), p. 162.
33. Sherwood, *Roosevelt and Hopkins*, p. 264, Gilbert, *Finest Hour*, p. 1031.
34. Davis, *FDR: The War President*, p. 105.
35. Sherwood, *Roosevelt and Hopkins*, p. 298 (italics in the original).
36. Sherwood quotes Hopkins, *ibid.*, p. 321.
37. *Ibid.*, pp. 327–45, and 343–44 for description of Stalin. During the long air journey from Scotland to Archangel, Hopkins nearly died in the PBY Catalina W 6416 because the plane was unheated and unpressurized. The pilots had not been forewarned of the serious state of Hopkins's health.
38. Sherwood, *Roosevelt and Hopkins*, gives the view as seen from the Oval Room, p. 366; Davis, *FDR: The War President*, p. 273.
39. Sherwood, *Roosevelt and Hopkins*, pp. 275–76.
40. *Hearings: Pearl Harbor Attack*, Part 1, SECNAV to SECWAR, letter dated January 24, 1941, p. 120.
41. Clark G. Reynolds, *Admiral John H. Towers. The Struggle for Naval Air Supremacy* (Annapolis: Naval Institute Press, 1991), pp. 217–18, 237–38.
42. *Hearings: Pearl Harbor Attack*, Part 12, pp. 45, 68, 72, 73; Dyer, *Amphibians*, pp. 167–68.
43. Dept. War Plans (DWP, Turner) to CNO (Stark), memorandum, July 19, 1941, U.S. Department of State, *Foreign Relations of the United States, 1941* (Washington, DC: U.S. Government Printing Office, no. 6325), vol. IV, pp. 839–40; Gerow (Army War Plans) and Turner, joint memorandum for President Franklin D. Roo-

sevelt, November 5, 1941, "Estimate Concerning Far Eastern Situation." Franklin Delano Roosevelt Library, Hyde Park, NY.

44. *Hearings: Pearl Harbor Attack*, Part 12, pp. 45, 68, 72–73; also Dyer, *Amphibians*, pp. 167–68: DWP (Turner) to CNO (Stark), OP-12-CTB, memorandum, July 11, 1941 (italics added).
45. Dyer, *Amphibians*, p. 188.
46. King was given a secret code name for this occasion, with the president's instructions to inform no one about this meeting. King was very good at keeping a secret—Thomas Buell, *Master of Sea Power: A Biography of Fleet Admiral Ernest J. King* (Boston: Little, Brown, 1980), pp. 142–43. On July 26, 1941, FDR froze all Japanese asssets in the United States—Davis, *FDR: The War President*, p. 263; D. Clayton James, *The Years of MacArthur*, vol. I: *1880–1941* (Boston: Houghton Mifflin, 1970), p. 590.

Chapter VI: "We Cannot Speculate with the Security of This Country"

1. Henry Stimson, Secretary of War, memorandum, October 2, 1940, in Henry L. Stimson and McGeorge Bundy, *On Active Service in Peace and War* (New York: Harper & Bros., 1948), p. 191.
2. Herbert Bix, *Hirohito and the Making of Modern Japan* (New York: HarperCollins, 2000), p. 227.
3. *Washington Post*, August 3, 1941, p. 3.
4. H. H. Arnold, *Global Mission* (New York: Harper & Bros., 1949), p. 246.
5. *Ibid.*, p. 247.
6. *Ibid.*, p. 248.
7. E.g., *Washington Post*, August 8–10, 1941, and *New York Times*, August 6–10, 1941.
8. Arnold, *Global Mission*, p. 248.
9. *Ibid.*, p. 249.
10. *Ibid.*, p. 250.
11. *Washington Post*, Thursday, August 7, 1941.
12. Arnold, *Global Mission*, p. 246.
13. *Ibid.*, p. 254. Hopkins had been given Captain Leach's spacious cabin and had been receiving blood transfusions ever since sailing from Scapa Flow.
14. George VI to President Roosevelt, August 3, 1941, Roosevelt Papers, Hyde Park, NY.
15. Arnold, *Global Mission*, pp. 82ff., 216ff. Arnold had been in England and France during World War I—*ibid.*, pp. 82ff.—and then again in April 1941 on air force business, pp. 216ff.
16. Arnold, *ibid.*, pp. 251–52, and Martin Gilbert, *Winston S. Churchill, 1939–1941*, vol. VI: *Finest Hour* (London: Minerva/Heinemann, 1989), pp. 1162ff.
17. Gilbert, *Finest Hour*, p. 1159.
18. Arnold, *Global Mission*, pp. 245, 251; Ed Cray, *General of the Army. George C. Marshall, Soldier and Statesman* (New York: W. W. Norton, 1990), p. 216. In 1940, the British government had ordered or held options for 20,000 planes and 42,000 engines—Arnold, *Global Mission*, p. 197.
19. Arnold, *Global Mission*, pp. 254–55.
20. Cray, *General of the Army*, p. 185.
21. Kenneth S. Davis, *FDR: The War President, 1940–1943* (New York: Random House, 2000), p. 166.

22. *New York Times*, Saturday, August 16, 1941.
23. *Washington Post*, Wednesday, August 13, 1941, p. 1. Eventually $750 million was later reinstated after a protracted battle. Stimson and Bundy, *On Active Service*, p. 257. Stimson gives U.S. Army strength on VE-Day as 8,300,000, exclusive of others no longer in the service or killed in action.
24. *Washington Post*, Wednesday, August 13, 1941, p. 1.
25. Arnold, *Global Mission*, pp. 244–45.
26. Diaries of Ian Jacob, August 11, 1941, Jacob Papers, Churchill Archives, Cambridge University.
27. *Washington Post*, e.g., Wednesday, August 13, 1941, p. 1. The cost of the new building was estimated at between $25 and $100 million when completed.
28. Cray, *General of the Army*, p. 207.
29. *Ibid.*, p. 209.
30. Stimson and Bundy, *On Active Service*, p. 185; Harold L. Ickes, *The Secret Diary of Harold L. Ickes,* vol. III: *The Lowering Clouds* (New York: Simon & Schuster, 1954), pp. 659–60.
31. Bix, *Hirohito*, pp. 406–07. Nagano advised Hirohito on July 21, 1941.
32. *Ibid.*, p. 413.
33. *New York Times*, Thursday, August 14, 1941, p. 1.
34. *New York Times*, Friday, August 15, 1941, p. 1.
35. *Ibid.*
36. *Washington Post*, Friday, August 15, 1941, p. 2.
37. Diary of Ian Jacob, August 19, 1941, summarizing their report, Churchill Archives, Cambridge University. This was the first time Roosevelt and Churchill had met as heads of state, but in fact they had met previously during World War I in England when Roosevelt was serving as assistant secretary of the navy—Elliott Roosevelt, ed., *The Roosevelt Letters, Being the Personal Correspondence of Franklin Delano Roosevelt* (New York: Duell, Sloan & Pearce, 1950), vol. 2: *1905–1928*, p. 286 for July 26, 1917, luncheon.
38. War Cabinet, No. 84, 1951 (August 19, 1941, 11.30 a.m.), "Cabinet papers, 65/19," Public Record Office, United Kingdom.
39. Bix, *Hirohito*, p. 417.
40. *Ibid.*, p. 421.
41. *Ibid.*, pp. 423–24.
42. *Ibid.*, pp. 423–25.
43. Paul Dull, *A Battle History of the Imperial Japanese Navy, 1941–1945* (Annapolis: Naval Institute Press, 1978), p. 10.
44. Bix, *Hirohito*, pp. 421, 430.
45. Tanaka Nobumasa, *Dokyumento Showā tennō, dai nikan* (Tokyo: Ryokufu Shuppan, 1964), p. 256; *Kido Kōichi nikki, gen*, p. 928; Nobutake Ike, ed. and trans., *Japan's Decision for War: Records of the 1941 Peace Conference* (Palo Alto, CA: Stanford University Press, 1967), p. 279.

Chapter VII: General Quarters!

1. Turner to Stark, January 24, 1941, quoted in George Carroll Dyer, *The Amphibians Came to Conquer: The Story of Admiral Richmond Kelly Turner*, vol. 1 (Washington, DC: U.S. Government Printing Office, 1972), pp. 177–79.
2. Herbert Bix, *Hirohito and the Making of Modern Japan* (New York: HarperCollins, 2000), p. 227.

3. CNO letter April 16, 1941, to SECNav, and memorandum then sent on for Roosevelt's signature.
4. DWP (Turner) to CNO (Stark), memorandum, July 11, 1941, in Dyer, *Amphibians*, p. 181.
5. Stark to Cooke, July 31, 1941, in Dyer, *Amphibians*, p. 181.
6. U.S. Congress, Joint Committee on the Investigation of the Pearl Harbor Attack, *Hearings: Pearl Harbor Attack* (Washington, DC: U.S. Government Printing Office, 1946), Part 26, p. 277 (italics added).
7. William F. Friedman, the head of the army's Signal Intelligence Service on February 20, 1939, was given the headache of cracking the new Japanese diplomatic code "Purple" which was now introduced. Frank Rowlett and a team of cryptoanalysts finally solved many of the problems, but it was a young MIT engineer, Leo Rosen, who actually invented the "Purple machine" required to decipher the new code, producing the decrypts code called "Magic" or "Ultra" on the third floor of the Munitions building in 1940—Stephen Budiansky, *Battle of Wits: The Complete Story of Codebreaking in World War II* (New York: Free Press, 2000), pp. 164, 216.
8. Official letter of June 1, 1941, in Appendix C, p. 1, prepared by Vice Admiral David C. Richardson, ed., *Pearl Harbor and the Kimmel Controversy: The Views Today*. Colloquium, Naval Historical Foundation, Washington, DC, December 7, 1999 (italics added).
9. *Ibid.*, Appendix C, pp. 1–2.
10. W. Jaspar Holmes, *Double-Edged Secrets: U.S. Naval Intelligence Operations in the Pacific During World War II* (Annapolis: Naval Institute Press, 1979), pp. 38–39; *Pearl Harbor and the Kimmel Controversy*, Appendix D by Captain Beach.
11. Some authors have erroneously attributed this decision to Turner, as well as the decision to send the remaining fourth Purple machine to England. Even Turner's superior, CNO Stark, lacked the authority to take such action.
12. Holmes, *Double-Edged Secrets*, pp. 48, 55.
13. *Ibid.*, pp. 25–26.
14. November 15, 1941, J-19 code, no. 111 (translated December 3); November 18, 1941, J-19 code, no. 113 (translated December 5), and November 18, 1941, J-19 code, no. 222 (translated December 6), followed on November 29 by another ship-movement request from Tokyo, J-19 code, translated by the navy—all in *Pearl Harbor and the Kimmel Controversy*, Appendix C.
15. November 4, 1941, Purple code, no. 736 (translated November 5)—David Richardson, *ibid.*
16. November 16, 1941, Purple (translated November 17)—Appendix C, pp. 4ff.
17. November 22, 1941, Purple 812, in *ibid.*
18. Stark to CINCAF and CINCPAC, November 24, 1941, WPD 4544-12 (italics added); Forrest C. Pogue, *George C. Marshall*, vol. 2: *Ordeal and Hope, 1939–1942* (New York: Viking Press, 1966), pp. 204–05. There is also the separate issue of the "winds message," a coded radio message to indicate which force would be striking at which objective. Washington never clearly understood the intent, and the information could not help either Kimmel or MacArthur. The confusion over this message is mentioned in *Pearl Harbor Hearings*.
19. Holmes, *Double-Edged Secrets*, pp. 25–26.
20. *Ibid.*, pp. 38–39; *Pearl Harbor and the Kimmel Controversy*, Appendix D by Captain Beach (italics added).
21. Quoted in *Pearl Harbor and the Kimmel Controversy*, Appendix D, "Operational," p. iii (italics added).

22. *Ibid.*, p. iv (italics added).
23. *Ibid.* See also Ed Cray, *General of the Army. George C. Marshall, Soldier and Statesman* (New York: W. W. Norton, 1990), p. 245, GCM to MacArthur, November 28, 1941, George C. Marshall Research Library, Lexington, VA.
24. *Pearl Harbor and the Kimmel Controversy*, Appendix D, p. iv.
25. *Ibid.*
26. *Ibid.*, p. v.
27. CNO to CINCAF, CINCPAC, Com 14 and 16, December 3, 1941, *Pearl Harbor Hearings*, Part 14, p. 1407. See also Forrest Pogue's coverage of this period in *Ordeal and Hope*, pp. 220–21. The Japanese first introduced code JN-25 in June 1939; by the fall of 1940, Major William Friedman and his team had cracked the code. SIS produced the first translation of Japanese Purple machine (diplomatic code) in September 1939—Budiansky, *Battle of Wits*, pp. 164, 216, and on. The Japanese altered their naval code, JN-25, in December 1941, and it was only in March 1942 that the U.S. Navy finally broke it.
28. Holmes, *Double-Edged Secrets*, pp. 27, 23–33, 53.
29. Dyer, *Amphibians*, p. 191; *Pearl Harbor Hearings*, Part 4, pp. 1869, 1984. Purple no. 867, dated December 2 (translated December 3–4), ordered Admiral Nomura to destroy some codes and one Purple machine.
30. Robert Dallek, *The American Style of Foreign Policy* (New York: Knopf, 1983), p. 309.
31. Kenneth S. Davis, *FDR: The War President, 1940–1943* (New York: Random House, 2000), p. 426.
32. *Ibid.*, pp. 416–17.
33. Cray, *General of the Army*, p. 252.
34. Pogue, *Ordeal and Hope*, p. 223.
35. *Ibid.*, pp. 225–28, Appendix 1, p. 432.
36. Stark to CINCPAC and CINCAF, November 6, 1941, *Pearl Harbor Hearings*, Part 14, p. 1408; Pogue also mentions this, *Ordeal and Hope*, p. 221.
37. For Purples 902 and 907, see *Pearl Harbor and the Kimmel Controversy*, Appendix C, p. 4.
38. Pogue, *Ordeal and Hope*, p. 228.
39. Stimson Diary, November 27, 1941, Sterling Memorial Library, Yale University, New Haven, CT.
40. For Stark and the events of December 7, see *Pearl Harbor and the Kimmel Controversy*, Appendix D, p. iv; B. Mitchell Simpson, *Admiral Harold Stark: Architect of Victory, 1939–1945* (Columbia, SC: University of South Carolina Press, 1989), chap. 15; and Pogue, *Ordeal and Hope*, p. 229.
41. Cray, *General of the Army*, p. 255; Radio no. 529, Secret, December 7, 1941, Washington, DC, to Lt. Gen. Walter C. Short—George C. Marshall, *The Papers of George Catlett Marshall*, vol. 3: *"The Right Man for the Job," December 7, 1941–May 31, 1943* (Baltimore and London: Johns Hopkins University Press, 1991), p. 7.
42. Radar was only turned on for three hours a day—Cray, *General of the Army*, pp. 257–58.
43. Pogue, *Ordeal and Hope*, p. 231.
44. Robert Sherwood, *Roosevelt and Hopkins, An Intimate History* (New York: Harper & Bros., 1948), pp. 430–31.
45. Henry L. Stimson and McGeorge Bundy, *On Active Service in Peace and War* (New York: Harper & Bros., 1948), pp. 195–96; and Godfrey Hodgson, *The Colonel: The Life and Wars of Henry Stimson, 1867–1950* (New York: Knopf, 1990), pp. 242–43.
46. Sherwood, *Roosevelt and Hopkins*, p. 431.

47. H. H. Arnold, *Global Mission* (New York: Harper & Bros., 1949), pp. 269–70.
48. *Ibid.*, p. 272.
49. E. B. Potter, *Nimitz* (Annapolis: Naval Institute Press, 1976), pp. 6–7.
50. Thomas Buell, *Master of Sea Power. A Biography of Fleet Admiral Ernest J. King* (Boston: Little, Brown, 1980), pp. 151–52.
51. Holmes, *Double-Edged Sword*, pp. 1–3.
52. Sherwood, *Roosevelt and Hopkins*, p. 431.
53. *Ibid.*, pp. 432–33.
54. Marshall, *Papers of George Catlett Marshall*, p. 8, for Radio no. 736.
55. Paul Dull, *A Battle History of the Imperial Japanese Navy, 1941–1945* (Annapolis: U.S. Naval Institute Press, 1978), pp. 10ff.; Samuel Eliot Morison, *History of United States Naval Operations in World War II*, vol. 3: *The Rising Sun in the Pacific, 1931–April 1942* (Boston: Little, Brown, 1948), pp. 88ff.
56. Holmes, *Double-Edged Secrets*, pp. 3ff.; Dull, *Battle History*, pp. 16ff.
57. Davis, *FDR: War President*, pp. 340–42; Sherwood, *Roosevelt and Hopkins*, pp. 430ff.; Morison, *The Rising Sun*, pp. 98ff.
58. Morison, *The Rising Sun*, pp. 98ff. Dull, *Battle History*, pp. 15–19, gives the most succinct coverage; see also Hashimoto Mochitsura, *Sunk: The Story of the Japanese Submarine Fleet*, trans. E. H. M. Colegrove (London: Cassell, 1954); John Toland, *Infamy: Pearl Harbor and Its Aftermath* (Garden City, NY: Doubleday, 1982); Husband E. Kimmel, *Admiral Kimmel's Story* (Chicago: University of Chicago Press, 1955); Simpson, *Admiral Harold Stark: Architect of Victory, 1939–45*; Elliott Roosevelt, *As He Saw It* (New York: Duell, Sloan, Pearce, 1946); and Maurice Matloff and Edwin L. Snell, *Strategic Planning for Coalition Warfare, 1941–42* (Washington, DC: Department of the Army, 1953).
59. Sherwood, *Roosevelt and Hopkins*, p. 436.

Chapter VIII: Two Admirals

1. *The Influence of the National Policy on the Strategy of a War*. Ernest King's thesis prepared for the Naval War College, 1932, cited in Thomas Buell, *Master of Sea Power. A Biography of Fleet Admiral Ernest J. King* (Boston: Little, Brown, 1980), pp. 94–95.
2. Buell, *Master of Sea Power*, pp. 152, 153; Kenneth S. Davis, *FDR: The War President, 1940–1943* (New York: Random House, 2000), pp. 347ff.; B. Mitchell Simpson, *Admiral Harold R. Stark: Architect of Victory, 1939–1945* (Columbia, SC: University of South Carolina Press, 1985), chap. 10 for Stark's position. Roosevelt officially relieved Stark as CNO, March 12, 1942, that title going to King as well—Executive Order 9096, Doc. 42-2195, Franklin D. Roosevelt Library, Hyde Park, NY.
3. George C. Marshall, *The Papers of George Catlett Marshall*, vol. 3: *"The Right Man for the Job," December 7, 1941–May 31, 1943* (Baltimore and London: Johns Hopkins University Press, 1991), p.21.
4. D. Clayton James, *The Years of MacArthur*, vol. II: *1941–1945* (Boston: Houghton Mifflin, 1975), first chapter.
5. Marshall, *"The Right Man for the Job,"* p. 15.
6. In the 1944 Pearl Harbor investigation carried out by Admiral Hart, the published Report of July 11, 1945, declared: "Admiral Stark and Admiral Kimmel were the responsible officers. . . . The derelictions on the part of Admiral Stark and Admiral Kimmel were faults of omission rather than of commission. . . . They indicate lack of

the superior judgment necessary for exercising command commensurate with their rank and their assigned duties. . . ." (The same could have applied to Marshall and MacArthur.) Buell, *Master of Sea Power*, pp. 3–8, 11, 154–61.

7. *Ibid.*
8. *Ibid.*
9. *Ibid.*, p. 24.
10. Clark G. Reynolds, *Admiral John H. Towers. The Struggle for Naval Supremacy* (Annapolis: Naval Institute Press, 1991), p. 44; Buell, *Master of Sea Power*, pp. 45, 55, 74, 79.
11. Buell, *Master of Sea Power*, pp. 86–88, 95.
12. *Ibid.*, pp. 96–97, 100.
13. *Ibid.*, pp. 375, 96–97, 100, 103, 106.
14. *Ibid.*, pp. 240, 110–11, 15, 123, 119, 123; J. L. McRea Papers, Franklin D. Roosevelt Library, Hyde Park, NY.
15. Godfrey Hodgson, *The Colonel: The Life and Wars of Henry Stimson, 1867–1950* (New York: Knopf, 1990), pp. 220ff.; Robert Sherwood, *Roosevelt and Hopkins, An Intimate History* (New York: Harper & Bros., 1948), p. 163. Special note: See also Ernest King and Walter Muir Whitehead, *Fleet Admiral King: A Naval Record* (New York: W. W. Norton, 1952), for all aspects of King's professional career. King's papers are in the Library of Congress, while official records are now mainly at the National Archives. Buell, like E. B. Potter, frequently fails to specify his source material from letters and interviews.
16. Buell, *Master of Sea Power*, pp. 132–33.
17. E. B. Potter, *Nimitz* (Annapolis: Naval Institute Press, 1976), pp. 22–23.
18. *Ibid.*, pp. 30, 55–56, 50, 61–62.
19. *Ibid.*, p. 141.
20. Roosevelt's diary, July 30, 1918—London, England, in Elliott Roosevelt, ed., *The Roosevelt Letters, Being the Personal Correspondence of Franklin Delano Roosevelt*, vol. II: *1905–1928* (New York: Duell, Sloan & Pearce, 1950), p. 314. At this stage FDR was very pro-French and strongly anti-German, referring to them in all his letters as "the Boches."
21. The first purpose-built oil tanker, *Murex*, with a capacity of 4,000 tons, was built in 1892 for Marcus Samuel, the founder of Shell Oil. He had it specially designed to be able to transit the Suez Canal, and within a few years had an entire fleet in service, including the *Conch, Clam, Elax, Bullmouth*, etc. built in West Hartlepool and later by Sir James Lang & Co. Ltd. of Sunderland and Armstrong Mitchell & Co in Newcastle-upon-Tyne—Robert Henriques, *Marcus Samuel: First Viscount Bearstead and Founder of the Shell Transport and Trading Company, 1853–1927* (London: Barrie & Rockliff, 1960), pp. 118–19.
22. Potter, *Nimitz*, pp. 150, 174, 175, 166. Potter's sources included comments from many dozens of interviews (non-dated) with naval personnel, and Nimitz's letters in the Office of the Naval Historical Center, Washington, DC. Potter also had hundreds of hours of interviews with Nimitz (few precise notes taken) while exchanging over one hundred letters with him. These are now in the Potter family. The Action Reports, CINCPAC papers, etc., are in the National Archives. Nimitz's two books do not cover this period, only the war: Chester Nimitz and E. B. Potter, *Sea Power: A Naval History* (Englewood Cliffs, NJ: Prentice-Hall, 1960), and Nimitz and Potter, *Triumph in the Pacific: The Navy's Struggle Against Japan* (Englewood Cliffs, NJ: Prentice-Hall, 1963).

Chapter IX: . . . and a General

1. William Manchester, *American Caesar: Douglas MacArthur, 1880–1964* (Boston: Little, Brown, 1978), pp. 182–83, quotes RG1, MacArthur to White, n.d.; Frazier Hunt, *The Untold Story of Douglas MacArthur* (New York: Devin Adair, 1954), p. 203.
2. D. Clayton James, *The Years of MacArthur*, vol. 1: *1880–1941* (Boston: Houghton Mifflin, 1970), pp. 88–89.
3. Manchester, *American Caesar*, pp. 30, 35.
4. James, *Years of MacArthur*, p. 23.
5. Manchester, *American Caesar*, p. 48; James, *Years of MacArthur*, pp. 31ff.
6. James, *Years of MacArthur*, pp. 67–84.
7. War Department, HR, G-2, Box 128, Nat. Arch.
8. Douglas MacArthur, *Reminiscences* (New York: McGraw-Hill, 1964), pp. 30–32; Major F. Freleth Winslow to CofS, August 7, 1908, Adjutant General's Office (AGO)-DF, Doc. 487448, Nat. Arch.
9. D. MacArthur to TAG (Adjutant General of the Army), July 28, 1908, AGO-DF, Doc. 487448. Major Judson's report in same file.
10. James, *Years of MacArthur*, p. 109.
11. *Ibid.*, pp. 125–26.
12. *Ibid.*, p. 130.
13. Henry J. Reilly, *Americans All: The Rainbow at War: Official History of the 42nd Rainbow Division in the World War* (Columbus, OH: F. J. Heer Printing Co., 1936), p. 6; MacArthur, *Reminiscences*, pp. 45–46; John J. Pershing, *My Experiences in the World War* (New York: Viking Press, 1931), vol 1, pp.15ff.
14. James, *Years of MacArthur*, p. 147.
15. Manchester, *American Caesar*, p. 88.
16. James, *Years of MacArthur*, p. 164.
17. Hunt, *Untold Story*, pp. 74–76.
18. James, *Years of MacArthur*, p. 176; MacArthur, *Reminiscences*, p. 57; Walter B. Wolf, *A Brief History of the Rainbow Division* (New York: Scribners, 1919), pp. 8–10; Thomas Shipley, *The History of the A.E.F.* (New York: Harper, 1920), pp. 78–79, 82ff.
19. Francis Duffy, *Father Duffy's Story* (New York: Harper, 1919), p. 130.
20. James, *Years of MacArthur*, p. 180; MacArthur, *Reminiscences*, pp. 58ff.; S. L. A. Marshall, *The American Heritage History of World War I* (New York: Knopf, 1964), p. 349.
21. MacArthur, *Reminiscences*, pp. 58, 70.
22. James, *Years of MacArthur*, p. 187; AGO-PF [Project File], Box 371, RG 407, MacArthur Memorial Bureau of Archives, Norfolk, VA, and Nat. Arch.
23. MacArthur, *Reminiscences*, pp. 60–61.
24. James, *Years of MacArthur*, p. 191; Gen. Order 51, 42nd Div, Hq, July 27, 1918.
25. Reilly, *Americans All*, pp. 547–48, 576–78; MacArthur, *Reminiscences*, pp. 63–64.
26. Reilly, *Americans All*, pp. 659–60; MacArthur, *Reminiscences*, p. 66.
27. MacArthur, *Reminiscences*, p. 67.
28. *Ibid.*, p. 63.
29. James, *Years of MacArthur*, p. 224; Reilly, *Americans All*, pp. 746–48.
30. Walter Wolf, *A Brief Story of the Rainbow Division* (New York: Harper & Bros., 1919), p. 52; Hunter Liggett, *Commanding An American Army: Recollections of the World War* (New York: Harper, 1925), pp. 229–30.
31. Manchester, *American Caesar*, p. 110.

32. MacArthur, *Reminiscences*, pp. 71–72; Faubion Bowers, "The Late General MacArthur, Warts and All," *Esquire* (January 1967).
33. Manchester, *American Caesar*, p. 135.
34. *Ibid.*, p. 136; Hunt, *Untold Story*, p. 117.
35. Manchester, *American Caesar*, p. 142, see note 60.
36. James, *Years of MacArthur*, p. 473.
37. Manchester, *American Caesar*, pp. 144–45.
38. MacArthur, *Reminiscences*, p. 99; James, *Years of MacArthur*, pp. 373–74.
39. James, *Years of MacArthur*, pp. 375–76.
40. Patrick Hurley, Sec. of War, to D. MacArthur, July 28, 1932, Bonus Riot File, Patrick J. Hurley Papers, University of Oklahoma Library, Norman, OK.
41. James, *Years of MacArthur*, p. 399.
42. See the *New York Times*, July 29, 1932, for interview of July 28.
43. James, *Years of MacArthur*, pp. 403, 406–07.
44. MacArthur, *Reminiscences*, p. 96.
45. Harold L. Ickes, *The Secret Diary of Harold L. Ickes* (New York: Simon & Schuster, 1954), vol. I: *The First Thousand Days*, p. 71.
46. MacArthur, *Reminiscences*, p. 101.
47. *Ibid.*
48. In 1931, the army and air force budget was down to $347 million; by 1934, it was cut to $277 million—MacArthur, *Reminiscences*, p. 99.
49. Manchester, *American Caesar*, p. 157.
50. MacArthur to Roosevelt, September 9, 1935; *New York Times*, September 4, 1935; War Dept. press release, September 18, 1935. MacArthur lied about this as well. In his *Reminiscences* (p. 102), he said that Roosevelt "offered me the most [as high commissioner] but that I declined because it involved my retirement from the Army," whereas in reality FDR had *withdrawn* the offer after discovery of MacArthur's deriding remarks about him behind his back—MacArthur, *Reminiscences*, p. 102.
51. Harry Woodring, Sec. of War, to FDR, January 21, 1938, President's Personal Files, Roosevelt Papers, Doc. 4771, Franklin D. Roosevelt Library, Hyde Park, NY.
52. *Annual Report of the President of the Philippine Commonwealth, 1939*, p. 10; *Annual Report of the President of the Philippine Commonwealth, 1940*, p. 4.
53. James, *Years of MacArthur*, p. 531.
54. Manchester, *American Caesar*, p. 182; letter, MacArthur to TAG, October 1, 1941, sub: Ops Plan R-5, WPD 417818; Louis Morton, *United States Army in World War II. The War in the Pacific: The Fall of the Philippines* (Washington, DC: Department of the Army, 1953), p. 65.
55. *Christian Science Monitor*, November 2, 1938 (italics added); Manchester, *American Caesar*, p. 185.
56. Gavin M. Long, *MacArthur as Military Commander* (London: Collins, 1969), p. 54.
57. Hunt, *Untold Story*, pp. 109–10.

Chapter X: The Philippines: "A Limit to Human Endurance"

1. Jonathan Wainwright, *General Wainwright's Story*, ed. Robert Considine (Garden City, NY: Doubleday, 1946), p. 122. The phrase comes from a letter from Wainwright to Roosevelt.
2. D. MacArthur to Joaquin M. Elizalde, February 1941, RG 1, MacArthur Memorial

Bureau of Archives, Norfolk, VA (cited hereafter as MMBA); D. Clayton James, *The Years of MacArthur,* vol. I: *1880–1941* (Boston: Houghton Mifflin, 1970), pp. 507–08, quoting MacArthur's April 1941 *Report on the National Defense of the Philippines*, pp. 21–22.

3. Wainwright, *Wainwright's Story*, p. 16.
4. Dwight D. Eisenhower, *At Ease: Stories I Tell to Friends* (Garden City, NY: Doubleday, 1967), pp. 230–32.
5. C. L. Sulzberger, *A Long Row of Candles: Memoirs and Diaries, 1934–1954* (New York: Macmillan, 1969), p. 672.
6. Elizalde to MacArthur, April 16, 1941, RG L, MMBA.
7. Kenneth S. Davis, *FDR: The War President, 1940–1943* (New York: Random House, 2000), pp. 429–33; Louis Morton, *Strategy and Command: The First Two Years* (Washington, DC: Department of the Army, 1962), pp. 189, 190; Forrest C. Pogue, *George C. Marshall: Ordeal and Hope, 1939–1942* (New York: Viking Press, 1966), pp. 247–48; Henry Stimson and McGeorge Bundy, *On Active Service in Peace and War* (New York: Harper & Bros., 1948), pp. 400–03; Eric Larrabee, *Commander-in-Chief* (New York: Harper & Row, 1987), p. 315, mentions the extortion paid by Quezon and the Philippine Treasury; see also pp. 213–17.
8. MacArthur to Elizalde, February 1941, RG 1, MMBA.
9. Douglas MacArthur, *Reminiscences* (New York: McGraw-Hill, 1964), p. 100.
10. Gerow to CofS, June 16, 1941, War Plans Department (cited hereafter as WPD) 3602-21.
11. MacArthur, *Reminiscences*, p. 100.
12. John Hersey's 1941 interview in *Men on Bataan* (New York: Knopf, 1942), pp. 287–91.
13. Marshall to MacArthur, June 20, 1941, Radio, Secret, Office of the Chief of Staff of the Army (cited hereafter as OCS), 20850-15.
14. MacArthur to TAG, July 27, 1941, RG 1, MMBA.
15. *Ibid*. (italics added).
16. Louis Morton, *The United States Army in World War II. The War in the Pacific. The Fall of the Philippines* (Washington, DC: Department of the Army, 1953), p. 65.
17. Gerow to CofS, July 30, 1941, WPD 4561-1; MacArthur to TAG, October 1, 1941, WPD 4178-18; Marshall to MacArthur, November 21, 1941, WPD 44002-112, and Clayton James's excellent discussion, in *The Years of MacArthur*, vol. I, pp. 590ff. Marshall quotes this to FDR, September 9, 1941, OCS 18136-48.
18. Marshall to MacArthur, Radio, Secret, OCS 8136-351. See also Gerow to CofS, July 17, 1941, WPD 3251-52; Stimson to FDR, July 25, 1945, OCS 181136-34.
19. James, *Years of MacArthur*, vol. I, p. 611; vol. II: *1941–1945* (Boston: Houghton Mifflin, 1975), vol. II, p. 28.
20. MacArthur's answers to Louis Morton's questionnaire of February 8, 1954—D. MacArthur, Miscellaneous, 201, Center of Military History, Fort McNair, Washington, DC.
21. MacArthur, *Reminiscences*, p. 128.
22. Samuel Eliot Morison, *The Two-Ocean War, A Short History of the United States Navy in the Second World War* (Boston: Little, Brown, 1963), p. 79. MacArthur protested his alleged bias against the navy: "I have always held that magnificent Navy, in the same administration and affection I feel for my own branch." Moreover, he added, "My brother and nephew died in the uniform of the Navy," although not in battle. In fact Douglas MacArthur's elder brother died of appen-

dicitis—*Reminiscences*, p. 102. S. E. Morison, *United States Naval Operations in World War II*, vol. III: *The Rising Sun in the Pacific, 1931–April 1942* (Boston: Little, Brown, 1948), p. 154.

23. MacArthur, *Reminiscences*, p. 121 (italics added).
24. *Ibid*.; MacArthur's radio message to Marshall, NA/RG 165 (OPD, Exec 8, Book 3, MacArthur File); George C. Marshall, *The Papers of George Catlett Marshall*, vol. 3: *"The Right Man for the Job," December 7, 1941–May 31, 1943* (Baltimore and London: Johns Hopkins University Press, 1991), pp. 101–02 (italics added); cf. p. 209.
25. Marshall to Sir John Dill, 22 May 1943, NA/RG 165 (OPD, Exec 8, Book 5).
26. See, e.g., Andrew B. Cunningham, *A Sailor's Odyssey* (New York: Dutton, 1951), which covers in great detail the very intense naval war in the Mediterranean, and later from his perspective as First Sea Lord. There were no ships to spare in the Atlantic or the Mediterranean, and this was clear to all those involved.
27. Winston S. Churchill, *The Second World War*, vol. IV: *The Hinge of Fate* (London: Cassell, 1951), p. 112.
28. James Dunningan and Albert Nofi, *Victory at Sea. World War II in the Pacific* (New York: Morrow, 1995), p. 177; William Manchester, *American Caesar: Douglas MacArthur, 1880–1964* (Boston: Little, Brown, 1978), p. 244, gives the figure of 206.
29. George C. Kenney, *General Kenney Reports. A Personal History of the Pacific* (Washington, DC: U.S. Government Printing Office, 1987), pp. 33, 151–53.
30. Robert L. Eichelberger, *Dear Miss Em: General Eichelberger's War in the Pacific, 1942–1945*, ed. Jay Luvaas (Westport, CT: Greenwood Press, 1972), p. 29.
31. Kenney, *General Kenney Reports*, pp. 26–27, 52–53.
32. See also Charles Willoughby and John Chamberlain, *MacArthur, 1941–1951* (New York: McGraw-Hill, 1954), p. 35. These authors are strongly biased in MacArthur's favor; see also Eichelberger, *Dear Miss Em*, p. 29, which is much more honest.
33. D. Clayton James, *The Years of MacArthur*, vol. II: *1941–1945* (Boston: Houghton Mifflin, 1975), p. 28.
34. James, *Years of MacArthur*, vol. I, p. 617, note 36.
35. James, *Years of MacArthur*, vol. II, p. 28.
36. James, *Years of MacArthur*, vol. I, p. 617. See also Wesley Craven and James Cate, eds., *The Army Air Forces in World War II*, vol. I: *Plans and Early Operations, January 1939 to August 1942* (Chicago: Chicago University Press, 1948), pp. 12, 191; Charles Willoughby et al., eds., *Reports of General MacArthur* (Washington, DC: Department of the Army, 1950), vol. I, p. 6; Romulo, *I Saw the Fall of the Philippines*, pp. 12, 26–28; MacArthur, *Reminiscences*, pp. 110ff.; Theodore Friend, *Between Two Empires: The Ordeal of the Philippines, 1929–1946* (New Haven: Yale University Press), p. 207; Morison, *Rising Sun in the Pacific*, p. 156; James, *Years of MacArthur*, vol. I, pp. 618–19; Maurice Matloff and Edwin Snell, *Strategic Planning for Coalition Warfare, 1941–1942* (Washington, DC: Department of the Army, 1959), pp. 77–78; David C. Evans and Mark R. Peattie, *Kaigun: Strategy, Tactics, and Technology in the Imperial Japanese Navy, 1887–1941* (Annapolis: Naval Institute Press, 1997), pp. 308–12; and Roberta Wohlstetter, *Pearl Harbor: Warning and Decision* (Palo Alto, CA: Stanford University Press, 1962), p. 396.
37. MacArthur, *Reminiscences*, pp. 112ff.
38. *Ibid*, p. 113

39. Wainwright, *Wainwright's Story*, p. 26.
40. *Ibid.*, p. 14.
41. *Ibid.*, p. 26.
42. MacArthur, *Reminiscences*, p. 114.
43. Wainwright, *Wainwright's Story*, p. 9.
44. *Ibid.*, p. 12.
45. MacArthur to TAG, 1 October 1941, sub: Opns Plans R-5, WPD 4178-18; memorandum, Marshall to MacArthur, 18 October 1941, sub: USAFFE, WPD 4175-18; letters, CofS (Marshall to CG [USAFFE, MacArthur]), 21 November 1941: US-British cooperation in the Far East, WPD 4402-112; letter, CG USAFFE to CG SLF, 3 December 1941 sub: Defense of Philippines, AG 381 (12-3-41), Philippine Records; letter order, CG USAFFE to CG V-MF, 3 December 1941, sub: Dfense of Phil., AG 381 (12-3-41), Philippine Records.
46. Wainwright, *Wainwright's Story*, p. 17.
47. Morton, *The Fall of the Philippines*, p. 79.
48. Morison, *Rising Sun in the Pacific*, pp. 168–69.
49. Morton, *The Fall of the Philippines*, p. 87.
50. MacArthur, *Reminiscences*, p. 120.
51. *Ibid.*
52. H. H. Arnold, *Global Mission* (New York: Harper & Bros., 1949), p. 272.
53. Morton, *The Fall of the Philippines*, p. 80.
54. Wainwright, *Wainwright's Story*, p. 20.
55. Morton, *The Fall of the Philippines*, p. 79.
56. Lewis Brereton, *The Brereton Diaries* (New York: Appleton-Century, 1946), p. 41.
57. Morton, *The Fall of the Philippines*, pp. 81, 86–87 (italics added).
58. *Ibid.*, pp. 81ff.; MacArthur to War Dept., Radio, to AGWAR no. 1133, 8 December 1941, and MacArthur to AGWAR, Radio no. 1135, 9 December 1941, both messages in AG 381 (11-27-41), Far East. See also Craven and Cate, eds., *The Army Air Forces in World War II*, vol. 3, pp. 200ff.
59. Morton, *The Fall of the Philippines*, pp. 85–87; Ernest Miller, *Bataan Uncensored* (Minneapolis: Hart Publications, 1949), p. 67; Pro CA Brig (A4), Rpt Opns, p. 3; Wainwright's final report, Annex IX, USAFFE, USMP, Rpt Gen. Sage, 28 February 1951.
60. Morton, *The Fall of the Philippines*, p. 87.
61. *Ibid.*, 88, 91.
62. Morison, *The Rising Sun in the Pacific*, p. 151.
63. Marshall, *"The Right Man for the Job,"* p. 15; Marshall to MacArthur, 11 December 1941, Radio, Secret, NA/RG 165 (OCS, Project Decimal File 1941–43, Philippines).
64. Letter to author by Admiral of the Fleet Sir Henry Leach, March 26, 2001.
65. Martin Gilbert, *The Second World War. A Complete History* (New York: Henry Holt, 1989), p. 276.
66. Wainwright, *Wainwright's Story*, p. 32; James, *Years of MacArthur*, vol. II, p. 23.
67. Wainwright, *Wainwright's Story*, p. 28.
68. Colonel Richard Mallonée, "Bataan Diary" (2 MS vols on 21st Infan. ops), vol. II, *1941–1942* (Center of Military History, Washington, DC), p. 76.
69. James, *Years of MacArthur*, vol. II, 63; William E. Dyess, *The Dyess Story*, ed. Charles Leavelle (New York: G. P. Putnam's Sons, 1944), pp. 47, 61.
70. MacArthur, *Reminiscences*, p. 125.
71. Robert Levering, *Horror Trek: A True Story of Bataan, the Death March, and Three*

and *One Half Years in Japanese Prison Camps* (Dayton, OH: Privately printed, 1940), p. 40.

72. *Ibid.*
73. General Wainwright's *Report of Operations of USAFFE and USFIP in the Philippine Islands, 1941–1942* (one copy at Departmental Records Branch, AGO; other at Center of Military History, Washington, DC), contains a series of separate reports on different subjects, to which are added twenty-eight annexes or appendices of great value. Here see Annex VIII, pp. 36–38; the Braly Diary, December 29–31, 1941; Benson Guyton Diary, December 25, 1941–May 3, 1942; Guyton Papers. Also the series of interviews with D. Clayton James, e.g., Wright Collier, Guyton, in James, *Years of MacArthur*, vol. II, pp. 814–15; William C. Braly, "Corregidor: A Name, A Symbol, A Tradition" (MS based on his diary, 1941–42), pp. 10, 24, Braly Papers; Wright, "To Hell and Back," 2, p. 21; and Levering, *Horror Trek*, pp. 222–23.
74. James, *Years of MacArthur,* vol. II, 32.
75. Sidney Huff, with Joe Morris, *My Fifteen Years with General MacArthur* (New York: Appleton-Century, 1964), pp. 43–44; *Manila Start Reporter,* June 8, 1945; Carlos Romulo, *I Saw the Fall of the Philippines* (Garden City, NY: Doubleday, 1942), pp. 100–01; Allison Ind, *Bataan, The Judgment Seat: The Saga of the Philippines Command of the United States Army Air Force, May 1941 to May 1942* (New York: Macmillan, 1944), p. 208; Bradford Chynoweth, "Visayan Castaways" (MS covering experiences 1941–45) (Center of Military History, Washington, DC), pp. 18–56.
76. See Wainwright, *Report of Operations*, Annex VIII, pp. 1–29, Rockwell Narrative, 2; James and William Belote, *Corregidor: The Saga of a Fortress* (New York: Morrow, 1967), p. 14.
77. Paul Hasluck, *The Government and the People, 1942–45* (Canberra: Australian War Memorial,1952), pp. 113–14; James, *Years of MacArthur,* vol. II, p. 66.
78. Marshall to FDR, 25 December 1941, NA/RG 166 (OPD, Exec, 8, Book 1). See also Maurice Matloff and Edwin Snell, *Strategic Planning for Coalition Warfare, 1941–42* (Washington, DC: Department of the Army, 1959), pp. 89–94; Marshall, *"The Right Man for the Job,"* pp. 37–38, 53; NA/RF 165 (OCS, Chronological Miscellaneous).
79. Marshall to MacArthur, Radio no. 932, Secret, 13 January 1942, NA/RF 165 (OPD, Exec 8, Book 2).
80. Marshall to King, memorandum, January 20, 1942, Marshall, *"The Right Man for the Job,"* p. 74; Marshall to FDR, February 4, 1942, Roosevelt Papers (PSF, Safe, Marshall), Franklin D. Roosevelt Library, Hyde Park, NY.
81. Marshall to FDR, memorandum, Secret, 26 January 1942, GCMRL/G C Marshall Papers (Pentagon Office, Selected); Marshall to Lt.-Gen. D. MacArthur, Radio, Secret, 11 December 1941, pp. 84–85, 15.
82. Wainwright, *Wainwright's Story*, pp. 45, 65.
83. *Ibid.*, pp. 50–51.
84. *Ibid.*, p. 54.
85. *Ibid.*, pp. 3–4.
86. James, *Years of MacArthur*, vol. II, p. 18.
87. *Ibid.*, 100–01.
88. *Ibid.*, pp. 101ff.
89. Wainwright, *Wainwright's Story*, p. 86.
90. *Ibid.*, p. 82.
91. Colonel Glen R. Townsend, "Defense of the Philippines" (MS on the 11th

Infantry) (Center of Military History), pp. 9–12; Operations Report of U.S. Army Forces in Far East and U.S. Forces in Philippines (Wainwright's main Report) (Center of Military History, microfilm, MSU), pp. 27ff.; Clark Lee, *They Call It Pacific* (London: John Long, 1943), pp. 71–90; Colonel Clyde Select, 71st Division (Philippine Army), Note (Center of Military History), pp. 57–58; and D. Clayton James, ed., *South to Bataan, North to Mukden: The Prison Diary of Brig. Gen. W. E. Brougher* (Athens, GA: University of Georgia Press, 1971), pp. 10–12. See also various interviews with Clayton by Collier, Milton Hill, etc., 1971; John Toland, *But Not in Shame: The Six Months After Pearl Harbor* (New York: Random House, 1961), pp. 110–13.

92. Wainwright, *Wainwright's Story*, pp. 117–18.
93. *Ibid.*, p. 118.
94. *Ibid.*, p. 119.
95. Morton, *The Fall of the Philippines*, pp. 572ff.; Wainwright, *Wainwright's Story*, pp. 142ff.
96. James, *Years of MacArthur*, vol. I, pp. 608–09.
97. Robert Hotz, ed., *The Way of a Fighter: Claire Lee Chennault* (New York: Putnam, 1949), p. 124; Edgar Whitcomb, *Escape from Corregidor* (Chicago: University of Chicago Press, 1958), p. 28; Francis Sayre, *Glad Adventure* (New York: Macmillan, 1957), p. 223.
98. James, *Years of MacArthur*, vol. II, pp. 4–5.
99. Manchester, *American Caesar*, pp. 182–83.
100. Morton, *The Fall of the Philippines*, p. 601.
101. The material that follows is all taken from William Dyess, *The Dyess Story: The Eyewitness Account of the Death March from Bataan and the Narrative of Experiences in Japanese Prison Camps and of Eventual Escape*, edited by Charles Leavelle, pp. 67–180. See also Wainwright, *Wainwright's Story*, and author interview with Major Burt Bank, AAF, September 21, 2001. The march began on April 10, 1942, ran sixty-five miles, Mariveles to San Fernando, seven miles by foot from Capers to O'Donnell, with a short section by train—*The Dyess Story*, p. 96; Morton, *The Fall of the Philippines*, p. 467; Colonel James V. Collier, Notebooks IV, p. 18, in MMBA.
102. Dyess attests to many Japanese atrocities. Lieutenant Jaspar Holmes read many of the captured Japanese diaries found on the battlefield. One discussed two American POWs who had tried in vain to escape. Their punishment: "A Japanese surgeon cut out their livers to see how long they would survive." There were no anesthetics—W. Jaspar Holmes, *Double-Edged Secrets: U.S. Naval Intelligence Operations in the Pacific During World War II* (Annapolis: Naval Institute Press, 1979), p. 123.
103. Wainwright, *Wainwright's Story*, p. 156.
104. *Ibid.*, p. 225.
105. *Ibid.*, pp. 194–95, 203–05.
106. Gilbert, *Second World War*, p. 297.
107. *Ibid.*, p. 282.
108. Pogue, *Ordeal and Hope*, pp. 254, 255.
109. Memorandum for the President, March 25, 1945, Marshall, *"The Right Man for the Job,"* p. 147; Pogue, *Ordeal and Hope*, pp. 253–54.
110. See Hampton Sides's article in the *International Herald Tribune*, Tuesday, May 29, 2001, p. 9, in which he, a former POW, mentions that there are now 46,417 former POWs living in the United States, totally forgotten by their government.

Chapter XI: First Washington Conference

1. Alex Danchev, *Very Special Relationship. Field-Marshall Sir John Dill and the Anglo-American Alliance, 1941–1944* (London: Brassey's Defence Publications, 1986), pp. 58–59.
2. Ed Cray, *General of the Army: George C. Marshall, Soldier and Statesman* (New York: W. W. Norton, 1990), p. 272.
3. Lord Moran, *Churchill: The Struggle for Survival, 1940–1965, Taken from the Diaries of Lord Moran* (Boston: Houghton Mifflin, 1966), p. 11.
4. *Ibid.*, p. 12; Martin Gilbert, *Churchill, A Life* (London: Heinemann, 1991), p. 713.
5. *Washington Post*, Thursday, December 25, 1941.
6. Moran, *Churchill*, p. 14; Kenneth S. Davis, *FDR: The War President, 1940–1943* (New York: Random House, 2000), p. 369.
7. Robert Sherwood, *Roosevelt and Hopkins, An Intimate History* (New York: Harper & Bros., 1948), p. 442.
8. Martin Gilbert, *Winston S. Churchill, 1941–1945*, vol. VII: *Road to Victory* (London: Heinemann, 1983), p. 23.
9. Charles de Gaulle, *The Complete Memoirs of Charles de Gaulle* (New York; Viking Press, 1965), p. 79.
10. J.-B. Duroselle, *L'Abîme, 1939–1944* (Paris: Imprimérie Nationale, 1986), pp. 334–35; and Davis, *FDR: War President*, pp. 377–79.
11. Moran, *Churchill*, p. 15.
12. *New York Post*, December 27, 1941; *Washington Post*, December 27, 1941.
13. Moran, *Churchill*, pp. 16–19.
14. *Washington Post*, Sunday, December 21, 1941. King had a terrible reputation, even in his own family. A young officer dating one of King's six daughters commented that he found King to be very temperamental. His daughter disagreed: "Oh, not at all, to the contrary, he is the most even-tempered man I know—he is *always* in a rage."
15. For background, see Danchev, *Very Special Relationship*. Lord Alanbrooke also gives background on Dill, who was a close friend of his: Lord Alanbrooke, *War Diaries, 1939–1945* (London: Weidenfeld & Nicolson, 2001); and finally the *Dictionary of National Biography*.
16. Cray, *General of the Army*, pp. 271–72.
17. Gilbert, *Road to Victory*, p. 35; Davis, *FDR: War President*, pp. 394–95.
18. Winston Churchill, *The Second World War*, vol. III: *The Grand Alliance* (London: Cassell, 1950), pp. 598–99; Gilbert, *Road to Victory*, pp. 39, 40; Washington Conference, memorandum no. 17, Annexes VI, VII and VIII of Cabinet Papers, 99/17; and the same group memorandum no. 17, Annex I, "American and British Strategy," which was prepared by the Combined Chiefs of Staff on January 14, 1942.
19. Churchill's toast: *New York Times*, Friday, January 2, 1942.

Chapter XII: Yamamoto's Great Offensive: Coral Sea and Midway

1. Operation MO (Yamamoto), The Japanese High Command in Port Moresby Operation, May 1942, vol. V, Subtitle: "May 1941. MO Operations," Doc. 18661, in Allied Translator and Interpreter Section (ATIS), South West Pacific Area, Nat. Arch.
2. January 5–18, 1942, submarines *Pollack*, *Gudgeon*, *Pompano*, *Tautog*, and

Plunger—Samuel Eliot Morison, *History of United States Naval Operations in World War II*, vol. III: *The Rising Sun in the Pacific, 1931–April 1942* (Boston: Little, Brown, 1948), pp. 258ff.

3. *Ibid.*, pp. 272, 273. See F. C. van Oosten, *The Battle of the Java Sea* (London: Ian Allan, 1975), for the best coverage of these "battles," including Dutch and Japanese sources.
4. Samuel E. Morison, *The Two-Ocean War: A Short History of the United States Navy in the Second World War* (Boston: Little, Brown, 1963), pp. 91ff; Kenneth S. Davis, *FDR: The War President, 1940–1943* (New York: Random House, 2000), p. 406.
5. Morison, *Two-Ocean War*, p. 100; Paul Dull, *A Battle History of the Imperial Japanese Navy, 1941–1945* (Annapolis: Naval Institute Press, 1978), pp. 62–63.
6. John Deane Potter, *Admiral of the Pacific: The Life of Yamamoto* (London: Heinemann, 1965), p. 3.
7. *Ibid.*, pp. 9, 11, 12, 14.
8. Potter, *Admiral of the Pacific*, pp. 15, 19, 24–25; David C. Evans and Mark R. Peattie, *Kaigun: Strategy, Tactics, and Technology of the Imperial Japanese Navy, 1887–1941* (Annapolis: Naval Institute Press, 1998), p. 532.
9. Evans and Peattie, *Kaigun*, p. 532.
10. Potter, *Admiral of the Pacific*, pp. 41, 44.
11. Mitsuo Fuchida and Masatake Okumiya, *Midway: The Battle That Doomed Japan* (Annapolis: Naval Institute Press, 1955), p. 79.
12. Commander Okumiya Masatake, February 1959, in *ibid.*, p. 18.
13. Admiral Chester Nimitz, CINCPAC Report, June 28, 1942—Nat. Arch.
14. W. Jaspar Holmes, *Double-Edged Secrets: U.S. Naval Intelligience Operations in the Pacific During World War II* (Annapolis: Naval Institute Press, 1979), p. 71; Samuel Eliot Morison, *History of the United States Naval Operations in World War II*, vol. IV: *Coral Sea, Midway and Submarine Actions, May 1942–August 1942* (Boston: Little, Brown, 1949), pp. 87ff.
15. Holmes, *Double-Edged Secrets*, p. 71. For radio dispatches: COMINCH (May 1942) 111245; CINCPAC (May 1942) 050321, 080252, 080346, 080402—Nat. Arch.
16. Holmes, *Double-Edged Secrets*, pp. 72–73.
17. Martin Gilbert, *Churchill, A Life* (London: Heinemann/Minerva, 1991), p. 719.
18. Dull, *Battle History*, pp. 117, 118.
19. *Ibid.*, p. 129–30.
20. *Ibid.*, pp. 124-26.
21. *Ibid.*, pp. 125-26.
22. Holmes, *Double-Edged Secrets*, pp. 85, 87, 89. HYPO, like OP-20-G in Washington, and the Army's SIS, was greatly assisted in sifting out the data sought through the use of huge IBM computers leased to the U.S. military using tens of millions of coded "punch cards" which IBM sold to these services. But what neither Nimitz, Layton, nor Holmes realized was that the patriotic chairman of IBM, Thomas Watson, and his senior legal counsel, Harrison Chauncey, were simultaneously leasing many hundreds of these same machines to Hitler's Third Reich. Indeed, Germany's extraordinary victories and "achievements" would have been inconceivable for the most part without Watson's IBM computers and punch cards, which made possible not only collating the population census of Germany and all its conquered countries but also pinpointing precisely every Jew in every country in Europe. Even the major concentration camps had these IBM machines,

which "sorted out" every prisoner and his/her background and applied a number to each individual, including babies and children. Moreover, IBM machines were responsible for operating Hitler's entire European rail network, and could locate any locomotive or freight car. The machines made possible the efficient transport of German troops to various occupied countries, and also catalogued the Third Reich's entire armaments for all military services. In brief, this same Thomas Watson who was aiding the American and Allied armed services was also actively aiding and abetting the enemy, and was in consequence responsible for thousands of American and Allied casualities. And yet, unlike many large American corporations placed on the State Department's Black List, such as Rockefeller's Standard Oil Corporation, Watson's IBM successfully escaped any stigma. Moreover, after the war, Watson demanded and received compensation through the U.S. government for lost and damaged IBM machines as well as for the revenues that he had lost when the vanquished Germans failed to pay IBM. This was possible because of Watson's astonishing influence with the government and State Department. For a detailed scholarly study of Watson's and IBM's activities, see Edwin Black's *IBM and the Holocaust: The Strategic Alliance Between Nazi Germany and America's Most Powerful Corporation* (New York: Crown Publishers, 2001). (Watson was entertained by Hitler, Göring, and Reichsbank president Hjalmar Schact in Berlin in June 1937, when he was awarded Hitler's Merit Cross of the German Eagle with Star.)

23. Holmes, Double-Edged Secrets, pp. 85–89. Radio dispatches: CINCPAC: outgoing (May 1942) 160307, 160325, 180357, 180403, 210137 (June 1942), 040014, 040245, 040715, 040801, 040811, 040959, 041847, 042331, 042340, 050052, 050129, 050335, 050611, 050915, 051134, 051203, 051225, 060315, 060831; incoming (June 1942) 041445, 041804, 041835, 042020, 042135, 042153, 042158, 042255, 05001—Nat. Arch.
24. Thomas Buell, *The Quiet Warrior. A Biography of Admiral Raymond Spruance* (Boston: Little, Brown, 1974), p. 183.
25. Holmes, *Double-Edged Secrets*, p. 23; E. B. Potter, *Nimitz* (Annapolis: Naval Institute Press, 1976), p. 83. Edwin Layton corroborates the events at this meeting as well as those that preceded it and then followed, but in even greater detail. See Edwin T. Layton, with Roger Pineau and John Costello, *"And I Was There": Pearl Harbor and Midway—Breaking the Secrets* (New York: Morrow, 1985), pp. 420–30.
26. Holmes, *Double-Edged Secrets*, pp. 95–96.
27. Thomas Buell, *Master of Sea Power. A Biography of Fleet Admiral Ernest J. King* (Boston: Little, Brown, 1980), p. 478.
28. Buell, *The Quiet Warrior*, pp. 139–40.
29. Morison, *Coral Sea, Midway*, pp. 104–05; Buell, *The Quiet Warrior*, p. 183.
30. Dull, *Battle History*, pp. 139–41.
31. Fuchida and Okumiya, *Midway*, pp. 160ff.
32. Theodore Taylor, *The Magnificent Mitscher* (New York: W. W. Norton, 1954), pp. 127ff.
33. Buell, *The Quiet Warrior*, p. 156.
34. Morison, *Coral Sea, Midway*, pp. 127ff.
35. Taylor, *Magnificent Mitscher*, p. 89; Morison, *Coral Sea, Midway*, p. 98.
36. Morison, *Coral Sea, Midway*, p. 103.
37. *Ibid.*, pp. 104–05.
38. *Ibid.*, p. 113.
39.. *Ibid.*, pp. 115, 117; Taylor, *Magnificent Mitscher*, p. 130.
43. Dull, *Battle History*, p. 158; Morison, *Coral Sea, Midway*, p. 135.

44. Morison, *Coral Sea, Midway*, p. 137.
45. *Ibid.*, pp. 149–50; Dull, *Battle History*, pp. 165–66; Taylor, *Magnificent Mitscher*, p. 136.
46. Morison, *Coral Sea, Midway*, pp. 156ff; Dull, *Battle History*, pp. 162ff; Morison, *Two-Ocean War*, p. 160; Potter, *Nimitz*, p. 107—Potter incorrectly states that the Japanese lost 2,500 men and 322 aircraft (although they only had 234 aircraft on the four carriers, according to Japanese figures given in Dull, *Battle History*, p. 140).
47. King and Muir, *Fleet Admiral King*, p. 380.
48. *Ibid.*; Potter, Nimitz, p. 107. "Had we lacked early information of the Japanese movements, and had we been caught with carrier forces dispersed," Chester Nimitz acknowledged, "the Battle of Midway would have ended differently"—CINCPAC Report, 28 June 1942, and Morison, *Coral Sea, Midway*, p. 158. One of the greatest injustices in the history of the U.S. Navy was about to take place. "Only Nimitz and a few close aides knew . . . that our strategic success in the action [Midway] was largely the result of Joe Rochefort's unique abilities to smell out 'something fishy' in the [Japanese naval] intercepts," Fleet Intelligience Officer Ed Layton commented. Commander Jack Redman of OP-20-G, although lacking any real experience as a crytanalyst himself, had early insisted to Admiral King that Commander Rochefort was absolutely wrong in saying that "AF" referred to Midway. "AF" referred to Johnston Island, he adamantly maintained. King for his part thought it might mean Fiji or New Caledonia. Most fortunately for the U.S. Navy and the outcome of the war, Chester Nimitz had much more faith in Rochefort's judgment and his long distinguished career in this field as a Japanese language expert and cryptanalyst. Accordingly, Redman's "feathers were ruffled" by Rochefort's independent and totally different assessment, acknowledged Ed Layton, who witnessed this sad fiasco. A by now desperate Jack Redman succeeded in sending out a coded alert to a co-conspirator, Commander Joseph Wenger: "Get rid of Rochefort at all costs." Layton then laid out how Jack Redman, his brother Captain Joseph Redman (director of naval communications in Washington), and Admiral Frederick Horne convinced Admiral King to have Commander Rochefort recalled to the States, to be replaced by Captain William Goggins, a competent communications officer but lacking knowledge or experience as either a cryptanalyst or a Japanese linguist. Indeed, Goggins had just been fired as head of OP-20-G in Washington after only seven weeks on the job. News of Rochefort's totally unexpected removal came as a real "blow to our morale," Jaspar Holmes attested. And to add to the despair at HYPO, none other than the newly promoted Captain Jack Redman was now posted to Pearl Harbor as Nimitz's staff communications officer, which further outraged Nimitz, who also discovered that Redman had tried to oust and replace Ed Layton. King, who had to admit that he had been completely wrong about "AF," had sought and gained his revenge. As for Commander Joe Rochefort, there was to be neither promotion nor Distinguished Service Medal—he deserved the Congressional Medal of Honor—but a transfer out of Naval Intelligience altogether, to assume command of a drydock at San Francisco. The secret file on "The Rochefort Affair" was only unearthed forty years later. See Admiral Edwin T. Layton, *Midway*, pp. 408–09, 466–68; Stephen Budiansky, *Battle of Wits: The Complete Story of Codebreaking in World War II* (New York: Free Press, 2000), pp. 22–23; and Holmes, *Double-Edged Secrets*, pp. 115–17.
49. Fuchida and Okumiya, *Midway*, p. 268.

50. *Ibid.*, pp. 16, 285.
51. *Ibid.*, pp. 285–86.

Chapter XIII: Australia–New Guinea

1. MacArthur to Sutherland, March 17, 1942, in Douglas MacArthur, *Reminiscences* (New York: McGraw-Hill, 1964), p. 145.
2. Quoted in Clark Lee, *They Call It Pacific* (New York: Viking Press, 1943), p. 289.
3. *Melbourne Herald*, December 27, 1941; Winston Churchill, *The Second World War*, vol. IV: *The Hinge of Fate* (London: Cassell, 1951), pp. 7, 8.
4. Churchill, *Hinge of Fate*, pp. 5, 6, 9–11.
5. *Melbourne Herald*, December 27, 1941.
6. Churchill, *Hinge of Fate*, pp. 7–8, 15.
7. Martin Gilbert, *The Second World War. A Complete History* (New York: Henry Holt, 1989), pp. 307, 361.
8. MacArthur, *Reminiscences*, p. 145.
9. Robert L. Eichelberger, *Dear Miss Em: General Eichelberger's War in the Pacific, 1942–1945*, ed. Jay Luvaas (Westport, CT: Greenwood Press, 1972), pp. 26, 30.
10. *Ibid.*, p. 4.
11. *Ibid.*
12. *Ibid.*, pp. 8–13.
13. Wesley Frank Craven and James Lea Cate, eds., *The Army Air Forces in World War II*, vol. IV: *The Pacific, Guadalcanal to Saipan, August 1942 to July 1944* (Chicago: University of Chicago Press, 1950), p. 7.
14. George Kenney, *General Kenney Reports. A Personal History of the Pacific War* (New York: Duell, Sloan & Pearce, 1949), p. 2.
15. *Ibid.*, pp. ii, 31.
16. *Ibid.*, p. 61.
17. *Ibid.*, pp. 65, 76.
18. *Ibid.*, pp. 151, 154.
19. MacArthur, *Reminicences*, pp. 164, 165; Eichelberger, *Dear Miss Em*, p. 62.
20. Kenney, *Reports*, p. 93.
21. *Ibid.*, pp. 84, 101, 110.
22. *Ibid.*, p. 103.
23. Craven and Cate, eds., *The Pacific*, p. 26.

Chapter XIV: "Sock 'Em in the Solomons"

1. Fuchida Mitsuo and Masatake Okumiya, *Midway: The Battle That Doomed Japan* (Annapolis: Naval Institute Press, 1955), p. 268.
2. COMINCH to C/SA, letter FFA/A16-3 (1), ser 00544, 25 June 1942, Subj. WATCHTOWER, Nat. Arch.
3. Thomas Buell, *Master of Sea Power. A Biography of Fleet Admiral Ernest J. King* (Boston: Little, Brown, 1980), p. 166.
4. Ike to Marshall, in Maurice Matloff, *Strategic Planning for Coalition Warfare, 1941–1942* (Washington, DC: Department of the Army, 1959), p. 157.
5. Buell, *Master of Sea Power*, p. 207; G. C. Marshall, *Papers of George Catlett Marshall*, vol. III: *"The Right Man for the Job," December 7, 1941–May 31, 1943* (Baltimore and London: Johns Hopkins University Press, 1991), pp. 269–70, where Marshall states that "it might be mighty popular throughout the U.S."; Kenneth S. Davis, *FDR: The*

War President, 1940–1943 (New York: Random House, 2000), p. 539. "The effect on Roosevelt was electric," quoting Davis, p. 539.

6. Alex Danchev, *Very Special Relationship: Field-Marshall Sir John Dill and the Anglo-American Alliance, 1941–44* (London: Brassey's Defence Publications, 1986), p. 35.
7. Buell, *Master of Sea Power*, p. 208 (italics in the original).
8. *Ibid.*, pp. 215–17.
9. *Ibid.*, pp. 218, 193, King to FDR.
10. Plan entitled "Limited Amphibious Offensive in South and Southwest Pacific"; Turner to Admiral Hepburn, memorandum, March 1943; COMINCH 231255; George Carroll Dyer, *The Amphibians Came to Conquer: The Story of Admiral Richmond Kelly Turner*, vol. 1 (Washington, DC: U.S. Government Printing Office, 1972), p. 272.
11. COMPHIBFORSCOPAC (Turner) to COMSOPAC (Ghormley) 192350 July 1942; COMSOPAC TO CINCPAC 210050 July 1942; Dyer, *Amphibians*, pp. 269–75.
12. Dyer, *Amphibians*, pp. 203–05; CNO to Commander Transport Train Atlantic, letter, OP-22-A; P16-3/S82-3/Ser 87722 of 27 September 1940, and CNO to Commander Train Atlantic and Commander Base Force Pacific, letter, OP-22-A (SC) P16-3/Ser 074422, 25, 41, Nat. Arch.
13. Capt. Roswell Daggett, USN (Ret), to Adm Dyer, letter, January 8, 1960, in Dyer, *Amphibians*, p. 206.
14. The APDs were naval auxiliary and cargo ships, redesignated APA and AKA, i.e., Attack Transports and Attack Cargo Ships. Types of landing craft: 30-foot lighters; 36-foot landing boats; some with bow ramps; 45-foot-long tank lighters, 47-foot tank lighters, and others for artillery. See Dyer's Chart, p. 209.
15. File no. FE23/Ae-1, serial 00342. *Secret Amphibious Force, South Pacific Force, Office of the Commander*: COMSOPAC to CINCPAC, memo signed by R. K. Turner; *Landing Operations Doctrine 1938*, Change no. 1, May 1941, which was a complete revision of FTP 167, and Change no. 2, 1 August 1942. Turner at Naval War College during amphibious ops of 1936, 1937, and 1938.
16. Alexander Archer Vandegrift and Robert Asprey, *Once a Marine. The Memoirs of General A. A. Vandegrift* (New York: W. W. Norton, 1964), p. 111.
17. COMSOPAC to King, 081012, 081017, 08110 20 July 1942; John Miller, *The United States Army in World War II. The War in the Pacific. Guadalcanal: The First Offensive* (Washington, DC: Department of the Army, 1949), p. 20.
18. COMSOPAC to CINCPAC, 1606 12 July 1942.
19. Dyer, *Amphibians*, p. 283.
20. Ghormley, Operation Plan no. 1-42, 16 July 1942; Miller, *Guadalcanal*, p. 28.
21. Miller, *Guadalcanal*, pp. 32–33.
22. *Ibid.*
23. Vandegrift and Asprey, *Once a Marine*, p. 103.
24. Dyer, *Amphibians*, pp. 282–83. On p. 295, he gives the figure of seventy-six ships.
25. Miller, *Guadalcanal*, pp. 45, 49.
26. *Ibid.*, p. 55.
27. Peyton interview with Dyer, *Amphibians*, pp. 302–03.
28. Fletcher interview with Dyer, May 25, 1963, in Dyer, *Amphibians*, p. 303.
29. Vandegrift and Asprey, *Once a Marine*, p. 120 (italics added).
30. *Ibid.*
31. Dyer, *Amphibians*, p. 308.

32. COMSOPAC (Ghormley) to TFs 61, 62, 63, 061040 August 1942.
33. Dyer, *Amphibians*, pp. 320–30, quoting staff logs.

Chapter XV: Guadalcanal

1. Rear Admiral Thomas Kinkaid, TF 61, 2330, 8 August 1942, War Diary.
2. Vice Admiral F. J. Fletcher, TF 61, in George Carroll Dyer, *The Amphibians Came to Conquer: The Story of Admiral Richmond Kelly Turner*, vol. 1 (Washington, DC: U.S. Government Printing Office, 1972), pp. 393–95.
3. Dyer, *Amphibians*, p. 358, quotes Turner in an interview.
4. Samuel Eliot Morison, *History of United States Naval Operations in World War II*, vol. V: *The Struggle for Guadalcanal, August 1942–February 1943* (Boston: Little, Brown, 1984), pp. 281–82; John Miller, *The United States Army in World War II. The War in the Pacific. Guadalcanal: The First Offensive* (Washington, DC: Department of the Army, 1949), p. 61.
5. Miller, *Guadalcanal*, p. 61; Alexander Archer Vandegrift and Robert Asprey, *Once a Marine. The Memoirs of General A. A. Vandegrift* (New York: W. W. Norton, 1964), p. 125.
6. Dyer, *Amphibians*, p. 353: Turner to Colonel James Webb, USMC 7th Marines, letter, August 20, 1942.
7. Dyer, *Amphibians*, pp. 351–53.
8. Miller, *Guadalcanal*, pp. 77–78.
9. Miller gives casualties, *Ibid.*, pp. 64–65.
10. *Ibid.*, pp. 73, 75.
11. *Ibid.*, p. 78.
12. *Ibid.*, p. 86; Morison, *The Struggle for Guadalcanal*, p. 292.
13. Paul Dull, *A Battle History of the Imperial Japanese Navy, 1941–1945* (Annapolis: Naval Institute Press, 1978), pp. 184–85.
14. Morison, *The Struggle for Guadalcanal*, p. 19.
15. Admiral Arthur Hepburn's *Report*, Annex T, dated May 13, 1943. Hudson pilot of A16/218, Search Mission FR623, Milne Bay.
16. The second pilot to sight the enemy, Hudson Flight A16/185, COMSOWESPACFOR Communication Officer, memorandum, February 19, 1943, naming the two pilots.
17. Dyer, *Amphibians*, p. 365.
18. The U.S. Navy had only sixteen of these AP transports in the entire Pacific at this time, not eighteen, and all sixteen were executing Watchtower at Guadalcanal—Dyer, *Amphibians*, p. 358, note 5.
19. Chester Nimitz, ed. E. B. Potter, *The Great Sea War. The Story of Naval Action in World War II* (London: George Harrap, 1961), p. 255; cf. David C. Evans and Mark R. Peattie, *Kaigun: Strategy, Tactics, and Technology in the Imperial Japanese Navy, 1887–1941* (Annapolis: Naval Institute Press, 1997), p. 267 for detailed techincal information.
20. Admiral Dyer has carefully unraveled this story, which Morison got somewhat confused (*The Struggle for Guadalcanal*, p. 25, and note 10)—Dyer, *Amphibians*, pp. 362–64.
21. *Hepburn Report* (on Pearl Harbor investigation), vol. 1, May 13, 1943, and Captain George Russell's review of it for Admiral King, as his flag secretary.
22. In all fairness to Fletcher, he did in fact specifically warn McCain to be unusually alert in such cases, concluding: "Note that enemy striking group could approach

undetected . . . by being to the northwest of sector 5 and north of sector 3" pertaining to an earlier operation plan. CTF 61 to CTF 63 (McCain), quoted in Dyer, *Amphibians*, p. 369.

23. Napoleon Bonaparte had of course abandoned the entire French army in Egypt in 1799 in the same manner, without even informing Kléber, his successor as commander in chief, until the former was already well away at sea. Napoleon likewise abandoned his defeated Grande Armée during the retreat from Moscow in 1812.
24. Dyer, *Amphibians*, p. 364.
25. Turner based this assumption on the report of two seaplane tenders, CTF to COMAIRSOPAC, 081055 August 1942, *Hepburn Report*, Annex T. MacArthur wrongly expected an "occupation of Bougainville and Buka," however. COMSOWESPACFOR to CINCPAC, 081055 August 1942.
26. Turner interview with Dyer, and Turner's subsequent official "Operations Reports" cover August 7–10, sent on to Ghormley, then to Nimitz and the CNO, viz. COMPHIBFORSOPAC to COMSOPAC and CINCPAC, letter A16 3(3)/, ser 231, 6 April 1943, forwarding copies of Turner's Operations Report to CTG 62.6 of 13 August 1942 on First Battle of Savo Island. See Dyer's own interview with Turner, *Amphibians*, pp. 400–01.
27. Dyer, *Amphibians*, pp. 365, 374.
28. Kinkaid's War Diary quoted by Admiral Dyer, *Amphibians*, pp. 390–93.
29. Turner interview with Dyer, *Amphibians*, p. 401.
30. COMSOPAC to CINCPAC, 090834 August 1942, *Hepburn Report* dispatches.
31. Fletcher interview with Admiral Dyer, 1960. In fact news of the actual battle there had reached his flagship by 0300 on August 9—Dyer, *Amphibians*, pp. 393–95.
32. For a detailed breakdown on each ship's fuel supply at this time, see Dyer, *Amphibians*, pp. 389–90. See also Morison, *The Struggle for Guadalcanal*, pp. 24, 27–78. Of the entire fleet, only destroyer *Grayson* was down to a three days' supply (39,520 gallons on August 8). Indeed, Fletcher did not even begin fueling until 1700 on August 10, so "critical" was his supply.
33. Alan Schom, *Trafalgar. Countdown to Battle, 1803–1805* (London/New York: Oxford University Press/Penguin Books, 1992), p. 292.
34. Clark G. Reynolds, *Admiral John H. Towers. The Struggle for Naval Air Supremacy* (Annapolis: Naval Institute Press, 1991), p. 399.
35. Morison, *The Struggle for Guadalcanal*, p. 58.
36. CTG 62.6 to CTF, 082211 August 1942, *Hepburn Report*, Annex T.
37. Turner to Director Naval History, letter, 1948, quoted in Dyer, *Amphibians*, p. 373.
38. CTG 62.6 to Admiral Helpburn, memorandum, February 21, 1943, *Hepburn Report*, Annex B.
39. Rear Admiral Turner to CINCPAC, official comment on *Hepburn Report*, January 8, 1943. Dyer quotes this paragraph, p. 381.
40. Morison, *The Struggle for Guadalcanal*, pp. 34ff.
41. Mikawa's Action Report, Central Intelligence Group "Solomons Naval Action, 7–10 August 1942," dated June 27, 1947, Nat. Arch.
42. Unlike U.S. heavy cruisers, those of the Japanese carried torpedo tubes. See Dull, *Battle History*, p. 187.
43. See comparative table of torpedoes in *ibid*., p. 60. The Japanese had a larger torpedo than either the United States or Great Britain. The Japanese Long Lance 24-inch could travel making little wake at 49 knots for 24,000 yards. It carried a 225-pound powder charge, compared to the U.S. 21-inch torpedo with a range of a mere 4,360 yards, at 48 knots, and only a 135-pound powder charge.

44. Morison, *The Struggle for Guadalcanal*, pp. 36ff.
45. *Ibid.*, pp. 39–41.
46. Dull, *Battle History*, pp. 188–90.
47. Morison, *The Struggle for Guadalcanal*, p. 42.
48. *Ibid.*, pp. 43–47.
49. *Ibid.*, pp. 50–51.
50. Dull, *Battle History*, p. 192.
51. Morison gives the figure of 111 Japanese casualties. Dull gives 69, but not including the *Aoba*—*Battle History*, p. 192. The *Canberra* had to be scuppered a few hours later.
52. Turner interview with Admiral Dyer, *Amphibians*, p. 408.
53. Dyer, *Amphibians*, p. 361. Radio dispatches: CINCPAC (August 1942) 962045, 070231, 090341, 0902033, 122025 (October 1942) 162359; COMSOPAC (August 1942) 082140, 090310, 090544, 090640, 131400; CTF 61 (Fletcher, August 1942) 090620, 131400; CTF 62 (Turner, August 1942) 090815, 090725; COMINCH (August 1942) 121250, Nat. Arch.
54. Thomas Buell, *Master of Sea Power. A Biography of Fleet Admiral Ernest J. King* (Boston: Little, Brown, 1980), p. 221.

Chapter XVI: Operation KA

1. Standing orders by Nimitz prior to the battle of Midway, CINCPAC to Commander Striking Force, *Letter of Instructions*, A16-3/A14-3 GG13 (16), ser. 0115 of 28 May 1942, Nat. Arch.
2. H. H. Arnold, *Global Mission* (New York: Harper & Bros., 1949), p. 342.
3. Paul Dull, *A Battle History of the Imperial Japanese Navy, 1941–1945* (Annapolis: Naval Institute Press, 1978), p. 195.
4. *Ibid.*, p. 195. Samuel E. Morison, *United States Naval Operations in World War II*, vol. V. *The Struggle for Guadalcanal, August 1942–February 1943* (Boston: Little, Brown, 1948), pp. 71–73.
5. Dull, *Battle History*, pp. 197 and 205.
6. Morison, *The Struggle for Guadalcanal*, p. 83, note 7.
7. *Ibid.*, p. 84.
8. Dull, *Battle History*, p. 200.
9. *Ibid.*, p. 201.
10. *Ibid.*
11. Morison, *The Struggle for Guadalcanal*, p. 96.
12. Dull, *Battle History*, p. 202.
13. *Ibid.*; Morison, *The Struggle for Guadalcanal*, pp. 96ff.
14. Sherman made no attempt to conceal his utter disdain of Fletcher.
15. Dull, *Battle History*, p. 203.
16. Samuel Eliot Morison, *The Two-Ocean War. A Short History of the United States Navy in the Second World War* (Boston: Little, Brown, 1963), p. 182.
17. See E. B. Potter, *Bull Halsey* (Annapolis: Naval Institute Press, 1988), p. 157.

Chapter XVII: The Open Slot

1. Alexander Archer Vandegrift and Robert Asprey, *Once a Marine. The Memoirs of General A. A. Vandegrift* (New York: W. W. Norton, 1964), p. 142.
2. Samuel E. Morison, *History of United States Naval Operations in World War II*, vol.

V: *The Struggle for Guadalcanal, August 1942–February 1943* (Boston: Little, Brown, 1948), pp. 75–76. On August 28, 1,250 men were landed; on the 29th, 750; on the 30th, 1,000; etc.—Paul Dull, *A Battle History of the Imperial Japanese Navy, 1941–1945* (Annapolis: Naval Institute Press, 1978), p. 210.

3. Morison, *The Struggle for Guadalcanal*, pp. 124ff.
4. Dull, *Battle History*, pp. 210–12.
5. See Vandegrift and Asprey, *Once a Marine*, pp. 154ff., for this period.
6. Morison, *The Struggle for Guadalcanal*, pp. 126, 129, note 4; John Miller, *The United States Army in World War II. The War in the Pacific. Guadalcanal: The First Offensive* (Washington, DC: Department of the Army, 1949), pp. 137ff.
7. Dull, *Battle History*, pp. 211, 212.
8. *Ibid.*, p. 214; Morison, *The Struggle for Guadalcanal*, p. 124, note; Miller, *Guadalcanal*, pp. 137ff.
9. Dull, *Battle History*, p. 214; Morison, *The Struggle for Guadalcanal*, pp. 131–33.
10. Dull, *Battle History*, p. 214.
11. Morison, *The Struggle for Guadalcanal*, p. 137, note 10.
12. Vandegrift and Asprey, *Once a Marine*, p. 166.
13. Morison, *The Struggle for Guadalcanal*, p. 141.
14. William Manchester, *American Caesar: Douglas MacArthur, 1880–1964* (Boston: Little, Brown, 1978), p. 325. MacArthur to Eichelberger, November 1942: "Bob, take Buna or don't come back alive." He later repeated that.
15. Dull, *Battle History*, p. 216. On October 10, 1942, U.S. bombers and torpedo planes attacked the Tokyo Express as it was returning to the Shortlands. The thousands of tons of munitions dropped once again resulted in only light damage.
16. Morison, *The Struggle for Guadalcanal*, pp. 149–50. Sent at Nimitz's orders to Ghormley on September 28, 1942, during the Nouméa conference—E. B. Potter, *Nimitz* (Annapolis: Naval Institute Press, 1976), p. 192.
17. Morison, *The Struggle for Guadalcanal*, p. 150.
18. *Ibid.*, p. 151.
19. *Ibid.*, p. 157.
20. Dull, *Battle History*, pp. 219–20.
21. Morison, *The Struggle for Guadalcanal*, p. 168.
22. *Ibid.*, p. 151.
23. Miller, *Guadalcanal*, p. 151.

Chapter XVIII: "A Goddam Mess"

1. George Carroll Dyer, *The Amphibians Came to Conquer: The Story of Admiral Richmond Kelly Turner*, vol. 1 (Washington, DC: Government Printing Office, 1972), p. 420. Letters of November 7 and 16, 1942, from Turner to Vandegrift and staff.
2. H. H. Arnold, *Global Mission* (New York: Harper & Bros., 1949), p. 348. Arnold of course was one of the recipients of the presidential memo.
3. E. B. Potter, *Nimitz* (Annapolis: Naval Institute Press, 1976), p. 264, note 1.
4. Samuel Eliot Morison, *History of United States Naval Operations in World War II*, vol. V: *The Struggle for Guadalcanal, August 1942–February 1943* (Boston: Little, Brown, 1948), p. 178; *New York Times*, October 17, 1942.
5. Potter, *Nimitz*, p. 264.
6. E. B. Potter, *Bull Halsey* (Annapolis: Naval Institute Press, 1988), pp. 160, 162.
7. Alexander Archer Vandegrift and Robert Asprey, *Once a Marine. The Memoirs of A. A. Vandegrift* (New York: W. W. Norton, 1964), pp. 181–82.

8. Potter, *Halsey*, p. 162.
9. Morison, *The Struggle for Guadalcanal*, p. 184.
10. Potter, *Halsey*, p. 163.
11. *Ibid.*, pp. 162–63
12. Clark G. Reynolds, *Admiral John H. Towers. The Struggle for Naval Air Supremacy* (Annapolis: Naval Institute Press, 1991), p. 403.
13. *New York Times*, October 25, 1942.
14. Reynolds, *Towers*, p. 403.
15. *Ibid.*, p. 410.
16. *Ibid.*, pp. 217–18; Archibald Turnbull and Clifford Lord, *The History of United States Naval Aviation* (New Haven: Yale University Press, 1949), pp. 78 and 151; Gwenfread Allen, *Hawaii's War Years, 1941–1945* (Honolulu: University of Hawaii Press, 1949), chap. 1; Robert G. Albion, ed. Rowena Reed, *The Makers of Naval Policy, 1918–1947* (Annapolis: Naval Institute Press, 1980), chap. 7; Scot MacDonald, *Evolution of Aircraft Carriers* (Washington, DC: U.S. Government Printing Office, 1964), pp. 230ff.; Clark G. Reynolds, *The Fast Carriers: The Forging of an Air Navy* (New York: McGraw-Hill, 1968), p. 280.
17. Nimitz in fact had once applied for flight instruction, at a time when there were no openings available.
18. Arnold, *Global Mission*, p. 348; Robert Sherwood, *Roosevelt and Hopkins, An Intimate History* (New York: Harper & Bros., 1948), p. 622–23.
19. Samuel Eliot Morison, *History of United States Naval Operations in World War II*, vol. III: *The Rising Sun in the Pacific, 1931–April 1942* (Boston: Little, Brown, 1948), p. 315.
20. Quoted in Morison, *The Struggle for Guadalcanal*, p. 189, from Imperial Headquarters Navy Staff Section Directive no. 135 (WDC = Nat. Arch. no. 216, 769).
21. Morison, *The Struggle for Guadalcanal*, p. 189.
22. Paul Dull, *A Battle History of the Imperial Japanese Navy, 1941–1945* (Annapolis: Naval Institute Press, 1978), p. 223.
23. Morison, *The Struggle for Guadalcanal*, p. 190; John Miller, *The United States Army in World War II. The War in the Pacific. Guadalcanal: The First Offensive* (Washington, DC: Department of the Army, 1949), p. 156.
24. Morison, *The Struggle for Guadalcanal*, p. 190; Miller, *Guadalcanal*, pp. 156ff.
25. The marines later buried some one thousand bodies there—Miller, *Guadalcanal*, pp. 163–67.
26. Morison, *The Struggle for Guadalcanal*, p. 198; Miller, *Guadalcanal*, p. 161.
27. Dull, *Battle History*, p. 226.
28. Dyer, *Amphibians*, p. 420.
29. Morison, *The Struggle for Guadalcanal*, p. 197.
30. Mitsuru Yoshida, *Requiem for Battleship Yamato* (London: Constable, 1985), pp. xv. The other ship was *Musashi*. The Japanese now had the largest and most powerful of any navy in the world. Battleships *Bismarck* and *Tirpitz*, for instance, displaced only 46,000 tons. In addition, Yamato had the most powerful guns afloat at 460mm (18.1 in.).
31. Dull, *Battle History*, p. 227.
32. *Ibid.*
33. For Japanese plane launches and strikes, see *ibid.*, pp. 229–30; for the American reaction, cf. Morison, *The Struggle for Guadalcanal*, pp. 208–09 and 221.
34. Morison, *The Struggle for Guadalcanal*, p. 323, note 12.
35. *Ibid.*, p. 215.

36. *Ibid.*, p. 213.
37. Dull, *Battle History*, p. 232.
38. Morison, *The Struggle for Guadalcanal*, p. 219.
39. Nagumo later transferred his flag and the emperor's portrait to *Zuikaku* at 1530, October 27, 1942—Dull, *Battle History*, p. 232.
40. Captain Charles Mason, *Report of Action 26 October 1942 Subsequent Loss of Hornet*, Nat. Arch.
41. Morison, *The Struggle for Guadalcanal*, p. 223.
42. Dull, *Battle History*, pp. 232–33.
43. Morison, *The Struggle for Guadalcanal*, p. 178. Nimitz comment, October 15, 1942.

Chapter XIX: "Friday the Bloody Thirteenth"

1. Clark G. Reynolds, *Admiral John H. Towers. The Struggle for Naval Air Supremacy* (Annapolis: Naval Institute Press, 1991), pp. 408–09.
2. Samuel Eliot Morison, *History of United States Naval Operations in World War II*, vol. V: *The Struggle for Guadalcanal, August 1942–February 1943* (Boston: Little, Brown, 1948), p. 286.
3. Reynolds, *Towers*, p. 408.
4. *Ibid.*
5. Morison, *The Struggle for Guadalcanal*, pp. 225–27.
6. E. B. Potter, *Bull Halsey* (Annapolis: Naval Institute Press, 1985); p. 168, Alexander Archer Vandegrift and Robert Asprey, *Once a Marine. The Memoirs of General A. A. Vandegrift* (New York: W. W. Norton, 1964), p. 196.
7. Potter, *Halsey*, p. 169.
8. J.-B. Duroselle, *L'Abîme, 1939–1944* (Paris: Imprimérie Nationale, 1986), p. 345.
9. *Ibid.*: "dire de ma part au général Patch que ni moi ni le Comité national français ne pourrions acceptons son ingérence dans une affaire française."
10. Potter, *Halsey*, pp. 184–86.
11. *Ibid.*, pp. 170–71; Vandegrift and Asprey, *Once a Marine*, p. 198.
12. David C. Evans and Mark R. Peattie, *Kaigun: Strategy, Tactics, and Technology in the Imperial Japanese Navy, 1887–1941* (Annapolis: Naval Institute Press, 1997), p. 527.
13. Paul Dull, *The Imperial Japanese Navy, 1941–1945* (Annapolis: Naval Institute Press, 1978), pp. 248–49. Dull includes here a chart of the complete command.
14. *Ibid.*, pp. 233–35.
15. *Ibid.*, p. 249, for the table of organization; and Morison, *The Struggle for Guadalcanal*, pp. 231–33.
16. Dull, *Battle History*, p. 239.
17. Morison, *The Struggle for Guadalcanal*, p. 238.
18. *Ibid.*, p. 239, based on later action report.
19. *Ibid.*, p. 241; John Miller, *The United States Army in World War II. The War in the Pacific. Guadalcanal: The First Offensive* (Washington, DC: Department of the Army, 1949), pp. 184ff.
20. Dull, *Battle History*, p. 239.
21. *Ibid.*, p. 240; Morison, *The Struggle for Guadalcanal*, p. 242.
22. Morison, *The Struggle for Guadalcanal*, p. 243.
23. Dull, *Battle History*, p. 240; Morison, *The Struggle for Guadalcanal*, p. 247.

24. Dull, *Battle History*, pp. 240–41; Morison, *The Struggle for Guadalcanal*, pp. 247–48.
25. Morison, *The Struggle for Guadalcanal*, p. 248.
26. Dull, *Battle History*, p. 242; Morsion, *The Struggle for Guadalcanal*, p. 253.
27. Dull, *Battle History*, p. 242; Morison, *The Struggle for Guadalcanal*, p. 257.
28. Morison, *The Struggle for Guadalcanal*, p. 262; Dull, *Battle History*, pp. 242–43.
29. Dull, *Battle History*, p. 243, for the precise movements of Mikawa's force; Morison, *The Struggle for Guadalcanal*, p. 263.
30. CINCPAC Action Report: "Pacific Counterblow," published by Headquarters, Army Air Force, as "Wings of War Series No. 2."
31. Dull, *Battle History*, p. 243.
32. Morison, *The Struggle for Guadalcanal*, p. 260; Dull, *Battle History*, p. 242.
33. Morison, *The Struggle for Guadalcanal*, p. 266.
34. CTF63, Action Report, CINCPAC Papers; *Enterprise*, Action Report, CINCPAC Papers, both in Nat. Arch.
35. Transports sunk, November 14: *Arizona*, *Shinanogawa*, *Sado*, *Canberra*, *Nako*, *Nagara*, and *Brisbane*.
36. Morison, *The Struggle for Guadalcanal*, p. 273.
37. Dull, *Battle History*, p. 243; Morison, *The Struggle for Guadalcanal*, p. 274, Action Reports, *Washington*, CINCPAC Papers, Nat. Arch.
38. Morison, *The Struggle for Guadalcanal*, pp. 274–77. The *Kirishima* sank off Savo Island at 0320 on November 15.
39. Action Reports, *Washington* and *South Dakota*, CINCPAC Papers, Nat. Arch.
40. Morison, *The Struggle for Guadalcanal*, p. 281; Dull, *Battle History*, pp. 244–47.
41. Upon his return Tanaka had a furious row with his superiors, and he was duly relieved of his command at the end of the Guadalcanal campaign, never again to take part actively in future operations of the war—Evans and Peattie, *Kaigun*, p. 535.
42. Dull, *Battle History*, p. 247. Commander Yamamoto Tadashi, Tanaka's communications officer, in U.S. Strategic Bombing Survey, *Interrogations of Japanese Officials* (Washington, DC: U.S. Government Printing Office, 1947), vol. II, p. 468.
43. Morison, *The Struggle for Guadalcanal*, p. 284.
44. Dull, *Battle History*, pp. 244–47.
45. Vandegrift, *Once a Marine*, pp. 199, 299; E. B. Potter, *Nimitz* (Annapolis: Naval Institute Press, 1976), pp. 206, 208.
46. Morison, *The Struggle for Guadalcanal*, p. 286.
47. Robert Sherwood, *Roosevelt and Hopkins, An Intimate History* (New York: Harper & Bros., 1948), p. 656.
48. The initial talks between Marshall and King, and subsequently with MacArthur, on the division of army/navy command around the Tulagi-Guadalcanal region had begun on June 26, 1942, with Marshall's secret memorandum to Ernest King of June 26, two more to King dated June 29, and George Marshall's secret Radio no. 306 message to MacArthur, also of June 29. Vandegrift's anticipated handing over of command to Army General Patch would conclude this process—George Marshall, *The Papers of George Catlett Marshall*, vol. 3: *"The Right Man for the Job," December 7, 1941–May 31, 1943* (Baltimore and London: Johns Hopkins University Press, 1991), pp. 252–56.
49. Morison, *The Struggle for Guadalcanal*, p. 294.
50. Dull, *Battle History*, p. 255.
51. "Battle of Tassafaronga," Allied Translator and Interpreter Section 16086; Dull, *Battle History*, pp. 255, 257.

52. Dull, *Battle History*, p. 257; Morison, *The Struggle for Guadalcanal*, p. 309.
53. Morison, *The Struggle for Guadalcanal*, pp. 309–10; Dull, *Battle History*, p. 257.
54. Morison, *The Struggle for Guadalcanal*, pp. 305, 310; Dull, *Battle History*, p. 257.
55. Morison, *The Struggle for Guadalcanal*, p. 307.

Chapter XX: A Troubled Hirohito

1. CINCPAC-CINCPOA Intelligence translation, ser. 4739, Nat. Arch.
2. Robert L. Eichelberger, *Dear Miss Em: General Eichelberger's War in the Pacific, 1942–1945*, ed. Jay Luvaas (Westport, CT: Greenwood Press, 1972), pp. 16, 50, 51. For the compliments that "I have not ever received, 'thank you dog,' from MacArthur and I do not expect to. . . ."—William Manchester, *American Caesar: Douglas MacArthur, 1880–1964* (Boston: Little, Brown, 1978), p. 304.
3. George Kenney, *General Kenney Reports: A Personal History of the Pacific War* (New York: Duell, Sloan & Pearce, 1949), p. 93.
4. *Ibid.*, pp. 84, 101, 103, 110.
5. *Ibid.*, pp. 125, 121; Wesley Craven and James Cate, eds., *The Army Air Forces in World War II*, vol. IV: *The Pacific: Guadalcanal to Saipan, August 1942–July 1944* (Chicago: University of Chicago Press, 1950), p. 26.
6. Myazaki's account in U.S. Strategic Bombing Survey, "Allied Campaign Against Rabaul."
7. Samuel E. Morison, *History of the United States Naval Operations in World War II*, vol. V: *The Struggle for Guadalcanal, August 1942–February 1943* (Boston: Little, Brown, 1948), pp. 318–19.
8. See biographical note in David C. Evans and Mark R. Peattie, *Kaigun: Strategy, Tactics, and Technology in the Imperial Japanese Navy, 1887–1941* (Annapolis: Naval Institute Press, 1997); Paul Dull, *A Battle History of the Imperial Japanese Navy, 1941–1945* (Annapolis: U.S. Naval Institute, 1978), pp. 345–47.
9. Morison, *The Struggle for Guadalcanal*, pp. 321–23; Dull, *Battle History*, p. 258.
10. Each 77-foot PT boat had three 4,050 hp Packard engines, four torpedo tubes, and four 50-caliber machine guns, two on each side.
11. Morison, *The Struggle for Guadalcanal*, p. 325.
12. Tokyo meeting, January 4, 1943: Solomon Tokyo Notes, and Allied Translator and Interpreter Section, from the Japanese "Southeast Area Operations Part I (Navy)"—Dull, *Battle History*, p. 259. Nagano had been one of the very senior naval officers to have opposed the surprise attack on Pearl Harbor in December 1941—Morison, *The Struggle for Guadalcanal*, p. 325.
13. Alexander Archer Vandegrift and Robert Asprey, *Once a Marine. The Memoirs of General A. A. Vandegrift* (New York: W. W. Norton, 1964), pp. 203–04; John Miller, *The United States Army in World War II. The War in the Pacific. Guadalcanal: The First Offensive* (Washington, DC: Department of the Army, 1949), pp. 218ff.
14. Miller, *Guadalcanal*, pp. 237ff. and 243ff.
15. *Ibid.*, p. 255.
16. *Ibid.*, p. 252.
17. *Ibid.*, pp. 260ff., 290, 332–35, 341ff.
18. Morison, *The Struggle for Guadalcanal*, p. 347.
19. *Ibid.*, p. 353, for a chart of the complete composition of TF 18 and its skippers.
20. *Ibid.*, pp. 356–57.
21. *Ibid.*, p. 359.

22. *Ibid.*, pp. 360–62.
23. Dull, *Battle History*, p. 259.
24. *Ibid.*
25. Morison, *The Struggle for Guadalcanal*, p. 369; Dull, *Battle History*, p. 259.
26. Morison, *The Struggle for Guadalcanal*, pp. 370, 371; Miller, *Guadalcanal*, p. 350. Dull, *Battle History*, p. 259, provides the first accurate figures for the number of Japanese troops; Radio, CG Cactus to COMSOPAC, 0718, 9 February 1943.
27. Dull, *Battle History*, p. 256.
28. Manchester, *American Caesar*, pp. 327–28.
29. *Ibid.*, pp. 149 and 29; E. B. Potter, *Nimitz* (Annapolis: Naval Institute Press, 1976), p. 214; Marshall to MacArthur, Radio no. 1171, 15 February 1943; Marshall memorandum to King, Secret, 16 February 1943; George Marshall, *The Papers of George Catlett Marshall*, vol. 3: *"The Right Man for the Job," December 7, 1941–May 31 1943* (Baltimore and London: Johns Hopkins University Press, 1991), pp. 551–52.
30. Miller, *The Struggle for Guadalcanal*, p. 350; Manchester, *American Caesar*, p. 328. Dull, *Battle History*, p. 260, states a total Japanese presence of 31,358 men. During the entire campaign, the Japanese lost 892 men and 1,882 pilots, according to Herbert Bix, *Hirohito and the Making of Modern Japan* (New York: HarperCollins, 2000), p. 461.
31. CINCPAC Action Report, 15 February 1943, CINCPAC Papers, Nat. Arch.
32. Bix, *Hirohito*, p. 456.

Permissions

Frank Hewlett lyrics from *General Wainwright's Story* (first published by Doubleday Publishing in 1946 and reprinted by Greenwood Publishing in 1986), by Jonathan Wainwright. Used by permission.

"Map of Guadalcanal" redrawn from *History of United States Naval Operations in World War II,* volume V: *The Struggle for Guadalcanal by Samuel Eliot Morrison.* Copyright © 1949 by Samuel Eliot Morison. By permission of Little, Brown, and Company, Inc.

"Battle of Midway" and "Map of the Pacific Ocean" redrawn from *History of United States Naval Operations in World War II,* volume IV: *Coral Sea, Midway and Submarine Actions* by Samuel Eliot Morison. Copyright © 1949 by Samuel Eliot Morison. By permission of Little, Brown, and Company, Inc.

"Merchant Ships Sunk by U-Boats in the Atlantic" redrawn from *The Two Ocean War* by Samuel Eliot Morrison. Copyright © 1963 by Samuel Eliot Morison; Copyright © renewed by Emily Beck, Elizabeth Spigarn, Catherine Morison Cooper. By permission of Little, Brown, and Company, Inc.

"Japanese Launch Attack against the Dutch East Indies" and "Detailed Map of Pearl Harbor" redrawn from *History of United States Naval Operations in World War II,* volume III: *The Rising Sun in the Pacific* by Samuel Eliot Morrison. Copyright © 1947 by Samuel Eliot Morison. By permission of Little, Brown, and Company, Inc.

"Papuan Operations," "Japanese Landings in the Philippines," "Japan's Defense Perimeter," "Battle of Savo Island," and "Japanese Thrusts" redrawn from *A Battle History of the Imperial Japanese Navy (1941–1945)* by Paul S. Dull. Copyright © 1978 by the U.S. Naval Institute, Annapolis, Maryland.

"Japanese Landings in the Philippines" and "Corregidor Island" redrawn from *Fall of the Philippines* by Louis Morton. Washington, D.C.: Office of the Chief of Military History, Dept. of the Army, 1953. Courtesy of U.S. Army.

Bibliography

Acheson, Dean. *Present at the Creation: My Years in the State Department* (New York: W. W. Norton, 1969).

Adams, Henry. *Harry Hopkins* (New York: G. P. Putnam's Sons, 1977).

Lord Alanbrooke. *War Diaries, 1939–1945,* ed. Alex Dancher and Daniel Todman (London: Weidenfeld & Nicolson, 2001).

Albion, Robert Greenhalgh. *The Makers of Naval Policy, 1878–1947,* ed. Reed, Rowena (Annapolis: Naval Institute Press, 1980).

———, and Robert Howe Connery. *Forrestal and the Navy* (New York: Columbia University Press, 1962).

The Allied Translator and Interpreter Section (ATIS), containing a complete set of publications gathered from General MacArthur's headquarters, is on file in the Office of the Center of Military History and with the Military Intelligence Library, Department of the Army for the Philippine campaign (Washington, DC).

Alsop, Joseph. *FDR 1882–1945: A Centenary Remembrance* (New York: Viking Press, 1982).

Arnold, H. H. *Global Mission* (New York: Harper & Bros, 1949).

Asukai, Masamichi. *Meiji taitei* (Tokyo: Chikuma Shobō, 1989).

Awaya, Kentarō, and Yoshida Yutaka, eds. *Kokusai kensatsukyoku (IPS) jimmon chosō, dai 8 and 42 kan* (Tokyo: Nichon Tasho Senta, 1993).

Baldwin, Hanson. *Great Mistakes of the War* (New York: Harper & Bros., 1950).

Barbey, Daniel. *MacArthur's Amphibious Navy: Seventh Amphibious Force Operations, 1943–1945* (Annapolis: Naval Institute Press, 1969).

Barnhart, Michael. *Japan Prepares for Total War. The Search for Economic Security, 1919–1941* (Ithaca, NY: Cornell University Press, 1987).

Belote, James H., and William M. Belote. *Corregidor: The Saga of a Fortress* (New York: Morrow, 1967).

———. *The Titans of the Seas: The Development and Operations of Japanese and American Carrier Task Forces During World War II* (New York: Harper & Row, 1975).

Benedict, Ruth. *The Chrysanthemum and the Sword: Patterns of Japanese Culture* (Tokyo: Kodansha International, 1990).

Beasley, W. G. *Japanese Imperialism, 1894–1945* (Oxford: Oxford University Press, 1987).

Best, Antony. *Britain, Japan and Pearl Harbor: Avoiding War in East Asia, 1936–41* (London: Routledge, 1995).

Bisson, T. A. *Japan in China* (New York: Macmillan, 1938; reprint Greenwood Press, 1973).

Bix, Herbert. "Japanese Imperialism and the Manchurian Economy, 1900–1931," *China Quarterly*, 51 (1972), pp. 425–43.

———. *Hirohito and the Making of Modern Japan* (New York: HarperCollins, 2000).

Black, Edwin. *IBM and the Holocaust; The Strategic Alliance Between Nazi Germany and America's Most Powerful Corporation* (New York; Crown, 2001).

Blair, Clay. *Silent Victory: The U.S. Submarine War Against Japan* (Philadelphia: Lippincott, 1975).

Blum, John Morton. *Roosevelt and Morgenthau* (Boston: Houghton Mifflin, 1970).

Brackman, Arnold. *The Other Nuremberg: The Untold Story of the Tokyo War Crimes Trials* (New York: Morrow, 1987).

Brereton, Lewis. *The Brereton Diaries* (New York: Morrow, 1946).

Brownlow, Donald Grey. *The Accused: The Ordeal of Rear Admiral Husband Edward Kimmel USN* (New York: Vantage Press, 1968).

Budiansky, Stephen. *Battle of Wits: The Complete Story of Codebreaking in World War II* (New York: Free Press, 2000).

Buell, Thomas. *The Quiet Warrior. A Biography of Admiral Raymond Spruance* (Boston: Little, Brown, 1974).

———. *Master of Sea Power. A Biography of Fleet Admiral Ernest J. King* (Boston: Little, Brown, 1980).

Burns, James MacGregor. *Roosevelt: The Soldier of Freedom* (New York: Putnam, 1970).

Butrow, Robert. *Tojo and the Coming of the War* (Princeton: Princeton University Press, 1961).

Byrnes, James F. *All in One Lifetime* (New York: Harper, 1958).

Calvocoressi, Peter, Guy Wint, and John Pritchard. *Total War: The Causes and Courses of the Second World War*, rev. 2nd ed. (Harmondsworth, UK: Penguin, 1995).

Cambridge History of Japan, ed. Peter Duus, vol. 6: *The Twentieth Century* (Cambridge: Cambridge University Press, 1988).

Casey, Hugh. *Engineers of the Southwest Pacific, 1941–1945*, 7 vols. (Washington, DC: U.S. Government Printing Office, 1947–53).

(British) Central Office of Information. *Among Those Present: The Official Story of the Pacific Islands at War* (London: HM Stationery Office, 1946).

Chan, Iris. *The Rape of Nanking: The Forgotten Holocaust of World War II* (New York: Basic Books, 1997).

Chennault, Claire Lee. *Way of a Fighter: The Memoirs of Claire Lee Chennault,* ed. Robert Bitlotz (New York: Putnam, 1949).

Chernow, Ron. *Titan: The Life of John D. Rockefeller, Sr.* (New York: Random House, 1998).

Chichibu, Princess Setsuko. *The Silver Drum. A Japanese Imperial Memoir,* trans. D. Guyver Britton (Folkestone, UK: Global Oriental, 1996).

Chichibu no Miya Kinenkai, *Yoshihito shinnō jiseki shiryō* (Tokyo: CNP, 1952).

Churchill, Winston S. *The Second World War.* Vol. I: *The Gathering Storm* (London: Cassell, 1948).

———. *The Second World War.* Vol. II: *Their Finest Hour* (London: Cassell, 1949).

———. *The Second World War.* Vol. III: *The Grand Alliance* (London: Cassell, 1950).

———. *The Second World War.* Vol. IV: *The Hinge of Fate* (London: Cassell, 1951).

Clark, Joseph James, and Clark G. Reynolds. *Carrier Admiral* (New York: David McKay, 1967).

Coffey, Thomas M. *Hap: The Story of the U.S. Air Force and the Man Who Built It, General Henry H. "Hap" Arnold* (New York: Viking Press, 1982).

Cole, Wayne. *America First: The Battle Against Intervention* (Madison: University of Wisconsin Press, 1955).

Colville, John. *Winston Churchill and His Inner Circle* (New York: Wyndham Books, 1981).

Cox, Alvin. *Nomonhan: Japan Against Russia, 1939* (Stanford: Stanford University Press, 1985).

Craven, Wesley Frank, and James Lea Cate, eds. *The Army Air Forces in World War II,* 7 vols. (Chicago: University of Chicago Press, 1948–50).

Cray, Ed. *General of the Army: George C. Marshall, Soldier and Statesman* (New York: W. W. Norton, 1990).

Crowley, James B. *Japan's Quest for Autonomy: National Security and Foreign Policy, 1930–1938* (Princeton: Princeton University Press, 1966).

Cunningham, Andrew B. *A Sailor's Odyssey* (New York: Dutton, 1951).

Daikichi, Irokawa. *The Age of Hirohito: In Search of Modern Japan* (New York: Free Press, 1995).

———. *The Age of Modern Japan* (New York: Free Press, 1995).

Dallek, Robert. *Franklin D. Roosevelt and American Foreign Policy, 1932–1945* (New York: Oxford University Press, 1979).

———. *The American Style of Foreign Policy* (New York: Knopf, 1983).

Danchev, Alex. *Very Special Relationship: Field-Marshall Sir John Dill and the Anglo-American Alliance, 1941–1944* (London: Brassey's Defence Publications, 1986).

Davis, Burke. *Marine! The Life of Lt. Gen. Lewis B. (Chesty) Puller, USMC (ret.)* (Boston: Little, Brown, 1962).

Davis, Kenneth S. *FDR: Into the Storm, 1937–1940* (New York: Random House, 1993).

———. *FDR: The War President, 1940–1943* (New York: Random House, 2000).

Daws, Gavan. *Prisoners of the Japanese: POWs of World War II in the Pacific* (New York: Morrow, 1994).

De Conde, Alexander. *Presidential Machismo: Executive Authority, Military Intervention, and Foreign Policy* (Boston: Northeastern University Press, 2000).

de Gaulle, Charles. *War Memoirs*. Vol. II: *Unity, 1942–1944*, trans. R. Howard (London: Weidenfeld & Nicolson, 1960; New York: Simon & Schuster, 1960).

Dower, John. *Embracing Defeat: Japan in the Wake of World War II* (New York: W. W. Norton, 1999).

Dull, Paul. *A Battle History of the Imperial Japanese Navy, 1941–1945* (Annapolis: Naval Institute Press, 1978).

Dulles, Allen Welsh. *The Secret Surrender* (New York: Harper & Row, 1966).

Dunnigan, James, and Albert Nofi. *Victory at Sea: World War II in the Pacific* (New York: Morrow, 1995).

Duroselle, Jean-Baptiste. *L'Abîme, 1939–1944*, 2nd rev. ed. (Paris: Imprimérie Nationale, 1986). Archives Ministère des Affaires Etrangères (Paris: MAE, 1940), Baudouin, Carton no. 14. T. 201–203, 20 September 1940, and T. 703–708 and T. 709–714, Arsène Henry, 22 September 1940.

Dyer, George Carroll. *The Amphibians Came to Conquer: The Story of Richmond Kelly Turner*, 2 vols. (Washington, DC: U.S. Government Printing Office, 1972).

Dyess, William. *The Dyess Story: The Eye-Witness Account of the Death March from Bataan and the Narrative of Experience in Japanese Prison Camps and of Eventual Escape*, ed. Charles Leavelle (New York: G. P. Putnam's Sons, 1944).

Eden, Anthony, Earl of Avon. *The Reckoning: The Memoirs of Anthony Eden, Earl of Avon* (Boston: Houghton Mifflin, 1965).

Eguchi, Keiichi. *Jūgonen sensō shōshi, shinpan* (Tokyo: Aoki Shoten, 1991).

Eichelberger, Robert L. *Dear Miss Em: General Eichelberger's War in the Pacific, 1942–1945*, ed. Jay Luvaas (Westport, CT: Greenwood Press, 1972).

———. *Our Jungle Road to Tokyo* (New York: Viking Press, 1950; Nashville: Battery Classics, 1989).

Eisenhower, Dwight D. *At Ease: Stories I Tell to Friends* (New York: Doubleday, 1967).

———. *The Eisenhower Diaries*, ed. Robert H. Ferrell (New York: W. W. Norton, 1981).

Endicott, Stephen, and Edward Hagerman. *The United States and Biological Warfare: Secrets from the Early Cold War and Korea* (Bloomington: Indiana University Press, 1998).

Evans, David C., and Mark R. Peattie. *Kaigun: Strategy, Tactics, and Technology in the Imperial Japanese Navy, 1887–1941* (Annapolis: Naval Institute Press, 1997).

Feis, Herbert. *The Road to Pearl Harbor: The Coming of the War Between the United States and Japan* (Princeton: Princeton University Press, 1950).

Fergusson, Bernard. *The Watery Maze: The Story of Combined Operations* (London: Collins, 1961).

Ferrell, Robert H. *George C. Marshall*. Vol. XV of *The American Secretaries of State and Their Diplomacy* (New York: Cooper Square Publishers, 1966).

Foreign Relations of the United States. U.S. State Department documents pertaining to peace and war, 1928–41, and the Far East, 1944–54 (Washington, DC: U.S. Government Printing Office).

Foreign Relations of the United States. Diplomatic Papers: The Conferences at Washington and Quebec, 1943 (Washington, DC: U.S. Government Printing Office, 1970).

Foreign Relations of the United States, Japan, 1931–1941 (Washington, DC: U.S. Government Printing Office, 1943).

Forrestal, James. *The Forrestal Diaries*, ed. Walter Millis (New York: Viking Press, 1951).

Forrestel, E. P. *Admiral Raymond A. Spruance, USN: A Study in Command* (Washington, DC: U.S. Government Printing Office, 1966).

Frank, Benis. *Halsey* (New York: Ballantine Books, 1974).

Freidel, Frank. *Franklin D. Roosevelt: A Rendezvous with Destiny* (Boston: Little, Brown, 1954).

———. *Franklin D. Roosevelt: Launching the New Deal* (Boston: Little, Brown, 1973).

Friend, Theodore. *Between Two Empires: The Ordeal of the Philippines, 1929–1946* (New Haven: Yale University Press, 1965).

Fuchida, Mitsuo, and Masatake Okumiya. *Midway: The Battle That Doomed Japan* (Annapolis: Naval Institute Press, 1955).

Fujiwara, Akira, "Dai Nihon teikoku kenpō," in Fujiwara, et al., *Tennō Shōwashi Shin Nihon Shinsho* (Tokyo: Shinnihon Shuppansha, 1986). On the connection between the right wing and the imperial court.

———. *Shōwa tennō no jūgonen sensō* (Tokyo: Aoki Shoten, 1991).

———. "Nitchū sensō ni okeru horyo gyakusatsu," in *Kikan sensōsekinin kenyū*, 9 (Autumn 1995), p. 23.

Fuller, J. F. C. *The Second World War, 1939–45: A Strategical and Tactical History* (London: Constable, 1948; New York: Duell, Sloan & Pearce, 1948).

Funk, Arthur. *The Politics of TORCH: The Allied Landings and the Algiers Putsch, 1942* (Lawrence, KS: University of Kansas Press, 1974).

Furuya, Keiji. *Chiang Kai-Shek: His Life and Times*, trans. Chun-ming Chang (New York: St. John's University, 1981).

Gilbert, Martin. *Winston S. Churchill.* Vol. VI: *Finest Hour, 1939–1941* (London: Heinemann, 1983).

———. *Winston S. Churchill.* Vol. VII: *Road to Victory, 1941–1945* (London: Heinemann, 1983).

———. *The Second World War. A Complete History* (New York: Henry Holt, 1989).

———. *Churchill: A Life* (London: Heinemann, 1991).

Glines, Carroll. *Doolittle's Tokyo Raiders* (Princeton: Van Nostrand, 1964).

Gold, Hal. *Unit 731: Testimony* (Tokyo: Yenbooks, 1996).

Gomer, Robert, John Powell, and B. V. A. Röling. "Japan's Biological Weapons, 1930–1945," *Bulletin of the Atomic Scientists* (October 1981), pp. 45–53.

Grew, Joseph C. *Turbulent Era: A Diplomatic Record of Forty Years, 1904–1945*, 2 vols. (Boston: Houghton Mifflin, 1952).

Griffith, Samuel. *The Battle for Guadalcanal* (Philadelphia: Lippincott, 1963).

Halifax, Earl of. *Fullness of Days* (London: Collins, 1957).

Halsey, William F., and Joseph Bryan. *Admiral Halsey's Story* (New York: Whittlesey House, 1947).

Hara, Kei. *Hara Kei nikki, dai hakkan* (Tokyo: Kangensha, 1950).

Harada, Kumao. *Harada nikki, Saionji kō to seikyoku*, vols. 1–9 (Tokyo: Iwanami Shoten, 1950–56). Diaries of Harada.

Harries, Meirion, and Susan Harries. *Soldiers of the Sun: The Rise and Fall of the Imperial Japanese Army* (New York: Random House, 1991).

Harriman, W. Averell. *America and Russia in a Changing World: A Half Century of Personal Observation* (Garden City, NY: Doubleday, 1971).

Harris, Robert, and Jeremy Paxman. *A Higher Form of Killing: The Secret Story of Chemical and Biological Warfare, 1932–45* (New York: Hill & Wang, 1982).

Harris, Sheldon. *Factories of Death: Japanese Biological Warfare, 1932–45, and the American Cover-up* (London: Routledge, 1994).

Hart, Robert. *The Great White Fleet: Its Voyage Around the World* (Boston: Little, Brown, 1965).

Haruko, Taya Cook, and Theodore F. Cook. *Japan at War: An Oral History* (New York: Free Press, 1992).

Hashimoto, Mochitsura. *Sunk: The Story of the Japanese Submarine Fleet, 1941–1945*, trans. E. H. M. Colegrave (London: Cassell, 1954).

Haslam, Jonathan. *The Soviet Union and the Threat from the East, 1933–41: Moscow, Tokyo and the Prelude to the Pacific War* (Pittsburgh: University of Pittsburgh Press, 1992).

Hasluck, Paul. *The Government and the People* (Canberra: Australian War Memorial, 1952).

Hata, Shunroku. *Rikugun, Hata Shuroku nisshi: Zoku Gendaishi shiryō*, 4 (Tokyo: Misuzu Shobō, 1983). Diaries of Hata.

Hayashi, Hiroshi, and Yamada Akira. *Kirwaado Nihan no senso banzai* (Tokyo: Yuzankahu Shuppan, 1997)

Hayashi, Saburo. *Kogun: The Japanese Army in the Pacific War*, trans. Alvin Cox (Quantico, VA: Marine Corps Association, 1959).

Hayes, Grace. *The History of the Joint Chiefs of Staff in World War II: The War Against Japan*. Vol. 1: *Pearl Harbor Through Trident* (Washington, DC: Joint Chiefs of Staff, 1953).

Heinl, R. D. *Marines at Midway* (Washington, DC: U.S. Marine Corps, 1948).

Henriques, Robert. *Marcus Samuel: First Viscount Bearstead and Founder of the Shell Transport and Trading Company, 1853–1927* (London: Barrie & Rockliff, 1960).

Hersey, John. *Men on Bataan* (New York: Knopf, 1942).

Higashino, Makoto, with Awaya Kentaro and Yoshida Yutaka. *Shōwa tennō futatsu no'dokuhakuroku* (Tokyo: Nihon Hoso Shuppan Kyokai, 1998).

Hodgson, Godfrey. *The Colonel: The Life and Wars of Henry Stimson, 1867–1950* (New York: Knopf, 1990).

Holmes, W. Jaspar. *Double-Edged Secrets: U.S. Naval Intelligence Operations in the Pacific During World War II* (Annapolis: Naval Institute Press, 1979).

Hopkins, June. *Harry Hopkins. Sudden Hero, Brash Reformer* (New York: St. Martin's Press, 1999).

Hosaka, Masayasu. *Chichibu no Miya to Shōwa tennō* (Tokyo: Bungei Shunjū, 1989).

Hotz, Robert, ed. *Way of a Fighter; The Memoirs of Claire Lee Chennault* (New York: G.P. Putnam's Sons, 1949).

House of Representatives, Subcommittee, Committee on Appropriations. *On Consideration of the Second Supplemental Appropriation Bill for 1942*. 77th Congress, 1st Session (Washington, DC: U.S. Government Printing Office, 1941).

Huff, Sidney, with Joe Morris. *My Fifteen Years with General MacArthur* (New York: Paperback Library, 1964).

Hull, Cordell, with Andrew H. T. Berding. *The Memoirs of Cordell Hull*, 2 vols. (New York: Macmillan, 1948).

Hunt, Frazier. *The Untold Story of Douglas MacArthur* (New York: Devin-Adair, 1954).

Ickes, Harold L. *The Secret Diary of Harold L. Ickes*, 3 vols. (New York: Simon & Schuster, 1954).

Ike, Nobutake, ed. and trans. *Japan's Decision for War: Records of the 1941 Peace Conference* (Palo Alto, CA: Stanford University Press, 1967).

Ind, Allison. *Bataan, The Judgement Seat: The Saga of the Philippines Command of the United States Army Air Force, May 1941 to May 1942* (New York: Macmillan, 1944).

Irie, Sukemasa. *Irie Sukemasa nikki*, vols. 1–6 (Tokyo: Asahi Shinbunsha, 1990–91). Diaries of Irie.

Isely, Jeter, and Philip Crowl. *The U.S. Marines and Amphibious War: Its Theory and Its Practice in the Pacific* (Princeton: Princeton University Press, 1951).

Itō, Hirobumi. *Commentary on the Constitution of the Empire of Japan*, trans. Itō Miyoji (London: Greenwood Press, 1978 [1906]).

Itō, Masanori. *The End of the Imperial Japanese Navy*, trans. Andrew Kuroda and Roger Pineau (New York: W. W. Norton, 1962).

James, D. Clayton. *The Years of MacArthur*. Vol. I: *1880–1941* (Boston: Houghton Mifflin, 1970).

———.*The Years of MacArthur*. Vol. II: *1941–1945* (Boston: Houghton Mifflin, 1975).

———. *The Years of MacArthur*. Vol. III: *Triumph and Disaster* (Boston: Houghton Mifflin, 1985).

———. ed. *South to Bataan, North to Mukden: The Prison Diary of Brig. Gen. W. E. Brougher* (Athens, GA: University of Georgia Press, 1971).

James, Lawrence. *The Rise and Fall of the British Empire* (New York: St. Martin's Press, 1996).

Jō, Eiichirō. *Jijubukan Jō Eiichirō nikki* (Tokyo: Yamakawa Shuppansha, 1982). Diary of Jō.

Jones, Francis Clifford. *Japan's New Order in East Asia: Its Rise and Fall, 1937–1945* (London and New York: Oxford University Press, 1954).

Jones, Jesse. *Fifty Billion Dollars: My Thirteen Years with the RFC, 1932–1945* (New York: Macmillan, 1951).

Kahn, David. *The Codebreakers: The Story of Secret Writing* (New York: Macmillan, 1967).

Kase, Toshikazu. *Journey to the Missouri* (New Haven: Yale University Press, 1950).

Kasza, Gregory. *The Conscription Society: Administered Mass Organizations* (New Haven: Yale University Press, 1995).

Kato, Masuo. *The Lost War: A Japanese Reporter's Inside Story* (New York: Knopf, 1946).

Kawahara, Toshiaki. *Tennō Hirohito no Shōwa shi* (Yokohama: Bungei Shunju, 1983).

———. *Hirohito and His Times. A Japanese Perspective* (Tokyo: Kodansha International, 1990).

Kawai, Yahachi. *Shōwa shoki no tennō to kyūchū jijuichō Kawai Yahachi nikki*, vols. 1–6, ed. Takahashi Hiroshi, Awaya Kentaro, and Otabe Yuji (Tokyo: Iwanami Shoten, 1993–94). Diaries of Kawai.

Kazuko, Tsurumi. *Social Change and the Individual: Japan Before and After Defeat in World War II* (Princeton: Princeton University Press, 1970).

Kenney, George. *General Kenney Reports. A Personal History of the Pacific* (New York: Duell, Sloan & Pearce, 1949).

Kimball, Warren. *The Most Unsordid Act: Lend-Lease, 1939–1941* (Baltimore: Johns Hopkins University Press, 1969).

———, ed. *Churchill and Roosevelt: The Complete Correspondence*, 3 vols. (Princeton: Princeton University Press, 1984).

Kimmel, Husband. *Admiral Kimmel's Story* (Chicago: H. Regnery, 1955).

King, Ernest J. *The Influence of the National Policy on the Strategy of a War*. Thesis prepared for the Naval War College, 1932.

———. *Our Navy at War: A Report to the Secretary of the Navy Covering our Peacetime Navy and our Wartime Navy and including Combat Operations up to March 1, 1944* (U.S. News, March 1944).

———, and Walter Muir Whitehead. *Fleet Admiral King: A Naval Record* (New York: W. W. Norton, 1952).

Kirby, Stanley Woodburn. *The War Against Japan* (London: HM Stationery Office, 1957–69). Vols. 1–5 of the *History of the Second World War; United Kingdom Military* series.

Kiyosawa, Kiyoshi. *A Diary of Darkness: The Wartime Diary of Kiyosawa Kiyoshi*, trans. Eugene Soviak and Kamiyama Tamie (Princeton: Princeton University Press, 1999).

Kobayashi, Hideo. "Ryūjōkō jiken o megutte: Ryūjōkō jiken rokujussūnen ni yosete," *Rekishigaku kenkyū*, 699 (July 1977), pp. 30–35.

Kobayashi, M. "Jekai Taisen to Tairiku seisaku no henyō," in *Reikishigaku Kenkyū*, 656 (March 1994).

Korjima, Noburo. *Tenno 1: wakaki shinnō* (Tokyo: Bungei Shunjusha, 1980, 1989).

Korman, Sharon, *The Right of Conquest* (Oxford: Clarendon Press, 1996).

Krueger, Walter. *From Down Under to Nippon* (Washington, DC: Combat Forces Press, 1953).

LaFeber, Walter. *The Clash: U.S.-Japanese Relations Throughout History* (New York: W. W. Norton, 1997).

Langer, William L., and S. Everett Gleason. *The Undeclared War, 1940–1941* (New York: Harper, 1953).

Large, Stephen. *Emperor Hirohito and Shōwa Japan: A Political Biography* (London: Routledge, 1992).

———. *Emperors of the Rising Sun: Three Biographies* (Tokyo: Kodansha International, 1997).

Larrabee, Eric. *Commander-in-Chief* (New York: Harper & Row, 1987).

Lash, Joseph. *Eleanor and Franklin* (New York: W. W. Norton, 1971).

Layton, Edwin, with Roger Pineau and John Costello. *"And I Was There": Pearl Harbor and Midway—Breaking the Secrets* (New York: Morrow, 1985).

Leahy, William D. *I Was There* (New York: McGraw-Hill, 1950).

Lee, Clark. *They Call It Pacific: An Eye-witness Story of Our War Against Japan, from Bataan to the Solomons* (New York: Viking Press, 1943).

Levering, Robert. *Horror Trek: A True Story of Bataan, the Death March and Three and*

One Half Years in Japanese Prison Camps (Dayton, OH: Privately printed, 1940; reprinted New York: Carlton Press, 1979).

Liddell Hart, Basil. *History of the Second World War* (New York: Putnam, 1970).

Liggett, Hunter. *Commanding an American Army: Recollections of the World War* (Boston: Houghton Mifflin, 1925).

Liu, F. F. *A Military History of Modern China, 1924–1949* (Princeton: Princeton University Press, 1956).

Lockwood, Charles. *Sink 'Em All: Submarine Warfare in the Pacific* (New York: Dutton, 1951).

Long, Gavin M. *MacArthur as Military Commander* (London: Collins, 1969).

MacArthur, Douglas. *Reminiscences* (New York: McGraw-Hill, 1964).

———. *Reports of General MacArthur*, ed. Charles A. Willoughby (Washington, DC: U.S. Government Printing Office, 1966).

McClain, James. *Japan: A Modern History* (New York: W. W. Norton, 2002).

MacDonald, Scot. *Evolution of Aircraft Carriers* (Washington, DC: U.S. Government Printing Office, 1964).

MacIntire, Ross T., with George Creel. *White House Physician* (New York: G. P. Putnam's Sons, 1946).

McMillan, George. *The Old Breed: A History of the First Marine Division in World War II* (Washington, DC: Infantry Journal Press, 1949).

MacMillan, Margaret. *Paris 1919: Six Months That Changed the World* (New York: Random House, 2002).

Mahan, A. T. *Naval Strategy Compared and Contrasted with the Principles and Practice of Military Operation on Land* (Boston: Little, Brown, 1911).

Makino, Nobuaki. *Makino Nobuaki nikki* (Tokyo: Chūō Kōronsha, 1990). Diary of Makino.

Malay, Armando J. *Occupied Philippines* (Manila: Filipiniana, 1967).

Manchester, William. *American Caesar. Douglas MacArthur, 1880–1964* (Boston: Little, Brown, 1978).

Marquardt, Frederic. *Before Bataan and After* (Indianapolis: Bobbs-Merrill, 1943).

Marshall, General George C. *Biennial Report of the Chief of Staff of the United States Army, July 1, 1941 to June 30, 1943, to the Secretary of War* (Washington, DC: U.S. Government Printing Office, 1943).

———. *George C. Marshall Interviews and Reminiscences for Forrest C. Pogue*, ed. Larry I. Bland (Lexington, VA: George C. Marshall Research Foundation, 1986).

———. *The Papers of George Catlett Marshall*. Vol. 3: *"The Right Man for the Job," December 7, 1941–May 31, 1943*, ed. Larry I. Bland and Sharon Ritenour Stevens (Baltimore and London: Johns Hopkins University Press, 1991).

———. *The Papers of George Catlett Marshall*. Vol. 4: *"Aggressive and Determined Lead-*

ership," June 1, 1943–December 31, 1944 , ed. Larry I. Bland and Sharon Ritenour Stevens (Baltimore and London: Johns Hopkins University Press, 1996).

———. *Selected Speeches and Statements of General of the Army, George C. Marshall*, ed. Harvey. A. DeWeerd (Washington, DC: Infantry Journal Press, 1945).

Matloff, Maurice, and Edwin M. Snell. *Strategic Planning for Coalition Warfare, 1941–1942* (Washington, DC: Department of the Army, 1953).

———. *Strategic Planning for Coalition Warfare, 1943–1944* (Washington, DC: Department of the Army, 1959).

Mayer-Oakes, Thomas F., ed. and trans. *Fragile Victory: Prince Saionji and the 1930 London Treaty Issue, from the Memoirs of Baron Harada Kumao* (Detroit: Wayne State University Press, 1968).

Mellnik, Stephen M. *Philippine Diary, 1939–1945* (New York: Van Nostrand Rheinhold, 1969).

Miller, Edward S. *War Plan Orange: The U.S. Strategy to Defeat Japan, 1897–1945* (Annapolis: Naval Institute Press, 1991).

Miller, Ernest. *Bataan Uncensored* (Brainerd, MN: Miller, Hart Publications, 1949).

Miller, John. *The United States Army in World War II. The War in the Pacific*. Vol. II: *Guadalcanal: The First Offensive* (Washington, DC: Department of the Army, 1949).

Miller, Nathan. *Theodore Roosevelt, A Life* (New York: Morrow, 1992).

Miller, Thomas. *The Cactus Air Force* (New York: Harper & Row, 1969).

Milner, Samuel. *Victory at Papua* (Washington, DC: Department of the Army, 1957).

Minobe, Tatsukichi. *Chikijō kempō seigi* (Tokyo: Yūhikaku, 1927).

Mitchell, Donald. *History of the Modern American Navy, from 1883 Through Pearl Harbor* (New York: Knopf, 1946).

Mitchell, George. *Matthew B. Ridgway: Soldier, Statesman, Scholar, Citizen* (Mechanicsburg, PA: Stackpole Books, 1999).

Moran, Lord (Charles Wilson). *Churchill: The Struggle for Survival, 1940–1965, Taken from the Diaries of Lord Moran* (Boston: Houghton Mifflin, 1966).

Morison, Elting. *Turmoil and Tradition: A Study in the Life and Times of Henry L. Stimson* (Boston: Houghton Mifflin, 1960).

Morison, Samuel Eliot. *History of United States Naval Operations in World War II*. Vol. III: *The Rising Sun in the Pacific, 1931–April 1942* (Boston: Little, Brown, 1948).

———. *History of United States Naval Operations in World War II*. Vol. IV: *Coral Sea, Midway and Submarine Actions, May 1942–August 1942* (Boston: Little, Brown, 1949).

———. *History of United States Naval Operations in World War II*. Vol. V: *The Struggle for Guadalcanal, August 1942–February 1943* (Boston: Little, Brown, 1949).

———. *The Two-Ocean War: A Short History of the United States Navy in the Second World War* (Boston: Little, Brown, 1963).

Morton, Louis. *United States Army in World War II. The War in the Pacific: The Fall of the Philippines* (Washington, DC: Department of the Army, 1953).

———. *Strategy and Command: The First Two Years* (Washington, DC: Department of the Army, 1962).

Murray, Williamson, and Allan Millett. *A War to Be Won: Fighting the Second World War* (Cambridge, MA: Belknap Press, Harvard University Press, 2000).

Nakajima, Michio. *Tennō no daigawari to kokumin* (Tokyo: Aoki Shoten, 1990).

Nakamura, Takfusa. *A History of Shōwa Japan, 1926–1989*, trans. Edwin Whenmouth (Tokyo: University of Tokyo Press, 1998).

Nakazono, Hiroshi. *Seitō naikaku-ki ni okeru Shōwa tennō oyobi sokkin no seijiteki Kōdō to yakuwari: Tanaka naikaku o chūsin ni*. Master's thesis, Aoyama Gakuin Daigaku Daigakuin, Tokyo University, 1992.

Newcomb, Richard F. *Abandon Ship!: Death off the USS Indianapolis* (New York: Henry Holt, 1958).

———. *Savo: The Incredible Debacle Off Guadalcanal* (New York: Holt, Rinehart & Winston, 1961).

Nezu, Masashi. *Tennō to Shōwashi, jō* (Tokyo: San'ichi Shobo, 1974).

Nimitz, Chester, and E. B. Potter. *Triumph in the Pacific: The Navy's Struggle Against Japan* (Englewood Cliffs, NJ: Prentice-Hall, 1963).

Okada, Seiji, and Hikuma Takenori. "Sokui no rei, daijōsai no rekishiteki kentō," in *Bunka hyōron*, 357 (October 1990).

Oosten, F. C. van. *The Battle of the Java Sea* (London: Ian Allan, 1975; Annapolis: Naval Institute Press, 1976).

Ostrower, Gary B. *Collective Insecurity: The United States and the League of Nations During the Early Thirties* (London: Associated University Press, 1993).

Otabe, Yuji, Hayashi Hiroshi, and Yamada Akira. *Kiwado Nihon no senso banzai* (Tokyo: Yuzankaku Shuppan, 1995). On casualty statistics during the war, i.e., more than 10 million Chinese killed, 1.5 million Indians, and so on.

Pearl Harbor and the Kimmel Controversy, The Views Today. Published Proceedings of the Symposium Held December 7, 1999, at the Navy Memorial, Washington, DC. (Naval Historical Foundation, 2000).

Peattie, Mark. *Ishiwara Kanji and Japan's Confrontation with the West* (Princeton: Princeton University Press, 1975).

Petillo, Carol Morris. *Douglas MacArthur: The Philippine Years* (Bloomington: Indiana University Press, 1981).

Pogue, Forrest C. *George C. Marshall: Ordeal and Hope, 1939–1942* (New York: Viking Press, 1969).

———. *George C. Marshall: Organizer of Victory, 1943–1945* (New York: Viking Press, 1973).

Pomeroy, Earl. *Pacific Outpost: American Strategy in Guam and Micronesia* (Stanford: Stanford University Press, 1951).

Potter, E. B. *Nimitz* (Annapolis: Naval Institute Press, 1976).

———. *Bull Halsey* (Annapolis: Naval Institute Press, 1985).

Potter, John Deane. *Admiral of the Pacific: The Life of Yamamoto* (London: Heinemann, 1965).

Prados, John. *Combined Fleet Decoded: The Secret History of American Intelligence and the Japanese Navy in World War II* (New York: Random House, 1995).

Prange, Gordon, Donald Goldstein, and Katherine Dillon. *At Dawn We Slept: The Untold Story of Pearl Harbor* (New York: McGraw-Hill, 1981).

Quezon, Manuel. *Annual Report of the President of the Philippine Commonwealth* (Manila: GPO, 1939).

———. *Annual Report of the President of the Philippine Commonwealth* (Manila: GPO, 1940).

———. *The Good Fight* (New York: Appleton-Century, 1946).

Reckner, James. *Teddy Roosevelt's Great White Fleet* (Annapolis: Naval Institute Press, 1957).

Records of the Joint Chiefs of Staff (Frederick, MD: University Publications of America, 1982).

"Records of the U.S. Department of State, Political Relations Between the United States and Japan, 1930–1939," reel no. 3, file no. 711.94/1184, Library of Congress.

Reilly, Henry J. *Americans All: The Rainbow at War. Official History of the 42nd Rainbow Division in the World War* (Columbus, OH: F. J. Heer Printing Co., 1936).

Reynolds, Clark G. *The Fast Carriers: The Forging of an Air Navy* (New York: McGraw-Hill, 1968).

———. *Admiral John H. Towers. The Struggle for Naval Air Supremacy* (Annapolis: Naval Institute Press, 1991).

Richardson, James O., and George C. Dyer. *On the Treadmill to Pearl Harbor: The Memoirs of Admiral James O. Richardson* (Washington, DC: Department of the Navy, 1973).

Rogow, Arnold. *James Forrestal: A Study of Personality, Politics and Policy* (New York: Macmillan, 1963).

Röling, B. V. A., and Antonio Cassesse. *The Tokyo Trial and Beyond: Reflections of a Peace Monger* (Cambridge: Polity Press, 1993).

Romulo, Carlos. *I Saw the Fall of the Philipppines* (New York: Doubleday, Doran, 1942).

Roosevelt, Eleanor. *This I Remember* (New York: Harper & Bros., 1949).

Roosevelt, Elliott. *As He Saw It* (New York: Duell, Sloan & Pearce, 1946).

Roosevelt, Franklin D. *The Public Papers and Addresses of Franklin D. Roosevelt,* ed. Samuel I. Rosenman, vols. VI, VII, IX (New York: Random House, 1938–50).

———. *The Roosevelt Letters, Being the Personal Correspondence of Franklin Delano Roosevelt,* ed. Elliott Roosevelt. Vol. 2: *1905–1928* (New York: Duell, Sloan & Pearce, 1950).

Roosevelt, James, with Bill Libby. *My Parents: A Differing View* (Chicago: Playboy Press, 1976).

Rosenman, Samuel I. *Working with Roosevelt* (New York: Harper & Bros., 1952).

Roskill, Stephen. *The War at Sea, 1939–1945*, 3 vols. (London: HM Stationery Office, 1954–61).

Sayre, Francis Bowes. *Glad Adventure* (New York: Macmillan, 1957).

Schultz, Duane. *Hero of Bataan: The Story of General Jonathan M. Wainwright* (New York: St. Martin's Press, 1981).

Seagrave, Sterling, and Peggy Seagrave. *The Yamato Dynasty: The Secret History of Japan's Imperial Family* (London: Bantam Books, 1970).

Senshi sōshō. Japan's official war history in 102 vols., ed. Bōeichō Bōei Kenshūjo Senshishitsu (Tokyo: Asagumo Shinbusha, 1966–80). A major source. See in particular:
Hawai sakusen (Hawaiian Operation), vol. 10 (1967).
Philippines-Marei hoomen kaigun shinkoo sakusen (Philippines-Maylay Area Naval Attack Operations), vol. 24 (1969).
N.E.I.-Bengaru hoomen kaigun shinkoo sakusen (N.E.I.–Bengal Bay Area Naval Attack Operations), vol. 26 (1969).
Chuubu taiheiyoo hoomen kaigun sakusen (Central Pacific Naval Operations), vol. 38 (1970).
Daihonei kaigunbu-rengoo kantaksi (Imperial General Headquarters–Combined Fleet), vol. 39 (1970).
Midooei kaisen (Midway Sea Battle), vol. 43 (1971).
Nantoo hoomen kaigun sakusen (Southeast Area Naval Operations to Guadalcanal reinforcement), vol. 49 (1971).
Chuubu taiheiyoo hoomen kaigun sakusen (Central Pacific Area Naval Operations after 1942), vol. 62 (1973).
Nantoo hoomen kaigun sakusen (Southwest Area Naval Operations to Guadalcanal evacuation), vol. 63 (1975).

Sherman, Frederick C. *Combat Command: The American Aircraft Carriers in the Pacific* (New York: Dutton, 1950).

Sherwood, Robert E. *Roosevelt and Hopkins, An Intimate History* (New York: Harper & Bros., 1948).

Shibuno, Junichi. "Taishō junen Kawasaki, Mitsubishi dai sōgi no bunken to kenkyū," *Rekishi to Kobe* (August 1967).

Shillony, Ben-Ami. *Politics and Culture in Wartime Japan* (New York: Oxford University Press, 1981).

Shipley, Thomas. *The History of the A.E.F.* (New York: George H. Doran, 1920).

Ship's Data, U.S. Naval Vessels, vol. IV (Washington, DC: U.S. Government Printing Office, April 15, 1945).

Smith, Holland M., and Percy Finch. *Coral and Brass* (New York: Charles Scribner's Sons, 1949).

Smith, R. Elberton. *The Army and Economic Mobilization* (Washington, DC: Department of the Army, 1959).

Stamps, T. Dodson, and Vincent J. Esposito. *A Military History of World War II*, 2 vols. (West Point, NY: U.S. Military Academy, 1953).

Steel, Ronald. *Walter Lippmann and the American Century* (Boston: Little, Brown, 1980).

Stettinius, Edward R. *Lend-Lease: Weapon for Victory* (New York: Macmillan, 1944).

———. *The Diaries of Edward R. Stettinius, Jr., 1943–1946*, ed. Thomas M. Campbell and George C. Herring (New York: New Viewpoints, 1975).

Stimson, Henry. *Diaries of Henry L. Stimson* (New Haven: Yale University Library, Archives).

———, and McGeorge Bundy. *On Active Service in Peace and War* (New York: Harper & Bros., 1948).

Strouse, Jean. *Morgan, American Financier* (New York: Random House, 1999).

Sulzberger, Cyrus. *A Long Row of Candles: Memoirs and Diaries, 1934–1954* (New York: Macmillan, 1969).

Supreme Commander for the Allied Powers, General Headquarters, International Prosecution Section. *Kokusai kensatsukyoku (IPS) jinmon chosho, dai 8 and 42 kan*, ed. Kentarō Awaya and Yoshida Yutaka (Tokyo: Nihon Tosho Senta, 1993).

Suzuki, Masayuki. *Kindai Tennōsei no Shibai chitsujo* (Tokyo: Azekura Shobō, 1986), part 2.

Takahashi, Fujitani. *Splendid Monarchy: Power and Pageantry in Modern Japan* (Berkeley: University of California Press, 1996).

Takahashi, Hiroshi, et al. *Shōwa shoki no tennō to kyuchu: Jijūjicho Kawai Yahachi nikki* (Tokyo: Iwanami Shoten, 1993–94). Diaries of Kawai Yahachi.

Takahashi, Yōichi. "Inoue Tetsujirō fukei/jiken sai Kō," in Terabaki, Masao, et al., eds., *Kindai Nihon ni okeru chi no bumpai to Kokunnin tōgō* (Tokyo: Dai Ichihōki Kik, 1993).

Takamatsu no Miya Nobuhito, with Hosokawa Morisada. *Takamatsu no miya nikki*, vols. 1–8 (Tokyo: Chūō Kōronsha, 1997). Diaries of Prince Takamatsu.

Tamaki, Nōrio. *Japanese Banking: A History, 1859–1959* (Cambridge: Cambridge University Press, 1995).

Tanaka, Nobumasa. *Dokyumento Shōwa tennō*, 8 vols. (Tokyo: Ryokufu Shuppan, 1984–93).

Tanaka, Yuki. *Hidden Horrors: Japanese War Crimes in World War II* (Boulder, CO: Westview Press, 1995).

Taylor, A. J. P. *The Origins of the Second World War* (New York: Fawcett Premier, 1963).

Taylor, Theodore. *The Magnificent Mitscher* (New York: W. W. Norton, 1954).

Terasaki, Hidenari, and Mariko Terasaki Miller, eds. *Shōwa tennō dokubakuroku: Terasaki Hidenari, Goyōgakari nikki* (Tokyo: Bungei Shunjū, 1991).

Theobald, Robert. *The Final Secret of Pearl Harbor* (New York: Devin-Adair, 1954).

Tinch, Clark. "Quasi-War Between Japan and the USSR, 1937–1939," *World Politics*, vol. 3, no. 2 (July 1951).

Togo, Shigenori. *The Cause of Japan*, ed. and trans. Togo Fumihiko and Ben Bruce Blakeney (New York: Simon & Schuster, 1956).

The Tokyo War Crimes Trial: The Complete Transcripts of the Proceedings of the International Military Tribunal for the Far East, 22 vols., ed. John Pritchard and Sonia Maganua Zaide (New York and London: Garland, 1981), vols. 8, 12, 13, 20, and 21 in particular.

Toland, John. *But Not in Shame: The Six Months After Pearl Harbor* (New York: Random House, 1961).

———. *The Rising Sun: The Decline and Fall of the Japanese Empire, 1936–1945* (New York: Random House, 1970).

———. *Infamy: Pearl Harbor and Its Aftermath* (Garden City, NY: Doubleday, 1982).

Tsurumi, Shunsuke. *An Intellectual History of Wartime Japan, 1931–1945* (London: KPI, 1986).

Tuchman, Barbara. *Stilwell and the American Experience in China, 1911–1945* (New York: Bantam Books, 1972).

Tully, Grace. *FDR, My Boss* (New York: Scribners, 1949).

Turnbull, Archibald, and Clifford Lord. *The History of United States Naval Aviation* (New Haven: Yale University Press, 1949).

Turner, Richmond Kelly. *Asiatic Annual Reports*, 1928, 1929.

U.S. Army Far East Command. *The Imperial Japanese Navy in World War II: A Graphic Presentation of the Japanese Naval Organization and List of Combatants and Non-Combatant Vessels Lost or Damaged in the War* (Tokyo: Military History Section, General Headquarters, Far East Command, 1952) (Japanese Operational Monograph Series No. 116).

U.S. Congress, Joint Committee on the Investigation of the Pearl Harbor Attack. *Hearings: Pearl Harbor Attack*, 19 vols. (Washington, DC: U.S. Government Printing Office, 1946).

U.S. Strategic Bombing Survey. *Interrogations of Japanese Officials*, 2 vols. (Washington, DC: U.S. Government Printing Office, 1947).

———. Pacific, Naval Analysis Division. *The Campaigns of the Pacific War* (Washington, DC: U.S. Government Printing Office, 1946).

Usui, Katsumi. *Nitchū sensō: Wahei ka sensen kakudai ka* (Tokyo: Chūō Korousha, 1967).

Vandegrift, Alexander Archer, and Robert Asprey. *Once a Marine. The Memoirs of General A. A. Vandegrift* (New York: W. W. Norton, 1964).

Vandenberg, Arthur. *The Private Papers of Senator Vandenberg*, ed. Arthur H. Vandenberg Jr., with Joe Alex Morris (Boston: Houghton Mifflin, 1952).

Van der Vat, Dan. *The Pacific Campaign: World War II. The U.S.-Japanese Naval War, 1941–1945* (New York: Simon & Schuster, 1991).

Varley, H. Paul. "Nanbokucho seijun ron," in *Kodansha Encyclopedia of Japan* (Tokyo: Kodansha, 1983), pp. 323–24.

Viorst, Milton. *Hostile Allies: FDR and de Gaulle* (New York: Macmillan, 1965).

Wainwright, Jonathan. *General Wainwright's Story. The Account of Four Years of Humiliating Defeat, Surrender and Captivity*, ed. Robert Considine (Garden City, NY: Doubleday, 1946).

———. *Report of Operations of USAFFE and USFIP in the Philippine Islands, 1941–1942*, including fourteen Annexes. Covers Wainwright's report and those of his commanders who survived. Located in the Departmental Records Branch, and at the Center of Military History (Washington, DC, 1945–46).

Watanabe, Toshihiko. "Nanajū ichi butain to Nagata Tesuzan," in *Chūō Daigaku* (Tokyo: Chūō Daiku Shuppanhu, 1993).

Waterford, Van. *Prisoners of the Japanese in World War II* (Jefferson, NC: MacFarland, 1994).

Watson, Mark. *Chief of Staff: Prewar Plans and Preparations* (Washington, DC: Department of the Army, 1950).

Wedemeyer, Albert. *Wedemeyer Reports!* (New York: Henry Holt, 1958).

Willoughby, Charles, et al., eds. *Reports of General MacArthur. The Campaigns of MacArthur in the Pacific* (Washington, DC: U.S. Government Printing Office, 1966).

———, and John Chamberlain. *MacArthur, 1941–1951* (New York: McGraw-Hill, 1954).

Wilson, Dick. *Zhou Enlai* (New York: Viking Press, 1984).

Wilson, Theodore. *The First Summit: Roosevelt and Churchill at Placentia Bay, 1941* (Boston: Houghton Mifflin, 1969).

Winant, John G. *Letter from Grosvenor Square* (Boston: Houghton Mifflin, 1947).

Wohlstetter, Roberta. *Pearl Harbor: Warning and Decision* (Palo Alto, CA: Stanford University Press, 1962).

Wolf, Walter. *A Brief Story of the Rainbow Division* (New York: Rand, McNally, 1919).

Yamanouchi, Yasushi, J. Victor Koschmann, and Ryūchi Narita, eds. *Total War and "Modernization"* (Ithaca, NY: East Asia Program, Cornell University, 1988).

Yoshida, Mitsuru. *Requiem from Battleship Yamato*, trans. Richard H. Minear (Seattle: University of Washington Press, 1985).

Yoshimi, Yoshiaki, and Matsumo Seiya. *Dokugasusen kankei shiryō* (Yokohama: Fuji Shuppan, 1997).

Young, Louise. *Japan's Total Empire: Manchuria and the Culture of Wartime Imperialism* (Berkeley: University of California Press, 1998).

Zokugendaishi shiryō Ho Rikugun, Hata Shunroyku nisshi (Tokyo: Misuzu Shoho, 1983).

Index

Page numbers in *italics* refer to maps.
Page numbers after 461 refer to end notes.